NATIONAl

ENGLISH PLACE-NAME SOCIETY

The English Place-Name Society was founded in 1924 to carry out the survey of English place-names and to issue annual volumes to members who subscribe to the work of the Society. The Society has issued the following volumes:

The volumes for the following counties are in preparation: *Berkshire, Cheshire* (Parts 2–5), *Dorset, Kent, Leicestershire & Rutland, Lincolnshire, the City of London, Shropshire, Staffordshire.*

All communications with regard to the Society and membership should be addressed to:

THE HON. SECRETARY, English Place-Name Society, University College, Gower Street, London w.c.1.

ENGLISH PLACE-NAME SOCIETY. VOLUME XLIV
FOR 1966–7

GENERAL EDITOR
K. CAMERON

THE PLACE-NAMES OF CHESHIRE

PART I

ENGLISH PLACE-NAME SOCIETY. VOLUME XLIV

THE PLACE-NAMES OF CHESHIRE

By
J. McN. DODGSON

PART I
COUNTY NAME, REGIONAL- &
FOREST-NAMES, RIVER-NAMES,
ROAD-NAMES,
THE PLACE-NAMES OF
MACCLESFIELD HUNDRED

CAMBRIDGE
AT THE UNIVERSITY PRESS
1970

Published by the Syndics of the Cambridge University Press
Bentley House, 200 Euston Road, London N.W. 1
American Branch: 32 East 57th Street, New York, N.Y. 10022

Printed in Great Britain
at the University Printing House, Cambridge
(Brooke Crutchley, University Printer)

The collection from unpublished documents of material for the Cheshire volumes has been greatly assisted by grants received from the British Academy

CONTENTS

PREFACE

THE *Place-Names of Cheshire* will occupy several volumes of *The Survey of English Place-Names*. The first volume contains the bibliography, the county-name, the river-names, regional-names, and road-names, and the place-names of Macclesfield Hundred. The place-names of the rest of the county, for the Hundreds of Bucklow, Northwich, Nantwich, Eddisbury, Broxton, Wirral and Chester, will appear in that order in the subsequent volumes. The last volume will contain the Introduction, notes on the dialect, the analyses of elements and personal-names, and the index.

It is a curious feature of the Society's procedure that the Introduction to a county survey should come last in publication. But this allows each part of the material to be printed and published without delay, and made available to members of the Society as soon as it is ready. If it were desired to put the Introduction in the first part published, the whole body of the work would have to be held back until the Introduction, analyses and index were ready. This is not difficult in a one- or two-volume county survey, but in a survey which occupies a longer series, delays would inevitably occur, for the apparatus sections cannot be composed until all the material is paginated.

The scope of the county surveys is constantly expanding in response both to the growing availability of documents and to the growing demands upon place-name research made by students in other fields. Whereas in former days a county might be covered in part of a volume, or in one or two volumes, it may now take three or four volumes, even more. The length of time required to finish the editing and publication of a county survey is correspondingly longer. The editors of the *Survey* are all sensitive to the patient demands of the members of the Society, and it would seem preferable to bring forward the parts of a county survey one by one as soon as they are ready, rather than to hold them back until the complete county survey is assembled. This publication by parts is artificial, for the county survey is one operation, and its result is one work of scholarship. The text of *The Place-Names of Cheshire* will not be paginated serially, so cross-references need part-numbers. But the method of publication entails the printing of the first part before the subsequent ones are paginated, and this makes it impossible to print accurate page references against allusions to place-names appearing in subsequent volumes. Back-references, of course, present no difficulty. To cope with the problem of forward references, each part of the county survey will contain a summary of forward-references, so that readers may catch up the appropriate page-numbers when the subsequent parts of *Cheshire* have been published.

By way of preface to this first part of *The Place-Names of Cheshire*, and in anticipation of the discussions which will be presented in the Introduction in a subsequent volume, a few remarks are offered to the reader to guide his appreciation of the material. It will be observed that the county of Cheshire occupies the angle between North Wales and North England, and forms the north-west corner of the English Midlands. It extends from the Peak to the Welsh hills, and from the Irish Sea to Yorkshire, Derbyshire and Staffordshire. It occupies a region which has been crucial in the ethnic and political history of England. Not only is it the scene of Welsh–English confrontation in the middle ages, but it saw in an earlier age the meeting of Angle and Briton, the emergence of Anglo-Saxon Mercia and the political confrontation of Mercia and Northumbria. The county coasts the Irish Sea whence came the settlements in the tenth century of the Vikings from Ireland and Man: it extends inland towards the Danelaw territory, hence the Danish influence in the place-names of East Cheshire. Of all the English counties, this one is as rich as any in place-names which commemorate the ethnic history of England and which suggest those courses of political history which are not recorded in documents. The place-names of Cheshire stand against a background devoid of early Anglo-Saxon archæological material by which historical inference may be checked. This is an acute problem, for it is difficult to stratify the English place-names without an archæological horizon. The place-names indicate that the British influence in Cheshire persisted down into the seventh century, i.e. until about the time when Mercia became a power. They suggest the nature of a changing relationship between the Welsh and the Angles at or before this time. Of course, the persistent medieval and modern Welsh influence in Cheshire life is illustrated in the place-names too, but it is their testimony to a more ancient course of events in the coming of the English which demands the most careful assessment.

In Cheshire the English place-names in -*ingham* are peculiar in form (with assibilated *ǧ* [-idʒəm, -indʒəm]), and the British and Welsh place-names and river-names are more than usually significant in form and distribution. The relationship between these is capable of an interpretation which goes beyond the familiar theory of *-ingas*, *-ingahām* which is used in the Society's volumes. It has been sketched in my article 'The English Arrival in Cheshire' LCHS 119 (1967), 1–37, and will be more thoroughly described in the Introduction, with such corrections as afterthought inspires. The Cheshire *-ingham* names will be discussed there, but in the meantime, readers are referred to my article 'The *-ing* in English Place-Names like Altrincham and Birmingham' BNF 2 (1967), 221–45, and its sequel in BNF 2 (1967), 296–325, BNF 3 (1968), 141–89. Interim reading about the Scandinavian settlements will be found in 'The English Arrival in Cheshire' *supra*, and in my article 'The Background of Brunanburgh', *Sagabook* 14 (1957–7), 303–16. Similarly, some discussion of the place-names of Cheshire will be found in my article 'Street-Names and Place-Names at Chester' forthcoming in CAS for 1968.

From the records of the Society, it would appear that *The Place-Names of Cheshire* was planned and to some extent in progress some forty-five years ago. Sir Allen Mawer was in correspondence in 1923 with Mr W. Fergusson Irvine and Mr R. Stewart Brown about Cheshire records and the collection of spellings from Plea Rolls, and with Dr W. J. Varley in 1935 about a study of place-names for a history of Cheshire. Mr W. Smith of Macclesfield and Mr J. E. Allison of Prenton were supplying notes in 1938 and 1939. Mr H. Alexander (author of *The Place-Names of Oxfordshire*, Oxford 1912) was interested in taking up the work in 1938, but it had already been put in the hands of Dr A. H. Smith early in that year, and he had constructed part of the gazetteer by autumn 1939. These papers and the Cheshire project were put in my hands in 1953. I have incorporated them in my collections but they proved too incomplete and occasional to serve as a basis for the survey, and a new gazetteer and a complete new collection were made as the basis of my M.A. thesis, 'The Major Place-Names of Cheshire' at London University 1957.

There have been many helpers with the work, in ways great and small, over the many years it has taken. Here it is my pleasant task and willing duty to express my personal gratitude and the thanks of

my predecessors and of the English Place-Name Society, to all these
following.

The late Professor A. H. Smith, Hon. Director of the Survey of
English Place-Names and Hon. Secretary of the English Place-Name
Society, 1949–67, was my teacher, master and friend, to whom I owe
many things which defy the fluency of my pen; his mark is upon this
book, and its author, in many ways, indelibly.

The late W. Fergusson Irvine, Esq., of Corwen, took an active and
lively interest in *The Place-Names of Cheshire* throughout the whole
course of the Society's existence, and indeed long before that; his
knowledge and kindness was the origin of many letters and words of
guidance, encouragement and information; even after his death, his
help continued, for the Venerable R. H. Burne passed on to me
Mr Irvine's collection of field-name maps for Wirral and West
Cheshire. Of all those who could not wait to see this book out, Mr
Irvine is the one most missed, for he waited patiently for many
decades, and his erudite enthusiasm deserves a better memorial than
this.

The late Dr F. T. Wainwright and the late Dr B. J. Timmer had
much to do with my education in the relevance of place-names to
archæology and philology; they were friends to me early in my career,
and their thoughts have informed many points of argument in this work.

Dr Geoffrey Barnes, of Bury, Lancs., formerly of Stockport, also
wrote *The Place-Names of Cheshire*—for his Ph.D. thesis at Sheffield
University 1960—and generously placed this work at my service
immediately after its completion. His book on my desk, and his
continued correspondence upon various problems and about the
difference between our solutions, have been a valuable help and
challenge. We have each seen some collections of documents which,
by various turns of circumstance, were not available to the other, and
in various parts of this book, his contribution will be seen. I have
acknowledged the use of his material in detail, and have presented
his arguments clearly wherever they were so different from mine as
to require comment or discussion. But for certain academic accidents
of time and place, it might well have been he who had the writing of
this preface.

Dr B. K. Blount made the Downes MSS available to me.

The Venerable R. H. Burne, archdeacon of Chester, gave me his
help and conversation over many years; I am grateful for his careful
rescue of Mr Irvine's field-name maps, and for his notes on Poosey.

J. E. Allison, Esq., of Prenton, was a correspondent of Allen Mawer's in 1937, and helped with the place-names of Tranmere and district in 1966–7.

Lady Lenette Bromley-Davenport gave information about Capesthorne.

Dr Arnold Brown, County Medical Officer of Health, Cheshire County Council, sent *A Cheshire Index*.

J. P. Dodd, Esq., of Frodsham, gave notes on Frodsham and district.

N. Ellison, Esq., of West Kirby, showed me Hilbre and Wirral from Grange Hill and told me about the fords of Dee.

K. S. Jermy, Esq., of Thelwall, gave information about Cheshire customs, local history, and Roman roads.

J. C. Jones, Esq., of Congleton, exchanged information about Congleton and district, and gave information about records and spellings in collections which I had not reached.

Sir Ernest B. Royden, Bt. of Frankby, gave copies of various estate maps and sent notes on Wallasey; he gave the Society a donation of £25 towards the cost of publication.

The late Walter Smith, Esq., of Macclesfield, gave Allen Mawer information and spellings thirty years ago, about Macclesfield and District, and made transcripts of documents in Birkenhead Public Library for him.

A. C. F. Tait, Esq., of Birkenhead, gave me notes about Bromborough and Wirral.

H. A. Trippier, Esq., of Poynton, gave notes on Poynton and district.

Dr A. G. C. Turner of Cheadle, sent me his notes on Celtic place-names in Cheshire, and permitted a preview of his article 'Some Celtic Traces in Cheshire and the Pennines' BBCS 22 (1967), 111–19.

Mr A. Young, architect, of Macclesfield, gave information about old buildings in that town.

Many people in Cheshire, whose names I do not know, answered daft questions with good manners and good humour in tap-rooms and at field-gates.

Mr G. A. McD. Wood, of Hyde, collected field-names in northeast Cheshire; and other students in the Department of English at University College, Mr L. Heap, Mr E. Domville and Mr D. J. Findlay, transcribed Tithe Awards.

The late Dr Liam Price, of Dublin, sent me notes on Irish place-names relevant to Noctorum.

The late Sir Frank Stenton, Professor Dorothy Whitelock, Professor B. Dickins, the late Dr P. H. Reaney, Dr J. P. Oakden (for help with Staffordshire place-names) and Professor K. Cameron (for help with Derbyshire place-names), my seniors in the Survey of English Place-Names, gave me helpful and restraining touches. Upon Professors Whitelock and Cameron especially has fallen the burden formerly carried by Sir Frank Stenton and Professor A. H. Smith. I am very grateful to them for their hard work in bringing my manuscript through to publication, and for the contributions to fact and argument which they have added as the work proceeded.

Major F. G. C. Rowe, and Mr B. C. Redwood, past and present County Archivists at Cheshire Record Office, Miss Elizabeth Beazley, and all the past and present members of staff there, gave me many hours of happy fellowship and shared scholarship, and numerous notes and transcriptions and investigations, corrections and checks, made for me willingly and courteously.

Dr Mary Finch, Miss Helen Boulton (now Mrs J. Parkinson) and Mrs E. K. Berry, past and present City Archivists at the City Record Office Chester, gave me patient and detailed help with my searches there. Dr Finch transcribed parts of the Assembly Books and Portmote Rolls for me.

Mr R. Sharpe-France, County Archivist at Lancashire Record Office, has been my mentor and friend for many years, and has played no small part in the direction of my career; to him and to all those past and present members of staff in that office who have borne with my doings as an honorary colleague long ago, and a demanding reader thereafter, I am grateful, for help and advice and instruction beyond what this book called for.

Mr Bruce Jones formerly of Lancashire Record Office, saw this work begin and had faith in its being finished while I had not yet dared look so far.

I thank Miss S. R. Chaplin, Secretary of Cheshire Community Council, and all those members of that organisation who helped in the preparation of a list of modern pronunciations of Cheshire place-names.

Miss H. Lofthouse, Librarian of Chetham's Library, Manchester, sent me lists of documents relative to Cheshire.

Mr M. P. Statham, County Archivist of West Suffolk Record

Office, and Mrs Margaret Statham his wife, helped me with the Bunbury MSS.

I am grateful to Miss W. D. Coates and Col. R. P. White, past and present Registrars of the National Register of Archives, and all those past and present members of staff there, who had to do with me; especially Messrs J. E. Armstrong and A. E. B. Owen, who helped me with this work and other enterprises, and shared various adventures with me in the process.

I was helped by the staff of the Reading Room, the Dept. of MSS, and the Map Room, at the British Museum; I am grateful especially to Mr P. D. A. Harvey for help with the physical problem of examining a large number of Additional Charters in a short time: and Mr Julian Roberts, whose bibliography of English place-names spared me many an hour to continue with Cheshire.

Mr R. H. M. Dolley of The Queen's University, Belfast, formerly of the Department of Coins and Medals at the British Museum, helped by Miss Elizabeth Pirie of the City Museum, York, helped me with the name-forms on the coins from the Chester mint. Mr Dolley prepared me a detailed and exhaustive schedule of the variant spellings from the entire known corpus of early Chester pieces, and so reduced to simple order a mass of information which would have confused me. I am proud to belong to that number which pays honour to his scholarship, and to add to that admiration my sincere gratitude for his help and friendship over many years.

The past and present members of the staff of the Public Record Office, Sir David Evans, Mr R. Ellis, Mr L. C. Hector, Mr D. B. Wardle (all these sometime my tutors), and Mr E. K. Timings, gave me much advice, many services, and helpful arrangements, and a deal of teaching. Their colleagues will forgive me for thanking very particularly Mr Hector for ascertaining difficult readings and Domesday Book forms, and Mr Timings for the trouble taken to give access to records in long series at a rapid rate.

The staff of Messrs Sotheby, auctioneers, of London, afforded facilities for the perusal of documents exhibited for sale in their auction rooms.

The Librarians of the Society of Antiquaries of London, the Institute of Historical Research, University of London, the University of London Library, the Guildhall Library, City of London, Westminster Public Library, and the City of Chester Public Library, gave patient and careful service.

b-2

Mr J. W. Scott, Librarian of University College London, and all his staff, my colleagues, did me many services, gave me constant help, showed me unchanging forbearance, and afforded me their scholarship over many years.

I thank Dr F. Taylor and his colleagues, and their learned porter, at the John Rylands Library, Manchester, for help with many documents and local histories.

I thank Mr G. Stratton, Librarian, Birkenhead Public Library, for lending to University College London Birkenhead's copy of Helsby's edition of Ormerod's *History of Cheshire*, on extended loan, for my convenient reference.

The former staff of the search room of the now defunct Tithe Redemption Commission's office, showed great kindness to me, my colleagues and my wife during many months of copying Tithe Awards.

Mr C. E. C. Burch, formerly Research Assistant to the late Professor A. H. Smith, did me many services and gave much generous assistance, especially in the transcription of Tithe Awards and other records.

Professor G. Melville Richards of Bangor, and Professor K. H. Jackson of Edinburgh, have examined the Celtic material, and Professor J. K. Sørensen of Copenhagen, Dr Olof von Feilitzen and Professor M. Löfvenberg of Stockholm, have examined the Scandinavian material. They have read over the work in typescript and proof, and have corresponded with the author, and his successive General Editors over a number of years. Their mark is made discreetly; acknowledgement at every point would have cluttered the page, so this modest but sincere acknowledgement has to suffice.

Miss G. Wotton, Mrs E. Garbutt, Mrs M. Boulton and Mrs L. Bose, have typed the manuscript and drafts for press. Upon their shoulders has fallen a great drudgery, carefully and patiently borne. I am especially beholden to Mrs Garbutt and Miss Wotton, who had the task of working from my manuscript notebooks. Mr A. Rumble and Miss P. Khaliq helped to check the typescripts.

My present and former colleagues at University College London and elsewhere, Dr Audrey Meaney, Dr C. Luttrell, Dr John Morris, Professor Arthur Brown, Professor J. F. Kermode, Mr A. D. Mills, Mr G. I. Needham, Professor C. R. Quirk, Professor J. R. Sutherland and Mr D. M. Wilson, Mr L. Gue and Mr R. L. Gregory, have given me all kinds of help in ways too many to list.

Dr J. E. Robinson, of the Department of Geology, University College London, advised and corrected me on the geology of Cheshire.

I am grateful to Professor H. C. Darby and Professor W. Mead, past and present heads of the Department of Geography at University College London, and the present and former members of that department, especially Dr Hugh Prince, Mr R. Versey, Mr K. Wass and Miss Ann Oxenham.

The late Mr G. Hobson of Pilling Lane, the late Mr F. J. Stafford of Poulton-le-Fylde, the late Mrs Ada Anyon of Preesall, and the late Mr J. Cottam of Knott End, to my regret, did not live to see this book, which came too late to satisfy their hopes or their curiosity.

I acknowledge my debt to Harry and Margaret Dodgson, my parents, for their patience, faith, foresight, and other virtues.

I affirm my loving gratitude to my wife Joyce Dodgson for her long labour in transcribing documents, sorting slips and organising indexes; for her acceptance throughout her married life, of all those inconveniences that this book has entailed; and most of all for that love and charity necessary to the wives of scholars, which have enabled her to share me with *Cheshire* and have inspired her to work patiently and hopefully by my side as fifteen years have slipped away.

I am glad to see *The Place-Names of Cheshire* off my hands at last, but my gladness at the event is tempered by a deep regret that it comes too late for those many friends and colleagues who did not live to see it, whose criticism would have prevented pride, and whose congratulation would have been my reward.

JOHN McNEAL DODGSON

University College London
Monday before St Andrews Day, 1968

ADDENDA AND CORRIGENDA

Items marked 'D.O.' are ex inf. Mrs Dorothy Owen. Items marked 'B.D.' are ex inf. Professor Bruce Dickins. Various addenda and corrigenda suggested by these colleagues and Dr von Feilitzen, Professor Sørensen, Professor Jackson, Professor Richards, Professor Löfvenberg, Professor Cameron and Mr Joseph Crabtree, have been silently incorporated in the typescript and proofs of Part 1; notes which were too late for inclusion are given here.

p. 21, s.n. R. DEE. The first el. in the form *Pifirdwy* is Welsh *Pefr*, cf. Peover Eye 38 *infra* (B.D.)

p. 22, l. 4. Professor Richards observes that the Archæologia form *Tyngued-fen* a misprint for *Tynghedfen*.

p. 22, s.n. R. DUCKOW. Professor Jackson dismisses the derivation offered. The *g-* in *glassjo-* appears as [ʒ] in PrWelsh, fifth-century and onwards, so cannot have appeared as OE [k]. Professor Richards agrees that there is some difficulty in understanding why **Duboglassjo* should give *Douglas* and *Doucles*, but on the other hand observes that PrWelsh *g* > *ʒ* does appear as English *k* in the p.n. Pembroke for PrWelsh **Penbrog* > **Penbroʒ* > Welsh *Penfro*. This may appear to be a chronological anomaly (see LHEB 458), but it is nonetheless an observed phenomenon. Unless there is some special distinction between the phonetic values of final PrWelsh *-g* > *-ʒ* and medial PrWelsh *-g-* > *-ʒ-*, it appears possible that the r.n. *Duckow* might indeed be, like *Douglas*, anomalously derived from **duboglassjo*.

p. 26, s.n. R. GOWY. Professor Jackson objects to this explanation on the grounds that, he says, the suffixed form *without* the suffixed '*-r-* extension' does not exist in any Celtic language, e.g. Welsh gwyr, Breton goar, Irish fiar (< IE **u̯eiro-*, Walde-Pokorny; OE *wīr*). He also dismisses the derivation from a stem **gwy*, because, he says, this would have been PrWelsh **wę̄*, becoming **wui* by late-7th, but hardly **gwui* so early (LHEB 434 f., 334 f.). [Professor Jackson insists upon borrowing from PrWelsh into OE, but this r.n. is not recorded early in English, and the form Gowy could be a borrowing into ModE from ModWelsh. West Ch is never free from Welsh influence, as may be seen in many modern f.ns. in Broxton Hundred.] Professor Richards agrees that **gwy* does not appear in Welsh independently of *gŵyr-o*, but observes the common acceptance of Welsh *caer* 'fort' as an *-r* derivative of *cae* 'shut, enclose'.

p. 69, s.n. HAMMERPOOL WOOD. B.D. suggests that this p.n. be associated with Furnacepool 1 68, alluding to an ironworker's forge powered by water from the pool, cf. *hammer* NED sb.1. 7, and Sx 255, 331, 344, 452. He notes that hammerponds were common in the Sussex Weald, though none are recorded in the Sx volumes.

p. 70, l. 6 from foot, s.n. Hickershaw. B.D. observes that the first el. might be **íkorni** 'a squirrel', cf. Ickornshaw YW **6** 13.

p. 140, s.n. SPULEY BRIDGE. B.D. observes that the occurrence of ME *ricande* in this p.n. makes unnecessary the editorial emendation of *rykande* Sir Gawain 2337 to *rynkande*.

p. 231, s.n. LINNEY'S BRIDGE, B.D. thinks the final el. is (**ge)hæg** rather than **ēg**.

p. 232, s.n. PIGGINSHAW. B.D. suggests the surname *Piggin*.

p. 243, s.n. GOOD MANS HEY. B.D. thinks that this type of name may refer to a bit of waste-land enclosed and left to the Devil.

p. 280, s.n. BEAR HURST. D.O. reports the modern name *Bears Wood*.

p. 303, s.n. HACKING KNIFE. D.O. points out that this is the NW face of Werneth Low 1 304.

p. 307, s.n. HATTERSLEY. Professor Löfvenberg observes that if Hattersley were a ME formation, the first el. might be ME *hattere* 'a hatter, a maker of hats' (Reaney s.n. *Hatter*, from 1212; Fransson 115, from 1268).

p. 307, s.n. APPLE ST. Perhaps part of the salters' road over Werneth Low, 1 50. (D.O.)

p. 308, s.n. TAULDLEY. D. O. reports a local pronunciation ([tɔləri].

p. 312, s.n. GALLOWS CLOUGH. Local pronunciation [gælʌskluf]. (D.O.)

p. 315, s.n. MUDD. D.O. notes that Mudd is on a high ridge, so the explanation may be unsatisfactory.

p. 315, s.n. WARHILL. Local pronunciation (wɔrl]. (D.O.)

p. 319, s.n. HEY HEADS. Local pronunciation [(h)ei edz]. (D.O.)

p. 322, s.n. CROWDEN. The local pronunciation is [krɔdn]. (D.O.)

ABBREVIATIONS AND BIBLIOGRAPHY

ABBREVIATIONS printed in roman type refer to printed sources and those in italic to manuscript sources.

a.	*ante.*
Abbr	*Placitorum Abbrevatio* (RC), London 1811.
AC	*Ancient Charters* (PRSoc 10), 1888.
acc.	accusative.
AD	*Catalogue of Ancient Deeds* (PRO), London 1890 and in progress, referred to by vol. and p. or by document number.
AD	Ancient Deeds in PRO, referred to by document number.
Add	Additional MSS. in BrMus.
AddCh	Additional Charters in BrMus.
AddRoll	Additional Rolls in BrMus.
adj.	adjective.
Adl	*Muniments of Legh of Adlington*, NRA 0917.
adv.	adverb.
AFr	Anglo-French.
al.	*alias.*
Alexander	*The Wars of Alexander*, ed. W. W. Skeat (EETS 47), London 1866.
Amerc	Fines and Amercements in the courts of the City of Chester, City Record Office, Chester.
AN	Anglo-Norman.
AncPet	Ancient Petitions in PRO.
Anderson[1]	O. S. Anderson, *The English Hundred-Names*, Lund 1934; sometimes referred to as EHN[1].
Anderson[2]	O. S. Anderson, *The English Hundred-Names; The South-Western Counties*, Lund 1939; sometimes referred to as EHN[2].
Anderson[3]	O. S. Anderson, *The English Hundred-Names; The South-Eastern Counties*, Lund 1939; sometimes referred to as EHN[3].
Angl	*Anglia*; Anglian; The Anglian dialect of OE.
AnglBeib	*Anglia Beiblatt.*
ANInfl	R. E. Zachrisson, *Anglo-Norman Influence on English Place-Names*, Lund 1909.
AnnCamb	*Annales Cambriae*, ed. J. Williams ab Ithel, London 1860.
AntIt	*Itinerarium Antonini Augusti*, ed. G. Parthey and M. Pinder, Berlin 1848; and in Codrington.
AOMB	Augmentation Office Miscellaneous Books in PRO.
APhSc	*Acta Philologica Scandinavica.*
ArchCamb	*Archaeologia Cambrensis.*
Arl	*Warburton Deeds*, property of the Viscountess Ashbrook of Arley, NRA 0011.
Arl	Warburton Deeds, property of the Viscountess Ashbrook of Arley, in John Rylands Library Manchester; cf. ArlB
ArlB	Forms from *Arl* ex inf. Dr Barnes and quoted in Barnes[1].
art.	article.

ASC The Anglo-Saxon Chronicle(s); *Two of the Saxon Chronicles Parallel*, ed. J. Earle and C. Plummer, Oxford 1892–9.

AScand Anglo-Scandinavian.

ASCharters *Anglo-Saxon Charters*, ed. A. J. Robertson, Cambridge 1939.

ASE F. M. Stenton, *Anglo-Saxon England, v.* Stenton.

Assem The Minutes of the City Council or Assembly of the City of Chester (The Assembly Books), City Record Office, Chester.

Aston MSS. of Aston of Aston Hall in Runcorn (*AddCh* 40000, 49770–51532) in BrMus; cf. *Catalogue of Additions to the MSS. in the British Museum* 1900–1905, London 1907, 411 ff.

ASWills *Anglo-Saxon Wills*, ed. D. Whitelock, Cambridge 1930.

ASWrits *Anglo-Saxon Writs*, ed. F. E. Harmer, Manchester 1952.

Atlas *The Historical Atlas of Cheshire*, ed. D. Sylvester and G. Nulty (Cheshire Community Council, Local History Committee), Chester 1958.

Ave. Avenue.

Bach A. Bach, *Deutsche Namenkunde*, Heidelberg 1952–6.

Bainb T. Bainbridge, *Plan of the Township of Oxton...belonging to the Rt. Hon. Charles, Earl of Shrewsbury, drawn by Thos. Bainbridge*, 1795, among W. Fergusson Irvine's maps (see W.F.I.).

Bardsley C. W. Bardsley, *Dictionary of English and Welsh Surnames*, London 1901.

Bark *MSS. of E. E. Barker, Esq.*, NRA 0406.

Barnes[1] G. Barnes, *The Place-Names of Cheshire* (unpublished Ph.D. thesis, University of Sheffield), 1960; (Barnes[1]) after a source reference indicates a form identified in Barnes[1] with the place in question; the references MainwB and ArlB are taken from this work, generously placed at the Society's disposal.

Barnes[2] G. Barnes, 'Early English Settlement and Society in Cheshire from the Evidence of Place-Names', LCAS 71 (1961), 43–57.

BBCS *The Bulletin of the Board of Celtic Studies*, University of Wales, Cardiff.

BCS *Cartularium Saxonicum*, ed. W. G. de G. Birch, London 1885–93.

Bd Bedfordshire; with p. reference, PN BdHu.

Bede *Historia Ecclesiastica* in *Venerabilis Bædae Opera Historica*, ed. C. Plummer, Oxford 1896.

Bk Buckinghamshire; with p. reference, PN Bk.

Blun Blundell of Crosby MSS. in LRO.

BM *Index to Charters and Rolls in the Department of MSS., British Museum*, London 1900–12.

BMFacs *Facsimiles of Royal and other Charters in the British Museum*, London 1903.

BNF *Beiträge zur Namenforschung.*

BodlCh *Calendar of Charters and Rolls in the Bodleian Library*, ed. W. H. Turner and H. O. Coxe, Oxford 1878.

Bowman M. W. Bowman, *England in Ashton-under-Lyme*, Altrincham 1960.

BPR *The Register of Edward the Black Prince* (PRO), London 1930–3.

BRA Publications of The British Records Association.

Bras *Calendar of the Muniments of Brasenose College Oxford* (NRA), Vol. 10 (Handbridge), Vol. 16 (Middlewich).

Bret	Breton.
BridgL	*The Great Leet Book of the Borough of Bridgnorth, Salop*; forms ex inf. R. W. Gregory, Esq.
Brit	British.
Brk	Berkshire; cf. PN Brk.
BrMus	Documents preserved in the British Museum.
Brownbill	J. Brownbill, *West Kirby and Hilbre, A Parochial History*, Liverpool 1928; Appendix 1, Allen Mawer, *The Local Place-Names.*
BRS	Publication of the British Record Society.
Brunner	K. Brunner, *Altenglische Grammatik nach der Angelsächsischen Grammatik von Eduard Sievers*, Halle 1942.
Bry	W. Bryant, *Map of Cheshire*, London 1831.
BT	*An Anglo-Saxon Dictionary* (based on the collections of J. Bosworth) by T. N. Toller, Oxford 1898.
BTSuppl	*Supplement* to BT, by T. N. Toller, Oxford 1921.
Bülbring	K. D. Bülbring, *Altenglisches Elementarbuch*, Heidelberg 1902.
Bun	The Bunbury MSS. in West Suffolk Record Office, Bury St. Edmunds.
Burd	P. P. Burdett, *A Survey of the County Palatine of Chester*, London 1777.
Burne[1]	R. V. H. Burne, *Chester Cathedral* (SPCK), London 1958.
Burne[2]	R. V. H. Burne, *The Monks of Chester* (SPCK), London 1962.
BW	The Baker–Wilbraham MSS. in CRO.
c.	*circa.*
C	Cambridgeshire; with p. reference, PN C.
Camd	Publications of the Camden Society.
Camden	W. Camden, *Britannia*, London 1590; *Britain*, transl. Philemon Holland, London 1610.
CampbCh	Lord Fred. Campbell's charters in BrMus.
Campbell	A. Campbell, *Old English Grammar*, Oxford 1959.
Campbell Brunanburh	*The Battle of Brunanburh*, ed. A. Campbell, London 1938.
CartAnt	*The Cartae Antiquae Rolls* 1–10 (PRSoc 17), 1939.
CAS	*The Journal of the Chester Archaeological Society*; CASNS indicates the New Series.
Celt	Celtic.
cf.	compare.
CGH	*Corpus Genealogiarum Hiberniae*, Vol. 1, ed. M. A. O'Brien, Dublin 1962.
Ch	Calendar of Charter Rolls (PRO), London 1903–27.
Ch	Cheshire.
Chaloner	W. H. Chaloner, *The Social and Economic Development of Crewe 1780–1923* (University of Manchester Economic History Series 14), Manchester 1950.
Chamb	R. Stewart Brown, *The Accounts of the Chamberlains and Other Officers of the County of Chester* (LCRS 59), 1910.
Chamb[1]	*The Account of the Chamberlain of Chester for 1301 in PipeRolls.*
ChancP	*Calendar of Proceedings in Chancery in the reign of Queen Elizabeth*, London 1827–32; *Index of Chancery Proceedings* PRO L & I 7, 24, 30), London 1896.
ChancW	*Calendar of Chancery Warrants* (PRO), London 1927 and in progress.

ChAttorn	Palatinate of Chester, Warrants of Attorney Rolls, in PRO.
ChCal	Palatinate of Chester, Calendar Rolls, in PRO.
ChCert	Palatinate of Chester, Returns to Writs of Certiorari, in PRO.
ChEss	Palatinate of Chester, Essoin Rolls, in PRO.
Chest	J. Tait, *Chartulary of the Abbey of St. Werburgh, Chester*, Parts I and II (ChetNS 79, 82), 1920–3; a fourteenth-century MS., with some seventeenth-century additions.
Chet	Publications of the Chetham Society of Lancashire and Cheshire; ChetNS indicates New Series, ChetOS Original Series, Chet³ Third Series.
ChEx	Palatinate of Chester, Exchequer Appearance Rolls, in PRO.
ChF	*Calendar of Fines, Cos. Chester and Flint, removed from Chester to the Public Record Office in* 1854 (DKR 28, appendix 5, pp. 6 ff.), London 1867.
ChFine	Palatinate of Chester, Fines and Recoveries, in PRO.
ChFineR	Palatinate of Chester, Fines and Recoveries, Enrolments, in PRO.
ChFor	Palatinate of Chester, Forest Proceedings, in PRO.
ChGaol	Palatinate of Chester, Gaol Files, Writs, etc., in PRO.
ChMisc	Palatinate of Chester, Miscellanea, in PRO.
Chol	The Cholmondeley Deeds in CRO; *Chol* refers to an orig., Chol(Boyd) refers to Boyd's MS. calendar in CRO, and Chol refers to the CRO typescript calendar.
ChQW	Palatinate of Chester, Pleas of Quo Warranto, in PRO.
ChRR	*Calendar of the Chester Recognizance Rolls* (DKR 36 appendix 2, DKR 37 appendix 2, DKR 39 appendix 1), London 1875–9.
City	*Selected Rolls of Chester City Courts*, ed. A. Hopkins (Chet³ 2), 1950.
Cl	*Calendar of Close Rolls* (PRO), London 1900 and in progress.
Cl	Close Rolls in PRO.
Cleanness	*Early English Alliterative Poems* etc., ed. R. Morris (EETS 1) 2nd ed., 1869.
Cleasby-Vigf	R. Cleasby and G. Vigfusson, *An Icelandic–English Dictionary*, Oxford 1874.
Clif	Clifton of Lytham MSS. in LRO.
ClR	*Rotuli Litterarum Clausarum* (RC), London 1833–44.
CMidl	Central Midlands.
Co	Cornwall.
Codrington	T. Codrington, *Roman Roads in Britain* (SPCK) 2nd ed., London 1905, cf. AntIt.
Coin(s)	Spellings taken from the legends of coins; ex inf. Mr R. H. M. Dolley and Miss Elizabeth Pirie.
CoLegh	MSS. of C. L. S. Cornwall-Legh Esq., (Legh of High Legh), preserved in John Rylands Library Manchester, cf. CoLegh.
CoLegh	*MSS. of C. L. S. Cornwall-Legh Esq.*, NRA 0604.
Comb	*The Book of the Abbot of Combermere* 1289–1529, ed. J. Hall (LCRS 31), 1895; a cartulary dated c.1524.
Comm	Exchequer Special Commissions in PRO.
comp.	comparative.
ContGerm	Continental German(ic).
Corn	Cornish.
Corp	Deeds of the Corporation of Chester in the City Record Office, Chester.

CorpMisc	Miscellaneous uncalendared deeds seen in the City Record Office Chester.
Cott.	The Cottonian MSS. in BrMus; *Cott.* Faustina B viii ff. 124–6, has been given a short date e12(1479) but it is more exactly dated a.1130(1279) (1476) (1478–9) (17), being a copy of an exemplification of a confirmation of an inspeximus of a grant.
CottCh	Cotton Charters in BrMus.
Court	*Calendar of County Court, City Court and Eyre Rolls of Chester,* 1259–1297, ed. R. Stewart Brown, (ChetNS 84), 1925.
c.p.	Civil Parish.
CRC	*Rotuli Chartarum* (RC), London 1837.
Cre	*MSS. of the Marchioness of Crewe,* NRA 1299.
CRO	(Documents preserved in) Cheshire Record Office.
Cross	Cross of Shaw Hall MSS. in LRO.
Crown	Files of the Crownmote Court in the City Record Office, Chester.
Crump	W. B. Crump, 'Saltways from the Cheshire Wiches', LCAS 54 (1940), 84–142.
CRV	*Calendar of Chancery Rolls, Various,* i, 1277–1326 (PRO), London 1912.
Ct	Court Rolls in PRO.
CtAugm	Records of the Court of Augmentations in PRO.
CtRequests	Records of the Court of Requests in PRO.
Cu	Cumberland; with page reference, PN Cu.
Cuer	The Cuerdon Hall MSS. in LRO.
Cumb	Cumbria(n).
Cur	Curia Regis Rolls (PRO), London 1923 and in progress.
CurR	*Rotuli Curiae Regis* (RC), London 1835.
d.	died.
D	Devon; with page reference, PN D.
DaGP	*Danmarks Gamle Personnavne,* ed. G. Knudsen and M. Kristensen, Copenhagen 1936 ff.
Dan	Danish.
Dane	*Documents Illustrative of the History of the Danelaw,* ed. F. M. Stenton, British Academy, London 1920.
DaSN	*Danmarks Stednavne,* Stednavneudvalget, Copenhagen 1922 ff.
dat.	dative.
Dav	MSS. in the Bromley Davenport Collection, in John Rylands Library Manchester.
DB	Domesday Book; ed. and transl. of Ch section in J. Tait, *The Domesday Survey of Cheshire* (ChetNS 75), 1916; cf. Tait.
DB	The Exchequer copy of Domesday Book in PRO.
Db	Derbyshire; with page reference, PN Db.
DbA	*Journal of the Derbyshire Archaeological and Natural History Society.*
decl.	declension.
Deed	Form taken from an orig. deed.
def.	definite.
Dep	Exchequer Special (Commissions and) Depositions in PRO.
DepEx	Depositions and Examinations in the City Courts in the City Record Office, Chester.
DEPN	E. Ekwall, *The Concise Oxford Dictionary of English Place-Names,* 4th ed., Oxford 1960.
dial.	dialect(al).

Dieul	*Chartulary of Dieulacres Abbey*, ed. G. Wrottesley (SaltNS 9), 1906; a seventeenth-century MS.
Din	Dines Moss Book, a MS. dated 1611, in Birkenhead Public Library, transcribed for Allen Mawer in 1939 by the late Walter Smith, Esq., of Macclesfield.
Dinnseanchas	*Dinnseanchas* (An Cumann Logainmneacha, Baile Atha Cliath: Irish Place-Name Society, Dublin), Vol. 1 (1964) and proceeding.
DKR	*Reports of the Deputy Keeper of the Public Records.*
DL	Records of the Duchy of Lancaster in PRO.
Do	Dorset; with page reference, PN Do.
Dow	The Downes MSS. in the possession of Dr B. K. Blount; *Downes MSS.*, ed. J. McN. Dodgson, (NRA), London 1958.
Du	co. Durham; with page reference, PN NbDu.
Du	Dutch.
Dugd	W. Dugdale, *Monasticon Anglicanum*, London 1817–30.
Duignan	W. H. Duignan, *Notes on Staffordshire Place-Names*, London 1902.
DuLa	*Calendar of Royal and other Charters of the Duchy of Lancaster* (DKR 31, 35, 36), London 1869–74.
DuLa	Duchy of Lancaster Deeds in PRO.
DuLaMinAcct	Duchy of Lancaster, Ministers' Accounts, in PRO.
e	early.
E	East(ern).
E	English.
E1, E2 etc.	Regnal date, t.Edward I, t.Edward II etc.; E1 1272–1307, E2 1307–27, E3 1327–77, E4 1461–83, E5 1483, E6 1547–53.
EAngl	East Anglia(n).
Earw	J. P. Earwaker, *East Cheshire*, London 1877.
EatonB	*Calendar of Charters at Eaton Hall*, ed. W. Beamont, 1872; forms quoted in Barnes[1].
ECy	East Country.
ed.	edition; edited by.
EDD	J. Wright, *The English Dialect Dictionary*, Oxford 1898–1905.
EDG	J. Wright, *English Dialect Grammar*, Oxford 1905.
EENS	*Early English and Norse Studies, Presented to Hugh Smith in honour of his Sixtieth Birthday*, ed. A. Brown and P. G. Foote, London 1963.
EETS	Publications of the Early English Text Society.
EFris	East Frisia(n).
e.g.	*exempli gratia.*
EHN	*v.* Anderson.
EHR	*English Historical Review.*
el.	(place-name) element.
Eliz	Regnal date, t.Elizabeth I, 1558–1603.
eME	Early Middle English.
EMidl	East Midlands.
eModE	Early Modern English.
EnclA	Unprinted Enclosure Awards.
E & P	*Two of the Saxon Chronicles Parallel, v.* ASC.
EPN	A. H. Smith, *English Place-Names Elements*, Parts i and ii (EPNS 25, 26), Cambridge 1956
EPNS	Publications of the English Place-Name Society.

ERY	The East Riding of Yorkshire; with page reference, PN ERY.
ES	*Englische Studien.*
E & S	*Essays and Studies by Members of the English Association.*
ESax	East Saxon.
esp.	especially.
Ess	Essex; with a page reference, PN Ess.
etc.	*et cetera*; and so forth; and the like.
et freq	*et frequenter*; and frequently (thereafter).
et seq	*et sequenter*; and subsequently.
Eyre	The Palatinate of Chester, Eyre Rolls of the Justice of Chester, in PRO.
Eyton	R. W. Eyton, *Antiquities of Shropshire*, London 1854–60.
f., ff.	folio(s).
FA	*Feudal Aids* (PRO), London 1899–1920.
facs.	facsimile.
Facs	G. Barraclough, *Facsimiles of Early Cheshire Charters*, Oxford for LCRS 1957.
Fees	*The Book of Fees* (PRO), London 1920–31.
Feilitzen	O. von Feilitzen, *The Pre-Conquest Personal-Names of Domesday Book*, Uppsala 1937.
Feist	S. Feist, *Etymologisches Wörterbuch der Gotischen Sprache*, Halle 1921–3.
Fellows Jensen	Gillian Fellows Jensen, *Scandinavian Personal-Names in Lincolnshire and Yorkshire*, Copenhagen 1968.
fem.	feminine.
ff.	folios; and thereafter; and the pages following.
Fiennes	*The Journeys of Celia Fiennes*, ed. C. Morris, London 1949.
Fine	*Calendar of Fine Rolls* (PRO), London 1911 and in progress.
FineR	*Excerpta e rotulis finium* (RC), London 1836.
Fitt	The Fitton Charters among the De Trafford MSS. in LRO.
Fl, Flints	Flintshire.
Fm	Farm.
f.n., f.ns.	field-name(s).
foll.	the following place-name.
For	Forest Proceedings in PRO.
Forssner	T. Forssner, *Continental-Germanic Personal-Names in England*, Uppsala 1916.
Förstemann	E. Förstemann, *Altdeutsches Namenbuch: Personennamen* (PN), *Ortsnamen* (ON), 3rd ed. by H. Jellinghaus, Bonn 1913–16.
FörsterKW	M. Förster, *Keltisches Wortgut im Englischen*, Halle 1921.
FörsterTh	M. Förster, *Der Flussname Themse und seine Sippe*, München 1941.
Fr	French.
France	*Calendar of Documents preserved in France* (RS), London 1899.
Fransson	C. Fransson, *Middle English Surnames of Occupation*, Lund 1936.
freq	frequent(ly), *frequenter*.
Fris	Frisian.
FW	Florence of Worcester; *Florentii Wigorniensis monachi Chronicon ex Chronicis* (MHB), London 1848–9.
G	German.
Gael	Gaelic.
Gaul	Gaulish.
gen.	genitive.

Germ	Germanic.
Gerv	Gervase of Canterbury; *Gervasius Cantuarensis, Mappa Mundi* (RS), London 1867–9.
Gir	Giraldus Cambrensis; *Giraldi Cambrensis Opera* (RS), London 1861–91.
Gl	Gloucestershire; with p. reference, PN Gl.
Goid	Goidelic.
Goth	Gothic.
Gough	*Facsimile of the Ancient Map of Great Britain in the Bodleian Library Oxford*, A.D. 1325–50 (O.S.), 1935.
Gr	Greek.
Greenwood	G. Greenwood, *Map of the County Palatine of Chester*, London 1819.
Gt.	Great.
GWPN	*A Gazetteer of Welsh Place-Names*, ed. E. Davies (Board of Celtic Studies), Cardiff 1957.
H1, H2 etc.	Regnal date, t.Henry I, t.Henry II etc.; H1 1100–35, H2 1154–89, H3 1216–72, H4 1399–1413, H5 1413–22, H6 1422–71, H7 1485–1509, H8 1509–47.
Ha	Hampshire; Mr J. E. B. Gover has permitted the consultation of his unpublished typescript on the place-names of Hampshire.
Hanshall[1]	J. H. Hanshall, *History of the County Palatine of Chester*, Chester 1817.
Hanshall[2]	J. H. Hanshall, *The Stranger in Chester*, Chester 1816.
Harl.	Harleian MSS. in BrMus.
HarlCh	Harleian Charters in BrMus.
Harrison	W. Harrison, *Description of Britain* in R. Holinshed, *The Chronicles of England*, London 1577, 1586.
H.A.T.	Spellings and information supplied by H. A. Trippier, Esq., of Poynton.
He	Herefordshire; with p. reference, PN He.
Hem	J. Hemingway, *History of the City of Chester*, Chester 1831.
Hesk	The Hesketh Muniments in LRO.
Hewitt	H. J. Hewitt, *Mediaeval Cheshire* (ChetNS 88), 1929.
Higden	Ranulph Higden's *Polychronicon* (RS), London 1865–86; cf. Trev, Higden(Anon).
Higden(Anon)	The anonymous translation (fifteenth century) of Higden's *Polychronicon*, from Harl.2261, published in Higden.
HMC	(Report of) the Historical Manuscripts Commission.
Ho	House.
Hogan	E. Hogan, *Onomasticon Goidelicum locorum et tribium Hiberniae et Scotiae*, Dublin 1910.
Holder	A. Holder, *Alt-Celtischer Sprachschatz*, Leipzig 1891–1913.
Hosp	*The Knights Hospitallers in England*, ed. L. B. Larking, (Camd 65) 1857.
HospCG	*Cartulaire général de l'ordre des hospitaliers de S. Jean de Jérusalem* 1100–1310, ed. J. D. le Roulx, Paris 1894–1906.
Hrt	Hertfordshire; with p. reference, PN Hrt.
Hu	Huntingdonshire; with p. reference, PN BdHu.
ib	*ibidem.*
Icel	Icelandic.
i.e.	*id est.*

IE	Indo-European.
Index	*A Cheshire Index* (County Health Dept., Chester), 1st ed., 1953, 2nd ed., 1955.
Indict	Palatinate of Chester, Indictment Rolls, in PRO.
inf.	infinitive.
Ingimund	F. T. Wainwright, 'Ingimund's Invasion', EHR 63 (1948), 145–69.
InqAqd	*Calendarium Inquisitionum ad quod damnum* (RC), London 1803; Inquisitions ad quod damnum (PRO, L & I 17, 22), London 1904, 1906.
inspex	An 'inspeximus'.
Ipm	*Calendar of Inquisitions Post Mortem* (PRO), London 1906 and in progress.
Ipm	Inquisitions Post Mortem in PRO.
IpmR	*Calendarium Inquisitionum post mortem sive Escaetorum* (*RC*), London 1802–28.
IPN	*Introduction to the Survey of English Place-Names* (EPNS I, i), ed. A. Mawer and F. M. Stenton, Cambridge 1924.
Ir	Irish.
Jas 1	Regnal date, t.James I, 1603–25.
J.C.J.	Spellings and information supplied by J. C. Jones, Esq., of Congleton.
J.E.A.	Spellings and information supplied by J. E. Allison, Esq., of Prenton.
JEGPh	*Journal of English and Germanic Philology*.
John	Regnal date, t.John, 1199–1216.
Jordan	R. Jordan, *Handbuch der Mittelenglischen Grammatik*, Heidelberg 1934.
Joyce	P. W. Joyce, *Irish Names of Places*, I, London and Dublin 1869, 1873; II, Dublin 1871, London and Dublin 1875; III, Dublin 1913.
JRC	R. Fawtier, H. Tyson, H. Taylor, *Hand-list of Charters, Deeds, etc....in the possession of the John Rylands Library*, John Rylands Library, Manchester 1925–37.
JRC	Charters etc., preserved in the John Rylands Library, Manchester.
JRL	*Bulletin of the John Rylands Library, Manchester*; JRL 32 (1950) 229–300 contains F. Taylor, 'Handlist of the Legh of Booths Charters in the John Rylands Library'.
K	Kent; with p. reference, PN K.
Karlström	S. Karlström, *Old English Compound Place-Names in -ing*, Uppsala 1927.
KCD	J. M. Kemble, *Codex Diplomaticus Ævi Saxonici*, London 1839–48.
Kluge	F. Kluge, *Nominale Stammbildungslehre der Altgermanischen Dialekte*, 3rd ed. by L. Sutterlin and E. Ochs, Halle 1926.
KPN	J. K. Wallenberg, *Kentish Place-Names*, Uppsala 1931.
Kt	Kentish.
l	late; in dates, with a number for the century, indicates the last quarter, e.g. l13 is 1275–1300.
L	Lincolnshire.
La	Lancashire; with p. reference, PN La.
La	Lane.

c

LaCh   *Lancashire Pipe Rolls; also Early Lancashire Charters*, ed. W.
              Farrer, Liverpool 1902.
Lacy   *Two Compoti of the Lancashire and Cheshire manors of Henry de
              Lacy, earl of Lincoln, 24 and 33 Edward I*, ed. P. A. Lyons
              (ChetOS 112), 1884.
Lat   Latin.
Lawton   *Map of the Birkenhead Estate...belonging to R. Price Esq.,
              January 1824, Surveyed May 1823, by William Lawton;*
              among the W.F.I. maps.
LCAS   *Transactions of the Lancashire and Cheshire Antiquarian Society.*
LCHS   *Proceedings and Transactions of the Historic Society of Lan-
              cashire and Cheshire.*
LCRS   Publications of the Record Society of Lancashire and Cheshire.
LCWills   *Lancashire and Cheshire Wills and Inventories at Chester*,
              ed. J. P. Earwaker and J. P. Rylands (ChetNS 3, 28, 37),
              1884–97.
Lei   Leicestershire.
Leland   *The Itinerary of John Leland*, ed. L. Toulmin Smith, London
              1906. Date 1536–9, but for economy c. 1536.
Leyc   P. Leycester, *Historical Antiquities*, London 1673.
LG   Low German.
L & I   *Lists & Indexes* (PRO).
Lib   *Calendar of Liberate Rolls* (PRO), London 1917 and in progress.
Life   *The Life of St. Werburge of Chester, translated into English by
              Henry Bradshawe*, ed. E. Hawkins (ChetOS 15), 1848, and
              C. Horstmann (EETS 88), 1887.
Lind   E. H. Lind, *Norsk-Isländska Dopnamn och Fingerade Namn*,
              Uppsala 1905–15; *Supplement*, Oslo 1931.
LindB   E. H. Lind, *Norsk-Isländska Personbinamn*, Uppsala 1920–1.
Lindkvist   H. Lindkvist, *Middle English Place-Names of Scandinavian
              Origin*, Uppsala 1912.
lit.   literally.
LLat   Late Latin.
Lloyd   J. E. Lloyd, *A History of Wales*, 2nd ed., London 1912.
LMS   *London Medieval Studies.*
Ln   London.
Löfvenberg   M. T. Löfvenberg, *Studies on Middle English Local Surnames*,
              Lund 1942.
Longnon   A. Longnon, *Les Noms de Lieu de la France*, Paris 1920–9.
LRMB   Land Revenue Office Miscellaneous Books in PRO.
LRO   (Documents preserved in) the Lancashire Record Office.
LRO   Documents preserved in Lancashire Record Office in various
              miscellaneous or artificial collections.
LSE   *Leeds Studies in English and Kindred Languages.*
Lt.   Little.
Luc   *Liber Luciani de Laude Cestrie*, ed. M. V. Taylor (LCRS 64),
              1912.
Luick   K. Luick, *Historische Grammatik der Englischen Sprache*,
              Leipzig 1914–40.
Lundgren-Brate M. F. Lundgren and E. Brate, *Personnamn från Medeltiden*,
              Stockholm 1892–3.
Lysons   D. and S. Lysons, *Magna Britannia*, London 1816.
m.   membrane.

m	In dates, with a number for the century, 'mid-century', e.g. m13 is 1225–75.
MainwB	MSS. of Mainwaring of Peover in John Rylands Library Manchester; forms quoted in Barnes[1] from J. H. Jeayes, *Catalogue of the Charters, Rolls, Letters*, [etc.] *at Peover Hall, belonging to...the family of Mainwaring* (John Rylands Library Manchester), unpublished; and R. Fawtier, *Handlist of the Mainwaring and Jodrell MSS. at present in the custody of the John Rylands Library*, John Rylands Library, Manchester 1923.
Map	Various printed maps.
Map	Unprinted, unpublished maps in various collections.
Map(Matth.Paris)	*Four Maps of Great Britain designed by Matthew Paris c.* 1250, BrMus, London 1928.
Margary	I. D. Margary, *Roman Roads in Britain*, Vol. II, London 1957.
masc.	masculine.
Mass	The Massey Charters among the De Trafford MSS. in LRO.
McClure	E. McClure, *British Place-Names in their Historical Setting*, London 1910.
MCorn	Middle Cornish.
Mdf	H. Middendorf, *Altenglisches Flurnamenbuch*, Halle 1902.
MDu	Middle Dutch.
ME	Middle English.
MED	*Middle English Dictionary*, ed. H. Kurath, University of Michigan, Ann Arbor, in progress.
MedAev	*Medium Aevum.*
MedArch	*Medieval Archaeology.*
MedLat	Medieval Latin.
MedWelsh	Medieval Welsh.
Merc	Mercian dialect of OE.
Mere	*The MSS. of Lt.-Col. R. P. Langford-Brooke of Mere Old Hall*, NRA 0131.
MGH	*Monumenta Germaniae Historica*, Hanover 1826–1913.
MHB	*Monumenta Historica Britannica*, London 1848.
MHG	Middle High German.
MidCh	*A Middlewich Chartulary*, ed. J. Varley (ChetNS 105, 108), 1941–4; an edition of a seventeenth-century MS., William Vernon of Shakerley's MS. book M among the Vernon–Shakerley MSS. in the custody of Sir Arthur Bryant.
Midl	Midland(s).
MinAcct	Ministers' Accounts in PRO.
MIr	Middle Irish.
Misc	*Calendar of Inquisitions Miscellaneous* (PRO), in progress.
MLG	Middle Low German.
MLR	*Modern Language Review.*
MNorw	Middle Norwegian.
ModE	Modern English.
ModEdial.	Modern English dialect(al).
ModWelsh	Modern Welsh.
mon.	Moneyer.
Mon	Monmouthshire.
Mont	The De Macclesfield Cartulary, known also as the Montalt.

	Cartulary, MS.*Cott.*Cleopatra D vi in BrMus; a fifteenth-century MS., c.1414–37.
Morris	R. H. Morris, *Chester in the Plantagenet and Tudor Reigns*, Chester 1894.
Morris-Jones	J. Morris-Jones, *A Welsh Grammar*, Oxford 1913.
Most	The Mostyn Papers, Library of the University College of North Wales, Bangor; forms collected by Professor G. Melville Richards.
MP	Matthew Paris, *Chronica Majora* (RS), London 1872–83.
MRA	*The Great Register of Lichfield Cathedral known as Magnum Registrum Album*, ed. H. E. Savage (SaltNS 25), 1924; a cartulary made 1317–28; referred to by entry numbers.
MS., MSS.	Manuscript(s).
MScots	Middle Scots.
MSwed	Middle Swedish.
MWelsh	Middle Welsh.
Mx	Middlesex; with p. reference, PN Mx.
n.	note; e.g. 'n.7' for 'note 7', '7n.' for 'note on p.7'.
(n)	New element, not in EPN.
N	North(ern).
Names	*Names* (Journal of the American Name Society).
Nat.Grid	O.S. National Grid references; the Grid References in this work consist of the 1″ OS 7th ed. sheet number followed by the four- or six-figure co-ordinates.
Nb	Northumberland; with p. reference, PN NbDu.
NCPN	B. G. Charles, *Non-Celtic Place-Names in Wales* (LMS Monograph 1), London 1938.
NCy	North Country.
n.d.	undated.
NE	North-East(ern).
NED	*A New Dictionary* (*Oxford English Dictionary* ed.), Oxford 1933.
NElv	O. Rygh, *Norsk Elvenavne*, Kristiania 1904.
NElvH	P. Hovda, *Norske Elvenamn*, Oslo and Bergen 1966.
Nennius	*Historia Brittonum cum additamentis Nennii* (MGH Auct. Antiq. 13, 111–222), Hanover 1898.
neut.	neuter.
NewC	The Newton Cartulary, *Add* 42134A in BrMus; date 1525.
Nf	Norfolk.
NFr	Northern French.
NG	O. Rygh, *Norske Gaardnavne*, Kristiania 1889–1936.
NoB	*Namn och Bygd.*
nom.	nominative.
Norw	Norwegian.
NotCestr	F. Gastrell, *Notitia Cestriensis, or Historical Notices of the Diocese of Chester*, Vol. 1, *Cheshire*, ed. F. R. Raines (ChetOS 8), 1845; the MS. dates from 1714–25.
NP	E. Björkman, *Nordische Personennamn in England*, Halle 1910.
NQ	*Notes and Queries.*
nr.	near.
NRA	The National Register of Archives; *Report of the National Register of Archives*, in progress.
NRY	The North Riding of Yorkshire; with p. reference, PN NRY.
NS	New Series.

Nt	Nottinghamshire; with p. reference, PN Nt.
Nth	Northamptonshire; with p. reference, PN Nth.
num.	numeral.
NW	North-West(ern).
NWM	F. T. Wainwright, 'North-West Mercia, AD 871–924', LCHS 94 (1942), 3–55.
NWMidl	North-West Midland(s).
O	Oxfordshire; with p. reference, PN O.
obl.	oblique case.
ObIR	*Rotuli de Oblatis* (RC), London 1835.
OBret	Old Breton.
OBrit	Old British.
OCelt	Old Celtic.
OCFr	Old Central French.
OCorn	Old Cornish.
ODan	Old Danish.
OE	Old English.
OEBede	*The Old English Version of Bede's Ecclesiastical History*, ed. T. Miller (EETS 95–6, 110–11) 1890–8.
OEDials	E. Ekwall, *Contributions to the Study of Old English Dialects*, Lund 1917.
OEScand	Old East Scandinavian.
OET	*Oldest English Texts*, ed. H. Sweet (EETS 83) 1885.
OFr	Old French.
OFrank	Old Frankish.
OFris	Old Frisian.
OG	Old German.
Ogilby	J. Ogilby, *Itinerarium Angliae*, London 1675.
OHG	Old High German.
OIcel	Old Icelandic.
OIr	Old Irish.
OLG	Old Low German.
ON	Old Norse.
ONb	Old Northumbrian.
ONFr	Old Northern French.
ONorw	Old Norwegian.
Ord	Ordericus Vitalis, *Historia Ecclesiastica*, ed. A. le Prévost (Société de l'Histoire de France), Paris 1838–55.
orig.	original document; originally.
Orig	*Originalia Rolls* (RC), London 1805–10.
Orm[1]	G. Ormerod, *History of Cheshire*, London 1819.
Orm[2]	G. Ormerod, *History of Cheshire*, ed. T. Helsby, London 1882.
O.S.	The Ordnance Survey.
OS	Original Series in a run of publications or periodicals.
OS	Ordnance Survey Maps; 1842 OS indicates the Original 1″ OS Map, 1″ OS indicates the 7th ed. OS 1″ Map, and 6″ OS indicates the 1910–14 eds. OS 6″ Map.
OSax	Old Saxon.
OScand	Old Scandinavian.
OSwed	Old Swedish.
Outl	Palatinate of Chester, Outlawry Rolls, in PRO.
OWelsh	Old Welsh.
OWScand	Old West Scandinavian.

p.	page.
p.	*post.*
(p)	Place-name used as a pers.n. or surname.
P	*Pipe Rolls* (PRSoc), in progress; M. H. Mills and R. Stewart Brown, *Cheshire in the Pipe Rolls* 1158–1301 (LCRS 92), 1938.
pa.	past.
Pal	*Palatinate Records* (PRO, L & I 40), London 1914.
Pap	*Calendar of Papal Registers* (PRO), London 1894–1961.
par.	parish.
para.	paragraph.
ParlSurv	Parliamentary Surveys in PRO.
par.n.	parish-name.
Par Reg	Parish Registers (various publications).
Par Reg	Parish Registers in various repositories.
part.	participle.
Pat	*Calendar of Patent Rolls* (PRO), London 1901 and in progress.
PatR	*Rotuli Litterarum Patentium* (RC), London 1835.
P(c)	Form taken from the Chancellor's copy of the Pipe Roll published in PipeRolls.
Peov	The Mainwaring of Peover MSS. listed at NRA.
pers.n., pers.ns.	personal-name(s).
p.h.	public house.
PipeRolls	M. H. Mills and R. Stewart Brown, *Cheshire in the Pipe Rolls* 1158–1301 (LCRS 92), 1938: cf. Chamb[1], P, P(c),
pl.	plural.
Plea	*Deeds, Inquisitions, etc., enrolled on the Plea Rolls of the County of Chester* (DKR 26–30), London 1865–9.
Plea	Palatinate of Chester, Plea Rolls, in PRO.
p.n., p.ns.	place-name(s).
PN BdHu	A. Mawer, F. M. Stenton, *The Place-Names of Bedfordshire and Huntingdonshire* (EPNS 3), Cambridge 1926.
PN Bk	A. Mawer, F. M. Stenton, *The Place-Names of Buckinghamshire* (EPNS 2), Cambridge 1925; occasionally this work has been referred to as PN Bu.
PN Brk	W. W. Skeat, *The Place-Names of Berkshire*, Oxford 1911; F. M. Stenton, *The Place-Names of Berkshire*, Reading 1911; M. Gelling, *The Place-Names of Berkshire* (EPNS), in preparation.
PN Bu	*v.* PN Bk.
PN C	P. H. Reaney, *The Place-Names of Cambridgeshire and The Isle of Ely* (EPNS 19), Cambridge 1943.
PN Cu	A. M. Armstrong, A. Mawer, F. M. Stenton, B. Dickins, *The Place-Names of Cumberland* (EPNS 20–2), Cambridge 1950–2.
PN D	J. E. B. Gover, A. Mawer, F. M. Stenton, *The Place-Names of Devon* (EPNS 8, 9), Cambridge 1931–2.
PN Db	K. Cameron, *The Place-Names of Derbyshire* (EPNS 27–9), Cambridge 1959.
PN Do	A. Fägersten, *The Place-Names of Dorset*, Uppsala 1933.
PN ERY	A. H. Smith, *The Place-Names of the East Riding of Yorkshire & York* (EPNS 14), Cambridge 1937.
PN Ess	P. H. Reaney, *The Place-Names of Essex* (EPNS 12), Cambridge 1935.

PN Gl   A. H. Smith, *The Place-Names of Gloucestershire* (EPNS 38–41) Cambridge 1964–5.
PN He   A. T. Bannister, *The Place-Names of Herefordshire*, Cambridge 1916.
PN Hrt   J. E. B. Gover, A. Mawer, F. M. Stenton, *The Place-Names of Hertfordshire* (EPNS 15), Cambridge 1938.
PN-ing[1]   E. Ekwall, *English Place-Names in -ing*, Lund 1923.
PN-ing[2]   E. Ekwall, *English Place-Names in -ing*, 2nd ed., Lund 1962.
PN K   J. K. Wallenberg, *The Place-Names of Kent*, Uppsala 1934.
PN La   E. Ekwall, *The Place-Names of Lancashire*, Manchester 1924.
PN Mx   J. E. B. Gover, A. Mawer, F. M. Stenton, S. J. Madge, *The Place-Names of Middlesex* (EPNS 18), Cambridge 1942.
PN NbDu   A. Mawer, *The Place-Names of Northumberland and Durham*, Cambridge 1920.
PN NRY   A. H. Smith, *The Place-Names of the North Riding of Yorkshire* (EPNS 5), Cambridge 1928.
PN Nt   J. E. B. Gover, A. Mawer, F. M. Stenton, *The Place-Names of Nottinghamshire* (EPNS 17), Cambridge 1940.
PN Nth   J. E. B. Gover, A. Mawer, F. M. Stenton, *The Place-Names of Northamptonshire* (EPNS 10), Cambridge 1933.
PN O   M. Gelling, *The Place-Names of Oxfordshire* (EPNS 23, 24), Cambridge 1953–4.
PN Sa   E. W. Bowcock, *The Place-Names of Shropshire*, Shrewsbury 1923.
PN Sf   W. W. Skeat, *The Place-Names of Suffolk*, Cambridge 1913.
PN Sr   J. E. B. Gover, A. Mawer, F. M. Stenton, A. Bonner, *The Place-Names of Surrey* (EPNS 11), Cambridge 1934.
PN Sx   A. Mawer, F. M. Stenton, J. E. B. Gover, *The Place-Names of Sussex* (EPNS 6, 7), Cambridge 1929–30.
PN W   J. E. B. Gover, A. Mawer, F. M. Stenton, *The Place-Names of Wiltshire* (EPNS 16), Cambridge 1939.
PN Wa   J. E. B. Gover, A. Mawer, F. M. Stenton, F. T. S. Houghton, *The Place-Names of Warwickshire* (EPNS 13), Cambridge 1936.
PN We   A. H. Smith, *The Place-Names of Westmorland* (EPNS 42, 43), Cambridge 1967.
PN Wirral   W. Fergusson Irvine, 'Place-Names in the Hundred of Wirral', LCHS 43–4 (1891–2), 279–304.
PN Wo   A. Mawer, F. M. Stenton, F. T. S. Houghton, *The Place-Names of Worcestershire* (EPNS 4), Cambridge 1927.
PN WRY   A. H. Smith, *The Place-Names of the West Riding of Yorkshire*, Parts 1–8 (EPNS 30–7), Cambridge 1961–3; referred to by part-number and p., e.g. WRY 2 10 indicates p. 10 of part 2, i.e. EPNS 31 p. 10.
PN Wt   H. Kökeritz, *The Place-Names of the Isle of Wight*, Uppsala 1940.
Polyolbion   M. Drayton, *Poly-Olbion*, London 1612.
Port   Rolls of Pleas of the Portmote Court, in the City Record Office, Chester.
Potter   S. Potter, 'Cheshire Place-Names', LCHS 106 (1955), 1–23.
Pr   Primitive.
PrCelt   Primitive Celtic.

prec.   the preceding place-name.
PremIt   B. Dickins, 'Premonstratensian Itineraries from a Titchfield
                       Abbey MS. at Welbeck', *Proceedings of The Leeds Philo-
                       sophical, Lit. & Hist. Society* 4 (1938), 349–61.
prep.   preposition.
Prep   A. H. Smith, *The Preparation of County Place-Names Surveys*
                       (EPNS), London 1953.
pres.   present.
PrGerm   Primitive Germanic.
PRO   (Record preserved in or published by) the Public Record Office,
                       London.
Problems.   A. Mawer, *Problems of Place-Name Study*, Cambridge 1929.
PrOE   Primitive Old English.
PrScand   Primitive Scandinavian.
PRSoc   The Pipe Roll Society.
PrWelsh   Primitive Welsh.
Ptolemy   *Claudii Ptolemæi Geographia*, ed. G. Parthey and M. Pinder,
                       Berlin 1860, ed. C. Mullerus, Paris 1883; cf. I. A. Richmond
                       and O. G. S. Crawford, 'The British Section of the Ravenna
                       Cosmography' under RavGeog *infra*.
QS   Quarter Sessions Files in City Record Office, Chester.
q.v.   *quod vide*.
R   Rutland.
R.   River.
R1, R2 etc.   Regnal date, t.Richard I, t.Richard II etc.; R1 1189–99,
                       R2 1377–99, R3 1483–5.
RavGeog   *Ravennatis Anonymi Cosmographia*, ed. G. Parthey and M.
                       Pinder, Berlin 1860; I. A. Richmond and O. G. S. Crawford,
                       'The British Section of the Ravenna Cosmography',
                       Archaeologia 93, 1–50.
RBE   *The Red Book of the Exchequer* (RS), London 1896.
RBES   R. G. Collingwood and J. N. L. Myres, *Roman Britain and the
                       English Settlements*, (Oxford History of England I), Oxford
                       1937.
RC   Publications of the Record Commission, London.
Rd.   Road.
Reaney   P. H. Reaney, *A Dictionary of British Surnames*, London 1958.
Redin   M. Redin, *Studies on Uncompounded Personal Names in Old
                       English*, Uppsala 1915.
Renaud   F. Renaud, 'Contributions to a History of the Ancient Parish
                       of Prestbury' (ChetOS 97), 1876.
Rental   Rentals in PRO.
RES   *Review of English Studies*.
RH   *Rotuli Hundredorum* (RC), London 1812–18.
RHistS   The Royal Historical Society.
Rich   *MSS. belonging to R. Richards Esq.*, NRA 1085.
Ritter   C. Ritter, *Vermischte Beiträge zur Englischen Sprachgeschichte,
                       Etymologie, Ortsnamenkunde, Lautlehre*, Halle 1922.
r.n., r.ns.   river-name(s).
RN   E. Ekwall, *English River-Names*, Oxford 1928.
RS   Rolls Series.
R.S.B.   Information transmitted to Allen Mawer by R. Stewart Brown,
                       Esq.

Runc	*The Foundation Charter of Runcorn Priory*, ed. J. Tait (ChetOS 100), 1939.
RyghGP	O. Rygh, *Gamle Personnavne i Norske Stedsnavne*, Kristiania 1901.
S	South(ern).
s.a.	*sub anno.*
Sa	Shropshire; with p. reference PN Sa.
Sagabook	*The Saga Book of the Viking Society.*
Salt	*Collections for a History of Staffordshire*, The William Salt Archaeological Society; SaltNS indicates the New Series in this publication.
Sandred	K. I. Sandred, *English Place-Names in -stead*, Uppsala 1963.
Sax	Saxon.
Saxton	C. Saxton, *Atlas of England and Wales*, London 1576.
sb.	substantive.
Sc	Scotland, Scottish.
Scand	Scandinavia(n).
ScandsCelts	E. Ekwall, *Scandinavians and Celts in the North-West of England*, Lund 1918.
Schönfeld	M. Schönfeld, *Wörterbuch der Altgermanischen Personen- und Völkernamen nach der Überlieferung des Klassischen Altertums*, Heidelberg 1911.
SCy	South Country.
SD	Symeon of Durham; *Symeonis monachi Opera Omnia: Historia Ecclesiae Dunhelmensis* (RS 75), London 1882–5.
SE	South-East(ern).
Seal	P.n. and pers.n. forms taken from seal-legends in transcription or reproduction.
Seal	Pers.n. or p.n. spelling taken from the legend of an orig. seal.
Searle	W. G. Searle, *Onomasticon Anglo-Saxonicum*, Cambridge 1897.
Sf	Suffolk.
sg.	singular.
Shav.	Shavington (Sa) records in SRO.
Sheaf	*The Cheshire Sheaf*; Sheaf[1] indicates the First Series (1878–85); Sheaf[2] the New Series (1895, 1 vol.); Sheaf[3] the Third Series (1903 and in progress); published at Chester at the office of *The Cheshire Observer* and formerly at the office of *The Chester Courant*; referred to by Series, volume and page, e.g. Sheaf[3] 6, 20, or by Series, volume and entry number, e.g. Sheaf[3] 6 (1290).
Sheriffs	Sheriffs Books, City Record Office, Chester.
Sir Gawain	*Sir Gawain and the Green Knight*, ed. J. R. R. Tolkien and E. V. Gordon, Oxford 1925 (corrected reprint 1949), 2nd ed. by N. Davis, Oxford 1967.
SMED	G. Kristensson, *A Survey of Middle English Dialects 1290–1350, The Six Northern Counties & Lincolnshire*, Lund 1967.
Smith	MS. notes on p.ns. near Macclesfield collected by the late W. Smith, Esq., of Macclesfield, c.1938–40, transmitted to Allen Mawer.
s.n.	*sub nomine.*
SNPh	*Studia Neophilologica.*
So	Somerset; Dr A. G. C. Turner has allowed the perusal of his unpublished Ph.D. thesis *The Place-Names of North Somerset.*

SocAnt Godley Charters preserved in the library of the Society of Antiquaries, London.

Sørensen J. K. Sørensen, *Danske Bebyggelsesnavne på-sted*, Copenhagen 1958.

Sotheby A Lot of Cheshire deeds bought at the saleroom of Messrs Sotheby, London, Monday 28 March 1960 (Item 126 in Sotheby's Sale Catalogue for that date); now in CRO.

SP State Papers Domestic in PRO.

SPCK The Society for the Promotion of Christian Knowledge.

Speed J. Speed, *The Theatre of the Empire of Great Britain*, 1611–12; *Map of Cheshire* 1610.

Sr Surrey; with p. reference, PN Sr.

SRO Salop Record Office, Shrewsbury.

St Saint.

St Staffordshire.

St. Street.

StdE Standard English.

Stenton F. M. Stenton, *Anglo-Saxon England* (Oxford History of England II), 2nd ed., Oxford 1947; sometimes referred to as ASE.

Stephen Regnal date, t.Stephen, 1135–54.

st.n., st.ns. street-name(s).

StNLn E. Ekwall, *The Street-Names of the City of London*, Oxford 1954.

Stowe Stowe MSS. in BrMus.

StoweCh Stowe Charters in BrMus.

str. strong.

Studies[1] E. Ekwall, *Studies on English Place- and Personal-Names*, Lund 1931.

Studies[2] E. Ekwall, *Studies on English Place-Names*, Stockholm 1936.

Studies[3] E. Ekwall, *Etymological Notes on English Place-Names*, Lund 1959.

Sund *References Relative to, and Maps of, Sundry Estates, Belonging to, Sir Richard Brooke Bart., Lying within the Townships of, Norton, Halton and Stockham. Surveyed in the Years*, 1806. 1811.; a MS. notebook, vii + 133 pp., with ink and wash MS. frontispiece, title and maps; made available for inspection by Mr B. Redwood, County Archivist, CRO.

sup. superlative.

Surv Surveys in PRO.

s.v. *sub voce.*

SvON *Sveriges Ortnamn.*

SW South-West(ern).

Swed Swedish.

SWMidl South-West Midland(s).

Sx Sussex; with p. reference, PN Sx.

t. *tempore.*

TA Tithe Awards, in PRO, formerly in the Tithe Redemption Commission's Office.

Tab *MSS. of the Leicester–Warren Family at Tabley House*, NRA 3636: the material is mostly seventeenth-century copy.

Tait J. Tait, *The Domesday Survey of Cheshire*, v. DB.

TAMap Maps accompanying Tithe Awards.

TAR	Treasurers' Account Rolls of the Corporation of Chester, City Record Office, Chester.
Tax	*Taxation Ecclesiastica Angliae et Walliae c.* 1291 (RC), London 1802.
Templar	*Records of the Templars in England,* ed. B. A. Lees, London 1935.
Tengstrand	E. Tengstrand, *A Contribution to the Study of Genitival Composition in Old English Place-Names,* Uppsala 1940.
Tengvik	E. Tengvik, *Old English By-Names,* Uppsala 1938.
Thuresson	B. Thuresson, *Middle English Occupational Terms,* Lund 1950.
Tourn	Palatinate of Chester, Sheriff's Tourn Rolls, in PRO.
Traff	The De Trafford MSS. in LRO.
transl.	translated by; translation.
TRE	*tempore Regis Edwardi,* the DB term for 'on the day that King Edward the Confessor was alive and dead'.
Trev	R. Higden's *Polychronicon,* transl. by J. Trevisa c.1387, in Higden; cf. foll.
Trev(Cx)	W. Caxton's version of J. Trevisa's transl. of R. Higden's *Polychronicon,* 1482, in Higden: cf. prec.
TRW	*tempore Regis Willelmi,* the DB term for 'during the days of king William I'.
U.D.	Urban District.
v.	*vide.*
ValeR	D. King, *The Vale Royal of England, or the County Palatine of Chester,* London 1656, and in Orm².
Varley	W. J. Varley, J. W. Jackson, L. F. Chitty, *Prehistoric Cheshire* (Handbooks to the History of Cheshire No. 1), Chester (Cheshire Rural Community Council) 1940.
vb.	verb.
VE	*Valor Ecclesiasticus* (RC), London 1810–34.
Vern	The Vernon Collection, the MSS. of Lord Vernon of Sudbury Hall, Derbyshire, in CRO.
v.l.	*varia lectio.*
VR	*The Ledger Book of Vale Royal,* ed. J. Brownbill, (LCRS 68) 1914; an edition of BrMus *Harl.* 2064, ff. 241–301, a copy made in 1662 of an orig. dated c.1338.
W	West(ern).
W	Wiltshire; with p. reference PN W.
Wa	Warwickshire; with p. reference PN Wa.
WCy	West Country.
Wd	Wood.
We	Westmorland; with p. reference, PN We.
Webster	G. Webster, 'Cheshire in the Dark Ages' CAS 38 (1951), 39–48.
Werb	*Annales Cestrienses, Chronicle of St. Werburg's Abbey,* ed. R. C. Christie (LCRS OS 14) 1886; a fifteenth-century copy of a thirteenth-century annals, the chronicle of St. Werburgh's Abbey, Chester.
W.F.I.	Information given, or documents made available, by W. Fergusson Irvine, Esq., of Corwen.
WFris	West Frisian.
WGerm	West Germanic.

Whall   *The Coucher Book of Whalley Abbey*, ed. W. A. Hulton (ChetOS 10, 11, 16, 20) 1847–9; a fourteenth-century MS.; the ed. contains *An Inventory of the Lands...of Whalley Abbey at its Dissolution*, dated 1553–4 (ChetOS 20).

White   F. White and Co., *History, Gazetteer and Directory of Cheshire*, Sheffield 1860.

Wil   *The late Major-General T. F. N. Wilson's Collection*, NRA 1203.

wk.   weak.

WM   William of Malmesbury, *Willelmi Malmesbiriensis Monachi De Gestis Regum Anglorum libri quinque* (RS), London 1887–9.

WMidl   West Midland(s).

Wo   Worcestershire; with p. reference, PN Wo.

Woll   Wolley MSS. in BrMus, *Add* 6666–718.

WollCh   Wolley Charters in BrMus.

Woulfe   P. Woulfe, *Irish Names and Surnames* (*Sloinnte Gaedheal is Gall*), Dublin 1923.

WP   A. Walde, *Vergleichendes Wörterbuch der Indogermanischen Sprachen*, ed. J. Pokorny, Berlin 1927–32.

WRY   The West Riding of Yorkshire; with p. reference, PN WRY.

WSax   West Saxon.

Wt   The Isle of Wight; with p. reference, PN Wt.

WW   T. Wright, *Anglo-Saxon and Old English Vocabularies*, ed. R. P. Wülcker, London 1884.

Y   Yorkshire.

YE   Occasionally used for ERY.

YN   Occasionally used for NRY.

YW   Occasionally used for WRY.

ZEN   E. Björkman, *Zur Englischen Namenkunde*, Halle 1912.

ZONF   *Zeitschrift für Ortsnamenforschungen*.

*   a postulated form.

~   cognate with; related to.

PHONETIC SYMBOLS

p	*p*ay	j	*y*ou	ɔ	p*o*t
b	*b*ay	x	lo*ch* (Scots)	ɔ:	s*aw*
t	*t*ea	h	*h*is	ɔi	*oi*l
d	*d*ay	m	*m*an	e	r*e*d
k	*k*ey	n	*n*o	ei	fl*ay*
g	*g*o	ŋ	si*ng*	ɛ	jam*ai*s (Fr.)
ʍ	*wh*en	r	*r*un	ɛ:	th*ere*
w	*w*in	l	*l*and	i	p*i*t
f	*f*oe	ʧ	*ch*ur*ch*	i:	b*ea*d
v	*v*ote	ʤ	*j*u*dg*e	ou	l*ow*
s	*s*ay	ɑ:	f*a*ther	u	g*oo*d
z	*z*one	ɑu	c*ow*	u:	b*oo*t
ʃ	*sh*one	a	m*a*nn (German)	ʌ	m*u*ch
ʒ	a*z*ure	ai	fl*y*	ə	ev*er*
þ	*th*in	æ	c*a*b	ə:	b*ir*d
ð	*th*en			ʔ	wa*t*er (Cockney, glottal stop)

Phonetic symbols are enclosed in square brackets: [huf]. The sign : indicates that the preceding vowel is long. The sign ˈ indicates that the following syllable is stressed, thus Altrincham [ˈɔ:triŋəm, ˈɔltriŋəm].

The symbols used in the expression of Brit and PrWelsh forms are those used in LHEB.

NOTES ON ARRANGEMENT

(1) The names in these volumes are arranged (after the county-name, regional-names, river-names and road-names) topographically by the old Hundreds and ecclesiastical parishes. The Hundreds are dealt with in order from east to west, Macclesfield, Bucklow, Northwich, Nantwich, Eddisbury, Broxton, Wirral, Chester. Within each hundred the ecclesiastical parishes are arranged in the order south to north or east to west so as to preserve as nearly as possible the geographical context. Within the ecclesiastical parishes the townships are arranged in alphabetical order. The boundaries of the townships are those in the 1911 edition of the O.S. 6″ map, occasionally adjusted to those shown in Bryant's map of 1831, or the Tithe Awards c.1840.

(2) The modern spellings of the place-names in these volumes are taken from the 1911 edition of the O.S. 6″ map.

(3) Each ecclesiastical parish name is printed in bold type as a heading, and is followed by a note on the extent and constitution of the ecclesiastical parish, and the modern disposition of its townships into civil parishes. Within each township section the names are arranged in the following categories and order: (i) the township name in small capitals with a reference to the appropriate sheet of the 7th ed .1″ O.S. map and a four- or six-figure National Grid reference to the location of the principal hamlet, followed by other major names (printed in small capitals), each treated separately; (ii) all minor names (printed in alphabetical order in small capitals), which are dealt with summarily in a single paragraph; (iii) field-names (which include other unidentified minor names) in small type, (*a*) modern field-names recorded since 1650 or 1700 (with any older spellings of these names) printed in lower case roman type, (*b*) medieval and early modern field-names which do not appear in the most modern extant field-name surveys of the township, and also other unidentified early names from before 1650 or 1700, printed in lower case italic type, the names in either group being arranged alphabetically. Street-names when they occur are treated as a separate section in small type immediately after the township name or the name of the hamlet in which they occur; existing street-names are printed in small capitals. As a rule, street-names not recorded before 1700 are excluded unless they bear some particular local interest or allusion.

(4) Place-names no longer current (that is, those not recorded on the current editions of 1″ and 6″ O.S. maps) are marked '(lost)'. This does not mean that the site to which the name refers is unknown. We are dealing with names and it is the name which is lost. Such names are printed in italic when referred to elsewhere in these volumes and in the index.

(5) Place-names marked '(local)' are those not recorded on modern maps but still current locally.

(6) The local and standard pronunciations of a name, when of interest and not readily suggested by the spelling, are given in phonetic symbols in square brackets after the map reference.

(7) In explaining the various place-names and field-names summary reference is made, by printing the elements in bold type, to the analysis of elements in the final volume, and more particularly (except when marked '(n)' in the list of elements) to *English Place-Name Elements* (EPNS xxv, xxvi). In many of the minor names and field-names the meaning is so obvious as to need no comment or so uncertain as not to warrant it. For personal-names which are cited without authority, reference should be made for Old English names to Redin, Searle and Feilitzen, for Old (Continental) German to FörstemannPN and Forssner, for Old Scandinavian to Lind, LindBN and DaGP, and for English surnames to Bardsley and Reaney.

(8) Unprinted sources of the early spellings of place-names are indicated by printing the abbreviation for the source in italics. The abbreviation for a printed source is printed in roman type. The exact page, membrane or folio reference is only given where the precise identification of an entry may be the subject of further argument.

(9) Where two dates are given for a spelling, e.g. 1285 (1450), the first is the date at which the document purports to have been composed, and the second is the date of the copy that has come down to us. Sources whose dates cannot be fixed to a particular year are dated by century (e.g. 12, 13 etc.), by regnal date (e.g. E1, H2 etc.) or a range of years (e.g. 1189–1217). Certain cartularies and similar compendia of documents which are often quoted are dated in the bibliography, so as to save print and space. Thus forms quoted from MidCh should always have '(17)' added to the date given, and forms from Chest should have '(14)' added, unless some different indication is made.

(10) The early spellings of each place-name are presented in the order 'spelling, date, source'.

(11) The sign '(p)' after the source indicates that the particular spelling given appears in that source as a person's surname, not primarily as a reference to the place.

(12) When a letter or letters in an early place-name form are enclosed in brackets, it means that spellings with and without the enclosed letter(s) occur. When only one part of a place-name spelling is given as a variant, it means that the particular spelling only differs in respect of the cited part from the preceding or following spelling. Affixes are usually given after the basic place-name form, and a hyphen is usually placed before or after to indicate whether the affix is suffixed or prefixed.

(13) Cross-reference to place-names in other townships is made by page number. Where no page reference is given, the references *supra* and *infra* indicate a place-name in the same township as the one in question.

(14) Putative forms of pers.ns. and p.n.els., which will appear asterisked in the analyses in Part 5, are not so marked in the text. There, an independently recorded pers.n. is introduced by "*the* OE pers.n....", whilst an otherwise unrecorded pers.n. is introduced by "*an* OE pers.n....".

(15) Attention is called to the addenda and corrigenda at the beginning of each volume, and to the explanation in the Preface of the order of publication and its effect upon the cross-references.

CHESHIRE

Legeceaster scir mɪɪ ASC(C) s.a. 980, *Civitatis Legionum provincia*
c.1118 FW s.a. 980, c.1130 SD s.a. 980

Cestriae provincia 1061–6 KCD 939, *provincia Cestriae* 14 Higden,
Cestrensis provincia c.1118 FW, *provincia Cestrensis* 14 Higden,
the provinces of Chestre 14 Higden(Anon), *þe province of Chestre*
1387 Trev

Ceasterscire 1085 ASC (E)

Cestre Scire 1086 DB *et freq* with variant forms *Cestre-, Cestra-,*
Cestri-, Cester(e)- Cestria-, (-ae-, -e-), Cestir-, sc(h)ir, -s(h)ir,
-s(h)yr, -c(h)ir, (-a, -ae, -e, -ia, -iae, -ie, -ye), -scr', -cyr, -ser, -s'r,
-cur, -sh', -sc', to *Cestreshyre* H8 Orm², *Cestresshire* 1301 (1344)
Pat, 1344 ib

Cestria c.1189–99 (1290) Ch, e13 Orm², *Chestre* 1536–9 Leland,
comitatus Cestrie 1237 Cl *et freq, passim* with variant forms
Cestriae, Cestr(e), Chestre (from 1361 Pat); *countee de Cester* Eɪ
(1666) Orm², *le Counte de Cestre* 1331 *Dow, the counte of Chestre*
1434 Sheaf *et freq* with variant forms *count(i)e, county(e),* and as
for Chester

Cestreyra 1250 Dieul

Chastirshir' 1313 Cl (p), Bardsley 175, cf. *Chastreschireford* 1337
Eyre

Chestershire 1326 Cl (p) *et freq* with variant spellings *Chester-,*
Chestre-, Chestur-, -ir-, -yr-, -s(c)hire, -chire, -shyr(e), to *Chester-,*
Chestreshir(e) 1536–9 Leland, *Chestershire...more short Cheshire*
1656 Orm², *þe schire of Chestre* 1387 Trev, *the shirez of...and*
Chestre 1486 AD

la conte de Wehestre 1427 Dav, co. *Westchestr'* 1505 *Dow, county of*
Westchester 1662 Sheaf, *-West-Chester* 1696 ib

Cheschire 1430 Eyre (p), *Chesshire* 1442 ChRR (p) *et freq* with
variant spellings *Che(s)shire, -s(h)ire, -s(c)hyr(e), -sheire, -sher,*
cf. *Chestershire, and by corruption, more short Cheshire* 1656
Orm² ɪ 129

county of Cicestre 1439 Cl 437

'The province of the city of Chester', *v.* scīr[1], Chester 330 *infra*. The emergence of this shire is discussed in Part 5. *Chastreschireford* was on the eastern boundary of the county, *v.* Derbyshire Bridge 173 *infra*.

REGIONAL-NAMES

LONGDENDALE, the valley of R. Etherow, in Ch and Db (Db 20, 69), appears more variously in Ch records than in those of Db, cf. Db 69 from which forms marked Db are taken.

> *Langedenedele* 1086 DB Db, -*dale* c.1153–81 (1318) Pat, *Lang(e)-den(e)dal(e)* c.1251 ChFor *et freq* to 1475 ChRR, (Db -*dal(a)*, -*dale* 1158 *et freq* to 1310)
> *Langedunedale* 1158 Db, -*done*- 1251 Misc, *Langdondale* 1574 MinAcct
> *Langedaladala* 1161 Db
> *Langedenehala* 1174, 1176, 1178, 1179 Db
> *Long(e)den(e)dale* 1181–1232 (1318) Pat, 1246 CRC *et freq* with variant forms *Longkedenedale* 1286 Court, *Longedene Dale* 1360 Rental, *Longdendale* from 1324 Fine, (Db -*dal(e)* 1245, 1275, 1285 *et freq*), cf. *Longedenedaleheved* 1285 ChFor
> *Londendale* 1189 (1845) ChetOS VIII, 1333 Cl
> *Langeden* 1251 Misc, 1285 For, *Langedene(heved)* 1285 ChFor
> *Langedenesdale* 1282 Cl
> *Longedene(heved)* 1285 ChFor, *Longeden* 1366 Eyre, *Longden* c.1620 Orm[2], 1760 Earw
> *Longedon Dale* 1332 Pat, *Longedonedale* 1332 Plea, *Longdondale* 1554, 1558 Pat
> *Longedale* 1386 Plea, *Longdale* 1423, 1507 MinAcct
> *Londondale* 1525 ChRR, 1554 Pat
> *Longdon* 1723 Earw

'The dale of *Longdene* (long valley)', from **lang** and **denu** with **dæl**[1], **dalr** added. *Longdene(dale)heved, Langedeneheved* 1285 ChFor, 'the head of *Longdene* valley' was near Woodhead 322 *infra*, *v.* **hēafod**. In *Langedaladala* the el. **dæl**[1] has been substituted for **denu** as well as suffixed. In *Langedenehala*, the el. **halh** (dat.sg. **hale**) appears suffixed instead of **dæl**[1].

THE LYME (lost), [laim], an old name for the uplands of the Pennine massif on the south-east border of La, the east and south-east

borders of Ch, and the north borders of St and Sa. The name appears
in Db, though at least one of the examples is probably quite inde-
pendent of *The Lyme*. It is found, however, in Ashton under Lyne,
Lyme Wood, Limehurst and Lyme Park in La (La 23, 29), Audlem,
Newbold-Astbury, Church Lawton, Great Moreton, Lyme Park (in
Lyme Handley) and Lyne Edge, and perhaps Lymford Bridge and
Lima, in Ch (329, 329, 330, 333, 198, 278, 56, 144 *infra*), Newcastle
under Lyme, Burslem, Whitmore, Chesterton (under Lyme),
Schertelyme, and perhaps Lymford, in St (DEPN, La 23, 263,
Lymford Bridge 56 *infra*), Betton (near Norton in Hales), Norton
in Hales, Market Drayton, in Sa (La 24, 263).

The following forms of *The Lyme* are taken from allusions in such
p.ns. as well as from specific references to the region.

-*iuxta nemus quod Lima dicitur* 1121–6 (Norton Sa), -*sub Lima* 1168
(Newcastle St), *Lima nemus* c.1195 Luc 65 (Cestria provincia,
Lime nemoris limite lateraliter clausa...), *Lima* (infra-, extra
Limam) c.1200 Dugd VI 314, Orm² II 845, 1216 Chest, 1249 Cl,
in bosco qui vocatur Lima 1297 Werb (s.a. 1259), *subtus Limam*
1305 ChFor (Ashton La)
-*under*-, -*subtus Lime* 1161–82, 1256, 1294 (Betton Sa), 1225
(Norton Sa), 1350 (Newbold Ch), *bosco de Lime* 1222–68 (Lyme
Wood La), *Limehurst* 1422 (Limehurst La), *Lime* 1690 to 1724
(Lyme Park Ch)
-*subtus Lymam* 1173 (Newcastle St), 1258 (Lawton Ch), 1289
(Moreton Ch), *Lyma* (infra-, extra *Lymam*) c.1216 (1299) Chest,
(1300) Pat, cf. Orm² III 390, *infra bosco de Lyma* 1249 Cl (1247–
61, p. 186, '...terras et boscos infra bosco de Lyma extra
dominicos boscos regis et forestam suam (de Maclefeud—
cancelled)')
-*subtus*-, -*under Lyme* 1243 (Whitmore St), 1259 (Drayton Sa),
1305, 1355 (Ashton La), 1316 (Betton Sa), *Lyme* 1312 *et freq*
(Lyme Park Ch), *boscus de Lyme* 1347 (id), *foresta de*- 1357 (id),
Lymehurst 1379 (Limehurst La), *Lyme Edge* 1842 (Lyne Edge
Ch), cf. *Schertelyme* (unid. St) and Newcastle-, Chesterton *under
Lyme* (St)
-*iuxta Lym'* 1305 (Lawton Ch), *boscus de Lym* (*in foresta de
Mackelesfeld*) 1354 to 1363 (Lyme Park Ch), cf. Lymford
(Bridge) (Ch, St)
-*subtus*-, -*under Lyne* 1319 (Ashton La), 1490, 1534 (Betton Sa)

-subtus Lynam 1350 (Newbold Ch)
-under Lynde 1400 PremIt (Newcastle St)
Line Edge 1831 (Lyne Edge Ch)
Limford Bridge 1831 (Lymford (Bridge) Ch, St)

The forms of the name *Lyme* as the final el. in compound place-names are seen in Audlem (329 *infra*) and Burslem St (La 23, DEPN, *-lim* 1086, *-lyme* 1242, *-lime* 1252, *-lym* 1297).

The distribution of the p.ns. containing *-under Lyme* follows the 400 ft. contour along the western edges of the Pennine-Peak massif, a steep escarpment which forms the geographical boundary of the lowland areas of Cheshire and Lancashire. This distribution, together with that of the localities in context with it in historical records, suggests that *The Lyme* was the region above the 400 ft. contour from south Lancashire to north Shropshire, and from east Cheshire to north and perhaps east Derbyshire. This represents The Peak and its environs. The greater number of instances of the name in the p.ns. on the western side of the hills is the result of survival fostered by two circumstances—first, that the western escarpment would have presented a more remarkable morphological feature than the eastern ranges of the massif as seen by the plainsman, and second, that this remarkably sharp geographical feature, a natural boundary, was almost co-incidental with the medieval limits of the palatinate county of Chester.

The geographical co-incidence of this region with the forests of Macclesfield and The Peak, and with the palatinate boundaries, leads to two important associations of meaning. In the records of the counties and duchies of Lancaster and Chester (more especially in the Chester records), the region-name is used as a boundary-term, cf. La 25, for 'the limit of the palatinate jurisdiction'—lands and privileges were held 'within the Lyme, without the Lyme'. Several major roads leading to the county boundary of medieval Cheshire are named after *The Lyme* in this sense, see 'Watling Street', King Street, *Lymestrete* (Bridgemere), 40, 43, 49 *infra*. But more significant was the association of *The Lyme* with a forest region. This is expressed in the licence to make approvements in the wood 'which is called *Lima*' 1259 (1297) Werb 76 and by the early descriptions in the p.n. forms listed *supra*.

The region, *The Lyme*, is one of wild upland moors now extensively covered with peat-bog, whose sides and valleys were covered in medieval times by forest in which oak was a prevalent tree, and whose heights are broken by the Millstone-Grit edges which form a distinctive geological feature.

The name is discussed at length by Ekwall (La 23–6) who takes it to be an ancient forest-name, derived from Brit *lemo- 'an elm' (cf. ERN 243–6, Jackson 278–82 esp. 282 and 278 (2), DEPN s.v. Lyme Hall Ch, and Db 241). He observes that the DB spelling supposes an OE *Līm, and explains the ME Line forms as a popular association with ME line 'a line, a boundary-line', due to the geographical accident described *supra*. But the -n- form appears e13, earlier than Ekwall reckoned with (La 24 note), and it ought to be considered an historical alternative form, OE *Līn. Db 241 refines upon Ekwall's etymology, from Brit *lemo- but in a derivative Brit *Lemia, PrWelsh *Liṽ, perhaps 'elmy place'. But the alternation of *m* and *n* in the English forms requires explanation. The PrWelsh form which the English borrowed must have been capable of interpretation into either of these nasals. It would seem that there must have been an -n- suffix upon the original British *lemo- stem. It would therefore seem that the origin of the p.n. *Lyme* is Brit. *lemo- or an ablaut form *lēmo- with an -n- suffix -n-o- or -n-ā-, in a name-formation Brit. *lemono-, *lemano-, or *lēmono-, *lēmano-. These would lead to PrWelsh *lliṽon, *lliṽan, or *llẹ̄ṽon, *llẹ̄ṽan. Because of the ambiguous *m/v* quality of PrWelsh ṽ < Brit *m*, these PrWelsh forms would be adaptable to OE *lifon, *lifan, *limon, *liman, or *lēfon, *lēfan, *lēmon, *lēman. The syncope of the *o/a* vowel in these forms would have to be ascribed to OE usage, because they were in stressed syllables in PrWelsh. In OE, the stress would be concentrated on the first syllable, leading to loss of stress on the final syllable. This would lead to OE forms *lif(e)n, *lim(e)n, or *lēf(e)n, *lēm(e)n, > *lifn (> līn), *limn > (līm), or *lēfn (> lēn), *lēmn (> lēm). By this derivation, *The Lyme* means 'the district of the Elm; the country where the elm tree grows; the district called after the elm tree or after a place where elms grow'. Dr A. G. C. Turner's study of the name ('Some Celtic Traces in Cheshire and The Pennines' in BBCS xxII, Part 2 (1967), 111–19) proceeds from an observation that the elm does not figure remarkably in the botanical history of the region, and offers an alternative derivation from PrWelsh *Līm(m) from Brit. *Lummio-, with some such sense as 'bare or exposed district' (he compares ModWelsh *llwm* 'bare, exposed, destitute, poor', ModIrish *lomm* 'bare'). He regards the -n- form, *Lyne*, as a ME reduction of an unstressed final nasal, not as an original alternative form. Professor Jackson observes, however, that Brit. *Lummio-* is not a credible basis, since there is no evidence at all for such an adjectival (or noun) form, from *lummo-* with -*ịo* suffix, in Welsh. Dr Turner's etymology represents an attempt to avoid the philological difficulties of the *lemo-* derivation and the apparent semantic irrelevance to the barren nature of the uplands called *The Lyme*. If Dr Turner's etymology were acceptable, it would suit the appearance of the moors of *The Lyme* in modern times, and probably also their condition 1500 years ago. But there is no need to set aside the 'elm' etymology because of the botanical evidence of a rarity of elms, since the rarity of that species in a district would cause any existing examples to be very notable and conspicuous phenomena. *The Lyme* might well have been named as the region in which there occurred a notable elm or a notable stand of elm in a country where that tree was rare—or even where any tree was rare.

THE MARSH (lost), *v.* Frodsham Marsh 331 *infra*.

WYCHEFELD (lost)

> *Wicesfeld* 1096–1101 (1280), c.1150, *Wyches-* 1096–1101 (1280),
> *Wisches-* 1096–1101 (1656), *Wysches-* 1096–1101 (1673) all Chest
> *Wyschefeld* (lit. *Wysthe-*), *Wische-* 1096–1101 (1280) Chest
> *Wichf'* 1175 Facs 3, (*le*) *Wichfeld* 1239 Tab, c.1240 MainwB,
>   *Wytchfeld* a.1260 Orm², *the Wychefeld* 1421 ib, *Wychefeld* 1437,
>   1445, 1440 *AddCh*, *le Wychefylde* 1439 Orm²

'The district around *The Wich* (i.e. Nantwich 333 *infra*)', *v.* wīc, feld. It included Worleston, *Wisterson*, Broomhall, Weston and Baddington 336, 336, 330, 335, 329 *infra*. Other contexts associate it with Nantwich proper (*le Wychefylde* 1439 Orm², *Schitshawe* 1462 *Sotheby*, *Shoteshawe or Wichefeld*, *Shoteshaws or Wicefield* 1564 *AddCh*, 'wood in a corner of land', *v.* scēat, sceaga), Minshull Vernon 333 *infra* (*Wytchfeld* a.1260 Orm²), Acton 329 *infra* (*the Wychefeld* 1421 Orm²), Stapeley 334 *infra* (*Wychefeld* 1437 *AddCh*, 'a meadow in Wychefeld beside Saltersiche', 'ten acres in Wychefeld and Stapeley' 1445 *ib*, *the great Wychfeilde* 1602 Sheaf). In some of these instances, the allusion is to smaller parcels of ground, 'field belonging to *The Wich*'.

WIRRALL

(on) *Wirhealum* s.a. 894 ASC (A), *-halum* 1002 (11) ASWills
(of) *Wirheale* s.a. 895 ASC (A), *Wirhale* 1096–1101 (1280) Chest
  et freq with variant spellings *Wyr-, Uyr-* to 1397 Pat, *Wyr-*
  Wirhal 1240, 1243 Cl *et freq* to 1362 Orm², 1724 NotCestr,
  Wyral 13 Whall, *Wiral* 1260 Court, *Wyrale* 1275 Misc, and 14x
  with variant spellings *Wyr-, Wir-, Uyr-, -al(e)* to *Wiral* c.1390
  AD, *Wyral(e)* 1536–9 Leland
Wirhalle 1096–1101 (1280) Chest *et freq* with variant spelling *Wir-,*
  Wyr-, -hall(e), -hallia to *Wyrhalle* 1404 Plea, *Wirhalle* 15 Higden
  (Anon); *Wirall'* 1096–1101 (1280) Chest, *Wyrall'* 1181–1232 ib
  et freq with variant spellings *Wir-, Wyr-, -all(e), -allia* to *Wyrall'*
  1581 ChRR, *Wyraul* 1536–9 Leland
Werul 1199 (1236) (1329) Pat
Werhall 1284 IpmR, *Werallia* 1309 AddCh, *Werall* 1309 Sheaf,
  1329 AD, 1454 Sheaf, 1460 ChRR, 1656 Orm², *Werrall* 1557
  Sheaf, 1561 ib, 1656 Orm², *Werral* 1656 ib, 1693 *Assem, Wereall*
  1690 Sheaf
Werhale 1361 BPR, *Werehale* 1407 Orm²
Wirehal' 1240 Lib, 1244, 1247 Cl, *Wyre-* 1253 Cl, 1391 ChRR,
  Wyrehale 1248 Cl *et freq* with variant spelling *Wire-* to *Wirehale*
  1463 ChRR, *Wyreale* 1387 Trev, *Wireal* 1512 Orm²
Wylihal 1244 Cl
Wirehall 1244 IpmR, 1286 Tab *et freq* with variant spelling *Wyre-,*
  -hall(e) to *Wyrehall* 1561 ChRR, *Wyreall* 1527 Orm²
Warall 1246–77 Chest
Wirnhal 1254 P
Wirral 1278 *ChFor*, 1309 ChRR, 1404 ib, 1579 Dugd, *Wyrral*
  1465 Pat (p)
Wirrall 1291 Pap, 1326 ChRR *et freq* with variant spelling *Wyrrall*
  to 1724 NotCestr, *Wirrhall* 1589 ChRR, 1724 NotCestr
Wyreshale 1298 P, 1468 *MinAcct*
Wyralegh' 1307–27 *JRC*
Wirrehale 1328 Cl
Whirhall 1351 Chamb, *Whirehall* 1471, 1472 ChRR
Wyerhall 1374 Cl
Wirrehall 1521 ChRR, 1535 VE, 1549 Orm², *Wyrre-* 1554 ib,
  1561 ChRR
Worall 1564 Sheaf, *Worrall* 1585 ib *et freq* with variant spellings

Wor(r)all, Worral to 1750 Sheaf, *Worrel* 1669 ib, *Worroll* 1739
LRMB 264
Woorrall 1580 Sheaf
Wearall 1699 Sheaf
Woirel 1709 *LRO*

'At the nook(s) where the bog-myrtle grows', *v.* wīr, halh (dat. pl.
halum). The significance of this name is not clear since the sense of
halh here is uncertain, and there is an interchange of singular and
plural form. In the plural it may mean 'the remote, secluded, places'
or 'the nooks, the corners', but it is not obvious what part of Wirral
gave rise to the name. In the singular, probably an analogical derivative of the plural, the sense is 'peninsula, corner of land, where bog-
myrtle grows', alluding to the whole peninsula, cf. Rossall La 158,
DEPN. The west side of Wirral is *De Side* 1536–9 Leland III 92,
v. sīde, R. Dee 21 *infra*. In 1918, R. Stewart Brown (Sheaf³ 15
(3566)) protested against the definite article in *The Wirral* which he
held to be an innovation since about 1860. Wirral is occasionally called
The Wirral in popular usage, presumably a short form for 'the Wirral
peninsula' etc. The Welsh name for Wirral is *Cilgwri* (*Cilgwri* l12,
Kilgwri 15, *Kill-gury* 1587, *Killgurry* 1621; ex inf. Professor Melville
Richards, cf. Camden *Britannia* (1587), 397, Webb's *Itinerary*
(Orm² II 359), and discussion by D. M. Ellis in BBCS XXI 30–7),
'Gwri's nook', from Welsh cil (Brit. *cūlo-) 'a nook, a corner' and
the OWelsh pers.n. *Gwri*.

FOREST-NAMES

FOREST OF DELAMERE, cf. Delamere Forest 331 *infra*

foresta 1086 DB

foresta de Mara 1153–60 Orm² *et freq* with variant forms *-Mare*
(from 1254 P), *-Maris* (1280 Cl), *-Maire* (1439 Pat), *foresta de la
Mare* 1233–7 Whall, 1240 Lib *et freq* with variant forms *-la
Mara, -la Mar'* to 1527 ChRR, *foresta delamar(e)* 1286 *ChFor*,
1332 *Chol, foresta de Lamare* 1470 ChRR, 1475 Orm²

foresta de Mor(a) 1239 P, Lib

foresta de Mere 1275, 1278 Misc, 1319 Pleas, 1359 Pat, *-la Mere* 14
Whall, 1354 BPR, Orm²

foresta de-, forest of Delamere 1308 Plea, 1312 Ch *et freq* with variant
spellings *Delamer'* (1536–9 Leland, 1656 Orm²), *Delamemere*
(1562 Pat), *forest' de Delamere alias de la Mare* 1527 ChRR

foresta iuxta Cestria 14 Higden, *þe forest bysides Chestre* 1387 Trev
the forest of Dalamere 1517 AD
forest of Delamare 1536–9 Leland, *forest De La Mar* 1647 *Chol*
Dallamore 1690 Sheaf
Dellamore Forest 1719 Sheaf
Dailameer Forest 1739 *LRMB* 264

'Forest at *The Mere*', *v.* mere[1] (MedLat form *mar(a)*), forest. The
forest would be named from one of the lakes near Eddisbury, either
Blakemere or Oakmere 329, 333 *infra*, probably the former. The
modern form arises from metanalysis, the Latin or French preposition
being compounded with the name, cf. *forest' de Delamere alias de la
Mare* 1527 ChRR. The jurisdiction of Delamere included the forest
of *Mondrem* 10 *infra*. The modern Delamere Forest lies in Manley,
Eddisbury, Delamere, Oakmere and Kingswood townships, cf.
Delamere Forest parish 331 *infra*, but the ancient Forest of Delamere
with *Mondrem* contained all Eddisbury Hundred and the townships
Church Minshull, Cholmondeston, Aston iuxta Mondrem, Worleston, Poole, and Stoke, in Nantwich Hundred, cf. Orm[2] II 107. Tarvin,
Kelsall and Hockenhull were in the liberty of the bishop of Coventry
and Lichfield's manor of Tarvin. Weaverham, Marton and Over were
in the liberty of the abbot of Vale Royal's manor of Weaverham.
Frodsham with its hamlets was a liberty of the earl of Chester.
Willington was a liberty of Whalley (*Stanlow*) Abbey. But all lay
within the forest, Orm[2] *loc. cit.* By Jas 1's time the extent of the royal
forest, mapped in *LRMB* 200, was reduced to that of the parish of
Delamere Forest.

FOREST OF MACCLESFIELD, *foresta de Maclesfeld* c.1153–81 (1318) Pat,
c.1190 *AddCh et freq* with variant forms as for Macclesfield and
Macclesfield Forest 113, 125 *infra*, cf. also Macclesfield Hundred 51
infra, *The Lyme* 2 *supra*, *v.* forest. This forest, now shrunk to the
extent of Macclesfield Forest township, occupied the parts of
Macclesfield Hundred south of R. Mersey, west of R. Goyt, north of
R. Dane, east of a line including North Rode, Gawsworth, Prestbury,
Adlington, Bramhall, Norbury, Bosden and Torkington. The ancient
boundaries of the Forest of Macclesfield are recorded in Orm[2] III
539n., Sheaf[3] 18, p. 19, *LRMB* 200 f. 180.

They are 1. Otterspool Bridge (101–937895) 263, 285 *infra*, 2. R. Mersey 31
infra, 3. R. Goyt 27 *infra*, 4. Goyt's Moss (111–0172) 173 *infra*, 5. Tinker-

spit Gutter (111–015708 to 017704) 162 *infra*, 6. Dane Bower (111–015700) 161 *infra*, 7. R. Dane 20 *infra*, 8. Cromwell Wood (110–887659) 59 *infra*, 9. Bramhallhill (110–882667) 59 *infra*, 10. Rodegreen (110–887677) 59 *infra*, 11. *le Churchgate, the Church Waye* (110–889678 to 889696) 71 *infra*, 12. Gawsworth (110–8969) 66 *infra*, 13. the direct road (110–886707 to 893735 to 101–900769, via Broken Cross 118 *infra*, cf. Gawsworth Road 122 *infra*) to Prestbury (101–9077) 212 *infra*, the direct road (the Macclesfield–Poynton–Stockport road) to 14. *Norbury Low* 288 *infra* (probably near Hatherlow (101–917867) 260 *infra*, 'lying beyond the house called Bullock-Smythy and on the west side of the said road', *v.* Hazel Grove (101–921869) 256 *infra*), 15. thence by the direct road (Hatherlow Lane, Chapel Street, Bean Leach Road, 101–919868 to 923873, 923865 to 926880), 16. 'leaving Robert Hanford's house within the forest' (perhaps Bosden Hall 101–923873), to 17. Poise Brook, descending this to 18. Barley Meadow (101–927885) 291 *infra*, in Offerton on the north bank of Poise Brook west of Bean Leach Road, thence to 19. *Saltersbridge* (about 101–927885) 292 *infra*, thence 20. by the direct road (through Offerton Green 101–930887), to 1. *supra*.

FOREST OF MONDREM (lost)

> *Mondreym* 13 *AddCh*, *-drem* 1284 Cl (lit. *Mou-*), l13 *AddCh et freq* with variant spelling *-dreme* to 1637 Sheaf, 1694 *Chol*, *-dram* 1312 IpmR (lit. *Mou-*), 1621 (1656), 1666 Orm², *-drein* 1347 BPR, *-dreyn* 1378 Pat (lit. *Mou-*)
> *la Mandrem* 1272–90 *ChFor*, *Mandrem* 1288, 1294 *ib*, ChF, 1351 BPR, *-dreme* 1332 *Chol*, *-dram* 1575 *ib*
> *Mondrun* 1313 Plea, 1462 ChRR
> *Modrem* 1320 Chamb, 1378 Pat
> *Mundrem* 1347, 1353 *ChFor*, 1351, 1352, 1357 BPR
> *Mondrom* 1347 BPR, *-drum* 1439 ChRR
> *Murdrem* 1351 BPR
> *Mundrum* 1356 *AddCh*
> *Mandrome* 1458 Pat
> *Mondremer* 1562 Pat
> *Mowndrem* 1630 *Chol*

'The pleasure-ground', from OE **man-drēam** 'happiness, pleasure, bliss'. Another example of an abstract-noun p.n. may be Witherwin 336 *infra*. *Mondrem* was part of the Forest of Delamere for administrative purposes. The actual extent of *Mondrem* within the forest of *Mare et Mondrem* is uncertain; but it is likely the *Mondrem* was approximately co-extensive with the bailiwick (c.1302–3 Orm² II 108) of one under-forester of Delamere forest in Church Minshull, Aston iuxta Mondrem, Poole, Cholmondeston, Calveley, Wettenhall and

Oulton Lowe, i.e. all that part of the whole *Mare et Mondrem* forest which lay in Nantwich Hundred, together with Wettenhall, Oulton, Calveley and Wardle townships in Eddisbury Hundred. This area, with Tiverton, Tilstone Fearnall and Alpraham, is not included in the boundaries of Sir William Troutbeck's claim, 115 Orm[2] 11 39, to the forestership in Delamere forest south of the Chester–Northwich road. Acton 329 *infra*, Aston iuxta Mondrem 329 *infra*, Mondrum *TA* in Cholmondeston 333 *infra*, *boscus de Mondrem* at *le hurst* in Worleston 332 *infra*, Woodgreen Fm in Church Minshull 336 *infra* are all named from *Mondrem* forest.

RUDHEATH (cf. Rudheath Lordship 333 *infra*)

> *Rudehez* 1181–1232 (1330) Ch, *Ruddeheth* 1208–17 Dieul, *-hez* 1270 (1427) Pat, *-het* 1271–4 Chest, *Rudeheth* c.1277 ib, *-heet* 1290 VR, *Rud(d)eheth* 1311 ChancW, 1312 Ch *et freq* with variant forms *Rude-* (to 1483 Sheaf), *Rudde-* (to 1440 ChRR), *-heth(e)*, *-hez*, *-het(gh)*, *-hed*'; *Ruddeheth More* 1359 Chamb
> *Ruddheth* 1270 Chest, c.1294 ChFor, 1328 (1338) VR, 1351 BPR, *Rudhethe* 1277 Dugd, (1350) VR *et freq* with variant spellings *-heth(e)* (to 1557 ChRR), *-het*, *-hethz*, *-eth*, *-heath(e)* (from 1357 ChRR, 1557 Pat), *-hith* (1423 Pat, 1441 ChRR), *-huth* (1441 Pat); *mora de Rudheth* 1311 Tab, *Rudhethe vastum* 1312 InqAqd, *mossa de Rudhet* 1323 Chol, 'the prince's moor of Rudheth' 1351 BPR, *Rudheth More* 1358 ChRR, 'the Moor, Heath & Turbary called Rudheth' 1450 Orm[2], *vasta de Rudheth* 1515 MinAcct
> *Rodeheth* 1287 Court (p), 1364, 1365 BPR, (*le*)*Rodehet* 1291–1316, c.1310 Chest, *Rodeheyth* 1318 AddCh, *Roddeheth* 1319 MidCh, *-het* 1328 Sheaf, *-hed*' 1332 Chol
> *Riddeheth* 1348 Tab
> *Rodheth* 1378 Pat

v. hæð 'a heath'. The first el. could be the OE pers.n. *Rudda*, but it is probably OE rūde the shrub 'rue', perhaps found also in Rudyard St (DEPN). DEPN also suggests ME *rud* 'marigold', which is not recorded before 14 NED. The extent of this heath may have been originally on the country contained by Peover Eye and R. Dane west of Twemlow, Goostrey and Barnshaw townships. The boundaries of the moor of Rudheath surveyed in 1346 (1662) are listed in VR 142, and include in whole or in part all the townships from Goostrey to Rudheath and Nether Peover to Byley.

They are 1. *Holden iuxta Shurlach*, The Holdings (110–676736, in Rudheath) 332 *infra*; thence north along the old boundary between Witton and Twambrook and Rudheath townships to 2. *Lostokebroke*, Wade Brook etc. (110–858688 to 110–6674) 37 *infra*, meeting it about 110–675739; thence east along Wade Brook to 3. *Loweforth* (Lostock Gralam) 332 *infra*; 4. *Portforth*, Portford (Allostock) 333 *infra*; 5. *Rynesforth*, an unidentified ford *Rismeford* (Nether Peover) 333 *infra*, perhaps at 110–731729 on the Allostock–Nether Peover boundary where a footbridge carried a footpath in alignment with Street Field (110–721701, Stublach) 334 *infra*, perhaps the true alignment of the supposed Roman Road from Byley to Bradshaw 110–720693 to 739720, route XX, 47 *infra*; 6. *Hardeshagheforth*, unidentified, perhaps a miscopied form of *Bradeshagheforth*, Bradshaw Bridge (110–738725, Allostock) 330 *infra*; 7. *Ormesforth*, unidentified, apparently in Nether Peover (*v.* 333 *infra*) but probably in Allostock (*v.* 333 *infra*) if 6. is at Bradshaw Bridge. However, the boundary may have left Wade Brook–Bradshaw Brook at 6., and 7. may be on Peover Eye, whence it returned to 8. *Lostokbrok*, Bradshaw Brook. Here the boundary turned southward to 9. *Rogereswey* (Barnshaw or Blackden) 333 *infra*; 10. *Shaghesyche*, Shear Brook (110–7769 to 760718, joins Bradshaw Brook) 35 *infra*; 11. *le Sondyforth*, probably at *Shaw Bridge* (110–769700, Goostrey), *v.* Shawcroft (Goostrey) 334 *infra*; 12. near *Chikenshagh in Rudheath*, *v.* 330 *infra*, not identified, presumably a tract of woodland in the south-west corner of Goostrey, towards Cranage and Allostock townships, and giving name to 10. *supra*, cf. Shear Brook 35 *infra*; 13. 'the Twemlow–Rudheath boundary', i.e. the perimeter of the detached part of Rudheath Lordship at No Town Fm (110–771687, Twemlow) 333 *infra*, near where should be located 14. *Goldewey* (Twemlow) 331 *infra*, 15. *Saghemor* (Twemlow) 334 *infra*, and 16. 'Thomas Hardy's house in Rudheath'. The latter may be No Town Fm. The next bound is 17. 'Twemlow wood', cf. The Wood 336 *infra*. The boundary wood must have been in the north-west corner of Twemlow township. Here the boundary turned westwards to 18. 'Cranage wood', cf. Wood Field (Cranage) 336 *infra*; 19. *Redlache* (Cranage) 333 *infra*; 20. *le Oldedyche* (Cranage) 333 *infra*; thence to 21. *Whystelhaghe*, Whishaw (Leese) 335 *infra*; 22. *Jurdanes-ryddyng* (Leese) 332 *infra*; 23. *Legheslone* (Leese) 332 *infra*, perhaps Byley Lane (Byley) 330 *infra*; thence to 24. *Byuelegh-lydeyate*, *v.* Yatehouse (Byley) 336 *infra*; 25. *le Bouhous* (Byley) 330 *infra*, perhaps near Byley Bridge 330 *infra*; 26. *Ravenscrofteslach* (Ravenscroft) 333 *infra*; 27. *Lynstrete*, King Street 43 *infra*. Here the boundary turned northwards along King Street, to 28. *le Hethlache*, Puddinglake Brook 34 *infra*, near Brook Ho (110–691698, Whatcroft) 330 *infra*; 29. *Alstan Thornsyche* 320 *infra*, and 30. 'the lane of *Woodhouses*' 336 *infra*, both unidentified but apparently along King Street; 31. *Pertreleghes* 333 *infra*, a tract of land on the Whatcroft–Drakelow boundary; 32. *le Whitesych* (Whatcroft) 335 *infra*; 33. *Whatcrofteslone*, Whatcroft Lane (110–690705, Whatcroft) 335 *infra*; 34. *Shipbrokesmos*, Moss Field (Shipbrook) 333 *infra*; 35. *Polsych* (Shipbrook) 333 *infra*; 36. *Shipbrokeslone*, Shurlach Lane (Shipbrook) 334 *infra*; 37. 'Walter Page's house', unidentified, in Shipbrook township; 38. 'Reginald Legg's grange', in Rudheath township; 39. *le Morstal*, Marstow (in Shipbrook) 333 *infra*; 40. *Simmesfeld* (Rudheath) 334 *infra*, 41. *Bradfordeswey* (Rudheath) 330 *infra*, 42. *le Lauedyfeld*, cf. Lady Hey (Rudheath) 332 *infra*, 43. 'Walter Page's marlpit', and 44. *Oldefeldesdyche* 333 *infra*, in Rudheath lordship; 45. *Bradefordesbrok* (in Bradford) 330 *infra*; 46. *Shurlach-dyche* (Shurlach) 334 *infra*; 47. *Bradeford Moor* (Bradford) 330 *infra*; 48. *Bradford*, Bradford Fm (110-682731) 330 *infra*; 49. 'the field of Bradford'; 50. *Goslache*, Gooseledge (Shurlach) 331 *infra*; 51. 'Stephen le Hunt's lane', unidentified; 52., 54., 'the boundary between Witton and Rudheath' (110-674735 to The Holdings at 1. *supra*); 53. *le Longacre*, cf. Long Acre (Rudheath) 332 *infra*; 1. *ut supra*.

FOREST OF WIRRAL (lost), *foresta de Wirehal* 1240 Lib *et freq* with spellings as for Wirral 7 *supra* to *foresta in loco qui vocatur Wirhale* 1376 Ch, *v*. forest. Wirral was afforested by Ranulph Meschines, earl of Chester 1119-28 (Orm² II 353), and was disafforested July 1376 (Pat 1376, p. 378), because of the numerous malefactors resorting there, cf. Sir Gawain 701-2.

MINOR HUNDREDS

CALDY HUNDRED (lost), *v*. 330 *infra*; HALTONSHIRE (lost), *v*. 331 *infra*; MALPAS HUNDRED (lost), *v*. 332 *infra*.

RIVERS AND STREAMS

The more important streams are listed here. Those named from places are included under the original p.n. unless the course is extensive or the location of the original p.n. uncertain. The names of tributaries are followed by the names of the waters into which they fall, e.g. Artle Brook (*joins* R. Weaver). A stream which changes its name is followed by (> the changed name), e.g. Arley Brook (*becomes* Waterless Brook[1]).

ARLEY BREEK (> Waterless Brook[1]), *Birch Brook* 1831 Bry, *v*. birce, brōc. The later name is from Arley 329 *infra*.

ARTLE BROOK (R. Weaver), 1842 OS, *aqua (de) Arcel* l13, 1328 MRA, (*aqua de*) *Arthull* 1342 AddCh, 1357 ChRR, *Hartle Brook* 1842 *TA* 194. The stream is probably named from a lost place, which may mean 'hart hill', *v*. heorot, hyll, brōc.

Ash Brook (R. Weaver), 1831 Bry, *Assebroke* 1217–32 VR, *Asschebrok* 1310 *AddCh*, and seven examples *ib*, AD, *ChFor*, with variant spellings *Asse-*, *Ass(c)he-*, *-brok(e)*, *-bro(o)c*, *-brock* to *Assebroke*, *-brock* 1338 VR, *The Ash* (commonly called *Ash-brooke*) 1656 Orm². 'Ash-tree brook', *v.* æsc, brōc. Forms for Ashbrook Bridge 329 *infra* show confusion of æsc with ēast 'east', or of *c* with *t*.

Ashton Brook (> Barrow Brook), 1812 Sheaf, *le Erw...brok* 1347 *ChFor*, from Ashton 329 *infra* and brōc, cf. Ark Wood 329 *infra*, Barrow Brook² 329 *infra*, *le Hee* 332 *infra*.

Bag Brook (>Peover Eye), *aqua de Chelleford* c.1238 (1595) ChRR, *Chelfordbroke* c.1529 Orm², *le Puctesbrok*, *Pygotes-*, *Pygotisbrok* 1318 *Dav*, *Bag Brook* 1831 Bry, cf. Bagbrook Bridge and Wood 72, 97 *infra*, *v.* brōc. The earliest name is from Chelford 75 *infra*. The second contains the ME pers.n. *Picot* (ModE *Piggot*). The later name is probably a back-formation from *Baggeford* 1342 Tab (p) at Bagbrook Bridge 97 *infra*, 'badger's ford', *v.* bagga, ford.

R. Bar (lost, R. Weaver) 1536–9 Leland, 1656 Orm², brook called *Hurlston* 1656 Orm² I 133. The old name was regarded as unauthentic in 1656 by ValeR (Orm² I 133). It is obviously a back-formation from Bar Bridge 329 *infra*. ValeR preferred the name *Hurlston* for this stream, cf. Hurleston 332 *infra*. It is formed by two tributaries at 110–605565 and joins R. Weaver at 110–663557.

Barnett Brook (R. Weaver), *rivulus de Burleya* e12 *Cott*. Faust. B viii, Dugd v 323, *the brook of Burley*, *Burlybrooke* 1133 (18) Sheaf³ 28, *Burley Brook* m13 (18) ib, *Barnett Brooke* 1609 Sheaf, 1621 ib, *-Brook* 1843 *TAMap* 145, *v.* brōc, cf. Burleydam 330 *infra*, Barnettbrook Bridge, Near Barnett and Barnettbrook 329 *infra*. The later name is taken from a lost p.n. *Barnett* 'land cleared by burning, burnt place', *v.* bærnet(t), probably near the hamlet Barnettbrook.

Barrow Brook¹ (R. Mersey), 1842 OS; *Barrow* could be bearu 'a grove', or bearh 'a barrow-pig'. There is another Barrow Brook 329 *infra*.

BEN BROOK (> Snape Brook).

BENSTALL BROOK (lost, Waterless Brook[1]), 1548 Tab, and 5 examples
ib, *Chol*, with variant spellings *Binstall-* (lit. *Bru-* 1565 Tab),
Benstall-, *-Brook(e)*, *-Broke* to Benstall Brook 1666 Orm[2], *v.* **stall**
'a fishery'.

THE BIRKET (Mersey estuary), *The Birkin* 1819 Orm[2], *The Birken*
1819 ib, 1823 Dugd, *The Main Fender* 1842 OS. *Birkin* is a back-
formation from Birkenhead 329 *infra*. Originally, the stream was
probably called *The Fender*, cf. The Fender *infra*, the south branch
of the stream, *v.* **fender** 'a drain, a (boundary) ditch'.

BIRKIN BROOK (R. Bollin), *Birkin* 1621 (1656) Orm[2], *Birken* 1860
White, *R. Birkin* 1831 Bry, a back-formation from Birkinheath 329
infra. ValeR, 1656 Orm[2] I 133, regards this as an unauthenticated r.n.
It seems that *Birkin* was the name of the stream through Knutsford
town 101–756781 to 764830, a branch of Birkin Brook (101–775786
to 748856). The old name of Birkin Brook is probably *aqua de
Wallebrock* 1300, 1301 JRL 32, *Wilbroc* c.1306 (15) ib, *Wylebrok* e14
ib, in Mobberley and Knutsford, *v.* **wella**, **wælla**, **brōc**, cf. Marthall
Brook *infra*, which joins Pedley Brook 32 *infra* to form Birkin Brook.

BLACK BROOK[1] (> Harrop Brook). BLACK BROOK[2] (lost), 1842 OS,
v. Day Brook *infra*. BLACK BROOK[3] (lost, 109–570523 to 578498,
R. Weaver), 1831 Bry, *le Blakebroc* 1305 *Chol*, *-brooke* 1385 (1619)
ib, *v.* **blæc**, **brōc**.

BOGART BROOK (Pettypool Brook), 'goblin stream', *v.* **boggart**, **brōc**.

R. BOLLIN (R. Mersey)
   Bolyne 1190–1208 (17) Orm[2], 13 ib, 1323 *Dow*, 1337 *Eyre*, c.1340
      Barnes[1] 10, c.1414, 1415 *Mont*
   Bolinn 1200–33 MidCh
   Bolin 1210 *Mass*, m13 *Fitt*, c.1280 ib, 1525 *NewC*, 1621 Earw
   Bolyn c.1220 Tab, 1250–88 Chest, 1284 (17) Sheaf *et passim* to
      1536–9 Leland
   Bolni 1268 Chest
   Bollin 13 Barnes[1] 10, c.1620 Orm[2], 1656, 1819 ib *et freq*
   Bollen 1577 Saxton, *R. Bollen* 1839 *TAMap* 268
   Bollein brooke water 1577 Holinshed

This r.n. is associated with Bollington 187 *infra*, 330 *infra*, Bollin Fee 220 *infra*, Bollin Hall 221 *infra*. The river is also named *Macclesfield Water* (*v.* Waters Green 121 *infra*), *Tegsnose Water* (1620 *Surv*, in Sutton, *v.* Tegg's Nose 152 *infra*), *Ringay flumen* (1610 Speed, from Ringway 333 *infra*), and Bollin Brook (> R. Bollin, the headstream in Sutton Downes and Macclesfield Forest). The name of Bollington 187 *infra* suggests that R. Dean was originally called *Bollin*. ValeR in 1656 describes this Bollington as on R. Bollin, cf. Orm² 1 133, and it may be that at that time R. Dean and Bollin Brook–*Macclesfield Water* were both known as *Bollin*. Bollin Brook Fm 216 *infra*, in Upton near Macclesfield, carries the r.n. down as far as Upton. In 1819, Orm² III 741, quoting Orm¹, states 'the town of Macclesfield is built on the bank of a principal feeder of the Bollin.'

Bollin is obscure in meaning and origin. Ekwall, RN 40, observes that the second el. may be hlynn 'a torrent, a noisy stream', but dismisses OE bōl 'eel' (BTSupp, a dubious gloss for MedLat *mūrenula* 'little eel or lamprey', dimin. of Lat *mūraena* 'the murena, a kind of eel') as first el. because it 'does not seem to go well with a word meaning a torrent'. This is not a valid objection. Parts of the course of R. Bollin are swift and noisy, so hlynn is apt; eels are taken at the eel-fare in quite turbulent streams. The real objection to OE bōl (whence its withdrawal in DEPN) must be the uncertainty of its meaning, see ES 40 (1909), 236–7.

BOLLIN BROOK, *v.* prec.

BOLLINHURST BROOK (> Norbury Brook), NORBURY BROOK (> Lady Brook) named from Bollinhurst 199 *infra*, Norbury 287 *infra*. From E1 (1611) *LRMB* 200 (f. 193, a survey) and 1370 *Eyre* (PRO Chester 17, 15 m.14d, coroner's inquest on a man drowned at Norbury), these two brooks are to be identified with *Bluntebroc* c.1217–29 (1287) Court, *Blentebrok* c.1217–29 (1288) *Eyre*, *Bluntesbroch* c.1217–29 (1353) *ChFor*, *Bluntisbroke* E1 (1611) *LRMB* 200, *Bluntesbrok* 1357 *ChFor*, (-*infra forestam de Maccl'*) 1366 *Eyre*, -*broke* 1579 *Dep*, *Blotisbroc* 1270 (17) Sheaf³ 18, *Bluncebroc* E1 *AddCh*, *Bluttesbrok* 1347 *Eyre*, *Blontesbrok* 1370 *ib* (at Norbury), 'Blunt's brook', from brōc and an OE pers.n. *Blunt* for which see Blundeston Sf (DEPN), Blunsdon W 30, Blunt's Hill Ess 300, and Bluntisham Hu (BdHu 204, Hrt xxxvii). Cf. *Cartelache infra*.

BRADSHAW BROOK (> Crow Brook), *Lostokbrok* 1280–90 Tab, 1346 VR, *-brouc* c.1290 Tab, *Lostoke brouk* c.1280–90 ib, *-broke* 1346 VR, *Lostock Broke* 1549 *Chol*, *The Lostok Water* 1656 Orm², *Bradshawe* 1619 Sheaf³ 22, *Bradshaw Brook* 1831 Bry, named from Lostock Gralam 332 *infra*, Allostock 329 *infra*, and Bradshaw 330 *infra*, cf. Bradshawbrook Fm 330 *infra* (*Bradshawbrooke* 1554–5 Orm² 1 505), *v.* brōc. *Lostock Brook*, the northern boundary of Rudheath 11 *supra*, comprises Bradshaw Brook, Crow Brook and Wade Brook *infra*.

BUTTON BROOK (lost, R. Mersey), 1842 OS, cf. Button Lane 237 *infra*. It was *Mill Stream* 1842 OS in Carrington, cf. Millbank Fm 333 *infra*. It ran from Button Lane in Northenden and Wythenshaw, across Ashton on Mersey, into Carrington.

CALDY BROOK (R. Dee), 'cold stream', *v.* cald, ēa, brōc, cf. *Caldewallemor*, Cald(e)y Shoots, Caldy Fd, 330 *infra*.

CALDWELL BROOK (Red Brook³), 1842 OS, *v.* cald, wella, brōc.

CARR BROOK¹ (Todd Brook). CARR BROOK² (Staly Brook), 1842 OS, 'marsh stream', *v.* kjarr, brōc.

CARTELACHE (lost, NORBURY BROOK), *Cartlach* 1202–29 (1611) *LRMB* 200, *-lache* E1 (1611) *ib*, *Kartelach* 1202–29 (1611) *ib*, *-lach(e)* 1270 (17) Sheaf³ 18, *Cartelache* 1208–29 (1608) ChRR, 1270 (17) Sheaf³ 18, 1290 *Eyre*, 1348 *ChFor* 'boggy stream in stony ground', probably a hybrid name from ON kartr and OE læc(c), though kartr could have replaced the cognate OE cært 'rough ground' as first el. It occurs as the name of two streams in the same vicinity, one the boundary between Norbury 287 *infra* and Poynton 207 *infra*, the other that between Torkington 299 *infra*, Heppales 299 *infra* and Norbury. Both fell into Norbury Brook *infra*. Local topography makes it unlikely these were one stream since it would have had to cross a watershed to form both boundaries. It is possible that the name *Cartelache* was extended to a district (cf. *Bluntesbroke* at Bollinhurst Brook *supra*, also Middle Wood 283 *infra*, Middlewood Rd 209 *infra*, Cartelachehurst 211 *infra*) from which two or more streams issued. Such a district gives rise to the surname of Richard de *Cartelache* 1290 Court 244. The problem of identification and distinction is aggravated by boundary changes. In c.1249 Richard de Vernon of Marple 'approved' land in Torkington and *Heppales* beyond 'a certain cartelache' at that time the boundary, and the modern boundary may not be original, cf. Torkington Lane 300 *infra*. In this instance, *Cartelache* is a common appellative, *quoddam cartelache* 1290 Court 246, and the stream-name ought to be regarded as a common stream-name type. It recurs elsewhere in Ch as Cartlidge Wood 55 *infra*, *Cartelache* 124 *infra*, 330 *infra*, Cartledge Fd 330 *infra*, -Moss 330 *infra*, Cart Lake 330 *infra*, in Db as Cartledge, Cartlidge Db 264, 88 and in YW in Cartledge Brook YW 1 232.

CHAPEL BROOK (> Midge Brook), 1831 Bry, *rivulum de Fenchawe* 13 *Dav*, *ductum de Merton* 1313 *ib*, cf. Finishaw and Marton Brook 65, 81 *infra*, Marton Chapel 82 *infra*.

CHECKLEY BROOK (> Forge Brook > Wybunbury Brook > Artle Brook), 1831 Bry, from Checkley 330 *infra* and brōc. ValeR (1656, in Orm² 1 133, III 290) describes two streams in this district, *Betley Water* 1621 (1656), *the Betley Water* 1656, and *the Lea Brook*, *the water Lee* 1621 (1656), *the Lea* 1656. The *Betley* is said to run from Betley near Wrinehill 329 *infra*, by Doddington, Wybunbury and Batherton into R. Weaver. The *Lea* is said to run by Lea and Wybunbury. These are the course of Checkley Brook except that Checkley Brook rises at Wrinehill Wood and Madeley St. The stream rising at Betley St also has a head at Cracow Moss (in Blakenhall 331 *infra* and Wrinehill St), and runs by Blackenhall, Chorlton, Weston, Basford, Gresty, Rope and Wistaston to Marshfield Bridge 333 *infra*, where ValeR (Orm² 1 133) says *the Lea* falls out. It looks as though the old name for Checkley Brook was *Lea Brook* (cf. Lea 332 *infra*). that *Betley Water* was the stream past Basford, and that ValeR has confused them.

CHEER BROOK (> Cheney Brook), 1831 Bry, perhaps 'winding brook', *v.* cearr(e), brōc, cf. also *Saltersich* 334 *infra*.

CHENEY BROOK (R. Weaver), *China Brook* 1831 Bry, named from the *Cheney* family, E1 to 19, in *Wisterson* 336 *infra*, cf. Willaston Cottage 335 *infra*, Cheny Brook Mdw 330 *infra*, Cheneybrook Bridge 330 *infra*, *Saltersich* 334 *infra*, also *Chayne Hall* 330 *infra*, Cheney Gate 59 *infra*.

CHESHIRE BROOK (Dane in Shaw Brook), 1795 JCJ, from brōc and the county-name, on the county boundary with Staffordshire, cf. Cheshire Brook Wood 330 *infra*.

CLOUGH BROOK (R. Dane), *Schut-, Shuclynglowebroc, -brok* 1337, 1350 *Eyre, Shotlynglowebrok* 1357 *ChFor, Bromecroft Water, Wilberclogh Water* 1503 *ChFor, v.* clōh, brōc, cf. Wildboarclough 159 *infra*, Shutlingsloe 160 *infra*, Broomycrofthead 126 *infra*.

CLOUTER BROOK (Midge Brook), *v.* brōc. *Clouter* is perhaps 'the noisy one, the clumsy one', cf. ModE dial. *clouter* 'to walk noisily or clumsily'.

COR BROOK (lost), *v.* Corbrook Ho 331 *infra*.

COW BROOK (R. Dane), 1831 Bry, *Colbrok* 1363 *ChFor*, 'cool brook' or 'charcoal brook', *v.* col[1], cōl[2], brōc, cf. Cowbrook 68 *infra*, Cow Bridge 60 *infra*.

R. CROCO (R. Dane)

> *doytum de Wico* e13 Dieul, *doetum Mediiwici* 1250–71 MidCh, *doetum Wici* 1315 ib, *le Wichebrooke* 1250–1300 ib *et freq* with variant spellings *Wych(e)-, Wich(e)-, -brook(e)* to *Wich Brooke* 1619 Sheaf, *torrens Mediiwici* 1362 MidCh, *le brook* 1309 ib, *rivulus* 1482 ib, *the brooke* 16, 17 ib.
> *Croco* 1621 (1656) Orm[2] I 131, III 9, *the Croc* 1819 Orm[2], *R. Crocker*, and *Croco or Allum Brook* 1831 Bry
> *Allum Brook* 1831 Bry, 1883 Sheaf

The first name was '(Middle-) Wich Brook', *v.* wīc, brōc, from Middlewich 333 *infra*. The third is from *Allom* and Dog Lane Fm (now Allum Brook Fm) 329, 331 *infra*. The r.n. *Croco*, dismissed by ValeR in 1656 as unauthentic ('that which they call the Croco', and 'the river, which some call Croco...', Orm [2] I 133, 138), goes back to before 1583 from which time ValeR reports it in 1621, *v.* Sheaf[3] 50 (9962). It may well be authentic. It would seem to be 'river with a crook', *v.* krókr, á, for the course has a pronounced bend northward at Middlewich. Etymologically identical and alluding to a bend in the course of the river, is the Norwegian river-name *Króká*, NG II 215, NElv 132.

CROW BROOK (> Wade Brook), 1831 Bry, *Lostock Brook* 1619 Sheaf, cf. Bradshaw Brook *supra*, and for the modern name Crowbrook Bridge 331 *infra*.

CUDDINGTON BROOK (Acton Brook), *the Black Brook* 1812 Sheaf, *Bog Lane Brook* 1831 Bry, *v.* blæc, brōc, cf. Cuddington 331 *infra*, Stony-ford Brook 334 *infra*, Bag Lane 329 *infra*.

R. DANE (R. Weaver)

> *Dauene* 12 *Dav, Dauen(e), Daven(e)* e13 ib, Chest, Dieul, 1270 (17) Sheaf, c.1300 *Dav et freq* to *Dauen* 1386 *MinAcct, Daven alias Dane* 1536–9 Leland, *Daven or Dane* 1724 NotCestr
> *Davere* c.1248 Dieul
> *Daane* 1295 *Chol*, 1392 *AddCh, Daan* 1393 *ib*, 1416 AD
> *Devene, Deuene* 1423, 1443 *MinAcct* (also lit. *Wende*)
> *Dane* 1443 *MinAcct*, 1487 *ib* (lit. *Dand*), 1503 *ChFor et freq, le Dane* 1503 *ChFor*
> *Dene* (lit. *Went*) 1487 *MinAcct*, (lit. *Wenc*) 1507 *ib, Dene* 1507 *ib*

This r.n. appears independently in Ch, at Danes Tenement 149 *infra* (*Dauenebonkes* c.1313 *Dow, Dane* 1503 *ChFor*, 1620 *Surv, Deane Eyes* 1611 *LRMB*, named from some stream near Nessit 155 *infra* a tributary of R. Bollin). Like the upper reaches of R. Dane, this is a fairly brisk water in a steep valley, which does not seem conformable with the etymology in RN 112–13, where Ekwall derives it from OWelsh *dafn* 'a drop, a trickle' with the sense 'slow river'. However, it would appear preferable to accept this derivation and to suppose a figurative, perhaps even ironic, quality for the r.n., rather than to attempt an alternative explanation, as in BBCS XXII, part 2 (1967).

DAY BROOK (lost, R. Bollin), 1831 Bry, or BLACK BROOK (lost) 1842 OS, *Daie Brooke* 1620 *Surv*, 'dairy brook', *v.* dey, brōc, cf. Day-brook St. (Hurdsfield) 107 *infra*. The other name is 'dark stream', *v.* blæc, brōc, perhaps to be identified with the forms *Blakebrok* 1341 *Eyre, Blacesbroc in foresta de Macclesfeld* 1347 *ib*, though the latter appears to contain the gen.sg. form of an OE strong masc. pers.n. *Blæc*.

R. DEAN (R. Bollin), *aqua de Honford* 1291 Earw, *Handforth Brook* 1831 Bry, *Deyne Water infra Wydford* 1552 Dav, *Deanwater* 1632

Earw, *Deanwater* (*House*) 1831 Bry, *Bolington Brook* 1686 *Dow*; cf.
Handforth 254 *infra*, Woodford 217 *infra*, Deanwater Bridge & Ho
217 *infra*, Bollington 187 *infra*, Danebent Fm 143 *infra*, R. Bollin
supra. This r.n. may be 'stream in a valley' from denu, or be a back-
formation from Dean Row 221 *infra*.

R. DEE

Δηοῦα c.150 (1200) Ptolemy (i.e. Chester)
Deva 4 (8) AntIt (i.e. Chester), 7 (13) RavGeog (i.e. Chester),
    Deva 1536–9 Leland
Diva c.1195 Luc
Deue 1370 RN
Dee 1043 (17) KCD 916, 1061–6 (17) KCD 939, 1096–1101 (1280)
    Chest, Ch, 1188–91 Chest, e13 Dieul *et freq*
De 1086 DB, 1096–1101 (1280) Chest, c.1130 SD (s.a. 973), 1150
    Chest, 1170 Peov, 1180–1216 *HarlCh et freq* to 1555 Sheaf
Dea c.1118 FW (s.a. 973), 1572 RN, (...in Latin) *Dea* 1656 Orm²
Deia 1191 (c.1200) RN, c.1214 (13), c.1212 (14) ib
Dhe e13 (1499) Sheaf, *flumen de Hee* 14 Higden
Dye 15 Higd–(Anon)
Dubr duiu 10 (c.1200) RN, *Doubyr Dviv* 12 (c.1200) ib
Deverdoeu 1191 (c.1100) RN, *Deverdoe, Devardoeu* c.1214 (13) ib,
    Glyndeuerdoe c.1214 (1400) ib, *Deuerdiw, -due* 1234 (1295) Ch,
    Deverdui 1236 (1295) Ch
Dyfrdwy 14 (?) RN
Dour douv. i. aquam Dei 1572 RN
Pifirdwy 1656 Orm² I 131
Funon Dourdroy 1656 Orm² I 131
Dyfrdwy id est aquam Devae 1731 RN

This is a Brit r.n., *Dēva*, 'the goddess, the holy one', cf. Lat *diva*,
sb. and adj., fem., 'holy, a holy one, a goddess'. The r.n. was
extended in Roman times to Chester, the city on its bank, 330
infra. For discussion of the etymology *v.* RN 118, Jackson, 375, 629,
Archæologia XCIII 31. Jackson 332–3 shows that the OE form *Dē*
must represent an older form *Dēw* borrowed from Brit *Dēua* before
the Welsh diphthong -*ui*- developed in -*Dwy* in the seventh century,
op. cit. 333. The prefix *Dubr-, Dever-, Dyfr-* in the Welsh forms is
Welsh *dyfr*, a weakened form of Welsh *dwfr* 'a river'. *Glyn-* is
Welsh *glyn* 'a valley'. *Funon-* is Welsh *ffynon* 'a spring, a well', the

head of R. Dee near Lake Bala in Wales. *Archæologia* and RN *loc. cit.* quote an alternative Welsh name *Aerfen*, which appears in early Welsh poetry and may represent R. Dee. This means 'battle goddess, goddess of war', from *aer-* 'battle', and *-men*, as in *Tyngued-fen* 'fate' (*Archæologia, loc. cit.*). Ekwall thinks *Aerfen* may be the original name of the river, and *Dee* a later, allusive name used because *Aerfen* was too sacred and potent a word for common use. He refers to the ancient tradition (from Giraldus Cambrensis) that the alterations of the river's course foretold the shifting fortunes of the wars between the Welsh and the English *v.* Addenda.

DIPPING BROOK (> Dood's Brook *infra*).

DOBBIN BROOK (R. Dean), *Dobbins Brook* 1840 *TA* 327. The first el. may be the common pers.n. *Dobbin, v.* brōc. Cf. 255 *infra.*

DOOD'S BROOK (> Dingle Brook[1]), 331 *infra.*

R. DUCKOW (R. Weaver), *Douclesbrooke* e12 *Cott.* Faust. B viii, *Doulebrooke* 1133 (17) Dugd v 323, *Doucklebrooke* 1134 (17) Sheaf, *Dockle-, Dokel brook(e)* 1133 (18) ib, *Docklewater* 1481 (1581) Sheaf, *the water of Dockle* 1537 (1581) ib, *Docle* 1299 (18) ib, *R. Duckow* 1831 Bry, a r.n. *Doucles* with brōc suffixed, in which the final *-es* has been taken as a gen.sg., and for which a new nom.sg. form *Douckle* (> *Duckow*) has been supposed. *Doucles* would be a r.n. of the type represented by Douglas La (RN 129, 131), 'dark stream', Brit **Duboglassio-, v.* dubo-, glassjo- (properly *glassjo-*) *v.* Addenda.

EDLESTON BROOK (R. Weaver), *le Smalebrock, Badileghbrock* 1298 *Chol,* identical with *le Smalebroke* 334 *infra,* 'narrow stream', *v.* smæl, brōc. Cf. Baddiley and Edleston 329, 331 *infra.*

EEL BROOK (R. Weaver), *Hell Brook* 1831 Bry, *v.* brōc, cf. *Helleclif* 332 *infra.*

ELDERSBRIAR BROOK (R. Dane), in Leftwich and Davenham.

ENGLESEA BROOK (> Valley Brook), *Inglesea Brook* 1845 *TA* 421, cf. Balterley Mere 329 *infra,* Englesea-Brook 331 *infra.* The brook flows from the mere and gives its name to the hamlet. The forms are too late for an etymology to be suggested.

R. ETHEROW (R. Goyt), *Ederau* c.1216–20 *AddCh*, *Ederou* c.1251 *For*, *R. Etherow* 1842 OS. This r.n. is discussed in Db 7, RN 156, where other forms quoted are *Ederhou* 1226, *Ederou* H3, 1285, *Edderowe* 1290, *Edrou* 1300, *Ederow* 1386, *Tedder* c.1600, *Etherow* 1767. Db 7 proposes that this river is called after 'a promontory by a river', from ēdre 'watercourse', and hōh 'a projecting ridge of land'. The second el. alternates with haugr 'a hill, a height'. An older name of this river may lie behind the p.n. Tintwistle 320 *infra*.

FAIRYWELL BROOK (Baguley Brook), 1842 OS, *Timperley Brook* 1831 Bry, named from *Fairy Well* 1838 *TA* 34, at Fairywell Wood 331 *infra* and brōc. Cf. also Timperley 335 *infra*. This brook joins Baguley Brook to form Sinderland Brook which joins Mersey as Red Brook[3] *infra* between Partington and Warburton. Redbrook Ho 333 *infra* in Timperley appears to extend this name back to Fairywell Brook.

THE FENDER (The Birket), 1844 *TAMap* 295, *the water of Ayne* 1522 Sheaf[3] 4 (613), *the Ford Brook* 1842 OS. This is a tributary of The Birket, which was *The Main Fender*. The term *fender* is here used of a drainage stream, with levée banks, and sluices to prevent tidal flooding, *v.* fender. In Sheaf[3] 6 (967) a definition is given from local usage that 'a fender is a bank raised to protect low-lying land from flood. The streams in Wirral are named from banks raised alongside them, the name for the banks being transferred to the streams', cf. ChetNS XLII 38. In 1585 Sheaf 'a good sufficient and able ditch and fender shall be made between the North and South meadows' (in Hoose 332 *infra*). In 1687 *Bun*, *The Fenders* refers to 'gutters' in Stoke 334 *infra*. In 1596 *Vern*, 'one sufficient Fender or Attachment in the ould brooke' was to divert and carry a watercourse to a mill at Hockenhull 332 *infra*. Cf. also Fender Meadow 255 *infra*. The Fender was known as *Ford Brook*, from Ford 331 *infra* and brōc. The form *Ayne* is supposed in Sheaf[3] 4 (613) to be from Welsh afon, but this is unlikely. Its etymology is unknown.

FINCHETT'S GUTTER (R. Dee), 1831 Bry, *le Pullesmouthe* 1327–8 Sheaf, *Portpool brook* 1703 *Assem*, 'the mouth of the creek', 'the brook at

Port Pool', *v.* pull, mūða, brōc, cf. *Port Pool* 333 *infra*. The modern name is from the surname *Finchett* and goter, cf. Elizabeth and Thomas *Finchett*, landowners in Chester 1711 *Corp*. The stream, carrying Flooker's Brook *infra* into R. Dee, became a drainage gutter when the R. Dee was canalised in the eighteenth century.

FINNAKER BROOK (R. Weaver), in Coole Pilate, Newhall and Hankelow.

FIR BROOK (> Stonyford Brook), *v.* brōc and cf. Firwood 331 *infra*.

FIRWOOD BROOK (R. Weaver), in Over 333 *infra*, 'brook at a fir wood', *v.* brōc.

FLENNEN'S BROOK (Worthenbury Brook Fl), *Flamings Brook* 1819 Orm[2], *Farning Brook* 1831 Bry, *Flennens Brook* 1842 OS, perhaps 'fugitive's brook', from flēming[1] and brōc. This is at the county boundary with Flintshire, at Threapwood 335 *infra*, a notorious no-man's-land for fugitives.

FLINDER (lost), *v. Flindow* 331 *infra*.

FLOOD BROOK (R. Weaver), 1712 *Chol, Pludbrok, -broc* c.1275 *ib*, *-brooke* 1650 *ParlSurv, Plidbrok* 1569 *Chol*, 'puddle brook, swampy brook', *v.* pludde, brōc. The name has been rationalised to flōd 'a flood'. This stream was *le Merebroc inter Halton' et Clifton'* c.1275 *Chol, v.* 333 *infra*.

FLOOKER'S BROOK (> Newton Brook)

> *Floker(e)sbroc* 1200–50, 1240–9 Chest, *Flokerrisbrook* 1291 *AddCh, Flokersbroke* 1339 (17) Orm[2], *Flokeresbrok* 1354 (1379) Ch *et freq* with variant spellings *Floker(e)s-, Flokars-, -brok(e), -Brouke, -brook(e)* to *Flokersbr(o)ok(e)* 17 Sheaf
> *Flookersbrook* 1539 Orm[2], *Flooker's Brook* 1557 Sheaf *et freq* with variant spellings *-brucke, -Brook(e), (the-)* 1656 Orm[2]
> *Folkers Broke* 1550 *MinAcct*, 1553 Pat
> *Flowkersbrook* 1571 Sheaf, *-brooke* 1594 Morris, 1641 Orm[2], *-bruck* 1573 Morris, *-brucke* 1600 Sheaf
> *Flutterbrooke* 1646 Sheaf
> *Flukersbrook* 1752 Sheaf

This name used to cover the whole course of Finchett's Gutter, Bache Brook and Newton Brook, down to R. Dee at *Port Pool* 333 *infra*. The stream anciently opened into the tidal estuary of R. Dee, and would itself be tidal in its lower reaches. This would make it a suitable place for flukeing, i.e. taking fluke (OE *flōc*, ON *flóki* 'a flat-fish'), a fishery still practised on the Irish Sea coast of Lancashire. As late as 1634–5, Orm² II 822 Roger Hurleton late of the city of Chester held several fisheries in R. Dee 'with *Flookenetts*, draught netts, stall netts, &c.' doubtless for taking fluke. Flooker's Brook, then, is 'the fluker's brook, the fluke-catcher's brook', from OE **flōcere*, ME **flokere* (ON **flókari* is formally possible) and **brōc**. Fransson and Thuresson do not note this occupational term. This stream is also referred to as *the Brooke* 1664 Sheaf, and as *a lake called in olde tyme St. Annes lake* 1573 Sheaf, Morris, *v.* lacu, cf. St Ann St. 334 *infra*, Hoole Rd 332 *infra*. ValeR, 1656 Orm² I 132–3, in an erroneous account of the lower reaches of R. Gowy, suggests that Flooker's Brook, or the boundary stream between Wirral and Broxton hundreds, was called *Wirral*, which is regarded as an unauthenticated name, 'Flooker's-brook...divideth Wirral from the rest of Cheshire, and therefore some imagine that it is called Wirral'. This is obviously a garbled report, cf. *Wervin Brook* 335 *infra*.

FLUELLENS BROOKE (lost, Hoolpool Gutter), *Lewunsbroc* 1307 *Chol* (F* 4, endorsed *Levensbroke* 16), *Leuyggisbroc* 1307–24 *ib*, *Old Lowent Brook* 1581 Sheaf, *Flulins brooke*, *Fluellens brooke* 17 ib, *Pynlors* 1581 Sheaf³ 5 (858). This stream was the boundary between Frodsham and Helsby crossing Frodsham Marsh to Hoolpool Gutter. A mill belonging to Helsby stood upon it in the fourteenth century. *Pynlors* cannot be explained. The earlier name means 'Lēofwine's brook', from the OE pers.n. *Lēofwine* and **brōc**. The pers.n. form changes to OE *Lēofing* and then to MWelsh *Llewellyn* anglicised *Fluellen*.

FOWLE BROOK (R. Wheelock), *Fulebrok* 1181–1232 (1285) Ch, *Fulbrook* 1621 Orm², *the-* 1656 ib, *Foul Brook* 1842 OS, 'dirty stream', *v.* fūl, brōc. In Haslington 331 *infra* the manor court rolls (*AddRoll* 6284–7) name it *the Mylne streame*, *le Mylne Brooke*, *le Milne Brooke* 1572 to 1609, *le Brooke* 1585, *Lie Brook(e)* 1588, 1590, *v.* le, myln, brōc, cf. Mill Fd 333 *infra*.

GAD BROOK (R. Dane), 1831 Bry, *Gadbroke* 1514 *ChEx*, 'gad-fly stream', *v.* gad, brōc, cf. Gadbrook Fm 331 *infra*.

GALE BROOK (Arley Brook), 1831 Bry, 'stream growing with bog-myrtle', *v.* gagel (dial *gale*), 'bog-myrtle', brōc.

GANDERS BROOK (lost, Arley Brook), 1831 Bry, cf. Ganders Bridge 331 *infra*. Perhaps 'gander's brook', *v.* ganra, brōc, but the first el. may be the surname *Gander*. This is also *Suthebroc* 335 *infra*.

GANDYS BROOK (> Snape Brook), *v.* 68 infra.

GOLBORNE BROOK (> Stonyford Brook), the stream gave its name to Golborne David and Golborne Bellow 331 *infra*, from which it is now named. It was *Milton Brooke* 1620 Sheaf, from Milton 333 *infra*.

GOOSE BROOK (Whitley Brook), *v.* gōs, brōc.

R. GOWY (Mersey estuary)

> *Tervin* 1209 Chest, (aqua de-, aqua que dicitur-) *Teruen* 1209, 1241, 1279 ib, Whall, 1290 *Bun*, aqua de *Teruein* 1265–91 Chest, cf. *le Teruen* 13 Whall (p)
> *aqua de Hokenhull* 1347 *ChFor*
> *Gowy* 1577 Holinshed, (*the*) *Gowy* 1656 Orm², *R. Goey* 1831 Bry
> *the Beeston Water* 1656 Orm², *Beeston Brook* 1671 Sheaf
> *R. Clotton* 1775 Sheaf

The various occasional names are from Hockenhull 332 *infra*, Beeston 329 *infra*, and Clotton 330 *infra*, cf. Beeston Brook 329 *infra*, Bunbury Brook 330 *infra*. The old name, which was extended to Tarvin 335 *infra*, is Welsh **terfyn** 'a boundary', i.e. 'the boundary river', *v.* RN 392, Jackson 488, 490, 494 n.4, cf. the Welsh p.n. Terfyn near Prestatyn Fl. Jackson dates the English sound-substitution of OE *f* for the PrWelsh lenition of *-m-* to *-v-* (Lat *terminus* > Welsh *terfyn*) as seventh century and later. This r.n. must have been borrowed into English in the lenited form in that period, cf. R. Dee *supra*. Presumably it was still the 'boundary-river' of a Welsh-speaking community down to the seventh century. The modern name *Gowy* is explained by Ekwall (RN 182) as the Welsh r.n. *Gwy* (English *Wye*), which is of uncertain origin, cf. Db 19, Jackson 452,

387 n.1, 434–5. Professor Melville Richards notes the connection between this r.n. and Welsh *gwyr-o* 'to curve, to bend', which is formally an *-r-* extension of a stem *gwy*. The r.n. probably means 'winding river' or 'river with a bend in it'. The name *Gowy* may have been quite recent when first recorded in 1577, for ValeR (1656, Orm² I 132–3) holds it unauthenticated, 'that which they call Gowy', and 'a river, which some call Gowy'. The pronunciation appears to have been [gu:i] > [goui] > [gaui] *v.* Addenda.

R. GOYT (> R. Mersey)

Guit 1208–29 (1608) ChRR, 1202–29 (1611) *LRMB* 200, 1244 Barnes¹ 15, *Guyt* c.1270 (17) Sheaf, 1284 Pat (p), 1304 ChF (p), 1354, 1370 Eyre, *Guyte* 1335 *Dow*, 1467 *MinAcct*, 1619 Earw *Goyt* c.1251 *For et freq*, le *Goyte* 1503 ChFor, *Goyt(e)* 1577 Saxton, 1611 *LRMB* 200, *Goit* 1577 Holinshed, *the Goit* (*-water*) c.1620, 1656 Orm²
(novus locus de) *Gwto* 1285 *For*

Other forms, in Db 8, are *Gwid*, *Gwyth* 1285, *Guyt* 1244, 1385, *Guyot* 1300. Related p.ns. are at Db 373 and Goyt's Bridge, Clough and Moss, Dale of Goyt, *Head of Goyt* 173 *infra*, Goite Hall 264 *infra*, *Gytehouses* 264 *infra*.

Db 8 refers to Jackson 387 n.1, and to Professor Jackson's objections on formal grounds to Ekwall's suggestion (RN 182–3 maintained in EStud (1959) 373) of Welsh *gwyth* 'channel, conduit, vein'. The principal objection is that Pr.Welsh forms never appear with initial *g-* in the English borrowed form except in late borrowings in Cornwall. The initial *g-* developed in the eighth century in Welsh, and is unlikely to appear in English borrowed forms before the ninth century: even so, the English appear to have rejected initial *gw-* and to have always taken it as *w-*. This argues against the observation by Dr A. G. C. Turner ('Some Celtic Traces in Cheshire and the Pennines', BBCS XXII, Part 2 (1967) 111–19), that this river-name ME *Guyt* might represent OE **Gȳt*, PrOE **Gūit*, going back to a Pr.Welsh **Gwui̯ð* < Common Celtic **U̯eido-*. Dr Turner's arguments would require a Welsh-speaking population surviving along R. Goyt down to the ninth century, and the borrowing of the river-name by the English in a form which would not have been developed by these Welshmen before the end of the eighth century. It would appear simpler to accept that the name *Goyt* represents OE **gyte** 'a rush of

water', *gote 'a watercourse, a gutter', as an anglicisation, or a
substitution, for some older British or Welsh river-name form.
The extent of this r.n. is debated. In e17 copies of e13 perambulations of the Forest of Macclesfield, (Orm¹ III 281, *LRMB* 200
f. 180) R. Goyt ends at its confluence with R. Etherow, where they
become R. Mersey. In 1842 OS also, the name Mersey extends up to
this confluence, but cf. Goite Hall and *Gytehouses* in Bredbury, from
1590 and 1441 respectively, and also White 868 which reports, in
1860, that some call the river *Goyt* all the way down to the confluence
with R. Tame.

THE GRIMSDITCH (lost), 1656 Orm² I 132–3, cf. NQ Ser i, IV 331,
a watercourse said to run from Grimsditch Hall 331 *infra* to R.
Mersey through Preston, Daresbury and Keckwick, though this
course is incredible. The stream-name is a back-formation from
Grimsditch Hall, erroneously applied to Keckwich Brook *infra*.

GUTTERS BROOK, *v.* 331 *infra*.

HARROP BROOK (R. Dean), from Harrop 138 *infra* and brōc. For an
old name *v.* Spuley (Bridge) 140 *infra*.

HAUGHTON BROOK (lost, R. Gowy), 1831 Bry, *Bonebur' Broc* e13 *Bun*,
ducta de Bonebur' 1310–50 *Chol*, *ducta de Lachecote* 13 *Bun, ductus de-*
13 (17) Sheaf, *Lachecote broc* 1312 *CoLegh, aqua que est diuisa inter
Halghton' et Bonebury* 1332 *Chol*; for the various names, cf. Haughton
331 *infra*, Bunbury 330 *infra*, Latch Cote Fd 332 *infra*, Green Lane
(Fm) 331 *infra*.

HENLAKE BROOK (R. Dee), cf. *Henlake* 1842 OS, a locality, probably
originally a watercourse-name, near Cheaveley Bridge 330 *infra*.
Henlake Brook carries Powsey Brooke into R. Dee at 109–415628
from 109–427614. From the run of the boundary between Huntington
and Buerton, Powsey Brook may formerly have joined Dee at Crook
of Dee, 109–424614.

HOGGINS BROOK (R. Wheelock), 1831 Bry.

HOLBROOK (lost, 109–530771 to 533784, R. Weaver) 1844 *TA* 173,
Holebroc c.1249 *Chol*, *-brocke* 1305 *AddCh, Hollebrok* c.1303 *ib*,

-broke 1340 *Chol, Holbrok* 1349 *ib, -broke* 1436 *ib, Howlbrooke* 1630
ib, Old Houlbrook 1754 *ib, Hollow Brooke alias Hole Brook* 1690 *ib*,
'brook in a hollow', *v.* hol², holh, brōc, cf. Holbrook 332 *infra*.

HOLDING BROOK (lost, perhaps formerly to R. Mersey), 1843 *TA* 378,
Holden Brook 1650 *ParlSurv*, 'brook in a deep valley', from hol² and
denu, with brōc, on the boundary of Halton and Norton 331, 333
infra. An earlier name for the part 109–542808 to 544814 on the
Stockton boundary was *Banalsiche* c.1200 Facs, *Banelsych* 1400
AddCh, le Banersiche 1506 *ib*, preserved in Banner Studge-, Bonner
Stitch Meadow 329 *infra*, (now locally *Bannersditch, Bannerstitch*
according to Facs 52). This is sīc 'a stream, a watercourse', and a
place- or stream-name *Banal-, Banel-*, perhaps from bana 'a slayer,
a killer' and wella, wælla 'a spring, a well', i.e. 'dangerous well' or
'killer's well'.

HOLFORD BROOK (lost, Ashton Brook), 1812 Sheaf, *Woodside Brooke*
Jas 1 *Map* (PRO, MR640), the boundary between Kelsall and
Delamere 332, 331 *infra*.

HOLYBROKE (lost, Poynton Brook), 1467 *MinAcct*, 1471 *ib*, 1560
Sheaf, *Holebroke* 13 (1611) *LRMB* 200, *-broc* 1270 (17) Sheaf,
Holbrook 1345 *Eyre, -broke* 1412 *Chol, Halebroke* 1508 *MinAcct*,
'brook in a hollow', *v.* hol², brōc. This is in Rams Clough 184 *infra*,
on the boundary of Adlington and Poynton, cf. *Merebroc* 187 *infra*.

HOLYWELL BROOK (Aldersey Brook), 1842 OS, cf. Holy Well 332
infra, Holywell Fm 332 *infra*, Holywell Fd 332 *infra*.

HOOLPOOL GUTTER (Mersey estuary), *Holpul* 1209 *Bun*, Chest, Whall,
le- 1279 *ib*, Chest, *Holpol* 1209 *ib, Holpol(e)-, -pul-, -pal-, -gote, -gate*
1351 Chamb, BPR, *MinAcct*, 1355 BPR, *Whole Poole* 1626 *Chol*,
Holepooll 1690 *ib*, the *Hole pool* 1799 Sheaf, *Holpool Gutter* 1842 OS,
Hoolpool 1844 *TA* 172, cf. Howpool 332 *infra*, Hole Pole Mdw 332
infra. 'Deep creek', from hol² and pol¹, pull, with gote, goter. There
was a sluice here, cf. '*the sluice of Frodesham*' 1351 BPR, *le Gote inter
manerium de Frodesham et manerium de Ines* 1351 Chamb. The higher
reaches of the stream are Hornsmill Brook, Moor's Brook, Peckmill
Brook 332, 32, 333 *infra*.

HOWBECK BROOK (Artle Brook), cf. Howbeck 332 *infra*.

THE HOWTY (R. Dane), *v.* 332 *infra*.

HURLSTON BROOK (lost), *v. R. Bar, supra*.

KEYS BROOK (lost, > Golborne Brook), 1842 OS, cf. Kay's-, Keys Brook Fd 332 *infra*, 'the cows' brook', *v.* cū, brōc.

KID BROOK (Budworth Mere), cf. Kidbrook 332 *infra*.

LADY BROOK (> Micker Brook), *Brame* c.1621 (1656) Orm² III 546, a back-formation from Bramhall 258 *infra*. The modern name is taken from Lady Bridge 250 *infra*.

LITTLE BROOK (lost), *v.* 205 *infra*.

LOACH BROOK (R. Dane), 1831 Bry, from OFr loche 'a loach', and brōc.

LOSTOCK BROKE (lost) *v.* Bradshaw Brook *supra*.

LOTHBURNE (lost), *v.* 332 *infra*.

LUMB BROOK¹ (R. Dean), cf. Lumb Fm 218 *infra*. LUMB BROOK² (R. Mersey), 1842 OS, *Lumbroc* 1190–9 Facs 15, *Lamb Brook* 1831 Bry, *v.* lumm 'deep hole in a stream', brōc.

MAG BROOK (Bradley Brook), 1831 Bry, *Madbrook* 1837 *TA* 245, cf. Mag Lane 332 *infra*.

THE MAR (lost, R. Bollin), 1656 Orm², 1819 ib, coming out of the mere by Mere Hall 333 *infra*, filling Rostherne Mere 333 *infra*, joining R. Bollin. This is Rostherne Brook 333 *infra*. ValeR (Orm² I 133) regards it as an unauthenticated name. It is a back-formation of The Mere 333 *infra*.

MARTHALL BROOK (> Birkin Brook), *doetum de Marthall* l13, *Wallebrock* 1300, 1301, *Wilbroc* c.1306 (15), *Wylebrok* e14 all JRL 32, cf. *Horse Bridge* 332 *infra* (*Wallbrooke Bridge* 1618), *v.* wælla, wella, brōc, cf. Marthall 333 *infra*, Birkin Brook *supra*, Pedley Brook *infra*.

MASSEY BROOK (> Thelwall Brook), 1831 Bry, from brōc and the surname *Massey*, cf. Massey Brook Fm 333 *infra*, Massey Hall, Thelwall Grange 333, 335 *infra*.

MERE BROOK (Coddington Brook), 1842 OS, *Mare Brook* 1831 Bry, on the boundary of Aldersey and Handley, *v.* (ge)mǣre, brōc.

MERE GUTTER (> Basford Brook), *Besley Mere Brook* 1831 Bry, *v.* brōc, goter, cf. Betley Mere 329 *infra* and in Betley St, Gutter Mdw 331 *infra*. Cf. also Basford Brook 329 *infra*, Checkley Brook *supra*.

R. MERSEY ['məːzi]

betwux...Mærse 1002 (11) ASWills
Mersham (acc.) 1086 DB
Mersam (acc.) 1094 (n.d.) RN, 1130, 1140 (n.d.), 1142 (n.d.), 1149 (1195) ib
Merse 1141–2 (n.d.) RN, 1154–60 (1329) Ch, c.1184 Chest, 1190–9 Facs 15, 1190–1211 *Cott.* Nero C iii *et freq* to 1499 *Eyre*
Mersey 1189–99 Orm[2], 1304 Barnes[1], 1316 JRL 32, 1361 Misc, 1365, 1499, 1519 ChRR, 1487 Plea, 1536–9 Leland *et freq*, *Merseie* 14 Higden, *Mersay* 1347 *ChFor*, 1422–71, 1445 AD, *Mersy* 1443 *MinAcct*, 1459 AD, 1499 ChRR.
Mereseie c.1200 (c.1260) RN, *Merese* 1228 Cl, 1295 Ipm, 1340, 1341 Pat, 1509 Orm[2], *Meres'* 1267 Pat, *Meresee* 1363 Fine, 1380 *Eyre*, 1394 Pat, *Mereses* 1397 ChRR, *Meresie* 15 Higden(Anon)
Mersee 1202–29 (1611) *LRMB* 200, (1608) ChRR, 1209, 1241 Whall, 1277 ib, Chest, 1290 *Bun et freq* to 1577 Saxton, *Mersea* 1387 Trev, 15 Trev(Cx)
Merc 13 Barnes[1], 1387 Trev, *the Merce* 1642 (17) Sheaf, *Mercee* 14 Higden, *Mercy* 1354 Plea, 1364 Pat, 1421 Plea, 1452 *MinAcct*, 1469, 1525 AD, 1633 Earw, 1660 Sheaf, 1793 *JRC* (Barnes[1]), *Mercey* 1383 *Eyre*, 1501 *JRC*, 1650 *ParlSurv*, *Mercie* 1387 Trev, 15 Higden(Anon), 1508 Sheaf, 1611 *LRMB* 200, 1659 Sheaf
Meresse 1276, 1298 RN, 1362 Pat, *Meressee* 1292 RN
Meersee 1309 Plea, *Meerse* 14 Higden, *Meersey* 1577 Earw
Mersce 1353 *MinAcct*
Mersse 1445 ChRR
Marsey 1536–9 Leland, c.1547 *Surv*, 1656 Orm[2], 1729 *Chol*, 1760 Sheaf, *Marsee* 1577 Saxton, *the Marsay* 1656 Orm[2]

Merzey 1621 (1656) Orm[2]
Marcum (acc.) 1653 Sheaf (Ashton super-)
'River at the boundary', *v.* (ge)mǣre, -es[2], ēa, cf. 333 *infra* and
RN 289. Before it received this English name, Mersey may have been
called *Tame*, *v.* R. Tame *infra*.

MICKER BROOK (R. Mersey), 1831 Bry, cf. *Micker Brook* (*site of*) 1844
TA 96, in Cheadle Bulkeley 246 *infra*. The first el. may be common to
this and to Michansedge 333 *infra*, Mecca Brook 333 *infra*.

MIDGE BROOK (> Swettenham Brook), 1842 OS, *Mugebroc* m13
Chest (p), 13 *Dav* (p), l13 Chest (p), *Magebrooke* 1283-8 ib (p),
Michebrock (lit. *Mithe-*) 1290 VR (p), *Miggebroke* 1351 Chamb (p),
1487 *Dav*, *Mygge-* 1464 *ib*, 'brook infested with midges', *v.* mycg,
brōc.

MILL BROOK[1] (R. Gowy), 1842 OS, *R. Twine* 1831 Bry, a mill-lade
to Stanney Mill in Little Stanney, *v.* myln, brōc. It is diverted from
and parallel to R. Gowy, *v.* ModEdial. *twin(e)* 'to separate, to make
two of'. MILL BROOK[2] (Fairywell Brook), perhaps *Enesebroc* 331
infra.

MOOR'S BROOK (> Peckmill Brook, Alvanley), 1842 OS.

NEWHALL CUT (> Sales Brook), *quadam sechetum versus austrum iuxta
inferius caput de le Nonnepoole* ('a certain watercourse towards the
south, next to the lower end of *le Nonnepoole*') e12 *Cott*. Faust.
B viii, *Combrus* 1621 (1656), 1656 Orm[2] I 133, III 289 (where ValeR
regards it as unauthenticated), *v.* cut, cf. Newhall 333 *infra*. *Combrus*
is a back-formation from Combermere 330 *infra*.

NORBURY BROOK (> Lady Brook), *le Mulnebrok'* c.1280 *Dow* (in
Poynton 207 *infra*), *v.* Bollinhurst Brook *supra*. Cf. Norbury 287
infra.

PARADISE BROOK (Wych Brook), 1831 Bry, *v.* paradis, brōc. The
location of this 'paradise' in Oldcastle or Threapwood, 333, 335
infra, is unknown.

PEDLEY BROOK (> Birkin Brook), *Peddeleghebroc* 13 (1611) *LRMB*
200, *Pedelegbroc* 1270 (17) Sheaf, *Marthall Brook* 1842 OS, cf.

Marthall Brook *supra* (on the other boundary of Marthall cum Warford), Pedley 182 *infra*, Pedley Ho 105 *infra*.

PEOVER EYE (> Wincham Brook)
  le Hey 13 Tab
  Peuerhee 13 *Chol*, RN, c.1270 *Chol*, c.1277, 1324 *ib*, *Peuer Hee* 1348
    Dav, *Puer'hee* c.1270 *Chol*, *Peu'hee* c.1290 Tab, *Peuerhe* 1280–
    1300 *Dav*, *Peueree* 1335, 1340 *Chol*, *Puer Eey* 1512 Sheaf, *Pever
    Ee* 1541 AD
  Peuerehe 13 RN, c.1308–17 *JRC*, *-hee* l13 RN, c.1300 *Chol*, c.1306
    JRC, *Puere ee* 1407 *Chol*
  Peuere 1276–7 RN, *Peuer* 1577 ib
  Pyuerehee 1330 *Chol*, *Pyverey river* 1536–9 Leland, *Piuerey* 1577
    RN, *Piuereie* 1577 ib
  Pevyr-eey c.1490 Sheaf
  Peever 1612 RN
  Peever Eye, or Holford Watter 1619 Sheaf, *Peever Eye* 1621 Orm²,
    Peever Brooke 1619 Sheaf
  Peover-Eye c.1620 Orm², *Peover Eye (River)* 1831 Bry, *Peover Eye*
    1842 OS
  The Peover 1819 Orm²
Cf. Peover Superior and Inferior, Nether Peover 333 *infra*. This is ēa 'a river', added to a Brit. r.n. *Pebro-, PrWelsh *Peƀr, Welsh *Pefr*, 'the bright one', cf. RN 322, Jackson 281. The river *Pever* gave its name to the district Peover, from which with ēa and brōc, the river was named again, cf. Golborne Brook *supra*.

PLUNGE BROOK (> Shoresclough Brook), 1842 OS, *v.* 145 *infra*.

POISE BROOK (R. Goyt), 1844 *TA* 186, *rivulum de Bosseden* 13 (17) Orm¹ III 281n., *LRMB* 200, *-Bosdon* 1619 Orm¹ III 281, *the Broucke of Bosden, Bosden Brooke* 1611 *LRMB* 200, *v.* brōc, cf. Bosden 256 *infra*. The modern name is discussed under Poise Bridge 300 *infra*. It is associated with Beanleach 256 *infra*. The lower reach of Poise Brook passes through Foggbrook 291 *infra* which may contain another name for the stream. Cf. Ochreley Brook 300 *infra*.

POTT BROOK (> Preston Brook, Chorley), 'brook at a hole' *v.* potte, brōc, the boundary of Over Alderley and Mottram St. Andrew 99, 202 *infra*.

POYNTON BROOK (Norbury Brook), *Holebroc* 1270 (17) Sheaf, *-broke* 13 (1611) *LRMB* 200, *-brok'* c.1280 *Dow*, 'brook in a hollow', *v.* hol², brōc.

PUDDINGLAKE BROOK (R. Dane), *Pudding Lake* 1831 Bry, 1842 OS; *le Hethlache* 1346 VR, 'boggy stream from a heath', *v.* hǣð, lǣc(c), cf. 12 *supra*. The later name means 'watercourse full of offal', probably denoting an open sewer, *v.* pudding (cf. StNLn 102), lacu, cf. Puddinglake 333 *infra*. Cf. also Shurlach 334 *infra*, which is on this stream and may represent its old name.

RED BROOK¹ (Peover Eye), *Radebroc* c.1300 Tab, *le Radebroke* 1337 *Chol*, *Radebrok* 1356 *ib*, *le-* 1357 *ib*, *Radbrok* c.1372 Tab, *le Reebrok* 1332 Orm², cf. Redbrook Fm 333 *infra* for other early forms, cf. also Red Eye Mdw 333 *infra*. RED BROOK² (R. Dean), *Redebrok* 1290 Court (p), *Radebrok* 1348 *Eyre*, *le Redbroke* c.1414 *Mont*, cf. Redbrook Bridge etc., 184 *infra*. RED BROOK³ (R. Mersey), *Whites Brook* 1831 Bry, *Wych Brook* 1842 OS, cf. Redbrook Ho 333 *infra*, Fairywell Brook *supra*. All three mean 'red brook', *v.* rēad, brōc.

SALES BROOK (R. Weaver), 1842 OS, cf. Salesbrook Bridge etc., 334 *infra*.

SALTERS BROOK¹ (R. Etherow), *v.* 325 *infra*. SALTERS BROOK² (Barrow Brook), 1831 Bry, *le Bromehill Broke* 1512 *Chol*, cf. *le Hee* 332 *infra*, cf. Saltersford (Bridge) 334 *infra*, Broom Hill 330 *infra*, Barrow Brook 329 *infra*.

SANDERSON'S BROOK (R. Croco), 1831 Bry, cf. Sanderson's Mdw 334 *infra*, presumably from a surname *Sanderson* and brōc. This stream was *doetum de Clayt(e)ford* 1260–82, a.1274 MidCh, *Claytfordbrooke* 1310 *ib* (cf. Cledford 330 *infra*), and *Hulmesbrok'* 1349 *Vern* (cf. Curtishulme 331 *infra*).

SANDYFORD BROOK (> Darley Brook), 1812 Sheaf, *a litle brooke caullid Sanddiford* 1536–9 Leland, cf. Sandyford 334 *infra*. This was also *le Brokh* 1360 ChRR, *Colbroke* (*Mylne*) 1476 *ib* (cf. Oulton Mill 333 *infra*), *Colebrooke* Jas 1 *Map* (*LRMB* 200), *Cole Brook* 1751 Sheaf, *Coatbrook* 1828 ib, *Cote Brook* 1831 Bry, *v.* Cote Brook 331 *infra*.

SHEAR BROOK (Bradshaw Brook), *Shaghesyche* 1346 VR, *Goostree Brooke* 1619 Sheaf, *Shay Brook* 1839 *TA* 405, *v.* sceaga, sīc, brōc, cf. Goostrey 331 *infra*, Chikenshagh 12 *supra*.

SLITTEN BROOK (> Sow Brook), *Dane* 1819 Orm² 1 580, cf. Danebank Ho 331 *infra*, Deansgreen 331 *infra*. This is probably named from the dingle in Lymm through which it runs, *v.* denu, and is the stream giving rise to the p.n. Lymm 332 *infra*. The meaning of the modern name is unknown.

SMALL BROOK¹ (Sanderson's Brook), 1831 Bry, *Smallebroc(k)* 1308 *Vern.* SMALL BROOK² (Crowton Brook), 1780 *EnclA* (Crowton 331 *infra*), *Smale Brooke* Jas 1 *Map* (*LRMB* 200), *Blake Mere Brook* 1812 Sheaf, 'narrow stream', *v.* smæl, brōc, cf. Fox Covert Lodge 331 *infra*, Blakemere (Moss) 329 *infra*.

SMOKER BROOK (Wincham Brook), a modern name for Waterless Brook¹ *infra* and Benstall Brook *supra* above their confluence with Peover Eye, taken from Smoker Inn in Plumley, cf. Smoker Brook, Hill and Wood 334 *infra*.

SNAPE BROOK (> Peover Eye), 1831 Bry, *aqua de Hasthal, -hul* c.1238 (1595) ChRR, *Astyll sych* 1441 Dav, *Siddington Brook* 1831 Bry, *v.* sīc, brōc, cf. Astle 76 *infra*, Snape 88 *infra*, Snape Brook Fm 87 *infra*, Siddington 84 *infra*, *Rauenkelesbroc* 88 *infra*.

SOW BROOK (R. Mersey), 1842 OS, *Little Saw Brook* 1839 *TA*, *v.* brōc. The first el. may be sugu 'a sow'.

SPENCER BROOK (R. Bollin), 1831 Bry, cf. Spencer Fd. 213 *infra*.

STANNEY BROOK (lost, in Bollington 330 *infra*), 1842 OS, *le Stanybrok'* 1318 JRL, 'stony brook', *v.* stānig, brōc, cf. Stoney Lake Mdw 334 *infra*.

STEER BROOK (> Shropshire Union Canal > Marbury Brook¹), *Stair-brook* 1724 NotCestr, cf. Steer Bridge 334 *infra*.

SUGAR BROOK (Mobberley Brook), *Ashley Brook* 1842 OS, from Ashley 329 *infra* and brōc, cf. Sugar Brook Bridge etc. 335 *infra*,

Sugar Hill 335 *infra*, and *Sugar Mill Brook* 1831 Bry a tributary of Sugar Brook on the Ashley–Mobberley boundary. The first el. may be **sugre** 'sugar, sweet'.

SWILL BROOK (Valley Brook), 1842 OS, probably 'brook which swills', i.e. with a tendency to flood, *v.* **swille, brōc.**

SWIM BROOK (> Mobberley Brook), 1847 *TA* 268, probably a brook with a swim in it, from ModE *swim* 'a stretch of water frequented by fish' or '-in which an angler fishes' (NED) and **brōc.** Another example is Swimbrooke 234 *infra*.

R. TAME (> R. Mersey), *Tome* n.d. (13) RN, 1292 ib, 1367 *Eyre, Thame* 13 Whall, *Tame* 1322 (15) RN, 1577 ib, 1656 Orm², 1842 OS, *Taume* 1622 RN, 1656 Orm², a Brit. r.n. *Tămā*, of unknown meaning (Ekwall suggests 'the dark water', but Professor Jackson thinks this very doubtful, *v.* RN 390, Jackson 487, cf. foll). *Tame* may have been the name of the whole Mersey before the latter became an English boundary-river; this head-water, not marking a boundary, would retain the old name, while the lower course, the boundary, would take the new one.

TAMYON BROOK (R. Tame), in Micklehurst 322 *infra*, probably named after R. Tame *supra*, of which it is a tributary, but the development is not known.

TIMBERS BROOK (R. Dane), *v.* Timbersbrook 335 *infra*.

TINKERS BROOK (lost), *v.* Todd Brook.

TODD BROOK (R. Goyt), *Toddesbrok* 1366 *Eyre*, 'fox's brook', *v.* **todd, brōc,** cf. *Tods Cliff* 141 *infra*. The lower course, now Toddbrook Reservoir in Taxal, was *Tinkers Brook* 1831 Bry, *v.* **tink(l)ere, brōc,** cf. Tynkar's Bancke 181 *infra*.

TOR BROOK, *v.* 128 *infra*.

TORKINGTON BROOK (R. Goyt), *Harper Brook* 1831 Bry. Cf. Torkington 299 *infra*.

VALLEY BROOK (R. Weaver)

Cruebrok 1335 *AddCh*

Wortʒorn (lit. *Westʒorn*, glossed *Westthorn*) 1406 Rich, *Wortyorn*
1450–60 *AddCh*, *Wortyorne* 1579 *ib*

Sloderhilbroke 1536 Sheaf, *Slaughter Hill Brook* 17 ib

Gory Brook 17 Sheaf

Wolwern Brook 1621 (1656) Orm², *Wulvarn* 1656 ib

*Valley (or South) Brook . . . sometimes dignified into the River Waldron
or Walvern* 1950 Chaloner

Another name is *Cartereslake* 330 *infra*. Associated with this stream
are Slaughter Hill 334 *infra*, The Valley, Valley Fm 335 *infra*,
Waldron's Lane 335 *infra*, Crewe 331 *infra*. The three remaining
names *Wortʒorn*, *Gory Brook* and *Wolwern Brook* are independent.
The first may possibly be OE *weorþ-georn* 'noble, excellent'. *Gory
Brook* is 'dirty brook', from gor, -ig³ 'dirty'; and *Wolwern* the same
compound as may appear in *Ollerpool(e)* 333 *infra* perhaps OE **hwalf-
ærn* 'house with a vault' or 'conduit-house'.

WADE BROOK (Wincham Brook), 1619 Sheaf, *Lostok(e)brok(e)* 1346
VR, *The Lostock Water* 1656 Orm², cf. Bradshaw Brook *supra*. *Wade*
is (ge)wæd 'a ford'.

WALTON BROOK (R. Mersey), 1843 *TA* 3, *Acton Yeard* c.1554 Whall,
Fenners Brook 1690 Sheaf, cf. Acton Grange 329 *infra* and Walton 335
infra, between which this was the boundary—'the rivulet which runs
between Acton and Walton' 1237–8 Whall, 'the rivulet running from
the flood-gate of the milldam of the mill called the Wood-mill of
Acton, as far as the old course of that water' c.1263 ib, 'the water
between the two mills . . . at . . . Acton Grange' 1286 Whall. The
geard refers to the mill-pond mentioned above. *Fenner* is probably a
surname.

WATERLESS BROOK¹ (Smoker Brook), 1842 OS, *Waterles* 1260–70,
1381 Tab, *Waterles-river* 1666 Orm², *Wateriles* 1260–70 Tab, *Water-
lesse* 1536–9 Leland, cf. Waterless Bridge 335 *infra*, from a p.n.
meaning 'the water(y) meadow', v. wæter, læs. It is Arley Brook in
1″ OS 7th ed. WATERLESS BROOK² (R. Gowy), 1831 Bry, cf. Waterless
Wood 335 *infra*.

R. WEAVER (Mersey estuary)

> *Weuer* c.1130 (1479) *Cott*. Faust. B viii, *Veuere* 1209–29 *AddCh*,
> *Wev-*, *Weuer(e)* c.1230–40 *JRC*, c.1240 Tab, 1240–50 *JRC*,
> c.1275 *Chol et freq* to *Weuere* 1468 *Sotheby*, *Wever* 1719 Sheaf,
> *Weuare* 1405 *AddCh*
> *Weever* 1133 (n.d.) Dugd, 1358 ChRR, 1546 *Chol*, 1602 *Sotheby*
> 1656, 1819 Orm[2]
> *Weure* 1190–1211 *Cott*. Nero C iii, c.1220 *AddCh*, *Weura* c.1220 *ib*,
> *Wevre* 1280 Ipm, 1289 RN, 1298 *Chol*, 1351 BPR
> *Wewir* c.1275 *Chol*
> *Wiure* 1284 VR
> *Wyvere* 1300 Sheaf, 1354 BPR, *Wiuere* c.1313 *AddCh*, 1314 *ib*,
> *Wyver* 1536–9 Leland, *Wiver* 1536–9 ib, 1570 *AddCh*, *Wiuer*
> 1577, 1586 RN
> *Weaver* 1341 Barnes[1], 1656 Orm[2]

'Winding stream', *v.* wēfer(e), cf. RN 445 and Weaver, Weaverham 335 *infra*. The form *Weuerhe* for Weaver township is the r.n.
with ēa 'a river', as may also be some of the spellings in *-e*.

R. WHEELOCK (R. Dane)

> *Quelok* c.1300 *Chol*, *Qwelok* 1321 AD
> *Whelok, -ocke* 1577 RN, *The Whelock, Whelock-water* 1621 Orm[2]
> *Wheelock Watter* 1619 Sheaf, *-Water* 1621 Orm[2], *-Brooke* 1619
> Sheaf, *Wheelock* 1656 Orm[2]

This stream was also *Sutton Watter or Brooke, Smallwood Brooke
& Lawton Brooke* 1619 Sheaf, from wæter, brōc, with Sutton 335
infra, Smallwood 334 *infra*, Church Lawton 330 *infra*. Early forms of
the r.n. Wheelock appear in Wheelock 335 *infra*, Wheelock St.
(Middlewich) 335 *infra*, Stanthorne Bridge 334 *infra*. This means
'winding river', Brit. *S̨uilāco-*, Welsh *chwylog* (Welsh *chwyl* 'a
turn, a rotation, a course', with *-og*, adj. suffix), cf. RN 455, Jackson
526. The latter describes the form as a seventh-century borrowing
from OWelsh to OE. Professor Melville Richards finds that Ekwall's
adjectival form does not exist in Welsh, and in LCHS cxi (1959), 199,
offers an alternative derivation from Welsh *chwil* 'beetle, chafer', in
an adj. compound *chwilog* 'abounding with beetles', assuming that
the English form *-ee-* [i:] represents Welsh [i:], that is OWelsh [i:] >
OE [i] > ME [ē] > ModE [i:]. But this etymology would suggest a

progression [iː] > [iː] > [iː] > [ai], producing a modern form
*Whylock [wailok] instead of Wheelock [wiːlok], and the spellings
do not support this. They indicate a progression OWelsh [i] > OE
[i] > ME [i, ę̄, iː] > ModE [iː], supporting Ekwall.

WHIM BROOK (Preston Brook, Chorley).

WHITLEY BROOK (> Cogshall Brook), *Street Lane Brook, Clatterwick
Brook* 1831 Bry, v. brōc, cf. Lower Whitley 335 *infra*, Street Lane 335
infra, Clatterwick 330 *infra*.

WINCHAM BROOK (R. Weaver), 1842 OS, *Witton Brook(e)* 1765 Tab,
1845 *TA* 442, v. brōc, cf. Wincham 336 *infra*, Witton 336 *infra*. This
is Peover Eye *supra*.

WYCH BROOK (Worthenbury Brook, Fl), *R. Elf* 1831 Bry, *R. Elfe* 1882
Orm[2]. The origin of *Elf(e)* is not known. ON *elfr* 'a river' seems un-
likely here. *Wych* refers to the saltwich at Wychough 336 *infra*,
Higher & Lower Wych 336 *infra*.

ROAD-NAMES

Few of the medieval roads in Cheshire bore one name throughout
their length, so the various names have been grouped under routes.
Information on the old roads in Cheshire is available in W. Harrison,
'Preturnpike Highways in Lancashire and Cheshire', LCAS IX
101–34, H. J. Hewitt, *Mediæval Cheshire*, Chet NS LXXXVIII, chap.viii,
W. B. Crump, 'Saltways from the Cheshire Wiches', LCAS LIV
84–142.

I. CHESTER–WREXHAM Fl, v. Wrexham Rd 336 *infra*. It extends in Ch
from Handbridge 109–4065 to Pulford 109–3759.

II. CHESTER-WEST KIRBY. *(le)Porteswaye* 1309 *Plea*, Sheaf[3] 25 (5753,
5762), at 109–319770 where Ness, Willaston and Little Neston meet,
cf. Chester Road Fd, Dam Head Lane 330, 331 *infra*, 'the road to a
(market-) town', v. port-weg.

III. CHESTER–WILLASTON–WALLASEY. *(le) Blakestret(e)* 1305 Chest,
1331, 1357 *ChFor*, 'dark road,' v. blæc, stræt, a road in Willaston and

Childer Thornton 330 *infra*, 109–337787 to 345771, cf. Street
Hey 335 *infra*. It was the east boundary of Willaston (1305 Chest) and
led from Chester to Wallasey Pool on the way to Liverpool (1357
ChFor). Perhaps it is Roman, for the surviving section is aligned upon
Northgate, Chester.

IV. CHESTER–TRAFFORD–FRODSHAM–LATCHFORD–WARRINGTON La.
Cf. The Street (6″) in Mickle Trafford, Hoole and Picton, 109–445702
to 425684, (*The*) *Street* 1842 OS, cf. Street Field 334 *infra*, *v.* strǣt.
This is designated Roman in the old 6″ OS map and in 1″ OS 7th ed.
The line from Chester to Trafford Bridge is followed by Newton
Hollow 333 *infra*. It may be supposed to continue north-eastward
from Trafford Bridge to Frodsham Bridge, perhaps as the modern
main road, but there was a medieval route through Manley, *v.* VI
infra. The east end of this route is the road 109–5781 to 101–6186, by
Sutton, Preston on the Hill, Daresbury, Walton, Stockton and
Wilderspool to Warrington, designated Roman by 1″ OS 7th ed.
Associated with this part are *Stanilode* c.1250 *LRO* ('stone or stony
passage', *v.* stān, stānig, (ge)lād) at Stockton 334 *infra*, and Chester
Lane 330 *infra*, Street Moors 335 *infra*, *Stretemore* 335 *infra*.
Chester Lane may not be the ancient route, which may have led from
109–575817 to 563816 to 553806, by Red Brow 333 *infra* in Preston,
Wood Lane 336 *infra* in Norton and Stockham, thence by alignment
on Frodsham Bridge.

V. HOOLE HEATH AND PICTON–SHOTWICK. A route branching off IV
supra at 109–437697, along Salter's Lane 334 *infra* and probably also
Acres Lane 329 *infra*, 109–437697 to 415700. The rest is lost, *v.* Hoole
Heath, *Salterway* 332, 334 *infra*. This was both a saltway (Crump 95)
and a military road.

VI. ?TRAFFORD–MANLEY–?NORTHWICH, *v.* Manley Lane, *Saltere-
strete* 333, 334 *infra*.

VII. CHESTER–STAMFORD BRIDGE–TARVIN–KELSALL–SANDIWAY–
NORTHWICH–CROSSFORD BRIDGE–MANCHESTER La. A Roman road,
Iter II in AntIt, cf. discussion under *Condate* 330 *infra*. It is desig-
nated 'Watling Street' in the old 6″ OS map and 1842 OS. The name

is not historical but rather an antiquarian extension to this road. It is associated with the p.ns. Tarvin Road 335 *infra*, Streetfield Ho, Stamford Bridge, Saltersbridge, Street Field Saltersford Bridge and Street Fm 334 *infra*, Kelsall Hill 332 *infra*, Stoney Lane and Sandiway 334 *infra*, Erbach Cross 331 *infra*, Chester Rd 330 *infra*, Castle St. (Castle Northwich) 330 *infra*, High St. (Northwich) 332 *infra*, Witton Street 336 *infra*, Condate 330 *infra*, Manchester Rd and *Over Street* 333 *infra*, Holford Street 332 *infra*, *Tabley Street*, and Street Meadow 335 *infra*, St Paul's Church 334 *infra*, *Strettelegh* 335 *infra*, Streethead 334 *infra*, Watlingford, Watling Ho, Washway Rd and Washway (Fm) 335 *infra*, Dunham Road, Highgate Rd 331, 332 *infra*, Shepherd's Brow and Street Acre 334 *infra*, Watling Gate and Washway Cottages 335 *infra*, Siddall's Bridge and Smith's Bridge 334 *infra*, Wash Lane and Washway Fm 335 *infra*, Street Field 334 *infra*, Cross Street and Crossford Bridge 331 *infra*, and with Stretford and Trafford La 32.

The stretch from Northwich to Tabley is alluded to by Leland iv 5 in 1536–9, 'a v. miles be cawse-way'. It was *regia via que ducit versus Mamcestriam* 1272–1307 MidCh, *via que ducit versus North Wycum* c.1313 Chol, *-Medium Wycum* 1330 *ib* (i.e. Manchester La, Northwich and Middlewich 333 *infra*); and *le Lynstrete* c.1277, c.1300 *Chol*, 1310 Tab, *Lynstrete* 1339 ib, c.1490, 1512 Sheaf, *le Lynt Strete* 1407 *Chol* ('road to *The Lyme*', i.e., 'to the borders of Cheshire', from stræt and *The Lyme* 2 *supra* in its sense 'the Cheshire frontier', cf. routes X, XXVII, *infra*). The stretch in Rostherne and Over Tabley was *le Salteresway*, *-is-* c.1300 JRL 32, *Salterestwaye*, *Salter-(e)sway(e)* 1339 Tab ('the salter's way', v. saltere, weg). Off it leads Ashley Rd 329 *infra*, formerly *Salter's Lane*. The name *Washway* 1831 Bry, is applied to the stretch in Ashton on Mersey, Sale, Dunham Massey and Altrincham, particularly at the traverse of Timperley Brook and Baguley Brook at Siddall's Bridge and Smith's Bridge in Timperley. The name is 'flooding road', from (ge)wæsc and weg, alluding to a liability to flood at these fords. Other old names for this road are *alta via* 1347 ChFor in Kelsall; *Harebachesty* (v. stīg, *Erbach Cross* 331 *infra*); *regalis via*, *le Kynges strete*, *regia strata* at Castle St. (Castle Northwich), High St. (Northwich), Manchester Rd 330, 332, 333 *infra* (v. cyning, stræt, cf. route X); *the Street* (cf. 334 *infra*), *Tabley Street* 335 *infra*.

VIII. CHESTER–EATON–ALDFORD–STRETTON–MALPAS–WHITCHURCH Sa. This was a Roman road, Iter II in AntIt, discussed under Stretton 335 *infra*. Associated with it are the p.ns. Eaton Rd 331 *infra*, Heronbridge 332 *infra*, Stretton 335 *infra*, Iron Bridge, Aldford, Hales Fd 332, 329, 331 *infra*, Redgate Fd, Stretton 333, 335 *infra*, Tilston Lane 335, *infra*, Malpas, High St. (Malpas), *Hintwike Yate* and *le Holxheway* 332 *infra*. The line of road between Aldford and Stretton is disused. It was *vetus strata de Etton* 1305 *AddCh* 49886 ('the old road from Eaton') at approximately 109–425580 to 430568, since a piece of heathland in that deed, belonging to Aldford manor, was bounded by *le Bruchis* 330 *infra* in Aldford, by the Churton–Edgerley road (109–425568 to 435569), and by the stream from Churton to this 'old street' (109–425565 to 425580). This line is continued to Barton township along the boundary between King's Marsh and Coddington (109–433564 to 436548). It was also called *le strete* 1257 *AddCh*, *alta strata que ducit de Malo Passu versus Cestr'* e14 *ib*, at Tilston (*v.* stræt, cf. Malpas, Chester 332, 330 *infra*); *Portwey* 13 *AddCh* at Coddington ('road to a (market-)town', *v.* port-weg), *le Portwey* 14 *ib*, Churton by Farndon (but this may be the Aldford–Farndon road); *via de Clavertone* 1292–3 Sheaf, in Claverton (*v.* Eaton Rd *supra*); *alta strata* 1341 Chol, High St. (Malpas) *supra*); *Red Gate* 1831 Bry, in Stretton (*v.* Redgate Fd *supra*).

This route declined in importance after the twelfth century, when the fords at Aldford and south of Malpas had become impassable, *v.* Aldford, Malpas 329, 332 *infra*. Alternative routes were developed, from Chester to Aldford by c.1200 via Great Boughton and Huntington (cf. Sandy Lane 334 *infra*), and to Whitchurch Sa, by 1315 at least, via Great Boughton, Huntington or Christleton, Handley, Broxton, Hampton, Macefen, Tushingham and Bradley (cf. Street Way 335 *infra*, Portersheath 333 *infra*, Stonyford 334 *infra*, Blake Street 330 *infra*). A further development took the route from Christleton over R. Gowy at Hockenhull Platts to route XXIV *v.* 48 *infra*.

IX. (MALPAS–) TARPORLEY–SANDIWAY (–ACTON–STRETTON). The medieval road from Tarporley to Northwich is noted from Sandyford (109–573657, 334 *infra*), as *via de Sondy-*, *Sondiford* (*ducens*) *versus Norwyc(um)* 1347 *ChFor*, northwards, and as *regia alta via inter le Sondyforde et Torpurley* 1503 *ib*, southwards 109–5765 to 5562. The stretch from 109–5765 to 110–6072, joining route VII near Sandiway, was *Peytevinnisti* 1275 Misc, *Peytevinnesty* 1275 Sheaf, *Peytvinnisty*, *Peytevinnestey* 1278 Misc, *Paytefynsty* 1359 VR, *Peytefynsty* 1359 Sheaf, 'the Poitevin's trackway', from stīg and the ME surname *Peiteuin* (AFr *Peitevyn* 'a man from Poitou'), possibly to be identified with Roger *Pictavensis* named in DB as formerly tenant of the land between Ribble and Mersey. A later name was *Padfield Way* 1699 Sheaf[3] 34 (7538), *-feild-* Jas 1 *Map* (*LRMB* 200). Street Field 334 *infra* (109–5051) is on a southward extension, and Street Lane 335 *infra*, (101–605775 to 614788, cf. Street Field 334 *infra*, Whitley Brook Bridge 335 *infra*, Whitley Brook 39 *supra*) in Dutton, Little Leigh and Lower Whitley, which forms with Booths Lane 330 *infra* a line of route from Stretton (101–620825) 335 *infra* to Acton Bridge on R. Weaver, leading to Cuddington and Sandiway, marks a northern extension. The whole route would connect Warrington La with Malpas and Whitchurch Sa, much as the modern A49.

X. WARRINGTON La–LATCHFORD–STRETTON–NORTHWICH–MIDDLEWICH–ELWORTH–CHURCH LAWTON–NEWCASTLE UNDER LYME OR CHESTERTON St. This would be a Roman road from a Roman station at Wilderspool 335 *infra* to *Condate* 330 *infra*, *Salinis* 334 *infra*, and Chesterton St. It is designated Roman and named *King Street* in 1″ O.S. 7th ed. at Stretton (101–620825), in Rudheath (110–695700) and at Elworth (110–745613), between which the line is fairly clear, cf. *Over Street* 333 *infra*; but between Elworth and Chesterton it is uncertain. It could proceed as the modern road via Sandbach, Rode Heath and Lawton Gate (110–809560, 332 *infra*, cf. route XI and *Salteresbache*, *le Stanweyeruding* 334 *infra*), to Red Street St (110–829510). Alternatively, it could have gone by Wheelock (110–752593) and Radway Green 333 *infra* (110–777543), i.e. a lost route abandoned in favour of the modern one. The south end of route X probably fell away as the corresponding part of route XI developed i.e. by c.1400 as PremIt No. 8. The Warrington–Middlewich–Newcastle road is *alta via que ducit de Werinton versus Nouum Castrum* 1321 MidCh, *via regalis ducens versus Novum Castrum* 1325 ib. The way from Warrington to Northwich is associated with the p.ns. Warrington Bridge 335 *infra*, Wilderspool Causeway 335 *infra*, Old London Rd 333 *infra*, London Rd, *Strethbrok* 332, 335 *infra*, Stretton 335 *infra*. The name *King Street* is an extension to this stretch from the Northwich–Middlewich section. The northern section was *via que descendit a Wyc ad Weryngton* 1307 *LRO*, (the right of way in 1354 is described in DKR xxviii, 55), and '*the high road that leads from*...*Warrington as far as Lyn-strete*' c.1490 Sheaf[1] 3, p. 77 (cf. route VII). It was called *le Saltlydehyate* c.1250 *LRO* (334 *infra*, in Stockton), *le Sale(lyde)yate* 1354 Plea (334 *infra*, in Appleton), *le Grenegate* 113 *LRO* (London Rd *supra*).

The way from Northwich to Middlewich is King Street 332 *infra* (*Kingstreete* 1609 *Rental, King or Kind Street* 1842 OS, *regalis via super Ruddehet* 1300–30 *Chol*, 'royal road, the king's road' *v.* cyning, strǣt, probably named from the royal demesnes at Drakelow). Another name is *le Linstrete* c.1300 *Chol, Lynstrete* 1346 VR, 1357 ChRR, BPR, 1356–8 Orm[2], *Lymstrete* E3 *Surv*, at Rudheath and Drakelow ('road to *The Lyme*', *v.* strǣt, *The Lyme* 2 *supra*, cf. routes VII, XXVII). Associated p.ns. are *Condate* 330 *infra, Over Street* 333 *infra*, King Street Hall & Fm 332 *infra*, Harbutt's Fd 331 *infra*.

The way from Middlewich to Elworth is Booth Lane 330 *infra*, London Rd 332 *infra*, (*Booth Lane* 1515 MidCh, (*le*) *Booth(e)lane* 1541 ib *et freq*), named from Bowfields 330 *infra*. An unproven Roman road from Middlewich south via Withinstreet Fm 336 *infra* may have led to Radway Green, cf. Street Field in Haslington 334 *infra*, also Atlas 13.

XI. NEWCASTLE UNDER LYME St–CHURCH LAWTON–HOLMES CHAPEL –KNUTSFORD–GRAPPENHALL–WARRINGTON La. The route is No. 8 in PremIt, c.1400, *Newcastel vnder Lynde*...(*inde usque Stopforde* deleted) *inde usque holme chapell xii ml*, (*inde usque prestkote* deleted), *inde usque Weryntone xii.*, cf. routes XII *infra*, X *supra*. The p.ns. associated with it are Cliff Lane 330 *infra*, Bradley Cross 330 *infra*, Street Field 334 *infra, Strettle* 335 *infra*, Warrington Common 335 *infra*, Street Lane (110–797602 to 809575) 335 *infra*, Forge Mill, *Styfordlone* 331, 335 *infra*, Lawton Gate *Salteresbache*, (*le*) *Stanwey(e)ruding(e)* 332 *infra*, 334 *infra*. The road is called *antiqua via* 13, *Stanystrete* 1352 (*v.* stānig, strǣt) at High Legh, *strata de Roda* 1184, *the Strete* 1604 at Street Lane (Odd Rode).

XII. NEWCASTLE UNDER LYME St–STOCKPORT. Itinerary No. 8 in PremIt shows that route XI *supra* superseded a route from Newcastle to Stockport. The details are not known, cf. foll.

XIII. STOCKPORT–CONGLETON. At Nether Alderley and Alderley Edge the road 101–843782 to 843763 was *Street Lane*, *v.* 98 *infra*, and may have been part of XII *supra*. At Marton (110–850680) is the lost road-name *le hyerlisweye*, *v.* 83 *infra*. An early route from Congleton to Stockport via Gawsworth, Broken Cross, Prestbury, Poynton and Hazel Grove appears to have been followed by the perambulations of the Forest of Macclesfield, 10 *supra*, cf. XVII *infra*.

XIV. STOCKPORT–TAXAL. Orm[1] III 536 reports the course of a supposed Roman road from Stockport to Buxton Db, via Bramhall, Adlington, Rainow and Taxal. The route is traced at Bramhall Lane 259 *infra* (101–893852 to 899890, designated Roman in the old 6″ O.S. map), or alternatively at Pepper Street 260 *infra* (101–905867 to 903859), *Street Fields* 260 *infra* (101–897854), Lumb Lane (*Hand Lane* 1842 OS) 260 *infra* (101–897843 to 900838). In Woodford township *alta strata* and *Derlingesyate* 1289 *ChFine* refer to the continuation of this route, which appears to leave Bramhall township southwards by *Hand Lane*, passing the field Great Darlingshaw (101–899838) on the Woodford boundary, to become the Woodford–Poynton boundary 101–900838 to 902836. *Derlingesyate* was probably a gate on this road at the Bramhall boundary near Great Darlingshaw. In Adlington township Street Lane 184 *infra* (101–913818 to 924817) may be on or near the line. In Rainow and Taxal, Ormerod observed the old road from Rainow Low (101–955772) to Saltersford 138 *infra* (101–983763), thence by Oldgate Nick 144 *infra* (101–995763), Embridge Causeway 173 *infra* (101–995766 to 000763), The Street 174 *infra* (111–005761 to 010760), to Goyt's Bridge (111–014751) and into Db. This stretch is *Oldegate* 1503 *ChFor*, *the Oldgate* 1782 Earw, *the Old Gate, The Street, Embridge Causeway* 1819 Orm[2], *Oldgate, Lower Street* 1842 OS, *v.* ald, gata. It may be associated with 'an old way in Rainow disused since ancient times, one leading from *blackwall* as far as the rivulet of *Hurdesbroke*' 1508 *MinAcct*, cf. Black Brook, *Hurdenbroke* 142, 147 *infra*. At Saltersford this route takes up a salt-way from Macclesfield into Db, Crump 135, 137.

XV. MACCLESFIELD–BUXTON Db. Cf. Crump 134–5. The p.ns. associated with this route are Windyway 123, 145 *infra*, Greenways 128 *infra*, Stonway 128 *infra*.

XVI. MACCLESFIELD–LEEK St. The existence of a medieval route here is supposed by the existence of a toll-passage in 1327 at Hug Bridge 55 *infra* (110–932636), but a direct line of lanes and tracks leads from Macclesfield to Dieulacres Abbey (110–980578) via Cleulow Cross 165 *infra* and Wincle.

XVII. MACCLESFIELD–CONGLETON. This may be the route of the road referred to in *le Strete* 1363 in Gawsworth 71 *infra*, but cf. XIII *supra*.

XVIII. CONGLETON–BUXTON Db. The only record of a route through Wincle & Wildboarclough may be traced in Stoneway Edge (110–991663) 162 *infra*, Sandyway (110–954672) 169 *infra*, Cleulow Cross 165 *infra*. A route from Congleton to Leek St was *Earlswaie* 1593 (*v.* Reade's Lane 333 *infra*, cf. *Hyerlisweye* route XIII *supra* and 83 *infra*).

XIX. NORTHWICH–MACCLESFIELD. There is no direct modern route between these towns. The course of the medieval route is observable from Northwich to Allostock and from Macclesfield to Broken Cross, cf. Crump 96. The middle course appears to have been divided. The western part of the route is *alta via de Maclesfeld usque ad vadum de Porteford'* 1291–1316 Chest, '*the street that leads from Macclesfield to Chester*' E3 Orm², c.1380–90 ChRR, at Hulse Lane 332 *infra* (110–700731 to 715728), perhaps *le Wyteweye* 336 *infra*. This follows a line from Broken Cross 330 *infra* (110–684732) on King Street (route X *supra*) to Portford 333 *infra* (110–717730), whence it proceeded as *Saltway* l13 Tab, 334 *infra*, to Bradshaw (110–739726) 330 *infra* and Cross Lanes Fm 331 *infra* (110–753724), by Hulme Lane (110–720731 to 732731) and Baker's Lane (110–732731 to 739725) 332, 329 *infra*. From Cross Lanes Fm the route may have proceeded by a more or less direct line to Siddington (110–845709) to join route XXI *infra* to Broken Cross 118 *infra* (110–893735, Chelford Road 122 *infra*, and Chestergate (Macclesfield) 115 *infra*. This stretch may be *Salteriswey* 334 *infra* unless this is route XXI. Alternatively, from Macclesfield and Broken Cross, the road proceeded to Chelford, 110–917737 to 818743, as *Pepper Street* 1842 OS 78 *infra*, in Henbury, and *le Portwey, Macclesfeld Strete* 77 *infra* in Chelford. From Chelford it could turn south to join the other line at 110–807719 near Withington Green, or it could proceed west to Cross Lanes Fm by joining Carter Lane 76, 330 *infra*, *Pepper Street* 333 *infra*. Carter Lane appears to be the vestige of a route from Alderley Edge, forming the boundary between Chelford and Snelson and Marthall cum Warford, and crossing Peover Superior by a direct line of lanes and paths 110–797745 to 783741 to 772732 to 760732, by Parkgate, Peover Hall and Longlane Fm, to Cross Lanes Fm.

XX. MIDDLEWICH–PEOVER. This is designated a Roman road in 1″ O.S. 7th ed., 110–723695 to 729709, *v.* Street Field 334 *infra*, cf. 12 *supra*.

XXI. MIDDLEWICH–MACCLESFIELD. A medieval route is traced as a salt-way, Crump 95–6, from Middlewich (110–705663) to Holmes Chapel (110–771673), thence by Saltersford 334 *infra* (110–772678), Forty Acre Lane 331 *infra* (110–788685 to 812687), Dicklow Cob 90 *infra* (110–815697), Salter's Lane 91 *infra* (110–815697 to 827701), Windyharbour 91 *infra*, Siddington (110–845709) and Broken Cross (110–893735), cf. route XIX *supra*. The Middlewich road is *alta via que ducit versus Macclesfield* c.1301 *Dav* 88 *infra* in Siddington (110–845709 to 867715), probably *le Sondifordestrete* and *le Stonwaye* 92 *infra* in Lower Withington, and perhaps *Salteriswey* 334 *infra* in Goostrey.

XXII. MIDDLEWICH–NANTWICH. The site of a Roman road is marked in 1″ O.S. 7th ed. at 110–700644 to 665560. The southern end of this line seems improbable. The line is feasible as far south as 110–679588, in line with Sutton Lane 335 *infra*, cf. Sutton Hollow 335 *infra*. The road may be *Menihincwey* 333 *infra*. Between Bradfield Green and Nantwich, the medieval route would use Marshfield Bridge 333 *infra*.

XXIII. MIDDLEWICH–KELSALL (–CHESTER). This route is mentioned as a salt-way in Crump 94. It proceeded from Chester Road (Middlewich) 330 *infra*, (*regia via que se ducit versus Cestriam* 1373), Middlewich Road, Station Road, Gravel Hill, 110–685667 to 656663, 333, 334, 331 *infra* (*The Gravel Road* 1831 Bry, *Gravel Lane* 1842 OS), to Winsford Bridge & High St. (Over) 336, 332 *infra* (*Wynesfordstrete* c.1230 (1400)). A branch proceeded through Clive (*redestrete* 333 *infra*, Rilshaw Lane 333 *infra*, Welsh Lane 335 *infra*), 110–660657 to 648648, and may have led south-westward towards Tarporley.

From Over, the route proceeds by *Saltereswey*, Salterswall 334, *infra*, (110–627670), and Chester Lane (110–627670 to 603668) 330, *infra*, (*Chester Lone* 1475), thence direct to 110–540687 to join route VII *supra*.

XXIV. STAMFORD BRIDGE–TARVIN–TARPORLEY–ACTON–NANTWICH. A salt-way in Crump 94. This route proceeds by Holme Street 332 *infra* (109–470674 to 485667, though an older line is probably 109–477668–491658–500657); Road Street (109–530637 to 553630), 1842 OS, named from the chapel of the Rood at Tarporley, *v. Hermitage* 332 *infra*, cf. Salters Well, High St. (Tarporley) 334, 332 *infra*; Watfield Pavement (109–592587 to 110–614568) 335 *infra*. At Tarporley, on this route and IX *supra*, was a toll-passage, *passagium de Torperlegh(e)* 1297, 1311, 1312 Ipm. Hockenhull Platts 332 *infra* (109–476657) joined this route to VIII *supra*, across R. Gowy.

XXV. NANTWICH–FARNDON. *Welshman's Street*, a medieval salt-way (Crump 95) from Nantwich (110–647524) to Farndon Bridge (109–412544), by Acton, Burland, Faddiley, Woodhey Hall or Hollywell Ho 336, 332 *infra*, Ridley Green, Bulkeley, Gallantry Bank, Peckforton Gap, Clutton and Barton. This was probably the most important trade-route from Nantwich into Wales. It gives name to Welsh Row (Nantwich) 335 *infra*, Welshman's Green & Lane 335 *infra*. The stretch 109–5544 to 4854, now Salter's Lane (Bickerton, etc.) 334 *infra* and Sandy Lane 334 *infra*, was *the high streete* 1250–1300 (1637) Rich, *-strete* 1312 (1637) ib, *le Walesmonwey, Walshmonstreet* 1314 (1596) *Chol, Walesmonsweye, Walchmonstreete* 1314 (1637) Rich, Orm², *le Walsemonnusstrete* 1316 *Chol, le Walschemonnis (s)trete* 1320 *ib, le Walschemon(n)es(s)trete* 1337, 1360 *ib, Saltersway* 1320 *ib,* 'the high road', 'the Welshman's road', 'the salter's way', *v.* hēah, Wels(c)h-man, saltere, strǣt, weg.

XXVI. NANTWICH–MARKET DRAYTON Sa. A medieval toll-passage at Swanbach 335 *infra* (110–655422) in Audlem indicates the existence of this route by 1274 Ipm, to Adderley and Market Drayton Sa. From Nantwich to Audlem it probably followed route XXVII *infra* by Broad Lane and Artlebrooke Bridge, thence by Hankelow.

XXVII. NANTWICH–WOORE Sa. This medieval route is discussed under the associated p.ns., *Saltersich, Saltford*, Broad Lane, Artlebrook Bridge 334, 334, 330, 329 *infra* (in Stapeley), Pepperstreet Moss, Hunsterson 333, 332 *infra*, Doddington, *Donnington* 331 *infra*, *Bruneshurst*, *Lymestrete*, Street Field 330, 332, 334 *infra* (in Bridgemere). The route reached Bridgemere either by Broad Lane, Artlebrook, Pepperstreet Moss, or by *Saltersich*, *Saltford*, Doddington. The road-name *Lymestrete* (*v. The Lyme* 2*supra*, strǣt) recurs in routes VII, X, *supra*.

XXVIII. MINOR ROUTES. (i) *le Portewey* 1270 (c.1340) *Bun*, *le Portwey* c.1278, 1279 Chest, (*le*) *Portway* 1278, 1279 Whall, a road from Whitby to Chester via Caughall, *Flindow* and Little Stanney 330, 331, 334 *infra*, cf. Butter Hill 330 *infra*, *Flag Lane* 1831 Bry 331 *infra*, *v.* ChetNS LXXIX 309, ChetOS XI 542, X 30. (ii) *le Portewey* c.1310 *Chol*, a road from Halton to Frodsham Bridge, at Clifton. (iii) *le Portway* 1279 Whall, -*wey* 1279 Chest, in Ince, the road to Chester, 'road to a (market-)town' *v.* port-weg. (iv) *Pepper Street &* Carter Lane, from Peover Superior towards Alderley Edge, *v.* route XIX *supra*, 333, 330 *infra*. (v) POWEY LANE, *Povey Lane* 1831 Bry, *v.* lane, extending across Wirral 109–366718 to 394737, Great Saughall to Little Stanney, forming the boundaries of Great Mollington, Capenhurst, Lea, Backford and Great Sutton.

XXIX. SALTWAYS. Crump, *op. cit.*, *supra*, identifies the following routes as salt-ways; VII (Northwich–Chester, Crump 94, cf. Salters Brook, Saltersbridge, Saltersford Bridge; he did not find it named a salt-way Northwich–Altrincham, Crump 99 (Saltway B), but note *Salteresway* 41 *supra*; he did not include Ashley Rd (*Salter's Lane*) 41 *supra*, 329 *infra*, cf. *infra*, carrying a salt-way off this road south of Altrincham, towards Cheadle, cf. Salter Riddings 253 *infra*, also Crump 102–3 (Saltways C, D at Northenden, to which add Salters Hey 238 *infra*); XXIII (ib 94, cf. Salterswall, *Saltereswey*); XXIV (ib 94, cf. Salters Well, also Southley 334 *infra*); XXV (ib 95, and also Salter's Lane); V (ib 95; with Salters Lane in Picton); XXI (ib 95–6); XIX (ib 96; and *Saltway*, *Salteriswey*); X (Northwich–Warrington, Crump 98 (Saltway A); to which add *le Saltlydehyate*).

Crump deduces that the Macclesfield–Whaley Bridge road was a salt-way from *Salter*-p.ns. in Db on the road to Chapel en le Frith Db, *v.* Crump 96, 135 (Saltway G), and that Saltersford 138 *infra* in Rainow marks the use of the east part of XIV as a salt-way from Macclesfield to Buxton Db, *v.* Crump 96, 137 (Saltway H). His

Salt-way F, which he traces or projects Altrincham–Stockport–Tintwistle–Woodhead (Crump 130–4, cf. Salters Brook 325 *infra*), should include Ashley Rd in Rostherne 329 *infra*, cf. *supra*, Salter Riddings in Cheadle 253 *infra*, *Saltersbridge* in Offerton 292 *infra*, Salters Lane in Romiley 294 *infra*, Salterslane and Saltersfield in Bredbury 265 *infra*, which produce a feasible line of route for a salt-way from south of Altrincham, eastward to miss that place and Stockport, along the ridge of Werneth Low to Mottram and Longdendale. Crump observes Saltersford in Barnton on R. Weaver, *v.* 334 *infra*, not on a recognisable route. He refers to route XV, and misses route VI, *supra*.

I. MACCLESFIELD HUNDRED

Hamestan, Hamstan(e) 1086 DB, *hundred' de Malcklesfeld'* 1242 Cl, -*Macclesfeld* 1249 IpmR, then as for Macclesfield 113 *infra*, 'Hāma's stone', from the OE pers.n. *Hāma* (as in Hamnish He (DEPN)) and *stān*, cf. *Homaston* 1473 ChRR (p). The site of the stone is unknown, but it may have been at Mutlow 81 *infra*. The meeting-place was later fixed at Macclesfield, the administrative centre of the royal Manor and Forest of Macclesfield, cf. *Hundredfeld* 119 *infra*. The hundred abuts upon La, YW, Db and St to north, east and south, where it is bounded by the rivers Mersey, Goyt and Dane, except that Longdendale is north of R. Mersey and R. Etherow. To the west it adjoins the hundreds of Bucklow and Northwich. The eastern part of the hundred is mountainous moorland on the Millstone Grit edges, formerly in the Forest of Macclesfield, containing the sources of the rivers Goyt, Dane, Mersey and Bollin, and rising to the greatest elevation in the county at Shutlingsloe 160 *infra*. The western part contains a lower, undulating terrain of glacial drift boulder-clay, sand and marl, except for an escarpment of Keuper sandstone protruding through the drift cover at Alderley Edge. The DB hundred was almost co-extensive with the later one, including the townships of Cranage, Twemlow, Swettenham and Kermincham, now in Northwich Hundred 333 *infra*, but did not include Snelson, Northenden and Great Warford 93, 234, 104 *infra*, which were in *Bochelau* (Bucklow) Hundred 330 *infra*.

The following unidentified p.ns. belong to this hundred: *Aschineladyn* 1345–7 *Eyre* ('ash-tree in the valley', v. æsc, in, la, denu); *le Askehurst* 1357 *ChFor* (v. askr, hyrst); *Astaneslegh* 1345 *Eyre*, *Hastanley* 1357 *ChFor* (p) (v. lēah. The first el. is probably a pers.n. such as OE *Hēahstān*, ON *Hásteinn* or OE *Æstān* (*Æðelstān*). The pers.n. may recur in Hastingshaw 146 *infra*); *Aynesargh* 1371 *Eyre* (p) (from erg 'a shieling' and a pers.n., probably a shortened form of an ON pers.n. in *Ein-*); *Barndeleesforde* 1286 Court (v. Brindleys 60 *infra*); *le Beredston* 1356 *Eyre* (a landmark, v. stān); *Bernardiscroft*

1286 Court (p) (from the ME pers.n. *Bernard* (OE *Beornheard* or OG *Ber(e)nard*) and croft); *þe Bernes* 1345 *Eyre* (p) (cf. *del Berne* 1360 *ib* (p), *v.* bere-ærn); *Berneslegh* 1360 *ib* (p) (perhaps 'glade at a barn', *v.* bere-ærn, lēah); *Bladehurst* 1287 Court (p), *-hirst* 1287 *Eyre* (p) ('leafy wooded hill', *v.* blæd, hyrst); *Borwik* 1347 *ib* (p) ('boar farm', *v.* bār², wīc); *Bothwghe* 1560 Sheaf³ 24 (5473) (a corrupt form, perhaps for Bollington 187 *infra*); *Bradeleghforde* 1357 *ChFor* ('ford at *Bradelegh* (*v.* brād, lēah)', perhaps at Bradleys Clough 100 *infra*); *Bradnok* 1503 *ib* ('at the broad oak', *v.* brād, dat. sg. brādan, āc); *Brekwellehurst* (*v.* 180 *infra*); *del Brendknol* 1351 *Eyre* (p) ('burnt hill', *v.* brende², cnoll); *le Brodhok* 1290 *ib*, *Brod(h)oke* 1304 Chamb, *le Brodok* 1342 ChRR, *le Brodhoc* 1347 *Eyre*, *Broodok* 1355 ChRR, (*le*) *Broodok* 1355 *ib*, 1356 *Eyre* all (p), 'broad oak', *v.* brād, āc, cf. Broad Oak 55 *infra*); *Brodhirst* 1287 Court, *le Brodehurst* 1352 *Eyre*, 1359 *ib*, *Brodehurst* 1574 *Dow*, *le Brodhurst* 1371 *Chol* all (p), *Brodhurst* 1503 *ChFor*, ('broad wooded-hill', *v.* brād, hyrst); *Brokenerze* 1287 *Eyre*, *Brokenerst* 1287 Court both (p) (probably 'broken wood, or -hill' from brocen and hyrst); *del Brugge* 1367 *Eyre*, *-Bruge* 1361 *Dow*, *del-*, *atte Brugge* 1397 ChRR all (p) (*v.* brycg); *le Bruggeende* 1345 *Eyre* (p) ('the end of a bridge', or 'the end of a town towards a bridge', *v.* brycg, ende¹); *le Bryndeyatefolde* 1503 *ChFor* (*v.* brende¹ or ², geat, fald); *Burybrokes* 1359 *Eyre* (p) (*v.* brōc); *Caluelegh*, *Caluirleg'* 1286 Court ('calves' clearing', *v.* calf, lēah, cf. Calveley 330 *infra*); *Carlisboth* 1287 Court, *Eyre* (p) ('peasant's hut', *v.* karl, bōth, cf. *Karlcotes* 294 *infra*); *del Causay* 1360 ib, *-Causey* 1366 *ib* both (p) ('the causeway', *v.* caucie): *del Cegge* 1369 *ib* (p); *Coddesburie* 1560 Sheaf³ 23 (5392) (a corrupt form, for some township in the Forest of Macclesfield); *Codlough* 1286 Court (p) (probably 'cold valley', from cald and clōh); *Coldelawe* 1286 ib (p) (*v.* cald, hlāw); *Coppedoneclyf* 1287 Court (p) ('(cliff at) the topped hill', *v.* coppede, dūn, clif); *Crowclaue*, *Crowcloue* 1347 *Eyre* (p) ('the mound', from crūc¹ *and* hlāw, a tautological compound like Crook Hill Db 124); *Cuddeclif* 1354 *ib* ('Cudda's cliff', from the OE pers.n. *Cudda* and clif. It is the site of a mill, and may be Cotcliffe 56 *infra*); *Cudynton iuxta Macclesfield* 1507 Plea (DKR XXIX, 97, perhaps a form for Tytherington 214 *infra*); *le Dokunesforde* 1357 *ChFor* (*v.* ford); *Doulak'* 1508 *MinAcct*, *Sowlake* 1560 Sheaf³ 24 (5467) (the latter an unreliable spelling, *v.* lacu); *Drameleg'* 1286 Court (p) (probably 'Drēama's glade', from an OE pers.n. *Drēama* and lēah); *le Echeneclif* 1347 *Eyre*, *le Echenesclyf* 1357 *ChFor* (*v.* clif); *del Endeschawe* 1286

Eyre (p) (*v.* ende[1], sceaga); *Erdeswyk* 1347 *ib* (probably 'herdsman's shed', *v.* hirde, wīc, but cf. Eardswick, Yeardsley 331, 176 *infra*); *del Fern* 1286 Court (p) (perhaps from fearn, in the sense 'a ferny place'); *le Fernyforde* 1337 *Eyre* (p), *le Ferniforde* 1347 *ib* (*v.* fearnig, ford); *Fernihalgh* 1347 *ib* (p) (*v.* fearnig, halh); *Foxbroke* 1503 *ChFor* (*v.* fox, brōc); *Gretewrthe* 1287 *Eyre* (p) (Court 231 reads *-wytht*, 'great enclosure', *v.* grēat, worð); *Haregreue* 1285 Court, *-grave* 1287, 1288 ib, *Hargreve* 1350 *Eyre*, *Hardgreue* 1461 *Dow* all (p) ('hoar grove', *v.* hār[2], græfe); *Hartenlegh* 1345 *Eyre* (*v.* lēah); *Haselhulm* 1285 Court (p) ('hazel marsh', *v.* hæsel, hulm); *Hasselegh'* 1341 *Eyre* ('hazel glade', *v.* hæsel, lēah); *Helleswode* 1287 Court (p) (*v.* wudu); *Hengilhulm* e14 *AddCh* (p) (*v.* hulm. The first el. may be ON *hengil*- 'hanging', used as a hill-name, 'overhanging hill', cf. Cleasby-Vigf s.v. *hengill*); *Hennegrave* 1288 Court ('hens' grove', *v.* henn, græfe); *Heppewod* 1337 *Eyre* (p) ('wild-rose wood, wood where hips grow', from hēope or hēopa and wudu); *Hewinnedene* 1286 Court 216 (probably 'Hēahwynn's valley', from an OE fem.pers.n. *Hēahwynn*, *v.* denu); *Hollecloutht*, *Holwes-*, *Howeliscloutht* 1287 ib 230 (p) (probably 'Howel's dell', from the OWelsh pers.n. *Houel* and clōh); *Holliden* 1560 *Sheaf*[3] 24 (5489) (an unreliable form); *Hondesdale* 1337 *Eyre* (p) ('hound's valley', *v.* hund, dæl[1]); *Hopeleg'* l13 *Fitt, Dow,* (p) ('glade in a valley', *v.* hop[1], lēah); *Horwell* 1348 *Eyre* (p) ('dirty well', *v.* horu, wella); *Hulmes* 1503 *ChFor* (*v.* hulm); *Judkynesrudyng* 1357 *ib* ('Judkin's cleared-land', from a ME pers.n. *Judkin* diminutive of *Judd(e)*, a shortened pet-form for *Jordan*, and ryding); *le Ker* 1287, 1288, 1290 Court, *le Caar* 1358 *Eyre*, *le Keer* 1361 *ib* all (p) (*v.* kjarr); *Kirkehouses* 1377 *ib* (p) (*v.* kirkja, hūs); *Knokeden(e)* 1365, 1366, 1367 *ib* (p), 1384 *Rental* (p) ('valley at a hill', *v.* cnocc[2], denu); *Kokenale* 1341 *Eyre* (p) (probably from an OE pers.n. *Cocca* and halh); *Lodelegap* 1373 *ib* ('Luda's clearing', from the OE pers.n. *Luda* and lēah, with gappe added); *apud Longum Egge* 1503 *ChFor* ('long hill-edge', *v.* lang, ecg. Perhaps Long Edge Db 99); *Lynales* 1351 *Eyre* (p), 1365 BPR (p) ('flax nooks', *v.* līn, halh); *Lynmora* 15 *Mont* (p) ('marsh where flax is grown', *v.* līn, mōr[1]); *Mogeleghes* 1350 *Eyre* (p) ('meadows at a heap, hill or stack', from mūga and lēah); *Narwedale* 1361 *ib* ('narrow valley', *v.* nearu, dæl[1]); *Northwell* 1366 *ib* (*v.* norð, wella); *Notehogh* 1354 *ib* (p) ('hill where nuts grow', *v.* hnutu, hōh); *Olrinleg'* 1283 *Dow* (p), *Olren(e)legh* 1287, 1290 Court, *Eyre* (p) ('alder wood', *v.* alren, lēah); *Ormelegh* 1285 Court (p) ('Ormr's wood', from the ON pers.n. *Ormr* and lēah, cf. *Ormesty* 271 *infra*);

Pekedon 1337 *Eyre* (p) ('peak hill', *v.* pēac, dūn); *Rudyng'* 1357 *ChFor*, *del Rudyng* 1361 *Eyre* (p) (*v.* ryding. There was a forge here in the Forest of Macclesfield, in 1357); *del Rodeforde* 1286 Court (p) ('ford with a cross', *v.* rōd², ford); (*del*) *Scole-*, *-Skoleclogh* 1337, 1347, 1350 *Eyre* (p) (*v.* skáli, clōh); *le Shirbrok* 1357 *ChFor* (from scīr¹ 'a district' or scīr² 'bright' and brōc); (*del*) *S(c)hore* 1351 *Eyre*, 1357 *ChFor*, 1358 Chamb all (p) ('the cliff', *v.* scora); *Shotton* 1560 Sheaf³ 24 (5489) (an unreliable form); *Shurbache* 1347 *Eyre* (*v.* bæce¹); *boscus de Stochale* 1286 *ib* ('dairy-farm nook', *v.* stoc, halh, cf. Stockerlane 334 *infra*); *Swynes-*, *Swynis-*, *Swinishurst* 1285, 1286 *ib*, Court, 1348 *MinAcct* ('swine's wooded-hill', *v.* swīn¹, hyrst. Court 226 reports a complaint in 1286 that the fuel in the Forest is much damaged by the pigs here); *Torfot* 1364 *Eyre* (p) ('foot of the rock', *v.* torr, fōt); *Wyt(e)-*, *Qwyt(e)-*, *Witfeld* 1285, 1286 Court (p) (*v.* hwīt, feld); *Wyndul* 1341 *Eyre* (p) ('windy hill', *v.* wind, hyll); *Worminehalh* 1286 Court (p) (perhaps 'nook where dye-plants grow', from halh and OE *wurma*, *wyrma* 'a purple dye, a plant from which dye was extracted'); *boscus de Wyringe* 1357 (1620) *Surv* (perhaps 'place where the bog-myrtle grows', from wīr and -ing²).

i. Prestbury

The townships of Bosley and North Rode are separated from the rest of Prestbury parish 181 *infra* by Macclesfield Chapelry 106 *infra* and Gawsworth parish 66 *infra*.

1. BOSLEY (110–9165) [bɔ:zli]

Boselega 1086 DB, -leg(h) 1275 Ipm, 1278 IpmR *et freq*, -le(e) 1286
    Court (p), 1313 Cl (p), -ley(e) 1314 Plea, 1351 BPR
Bozeley 1275 Ipm
Bothis-, le Botesleg' 1286, 1287 Eyre (p), Botesle 1322 Cl
Boslee 1305 Plea, -ley(e) 1306 ChF, 1375 Pat, -legh' 1337 Eyre, -le
    1396 Plea
Beselee 1382 Pat
Baseley 1471 *MinAcct*
Bosseley H8, 1551 Sheaf

'Bōt's wood or clearing', from an OE pers.n. *Bōt and lēah, cf. Bostock 330 *infra*, Bossall YN 36. The AN spellings with -s- and -z- represent [-ts-].

BOSLEY MINN (110–940660), MINNSIDE 154 *infra*, SUTTON COMMON
155 *infra*, WINCLE MINN 170 *infra*, le *Miyen* 1363 *ChFor*, le *Mynde*
1471, 1560 Sheaf, le *Mynnd* 1520 Plea, *the Minde(s)* 1611 *LRMB* 200,
(the) Mind(e) Lees 1611 *ib*, *(the) Mind (Common)* 1620 *Surv*, le *Mynne*
1516 ChRR, *Boseleigh Comon* 1611 *LRMB* 200, *Bosley Minn* 1842
OS. This is OWelsh minid (Pr.Welsh *mɵniδ*) 'a mountain', with
lǣs and commun. It is a ridge of moorland on the boundaries of
Sutton, Wincle, Gawsworth and Bosley. Cf. *Schuseg' infra.*

DAVEN WOOD (lost, 110–943642), 1831 Bry, 1848 *TA*, *boscus de
Dauene, -Davene* 1286 *Eyre*, Court, 1357 *ChFor*, *Dauen(e)wod(e)* 1347
Eyre, 1357 *ChFor*, 'wood by the R. Dane (20 *supra*)', v. wudu.

FAIRYHOUGH, 1848 *TA*, le *Fairehalw*, le *Fayrehalch* 1270 (17) Sheaf,
le *Fayre halyge de dominicis de Gowsworthe*, le *Fayr Halph* 13 (1611)
LRMB 200, 'the fair nook', v. fæger, halh.

HUG BRIDGE, 1842 OS, *Huggebrigge* c.1248 Dieul, (passagium de-)
1327 ChRR, *-brugge* 1318 *Eyre* (p), *Hokebrugge* 1431 ChRR, perhaps
the origin of the surname *de Hogge Brugge* c.1280 *Chol*, *Huggebru(g)g'*
1315, 1331 Tab, *Luggebrigge* 1315 ib, in Bexton 329 *infra*, v. brycg.
This bridge crosses R. Dane and was a medieval 'passagium' or
toll-road, cf. ChetNS LXXXVIII 71n. The first el., which may recur in
Huggehee 109 *infra*, is obscure. Similar forms in Hugset YW 1, 306
are explained as from the rare ODan by-name *Hugger* recorded in
15th (cf. Dan. *hugger* '(wood-, stone-) cutter'). A ME pers.n. *Hugge*
appears in *Huggeruydin, -ruding* 332 *infra*, and may be common to
the Ch p.ns. Cf. in the ME pers.n. *Hugge* Reaney s.n. *Hug*.

ALDERLEES WOOD, *Elder Lees (Wood)* 1848 *TA*, v. ellern, lēah.
BALL CLOUGH, *Bull Clough* 1842 OS, v. bula, clōh, cf. Bullgate *infra*.
BIRCHES WOOD, *Birch Wood* 1831 Bry.   BLAKEFIELD, 1848 *TA*,
v. blæc, feld.   BOGGINSHILL, perhaps 'boggart hill', v. boggin,
hyll.   BOSLEY BRIDGE, cf. *del Brugge* 1345 *Eyre* (p), v. brycg.
BOSLEYBROOK, 1842 OS, a stream and hamlet.   BOSLEY WORKS,
1831 Bry, a hamlet named from a factory.   BROADOAK, 1831 ib,
cf. *Brodhok* 52 *supra*, Greatoak *infra*.   BULLGATE, 1831 ib, *Ball-
gate* 1842 OS, cf. Ball Clough *supra*, v. bula, gata.   CARTLIDGE
WOOD, *Cartridge Wood* 1831 Bry, 1848 *TA*, possibly of similar origin
to the lost stream-name *Cartelache* 17 *supra*, but the older form

suggests 'ridge of rough ground', from **kartr** and **hrycg**, cf. Carterage
Fd 330 *infra*.   CHAFF HALL, *v*. **ceaf**, **hall**.   CLOSE WOOD.
COTCLIFFE ISLAND, 1831 Bry, perhaps 'cliff with a hut', from **cot** and
clif, but cf. *Cuddeclif* 52 *supra*.   DANE MILLS, 1860 White,
Bosley Mill 1842 OS, *v*. **myln**, R. Dane 20 *supra*.   DUMBERS,
Dumbles 1848 *TA*, 'the hollows' *v*. **dumbel**.   FLASH WOOD, *les
Flaskes* 1414 *Mont*, cf. *Flash Field & Ley* 1848 *TA*, 'the swamp',
v. **flask**.   FOLD, *Folds* 1831 Bry, *Fould* 1860 White, *v*. **fald**.
FOXCROFT WOOD, *Fox Croft* 1848 *TA*.   GOLDEN SLACK, 1831 Bry,
cf. Golden Slack 169 *infra*.   GOODWIN'S HOLE, a place in R. Dane,
v. **hol**[1].   GREATOAK FM, *Great Oak* 1860 White.   HARRINGTON
Ho, named after the earls of Harrington, local landowners, cf. also
69 *infra*.   HIGHFIELD, *High Field* 1848 *TA*, *v*. **hēah**, **feld**.
HIGH WOOD, 1831 Bry, cf. Lowerhouse Wood *infra*.   THE
HOLLINS, *Hollins* 1831 ib, *-ings* 1842 OS, 'the hollies', *v*. **holegn**.
KEYCLIFF WOOD, *Cliff Wood* 1842 ib, *v*. **clif**; *Key-* may have been
added from Keygreen (foll.).   KEYGREEN, HIGHER & LOWER, *Key
Green* 1831 Bry, (*Higher*, *Lower*) 1842 OS, 'cow green', *v*. **cū** (pl.
cȳ, dial. *kye*), **grēne**[2], cf. 332 *infra*.   KILNHILL, 1831 Bry, *v*. **cyln**,
hyll.   LEWINSHILL WOOD, *Lewin Hill* (*Wood*) 1848 *TA*, from the
ME pers.n. *Lewin* and **hyll**.   LOWER HO, 1831 Bry.   LOWER-
HOUSE WOOD, *Lower Wood* 1831 ib, cf. High Wood *supra*.   LYM-
FORD BRIDGE, *Limford Bridge* 1831 ib, crossing R. Dane to Lymford
St., perhaps derived from *The Lyme* 2 *supra*, *v*. **ford**.   MADCROFT
WOOD, cf. *Mad Croft* 1848 *TA*.   MARSHHEAD, 1848 *ib*, *v*. **mersc**,
hēafod.   MILLHOUSE, 1860 White, near Old Mill *infra*, *v*. **milne-
hous**.   MINNEND, HIGHER & LOWER, *Low Min End* 1831 Bry,
Minn End 1842 OS, *Higher-*, *Lower Minden* 1860 White, from Bosley
Minn *supra* and **ende**[1].   MORRISGREEN, 1842 OS, *Moores Green*
1831 Bry, *v*. **grēne**[2].   MORTAR MILL HO.   OLD MILL, 1860
White, *Bosley Mill* 1831 Bry, *molendinum aquaticum* 1400 *Mont*.
PECKER POOL, a place in the R. Dane, *v*. **pōl**[1].   PENN BRIDGE.
PRIMROSEBANK, 1831 Bry, *v*. **banke**.   PYEASH, 1842 OS, *v*. **pīe**[2]
'magpie', **æsc**.   RED POOL, a place in the R. Dane, 'red pool',
v. **rēad**, **pōl**[1].   RINGOTT, cf. *Ringate Lane* (*Wood*), *Ringate Meadow*
(*Head*) 1848 *TA*.   ROYLES FM, *Royleys* 1831 Bry, *Royles* 1860
White, *v*. **ryge**, **lēah**.   SLACK WOOD, *v*. **slakki**.   SMITHYGREEN,
1831 Bry, *v*. **smiððe**, **grēne**[2].   SOURBUTTS, 1831 ib, *v*. **sūr**, **butte**.
SPOUT WOOD, cf. *Spout Croft* 1848 *TA*, *v*. **spoute**.   STILES-
MEADOW, formerly *Broughs* 1831 Bry, *-Tenement* 1842 OS, from the

surname *Brough*.   STONYFOLD (WOOD), *Stony Fold* 1831 Bry, *Stony Folds Wood* 1848 *TA*, v. stānig, fald.   STYE, 1831 Bry, *Lower Style* 1860 White, v. stīg 'path'.   SWALLOWDALE, 1831 Bry, v. dæl[1] 'a valley'; the first el. may be swalg 'a pool', as two streams converge sharply upon the place.   SWANSLAKE, 1842 OS, *Swanlake* 1831 Bry, v. swan[1], lacu.   TURNHURST, 1831 ib, *Turn Horse* 1860 White, 'round wood', v. trun, hyrst.   UPTON FOLD, formerly *Young's Folly* 1842 OS, *Upton's Folly* 1860 White, cf. *Youngs Close* 1848 *TA*, from the local surname *Young* and folie.   WHITEMOOR HILL, cf. Whitemoor 69 *infra*.

FIELD-NAMES

The undated forms are 1848 *TA* 61. Of the others, 1270 (17), H8 are Sheaf, 13 (1611) *LRMB* 200, 1305 Plea, Orm², 1347, 1348 *Eyre*, 1357, 1363 *ChFor*, 1400, c.1414 *Mont*, 1831 Bry, 1842 OS, 1860 White.

(a) Acre; Andrews Fd; Ashen Flatt (v. æscen, flat); Asker Mdw (dial. *asker* 'a lizard'); Back Gutters (v. back, goter); Back o' th' Barn Mdw; Bank Fd; Bard Flatt (v. flat); Barley Stubble (v. bærlic, stubbil); Bean Clough (v. clōh); Bent, -Wd (v. beonet); Birch Fd & Flatt; Blake Lake (v. blæc, lacu); Booth Croft (v. bōth, croft); Bottoms (v. botm); Briary Croft; Broad Fd & Lee (*le Brodefeld* 1400, c.1414, v. brād, feld, lēah); Brownsley Wd; Calf Croft; Carr Croft (v. kjarr); Champion Fd & Mdw (*Champion Wood* 1831, named from the local *Champion* family, cf. Orm² III 703n., and wudu); Clay Flat (v. clæg, flat); Clough, Clough House Wd (cf. *Clough House* 1831, 1842, v. clōh, hūs); Cot Croft, Fd & Mdw (v. cot); Cockshades Mdw (v. cocc-scyte); Cockin Hitches & Mdw ('pens and meadow where cock-fights are held', from dial. *cocking* 'a cock-fight' and hiche, mǣd); Corner; Cow Hey & Ridding (v. cū, (ge)hæg, ryding); Croft Green (v. croft, grēne²); Cromwell Fd (cf. Cromwell 59 *infra*); Crow Bottom (v. botm, and foll.); Crowholt Wd 1831 (v. crāwe, holt); Cushy Bank ('wood-pigeon bank', v. cūscote, banke); Daisey Bank; Higher & Lower Dam (v. damme); Daven Mdw (cf. *Daven Wood supra*); Four, Ten, Three & Two Day Work (v. day-work); Egg Croft (perhaps dial. *egg* 'the snowberry'); Elmets Croft; Emm Mdw; Eye Mdw, Eyes (v. ēg); Ferry Fd; Fox Fd; Gilliam; Gorsey Bank (v. gorstig, banke); Green (v. grēne²); Green Eye (1831, v. grēne¹, ēg); Hall Fd, Mdw, Ridding & Wd (cf. foll.); Hall Lees (-*Leys* 1831, v. hall, lǣs); Long & Rough Halsteads (v. stede, first el. uncertain, cf. Hallstead 70 *infra*); Hare Ridding (v. hara, ryding); Hay, Hey (v. (ge)hæg); Hazle Butts (v. hæsel, butte); High Flatt (v. hēah, flat); Hill (-Fd); Hollingsheads Croft (from the surname *Hollingshead*, cf. Hollinset 150 *infra*); Hollin Knoll (v. holegn, cnoll); Hollow Mdw (v. holh, mǣd); Horse Pasture; House Fd; Huckday Math ('Hocktide mowing' v. mǣð); Hurst (v. hyrst); Ingsey; Intake (v. inntak); Jobs Piece; Kenners Bank; Kiln Croft; Kitchen Crofts; Knoll (-Wd) (v. cnoll, wudu); Lane End 1831; Leek Bank (v. banke, cf. Leek

St); Lees Bank (from l͞æs or the surname *Lee* and banke); Legs Fd (*v.* dial. *leg* 'the body of a stack'); Light (*le lyght*' c.1414. 'the light place, the glade', *v.* līhte, cf. Raby Lights 333 *infra*); Limed Fd; Little Rough (*v.* lȳtel, rūh); Long Butts (*v.* lang, butte); Long House (Clough) (*v.* clōh); Long Moor; Long Shoot (*v.* scēat); Lower End 1860; Lumber Fd & Holme (*v.* lumber, feld, holmr); Luxington Croft; Marl Butts, Croft & Fd; Marlheap (*v.* marle, hēap); Marld Fd (*v.* marlede); Marsh (*v.* mersc); Micha Mdw; Mill Fd; Moor a Dean; Moor House Clough 1842 (*v.* mōr[1], hūs, clōh); Muck Earth (*v.* muk, eorðe, or erð); Nabb ('knoll', *v.* nabbi); Neppers Hill; New Fd, Mdw & Piece; Now Ridding (*v.* cnoll, ryding); Nutts Fd; Oaks; Old Mdw; Over Croft & Fd (*v.* uferra); Ox Hey Mdw (*v.* oxa, (ge)hæg, mǣd); Park Mdw; Pease Butts (*v.* pise, butte); Pedlers Croft (*v.* pedlere); Pica Wd; Picket Eyes (*v.* ēg); Pilsbury Close; Pingate (*v.* pingot); Great Pit Fd (*v.* pytt); Poolstead (*v.* pōl-stede); Priest Fd; Proctor Fd; Ridding, Riddings Head (*v.* ryding, hēafod); Rough (*v.* rūh); Rough Bottom (*v.* rūh, botm); Round Bank & Knoll (*v.* rond, banke, cnoll); Rowley Mdw (possibly 'rough clearing', *v.* rūh, lēah); Rushy Croft; Rye Croft; Ryleys Croft (*v.* ryge, lēah, cf. Royles Fm *supra*); Saint Marys Hey (*v.* (ge)hæg. The church is dedicated to St Mary, but the f.n. may be a rationalisation of *Maryheye infra*); Shale Bank; Shepherds Fd & Hill; Short Flatt; Slang (*v.* slang); Sparrow Fd; Spencers Meadow (the *Despencer* family were lords of nearby Rushton St); Springs (*v.* spring); Stirkhouse ('calf house', *v.* stirc, hūs); Stoney Close; Thorp-, Throp Wd (*boscus vocat*' *Tropwo*(*o*)*d* 1305, 'wood near or belonging to an outlying farm', *v.* þrop, wudu); Tinkers Flatt (*v.* tink(l)ere, flat); Tom Fd (*v.* toun); (Great) Twamlow ('at the two mounds', *v.* twēgen, hlāw, cf. Twemlow 335 *infra*); Tyron Head, Lower & Middle Tyron (cf. Tyrant 335 *infra*); Wall Bank & Croft (*v.* wælla); Way Fd; Well Croft, Fd & Mdw; Wet Fd; Wheat Butts (*v.* hwǣte, butte); Wheat Field Clough; White Croft; Great, Little & Middle White Hurst Fd & Wd (*White Hurst Clough & Fields* 1842, 'white wood' *v.* hwīt, hyrst, clōh); Wicken Croft ('mountain-ash croft', *v.* cwicen, croft); Woody Clough (*v.* wudig, clōh); Worsley (perhaps connected with John de *Wordisleg*' 1287 Court (p), *v.* lēah. The first el. may be a genitival form of worð (*v.* -es[2]), but it could be an OE pers.n. *Weorð, Wurð*, discussed in Reaney s.n. *Worthing*).

(b) *Bosleheye* c.1414 (*v.* (ge)hæg 'fenced-in enclosure'); *Boselegh Wode* 1347, *boscus de Boseleye* 1363, *Bos*(*se*)*ley Wods, the Wodds of Bosley* H8 (*v.* wudu); *Hawkescloughe* 13 (1611), *Le Haukis-kliffe* 1270 (17) ('hawk's valley', *v.* hafoc, clōh, probably between Cartlidge Wood *supra* and Barleyford 168 *infra*, cf. Hawkslee, *Hawkesyord* 166, 166 *infra*); *le Houereuese quod boscus est in Bosley* 13 (1611), *le Overest* 1270 (17) ('wood-edge on a hill', *v.* ofer[2], efes); *Maryheye* 1400, *le Mareheye* c.1414 (from mere[2] 'a mare', and (ge)hæg 'enclosure', cf. St Marys Hey *supra*); *Schuseg*' 13 (1611), *Schoseg, Chuseg* 1270 (17), *Sheueegge* 1348, *boscus de*- (at *Dauenewode*) 1357 ('boundary edge', *v.* scēað, ecg, apparently along the Bosley and Wincle boundary along Bosley Minn *supra*, cf. R. Sheaf Db 16, RN 360); *le Weueknoll*' 1400 ('yew hillock', *v.* īw, cnoll, cf. *le We*(*w*)*es* 335 *infra*).

2. NORTH RODE (110–8966)

Rodo 1086 DB

Rode 1259 Plea *et freq*, (*-iuxta Gawseworth*) 1460 ChRR, *Rod* 1348
Eyre, *Roede* 1384 *Surv*, *Roode* 1397 ChRR, *Rowde* 1413 Orm²,
Roade 1611 *LRMB* 200

Northrode c.1284 *ChFor et freq*, (*Norht-*) c.1312 AddCh, *North-
roude* 1313 Cre, *-Roode* 1356 Plea, *-rood* 1507 *MinAcct*, *-road(e)*
1580, 1585 Cre, *-Rhode* c.1620 Orm²

'The clearing', *v.* rod¹. The affix norð 'north' distinguishes the
place from Odd Rode 333 *infra*.

BRAMHALLHILL (110–882667), 1619 Orm², 1831 Bry, *v.* hyll. *Bramhall*
may be analogous with Bramhall 258 *infra*, or a surname derived
from it, but cf. Bramhall Hill 82 *infra*. This place was on the boundary
of the Forest of Macclesfield, *v.* 10 *supra*.

CROMWELL WOOD (110–887659), *Crumbwell* 13 Dieul (p), Orm², 1831
Bry, *Crumbewell* c.1270 (17) Sheaf, *Crumwall* 1286 *Eyre*, *-well* 1611
LRMB 200, 1619 Orm², *Crombewelle* 1344 *Eyre* (p), *le Crombewell*
1531 *AddCh*, cf. Cromwell Fd 57 *supra*, 'spring at a river-bend',
v. crumb, wella, wælla. This place lies at a bend of the R. Dane,
cf. Cromwell Nt 185, and was on the boundary of the Forest of
Macclesfield, *v.* 10 *supra*.

RODEGREEN (110–887677), *villa de Rode* 13 (17) Orm², *Roade* 1611
LRMB 200, *Rode Greene* 1619 Orm², *-Green* 1831 Bry, (*North-*) 1842
OS, 'village green of Rode', *v.* grēne², cf. North Rode *supra*. This
was on the boundary of the Forest of Macclesfield, *v.* 10 *supra*.

BANK FM & LANE, (*The*) *Bank* 1831 Bry, 1842 OS. BEANCROFT
WOOD, *Bean Croft* 1848 *TA*. BIG WOOD, 1848 *ib*. OLD
BRICKBANK WOOD, *Break Bank* 1848 *ib*, probably from bryke 'a
brick' and banke, a source of brick-clay, cf. Brickbank Cottage 61
infra. BULLGATE LODGE, *v.* Bullgate 55 *supra*. CHENEY GATE
(p.h.), 1842 OS, *China Gate Inn* 1831 Bry, *v.* geat and dial. *cheeny*
'china (-ware)' confused here with the surname *Cheney*, cf. Cheney
Brook 18 *supra*. CHURCH LANE. COLLEYMILL (BRIDGE),
Colley Bridge 1619 Sheaf, *-Mill* 1831 Bry, cf. *Colley* 1848 *TA*,
perhaps 'charcoal-wood or -glade', from col¹ and lēah, with brycg,

myln, cf. Cowley 67 *infra*.   Cow Bridge, named from Cow
Brook 19 *supra*.   Damhead Wood, at the head of an artificial lake,
v. damme, hēafod.   Dobford (Bridge), *Dobford* 1831 Bry, at a
ford on Cow Brook 19 *supra*.   Big & Little Dog-Bottom
Wood, *Dog Bottom* 1848 *TA*, *v.* botm. The first el. may be docce or
dogga, cf. *Docklacheseche* 88 *infra*.   Ethel's Green, *Wheat Sheaf*
1842 OS, *v.* grēne². Farsidegreen Wood, *-Plantation* 1842 ib,
v. feor, sīde, grēne². Fernybank Wood, *v.* fearnig, banke.
Fine Wood (*Little*) *Fine Woods* 1848 *TA*.   Furze-Acre Wood,
v. fyrs, æcer.   Garden Wood.   Gaws Wood, *v.* gorst.
Gooseberry Pool, a place in R. Dane.   The Grange, *North Rode
Farm* 1842 OS, *The Farm* 1860 White.   Hungerhill Wood,
Hungerhill (*Wood & Bottom*) 1848 *TA*, *v.* hungor, hyll.   Intac
Wood, *v.* inntak.   Ladderstile, 1831 Bry, *v.* hlǣd(d)er, stigel.
Little Kennel Wood, *v.* kenel 'a dog-kennel'.   Manor Ho,
North Rode Cottage 1842 OS, *The Cottage* 1860 White.   Marton
Lane (Fm), a lane running into Marton 80 *infra*.   Moss Wood,
Mosses Plantation 1842 OS, *v.* mos.   Park Wood.   Pecker
Pool (Wood), *v.* 56 *supra*.   Pexall Road, *Pexhill Lane* 1831 Bry,
cf. *Lounds & Lower Pexhill* 1848 *TA*, cf. Pexall 78 *infra*.   Pipe
Wood, *v.* pipe² 'a small dingle' or 'a decoy'.   Rode Hall, 1860
White, *North Rode Hall* 1842 OS, *v.* hall.   Rode Heath, 1831 Bry,
v. hǣð.   Scissorcroft Wood.   Toot Hill Lodge (lost,
110–890671), 1831 ib, in North Rode Park, *v.* tōt-hyll.   Wild-
forest Wood, *Wild Forest* 1848 *TA*.   Yew Tree Fm, *-House*
1842 OS.

FIELD-NAMES

The undated forms are 1848 *TA* 338.

(*a*) Acre, -Hill; Ash Heys & Riddings (*v.* æsc, (ge)hæg, ryding); Barkers
Croft; Barn Stead (*v.* bere-ærn, stede); Birchen Bye ('birchen corner',
v. bircen², byge¹); Blake Fd (*v.* blæc, cf. dial. *blake*); Bradford Ley (*v.* lēah);
Briary Croft; Brindleys (this may be from a surname *Brindley*, but 'burnt
clearings' is possible, *v.* brende², lēah, and cf. *Barndeleesforde* 1286 Court 225,
a lost place in the Forest of Macclesfield, '(ford at) the burnt clearing(s)',
v. berned, lēah, ford); Brook Platt (*v.* brōc, plat²); Brooms Mdw; Butty Parts
(*v.* butty, part); Bye Flatt (*v.* byge¹, flat); Coble Dock (probably from the
plant-name *keddle-dock*); Carr (*v.* kjarr): Chemistry; Cockshut (*v.* cocc-
scyte); Coney Green (*v.* coninger); Cord Hay; Cote Fd; Cow Hey (*v.* cū,
(ge)hæg); Cross Fd; Dane Close (*v.* clos, cf. R. Dane 20 *supra*); Dig Croft
& Fd (*v.* dīc); Dingle Wd (*v.* dingle); Edge Fd (*v.* ecg); Far Piece; Flash, -Fd
& Mdw (*v.* flasshe); Fox Holes (*v.* fox-hol); Foxley (*v.* fox, lēah); Gig Hole

(*v.* **gigge, hol**[1]); Gorsey Fd & Hey (*v.* **gorstig, feld, (ge)hæg**); Hall Mdw;
Hare Berry; Hay Dowell; Hayes (*v.* **(ge)hæg**); Heath Croft; Heathy Hey
(*v.*hǣðig, **(ge)hæg**); Hollin Knoll (cf. *William de*(*l*) *Holines* 1309, 1312 *AddCh*,
v. **holegn, cnoll**); Horse Close; House Croft ('croft next the house', *v.* **hūs,
croft**); Jay Hay ('jay enclosure', *v.* **jay, (ge)hæg**); Kiln Croft; Little Clough
(*v.* **lȳtel, clōh**); Lowndes Croft (from the surname *Lowndes*, cf. *Lounds
Pexhill* s.n. Pexall Rd *supra*); Marl Fd; Big & Little Moor; New Fd &
Piece; Old Lane; Ottery Hedge; Outlett (*v.* **outlet**); Ox Hey (*v.* **oxa, (ge)hæg**);
Peas Croft (*v.* **pise**); Pingle (*v.* **pingel**); Pink Ridding (*v.* **ryding**); Pit Fd;
Prison Bar Fd ('field where the game "prisoner's base" is played', *v.*
prison-bars); Push Fd; Range Mdw (*v.* **rang**); Red Bank & Hill (*v.* **rēad,
banke, hyll**); Riddings (*v.* **ryding**); Rode Heys; Rough Wd(s); Round Knoll
(*v.* **rond, cnoll**); Rushy Lake (a meadow, *v.* **riscig, lacu**); Rye Hill; School
Croft; Shads Clough; Smallwoods Mdw; Sparton Mdw; Spoil Bank (*v.*
spoil-bank); Stubble Fd; Swanley Mdw; Swine Park (*v.* **swīn**[1], **park**); Tit
Croft; Triangle Croft; Water Falls (a pasture, not on a stream); Weaser
Heys (probably 'weasel enclosures', *v.* **wesle, (ge)hæg**); Weavers Hey; Well
Banks; Wet Fd & Heys; Wheat Bank & Eyes (*v.* **hwǣte, banke, ēg**); Whit
Croft (*v.* **hwīt, croft**); Whittle (cf. *Wyghthull* 1361 *Eyre* (p), 'hill at a bend',
v. **wiht, hyll**, cf. Whitehill O 286); Wood Fd & Heys (cf. *boscus de Rode*
1286 *Eyre*, 1363 *ChFor*, *v.* **wudu, feld, (ge)hæg**).

(*b*) *le Merelache* 1359 *Eyre* (p) ('boundary stream', *v.* (*ge*)mǣre, lǣc(c)).

ii. Astbury

The rest of Astbury parish is in Northwich Hundred.

1. EATON (110–8765)

    Yei-, *Yeyton* c.1262 *Dav*, *-under Lime* 1318 Cl, *Yay-*, *Yaiton* 1327
      Pat, *Yayton* 1394 Orm[2], *Yeaton* 1370 ib, *Yaton* 1384 *Eyre*, *Yeton*
      1516 Sheaf, *Yaeton* 1611 Orm[2]
    Geyton 1286 *Eyre*
    Yatton 1361 Orm[2]
    Ȝaton 1384 *Eyre*
    Ayton 1365 *Eyre*, *Eton* 1549 ChRR, *Eaton alias Yayton* 1666 Orm[2]

'Farm at the river', from ēa and tūn. The place is on R. Dane. The
Y- spellings express a stress-shift in the initial diphthong ēa-.

HAVANNAH, cf. *Higher & Lower Havannah* 1839 *TA*, *v.* 332 *infra*.

BELL FM, 1831 Bry, cf. *Bell Croft* 1839 *TA*. BIG PLANTATION,
Moss (*Plantation*) 1831 Bry, *v.* **mos**. BRICKBANK COTTAGE, cf. Old
Brickbank Wood 59 *supra*. CRANBERRY MOSS, *Moss* 1839 *TA*,

v. cranberry, mos.   EATON BANK, 1691 (J.C.J.), *Bull's Bank* (Samuel Bull, proprietor) 1820 (J.C.J.), *Dane Bank* 1831 Bry, cf. Dane Bank 331 *infra*.   EATON COTTAGE, 1831 ib.   EATON HALL, 1667 Orm², *aula de Yayton* 1364 *Eyre*.   EATON MILL.   FRIENDS' BURIAL GROUND, cf. *Quaker Field & House* 1839 *TA*.   GORSEY-MOOR, 1831 Bry, *Gorsty-* 1839 *TA*, v. gorstig, mōr¹.   HEATHSIDE, 1831 Bry, v. hǣð, sīde.   HILLMOOR FM, *Hill Moor* 1831 ib, cf. *Newhall Wood*, Yewtree Fm *infra*.   JACK FIELD'S FM, *Jack Fields* 1831 ib, 'odd bits of unused land', v. jack, cf. Jack Croft & Gate 186 *infra*.   KENNEL WOOD.   LANE END, 1831 ib.   MAYPOLE FM (lost, 110–861649), 1831 ib, 1842 OS, v. may-pole.   MIDWAY HO, 1831 Bry.   MOSS FM, cf. Cranberry Moss *supra*.   NEWHALL WOOD (lost, 110–877657), 1842 OS, cf. *Newehall* 1402 ChRR (p), *Newall* c.1602 *Chol*, v. nīwe, hall; the wood is near Hillmoor Fm, which may be the site of the hall.   LT. RODE HEATH, *Rode Heath Field* 1839 *TA*, cf. Rode Heath 60 *supra*.   SMITHY FARM, v. smiðð e.   STANWAYS (lost, 110–871663), 1842 OS, either 'stone ways' from stān and weg, or a surname *Stanway*.   TANHOUSE, 1840 *TA*, v. tan-hous.   YEWTREE FM, *Little Hill Moor* 1842 OS, cf. Hillmoor Fm *supra*, v. īw, trēow.

FIELD-NAMES

The undated forms are 1839 *TA* 156.

(a) Acre; Aspin Croft; Back Lane; Bank Fd; Far-, Near Bent (v. beonet); Birch Fd; Black Fd and Mdw (*Blackfield* 1582, *-feild* 1593 (J.C.J.), v. blæc, feld); Blake Fd (v. blæc, cf. dial. *blake* 'bleak, colourless', cf. bleikr, blāc); Brick Kiln Fd; Briery Flat (v. brērig, flat); Broad Flat; Broom Fd (v. brōm); Brow (v. brū); Butchers Mdw; Calf Croft; Carr Mdw (v. kjarr); Great & Little Cathill Low ('mound called *Cathill*', v. cat(t), hyll, hlāw); Chapel Fd & Leys (v. chapel(e), lēah); Clay Flat (v. clǣg, flat); Close Mdw; Common Piece; Corner Bit; Cote Croft (v. cot); Crabtree Fd; Daisey Fd; Dane Fd (named from R. Dane); Day Math ('one day's mowing', v. day-math); Four-, Three-, Two Days Work (v. day-work); Dole (v. dāl); Drakes Mdw; Ash-, Deaf-, Long Eye (cf. *the Wheat Eye, the Ash Eye, the Plaster Eye, the Bridge Eye* 1691 (J.C.J.), from ēg 'a meadow', with æsc, dial. *deaf* 'barren', lang, hwǣte, pleg-stōw, brycg); Files; Fish Fd; Flat Fd (v. flatr); Flaxbutt (v. fleax, butte); Garden Fd; Gors(t)y Croft, Gorsy Knowl (v. gorstig, croft, cnoll); Grass Flatt; Greenway Fd (v. grēne¹, weg); Gristley Ho; Hand Fd; Handkerchief (v. 331 *infra*); Haw Hill; Hollin Hay (v. holegn, (ge)hæg); Intake (v. inntak); Kelsall Mdw; Long Shute (v. lang, scēat); Long Slang ('a long, narrow strip', v. lang, slang; the type is common in Ch); Marlage ('marleing place', v. marlage, cf. marle, -age); Marl Pit Leasow (v. marle-pytt, lǣs); Marton (Head) Croft (named from Marton 80 *infra*, *v.* hēafod, croft); Matley Croft (cf. Mutley *infra*); Mill Eyes (*v.* myln, ēg); The Moor; Moss Piece & Room (*v.* mos, pece, rūm[1]); Mutley Croft (perhaps 'glade where meetings are held' from mōt and lēah, cf. Mutlow, in the adjacent township, 81 *infra*); New Mdw; Old House Fd; Old Knowles (*v.* ald, cnoll); Ozier Flatt (*v.* oyser, flat); Park; Parsons Ease; Pingle, Pingot (*v.* pingel, pingot, the latter is common in Ch f.ns.); Barn & Far Plat (*v.* plat[2]); Plough Mdw; Poor Piece; Round Fd & Heath; Rushy Lake ('rushy stream' *v.* riscig, lacu); Sand Hole Fd; Sheep Fd; Shop Fd; Stone Fd; Swain Croft; Three Nooked Piece (*v.* three-nooked, pece), Town Croft (*v.* toun); Turn Croft (*v.* trun); Warth (*v.* waroð); Well Fd; White Fd; Winlow Fd ('gorse hill', *v.* hvin, hlāw); Wood Bank & Mdw, Little Wd; (The) Yeld (*v.* helde).

(*b*) *Brondyarth* 1593 (J.C.J.) ('burnt ground', *v.* brende[2], eorðe); *del Hokes* 1373 *Eyre* (p) ('the oaks', *v.* āc); *Soot Field* 1698 (J.C.J.) (*v.* sōt).

2. SOMERFORD BOOTHS (110–8366)

Sumreford 1086 DB, *Somerford* 1278 Ipm, *-iuxta Merton* 1288 Court, *-Marton* 1335 Orm[2], *-iuxta Marton alias Somerford Boothes* 1630 ib, *-prope Swetenham* 1378 Tab, *Somereforde iuxta Morton* 1321 Dav, *Over Somerford(e)* 1510 ChRR, *-forth* 1524 AddCh, *Sommerford-Ultra alias Somerforde iuxta Marton* 1597 ChRR

le Bothys, *-es* c.1270, 1313 *Dav*

Somir-, *Somerfordebothis*, *-es* c.1270 Dav, *Somerfordboth'*, (*-us*) 1313, 1353 ib, *-boothes* 1571 ib, *-Booths* 1724 Not Cestr

Somerton (*Marton iuxta-*) 1374 *Eyre*

'The Booths of Somerford', *v.* bōth, cf. Somerford, Marton, Swettenham 334, 80, 335 *infra*. The type appears elsewhere in Ch, in Knutsford- and Lymm Booths, and Bowfields 332, 332, 330 *infra*. Somerford Booths represents old out-pastures of Somerford, from which it is separated by R. Dane (hence the suffix *-Ultra*). *le Bothys*, *-es* refer to the Old Hall *infra*. The form Somerton suggests an alternative name 'summer farm', *v.* sumor, tūn. It is not certain whether the DB form belongs to Somerford Booths or to Tranmere 335 *infra*. In DB f.267b, the entry *Sumreford* follows immediately after that for Storeton 334 *infra*, without further hundred-rubric. Tait 209 assumes the rubric for *Hamestan* (Macclesfield) hundred has been omitted, and he inserts it. Orm[2] II 450–1 reads *Sumreford* into *Wilaveston* (Wirral) hundred, as DB has it, and, since it is recorded next to Storeton and has a similar tripartite manorial division to that of Tranmere, he identifies it with Tranmere. Tait's handling is preferable.

HOLLY BANKS, FM, & HEATH, *Holey(e)* 1262, 1270 *Dav*, 1315 Orm[2] (p), (*bruar' de*) *Holay* 1313, 1379 *Dav*, 'clearing on a ridge', *v.* hōh, lēah. The district is on the ridge between R. Dane and Midge Brook. Holly Banks is *Dwarf Wood* 1831 Bry.

SHANNOCK, *Schauinwyk, -wyc* 13 *Dav, Schauinwike* l13, 1313 *ib, Shan(e)wyk(e), -wike* 1450, 1525 ChRR, Orm[2], *Shanewik* 1471 *MinAcct, -wick* 1450 Orm[2], (-*Farm*) 1831 Bry, *Shannock Farm* 1839 *TAMap*, probably 'wīc called after Scēafa', from the OE pers.n. *Scēafa*; but also possible is 'buildings where planing or scraping is done', from OE *sceafa* 'a plane, a scraper' (OE *sceafan* 'to scrape') with -ing[1], wīc. Cf. Shannock Big Wood, Shavington and *Shauintonfeld* 334 *infra*.

WORNISH NOOK, 1842 OS, *Superior Walnedis iuxta Hulm* l13 *Dav, Wallnish Nook* 1831 Bry, *Wall Nitch* 1839 *TA*. The first el. may be an oblique-case or plural form of wælla 'a well-spring'. The second is edisc 'an enclosure', with nōk and ModE niche 'a niche', cf. *Westedis infra*.

BANCROFT WOOD, 1839 *TA, Bank Roughs* 1831 Bry, *v.* banke, rūh. BRIERY BANK 1831 ib, *v.* brērig, banke.   BROOMFIELD FM, *Broomfields* 1839 *TAMap, Broom House* 1842 OS, *v.* brōm, feld.   BUNISTER WOOD, *Bunnistar* (a pasture) 1839 *TA*, a hybrid p.n. 'reedy place', from bune and storr[2], star.   CLOUTER WOOD, *v.* 330 *infra*, cf. Clouter Brook 19 *supra*.   CRABMILL FM, 1831 Bry, *v.* crabmill.   DAIRYHOUSE FM, *v.* deierie, hūs.   FIELDHOUSE FM, *Field-House* 1839 *TAMap*.   HALLGREEN LANE, *Hall Green* 1831 Bry, *v.* hall, grēne[2].   MIDGEBROOK FM, 1839 *TA, Tan Yard* 1831 Bry, cf. Midge Brook 32 *supra, v.* tan-yard.   MILLBANK FM, 1831 ib, cf. Somerford Booths Mill *infra*.   NEWPOOL INN, *New Pool House* 1831 ib.   NEWSBANK, 1831 ib.   OLD HALL, 1831 ib, *le Bothys, -es* c.1270, 1313 *Dav, v.* Somerford Booths *supra*.   OLDHALL WOOD, *The Bottoms* 1831 Bry, *v.* botm.   PARK COTTAGES, *Little London* 1831 ib.   RADNOR BRIDGE, 1831 ib, cf. Somerford Radnor 334 *infra*.   SCAR WOOD, *v.* sker.   SCHOOLPOOL BROOK (Midge Brook).   SOMERFORD BOOTHS HALL, *Somerford Booths* 1839

TAMap, cf. Old Hall *supra*. SOMERFORD BOOTHS MILL, 1831 Bry. SWETTENHAM RD, *Out Lane* 1831 ib, *via que ducit ultra bruar' de Holay usque ad le Bothes* 1313 *Dav*, *v.* ūte, lane, cf. Swettenham 335 *infra*, Hollybanks, Old Hall, Somerford Booths *supra*. TANYARD FM, 1842 OS, *v.* tan-yard.

FIELD-NAMES

The undated forms are 1839 *TA* 359, 1831 Bry, and the rest *Dav* unless otherwise indicated.

(a) (The) Acre(s); Allenshed; Balsom Low (*v.* hlāw); Banky Fd; Black Croft & Fd; Blake Fd (*v.* blæc); Bleak Fd (*v.* bleikr); Boggy Fd; Broad Fd; Brook Fd; Broomy Bank (*Broomy Wood* 1831 *v.* brōmig, banke, wudu); Brown Fd; Brund Yard (*v.* brende², geard); Budge Bit; Bunts Fd; Butts, Butty Croft (*v.* butte, butty); Common Piece; Corner Croft; Court Fd; Cow Hay (*v.* cū, (ge)hæg); Croutches (*v.* crouche); Dane Mdw (named from R. Dane 20 *supra*); Four-, Seven-, Two Day(s) Work (*v.* day-work); Derrilake (*Derry Lake* 1831, *v.* lacu); Dial Croft (*v.* dial); Dig Fd (*v.* dīc); Dingle (*v.* dingle); Dole, Dow Bank, Dows (*v.* dāl); Drumble (*v.* drumble 'a wooded hollow, a dingle, a ravine', cf. dumbel; the type is common in Ch, and occurs in Sa and St); Eases Lane 1831; Edmunds Eye (*v.* ēg); Elderley Fd (*v.* ellern, lēah); Finishaw (*Fenchawe* 13, 'fen copse', *v.* fenn, sceaga, cf. Chapel Brook 18 *supra*, upon which these fields abut. Cf. also Finney 331 *infra*); Fishery; Folly Fd (*v.* folie); Gailey Piece (*v.* gagel, lēah, pece); Gorsey Croft (*v.* gorstig); Great Harry; Grind Stone Fd (*v.* grindel-stān); Big Harret Acre, Long Harret Fd (*v.* heriot); Hemp Croft; Hill Top (*v.* topp); Horse Pasture; Intake (*v.* inntak); Kiln Croft; Landers Fd; Lane Croft; Big & Little Lincoln; Linney Mdw (*terra de Liney* m13, cf. Lynney 332 *infra*, perhaps 'flax meadow', from līn and ēg); Long Shute (*v.* lang, scēat); Lower Eye (*v.* ēg); The Lunt (*v.* land); Mill Croft, Fd & Mdw (cf. Somerford Booths Mill *supra*); Moorish Mdw; Moss Bottom (*v.* mos, botm); Night Pasture; Nook Fd; Big Nut Hatch (possibly 'nut-tree gate', *v.* hnutu, hæc(c)); Orchard Croft & Fd; Ox Hey & Pasture (*v.* oxa, (ge)hæg, pasture); (High) Park (*v.* park); Partridge Hill; Patch; Peas Fd (*v.* pise); Pool Croft, Fd & Mdw; Pool Pipes ('decoy channels off a pool' *v.* pōl¹, pipe²); Red Sitch (*v.* rēad, sīc); Rib Croft (*v.* ribbe); Ridding (*v.* ryding); Rye Croft (cf. *Ru(e)croft infra*); Sand Fd; Slang Fd (*v.* slang); Snelsons Mdw (contains the surname from Snelson 93 *infra*); Soon Fd (*v.* sand); Spark Fd & Mdw (*v.* spearca); Square Mdw; Stable Mdw; Strines (*v.* strind, cf. Strines 268 *infra*, Db 152); Tan House Fd (*v.* tan-hous); Tan Yard (*v.* tan-yard); Wemish Fd (possibly from cwēme 'sheltered, convenient'); Wet Fd; The Wharf (*v.* waroð 'marshy meadow by a stream'; the form is a ModEdial. treatment of ME *warth*, with substitution of *f* for *th*, and association by popular etymology with hwearf 'an embankment, a shore, a wharf, cf. also Wath(s) 113, 171, 175 etc., *infra*'); White Fd; Willows; Wimberry Low (*v.* winberige, hlāw); Womans Fd; Wyer Mdw (*v.* wīr).

5

(b) *Bothefeld* c.1300 (v. bōth, feld); *le heyeloundis* 13 ('hay selions' v. hēg, land); *Longey(mor)* 1262, *Longeyhorne, Loncheyhorn* l13 ('(moor and projection at) the long water-meadow', from lang and ēg, with mōr[1], horn); *Olrinschae* 1313 (v. alren, sceaga); *Ru(e)croft* 1262, *Ruecrot* 13, *Ruy(e)croft* l13 *Rucroftisclok* c.1270, *Ruyecroftismor* l13 ('the rye croft', from ryge and croft, with clōh 'a dell', and mōr[1] 'a moor'. The clough descends to R. Dane southwest of Holly Fm, 110–819658, cf. *Westedis infra*); *Threphurstisclok, Therphurstclok* 13 ('(dell at) the disputed wood', v. þrēap, hyrst, clōh. This was on the boundary of Swettenham 335 *infra*); *sepis de Westedis* 1262, *Westhedis* c.1300, *Westedish* 1317 Plea (p), *-dych* 1350 Eyre (p), *Westedisclok, Westedisclokis-, -clo(h)isheuid, Westedisc(h)iche, Westedissiche* 13, 1262, *le Schiche* 1262 ('the western park or enclosure', v. west, edisc, with clōh, hēafod, sīc, cf. Wornish Nook *supra*. The clough descends to R. Dane on the Swettenham boundary, *le clog qui cadat in dauene inter scitfoldeley* (Shutfallow 334 *infra*) *et Ruecrot (Ruecroft supra)* 13 *Dav*; *Wymundiscroft* 1313, *-es-* 1457 ('Wīgmund's croft' from the OE pers.n. *Wīgmund* and croft); *rivuulum del Wytelache* 1313 (v. hwīt, læcc); *le Quitestol, -stob* 13 ('the white tree-stump', v. hwīt, stobb; the *-stol* spelling is a scribal error).

iii. Gawsworth

Gawsworth was a chapelry of Prestbury parish c.1265–89, and became independent in 1382, Orm[2] III 556. Mutlow (81 *infra*) in Marton township, was in Gawsworth ecclesiastical parish.

GAWSWORTH (110–8969) [gɔːzwərþ]

Govesurde 1086 DB, *-wrthe* 1238 *Dav* (p)

Gous(e)worth c.1130 (1580) (17) Sheaf, c.1265 Chest *et freq*, *-wurthe* e13 Dieul, *wrth(e)* m13 *Dav*, *-wrtht* 1285 *Eyre, Gouze-worthe* 1301 Sheaf, *Goues-* 1351 BPR, *Gousseworth* 1365 *Eyre*

Goweswurth m13 Adl, *-worth* 1274 Orm[2], *-word* 1312 Plea, Court, *Gows(e)worth* 1285 ib, *-wourthe* 1569 Wil, *Gouwesworth* 1357 ChRR

Goseworth c.1270 (17) Sheaf, 1558 *AddCh, -w(o)rd* 1290 Ipm, Cl, *Gosse-* 1476 ChRR, *Gos-* 1514 *ChEx, Goosworth* 1580 ChetOS VIII

Gaus(e)worth(e) 1279 Adl, *Gaws(e)worth(e)* 1389 ChRR *et freq*, *-wourth* 1553 Pat, *Gawesworth* 1457 ChRR

Goghesworthe 1341 *Eyre*

Gouselworth 1386 ChRR

Gorysworth 1445 Pat

Gaseworth 1460 ChRR, *Gays-* 1694 ChetOS VIII

Godsworth 1503 Plea

'Smith's enclosure' from PrWelsh *goƀ, OWelsh *gob, MWelsh gof 'a smith' and worð, cf. Gawton, Goveton D 223, 318. The first el. may be used as a pers.n. here, cf. the surnames Goff(e), Gough, v. DEPN and ES 64, 221.

BAILEY RIDDING, bayllysrudyng' 1363 ChFor, Rydeing 1584 Dav, Baylie Ridding 1638 Sheaf, 'bailiff's clearing', v. baillie, ryding, named from the bailiffs of Macclesfield, cf. Moss Terrace infra, Baillebut 124 infra.

COWLEY, 1831 Bry, Collegh' in Gouseworth 1286 Eyre, Coulegh 1398 ChRR (p), 'charcoal glade', v. col[1], lēah, cf. Colleymill 59 supra.

DANES MOSS, 1831 Bry, Dunismosse c.1270 (17) Sheaf, Dunnes-, Donnesmos(se) 1290, 1347 Eyre, Dinnysmoss l13 Smith, Dines Moss 1509, 1658 ib, Dinsmosse 1620 Surv, Dins Moss 1825 Smith, Dindesmosse 1611 LRMB 200, Densmoss 1762 Smith, 'the moss of Downes' from mos and Downes 148 infra, cf. Moss Lane 122 infra.

HIGHBIRCH, -COTTAGE & WOOD, Great & Little High Birch, High Birch Wood 1842 OS, cf. Hegebirches m13 Adl, 'the high birches', v. hēah, birce.

MILL END, 1724 NotCestr, and MILLHOUSE, 1842 OS, Mylnehouse 1536 Plea, named from GAWSWORTH MILL, 1831 Bry, molendinum de Gouswrthe m13 Dav, 'the district around-, the house at-, the mill', v. myln, ende[1], milne-hous.

MOSS TERRACE is named from le mosse 1347 Eyre, -atte Parkheued 1363 ChFor, Moss 1842 OS, Bailey Ridding Moss 1831 Bry, v. mos, park, hēafod, cf. Bailey Ridding supra, Macclesfield Park 120 infra.

SHELLOW, 1831 Bry, Little Shellow 1847 TA, GREAT SHELLOW (lost), 1847 TA, Old House 1831 Bry, Shellow 1842 OS, SHELLOW LANE, and SHELLOW WOOD, Shellow Moss 1831 Bry, Shellow Heath 1847 TA, comprised the hamlet SHELLOW END (lost), 1724 NotCestr, 1831 Bry, cf. Hugh & William de Celdelawe 1289 Court, probably 'mound at a shelter', from sceld and hlāw, v. ende[1], lane, mos.

SHIPLEY (lost), vadum de Schep-, Shepeleg(he) 13 (1611) LRMB 200, c.1270 (17) Sheaf, Shep(pe)legh 1364, 1380 Eyre (p), Far Shipley 1847 TA, 'sheep clearing', v. scēap, lēah. The ford is probably that shown in the old 6" OS, on Cow Brook at 110–909687.

STUBS-END (lost), 1724 NotCestr, *le Stubbys* 1286 *Eyre, le Stobbes* 1288 *ib* (p), *Stobbes* e14 *AddCh,* (*le*) *Stubbes* 1328 *Fitt, -iuxta Gouseworth* 1338 Plea, 'the tree stumps', *v.* stubb, ende[1], cf. *Stubbes* 125 *infra.*

TIDNOCK, *Tydenac* e14 *AddCh,* Tyd-, *Tidenak* 1364 *Eyre* (p), *Tydenacbothes* 1356 Orm[2], *Tytnake* 1525 ChRR, *Tidnock* 1506 *Dav, Tidnacke Boothes* 1613 Orm[2], *Gt. Tidnock* 1831 Bry, LT. TIDNOCK, 1831 ib, TIDNOCK WOOD, *Tidnock Moss* 1831 ib, *-Plantation* 1847 *TA,* comprised the hamlet TIDNOCK-END (lost), 1724 NotCestr, 'Tīda's oak' from the OE pers.n. *Tīda* and āc, with ende[1], bōth, mos.

WOODHOUSE, (-END & -GREEN), *Woodhouse-end* 1724 NotCestr, *Wood House* (*Green*), *Wood End Lane* 1831 Bry, cf. *Gouesworthwode* 1363 *ChFor, v.* wudu, hūs, ende[1].

ASHTONHOLE WOOD, *Ashton Hole* 1831 Bry.   BEAUMONTS, *Beamons Place* 1842 OS.   BRERETONS, 1842 ib, *Saw Pit Farm* 1831 Bry, *v.* saw-pytt.   BROOK HO, *Brook* 1860 White, from Ben Brook 15 *supra.*   BROWNHILLS, 1842 OS, *Brownehill* 1565 Sheaf, *v.* brūn[1], hyll.   BUTTYMOSS (WOOD), 1831 Bry *v.* butty, mos.   COWBROOK, 1831 ib, cf. Cow Brook 19 *supra.*   CRAB(TREE)MOSS, *Crabtreemoss* 1831 ib, *Crabtree* 1842 OS, *v.* crabbe, trēow, mos, cf. Crabtreemoss 86 *infra.*   CROWHOLT, 1831 Bry, *v.* crāwe, holt.   DALEHOUSE, 1831 ib, *v.* dæl[1], hūs.   DARK LANE, 1831 ib.   DEANS, cf. *Deans Bottoms & Fleet* 1847 *TA,* from a surname *Dean, v.* botm, flēot.   THE DIGHILLS, DIGHILL BROOK & WOOD, *Dighill Brook* 1831 Bry, *Dighill Nursery* 1842 OS, *Diggles* 1847 *TA,* perhaps 'dike hills', *v.* dīc, dík, hyll. The brook becomes Chapel Brook 18 *supra.*   DOB FORD BRIDGE, cf. Dobford 60 *supra.*   DRYHEATH WOOD, *Dryheath* 1842 OS, *v.* drȳge, hǣð.   FODENS, from the surname *Foden,* cf. Foden Bank, *Fodon* 153, 331 *infra.*   FOOLS NOOK (lost), 1831 Bry.   FURNACEPOOL, 1831 ib, *v.* furneis, pōl[1].   GANDYSBROOK, 1842 OS, *Gandy Brook* 1860 White, a hamlet named from GANDYS BROOK (Snape Brook 35 *supra*), *Gandy Brook* 1831 Bry, apparently from the surname *Gandy* (cf. Thomas *Gondi* 1287 Court) and brōc.   GARDENS, *Gawsworth Gardens* 1831 Bry.   GASKELLS, cf. *Gaskel's Moss* 1847 *TA,* from the surname *Gaskell* and mos.   GAWSMOOR HILL, *v.* mōr[1], hyll; the first el. is either gorst or that in Gawsworth *supra.*   GAWSWORTH COMMON, 1831 Bry.   GOOSETREES, 1842 OS, 'gorse bushes', *v.* gorst-trēow, cf. Goostrey 331 *infra.* HAMMERPOOL WOOD, 1847 *TA, Andertons Wood* 1842 OS, from the surname *Anderton* and **wudu**; '(yellow)-hammer pool', *v.* **amore, pōl**[1], but *v.* Addenda. HARRINGTON ARMS INN, 1831 Bry, cf. *Harrington Hill* 1847 *TA, v.* **hyll**, named from the lords Harrington, landowners here, cf. 56 *supra.* HARROPS (lost), 1831 Bry, probably from the surname *Harrop*, cf. Harrop 138 *infra.* HIGHLANE, 1831 ib. HIGH PARK CORNER (lost), 1842 OS, cf. Old Park *infra.* HIGH WOOD, 1842 ib. LARK HALL (lost), 1831 Bry, 1842 OS. LOWES, *Old Close* 1831 Bry; the modern name is from the surname *Lowe.* MAGGOTY JOHNSON'S GRAVE, MAGGOTY WOOD (110–889702), associated with Samuel Johnson (c.1691–1773), resident buffoon at Gawsworth Hall, author of *Hurlothrumbo, or the Supernatural* (1729), who planned to bury a devoted woman-servant in Maggoty Wood and, being thwarted, had himself buried there, hence his nickname, and the grave, *v.* Orm[2] III 554n, and R. Brown, *Gawsworth and its Worthies* (3rd ed., 1927). MALYPOLE FM, *Mayley Poles* 1842 OS. MOATS HO (lost), 1831 Bry, *v.* **mote.** MOLLARDS, 1831 ib. MORTON COTTAGE, 1831 ib, *Moreton House* 1842 OS. MOSSHEAD, MOSS HOUSES, 1831 Bry, named from Danes Moss *supra.* NEWBARN, *-Inn* 1831 ib. NEW HALL, *the Hall* 1724 NotCestr, erected in 1712, cf. Old Hall *infra.* OAKES (lost), 1842 OS, cf. *Oakes's Close* 1847 *TA,* from the surname *Oakes.* OLD HALL, 1842 OS, *Gauseworth Hall* 1724 NotCestr, cf. New Hall *supra.* OLD PARK (lost), 1842 OS. OLD PARKS, 1831 Bry. OVERBANK, 1831 ib, 'above the hill-side', *v.* **ofer**[3], **banke,** cf. Underbank *infra.* PARK CLOUGH, *v.* **park, clōh.** PARKHOUSE, 1831 ib. PASTURES, *Swains Pasture* 1831 ib, *(The) Pasture(s)* 1842 OS, 1860 White. PINFOLD HO (lost), 1842 OS, *v.* **pynd-fald.** POOL WOOD, cf. Thornycroft Pools *infra.* PYETHORNE WOOD, *le Pyethorne* c.1503 Orm[2], *Pithorn* c.1527 ib, 'magpie thorn', *v.* **pīe**[2], **þorn.** RANKER'S FORD, 1847 *TA.* RIDDINGS (lost), 1831 Bry, 1842 OS, *v.* **ryding.** ROUGH-HAY, 1842 ib, *-Hey* 1831 Bry, *v.* **rūh, (ge)hæg.** ROUGHPLACE, 1842 OS. SANDY LANE. SLOPE PLANTATION, *v.* **slope.** THORNYCROFT POOLS, *v.* 85 *infra.* UNDERBANK, 1831 Bry, *v.* **under, banke,** cf. Overbank *supra.* (LITTLE) WALKERSHEATH, 1842 OS, *Walkers* 1831 Bry. WALLEY WOOD, 1831 ib, *v.* **wælla, (ge)hæg.** WALL POND. WARREN, *The-* 1842 OS, cf. *Warren Brow* 1847 *TA, v.* **wareine, brū.** WHERETON. WHITEGATE, 1860 White, *Hammonds* 1831 Bry, *Butchers Place* 1842 OS. WHITEMOOR, WHITEMOOR HOLLOW & WOOD,

Whitemore 1402 ChRR (p), *White Moor* 1831 Bry, *-Plantation* 1847
TA, *v.* hwīt, mōr¹, cf. Whitemoor Hill 57 *supra.*   YEWTREE FM,
Yewtree House 1842 OS.

FIELD-NAMES

The undated forms are 1847 *TA* 175. Of the others, 13 (17) is Orm², Sheaf,
13 (1611), 1611 *LRMB* 200, 1270 (17) Sheaf, 1347 *Eyre*, 1349 *MinAcct*,
1357, 1363 ChFor, 1506 Dav, c.1527, 1619 Orm², 1561 ChRR, 1831 Bry,
1842 OS.

(*a*) Adam Mdw, Great Adams Piece; Aken Fd, -Nook (*v.* ācen, nōk);
Balshaws (perhaps from a surname, but it may be a p.n. analogous with
Balshaw La 7, 'rounded wood' or 'wood at a rounded hill', *v.* balg, sceaga);
Barn End; Bean Mdw; Little Bents (*v.* beonet); Benty Work (*v.* benty,
(ge)weorc); Berry Lawton; Black Croft & Fd; Black Marsh; Blake Fd,
Blakeley (*v.* blæc, feld, lēah); Booth Croft (from bōth or the surname *Booth*);
Bottoms (*v.* botm); Breckridge (*v.* brekka, hrycg); Brick Kiln Fd; Brock Hole
('badger hole', *v.* brocc-hol); Brood Fd; Brook Side; Broomy Croft
(*v.* brōmig); Bull Lane Mdw; Burnt Knoll (*v.* brende², cnoll); Butty Fd
(*v.* butty); Carr, Carr Mdw (*v.* kjarr); Carry Knoll (*v.* kjarr, -ig³, cnoll);
Cheney Croft (cf. Cheney Gate 59 *supra*); Church Fd & Hill; Cicily
Thorn; Clay Flatt (*v.* clæg, flat); Close Hedge Fd; Clough Mdw; Coat Fd
(*v.* cot); Cobb Fd (*v.* cobb(e)); Coppice Wd 1831; Cork Hill (possibly 'coke
hill', *v.* dial. *coke, cork*); Cow Hey Mdw (*v.* cū, (ge)hæg); Cranberry Dale
('an allotment where cranberries grow', *v.* cranberry, dæl²); Crewd Fd (*v.*
crew 'a coop or pen'); Cuckoo Thorn; Dale Heap (*v.* deill, dæl², hēap);
Demain Fd (*v.* demeyn); Dingo (*v.* dingle); Dodige Hill: Dove Mdw:
Drumbow (*v.* drumble 'a wooded ravine', cf. dumbel); Dunnocks Hill
(*v.* dunnoc); Fairyhaugh (*v.* Fairyhough 55 *supra*); Fenders Fd (*v.* fender);
Fernay Fd (*v.* fearn, (ge)hæg); Ferret Croft; Fittons Moss 1842 (from the
surname *Fitton* and mos); Flagwire Croft ('reed-stalk croft', from flagge
'a reed', wire 'a stalk'); Flash Fd (*v.* flasshe); Forty Penny Mdw (presumably bought or rented for that sum); Fox Hey (*v.* fox, (ge)hæg); French
Brow (*v.* brū); Gailey Piece (*v.* gagel, lēah, pece); Gosport Hill; Granny Fd
(probably dower-land); Hallstead (*v.* stede; the first el. may be hall, cf.
hall-stede, Halsteads 57 *supra*); Hanging Side (*v.* hangende, sīde); Hare
Bryer; Harlow Fd (*v.* hār², hlāw); Hawshead, -Wd (*v.* Hawkshead 154
infra); Hazlehurst (*v.* hæsel, hyrst); Heath Stack Yard ('enclosure in which
heath is stacked (for fuel)' *v.* hǣð, stak-ʒard, cf. Gorse Stacks 331 *infra*);
Hebrow Hill; Hell Hole (*v.* hell, hol¹); Henbury Fd & Plain (named from
Henbury 78 *infra*, *v.* plain); Hermitage Wd; Hickershaw (*v.* sceaga; the
first el. may be hicol 'a wood-pecker'); Hollin Hey (*v.* holegn, (ge)hæg);
Hollin Knoll (*le Holynknol* 1347, *v.* holegn, cnoll); Holme Mdw (*v.* holmr);
Horse Coppy (*v.* copis); Hotch Potch (*v.* 332 *infra*); Hovel Croft (*v.* hovel);
Kasker Wd; Kid(d) Fd (*v.* kide, possibly here meaning 'a sucking calf' as
in dial. *kidcrow* 'a calf crib'); Kiln Croft; Kirk Fd (cf. Church Fd *supra*);

Laughing Croft; Limed Fd; Lodge Bank; Long Butts (*v.* lang, butte); Loond Hey (*v.* land, (ge)hæg); Lower Bottoms (*v.* botm); Martha Bank; Mellow Pool; Mexo Close, Mexons (*v.* mixen); Milking Fd; Moss Close & Hill; Mow Fd (*v.* mūga); New Close; Newer; Nook Fd; Oat Hey (*v.* āte, (ge)hæg); Oulers (*v.* alor); Ouzle Croft (*v.* ōsle); Ox Hey (*v.* oxa, (ge)hæg); Petersham Bank; Pexel Fd & Nook (*v.* nōk, cf. Pexall 78 *infra*); Pike Moor (*v.* pīc[1], mōr[1]); Pingate, Pingle (*v.* pingot, pingel); Pit Stead (*v.* pytt, stede, cf. pōl-stede); Pokas Fd; Pool Head; Little Pushing (probably referring to push-ploughing); Rawmersley (*v.* lēah. The basis of this name might be a p.n. like Rawmarsh WRY 1 175, 'red marsh', *v.* rauðr, mersc); Red Bank; Revel End; Ridding Bottom (*v.* ryding, botm); Robins Croft; Rough Close, Gate & Knoll (*v.* rūh, clos, gata, cnoll); Rough Mutton; Rowel (*v.* rūh, hyll); Great Rowley (*v.* rūh, lēah); Rushy Bottom & Fd (*v.* riscig, botm); Rye Hill; Severn; Shaws Fd; Sheep Fd; Shewds (*v.* scēod, dial. *shood* 'a husk'); Slack Fd (*v.* slakki); Slipperley ('slippery clearing', *v.* slipor, lēah); Snelsons Hill (from hyll and the surname from Snelson 93 *infra*); Soond Fd (*v.* sand); Soot Fd (*v.* sōt); Spring (*v.* spring); Stack Fd (*v.* stakkr); Stanhope Hey; Stirkhouse Hey (*v.* stirc, hūs, (ge)hæg); Old Stubbing (*v.* ald, stubbing); Suggs (*v.* sugga); Swine Hall, -Bottom (*v.* swīn[1], hol[1], botm); Tagg; Tan Croft; Thornley Thorns (*v.* þorn, lēah); Thorney Arbour (*v.* þornig, here-beorg); Thorpe (*v.* þorp); Timber Brow (*v.* timber, brū); Timber(e)ous; Toad Hole & Lake (*v.* tāde, hol[1], lacu); Turf Banks (cf. *Turberhurste* 1561, *v.* turf, OF turberie (MedLat *turbaria*), banke, hyrst); Watershead, Watry Shead ('watershed', *v.* wæter, scēad, cf. *watershed* NED c.1800, though Watry Shead suggests a ME form < OE **wæter-gescēad*); Way Bitt (*v.* weg, bita); Well Bank; Wet Croft; White Fd & Flatt (cf. *Whitecroft* c.1527, *v.* hwīt, croft); Wilkin Ridding (from the ME pers.n. *Wilkin*, diminutive of *William*, and ryding); Willets Heath; Winberry Hill (*v.* winberige); Windle Straw Fd (*v.* windel-strēaw, dial. *windle-straw* 'coarse grass', BT, EDD); Woody Clough (*v.* wudig, clōh); Yell Bank (*v.* helde, banke).

(b) *Blakelowe* 1270 (17), *le Lowe* 13 (1611), 1349 (p) (*v.* blǣc, hlāw); *le Churchgate* 13 (17), 1619, *the Church Waye* 1611 (*v.* cirice, gata; the track 110–889678 to 889696 from Rodegreen 59 *supra* to Gawsworth church, the boundary of the forest of Macclesfield, *v.* 10 *supra*); *le Cressefeld* 1363 (*v.* cærse, feld); *le Grene* 1357 (*v.* grēne[2]); *Ladybrugge* 1347 ('lady's bridge', *v.* hlǣfdige, brycg); *Loncull* c.1527 ('long hill', *v.* lang, hyll); *the Mershfild* 1506 (*v.* mersc, feld); *the newfoxholez* 1506 (*v.* nīwe, fox-hol); *Northurste* 1270 (17) (*v.* norð, hyrst); *le Rotindebroke* 13 (1611) ('roaring brook', from rotinde, the pres. part. of ME *routen* 'to roar' (ON *rauta*), and brōc); *le Strete* 1363 (*v.* strǣt, cf. 46 *supra*); *Turneschaghe* 1347 ('round copse', *v.* trun, sceaga).

iv. Prestbury

For the rest of Prestbury parish *v.* 54 *supra*, 181 *infra*.

3. BIRTLES (110–8674)

Now included in Henbury c.p., except for Whirley Hall 101 *infra* now in Over Alderley c.p.

> *Bircheles* m12 Tab, *Byrchlis* 1240–57 *AddCh* (p), *Birch(e)l-*, *Birchiles*, *-is* m13 *Dow* (p), *Dav* (p), *Fitt* (p), Chest, *Birchelis* e14 *AddCh*, *Burch(e)l-* 1291 Pat (p), *Byrcheles* 1295 Lacy, 1306 *MinAcct*, *Byrchels* 1305 Lacy, *Byrchelis* 1341 *Eyre*, *Birchel(l)* 1267 Chest, *-iuxta Hemdebur'* 1289 Plea, *Birchal'* 1269 Adl (p), *Byrchells* c.1283 (17) Chest, *Birchulles*, *-illis* 1287 Court (p), e14 *Fitt* (p)
>
> *Birtles*, *-is* c.1235 (1621) ChRR, 1324 Orm², 1392 Fine (p), *Byrt-*, *Bertles* 1374 *Eyre*, 1657 Sheaf, *Byrtel-*, *Birtulus* 1349, 1377 *Eyre* (p), *Birteles* 1389 ChRR (p), *Birtils* 1550 *Dow*
>
> *Byr-*, *Birthel-*, *-is*, *-es* 13 *Dav* (p), 1289 Plea (p), *Birthelees* 1418 Bark (p)
>
> *Birclis*, *-lie* l13 *Fitt* (p), *Bircles* 1327–77 *AddCh*
>
> *Birches* 1286 *Eyre*, Court 217
>
> *Brit-*, *Bryt-*, *Brittles* 1418 Cl (p), 1515 Plea, 1592 Sheaf, *Britte-*, *Brytheles* 1440 *Eyre* (p), 1514 Orm²

This p.n. is analogous with Birchill Fm Db 110, The Birtles 329 *infra*, Birch Hall Fd 329 *infra*. It is 'little birches' from an OE **bircel*, diminutive of birce 'a birch-tree'; cf. Birtle La 54. The spelling *Birchelegh* 1289 Court appears to be an incorrect expansion of the form *Birchel'* 1289 Plea (DKR xxvi 39), due to confusion with the reduced forms of hyll, lēah, *v.* LMS i, i, 48. The transition from *Birc(h)-* to *Birt-* is obscured by the palæography of *-t(h)-*, *-c(h)-*, undistinguishable in many sources. The name appears at Birtles Hall, Whirley Hall 100, 101 *infra*.

BAGBROOK BRIDGE, 1842 OS, named from Bag Brook 14 *supra*. BATHHOUSES WOOD, *v.* bath-house. BIRCHTREE, *Birch Farm* 1842 OS. BIRTLES BRIDGE. BIRTLESHILL, *Birtles of the Hill* 1819 Orm¹, 1842 OS, *-on the Hill* 1831 Bry, cf. *John Birtles, of the Hill* 1624 Earw, named after a branch of the Birtles family (Orm² iii, 709, 724), cf. Pale 79 *infra*, *v.* hyll. BIRTLES LAKE. BIRTLES MILL, 1860 White. HIGHLEES WOOD, *v.* 101 *infra*. MILL HOUSE, 1831 Bry, *v.* milne-hous, named from Birtles Mill. OLD HALL, 1831 *ib*, cf. Birtles Hall 100 *infra*. POOLSTEAD WOOD, *v.* pōl-stede, wudu, named from the mill-pool of Birtles Mill. ROUGH-HEY, *Henbury* 1842 OS, (possibly a misplaced name for Henbury 78 *infra*), *v.* rūh, (ge)hæg.

FIELD-NAMES

The undated forms are 1848 *TA* 52.

(*a*) Ben Fd (*v.* bēan); Black Hill; Brook Croft; Great Hill; Henbury Wood Land (cf. Henbury 78 *infra*); Marl Fd; Moss Fd, Mdw & Wd; Near Hey Moss (*v.* (ge)hæg, mos); Neather Mdw (*v.* neoðera, mǣd); Old Mdw; Pease Fd (*v.* pise); Spring Fd ('plantation field', *v.* spring).

4. CAPESTHORNE (110–8472), CAPESTHORNE HALL & PARK
Now included in Siddington c.p.

> *Copestor* 1086 DB
> *Capestorn'* 1238 *Dav* and 9 examples *ib*, *AddCh*, Court, *Dow* with variant spellings *Kapes-*, *-torn(e)*, *-tor(na)* to 1331 *Dav*, *Capestorne* 1551, 1565 *Dow*, 1571 *Dav*, *Capistorn'* 1283 *ib* and 9 examples *ib*, Court with variant spellings *Capys-*, *-torn(e)*, *-tourn* to 1323 *Dav*, 1500 *ib*, *Capistorin* 1287 *Eyre* (p), *Capustorn* 1318 *Dav*, 1323 *ib*, *-torne* 1386, 1403 *ib*
> *Capesthorn* 1288 Court (p), *-thorne* 1296 *Dav et freq* with variant spellings *-thorn*; *Capisthorn* 1320 *Dav* and 7 examples with variant spellings *Capys-*, *-thorne* to *Capisthorn* 1580 ChRR; *Capusthorn* 1365 *Eyre*, *-thorne* 1421, 1489 *Dav*
> *Cappesthorn* 1290 Court (p), 1345 *Eyre*
> *Capsthorn* 1290 Court (p)
> *Capisstorne* 1l3 *Dav* (p), *-tor'* c.1301 *ib* (p), *-torn* 1323 *ib*
> *Capesturn*, *-trun* 1322 *Dav*
> *Capist(t)ron* 1323 *Dav*
> *Capethorn* 1379 *Eyre*
> *Capisshethorne* 1541 Orm²
> *Capstorne* 1548 Orm²
> *Capeston or Capesthorne* 1724 NotCestr

The second el. is OE or ON þorn 'a thorn-tree'. The first el., not explained in DEPN, may be the gen.sg. of an OE by-name **Capp*, **Cæpp* derived from OE *cappa*, *cæppe* 'a cap, a cope, a hood' (BT), cf. *Cappe* DB a variant of the by-name of Algar *Cabe* (Feilitzen s.n.,

Tengvik 389); or alternatively, from an OE by-name *Cāp* derived from OE *cāp* 'a cope' (as in *cantelcāp* BT and BTSuppl, and cf. Reaney s.n. *Cape*); but 'thorn-tree at the scene of a battle', from ON *kapp* 'a match, a battle, a contest', is suggested by the lost f.n. in this township, *the Fexulfildes* 1571, *Feghtilfild* 1500, *Fectulmos* 1320 *Dav*, 'fight-hill', from (ge)feoht and hyll, with feld, mos. The lost f.n. *Cappis feld* in Storeton, 330 *infra*, appears analogous. CAPESTHORNE HALL is (*The*) *Hall* 1831 Bry, 1842 OS. The medieval hall was at 110—843726.

MILL LANE & WOOD, MILL LANE FM, *Mill Wood & Meadow* 1848 *TA*, cf. *Mill* (lost, 110–837727) 1831 Bry, 1842 OS, *le milne* 1313 *Dav*, *molendinum aquaticum* 1403 *ib*, v. myln.

BRICKBANK COTTAGE, v. bryke, banke.   CAPESTHORNE CHAPEL, *a new Chappell, lately built* 1724 NotCestr. The old one was at 110–843727.   CRANSHAWES, *Cronksheds* 1842 OS, cf. Richard *Cronk-shawe* 1451 Pat, probably from Cronkshaw La 83.   DOGKENNEL WOOD, cf. The Kennels *infra*.   HACKNEYPLAT BRIDGE, 1831 Bry, 'horse bridge', v. hakenei, plat[1].   HOME FM, *Capesthorne Farm* 1842 OS.   THE KENNELS.   LEY PLANTATION, *the legh* c.1500 *Dav, Ley Park Plantation* 1848 *TA*, v. lēah.   MASSEYS MOSS, 1842 OS, *Massey Moss* 1831 Bry, from the surname *Massey* and mos.   PARK FM & PLANTATION, cf. Capesthorne Park *supra*.   REDES MERE, a lake in Siddington, Capesthorne and Henbury townships, *le Redemor'* c.1318 *Dav, Redemere* 1441 *ib, the Rede mer, Capistorn Mer* c.1500 *ib, Reeds Meer* 1831 Bry, 'marsh-, lake at a reedy place', v. hrēod, mōr[1], mere[1], cf. Redesmere Fm, etc. 86 *infra*.   THE ROUGH, 1842 OS.   WALKERS BOTTOMS (lost), 1842 *ib*, v. botm.

FIELD-NAMES

The undated forms are 1848 *TA* 92, the rest are *Dav*.

(*a*) The Acre (*the Acurs* c.1500, *the lower Acre* 1638, v. æcer); Badge Fd (*v.* bæce[1]); Bakehouse (*v.* bæc-hūs); Barn Fd (cf. *the Barne Crofte* 1638); Bottoms (*v.* botm); Brickiln Fd; Calf Croft; Coney Croft (*v.* coni); Coplow Mdw (*Coppelouwe* 1318, *le Copelowes* c.1500, *Coplowes* 1638, 'peaked mound', *v.* copp, hlāw, cf. Coploe C 95, Coplow Wa 222); Double Ploughed Fd; Heath Fd (*v.* hǣð); Holme Croft (*v.* holmr); Long Butts (cf. *le hare-, le bromibuttes* 1313, *v.* lang, hara, brōmig, butte); Long Mdw (*the longe meadowe* 1586); Mere Moss (named from Redes Mere *supra*); Middle Pool;

New Piece(s); Old Mdw; Outlet (*v.* outlet); Pig Moss; Pool Fd; Queens Shaw (*v.* sceaga); Rookery Wd; Sand Fd; Sand Hole Croft; Well Croft; Wood Fd; Woody Rough (*v.* wudig, rūh); Worth (*v.* worð or waroð).

(*b*) *Alen Crofte* c.1500 (from the ME pers.n. *Alein* and croft); *le Blakehalg-feld* c.1500 ('dark nook field' *v.* blæc, halh, feld); *campus voc' Briddeshus* 1313 (*v.* bridd, hūs); *Brodemoreshefd* 1349 ('(the head of) the broad moor', *v.* brād, mōr[1], hēafod); *the Burnt Gorse* 1638 (*v.* brende[2], gorst); *Capistornebrok* c.1318 (*v.* brōc); *ye clamme Croftes* c.1500 ('sticky crofts', *v.* clǣme, cf. clām and ME and ModEdial. *clam*); *Couheye* 1320 (*v.* cū, (ge)hæg); *le Crouweholre* 1318 ('crow's alder', *v.* crāwe, alor); *Farneschawecroftes atte Brodemoreshefd* 1349 (*v.* croft, cf. Fanshawe 79 *infra*, cf. *Brodemoreshefd supra*); *Fexulfildes* (*v.* Capesthorne *supra*); *the Gesling Croft* 1638 (*v.* gesling 'a gosling'); *graymerch* 1313, *Grey-*, *Graymersh*(*e*) 1451 *v.* grǣg[1], mersc); *Haywod feld* c.1500 (*v.* (ge)hæg, wudu, feld); *the Hempe Crofte & Fould* 1638 (*v.* hænep, croft, fald); *Henshaw Hills* 1609 (*v.* hyll, cf. Henshaw 84 *infra*); *le Heuwes-feld* 1318 (probably 'the domestic servant's field', *v.* hīwan, cf. *hewe* NED); *le holewaye* c.1320 ('way in a hollow', *v.* hol[2], weg); *Hulfordhet* 1313 ('(heath at) the hill ford', *v.* hyll, ford, hǣð, cf. *le Wayndore infra*); *the intack* c.1500 (*v.* inntak); *Karlingescroft* 1313 ('old woman's croft', *v.* kerling (cf. *carline* NED), croft); *the littlebrookes* 1571 (*v.* lȳtel, brōc); *lomiforde* 1313 ('clayey ford', *v.* lāmig, ford); *the Marled Crofte* 1638 (*v.* marlede, croft); *le marlputte* 1313 (*v.* marle-pytt); *le Merestall(luscroft)* 1322 '(croft near) a pond', *v.* mere-steall, croft, cf. Redes Mere *supra*); *the Mosse feild* 1638 (*v.* mos); *nouus campus* 1318, *the Newefeld* c.1500 (*v.* nīwe, feld); *the Newe Intacke* 1638 (*v.* nīwe, inntak); Pilatelond 1313 (*v.* pil-āte, land); *le plattes-chaye* 1313 ('copse at a plot of ground', *v.* plat[2], sceaga); *le Schaweruding* 1318 *v.* sceaga, ryding); *le Schertecrofte* 1313 (*v.* sc(e)ort, croft); *le schorte ferni-forlong* 1313 (*v.* sc(e)ort, fearnig, furlang); *The Slackfeild* 1638 (*v.* slakki, feld); *Sondul* 1296 (p) (*v.* sand, hyll); *Warynsamhillis* 1500, *le Warencham hills* 1515 (from hyll 'a hill', and a form of the p.n. Warmingham 335 *infra*); (*campus voc' Hulfordhet super*) *le Wayndore* 1313 (the form suggests 'waggon gate' *v.* wægn, duru, but the context suggests that this is the name of a stream, perhaps 'white stream', from winn[3] and dubrā, as in Wendover Bk); *le yate* e14 (*v.* geat).

5. CHELFORD (110–8174)

Celeford 1086 DB, *Chelle-* c.1200 Facs, *Cheleford* c.1250 Chest, -*furth* 1286 Court (p), *Chel-* 1210 Dieul, (lit. *Clel-*) 1285 Court 208, *Chelforde* (lit. *Chetforde*) 1489 ChRR, *Chellford* 1267 ChetOS VIII 288, *Chelford cum Withington* 1724 NotCestr, *Chelford Green* 1789 (1848) TAMap

Cholleford c.1250 Chest *et freq*, -*forth* 1337 Eyre, *Cholford* 1341 *ib*, *Cholle'* 1351 *ib*

Shelford 1467 MinAcct

Salford 1508 *MinAcct*

'Ceola's ford', from the OE pers.n. *Cēola* or *Ceolla* and **ford**. OE **ceole** 'throat', in a topographical sense, may have applied to the original site of this ford, cf. *ad vadum aqueductus subtus molendinum de Chelleford* c.1271 Chest (ChetNS LXXXII 570), a point on the Snelson boundary about 110–813740, from which the bounds ascended Mere Clough (110–809745) *infra*. The lakes at Astle Park have altered the clough, and the topographical interpretation cannot be proved.

ASTLE (110–829738)

> *Asthul* 1190–1210 Facs, -*hull* c.1245 Chest *et freq*, -*e* c.1540 Dugd,
>   *Hasthul* c.1238 (1595) ChRR, *Astehul*(*l*) c.1300 Cre (p), c.1310
>   Chest
> (*H*)*Esthul* 1210 Orm² (p), Dieul, *Esthult* c.1220 ib
> *Astul*(*l*) 13 *Dav*, c.1250 Adl, 1288 *Eyre*, 1349 *AddCh* (p), -*ell*(*e*)
>   1357 Orm² (p), ChRR (p), -*yll*(*e*) 1395 JRL 32 (p), 1437 ChRR
>   (p), -*ill*(*e*) 1425 MidCh (p), 1440 JRL 32 (p), -*all* 1724 NotCestr
> *Hasthal* 13 (1594) ChRR, *Asthall* 1546 Dugd
> *Ashtul* 1313 *SocAnt* (p)
> *Astleye* 1560 Orm²
> *Astle* 1571 ChRR *et freq*

'East hill', from **ēast** and **hyll**. The place is east of Chelford.

ASTLE HALL (110–8173), 1831 Bry, *Milne-house nigh Chelford* 1499 (1666) Orm², *Mylnehowse* 1536 ib, *the Milnehouse* 1660 ib, cf. *molendinum de Chelleford* c.1245, c.1271 Chest, *v.* **milne-hous**. The old house was replaced in the eighteenth century, *v.* Orm² III 715.

ASTLE PARK.   ABBEY FM, probably refers to the possessions of Chester and Dieulacres Abbeys in this township.   BRICK HILLS. BROOK FM, named from Bag Brook 14 *supra*.   CALLWOOD'S MOSS, *Kennerleys Rough* 1842 OS, *v.* **rūh**, **mos**, cf. James *Callwood* of Firtree Farm, Little Warford, 1860 White.   CARTER LANE, *v.* 330 *infra*.   CHAPEL WOOD, named from *Chelford Chapel*, *v.* St John's Church *infra*.   CHELFORD BRIDGE.   CHELFORD HEATH, 1842 OS. CHURCH HOUSES, near St John's Church.   DALEFIELDS, *Far-*, *Near Dale Fields* 1848 *TA*, *v.* **deill**, **dæl²**.   DAVENPORT HALL (lost, 101–813754), 1842 OS, from the surname *Davenport* and **hall**. HOLLOWACRE WOOD, *Oak Plantation* 1842 ib, *v.* **holh**, **æcer**.   HOME

Fм.   Line Pits, v. pytt; perhaps named from the railway line alongside.   Manor Ho, 1860 White, cf. *manerium de Chelleford* 1358 *MinAcct*.   Mere Hill (lost, 101–808752), 1842 OS, a hamlet on the boundary with Marthall cum Warford, v. (ge)mǣre, hyll. Promontory Wood, in the promontory between Bag Brook and Snape Brook.   Roadside Fм.   St John's Church, the site of *Chelford Chapel* (Sheaf[1] 1, 360), *capella de Chelleford* 1267 Chest, cf. Adam *del Kirke* of Chelford 1350 *Eyre*, v. chapel(e), cirice, kirkja. Sunny Bank.   Willow Gaff, a wood.

FIELD-NAMES

The undated forms are 1848 *TA* 99. Of the others, c.1230–50, 1267, c.1271, l13 are (14) Chest, 1267 (1285) Ch, 1351, 1355 *Eyre*, 1401, 1529 Orm[2], 1779 *AddCh*, 1831 Bry, 1842 OS.

(a) Barn Croft; Creek Moss (*campus de Crakemers* c.1230–50, l13, 'raven's marsh', v. kráka, mersc, cf. Crakemarsh St and DEPN); Cross Croft; Driving Lane 1831 (a cow-lane or drove-way from 110–830738 to 834738); Fulshaw Mdw (cf. Fulshaw 227 *infra*); Furlong (v. furlang); Gibb Croft (perhaps from the pers.n. *Gibb*, for *Gilbert*, but v. gibbe[2] 'a tom-cat, a male ferret', cf. WRY 7 193); Hitch Lowes 1779 ('hillocks at hurdle-pens', v. hiche, hlāw); Hobbarding; Intake (v. inntak); Longshoots 1842 (v. lang, sceāt); Mere Clough (*le Merecloh* c.1271, cf. *Mereclogh* 1365 (p), Thomas *del Clogh* 1401, 'boundary valley', v. (ge)mǣre, clōh, cf. Chelford *supra*); Mill Lane 1831 (110–818744 to 810740, cf. Astle Hall *supra*); Slade or Sledge Mdw (v. slæd); Town Fd; Wheat or Gorsty Moss (v. hwǣte, gorstig, mos).

(b) Leylache (*ubi diuise de Chelleford et de Faudon et de veteri Werford sibi invicem obviant* 'where the bounds of Chelford and of *Fodon* and of *Old Warford* in turn meet it') c.1271 (the final el. is læc(c) 'boggy stream'; the first could be lēah, hence 'boggy stream at a woodland glade or pasture', or alternatively it could be lǣge, dat. sg. of lagu, 'a water, a stream, a pool', hence 'boggy stream-, bog-, at a water'; cf. *Fodon* 331 *infra*, *Old Warford* 335 *infra*); Longefordecrofte 1267 (1285), 1267, cf. *Longeforde* 1351 (p) (v. lang, ford, croft); *profundam mossam* c.1271 ('deep moss', identified with Sossmoss 97 *infra*, in ChetNS LXXXII 328, but that place is distant, cf. Stockin Moss 334 *infra*); *Macclesfield Strete* 1529 ('road to Macclesfield', v. strǣt, cf. 46 *supra*, Orm[2] III 715, Macclesfield 113 *infra*, *le Portwey infra*); *le Portwey* 1529 ('road to a (market-) town', v. port-weg, cf. prec., 46 *supra*); *Puttes* (*unum croftum extra campum de Crakemers veteri quadam fossa circumdatum* 'a croft outside the field of Creek Moss surrounded by a certain ancient ditch') l13 (v. pytt, cf. Creek Moss *supra*): *the Wodhey* 1529 (v. wudu, (ge)hǣg).

6. HENBURY CUM PEXALL, *Endesbyre et Pexhille* 1295, 1305 Lacy, *Ende(s)byr et Pexhill(e)* 1306 *MinAcct*, *(H)Endeburypex(h)ull* 1355 *Eyre, Hendburypexhull* 1374 *ib*, *Hen(ne)bury Pexhull* 1417 ChRR and thereafter as in Henbury, Pexall *infra*.

HENBURY (110–880736)

> *Hameteberie* 1086 DB, *Hamedeberie* 1086 ib, *-bury* c.1301 *Dav* (p),
>   *Hemdebur'* l13 *Fitt* (p), 1285 *Eyre*, *-bury* 1285 Court
> *Hembur'* 1286 *Eyre* (p), *-bury* 1517 *ChEx*
> *Hendebiry* 1288 *Eyre*, *-bur'* 1296 *Dav* (p), *-bury* 1307 Plea *et freq*
>   to 1478, *Endebyr'* 1306 *MinAcct*, *-bury* 1356 *Eyre, Hendburie, -ye*
>   1341 *ib*, *-bury* 1374 *ib*
> *Endesbyre* 1295, 1305 Lacy, *-byr'* 1306 *MinAcct*
> *Henbury* 1383 Cre *et freq*, *-e* 1559 Pat, *-burie* 1545 *Dow*, *-byri*
>   c.1536 Leland, *Hennebury* 1417 Plea, ChRR, *Henebury* 1490
>   *Dow*

From hǣmed and burh. The name may mean 'manor-house or stronghold where people live together; where a community lives'. The el. hǣmed appears in Presteigne Sa (DEPN) with prēost, and is there interpreted 'household of priests', but since it is recorded in OE only with the meaning 'sexual intercourse, cohabitation', there may be indelicate connotations to these p.ns. The hamlet of Henbury is referred to in Orm² as *Henbury Green* (cf. Hamo *del Gren* 1343 Orm², *del Grene de Endebury* 1362 *Eyre* (p), *v.* grēne²), and is marked *Pepper Street* 1842 OS (*v.* Pepper Street 333 *infra*, cf. 46 *supra*) in which map the name *Henbury* is erroneously placed upon Rough-Hey in Birtles (73 *supra*).

PEXALL (110–877721)

> *Pexhull* 1274 Orm² *et freq*
> *Pexhille* 1295, 1305 Lacy, *-hill(e)* 1306 *MinAcct*
> *Pexul* l13 *Fitt* (p), 1285 *Eyre*, *-ull* 1356 *ib*
> *Pesall* 1454 ChRR (p)
> *Pexsell* 1536 Plea
> *Pexhall* 1724 NotCestr, 1953 Index
> *Upper Pexhill* 1831 Bry, 1842 OS

'Hill called *Pēac*; *Pēac* hill', from pēac 'a hill', -es² and hyll. The name appears again in Pexall Rd 60 *supra*, Pexel Fd & Nook 71 *supra*.

LOWER PEXALL, *Pexall Yate* 17 *Chol, Pexal(l) Gate Farm* 1860 White, *Lower Pexhill* 1831 Bry, 'gate leading to Pexall', *v.* geat, cf. prec.

BEARHURST, 1831 Bry. BIG WOOD, *Smithy Brow, Moss Wood* 1831 ib, *Long Shoot Wood, The Coppice* 1842 OS. BRICKBANK, *-Farm* 1842 ib, 'bank where brick-clay is got', *v.* bryke, banke. BROOM-FIELD, *-House* 1842 ib. COCK WOOD, *v.* cocc², wudu. DAVEN-PORT HAYES, from the surname *Davenport* and (ge)hæg. FAN-SHAWE (LANE), FANSHAWE BROOK (FM), *Fanshawe (Brook)* 1831 Bry, cf. *Farneschawecroftes* 1349 *Dav,* 75 *supra,* '(crofts at) the ferny wood', *v.* fearn, sceaga, croft. The brook becomes Snape Brook 35 *supra.* GRAVELHOLE WOOD, cf. *Gravel Hole Field* 1848 *TA.* HENBURY HALL, *the hall of Henbury* c.1558 Orm². HENBURY LODGES, *New Lodge* 1842 OS. HENBURY MOSS, 1831 Bry. HENBURY SMITHY, 1831 ib. HIGHTREE, cf. *High Tree Field* 1848 *TA.* HORSESHOE, *-Farm* 1831 Bry. HUNTLEY WOOD, 1842 OS. LINGARDS, 1831 Bry, from the surname *Lingard* found also in Lingerds 154 *infra,* cf. Robert *Lyngard* (of Hurdsfield 106 *infra*) 1287 Court. LODGE FM, *Henbury Lodge* 1831 Bry. MARL-HEATH, *Merleheath* 1558 JRC, *Marlearth* 1831 Bry, 1842 OS, *v.* marle, hæð. MOSS COTTAGES, named from Longmoss 119 *infra.* PALE (110–865738), *the parke pale* 1558 JRC, *Birtles of the Pale* 1819 Orm¹, *-at the Pale* 1831 Bry, *Pale Farm* 1860 White, the home of a branch of the Birtles family, cf. Orm² III 709, Birtles, Birtleshill 72 *supra, v.* pale 'a park-pale', park. PARK FIELDS (lost), PARK HO, 1831 Bry, cf. *Henbury Park* c.1558 Orm², cf. prec. PEXALL WOOD, *Pexhulwode* 1413 ib. POOL WOOD, cf. Thorneycroft Pools *infra.* REDES MERE, *v.* 74 *supra.* SANDBACH, *-Fm* 1860 White, *Sand-baches* 1842 OS, from the surname from Sandbach 334 *infra.* SMITHY WOOD, cf. Henbury Smithy *supra.* THORNYCROFT LODGE & POOLS, cf. Thorneycroft Hall 85 *infra.* WOOD HOUSE (lost), 1842 OS. YEW-WOOD, *Ruewood Farm* 1842 ib, *Hough Wood* 1860 White.

FIELD-NAMES

The undated forms are 1848 *TA* 200. Of the others 1286 is Court, 1296, 1702 *Dav,* 1374 *Eyre,* 14 Orm², 1536 Leland, 1558 JRC, 1842 OS.

(a) Acre; Banky Fd; Birch Wd (cf. *Bircholt* 1286 (p), *-old* 1296 (p), *one woode called hye byrcholte, bromyrcholte* (? for *brom(y)byrcholte), byrcholte meadow* 1558, *v.* birce, holt, hēah, brōmig); Black Mdw; Brick Kiln Mdw; Clover Croft; Cow Hey (cf. *Oxehaye* 1558, *v.* cū, oxa, (ge)hæg); Crumpback

Fd ('hunchback field', v. dial. *crump* 'crooked, hunched', cf. crumb, bæc, here probably topographical); Dam Fd (v. damme); Rough Henbury, Henbury Fd (cf. Henbury *supra*, v. rūh); Horse Pasture; Jay Fd; Little Butts (v. butte); Lodge Fd & Ground; Lowns's Fd (perhaps from the surname *Lowndes*); Marlhole Fd, Marlhurst (v. marle, hol[1], hyrst); Megs Fd (from the fem. pers.n. *Meg* from *Margaret*); Moss Fd (*Mosse-* 1558, cf. Henbury Moss *supra*); Old Mdw; Pingot (v. pingot); Robins Cob (from the pers.n. *Robin*, diminutive of *Robert*, with cobb(e) 'a round lump', or 'a tumulus' as in Dicklow Cob 90 *infra*); Round Wd (*Round Plantation* 1842); Sandhole Fd (v. sand, hol[1]); Shippon Fd (v. scypen); Spike Fd; Tadmore Croft 1842 (perhaps 'croft at toad-marsh', v. tāde, mōr[1], croft); Well Fd; Wood Fd.

(b) *byrchen greate meadowe* 1558 (v. bircen[2]); *Flaxhalflond* 14 ('half-selion under flax', v. fleax, half-land); *gosperlandes* 1558 (v. land; the first el. may be gospel); *hall croft meadowe* 1558; *greit-, litle mo(o)re field* 1558 (v. mōr[1]); *the poole head, poole meadowe* 1558 ('at Henbyri is a greate poole' c. 1536 Leland, v. Orm[2] III 706); *pynehyn grene meadowe* 1558; *Redde broke haye* 1558 ('(enclosure at) the reedy stream', v. hrēod, hrēoden, brōc, (ge)hæg); *the lower Shepe pasture* 1558; *the Six Day Math* 1702 ('six days' mowing', v. day-math); *Small Furlong* 14 ('narrow furlong', v. smæl, furlang); *le Sych inter Byrtles et Hendbury* 1374 (v. sīc; the watercourse from 110–870739 to 860738 formerly the boundary of the township, near Pale *supra*).

7. MARTON (110–8568)

Merutune 1086 DB

Mereton 1086 DB, *Merton* m12 Orm[2] *et freq* to 1612 ChRR, (*-iuxta Mutlowe*) 1370 Orm[2], (*-Gouseworth*) 1383 Plea, (*-Davenport*) c.1533 ib, *Mertona* l13 Dav, *-tun* c.1307 *ib*, *maner de Merton* 1353 *ib*

Marton l13 MidCh (p), 1551 ChRR *et freq*, (*-iuxta Somerton*) 1374 Eyre

Marton Chapel 1581 Cre

'Lake farm', from mere[1] and tūn. There was a lake here, cf. Mere Fm *infra*. *Meru-* might suggest confusion with (ge)mǣre 'a boundary' but there is no historical evidence to support that etymology. It could be a reduced form of OE dat.pl. *merum* 'at the lakes', (cf. Mareham L (DEPN)), a simplex p.n. to which tūn has been added; but there is no record of more than one lake here. The *Meru-* spelling looks like a scribal anticipation of the *u* in *-tune*. Marton adjoins Mutlow *infra*, Gawsworth 66 *supra*, Davenport 331 *infra*, Somerford Booths 63 *supra*. *-iuxta Somerton* refers to the latter. The suffix *chapel* is from St James's Church *infra*, v. chapel(e).

MUTLOW (110–860677), a part of Marton township in Gawsworth ecclesiastical parish, including MUTLOW (*Higher Mutlow* 1831 Bry, *High Mutlow* 1842 OS, *Middle Mutlow* 1860 White), HIGHER MUTLOW (*Old Mutlow* 1831 Bry, *Mutlow* 1842 OS, *Great Mutlow* 1860 White), MOSS BANK (*Rughmutlow(e)* 1525 ChRR, Orm², *Rough Mutlow* 1831 Bry, *Lower Mutlow* 1860 White, *v.* rūh), and BLACK WOOD (*Mutlow Moss* 1842 OS, *v.* mos).

> *Motlau* e13 Dieul, *-lawe* c.1232 Dugd (p), c.1300 JRL 32 (p),
> *-low(e)* c.1296 Orm² (p), 1313 *Dav*, *-lows* 1482 ChRR (p),
> *Mothelawe* c.1262 *Dav* (p) *et freq* to c.1290 *ib*, 1371 MidCh (p),
> *Motthelawe* c.1318 *Dav* (p), *Mothlowe* 1360 MidCh (p), *Mote-lowe* 1318 Cl (p), *-low* 1488 ChRR (p), *Mottelowe* c.1320 *Fitt* (p),
> *Mhotlowe* 1321 *Dav* (p), *Mottlelowe* 1394 ChRR (p)
> *Matlow* c.1233 Tab (p)
> *Muttelawe* 1288 Court (p), *del Muttelowe* 1354 Chamb (p), *Mutlowe* 1429 ChRR (p), *-law* 1724 NotCestr
> *Modlowe* 1323 *Dav* (p)
> *Moutlouwe* 1331 Tab (p), *-lowe* 1353 *Dav* (p)

'Assembly mound', *v.* mōt, hlāw. This may have been the meeting-place for *Hamestan* hundred, but it is not central.

BANK FM, *Bank* 1848 *TA*. BOTTOMEND, cf. *Big-*, *Little Bottom* 1848 *ib*, *v.* botm, ende¹. BOUNDARY FM, cf. Boundary Fm 90 *infra*, on the Lower Withington boundary. BRICKYARD FM. BUNCE LANE (FM), *Bunce Lane* 1831 Bry, may contain the surname *Bunce* cf. Bunse St. (Chester) 330 *infra*. CHAPEL BRIDGE, crosses Chapel Brook near St James's Church. CHAPELBROOK COTTAGES, cf. Chapel Brook 18 *supra*. CHURCH FM, *Chapel House* 1860 White, cf. St James's Church *infra*. COCKMOSS COTTAGE, FM, RD, & WOOD, *le mos* c.1262 *Dav*, *Cock Moss* 1831 Bry, *Cocks Moss*, *Moss Fm* 1842 OS, 'moor-cock moss', *v.* cocc², mos. DAIRY FM (lost), 1842 *ib*, *v.* deierie. DAISYBANK FM. DAVENPORT LANE, cf. *Davenport Hey* 1848 *TA*, from the surname *Davenport*, *v.* (ge)hæg, lane. FERN FM. GORSLEY GREEN (FM), HIGHER GORSLEY, *Gosling Green* 1831 Bry, *Gorsley Green*, *Gorsey Green Farm* 1842 OS, 'green at gorse clearing', *v.* gorst, lēah, grēne². The farm was *Masseys* 1831 Bry, from the surname *Massey*. HOLLY BANK (110–853692), *Holling House* 1831 *ib*, *Lower Pikelow* 1842 OS, *v.* holegn, cf. Pikelow *infra*. MARTON BRIDGE. MARTON BROOK

(> Redlion Brook 91 *infra*), cf. *ductum de Merton* 1313 *Dav* perhaps Chapel Brook 18 *supra*, v. brōc.   MARTONGATE, 1831 Bry, 'gateway to Marton', on the boundary with Gawsworth and Siddington, v. geat.   MARTON HALL, 1831 ib.   MARTON HEATH (WOOD), *Marton Heath* 1831 ib.   MARTON LANE. MARTON MERE (lost, 110–850685), MERE COTTAGES & FM, *The Mere* 1819 Orm[1], *Marton Mere* 1848 *TA*, v. mere[1]. The mere was drained 1848–9 (Orm[2] III 726) and formerly covered about 14 acres (White 762).   MILL HO (lost, 110–844673), 1848 *TA*, *molendinum de Mertun* c.1307 *Dav*, *Marton Mill* 1831 Bry, v. milne-hous. MILLBANK COTTAGES (110–843673), *Mill Bank* 1831 ib, cf. prec. MOSS COTTAGES, v. mos.   OAK FM, 1860 White, named from the celebrated Marton Oak, Orm[2] III 726n.   PIKELOW (110–856690), 1831 Bry, (*Lower*) *Pikelow* 1842 OS, 'pointed mound', v. pīc[1], hlāw, cf. Holly Bank *supra* perhaps incorrectly named in 1842 OS.   ST JAMES'S CHURCH formerly MARTON CHAPEL, *capella de Merton* 1370 Orm[2], *the late chantry or free chapel of Merton* 1549 Pat, *Marton Chapel* 1581 Cre *et freq* to 1848 *TA*, built c.1343 (White 761, cf. Orm[2] III 726).   SANDPIT FM, *Sand Pit* 1842 OS, v. sand, pytt. SNOW BALL HO (lost), 1842 ib.   YEWTREE, cf. *Yew Tree Field* 1848 *TA*.

FIELD-NAMES

The undated forms are 1848 *TA* 258; 1842 is OS, the rest *Dav*.

(a) Acorn Fd & Ley (v. æcern, feld, lēah); Acre(s); Adams Corner; Bake House Croft (v. bæc-hūs); Baleys Mdw (v. baillie); Barbers Fd; Basine Croft ('basin croft', v. bacin, croft); Bean Fd & Yard, Bean Pit Fd; Bent (v. beonet); Birchen Croft (v. bircen[2], croft); Black Croft & Fd; Black Pit Fd; Blake Fd, Blake Field Bent (v. blæc, feld, beonet); Blake Low (*le Blakelowe* c.1262, *Le Lyttil-*, *le Mucleblakelowis, -us* l13, 'dark mound(s)', v. blæc, hlāw, lӯtel, mycel); Bramhall (Hill) (*Bro(m)hul* l13, 'broom hill', v. brōm, hyll, cf. Bramhallhill 59 *supra*); Brick Bank (v. bryke, banke); Brick Kiln Fd, Bricken Croft (v. bryke-kyl); Broad Fd and Mdw; Brook Strip(e)s (v. brōc, strīp); Broom (v. brōm); Brown Fd: Butty Mdw (v. butty); Calf Croft; Calvey Croft (v. calf, (ge)hæg, croft); Carr Mdw (v. kjarr); Cherry Barrow (*Churubaruhe* l13, 'cherry-tree wood', v. chiri, bearu, cf. 233 *infra*); Church Fd; Cinder Hill (v. sinder, hyll); Common Fd; Coney Greave ('rabbit warren', v. coninger); Copice (v. copis); Cow Hey (v. cū, (ge)hæg); Cross Fd (v. cros 'a cross'; there is an ancient stone cross at 110–850680 near the church); Crow Bottom (v. crāwe, botm); Four, Seven, Ten, Eight & Five Day Work (v. day-work); East Fd; Eels Moss (v. ēl[2], mos); Fairy Fd (v. faierie); Fall (v. (ge)fall); Fernyshaw ('ferny copse', v. fearnig, sceaga); Flat Carrots; Fowl Fd; Furry Fd; Goody Croft; Gorse Low (*le Gorstilowe* 1313, 'gorse-grown mound', v. gorstig, hlāw); Gravel Bank; Old Green; Green Lane ('grassy lane', v. grēne[1], lane); Hales Fd & Hey (v. halh, feld, (ge)hæg); Hall Croft, Flatts, & Lane (v. hall, croft, flat, lane, cf. Marton Hall supra); Handforth Hey (probably named from Handforth 254 infra where the Davenport family also had estates, v. (ge)hæg, cf. Davenport Lane supra); Hatch Fd (v. hæc(c)); Heath Hay (v. hǣð, (ge)hæg); Hemps Yard (v. hemp-yard); Hill; Hodge Fd (cf. Hodg Croft 158 infra); Hole (v. hol[1]); Hollin (v. holegn); Hollow(s) (v. holh); Horse Pasture; House Mdw; Kiln Croft; Kith Croft (v. kide); Knaves Acre ('boy's acre', v. cnafa, æcer); Land Lees ('strip meadow', v. land, lǣs); Lanthorn Fd (probably 'tall thorn-tree', v. lang, þorn); Laughing Croft (v. 332 infra); Lime Piece; Long Shoot (v. lang, scēat); Mare Fd (v. mere[2]); Marl Fd; Marl Pit Bank (v. marle-pytt, banke); Marsh, Marsh Lane; Meadow Top; Meg Croft (v. meg); Missick (v. mizzick); Moor Heyes (v. mōr[1], (ge)hæg); Morris ('marsh', v. mareis); Moss End; Nick Acre (v. nick(e)); Oller (Fd), Oller Hey (v. alor, (ge)hæg); Oven Fd, Oven House Croft (v. ofen, hūs); Ox Close (v. oxa, clos); Partridge Hill; Patch; Pinfold Piece (v. pynd-fald, pece); Pingot (v. pingot); Pink Croft; Plumb Park ('plum-tree plot', v. plūme, park); Pool Stead (the name of three fields adjoining the mill-pool at Marton Mill, v. pōl-stede); Potts Fd (perhaps from the surname Pott from Pott Hall 130 infra, cf. potte); Priest Mdw; Prison Bar Bank & Mdw (probably from the game of 'prisoner's-base', v. prison-bars); Quick Hills ('couch grass', v. cwice, hyll); Ridding (v. ryding); Roscins; Ruxley Hill; Rye Croft; Sand Fd; Saw Pit Croft (v. saw-pytt); Senichar ('seven acre', v. seofen, æcer); Shippon Croft (v. scypen); Sing Pool Mdw ('meadow with a sump-hole', v. sinke, pōl[1], mǣd); Smithy Fd; Soond Hill Fd, Soond(s) ('sand hill, sand(s)', v. sand, hyll); Sour Mdw; Sparrow Croft; Steansley (croftum vocatum vetus steynisleg' 113, vetus-, paruum Steynisleg' 1307, Steӡnisleg' 1313, 'Steinn's clearing', from the ON pers.n. Steinn and lēah, with ald, lȳtel); Sun Fd (v. sunne); Sweet Grass (v. gærs); Tentry Fd ('tenter field', v. tentour); This(t)ley Fd; Thorn Hill; Tinkers Fd (v. tink(l)ere); Turf Coat Croft ('hut built of turf', (v. turf, cot, croft); Twin Moor; Two Day Math (v. day-math); Underbank (v. under, banke); Vetchey-, Vitchey Fd (v. fecche, ficche); Wall Flat(t) (v. wælla, flat); Wards Nook; Well Nook; Welshaw Mdw (probably 'well copse', v. wella, sceaga); White Hill (3x) (le Quitehullis 113, 'white hills', v. hwīt, hyll); White Meres (v. hwīt, mere[1]); White Moss 1842; Wicken ('mountain-ash tree', v. cwicen); Wift Fd; Within Flatt (v. wiðign, flat).

(b) Blakedene 1353 (v. blæc, denu); le Blakelache 1313 ('black stream', v. blæc, læc(c)); Chynnaleheuid 1313 (v. cinu, halh, and hēafod); Gosemere-seche c.1262 ('(stream at) the goose-lake', from gōs and mere[1], with sīc); (nemus de) Harewode 1300, 1307, 1313 ('hoar wood', v. hār[2], wudu); Hullecroft 113, (nemus de) Holecroftismor 1300, 1307 ('hill enclosure, moor at the hill-croft', v. hyll, croft, mōr[1], cf. hol[1, 2]); Hosseberneruding 113, Hosebern-, Hosebarnisruding 1307, 1313 ('Ásbiǫrn's clearing', from the ON pers.n. Ásbiǫrn and ryding); alta via que vocatur le hyerlisweye 1313 ('the high earl's-way', v. hēah, eorl, weg, cf. 45 supra and Reade's Lane 333 infra); le Quitehockes 1313 ('the white oaks', v. hwīt, āc).

8. SIDDINGTON (110–845709)

Now a c.p. including Capesthorne 73 *supra*.

> *Sudendune* 1086 DB, *Sudindun, -don* m13 *Dav* (p), 1249 Earw,
>   *Sudingdon(e)* 1286, 1288 Court (p)
> *Sydent'* e13 Dieul, *Sydenton* c.1300 Orm², *Sidentun* 1313 *Dav* (p)
>   *Sidinton* 1269 Tab, *-tun* c.1300 Orm², *Sydinton(a)* l13 *Dav* (p),
>   1304 Chamb (p), *-tun* c.1300 Orm², *Sydynton'* 1311 *Dav et freq*
>   to 1518 Plea, *Sidyn-, Sydunton* 1318 *Dav* (p)
> *Sydyndon'* m13 *Dav, Sidindun'* 1286 *Eyre, -don* 1323 *Dav, Sydindon*
>   c.1300 Orm², *Sidendon* c.1301 *Dav* (p)
> *Suddinton* 1278 Ipm, *Sudington'* 1286 *Eyre*, 1353 Orm² (p),
>   *Sudinton(a)* 1296 (p), c.1300 *Dav*
> *Sidindam* 1286 *Eyre* (p)
> *Sudindam* 1286 *Eyre* (p)
> *Sotington* 1290 Court (p)
> *Sidington* 1335 Pat, *Sydyng-* 1357 ChRR (p), *Sidyng-, Syding-* 1361
>   BPR (p), Orm², *Siddington* 1383 ChRR (p), 1694 *AddCh et freq*,
>   *Syddington* 1548 Orm²
> *Sythington alias Siddington* 1694 *AddCh*

'(Place) south of the hill', from sūðan and dūn. It is not clear which hill this refers to, for this is undulating country. The final el. is replaced by tūn, which misled BdHu 110, Wo 60 into suggesting analogy with Sodington Wo (cf. DEPN).

LE BYRREHYLL (lost), c.1500, (*le*) *Byrellis* l13, (*le*) *Burellis, -ys* 1301, 1311, *Borelles* 1310, *berihullis* 1318 all *Dav*, 'burial-place', *v.* byrgels, cf. *Burying Field infra*. In 1311, *Dav* 1/24:61 locates *le Burellys* 'iuxta rivulum currentum et metas de Capistorn', i.e. between Snape Brook and the Capesthorne boundary, about 110–835720.

HENSHAW HALL (110–861705)

> *Henneschæ* m13 *Dav, -schage, -s(c)hawe, -shagh(e), -sahe, -scawe* l13
>   *ib*, 1288 *Eyre* (p), c.1300 Orm², *Hennesshawe* 1423 *Dav* (p),
>   *Hennishage* 1287 *Eyre* (p), *Hemigshawe* 1288 *ib* (for *Hennig-*)
> *Henesahe* 13 *Dav, -schaghe* 1351 *Eyre* (p)
> *Hensha* 1289 Cre (p), *-shaw(e)* 1355 *Eyre* (p), 1443 ChRR (p),
>   *-shagh* 1409 ib (p), *Henshaw Hall* 1860 White
> *Hendshagh* 1377 *Eyre* (p)
> *Hanshagh* 1441 ChRR (p)

Heynshagh 1525 *ChEx*
Henshall Hall 1831 Bry, 1842 OS

'Hens' copse', from the gen.pl. of **henn** and **sceaga**. These hens would be wild birds, such as woodcocks or partridges.

NORTHWOOD (110–849697), *Nordwode* 1278 Ipm, *Nortwode* 1296 *Dav* (p), *Norwod(e)* 1286 Court (p), 1301 *Dav* (p), *Northwode* 1288 *Eyre*, *-wod* 1386 *Dav* (p), *-wood* 1730 *ib*, 'north wood', *v.* **norð, wudu**. The place is north of Marton 80 *supra*.

THORNYCROFT HALL & POOLS (110–869729)

> *Thornicroft* l13 *Dav* (p), *Thornnicroft* 1361 Orm² (p), *Thornicrofte near Goseworth* c.1703 *Chol*, *Thornycroft* 1349 *Eyre* (p), *-e* 1423 *Dav* (p)
> *Thornecroft* 1413, 1430, 1503 Orm² (p)
> *Thorneycroft Hall* 1831 Bry

'Thorny croft' from **þornig** and **croft**. The pools are *Higher & Lower Pool* 1838 *TA*, *v.* **pōl**¹.

TURNOCK (110–838703)

> *Tornoc* 13, c.1300 *Dav*, *ok-*, (*aula de*) *Tornock*, *Tornockgrene* c.1301 *Dav*
> *Turnoc* c.1260, 1323 *Dav*, *-ok* c.1300 Orm², *-ock* c.1301, 1730 *Dav*

The place is at the west end of the higher ground south of Siddington village, and is not on a stream. The etymology of the name is uncertain. It might be of Celtic origin, a word formed with the PrW suffix *-ǫg*, *v.* **-āco-**, but a more obvious meaning would be 'thorny place', from OE **þurnuc, *þornuc* (*v.* **þorn, -uc**), analogous with Rushock, Rushwick Wo 255, 94 and xliii, *v.* **riscuc**, cf. Tarbock La 113, 263. For *þ-* > *t-* cf. DEPN s.nn. Turnaston He, Turnworth Do.

WHISTERFIELD (HO & RD) (110–829713)

> *Quitstanisfeld* c.1260 *Dav*, *-es-* 1341 *Eyre*
> *Wistannisfeld* 13 *Dav*, *Qui-*, *W(h)i-*, *W(h)ystan(e)s-*, *-isfeld* c.1301 *ib*, 1337, 1347, 1348 *Eyre*, 1358 Chamb (p), 1402 ChRR (p), 1425 MidCh (p), *Qui-*, *Whyston(u)sfeld* 14 *Dav*, 1400 ChRR, *Qui-*, *Quystenesfeld* 1365, 14 Tab

Whi-, Whystan(e)feld 1365 Pat, 1371 *Eyre*, 1428 *Dav, Whistonn-feld* 1381 *Eyre*

Whisterfelde 1353 Orm² (p)

'Open land near a white stone', *v.* hwīt, stān, -es², feld. This may refer to a boundary-stone, as the place is on the township boundary. For the development *-stan(e)s-, -ster-* cf. Austerson 329 *infra*. Whisterfield is in Siddington and Lower Withington townships.

ALL SAINTS' CHURCH formerly SIDDINGTON CHAPEL, *capella de Sydinton* 1337 *Eyre, Sydynton Chapell* 1415 Earw, *Siddington chapel* 1724 NotCestr (ChetOS VIII 297), cf. *the Chappel house* 1730 *Dav, Chapel Croft & Field* 1848 *TA.*   BLAKEHOUSE FM, *the Black(e) house* 1638, 1730 *Dav*, Blake House 1831 Bry, 'black house', *v.* blæc, hūs.   THE BOTTOMS, 1848 *TA, v.* botm.   BOUNDARY FM, on the township boundary.   BROADOAK, 1831 Bry.   BUCK'S HILL, cf. *The Buck, Bucks (Field & Meadow)* 1848 *TA*, probably 'the bush(es)', *v.* buskr, dial. *busk*, with metathesis leading to a new sg. form by analogy.   CARDITCH, 'marsh ditch', *v.* kjarr, dīc. COLSHAW WOOD, perhaps 'charcoal copse', *v.* col¹, sceaga, wudu. CRABTREEMOSS, *Far Crabtree Moss* 1842 OS, cf. Crabmoss 68 *supra.* ETTILY WOOD, 1848 *TA*, cf. Ettiley Heath 331 *infra.*   FANSHAWE LANE, *v.* 79 *supra.*   FLOATING ISLAND (lost, 110–849717), 1842 OS, an island in Redes Mere which floated about the lake, *v.* White 771.   GARDEN WOOD, 1848 *TA.*   GORSEYKNOWL, *v.* gorstig, cnoll.   HAZELWALL (WOOD), 1842 OS, *Haslewall* 1730 *Dav, Hazle Wood, Hazle Walls* 1831 Bry, 'hazel spring', from hæsel and wælla, with wudu.   HESKEY WOOD, 1848 *TA*, probably 'ash-tree enclosure', *v.* æsc, (ge)hæg, cf. esc, eski.   HILLSGREEN, 1831 Bry, cf. *the lagher hillez* 1542, *the hier hilles* 1571, *the Hill Top* 1730 all *Dav, v.* hyll, grēne².   HODGEHILL, 1831 Bry, *v.* hyll, cf. 91 *infra*, from hogg 'a hog', or the pers.n. *Hodge* (ME *Hogge*), cf. *Hodg Croft* 158 *infra*, Hodge Croft, Rogers Croft *infra.*   HORSE WOOD, 1842 OS.   LONGFOLD, *v.* lang, fald.   MANOR HOUSE, 1842 OS. MARTON BRIDGE, *v.* 81 *supra.*   MILLHOUSE, *v.* milne-hous. MERE MOSS (110–841698), 1842 OS, *v.* mere¹, mos.   MOSS FM & WOOD, cf. Siddington Moss *infra.*   NURSERY LANE, cf. *Nursery Croft* 1848 *TA.*   PYETHORNE WOOD, *v.* 69 *supra.*   REDESMERE FM & LANE, named from Redes Mere 74 *supra.*   SIDDINGTON BANK, *Simpson's Brow Farm* 1842 OS, *v.* brū.   SIDDINGTON BRIDGE.   SIDDINGTON HALL, 1831 Bry.   SIDDINGTON HEATH,

1842 OS, *le Het* 1323 *Dav, v.* hǣð. SIDDINGTON MILL. SID-
DINGTON MOSS, 1831 Bry, cf. *le Mos* 1323 *Dav, v.* mos. SIMON'S
WOOD, SIMONSWOOD FM, *Simons Wood* 1831 Bry. SNAPE
BROOK FM, cf. Snape Brook 35 *supra.* SPORDS FM, cf. *Spodes
Croft* 1848 *TA*, from the surname *Spode.* TOLLBAR FM.
WICKENHALL, *Wicken Hall* 1842 OS, *v.* cwicen 'mountain-ash', hall.

FIELD-NAMES

The undated forms are 1848 *TA* 356; if not otherwise ascribed, the rest
are *Dav.*

(*a*) Ashen Flatt (*v.* æscen, flat); Bakehouse Croft (*v.* bæc-hūs); Barn Field
Lane & Wd; Bend Lands, Bent Fd (*v.* beonet); Big Fd (cf. *the great field*
1745); Big Garden; Big Meadow Bottom (*v.* botm); Birchall Croft; Birch
Hill; Birchen Croft (*the Birchen Crofte* 1638, *v.* bircen[2], croft); Birches;
Birtles Croft (cf. Birtles 72 *supra*); Black Croft (*the Blake Crofte* c.1500,
v. blæc, croft); Black Fd (*le blacke fylde* 1552, *the Blakefield* 1745, *v.* blæc,
feld); Blackden (*Blake*(s)-*den*(*e*) 1312–18, messuage or tenement called
Blackden 1580, 'Black's valley', from a ME pers.n. *Blake* (cf. OE *Blaca*,
*Blæc) and denu); Brick Kiln Fd; Brook Hole (*v.* brōc, hol[1]); Broom (*v.*
brōm); Bull Hill; Burying Fd (*v.* burying, feld, cf. *le Byrrehyll supra*,
Burying Fd 156 *infra*); Calf Croft Wd; Calves Knowl (*v.* calf, cnoll); Carr
(*v.* kjarr); Clatten Bridge (perhaps 'noisy bridge' or 'causeway of loose
stones', from clater and brycg, assuming -*n* substituted for -*r* as in Withinger
infra); Clay Bank, Fd & Wd; Common Fd, Moss & Piece; Con(e)y
Gr(e)ave(s) (*v.* coninger); Crabtree Fd,Crabtree Little Ruloe ('field at a
crab-tree' and '(field called) "little rough mound" at a crab-tree', *v.* crabbe,
trēow, lȳtel, rūh, hlāw, cf. Low *infra*); Cross Hill (*v.* cros, hyll); Crow Park(s)
(*v.* crāwe, park); Dallingreave (*Dalingreue*, croft vocat' *Dalyngreue iuxta
Tornok* 1301, *Dalingreues* 1730, 'Dealla's, or Dealing's, wood', from grǣfe
with the OE pers.n. *Dealla* and -ing-[4], or with the OE pers.n. *Dealing*);
Dirty Fd; Dowse Bank & Mdw (*v.* douce, banke, mǣd); Drumble ('wooded
dingle', *v.* drumble); Eels Moss (*v.* ēl[2], mos); Fanshawe Garden (cf. Fanshawe
79 *supra*); Findlow ('heaped mound', *v.* fīn, hlāw); Flash Piece (*v.* flasshe,
pece); Footway Fd; Forty Acre; Fox Holes (*v.* fox-hol); Gallows Hill (*v.*
galga, hyll); Goodiers Fd (cf. *Goodyers tenement* 1730, from the surname
Goodier); Gorse Croft; Gorsey Bank, Gorsty Croft (*v.* gorstig, banke, croft);
(Top o'th') Green (cf. *the Green Tenement* 1730, *v.* grēne[2]); Gutter Croft
(*v.* goter); Hays (*v.* (ge)hæg); Hemp Yard (*v.* hemp-yard); Hermitage Wd;
Hodge Croft (cf. Hodgehill *supra*); Hollin Croft, Hollingreave (*v.* holegn,
croft, grǣfe); Horse Hill; Intack, Intake (*v.* inntak); Jacks Croft; Keddle
Dock Fd (*v.* keddle-dock); Knowl (-*e* 1745, *v.* cnoll); Lane Fd; Lime Fd;
Long Croft (1745, *v.* lang, croft); (Further & Rough) Low (*v.* hlāw, cf.
Crabtree *supra*); Lowthorne Lodge; Mad Cross; Marl Fd & Piece (cf. *le
Marlidcroft, le Marledecroftesyherd* c.1301, *v.* marlede, croft, geard); Marton

Mdw (*v.* Marton 80 *supra*) Masters; Mattock Fd; Mear-, Mere Fd, Croft
& Flat (cf. *le mereruding* c.1307 *v.* mere[1], ryding, cf. Mere Moss *supra*,
Redes Mere 74 *supra*); Mile Wood (*v.* mīl); New Piece; Oak(s) Croft; Old
Betty's Piece (from *Betty*, a pet-form of *Elizabeth*); Old Years (cf. Blackeyer
265 *infra*); Orchard Wd; Outcote ('the outlying cottage', *v.* ūt, cot); Oven
Croft (*v.* ofen); Pasture Fd (cf. *the Over Pasture* 1513 Orm[2], *v.* uferra,
pasture); Pearl (-Lane) (*Pearlfield* 1729 Sheaf, from pyrl(e) 'a bubbling
stream', and feld, lane); Peartree Fd; New Pickow (*v.* nīwe, pichel); Pillows
Croft (*v.* pil-āte); Pingot (*v.* pingot); Plumtree Croft & Moss; Pool Ford
(*v.* pōl[1], ford); Pretty Fd; Rogers Croft (Wood) (from the ME pers.n. *Roger*
and croft, wudu, cf. Hodgehill *supra*); Rough Ridding (Spink) ('plantation at
rough clearing', *v.* rūh, ryding, spring); Rushy Fd; Sand (Hole) Fd; School
Fd; Shippon Fd (*v.* scypen); Short Lands (*v.* sc(e)ort, land); Siddington Fd
& Mdw; Six-, Two Days Work (*v.* day-work); Sledge Fd; Smithy Fd;
Snape (*v.* snæp, cf. Snape Brook 35 *supra*); Somerless Knowl, Long
Somerless (*the Somerlesowe* 1506, 'summer pasture', *v.* sumor, lǣs); Spout
Fd (*v.* spoute); Square Croft; Stave Gate Fd; Little Stones; Thistley Fd
(*v.* þistlig); Tile Bank (*v.* tigel, banke); Wall Gate Hole Mdw, Wall Gate
Water Bank (*v.* wǣlla, gata); Well Bank; Wet Fd; White Fd(s); Will
Gorse; Winnowing Bank; Withinger(s), Withingen (*Witheneker* 113, 1301,
Wi-, *Wythinker* 1301, *Withingers* 1730, 'the willow marsh', *v.* wiðign, kjarr;
-n is substituted for *-r* as in Clatten Bridge *supra*).

(*b*) *le depelache* c.1301 (*v.* dēop, lǣc(c)); *Docklacheseche* c.1301 ('(drain
through) the dock-ridden bog', *v.* docce, lǣc(c), sīc); *le Grenelache* c.1301
('green bog', *v.* grēne[1], lǣc(c)); *alta via que ducit uersus Macclisfeld* c.1301
(part of the salt-way from Middlewich to Macclesfield, *v.* 47 *supra*); *le
Louyndgreues* c.1301 ('copses where courting is done', from the pres. part.
of ME *luvien* 'to love', and grǣfe); *le meresiche* c.1307 (*v.* mere[1], sīc); *le
Okenestobbe* c.1301 ('the oak-stub', *v.* ācen, stubb); *Rauenkelesbroc* m13
('Hrafnkell's brook', from the ON pers.n. *Hrafnkell* and brōc. This is Snape
Brook 35 *supra*. The pers.n. appears among the TRE tenants of Ch,
Feilitzen 293); *Roolegheslawne* 1552 ('(pasture at) the rough clearing', *v.* rūh,
lēah, launde); *yelildelawebroc* m13, *Yillowe* c.1503 Orm[2] ('(brook at) Æðel-
hild's mound', from the OE fem pers.n. *Æðelhild* and hlāw, with brōc; cf.
Feilitzen 103 for the pers.n. forms).

9. LOWER WITHINGTON (110–8170)

Now included in Withington c.p., with Old Withington 92 *infra*.

Widinton, *-enton* 1185, 1186 P, *Wydinton* 1240 ib (p), *-ynton* 1277
VR (p), *-ington* 1289 Cl

Withinton, *-enton* 1210 Dieul, e13 Adl (p), *-ington* 1249 IpmR,
(*-iuxta Merton*) 1347 Dav, *Wythynton* c.1238 (1595) ChRR (p),
-yngton 1447 Eyre, *-inton* 1240 P (p), *-a* c.1271 Chest, *-ington*
1267 (1845) ChetOS VIII, (*Lower-*) 1598 ChRR, *Withyngton*
1290 Court (p), *-ynton* 1354 Chol, *Whithinton* 1210 (17) Orm[2] II

864, c.1245 Chest, -*ington* 1440 MidCh, *Whythinton* 1267 (17)
Chest, -*ynton* 1341 *Eyre*, *Whithynton* 1535 VE
Wit- 1239 P, *Wytinton* 1267 (1285) Ch, *Wytt*-, *Wittington* 1540
Dugd, 1547 *MinAcct*, *Lower Wittington* 1694 *AddCh*, *Whit*-,
Whytinton 1337 Plea (p), ChRR (p), *Whytynton* 1343 Plea (p),
-*yngton* 1429 ChRR (p), *Whyttyngton* 1554 *MinAcct*
Weþnton 1337 *Eyre*, *Wethinton* 1354 *Dav*, -*yngton* 1510 ChRR
Wyvinton 1341 AD (p)

'Willow farm', *v.* wiðign, tūn, cf. Old Withington 92 *infra*, and
Hungrewenitune infra.

BROAD HILL (110–817688), 1848 *TA*, *Tunstude* m13 Dav, -*stud* 1349
Eyre, -*sted* m13 Orm², 1314 *Dav*, *le Tunstede infra metas de Wythinton*
& *campus del Tunsted* 1312–18 *Dav*, *a singular hill called Tunsted* 1819
Orm[1,2], *le tonstede* l13, 1347 *Dav*, (-*mulne*) 1337, 1347 *Eyre*, *le
Tounstud* 1349 *ib*, 'site of a farm', *v.* tūn, stede, styde, cf. *croftum
quod vocatur tuncroft* 1248, *fossatum antiqui curtilagii* 1312–18 *Dav*,
'croft called Tuncroft', 'the ditch of an old curtilage', (*v.* tūn, croft),
which suggest an old habitation-site perhaps that of *Hungrewenitune
infra*, and cf. Welltrough *infra*.

HUNGREWENITUNE (lost), 1086 DB, *Wi*-, *Wyni(n)gt(h)on* 1286 *Eyre*,
Court, *Wininton* c.1310 Chest, 'Wine's farm', from the OE pers.n.
Wine and ingtūn (cf. Winnington 336 *infra*). The prefixed hungor or
hungrig 'hunger, hungry' probably alludes to barren land (DB says
the place 'was and is waste'), which would explain the disappearance
of the p.n. The location of this place is uncertain. It has been
identified with both Lower- and Old Withington (*v.* ChetNS LXXV, x
and 115), neither of which is named in DB (Orm² III 717). Then and
later, Old Withington was part of the manor of Chelford, and Lower
Withington has no separate manorial history until c.1217–29 (Orm²
III 720). However, a location in Lower Withington is indicated if
(*le*) *hewode infra* is identical with *Hewode in Wini(n)gton* 1286 *Eyre*,
Court 217. It would then be feasible to place *Hungrewenitune* at
Broad Hill *supra*.

WELLTROUGH HALL (110–817689)

Wultrok m13 *Dav*
Weltrok m13 *Dav*, -*trogh* 1354 *ib*, -*trough* 1589 MidCh, (*Hall*) 1860
    White

Wheltrogh 1272 Plea *et freq* to 1512 *ChEx, Qweltrogh* 1353, 1430
   Eyre, Wheltrough 1381, 1390, 1606 ChRR
Whaltrogh 1431 ChRR
Whelstrogh 1453 (17) Sheaf

From **hwēol** 'a wheel, something circular' and **trog** 'a trough'. The
significance at Welltrough is not apparent. It may refer to a mill-
stream, or some winding ditch or circular trench, since Broad Hill
supra is nearby, cf. *le Hallefeld infra.*

WITHINGTON GREEN, 1842 OS, (*Further-*) 1848 *TA, Lower Withington*
1831 Bry, cf. Lower Withington *supra*, in which this is the hamlet,
v. **grēne²**.

BADGERBANK, 1842 OS, *Dingle Bank* 1831 Bry, *v.* **dingle, banke,** cf.
Dingle Brook 93 *infra*.   BEECHWOOD FM.   BIG WOOD, (*Field*)
1848 *TA*.   BLACK SWAN (p.h.), *The Swan* 1831 Bry, *The Black
Swan, now more commonly called the Trap Inn* 1860 White 778, said
by White to have been named 'The Trap' about 1810 by one John
Peak who was induced to waste his time there drinking, while he was
building cottages nearby, which are therefore called Trap Street
(*v. infra*).   BODKIN.   BOMISH LANE (110–803718 to 795717) &
WOOD (110–795720), *Bullmarsh Wood* 1831 Bry, *Bomish Wood* 1842
OS, *v.* Bellmarsh Ho 329 *infra*.   BOUNDARY FM, *Baguleys* (*tenement*) 1730 *Dav*, 1831 Bry, from the surname *Baguley* of its eighteenth-
century tenant, and its position on the Marton boundary, cf.
Boundary Fm 81 *supra*.   BROAD HALL, *Fodens Cottage* 1730 *Dav,
Fodens Farm* 1831 Bry, from the surname *Foden* (cf. Fodens 68
supra), and later from Broad Hill *supra*.   BROOK FM, cf. Dingle
Brook 93 *infra*.   CATCHPENNY LANE, no doubt named from the
collecting of tolls at the toll-gate shown 1842 OS at 110–805713,
cf. *Toll House* 1848 *TA*.   CHAPEL LANE, from a Methodist Chapel.
CLAYHILL, 1831 Bry.   DEANS ROUGH, 1842 OS.   DEANS-
ROUGH, *Diglake* 1831 Bry, 'watercourse-ditch', from **dík, díc** and
lacu, the modern name being taken from Deans Rough *supra*.
DICKLOW COB & FM (110–814697), *Withington Heath* 1831 Bry, 1848
TA, 'mound called Dicklow', *v.* **cobb(e)**. The etymology of *Dicklow*
is unknown.   DOOLEY'S FM & GRIG, 'heath', *v.* **grig²** 'heather'.
GLEADS MOSS (a wood), GLEADSMOSS (a hamlet), *Glead Moss* 1831
Bry, 'hawk moss', *v.* **gleoda** (dial. *glead*), **mos**.   HAROPGREEN,
from **grēne²** 'a green', cf. Harropgreen 183 *infra*, Harrop 138 *infra*.
HAZLEHURSTS (lost, 110–799720), 1831 Bry, from the surname

Hazlehurst. HODGEHILL (COTTAGES), (*Big-*) *Hodge Hill* 1848 *TA*, cf. 86 *supra.* HOME FM. HORNPIPE HALL. JONES'S WOOD. LONG SHOOT RD, cf. *Long Shoot* 1848 ib, v. lang, scēat. MIDGLEY BROW (lost, 110–829706), 1842 OS, v. brū. NUT WOOD, v. hnutu, wudu. OLD FM. PARADISE FM, -*Cottage* 1831 Bry, perhaps from paradis 'pleasure garden', but it may be ironic. PITT FM. PORTERS WOOD. REDLION BRIDGE & BROOK (FM), *Redlion Brook* 1831 Bry, named from the *Red Lion* 1831 ib, a public house by the stream. RULOW WOOD, *Rulow* 1848 *TA*, 'rough mound', v. rūh, hlāw. SALTERS LANE (110–815697 to 827701), SALTERSLANE FM, part of a salt-way from Middlewich to Macclesfield, v. saltere, lane, cf. 47 *supra.* SHELLMOREHILL, *Scheldmor* 1333 *Dav*, *Skilmar Hill* 1848 *TA*, 'moor at a shelter', from sceld and mōr[1], with hyll. SMITHS GREEN, 1842 OS. STRAWBERRY WOOD. TITHEBARN. TRAP STREET, 1842 ib, cf. Black Swan *supra*, Trap Rd 335 *infra.* WHISTERFIELD, v. 85 *supra.* WHITE-CROFT HEATH, *quitecroft* 113 *Dav*, *Whitcroft Heath* 1831 Bry, v. hwīt, croft. WINDYHARBOUR (110–827701), 1831 ib, 'windy shelter', v. windig, here-beorg, a common and a cottage on Salters Lane *supra.* WITHINGTON HO, 'the house in Withington', on the Siddington boundary at Whisterfield. WOOD HO, twice, from Big Wood and Jones's Wood *supra.*

FIELD-NAMES

The undated forms are 1848 *TA* 443. Of the others, 13 (17), m13 (17) are Orm[2], 1375, 1447 *Eyre*, and the rest *Dav*.

(*a*) Acre; Acre Nook (cf. Acre Nook 93 *infra*); Alder Intake (*v.* alor, inntak); Ash Croft (*the Ashe Crofte* 1638, 'ash-tree croft', *v.* æsc, croft); Back House ('field at the back of the house', *v.* back, hūs); Backside ('field at the back-side', *v.* ba(c)ksyde); Bailey Croft (*v.* baillie); Ball Flatt; Bell House Croft (*v.* bell-hūs, but the history is uncertain); Birch; Birchen Croft (*v.* bircen[2]); Black Croft; Blake Fd (*v.* blæc); Bottom (*v.* botm); Brook Fd, Brook Field Pingot (*v.* brōc, feld, pingot); Brook Smalley (*v.* Smalley *infra*); Broom(y) Fd (*v.* brōm(ig)); Brow Fd (*v.* brū); Brown Edge; Buckley Fd; Burley Moor; Canters Hey; Further & Little Cinder Hill (*le Sinderhulles* 1337, *v.* sinder, hyll); Clemley (cf. Clemley 330 *infra*); Close Fd; Cockshoot (*v.* cocc-scyte); Croft (*freq*, cf. *le croftes* 1337, *v.* croft); Dales Croft; Fallow Fd; Flash (*v.* flasshe); Flat(t)s (*v.* flat); Fold, Fold Croft (cf. *le fold, le foldyorth* 1312–18, *v.* fald, eorðe); Foxhall Fd (*v.* fox-hol); Goose Hey (*v.* gōs, (ge)hæg); Gorsey Brow (*v.* gorstig, brū); Harding Croft & Mdw; Head Hill (*v.* hēafod, hyll, referring to headlands in a common field); Hemp Yard (*v.* hemp-yard); Big Hignell; Hill Fd (cf. *Hull* 1312–18, *v.* hyll); Hollin

Wood (*v.* holegn); Horse Pasture; House Croft, Fd & Mdw ('adjoining the house', *v.* hūs); Intack, Intake (*freq, v.* inntak); Kiln Croft; Kitchen Fd & Mdw; Knowl Small Hey (*v.* Smalley *infra*); Land Croft (*v.* land); Lane Croft, Lanes; (Rough) Leach (*v.* rūh, lᵫc(c)); Ley (*v.* lēah); Lime Fd; Long Loons (*v.* lang, land); Mare Fd; Marl Fd; Meadow End; Mill Fd & Mdw (cf. *molendinum de Withington* 1281–1300, *Milnehous* 1447, *v.* milne-hous); Moat Mdw (*v.* mote); Moss (*v.* mos); the New Work; Nooked Cake; Oak Intake (*v.* āc, inntak); Ocean Croft; Old Mdw; Outlet (*v.* outlet); Ox Hey Croft (*v.* oxa, (ge)hæg, croft); Patch; Pickers; Pingot (*v.* pingot); Pit Fd; Pot Croft (*v.* pott); Privy Croft; Riddings (cf. *le Brode Riddings* 1312–18, *le Broderudding* 1337, 'broad clearings', *v.* brād, ryding); The Roughs (*v.* rūh); Round Mdw; Rush Croft; Sand Fd; Saw Pit Fd (*v.* saw-pytt); Ship Hey (*v.* scēap, (ge)hæg); Shippon Fd (*v.* scypen); Sickow Flat; Slack Croft (*v.* slakki); The Slade (*v.* slæd); (River- & Road-) Slang ('long, narrow strip of land', *v.* slang); Sludge Fd (*v.* sludge); (Brook- & Knowl-) Smalley, Small Hey (*placea terre vocat' Smallegh* 1312–18, cf. *Smallegforth* 1312–18, 'narrow glade' from smæl and lēah, with ford, brōc, cnoll); Stone Bridge Croft; Stump Fd; Sun Fd (*v.* sunne); Ten Day Work (*v.* day-work); Thistle; Three Nook(s) ('three-cornered', *v.* nōk); Twelve penny piece; Twistle ('fork', *v.* twisla (dial. *twizzle*), cf. Tintwistle 320 *infra*); Warchew (Nook) (*Wardesahe* m13, *Wardshaw* 13 (17), *Wordeschae(heued)* 1312–18, 'watch copse', from weard and sceaga, with nōk, hēafod); Water Gee ('crooked field at the water', *v.* gee); Wood Croft.

(b) *buterlehe* m13, *Boterlegh* l13 (*v.* butere, lēah); *le Castelwey* 1312–18 ('castle way', *v.* castel(l), weg, presumably referring to an earthwork); *Coterelleswaye* l13 ('Coterel's way', from the OFr surname *Coterel* and weg); *gateford* l13 ('ford carrying a road', *v.* gata, ford); *le Hallefeld apud le Tunsted* 1312–18 (*v.* hall, feld, cf. Broad Hill, Welltrough Hall *supra*); *le hallehurst* l13 (*v.* hall, hyrst); (*le) hewode* m13, l13 ('high wood', *v.* hēah, wudu, cf. *Hungrewenitune supra*); *Kocshawemershe* 1348 (*v.* cocc², sceaga, mersc); *Linenehok* 1312–18 ('corner growing with flax', *v.* līnen, hōc); *louerichelache* l13 ('lark bog', *v.* lāferce, læc(c)); *Lundrys* m13, *-is* m13 (17) ('grove shrubs', *v.* lundr, hrís); *le Mers* m13 (*v.* mersc); *Pilotcroft* l13 (*v.* pil-āte, croft); *le Rypuhhul* 1312–18 ('rye croft', *v.* ryge, pighel); *le Sondifordestrete* l13 ('(paved road to) the sandy ford', *v.* sandig, ford, strᵫt); *le Sedulheth* 1354 ('heath where the house stands', *v.* sedl, hǣð); *le Snape* m13 (*v.* snæp); *le stodmar'siche* 1312–18 ('the stud-mare watercourse', from OE stōd-mere 'a brood-mare' and sīc); *le Stonwaye* l13 (*v.* stān, weg); *Withiford* 1375 (*v.* wiðig, ford).

10. OLD WITHINGTON (110–8172)

Now included with Lower Withington 88 *supra* in Withington c.p.

Widinton, -enton 1185, 1186 P, *Withinton* 1210 Dieul and subsequently spellings as for Lower Withington 88 *supra*, (*Chelford cum*) *Withington* 1724 NotCestr

Oldewethynton 1462 Plea, *Old Withington* 1618 Sheaf

'Old Withington', *v.* ald, as distinct from Lower Withington which was separated in the thirteenth century, cf. 89 *supra*.

ACRE NOOK, 1842 OS. BRICK KILN WOOD, *v.* bryke-kyl. BROOK HO, named from Snape Brook 35 *supra*. BURNT ACRE, 1842 OS, *v.* berned, æcer. COLT HOVEL WOOD. DAIRY FM, *Dairy House* 1831 Bry, *v.* deierie, hūs. DINGLE BROOK & SMITHY, *Dingle Smithy* 1842 OS, cf. Badgerbank 90 *supra*, 'deep valley', from dingle, with smiðõe, brōc. The brook joins Peover Eye 33 *supra*. HACKNEYPLAT BRIDGE, *v.* 74 *supra*. HOLLOWACRE WOOD, *v.* 76 *supra*. HOME FM. LAPWING HALL, 1831 Bry. THE MOSSES, 1831 ib, *Bradfords Moss* 1842 OS. *Bradford* is probably a surname. NOOK RD. NORFOLK, *Mount Pleasant* 1831 Bry. OAK WOOD, *Oak Nursery* 1831 ib. OLDPOOL WOOD. PIGOTT-HILL, -*s* 1842 OS, *Bigot Hill* 1831 Bry. PRIVET WOOD. WILLIE'S WOOD, *Willeys Wood* 1831 ib, 'the willows', *v.* wilig, wudu. WITHINGTON HALL, *Old Withington Hall* 1819 Orm². WITHINGTON PARK & POOL.

FIELD-NAMES

(a) Lords Pits 1842 OS; Spout Lane 1831 Bry (*v.* spoute, lane); Walkers Pits 1842 OS; The Warren 1842 ib (*Warren Wood* 1831 Bry, *v.* wareine); Willow Beds 1842 OS (*v.* wilig, bedd).

(b) *le Barned Erthe* 1312–18 Dav ('ploughland cleared by burning', *v.* berned, erð).

v. Over Peover Chapelry

The rest of this chapelry, and its parent parish of Rostherne, is in Bucklow Hundred. This portion was included in Bucklow Hundred in DB.

1. SNELSON (110–8074)

Senelestune 1086 DB, *Senellest'* 1202–17 Orm²
Snelleston 1209 Tab *et freq*, (-*iuxta Chelleford*) 1369 Plea, -*e* 1364 ChRR (p), -*thorn* 1398 Plea, *Snelestun* 113 Orm² (p), *Snel(l)iston* 1276 Ipm, IpmR, *Scnelliston* 1323 Dav (p)
Snelstun 1322 Dav (p), -*ton* 1414 ChRR
Snelson 1501 MidCh (p) *et freq*

'Snell's farm', from the OE pers.n. *Snell* and **tūn**, cf. Snelson Bk 10, Snelston Db 602, Snailston Pembrokeshire, NCPN 58. The hamlet was known as *Snelson Lane* 1860 White, *v.* lane, cf. *Pepper Street* 333 *infra*.

AINSWORTH FM, probably from the surname *Ainsworth*.   ASTLE COTTAGE, cf. Astle 76 *supra*.   THE COMMON WOOD, *Snelson Common* 1847 *TA*.   HEATH COTTAGE, cf. *Snelson Heath* 1831 Bry. HIGHFIELD FM & HO.   IVYGREEN FM.   KENNEL BANK, *Dog Kennel Wood* 1847 *TA*.   MANOR FM.   SNELSON COVERT, *Covert* 1842 OS.   SNELSON'S FM, from the surname *Snelson*, cf. Adam de *Snelestun* l13 Orm². WOODEND FM.

FIELD-NAMES

The undated forms are 1847 *TA* 358, and 1831 is Bry.

(*a*) Black Fd; Bone Dust Fd (*v.* bone-dust); Bottoms (*v.* botm); Broom Fd; Burnt Acre ('ploughland cleared by burning', *v.* berned, æcer); Chapel Croft; Drumble Fd (*v.* drumble); Flatt Fd (*v.* flat); Gorst Fd (*v.* gorst); Green Lane; Intack (*v.* inntak); Lime Close; Marl Fd; Mill Lane 1831 (cf. 77 *supra*); Mills Fd; Moss Brow (*v.* brū); Moss Room ('allotment in the moss', *v.* mos, rūm¹); Mountain; Odd Fd (*v.* odde); Outlet (*v.* outlet); Oven Croft; Peover Heath Fd (cf. Peover Heath 333 *infra*); Poor House Croft; Pound Fd (*v.* pund); Sand Fd; Sandback ('sand ridge', *v.* sand, bæc); Shippon Mdw; Sweet Field; Tentry Fd (*v.* tentour); Way Fd (*v.* weg); Whitlows Mdw.

vi. Alderley

Anciently a parochial chapelry of Prestbury parish, it was independent by 1328, *v.* Orm² III 565, 568, ChetOS VIII 268.

1. NETHER ALDERLEY (101–8476)

Aldredelie 1086 DB, *-lega* c.1208 (14) Dieul, *-leia* H3 Orm², *Aldredel'* 1220–30 AddCh, *-legh* l13 Adl, 1364 BPR, (*Nether-*) 1315 Plea, *-ley*, *-lg'* c.1300 JRL 32, *-lay* 1305 Lacy, *-le* 1347 BPR
Aldrideleg' l12 Facs, *-ley* c.1280 Chol (p), *-li* 1285 Eyre, *-legh* 1290 *ib*, *-ll'* c.1245 Chest (p), *Aldridel'* (*Inferior*) 1285, 1286 Eyre, *Aldritdeleg'* 1290 *ib*, *Aldrudeleg'* 1285 *ib* (p)
Aldredis c.1208 (17) Sheaf
Aldirdelegh' 13 AddCh, *-leg'* 1287 Eyre, *Aldurdelee* 1255 Plea (p), *-legh'* 1337 Eyre, *-ley* 1375 *ib*, *Alderdeley(e)* 1275 Ipm, 1309

InqAqd, *-leg(h)* 1286 *Eyre*, l13 *Fitt*, (*Nether-*) 1359 *Eyre*, *-leygh*
1312 Pat, *Halderdeleg* 1275 Cl
Aldurleya e13 (17) Orm², *-lee* 1260 Court (p), *-leg* 1323 *Dav* (p),
-ley 1419 *SocAnt*, *Alderlegh* 1275 IpmR, (*Nether-*) 1341 *Eyre et
freq* to 1653 Sheaf, *-le(ighe)* 1329, 1333 IpmR, *-ley* 1342 Tab,
(*Nether-*) 1423 ChRR, *-leygh* 1559 Pat, *-leigh* 1602 ChRR,
Aldyrlegh l13 Tab (p), *Aldirlegh* 1358 *MinAcct*
Aldrel' 1238 (1623) ChRR (p), *Aldrelegh* l13 *Fitt* (p), (*Nether-*) 1315
Plea, *-leigh* 1313 *SocAnt* (p)
Audredeleg' m13 *Dav* (p), 1254 Pat, *-leigh*, *-ley* 1254 CRC,
Audridel' 1260 *Eyre* (p), *Auderdel'* 1262 *Dav* (p)
Aldridley 1274 Orm² (p), *Aldredley* 1295 Lacy, (*Nether*) *Aldredlegh*
1315 Plea, *Alderedlegh* c.1320 *Chol*, *Alderdlegh* 1380 *Eyre*
Aldeldeleg' 1286 *Eyre*
Aldireleg' 1288 Court (p)
(*Nether*) *Aldelegh* 1380 *Eyre*, 1476 ChRR, 1539 Dugd, *-ley* 1527
ChRR
Orderly 1727 Sheaf

'Alðrȳð's clearing', from the OE fem. pers.n. form *Alðrȳð* and
lēah, with neoðera, inferior. The pers.n. form may represent OE
Ælfðrȳð, *Æðelðrȳð* or *Ealhðrȳð*, *v.* Feilitzen 153. Cf. Over Alderley
99 *infra*.

ALDERLEY EDGE, 1842 OS, *le Hegge* e14 Tab, *l'Egge* 1352 *Eyre*, 'the
edge', *v.* ecg, referring to the abrupt escarpment which gives name
to the township of Alderley Edge 225 *infra*.

BRADFORD HO, LANE & LODGE (101–853766), *Bradeford* c.1208 Dieul,
1287 *Eyre* (p), *Bradford* 1391 ChRR (p), 'broad ford', *v.* brād, ford.

CORBISHLEY (101–827757)
Curbichley c.1200 (17) Orm¹, *Curbicheleg(h)* c.1200 (17) Orm²,
Earw, 1381 *Eyre*, *-bychelegh'* 1345 *ib* (p), *Kurbychley* 1427 ChRR
(p)
Surbrechelegya e13 *Fitt*
Curbrecheleg' c.1280 *Fitt* (p), Orm²
Curbrugg' 1288 Court
Corbishley 1831 Bry

'Cur-bitch clearing', *v.* curre, bicce, lēah. The spellings *-breche-*,

-brugg' indicate confusion of *-brich-* (with intrusive *-r-*) with brēc, bryce or brycg. *Sur-* may be due to Anglo-Norman influence (ANInfl 39), but cf. Bowdon 330 *infra*. In the early references the, place is part of Wilmslow and Fulshaw, cf. Oak Fm 232 *infra*, a seat of the *Corbishley* family (Earw II 138). *Carbishley Brook* 1831 Bry is the same as *Bentley Brook* 1831 ib, 'brook at a grassy clearing', *v.* beonet, lēah. It joins Pedley Brook 32 *supra*.

DEAN GREEN, *Deans-* 1841 *TA*, *Dane-* 1842 OS, *le Dene* 1335 ChRR (p), 1336 *Mass et freq*, '(green at) the valley', *v.* denu, grēne².

FALLOWS HALL (110–834741)

> *le Falwitz* 1199–1216 Orm², *Faluis* 1274 ib (p), *Falewys* 1285 *Eyre* (p)
> *le Falghes* m13 *Dav* (p), *(le) Faleg(h)es* 1287 Court (p), 1288 *Eyre*, *Faleis* 1313 Orm² (p), *Falughes* 1401 ib (p)
> *(le) Fallowes* 1364 *Eyre* (p), *-Hall alias þe Hall of Fallowes* 1697 Orm², *Falowes* 1516 *ChEx* (p)
> *þe Faloos* 1450 Orm²

'The ploughed lands', *v.* falh. *le Falwitz* is an Anglo-Norman spelling for *Falwis* (cf. ANInfl 37).

FERNHILL, *Fernhull'* 1287 *Eyre* (p), *Farnhull* 1287 *ib* (p), 1341 *ib*, 'fern hill', *v.* fearn, hyll.

HEAWOOD HALL, *Heywode* 1286 *Eyre* (p), *-wood* 1681 *Dow*, *(Hall)* 1819 Orm¹, *Haywod(d)e* 1286, 1375 *Eyre*, *Heawood* 1663 Earw, 'wood at a fenced-in place' or 'fenced-in wood', *v.* (ge)hæg, wudu.

MONK'S HEATH (110–8474), MONKSHEATH HALL, *Munkesheth* c.1389 Orm², *Munk(e)sheath* 1632 Sheaf, 1651 *Dav*, *Munckes-* 1634 *AddCh*, *Monk(e)she(a)th(e)* 1565 *Dow*, 1571 Earw, c.1620 Orm², 'monk's heath', *v.* munuc, hǣð. Dieulacres Abbey owned estates in this district. It may be the land called *Wethull* granted to Poulton Abbey c.1216 Orm² II 77 ('wet hill', *v.* wēt, hyll), but *v.* *Wetehull* 335 *infra*.

SANDLE HEATH (101–828752), 1618 Sheaf, *Sandhul* c.1208 Dieul, *-hull'* 1288 *Eyre*, *Sondul* 1296 *Dav* (p), *-ell* 1421 Plea (p), 'the sand-hill', *v.* sand, hyll and hǣð, cf. Yarwoods *infra*.

SOSSMOSS HALL & WOOD (101–828759), *Sostemosse* 1389 Orm², *Soss Moss* 1619 Earw, (*Hall*) 1819 Orm², (*Wood*) 1831 Bry, *v*. mos 'a swamp'. The fourteenth-century form is too late to be reliable, but the first el. may be connected with dial. *soss* (EDD) 'wet, sloppy mess, soaking'. Cf. Soss 253 *infra*. The same el. may appear in Sussgreaves 234 *infra*. This place has been identified with the *profundam mossam* of the bounds of Chelford and Snelson, but cf. 77 *supra*.

ALDERLEY BEACON, 1831 Bry, the site of a beacon in 1622 (LCAS xv 45, Orm² III 545). ALDERLEY CROSS, 1831 Bry, a stone cross at a cross-roads. ALDERLEY MILL, 1831 ib, cf. *molendinum aquaticum* 1391 ChRR, *v*. myln. ALDERLEY PARK, 1831 Bry, perhaps the site of *boscus de Aldredeleg'* c.1208 Dieul, *-Aldeldeleg'* 1286 Eyre (*v*. wudu), gives name to the house Alderley Park (1842 OS), *The Parke, Parke-house* 1693 Orm² III 715, *The Parks, Park House* 1724 NotCestr, *v*. park, though the plural form may indicate pearroc 'paddock'. BAGBROOK BRIDGE & WOOD. The bridge may be at *Baggeford* 1342 Tab (p), *v*. bagga, ford, cf. Bag Brook 14 *supra*. BARNFIELD, cf. *Barn Field* 1841 *TA*. BEECH WOOD, 1842 OS, *Sheffield Wood* 1831 Bry. BIRTLES CROFT (lost), 1831 ib, cf. Birtles 72 *supra*. BOGGART WOOD, 'haunted wood', *v*. boggart. BOLLINGTON HO & PITS, *Bollington House* 1831 ib, *Bollington Grange & Pits* 1842 OS, *v*. grange, pytt, cf. Bollington 187 *infra*. BRIDGE WOOD. BRYN-LOW, *Brinlow* 1831 Bry, *Brunley* 1842 OS, cf. *Brunlegh* 1345 Eyre (p) (at Adlington), 'brown wood', *v*. brūn¹, lēah. THE BUTTS, 1841 *TA*, *v*. butte. CHANDLER'S FM, *Chantlers* 1831 Bry, cf. John *Chantler* 1654 *Dow*. COACH PASTURE POND, cf. *Great Coach Pasture* 1841 *TA*, *v*. cwice, dial. *couch*, 'couch grass'. CORBISHLEY BRIDGE, 1831 Bry. DOG HOLE WOOD, *Dogholes* 1841 *TA*, *v*. Dog Hole 331 *infra*. DUMVILLE'S FM. FINLOW HILL WOOD, *v*. 100 *infra*. FROG LANE. GATLEY GREEN, 1831 Bry, *Gatiler* 1391 ChRR (p), 'goat clearing', *v*. gāt, lēah, grēne²; *Gatiler* is probably an error for *Gatiley* since a toponymical surname in -(*i*)*er*, 'man from Gatley', is not likely in this part of England at this date (Fransson 193). GREYSTEAD. GROGAN COTTAGE, *Grogrum, Gogram Mea-dow* 1841 *TA*. THE HAGG (lost), 1831 Bry, *v*. hǫgg 'a felling of trees'. HOLY WELL. IRON GATES (lost), 1831 ib. KNOWSLEY, *Nowsley House* 1831 ib. LOMAS'S BOTTOMS, *v*. botm. MERE FM. MOTTRAM HO, 1831 ib. MOUNT PLEASANT (lost), 1842 OS. OAKWOOD. OLD HALL (101–844763), 1831 Bry, the house was destroyed by fire in 1779 and only the offices remained, Orm[1] III 301.   PAINTERS EYE, a wood.   PARKHEAD POND, cf. *Park Head* 1831 Bry and Alderley Park *supra*.   RADNOR MERE, 1819 Orm[1], *v.* mere[1] 'a lake'. The origin of Radnor is unknown.   ROADSIDE FM.   STREET LANE FM (lost, 101–843778), 1831 Bry, STREET LANE (lost, 101–843782 to 843763), 1842 OS, *v.* strǣt, lane, cf. 45 *supra*. This is now Alderley Road 225 *infra*, and gave name to *Street Lane Ends* 226 *infra*.   THE TOPPS, *Topps* 1841 *TA*, *v.* topp.   WALTON FM.   WELSH ROW, 1831 Bry, *Welch-* 1841 *TA*, *v.* Welisc, rāw, 'Welsh(man's) row', a row of houses, cf. Welsh Row (Nantwich) 335 *infra*.   WHITE BARN, 1831 Bry.   WHITLOW WOOD (110– 836740), perhaps 'white mound', *v.* hwīt, hlāw, from the tumulus (1842 OS) at 110–842739.   WINDMILL WOOD.   THE WIZARD OF THE EDGE, (p.h.), 1860 White, *Miners Arms* 1831 Bry, cf. Wizard's Well 223 *infra*.   WYCHE'S FM, named after the *Wyche* family, *v.* Orm[2] III 568, cf. Thomas *Wiche* l16 *Dow* 468.   YARWOODS, 1842 OS, *Sandle House* 1831 Bry, cf. Sandle Heath *supra* and Randle de *Yarwode* 1441 ChRR.   YEWTREE, 1831 Bry.

FIELD-NAMES

The undated forms are 1841 *TA* 7. Of the others, e13 is Orm[2], c.1208 Dieul, 1368, 1651 *Dow*, 1391, 1406 ChRR, 1618 Sheaf, 1831 Bry.

(*a*) Acre; Alder Mdw (*v.* alor); Baddeley Croft (cf. John *Baddeley* 1651); Bailiff Mdw; Bain Fd; Bank Mdw; Barn Hey; Birch Knott (*v.* knǫttr); Birches; Black Fd; Blue Button Fd (from dial. *Blue-Button* '*Scabiosa succisa*, devil's bit'); Bollington Lane (cf. Bollington Ho *supra*); Bongs (*v.* banke); Bottoms (*v.* botm); Bow Greaves; Bradcroft (*v.* brād); Bradley (*v.* brād, lēah); Broad Fd; Broom Fd; Bucketts; Burnt Butts, Earth & Fd (*v.* berned, butte, eorðe or erð, cf. *le Barned Erthe* 93 *supra*); Butter Fd (*v.* butere); Calf Croft; Carr Mdw (*v.* kjarr); Castle Stone Fd ('heap of stones', *v.* castel(l), stān); Church Fd; Cinder Hill (*v.* sinder); Colley Hey (*Collye heys* 1618, *v.* colig, (ge)hæg); Common (Fd & Piece); Copy (*v.* copis); Cow Hay, -Hey, -Lane; Crabtree Hill; Croft Green (*v.* grēne[2]); Cross Flat (*v.* cros ME 'athwart', flat); Dale Fd (*v.* dæl[1]); Dean Fd (cf. Dean Green *supra*); Down Shut ('hill corner', *v.* dūn, scēat); Edge Croft (cf. Alderley Edge *supra*); Fishpond Fd; Flat Fd (*v.* flatr); Garden Hill; Glade; Green (*v.* grēne[2]); Grow Croft (possibly from dial. *graw, grew* 'grime, filth'); Hall Fd; Heald (*v.* helde); Hoblington Mdw (perhaps a lost -ingtūn p.n.); Hodge Fd (*v. Hodg Croft* 158 *infra*); Hollin Mdw (*v.* holegn); Holly Knowl; Intake; Kiff Lands; Kiln Croft; Kinnerley Croft (cf. Kennerley Fd 105 *infra*, probably from the surname *Kennerley*); Kitchen Croft; Knowl; Land Fd; Lawton Croft; Lee (*v.* lēah); Lime(d) Fd & Mdw; Lingot Mdw; Long Hey,

-Leach & -Ley (v. (ge)hæg, læc(c), lēah); Maggots Hey; Marl Fd; Fir-, Great- & Long Marsh (*Fir-* is dial. *fur(r)* 'farther'); Cross- & Far Mawshaws; Mean Hey & Ley (v. (ge)mǣne 'common', cf. *Menelegh* 113 *infra*); Mere Hey (v. mere[1]); Mickle Hey (v. micel, (ge)hæg); Middle Shaw ('the middle copse', v. middel, sceaga); (Great) Moss, Moss Fd, Mdw & Room (v. mos, rūm[1]); Mountain of Poverty (v. 329 *infra*); New Fd, Green & Hay (v. grēne[2], (ge)hæg)); Oak Fd; Oldham (cf. Oldham's Wood 102 *infra*); Old Mdw; Outlet (v. outlet); Oven Croft & Yard, Oven House Mdw (v. ofen, oven-house, geard); Owler Mdw (v. alor); Ox Hey (v. (ge)hæg); Oxter (probably dial. *oxter* (OE *ōhsta*) 'armpit', here used either topographically, or figuratively for 'dower land, gift land', v. *oxter* EDD); Paddle Mdw; Park White Fd ('white field in the park', cf. Alderley Park *supra*); Parsons' Croft; Patch; Pease Fd (v. pise); Great Pedley Hill, Pedley Mdw (cf. Pedley 182 *infra*); Petty Croft & Intake (v. pety 'little'); Pool Croft & Wood Fd; Quarry Fd; Ridding(s), -Orchard (v. ryding); Round Croft & Mdw; Rugriffs Hall; Rush(y) Fd, Croft & Hey; Rye Fd; Sand(y) Fd & Croft; Great & Little Sandhole, Sandle Inclosure (cf. *croftum iuxta Sandhul* c.1208, v. Sandle Heath *supra*); Sheep Fd; Shifting Lands; Shippon Croft; Slack Hey ('enclosure at a hollow', v. slakki, (ge)hæg); Smalleys; Smithy Bank; Square Fd; Stable Mdw; Stackley Hey; Stoney Rough; Great Stubble; Swine Yard (v. swīn[1], geard); Tan Yard; Tenter Croft (v. tentour); Thier Wood 1831 ('the higher wood');Thistles Clough (v. þistel, clōh); Great Tid Croft; Time of Day (v. 335 *infra*); Town Fd; Wantley Pits; Wantlings; Wauving Hill; Little Weather Fd; Well Croft & Mdw; White Fd; Windy Croft; Wood Fd; Worthington Fd (cf. Richard *Worthington* 1623); Yeld Bottoms (v. helde, botm); Yellow Croft; Yew Acre.

(b) del *Lowe* 1368, 1391, 1406 ('the mound', v. hlāw); *Wethull* e13 (v. Monk's Heath *supra*).

2. OVER ALDERLEY (101–8675)

Now a c.p. including part of Birtles 72 *supra* from Chelford Chapelry.

Aldredelie 1086 DB and other spellings as in Nether Alderley 94 *supra*

Superior Aldredeleg' l12 (17) Orm[2], *-Aldredelegh* 1310 Tab, *Oure Aldredeleg'* 1281 Court, *Ouer Alderedelegh* 1350 VR, *-alderdelegh* 1337 Plea

Superior Aldereleia l12 (17) Orm[2], *Alderelegh Superior* 1288 Court

Superior Alderlegh 1294 Tab, *Overalderlegh* 1332 Ipm *et freq*, *(le-)* 1352 Orm[2], *-leigh(e)* 1333 IpmR, 1557 ChRR, *-ley* 1342 Tab *et freq*, *Alderlegh Superior* 1370 *Eyre*

Aldridel' Superior 1285 Court

Over Aldirlegh 1289 Court

Over Aldurdelegh 1338 Orm[2]

Oueraldredlegh 1341 *Eyre*
Oueraldrelegh 1341 *Eyre*

v. uferra, superior, cf. Nether Alderley 94 *supra.*

ACTON FM, *Hacton Farm* 1842 OS, *Acton* 1352 Orm² (p), *Aketon* 1366
Eyre (p), *-don* 1391 ChRR (p), 'oak farm', *v.* āc, tūn, but the p.n.
may be manorial, since the early references are surnames, cf. Orm²
III 574, 580.

ADSHEAD GREEN (101–868767), 1831 Bry, cf. *Addeshed* 1337 *Eyre* (p)
et freq, *Addresheued* 1361 *ib* (p), *Adsedd* 1453 *Dow* (p), The final el.
is hēafod 'a head' or 'the top of something, a hill'. The first el. could
be the OE pers.n. *Ēadhere*. The place is close to Adder's Moss *infra*
(*v.* mos), which is probably related.

BIRTLES HALL (110–858746)

>   *Ulm* 112 Orm², *Hulme* 1275 Ipm, 1352 *Dow* (p) *et freq* to 1414 ib,
>   *Hulm* 1288 Court, 1290 ib (p), *Holm* 1275 Cl, 1335 *Mont*, *-e* 1275
>   Ipm
>   *Hulme House now called the Pasture(s)* 1666 Orm², (*The*) *Pasture*
>   1681 *Dow et freq* to 1841 *TA*, (*le*) *Pastur* 1684 *Dow*
>   *Birtles New & Old Hall* 1750 Sheaf³ 11, *New Hall* 1831 Bry

'The water-meadow', 'the pasture', *v.* hulm, pasture. The later
name arises because c.1800 this house superseded Birtles Old Hall
73 *supra* as the seat of the manor of Birtles, *v.* Orm¹ III 304. The
original name appears in *Hum Covert* and Hulmes *infra*.

BRADLEY'S CLOUGH, cf. *saltum quod dicitur Bradele* c.1208 Dieul,
Bradil' 1288 Court (p), *Bradelegh* 1326 *Dow* (p), *-ley* 1439 ChRR,
Bradlegh 1370 *Eyre* (p), 'broad clearing', *v.* brād, lēah, and clōh.
This may be the location of *Bradeleghforde* 52 *supra*.

CLINTON HILL, *Clinton* 1275 IpmR, *Clynton* 1308 Whall (p), 1367
ChRR, perhaps 'farm at a rocky hill', *v.* klint, tūn, but it could also
be a hill-name *Klint-dūn* 'klint-hill', from dūn, in which the *d-* of
dūn has been assimilated with the *-t* of klint in the consonant-group
-ntd-.

FINLOW HILL (101–860766), 1654 *Dow*, 'heaped mound', *v.* fīn,
hlāw. This is the origin of the surname *Fynlawe* 1342 Tab, *-lowe* 1369

Eyre, Findlow 1688 Tab, in Finlows Ho (101–863782), *Finlow's* (*Living*) 1737, 1800 *Dow* (*v.* living).

FITTONTOWN (101–879755), 1831 Bry, *v.* toun; identified by Helsby with an estate granted e14 by John de Arderne lord of Alderley to John son of Edmund *Ffyton.* The grant is imperfectly recited in Orm² III 584. The original is now *Fitt* Bundle 7, 10, c.1300–30, in which one of the bounds is *Ffytonnestrystre* (Orm² reads *Fytoune-strystre*), cf. *Tristria Fyton'* 1384 *Rental,* 'Fitton's hunting-station', *v.* trystor.

HAREBARROW FM formerly OLD HARBOROUGH (101–881760), LOWER (101–883751) & NEW HAREBARROW (101–878757), HAREBARROWLAKE (101–886759), *Harebarwe* c.1220 Chest, *-barwe* 1364 *Eyre* (p), *-borowe* 1376 Tab, *Harborowe* (*Hall*) 15 Orm², *New & Old Harbarrow, Harbarrow Lake* 1831 Bry, 'hoar wood', from hār² and bearu, with hall, lacu, cf. Big Wood *infra.* The district is on the Prestbury boundary and its earliest appearance is in the bounds of land called *Bothes* in Prestbury 213 *infra.*

HIGHLEES (WOOD), *High Leys* (*Wood*) 1831 Bry, cf. *Hegheleghes* 1320 Chamb, (*le-*), *Hegleghes* 1345 *Eyre,* 'high clearings', *v.* hēah, lēah.

WHIRLEY (HALL) (110–877748), *Whirley Farm & Hall* 1831 Bry, *Wyrlegh* 1348 *Eyre* (p), *-ley* 1353 *ib, Wirleye* 1362 BPR (p), *Wherlegh'* 1508 *MinAcct,* 'bog-myrtle clearing', *v.* wīr, lēah, cf. Whirleybarn etc. 121 *infra.* Whirley Hall was in Birtles township in 1831, and is described as *the Higher Hall* of Birtles in 1882 Orm² III 709n.

ADDER'S MOSS (101–867768), 1831 Bry, *v.* Adshead Green *supra.* BAGLEY FM (lost), 1842 OS, cf. *Baguley* (*Meadow*) 1841 *TA, v.* bagga, lēah, cf. Baguley 329 *infra.* BENT'S WOOD, *v.* beonet. BIG WOOD (101–888757), *Harbarrow Copse* 1842 OS, *v.* Harebarrow *supra.* BROADHEATH, *Brodhetht* 1287 Court (p), *Brodheath* 1578, 1638 Tab, 'broad heath', *v.* brād, hæð. BULGAMY WOOD, cf. *Bulgany Croft* 1841 *TA.* CLOCK HOUSE, 1831 Bry. DANIEL HILL, 1831 *ib.* DEVILS LANE (lost, 101–855759 to 860766), 1831 *ib.* DICKENS FM & WOOD, *Dickens Wood* 1841 *TA.* DUNGE COTTAGE & FM, *Dunge* 1545 *Dow,* 'the dung heap', *v.* dynge, cf. Dunge III *infra.* EDGE HO, 1831 Bry, cf. Alderley Edge 95

supra.   FINLOW'S HO, *v.* Finlow Hill *supra.*   GLAZE HILL, 1831
Bry.   GOLDEN STONE, a boundary-mark between Nether- and
Over Alderley.   GREYHOUND HO, *The Black Greyhound* 1831 ib,
a p.h.   HAREHILL, *-s* 1831 ib, *Hareshill* 1842 OS, *v.* hara, hyll.
HAYMAN'S FM, *Byrons* 1831 Bry, from the surnames *Hayman, Byron.*
HEATHERLEY WOOD, *Heatherly, Yeatherley* 1841 *TA*, perhaps *le
Hethel'* 1285 *Eyre* (p), *Hethileg'* 1286, *-legh* 1290 Court (p), 'heathy
clearing', *v.* hæðig, lēah, cf. Heaviley 296 *infra.*   HIBBERT'S
HEATHERLEY, named after Robert *Hibbert* 1791 Orm², cf. prec.
HIGHER HO, *Roger Simpcocks Higher House* 1841 *TA*.   HIGHER
PARK FM.   HILL TOP, 1831 Bry.   HOCKER LANE, 1831 ib.
HUM COVERT (lost, 110–862749), 1842 OS, *v.* hulm and Birtles Hall
supra.   JENKINS HAY WOOD.   MOSS PLANTATION.   THE
MOUNT.   NOAH'S ARK, 1841 *TA*, a wood.   OLDHAM'S WOOD
(101–867766), cf. Oldham 99 *supra*, perhaps *Oldum* 1337 *Eyre* (p),
Oldhum 1356 *ib* (p), *Holdum* 1363 *ib* (p), either 'old water-meadow',
(*v.* ald, hulm) or a surname from Oldham La 50; cf. also Oldham's
Hollow 215 *infra.*   RIDLEY LANE (lost, 110–877745 to 101–
876755), 1831 Bry.   SADDLEBOLE, 1831 ib, a prominence of
Alderley Edge at 101–860781, probably named from its fancied shape,
cf. *le Sadel infra*, Saddle Brow 224 *infra.*   SHAW CROSS, 1831 ib,
cf. Robert *del Shaghe* 1397 Plea, '(cross at) the copse', *v.* sceaga,
cros.   SLADEGREEN, 1831 Bry, *v.* slæd, grēne².   SNUG HALL
(lost), 1831 ib.   STORMY POINT, a rocky outcrop on Glaze Hill, at
Alderley Edge.   TRUGS I' TH' HOLE FM, 1831 ib, *Troughs in the
Hole* 1842 OS, 'troughs in the hollow', *v.* trog (dial. *trig, trug*), hol¹,
cf. 184 *infra*, Howlanehead 195 *infra.*   VARDENTOWN, cf. *Varden
Field & Meadow* 1841 *TA*, Verdon Ho 233 *infra*, and Fittontown
supra, v. toun.   WATERFALL WOOD.   WINDMILL FM, 1831 Bry.
HIGHER YEWTREE, *Peacock House* 1831 ib, cf. foll.   LOWER YEW-
TREE, *Yew Tree House* 1842 OS.

FIELD-NAMES

The undated forms are 1841 *TA* 7. Of the others, 12 is Cre, e14 *Fitt*, 1347²
Plea, 1366 *Eyre*, 1376 (17), 1521 Tab, 1384 *Rental*, 1602, 1654 *Dow*, and the
rest Orm².

(*a*) Ash Fd (*v.* æsc); Back Lane Fd; Bank; Bean Croft; Bent Rutland;
Bilberry (Hill); Birch Fd (*the Birchfield* 1654); Birch Moss; Birchin Hill
(*v.* bircen²); Black Croft & Earth; Blake Fd (*v.* blæc); Bloomy Wd; Bottom
Fd, Far Bottoms (*v.* botm); Bowling Green; Box; Bramhall Croft; Brickiln

Wd; Broadstone Fd, Higher Broadstone Wd (v. brād, stān); Broken Cliff
(v. brocen, clif); Brook Fd; Broom Hey (v. brōm, (ge)hæg); Brows (v.
brū); Brown Fd; Bull Yard; Burnt Earth; Butts Croft (cf. *the short buts* 1654,
v. sc(e)ort, butte); Calves Wd; Caper Croft (from dial. *caper* 'the plant
Euphorbia Lathyris'); Little Carr, Carr Fd (v. kjarr); Clough (Mdw) (v.
clōh); Common Piece; Cow Hey; Crab Tree Lands (v. land); Cross Fd;
Daving-, Delving Ditch; Fallow Fd; Farmost Fd (v. dial. *farmost* 'further-
most'); Farthing Flatt (v. fēorðung, flat); Fish Pond Bank; Folley (v. folie);
Four Day Work (day-work); Foxley (v. fox, lēah); Gate Fd; Gee Fd (v. gee
'crooked'); Gods Knowl (*the gorst knowes* 1654, 'gorse hillocks', v. gorst,
cnoll); Grange(s) Croft & Fd (v. grange); Great Mdw (*the-* 1654); Great
Rough; Green Fd; Haddon (perhaps 'heath hill', v. hǣð, dūn); Hall Mdw;
Hannakin Mdws; Hare Knowle (v. hara, cnoll); Heathy Fd; Heywoods
(probably from the surname from Heawood 96 *supra*); High Fd (*the-* 1654);
High Knowl; High(er) Moor; Hill Fd (*le Hullefeld* 1366, v. hyll, feld); Brow-,
Great- & Little Hill Ho; Hodkinsons Croft (cf. Roger *Hodgekynson* 1602);
Holland Knowl (cf. John *Holland* 1672, v. cnoll); Hollin(s) Croft (v. holegn);
Hollow Fd; Hough Mdw, Houghs Dunge Park (v. hōh, dynge, park); House
Croft & Fd; House Steads (v. hūs-stede); Hulmes (v. hulm, cf. Birtles Hall
supra); Humphrey Bank; Intake; Josen Croft; Kiln Croft; Knowle (v.
cnoll); Lane Croft; Lime Fd; Linnershawe Mdw (perhaps an old p.n. in
sceaga 'a wood'); Long Butts (v. butte); Long Corner; Low Hill; Marl Fd
(*the Marlfield* 1654); Marsh (Mdw); Meadow Ransor (this may contain a
form of *Raveneshurst infra*); Middle Hey (*media haya* 1384, v. middel,
(ge)hæg); Moss (*Alderley Mosse* 1556, v. mos); Mouse Riding ('mouse-
infested clearing', v. mūs, ryding); New Field Park; Oak Fd; Oaken Wd;
Old Croft; Oven Fd; Owler Fd (v. alor); Ox Mullock ('ox midden', from
oxa and dial. *mullock* '(a heap of) dirt, rubbish, filth'); Pack Saddle Fd
(v. pakke-sadil); Pingot (Fd) (v. pingot); Pit Close & Fd; Poolstead (v. pōl-
stede); Quick Fd; Ridding (v. ryding); Rigley Mdws (v. Wrigley *infra*);
Rough Brow & Hey; Round Fd; Royle ('rye hill', v. ryge, hyll); Rushy Fd;
Rye Croft & Hill (cf. Royle *supra*); Little Shut (v. scēat); Slow (v. slōh);
Smith Fd; Smithy Fd; Sough Mdws (v. sogh); South Park; Springs (v.
spring 'a young plantation'); Square (v. squar(e)); Stable Fd; Stack Garth
(v. stakk-garðr); Stitchings ('the pieces' from OE *styccing, v. stycce, -ing[1],
cf. Stychens Sr 310); Stock Fd; Stoney Bank; Sun Fd (v. sunne); Swan
Mdw; Swindells (Croft) (*Swyndel(fs)* 1520, *Swindels* 1602, 'swine pits',
v. swin[1], (ge)delf); Swine Ridding (v. swin[1], ryding); Tear Hill; Tenter Fd
(v. tentour); Tongue (v. tunge); Ton Hey (v. toun, (ge)hæg); Top o' th'
Brow; Triangle; Videser; Wetley Hey; Great Whet Fd; Whiley Hey (cf.
Whirley *supra*); White Fd; Wicken Mdws (v. cwicen); Widow Heys (v.
widuwe, (ge)hæg); Wood Fd; Wrigley, Rigley Mdws.

    (b) *Auardeshacche* e14, *Avardeshache* e14[2] ('Ælfweard's gate' from the OE
pers.n. *Ælfweard* and hæc(c), cf. *Awardus* de *Fuleshae* (Fulshaw 227 *infra*)
12 Cre); *le Birchenegrof* e14, *-gros* e14[2] ('the birch grove', v. bircen[2], grāf);
Bromlegh 1353 (p), del *Bromyleghes* c.1390 (p) ('the broom(y) clearing',
v. brōm(ig), lēah); *le Colefeld* 1353 ('the cabbage field', v. cāl, feld); *the*

Cowper Croftes 1654 (from the surname *Cooper* and croft); *Gosecroft* 1528 (from gōs or gorst and croft); (*le*) *Heyeruding* 1347, *le Heghrudding* 1366 (*v.* hēah, ryding); *le Irissebrugelegh* 1353 ('(clearing at) Irish(man's) bridge', *v.* Irische, brycg, lēah); *le Pykedelowe* e14, *le Pykedlowe* e14[2] ('the pointed mound', *v.* piked, hlāw); *Raveneshurst in Aldredelegh* 13, *Ravenhurst* 1347[2] (p), (*le*) *Ravenshurst* 1352 *et freq* ib to c.1424, ('Hræfn's wooded-hill', from hyrst and a shortened form of the surname of a local family, *Waleran, Walraven(e)* 12, e13 Orm[2] III 579, 1294 Court, 1338 Orm[2], from the OE pers.n. *Wælhræfn* (Feilitzen 409)); *le Rav'feld* 1397; *Rogerisheye* 1352, *Rogers Heye* 1376 (17), 1521 (from the ME pers.n. *Roger* and (ge)hæg); *le Sadel* e14 (a bound of the Fitton estate, cf. Fittontown *supra, v.* sadol, cf. *Saddlebole supra*); *Seuanesty* e14 ('Sven's path', from the ODan pers.n. *Sven* and stig, stigr); *the great Shakoe flat* 1654; *Tykhouse* c.1536 Orm[2] II 867; *Wlfgreneockes* e14, *Elfgrenhoks* e14[2] ('(oaks at) the wolf green', from wulf and grēne[2], with āc); *Wymundshurst* 1376 (17) ('Wīgmund's copse', from the pers.n. OE *Wīgmund*, ON *Vígmundr* (Feilitzen 413) and hyrst).

3. GREAT WARFORD (101–8077)

Wareford 1086 DB
Wereford e13 Dieul *et freq* to 1525 ChRR, (*Magna-*) 1288 Court, *-e* 1285 ib, *Werford* 1285 ib (p) *et freq* to 1557 ChRR, (*Magna-*) 1287 Court, JRL, (*Magnum-*) 1411 *Chol*, (*Mucle-*) 1317 Plea, *Qwerford* 1286 *Eyre* (p)
Warefeld 1471 *MinAcct*
(*Great*) *Warford* 1511 ChRR, (*-Magna*) 1710 *Dow*, *-fort* 1529 Plea, *-furthe* 1554 *MinAcct*.

'Weir ford', from wer (wær[1], waru[1]) and ford, with magna, micel, grēat. This township represents one of the three divisions of the DB manor of *Wareford* (cf. Little- and *Old* Warford 335 *infra*), which was then in Bucklow Hundred, *v.* Orm[2] I 487. The location of the ford is uncertain, but it may have been at Sandle Bridge 334 *infra*. Part of Great Warford formerly abutted upon Ollerton (cf. *Old Warford*), because *situm molendini in villa de Magna Werford* and *molendinum de Magna Werford* c.1280, c.1290 JRL are described as 'a watermill in the township of *Magna Werford*, with the site of a mill-dam made or to be made, for the diversion of water to the mill, upon the stream between *Magna Werford* and *Holreton*' 1319 Orm[2] III 585, and this can hardly be Colthurst Mill 330 *infra*.

ANTROBUS BRIDGE, cf. Antrobus Hall 329 *infra*.   THE ASH.
BEECH HO.   BLUEBALL, cf. *Blue Ball Meadow* 1841 *TA*.   BOSTOCK
BARNS, *Earls Farm* 1831 Bry, *Bostock* 1841 *TA*.   BROOK, *-House*

1831 Bry, near a tributary of Whim Brook. BROOK COTTAGE &
HO. BROWNFIELD HO (lost), 1831 ib, cf. Stanley Cottage *infra*.
FOLLY HOUSES, *v.* folie. HEATHGATE, *Heath Gate* 1842 OS, cf.
(*Warford*) *Heath* 1841 *TA*, *v.* hǣð; the second el. is either geat or
gata. KILLOCKS. LINDOW END, 1831 Bry, cf. *Lindow* 1841
TA, *v.* ende[1], cf. Lindow 230 *infra*. LITTLEMOSS, 1842 OS, *v.*
lȳtel, mos, cf. The Moss, Little Mosses 226 *infra*. MANOR HO,
1842 ib, 'adjoins a disused graveyard, probably...a burial place of
the Quakers of the seventeenth century', Orm[2] III 585, but cf. White
659, where, erroneously, this 'is supposed the site of a chapel, St
Chad, standing here 780 A.D.'; Manor Ho is named *Norbury* in 1831
Bry. MERRYMAN'S LANE, *Merryman Lane* 1842 OS. NOONSUN
-*Farm* & *Lane* 1831 Bry, cf. Warford Ho *infra*. NORBURY
COTTAGE & HO, *Norbury Houses* 1831 ib, cf. Manor Ho *supra*.
PEDLEY BRIDGE & HO, PEDLEY LANE (lost), 1831 ib, named from
Pedley Brook 32 *supra*, cf. Pedley 182 *infra*. POWNALL BRIDGE &
BROW, 1831 ib, cf. Pownall 229 *infra*. SANDPIT FM. SPRING-
FIELD. STANLEY COTTAGE, *Brownfield Cottage* 1842 OS, cf. Brown-
field Ho *supra*. SWANBANK, 1842 ib. WARFORD COVER (*Cover*
1831 Bry), HALL, LANE & LODGE. WARFORD HO, *Noon Sun* 1842
OS, a house-name extended to Noonsun *supra*.

FIELD-NAMES

The undated forms are 1841 *TA* 7.

(*a*) Appletree Flat (*v.* flat); Barsey Fd; Bear Fd; Big Rice ('brushwood',
v. hrīs, dial. *rise*); Birch Fd; Birchin Acres (*v.* bircen[2]); Black Croft & Hey;
Boar Fd (*v.* bār[2]); *the Bootiefeild* 1654 Tab (*v.* botye); Bottoms (*v.* botm);
Breeches Croft (*v.* brēc); Brickiln Fd; Broad Fd; Brook Yard (*v.* geard);
Brow Fd; Brunt Yard (*v.* brende[2], geard); Cappers Fd; Carr (Riding)
(*v.* kjarr, ryding); Chapel Fd; Clay Fd; Coppuck House Fd (cf. Coppock
Ho 330 *infra*); Cow Hill; Cronks Hill (*v.* cranuc); Crook Flatt (*v.* krókr,
flat); Dig Weeds; Dirty Croft & Mdw; Dry Croft; Flash (*v.* flasshe); Flatts
(*v.* flat); Gorsey Fd; Green Grass; Half Acre; Half Mdw; Hazlehold (*v.*
hæsel, holt); Hill Fd; Hob Fd (*v.* hobb(e)); Holland; Hoop Hey; House Fd;
Irons (the plural of the dial. form of hyrne 'a corner', cf. Heronbridge 332
infra); Kennerley Fd (cf. Kinnerley Croft 98 *supra*); Knowl; Lane Fd;
Lime Fd; Long Hey (*v.* (ge)hæg); Long Shoot (*v.* scēat); Marl Park (*v.*
marle, park); Marsh Croft & Fd; Middle Hill; Moss (Patch); New Hey;
Old Orchard; Outlet (*v.* outlet); Oven Croft; Pasture Fd; Patch; Pica Mdw;
Pingot (*v.* pingot); Pit Croft & Fd; Poor Pipes (*v.* pipe[2] 'a decoy channel');
Pump Mdw; Push Ploughed Fd (*v.* push-plough); Rape Fd; Redmanhay
(*Redmans Heys, Redman's Hayes* 1654 Tab, *Redmen's Heyes* 1665, *Redman-*

heye 1677 ib, from (ge)hæg and the surname *Redman*); Ridding (*v.* ryding); Riddow; Road Flash (*v.* flasshe); Rough Hostage; Round Fd; Rulow (perhaps 'rough mound', *v.* rūh, hlāw); Rye Croft; Sand Fd; Sandhole Fd; Short Butts (*v.* sc(e)ort, butte); Smith Fd; Smithy Fd; Sound Fd (*v.* sand); Special Croft; Spout Mdw (*v.* spoute); Stable Mdw; Stubble Fd; Sun Fd & Mdw (*v.* sunne); Three Corner'd Fd; Two Acres; Vetch Croft (*v.*fecche); Well Fd (cf. *The Wellcroft* 1654 Tab); Wem (*v.* wemm); Wheat Fd; Withy Croft.

(*b*) *Aspowe* c.1316 Orm² (may contain æspe 'aspen'); *Brucshut* 1547 *Dav* (*v.* brōc, scēat).

vii. Macclesfield Chapelry

A parochial chapelry of Prestbury parish 181 *infra*, founded in 1278, *v.* Orm² III 751, it contained the townships 1. Hurdsfield (*v.* Macclesfield *infra*), 2. Kettleshulme, 3. Macclesfield (now a municipal borough including Tytherington 214 *infra* and Upton 216 *infra* from Prestbury parish, and parts of Hurdsfield *supra* and Sutton Downes *infra*), 4. Macclesfield Forest, 5. Pott Shrigley, 6. Rainow, 7. Sutton Downes (*v.* Macclesfield *supra*), 8. Wildboarclough, 9. Wincle.

1. HURDSFIELD (110–9274)

This township originally comprised Hurdsfield and Higher Hurdsfield. The former is included in Macclesfield municipal borough and c.p., but is dealt with here for historical convenience, the place-names contained in that part being marked +.

Hirdelesfeld 13 Chest, m13 Adl

Hyrdesfeld m13 Adl, 1286 *Eyre*, (*utraque-*) c.1301 *AddCh*, (*Magna-*) 1384 *Rental*, *Hyrdisfeld* 1286 *Eyre* (p), l13 *AddCh*, Hirdis-, *Hirdesfeld* 1285, 1286 *Eyre*, l13, c.1301 *AddCh*, *Hirdisfeld Inferior* l13 ib, Herdis-, *Herdesfeld* 1285, 1355 *Eyre*, (*utraque*) *Hurdesfeld'* 1301 Sheaf *et freq*, (*Magna-*) 1356 Orm², 1369 *AddCh*, -feild 1602 MidCh, *Hurdisfeld* 1288 Court (p) (lit. Hundis-), c.1303 BM, -filde 1560 Sheaf, *Hurdsfield* 1724 NotCestr *et freq*

Huderisfeld 1287 Court, *Hydresfeld* c.1310 Chest, *Huddesfeld* 1503 Plea, *Hudsfield* 1686 *Dow*, *Hudderfelde* 1550 *MinAcct*

Hurdefeld 1416 Plea, -fyld 1518 ChRR, *Hurd(e)feild* 1650 *Dow*

Hurdeswell 1467, 1471, 1508 *MinAcct*, *Hardeswell* 1560 Sheaf

Hurdelfeld 1471 *MinAcct*

Yeardsfield 1501 Earw

Hursfeude 1560 Sheaf, *-field* 1724 NotCestr
Hardefeild c.1639 *Chol*

'Open land at a hurdle', *v.* hyrdel, -es², feld, cf. Hurleston 332 *infra*. The name may refer to a hurdle-fence. Ekwall (DEPN) proposes the OE pers.n. *Hygerēd* for the first el., but this does not support the *Hirdeles-* forms, identified with Hurdsfield by *grangia aedificata...in Hirdelesfeld* 13 Chest (ChetNS LXXXII 591) and *grangia de Hirdelesfeld, grangia aedificata apud Hyrdesfeld* m13 Adl (NRA 0917, 48), all referring to the same barn. Dr von Feilitzen maintains that the original form of the p.n. might be that containing the pers.n., the *Hirdeles-* form being due to a later association with a *hyrdel*.

HIGHER HURDSFIELD, *Parua Hirdesfeld* l13 *AddCh*, *-Hurdesfeld* 1369 *ib*, *Litelhyrdesfeld* 1385 *Rental*, cf. *utraque Hyrdesfeld* c.1301 *AddCh*, *-Hurdesfeld*' 1301 Sheaf, *v.* lȳtel, cf. Hurdsfield *supra*.

STREET-NAMES. ARBOURHAY ST., +, 1860 White, probably named from a f.n. *Arbourhay*, cf. *Narbur(e)y* 1686, 1688 *Dow*, 'at the sheltered enclosure', *v.* atten, here-beorg, (ge)hæg; DAYBROOK ST., +, 1860 White, named from Day Brook 20 *supra*; FENCE ST., +, 1860 *ib*, named from Fence *infra*; HIGHERFENCE RD., +, 1860 *ib*, *v.* Higherfence *infra*; HURDSFIELD RD., +, 1860 *ib*, *via que ducit versus Hurdesfeld* 1381 *Mont*.

CLIFF FM, HILL & LANE, *la Cluffe* 1386 *Chol* (p), *the (Millstone) Clyffe* 1611 *LRMB* 200, *The Clifte* 1620 *Surv*, *v.* clif, myln-stān, cf. Cliff Hill 143 *infra*.

THE FENCE+ (lost), HIGHERFENCE (FM)+

   haia de Macclesfeld e13 Orm², *quadam haia vocata le Wodehaue* 1471 *MinAcct*, *le Wodeheye* 1508 *ib*, *the Woodhey* 1560 Sheaf *boscus qui dicitur le Fens* 1337 *Eyre*, (*boscus de*) *Fens* 1358 BPR, *le Fence* 1467 *MinAcct*, (*de Macclesfeld*) 1513 Orm², *The Fence* 1560 Sheaf, *Fence* 1831 Bry
   le Fencer 1508 *MinAcct*

'The wood-enclosure', 'the fence', *v.* wudu, (ge)hæg, haga, fence. Cf. Fence St., Higherfence Rd., *supra*.

SHRIGLEYFOLD FM, *Shrigley Fold* c.1788 *Dow*, *Sigley* 1842 OS, the home of Robert *Shrygeley* 1545 *Dow*, cf. Shrigley 130 *infra*, *v.* fald.

(HIGHER & LOWER) SWANSCOE (101–937753), SWANSCOE COTTAGE, HALL, PARK FM & WOOD

> *Swanneshogh* 1357 *ChFor et freq*, *-e* 1523 Orm², ChRR, *Swanneshog(h)hill* 1503 *ChFor*, *Swaneshogh* 1446 ChRR (a messuage)
> *boscus de Swainnehooh* 1357 (1620) *Surv*
> *Swanscoe, Swanescough* 1611 *LRMB* 200, *Swansco(w)* 1686 *Dow*, *Higher & Lower Swanscoe* 1831 Bry
> *Swainscoe* 1666 Orm²

Probably 'herdsman's hill', from swān² and hōh, with hyll. The first el. could be an OE pers.n. *Swān*. The second has been confused with skógr 'a wood'. Here was *Swanneshogh Pool* 1505 (117) *Dow*, *v.* pōl¹.

BARCROFTE HO (lost), 1611 *LRMB* 200, *Berecroft* 1286 *Court* (p), c.1301 *AddCh* (p), 1506 *Dow*, *the-* 1509 *ib*, 'barley croft', *v.* bere, croft; also referred to as *Clarkhouse* 1611 *LRMB* 200, the home of Thomas *Clark*.   BROOKSIDE HO, named from Shores Clough Brook *infra*.   CLOSE HO, 1831 Bry.   COMMONSIDE, cf. *Hurdesfield Common, the Comon* 1611 *LRMB* 200, also beside Macclesfield Common 122 *infra*.   DODGEMORE WELL, probably '(well at) the dog's marsh', from dogga 'a dog', and mōr¹, with wella, cf. *Hodg Croft* 158 *infra*.   DONCASTERHILL, c.1788 *Dow*.   HIGHER- & LOWERFOLD, *Higher Fold* 1842 OS.   HALLE FIELDS (lost), *v.* 118 *infra*.   HURDSFIELD HO, 1831 Bry.   JANNEY'S FM, *Janneys* 1831 ib.   LOWER MARSH, 1860 White.   OLDHAM'S HOLLOW, *v.* 215 *infra*.   PARADISE+, 1831 Bry, 'pleasure garden', *v.* paradis.   RED HOUSE FM+, *Lower Clough* 1831 ib, *v.* clōh.   ROCK WOOD.   ROEWOOD HO, *Roughwode* 1357 BPR, *Roewood Gate* 1831 Bry, 'rough wood', *v.* rūh, wudu, geat.   THE ROUGH.   SHORES CLOUGH (BROOK), *Shores Clough* 1831 ib, (*Brook*) 1842 OS, cf. *aqua decurrens inter Maccl' et Tyderynton* 1369 *Eyre*, 'clough at a steep slope', *v.* scor(a), clōh. The brook joins R. Bollin 15 *supra*.   SWANSCOE COTTAGE, 1860 White, *Swanscoe Lodge* 1766 *Dow*.   SWANSCOE HALL, *Swaneshogh* (a messuage) 1466 ChRR.   SWANSCOE PARK FM, cf. *parcum vocatum Swanneshogh' parke* 1503 *ChFor*, *palusia de Swanneshogh* 1505 *Dow*, *v.* park.   SWANSCOE WOOD.   WOODEND COTTAGES, cf. *le Wode* 1492 *Dow*, cf. prec.

FIELD-NAMES

The undated forms are 1849 *TA* 214. Of the others 113, c.1301 are *AddCh*, 1325, 1390, 1397, 1402, c.1414 (15) *Mont*, 1467, 1471, 1508 *MinAcct*, 1501 *Earw*, 1560 *Sheaf*, 1611 *LRMB* 200, 1620 *Surv*, and the rest *Dow*.

(a) Baines Brow (v. brū); Big & Little Clough (v. clōh); Cockers Close Brow; Corken Croft; Dyehouses Yard (v. dye-house); Far Brow (v. brū); Holly Wd; Honey Fd (v. hunig); Lodge Brow Bottom (v. loge, brū, botm); Ox Close; Pingot (cf. *the Furr Pingot* 1611, v. pingot); Pool Mdw; Ryla Croft; Spoil Banks; Summer House Fd; Three Nook's Fd; Well Bottoms (cf. *Far & Nar Bothams* 1688, v. botm); Whitening Croft.

(b) *Barne meadow* 1688, cf. *Berne feld* 1506; *Birchfield (Rough)* 1611; *le Blakehey* 1492 (v. blæc, (ge)hæg); *Blakyearthes* 1611 (v. blæc, eorðe or erð); *Broadhey* 1611; *the Browne-hill* 1501, *great & little brownehill, brownehill peece* 1611 (v. brūn[1], hyll, pece; here the boundaries of Bollington, Hurdsfield and Tytherington met); *Calcroft* 1508, *Calfe Crofte* 1611, 1688, *Calfehey* 1611 (c. calf, croft, (ge)hæg); *Far- & Narcocke Meadowe* 1611; *Cornefield* 1611; *Cowley meadowe, Lower Cowley* 1611 (v. cū, lēah); *Deyhiren* 1508, *Hyron, the hiron* 1611 ('the dairy nook', v, dey, hyrne, cf. Heronbridge 332 *infra*); *The Eyes* 1611, 1620 (cf. *le Brode Eye* 1323, *(le) Huggehee* 1325, 1369, *aqua que vocatur le Goseeghe* 1396, *le Goseghe* 1397, *le Gosegh* 1402, *the Goose Eye* 1620, 'the water-meadows', from ēg (alternatively ēa 'a stream') and brād 'broad', gōs 'goose', cf. Waters Green 121 *infra*. For *Hugge-* cf. Hug Bridge 55 *supra*); *fourty peniworth* 1611, 1686 (v. peni(n)g-weorð); *Gorsey field* 1688; *greatfield* 1611; *Greenefield* 1611; *Harfield* 1686 ('higher field', v. hēarra); *Heycroft* 1686 (v. hēg, croft); *Hey-, High Readinge* 1611 (v. hēah, ryding); *Heghfilde* 1502, *the Harr-, the Lower Highfield* 1611, *les Highfieldes* 1631, *far-, lower highfield* 1686 (v. hēah, hēarra, feld); *the Hollin knowe* 1611, *holin know* 1686 (v. holegn, cnoll); *placea terre vocata le houstude* 1323, *the Houstides (Carre)* 1611 ('the house site', v. hūs-stede, kjarr, the *carr* being partly in Bollington 187 *infra*); *lower Howland* 1686; *Hutton Crofte* 1611; *the Kilne Crofte & -field* 1611, *Killne croft* 1686; *the knowle, the know(le)-f(e)ild* 1611, *great, little & nar know* 1686 (v. nēarra, cnoll); *Kooheg* 1506, *the Cowhey* 1611 (v. cū, (ge)hæg); *the Lane Croft* 1611; *the Ley-buttes* 1611 (v. lēah, butte); *the longshutt* (v. scēat); *the Lordes close* 1611 (v. hlāford, clos); *the Lowerfield Spring* 1611 (v. spring); *Manyfold field* 1611; *Marled Crofte & Field* 1611, *Marle field* 1686, 1688 (v. marlede); *Moss(e)field, Mosspittes* 1611; *the Muck Crofte* 1611 (v. muk); *narrow field* 1686; *new Fyeld* 1611, *(far)* 1686; *the Old Marled Earth* 1611 (v. marlede, eorðe); *the Orchard* 1611; *the Oxeheys* 1611 (v. oxa, (ge)hæg); *Pingle* 1686 (v. pingel); *Pitt know(e)* 1686, 1688 (v. pytt, cnoll); *great rishey field* 1686 (v. riscig); *Rowhey* 1467, *the Roe hey* 1611 (v. rūh, (ge)hæg); *Roodes Meadow* 1611 (v. rod[1]); *Round Hey* 1611; *Rowley* 1471, 1508, *Rawley* 1560 (v. rūh, lēah, cf. *The Isinge* 119 *infra*); *the Rye Route* 1611 (cf. *Ryeroote* 159 *infra*); *Sanderpingate* 1611 (probably 'Sander's little plot', from the ME pers.n. *Sander*, a short form of *Alexander*, and pingot, cf. *Alysandrebanke* 124 *infra*); *le Schidyord* c.1301 (p) ('(en-closure with) a wooden fence', v. scīdgeard); *skinpit botham(s)* 1686, 1688 ('(bottoms near) pits where skins are steeped for tanning', *v.* botm); *the Springe* 1611 (a wood, *v.* spring); *Stonyards lands* 1686; *Thistle Croft* 1611; *thorny Crofte* 1611; *Trough meadowe* 1611 (*v.* trog); *Wilkyn(s)feld(e)* 1506, 1508, *Will Akers* 1611 ('Wilkin's, Will's field', from *Wilkin*, *Will*, diminutive and shortened forms of *William*, and feld, æcer); *Wliethishehe* 113 ('Wulf-gēat's water-meadow', from the OE pers.n. *Wulfgēat* and ēg); *le Wod(e)hous* 1390, 1392, c.1414 (*v.* wudu, hūs).

2. KETTLESHULME (101–987797)

    Ketelisholm 1285 *Eyre* (p), *Ketelesholm(e)* 1357 *ChFor*, 1358 *MinAcct*, *Ketelsho(l)m'* 1467 *ib*, *Kettelsholme* 1539 ChRR, *-home* 1582 *Dow*, *Ketilesholme* 17 *ib*, *Ketils-* 1492 *ib*, *Ketyls-* 1528 *ib*, *Ketuls-* 1567 *ib*

    Keteleshulm 1285 *Eyre*, *-hulme* 1357 *ChFor*, 1358 *MinAcct*, *Ketelleshulm* 1367 *Eyre*, *Ketelshulme* 1536 ChRR, *Ketilleshulme* E3 *Surv*, *Ketilshulm* 1375 *Eyre*, *-hulme* 1465 ChRR, *Ketyls-* 1536 *ib*, *Ketulles-* c.1494 *Dow*, *Ketuls-* 1503 *ChFor*

    Ketleshulm 1337 *Eyre*, *Kettles-* 1347 *ib*, *Ketlushulme* 1370, 1381 *ib*

    Ketleshom 1345 *Eyre*, *-holm* 1384 *Rental*, *Kettlesholm* 1724 NotCestr *Ketlusholm(e)* 1370, 1381 *Eyre*, *Ket(t)les(h)ome* 1738 *Dow*

    Keteleshull' 1348 *Eyre*

    Kettesholm 1364 *Eyre*, *-holme* 1471 *MinAcct*, *Ketesho(l)me* 1467 *ib*, *Ketisholme* 1471 *ib*

    Kattes-, *Cattesholme* 1508 *MinAcct*

    Cottesholme 1508 *MinAcct*, *-ham*, *Cotteholme* 1560 Sheaf

    Ketelholme 1519 ChRR, *Kettle Holme* 1671 *AddCh*

    Ketushulme 1548 ChRR

    Kydils-, *Kedilsham* 1550 *MinAcct*

    Kedylson 1550 *MinAcct*

'Ketil's water-meadow', from the ODan pers.n. *Ketil* and hulm. Many of the spellings show the influence of late OE *holm* (< ON holmr) but those in *-hulm(e)* preponderate.

THE CAPLES LAW (lost), 17 (1738) *Dow*, 'a place with an allowed right of way for a horse', as the context makes clear, '........ Roger Pott of *Churleshead* (Charles Head 143 *infra*) is alowed a way to goe with loaden Horses through a parcell of Land the wch is called *the Caples Law*' *Dow* 404, *v.* kapall (ME capel), cf. *Capel Gate* (Chester) 330 *infra*. *Law* here may be ModE *law* 'an allowance, an indulgence' (NED), but it is used geographically in the same way as ON lǫg 'law, law-district' (Cleasby–Vigf), cf. býjar-lǫg.

DUNGE FM & CLOUGH (101–989777), *Dunge* 1545 *Dow, the-* 1611 *LRMB* 200, *the Dounge* 1562 Orm², *Dung(e)he(a)d* 1611 *LRMB* 200, 1620 *Surv, Dunge Alley* 1831 Bry, 'the dung-heap', *v.* dynge cf. Dunge 101 *supra. Dunge Alley* was the farm at 101–988773 on a track leading to Dunge, *v.* aley. *Dungehead* was a common at 101–994773, the head of Dunge Clough, *v.* hēafod.

TUNSTEADKNOLL (101–987783), 1842 OS, *Tunsteed-, Tunstide Knowle* 1611 *LRMB* 200, *the Stunstid knowle* 1620 *Surv, Turnside Knowl* 1831 Bry, '(hill at) the farmstead-site', *v.* tūn-stede, cnoll.

WALKER BROW & FM, *le Wallecor* 1283 *Dow* (p), *(le) Walleker* 1286 *Eyre* (p), Court (p), 1355 *MinAcct*, 1384 *Rental, the Walker* 1611 *LRMB* 200, 1620 *Surv, Walker Brow* 1831 Bry, 'marsh at a spring', *v.* wælla, kjarr.

WINDGATHER COTTAGE, WINDGATHER ROCKS (101–995784, the rocks are also in Taxal 175 *infra*), *campus qui vocatur Gederwynd* 1355 *Eyre*, close called *the gather wynd* 1611 *LRMB* 200, *Wine Cader Hill* 1656 Orm², *Windcather* 1720 (1819) *Dow, Wind Gather-, -Kather Rock, Wind Hather-, -Kather Tor(r), Tor(r) Top(p)* 1738 *ib*. Derivation from cadeir and winn³ is ruled out by the word-order. The name is 'gather-wind', an exposed place which seems to attract winds, from ME *gæderien, gederen* (OE *gaderian*) 'to gather' and wind¹, with roke 'a rock'. cf. Gather Wind 217 *infra*.

BENTHALL, *the Bent (fieldes)* 1611 *LRMB* 200, *Bents* 1842 OS, 'grass-land', *v.* beonet. BLACKHILLGATE, 1831 Bry, *the Black(e)hill* 1611 *LRMB* 200, 1620 *Surv*, '(gateway to) the black hill'. BOGGART HO, 'haunted house', *v.* boggart. BROADCARR, *(the) Broad(e)-carr(e)* 1611 *LRMB* 200, 1620 *Surv*, 'broad marsh', *v.* brād, kjarr. BROOKBOTTOM, cf. *Brook Bottoms* 1848 *TA, v.* botm. BROWTOP, 1831 Bry. NEAR CARR, CARR BROOK & CLOUGH, *v.* kjarr, brōc, clōh. CHAPEL HO. CLAYTONFOLD, 1831 Bry, *Hugh Clayton's* 1738 *Dow*, cf. George *Cleyton* 1602 *ib, v.* fald. CLOUGH FM, *Clough* 1831 Bry, cf. *the Clough pasture* 1611 *LRMB* 200, *v.* clōh. COALHURST, *-hirst* 1831 Bry, *v.* col¹, hyrst. COOPERSHAW.

DALES FM.   FIVELANE-ENDS, 1831 Bry.   GAP HO, 1831 ib, *del Gappe* 1362 *Eyre* (p), named from the gorge at 101–805997 below Kishfield Bridge *infra*, *v.* gap.   GREENDALES FM.   GREEN HEAD FM, *v.* grēne², hēafod.   HARDY GREEN.   HODGEL BROOK, cf. *Hodghill* 1611 *LRMB* 200, 1620 *Surv*, the high ground adjoining Pym Chair 174 *infra*, from hogg 'a hog' or the ME pers.n. *Hodge* and hyll; cf. *Hodg Croft* 158 *infra*.   HOLLOWCOWHEY, *Hollow Carr Hey* 1831 Bry, *v.* holh, kjarr, (ge)hæg.   KIRKY CLOUGH, *Kirkey-* 1831 ib, *v.* clōh; *Kirky* is perhaps 'enclosure belonging to a church', from kirkja and (ge)hæg, cf. Priest Fm *infra*.   KISHFIELD BRIDGE & FM (101–994807), *Kiss Field* 1831 ib, cf. *the Kisfieldes head* 1611 *LRMB* 200, 'field in a valley', *v.* kjóss, feld, cf. Kiss Arse 146 *infra*. Kishfield is at a recess at the top of the narrow valley on Todd Brook, cf. Gap Ho *supra*.   LAPWING FM, *Lapwing* 1831 Bry.   LUMBHOLE MILL, 1831 ib, 'deep hole', *v.* lum(m), hol¹, myln.   MANGERS CARR, *Mangescarr(e)* 1611 *LRMB* 200, 1620 *Surv*, *v.* kjarr.   MEADOWS FM.   NEEDHAM FM, cf. *Needham Field* (2 ×) 1848 *TA*, probably from the surname *Needham*.   NEIGHBOURWAY.   OLD MAT'S FM.   PADDOCK, *v.* pearroc.   PRIEST FM, cf. *Priestes meadowe* 1611 *LRMB* 200, perhaps denoting the Kettleshulme lands of the chantry foundation of Downes chapel at Pott Shrigley, as in *Dow* 165, *v. The Library*, 5th ser., xv, 48.   PYMCHAIR FM, cf. *Pim Chair Piece* 1848 *TA*, *v.* Pym Chair 174 *infra*.   REDFERN, cf. John *Redferne* 1582 *Dow*.   REED BRIDGE, *v.* 200 *infra*.   ROUNDKNOLL. SHEPHERDS BANK.   SIDE-END, cf. *the syd(e), the sydd* 1611 *LRMB* 200, 1620 *Surv*, 'the (hill) side', *v.* sīde, ende¹.   SLATER'S FM, *Slaters* 1831 Bry, from the surname *Slater*.   SPONDSBOTTOM, in the valley of Todd Brook, opposite Back Sponds 200 *infra*, *v.* spann¹, botm.   SPOUT HO, *v.* spoute.   STOCKSBANK, *v.* stocc, banke. SWAN INN, 1848 *TA*, *Swan with Two Necks* 1860 White.   TAXAL EDGE, *v.* 174 *infra*.   THORNEYCROFT, 1831 Bry.   TOWNFIELD, 1831 ib, cf. *the lower & the over townefield* 1611 *LRMB* 200.   WELL HO.   WOOD BANK.

FIELD-NAMES

The undated forms are 1848 *TA* 221. Of the others, E3, 1620 are *Surv*, 1384 *Rental*, 1467, 1471, 1508 *MinAcct*, 1357, 1503 *ChFor*, 1560 Sheaf, 17, 1738 *Dow*, 1611 *LRMB* 200.

(a) Back Brow; Bulls Head Croft; Calf Croft; Castle Fd (*v.* castel(l)); Clay Holes; the Clo(o)se Yate, -Gapp 1738 ('the narrow gateway', an access to Kettleshulme common, v. clos adj. 'close', geat, gap); Kettlesho(l)m Common 1738 (being enclosed at this date, Dow 421); Corn Fd; Dye House Mdw (v. dye-house); the Edge End (from Taxal Edge 174 supra); Ely Mdw; Goodier-, Goodser Well 1738 (v. wella; perhaps from Godeshagh 1367, 'good wood', v. gōd[2], sceaga); Gorsey Brow & Knowl; the Greenelowehead 1738 (the greene lowe 1611, 1620, v, grēne[1], hlāw, hēafod); Hey Fd (v. (ge)hæg); Hog (the Hogghey pasture 1611, 'hog enclosure', v. hogg, (ge)hæg); Hollow Fd & Mdw; Lamb Croft; Lime Fd; Little Holes (v. hol[1]); the longe Lane 1738; Long Slip (v. slipe); Meadow Head Fd; New Close & Hey (cf. New Crofte 1611); the Overforde 1738 (v. uferra, ford); Pasture Fd; Pig Fd (cf. Hog supra); Red Rose; Rough Fd; Rye Croft; Sandy Gutter 1738 (v. goter); Shepton Croft ('sheep farm or enclosure', v. scēap, tūn); Shotten Fd ('spent field', v. shotten); Spars, Long Sparks Fd (the Spart(e)s 1611, 1620, 'rushes', v. spart); Spring Mdw (v. spring 'a well-spring'); Long Swan, Swan(n) Meadoe & Fd (perhaps from the Swan Inn supra); Taxall Way 1738 (to Taxal 172 infra); Top Knowl; Waths ('water meadows', v. waroð, here confused with vað, cf. Wharf 65 supra); Well Fd; Wett Fd (v. wēt); Wheat Croft.

(b) the banckend 1611 (v. banke, ende[1]); the Black earth 1611 (v. blæc, eorðe); the Borne meadowe 1611; Brekwellehurst (v. 180 infra); the Bridgfield 1611; Browne Kno(w)le 1611, Broome knowle 1620 (v. brūn[1], brōm, cnoll); the Buttes 1611 (v. butte); le Chesehurst E3, little-, newe- & old Cheesehurst 1611 ('gravel wood-bank', v. cis, hyrst, cf. Chislehurst KPN 300); the Corfetweyer 1611; Cothursfeild 1611 (perhaps from cot and hyrst); Cottwaye-head, great- & over Cottwaye 1611 (v. cot, weg, hēafod); the dowry meadowes 1611 (v. dowarie); the Heild 1611 (v. helde); the horseflatt 1611 (v. hors, flat); the Marestowes 1611 (probably places where boundaries meet, from (ge)mǣre and stōw although the second el. might be stall and the p.n. may mean 'the positions of the boundary (-markers)'); the Meare 1611 (v. (ge)mǣre); Mellars wyves Crofte 1611 ('Mellor's wife's croft' from the local surname Mellor, v. Db 144); Menelegh 1357 ('common woodland', v. (ge)mǣne, lēah, cf. Mean Ley 99 supra); Normonwode 1384 ('Norwegian's wood', v. Norðman, wudu, cf. Normans Hall 134 infra); Oldegate 1503 ('old road', v. ald, gata, Oldgate Nick 144 infra); the Parke 1611 (v. park); the Rishie field, the Rushe feild (v. risc, riscig); the further & nearer Rossawe 1611: the Rydding 1611; Silkenwale 1611; the Stonnenflatt 1611 ('stony plot', v. stænen, flat); Treleighe 1560 (v. lēah); the White acre 1611.

3. MACCLESFIELD (110–9173) [mækəls-]

Maclesfeld 1086 DB, c.1096 (1150) Chest, Macclesfeld c.1096 (1280) ib et freq with variant spellings Mac(c)les-, -is-, Ma(c)kles-, Makkles-, Macckles-, Maclys-, -us-, Maklis-, -feld (e, -ia, -a), -felt, -feud, -fild, -fell, -feild(e), -field to Macklesfield 1656 Orm[2], Macclesfield 1548 ChRR et freq
Maschesfeld c.1096 (1280) Chest

8

Masclesfeld c.1096 (1280) Chest

Makelesfeld 1182 P *et freq* with variant spellings *Makeles-, -is-, Macheles-, -is-, Ma(c)keles-, Mackelles-, Makkeles-, Mackiles-, -feld(e), -feud, -fed', -fild(e), -feild* to *Makelesfild(e)* 1564 Sheaf, *Mackelsfeld* 1310 ib (p), *Makels-* 1493 ib, *Maculs-* 1400 JRL

Makesfeld' 1183 P, *Mak(k)esfeld* 1284 Pat, 1285 *For et freq* Pat to 1393, *Mackesfeld* 1303 Cl, *-feild* 1596 *Dow*

Makerfeld' 1184 P

Maxfeld 1237 Cl (p), 1325 Pat, Gough, 1373 *AddCh*, 1397 ChRR, 1656 Orm², *-e* 1582 *Dow*, *-field* 1356 Tab, *-e* 1554 Sheaf, *-feild* 1662 *AddCh*, *Maxefeld* 1395 Pat (p)

Makefeld', -feud 1237 P *freq* to 1250 ib, 1294 ChancW (p), *Machefeld* (lit. *Mathefeld*) 1241 Lib, *Mackefeud'* 1247 P, *Makfeld* 1294 ChancW, *Macffield* c.1662 *Surv*

Makeld' 1240 P

Maclef' 1241 Lib, *Maclefeud* 1270 Pat, *Makle-* 1252 Cl, *Macklefeld* 13 Dieul, *Macclefeld* 1259 Pat, *-e* 1507 MinAcct, *Makklefeld'* 1365 *Dow*, *Makelefeld, -feud* 1254 P, *Mackelefeld* 1357 BPR, *Maclifeld* 1260 Court

Maglisfeld 13 AD

Malcklesfeld 1242 Cl

Matlesfeud 1247 P

Makonefeld 1248 Lib

Makerisfield 1327 Pat

Maxwelle c.1536 Leland

The final el. is feld 'open country'. For the first el., Ekwall (DEPN) suggests a p.n. analogous with Mackley Db 610, 'Macca's clearing', from an OE pers.n. *Macca* (as in Mackworth, Makeney Db 479, 589, Maxstoke Wa 87) and lēah. Macclesfield would then mean 'open tract at Macca's clearing'. On the other hand, an OE pers.n. *Maccel*, an *-el* diminutive from the same stem as *Macca*, has been suggested, cf. Sheaf³ 4 (551, 564). This pers.n. is not independently recorded, but it would suit the spellings and it is a feasible formation. There is in DB a pers.n. form *Machel*, probably representing OG *Maghelm*, v. Feilitzen 323, Forssner 180, which is unlikely to appear in this p.n. Macclesfield would then mean 'Maccel's open land'. Certain spellings point to confusion with Makerfield La 93.

STREET-NAMES

BACK WALLGATE, 1819 Orm², *the Backstreete* 1620 *Surv, Backe Street* 1652 *ParlSurv*, 'street at the back (of Wallgate)', *v.* back, strǣt, cf. Wallgate *infra*.

CHESTERGATE, *Chastergate* 1272–1307 *AddCh, Chestur-* 1332 *Mont, Chestre-* m14 *Dav et freq* with variant spellings as for Chester, *Jastergate* 1364, 1366 *Mont, Chester Street* 1453 (17) Sheaf, 'the road to Chester', *v.* gata, strǣt, cf. Chester 330 *infra*.

CHURCH ST., 1860 White, *Churchwallgate* 1819 Orm², beside the parish church, cf. Wallgate *infra*, and *the Chirchyardwalle* 1573 (1620) *Surv, (the) Church Yard Side* 1611 *Din, -syde* 1620 *Surv, Church Side* 1860 White, *v.* cirice, chirche-ȝeard, wall, sīde. The name Church St. has been extended to the whole of Wallgate.

COPPER ST., from an eighteenth-century copper-smelting industry, *v.* White 720.

COW LANE, a driving road on to the Moss, *v.* cū, lane.

CUCKSTOOLPIT-HILL (lost), 1880 Earw, 1860 White, *the Cuckstool and the Cuckstool Pit* 1664 Earw, from cucke-stole 'a ducking-stool', pytt, hyll.

DAMS, 1860 White, *le dam(-me infra parcum)* 1467, 1471 *MinAcct, The Dammes* 1620 *Surv*, from damme 'a dam', probably referring to fishponds.

DERBY ST., *Derby Gate* 1860 White, after the earls of Derby, *v.* gata.

EAST GATE, 1860 White, leading eastwards into *Fence* 107 *supra*, *v.* ēast, geat.

GUNCO LANE, *Guneker* E3 *Surv, Gunker* 1467 *MinAcct, -Lane* 1860 White, *Gunncarr (Lane)* 1620 *Surv*, 'Gunni's marsh', from the ODan, ON pers.n. *Gunni* and kjarr.

HIBEL RD [ˈhaibəl], 1860 White, cf. *Hible Hole* 1620 *Surv*, possibly dial. *hibbal* 'a head, a hillock', with hol¹ 'a hole, a hollow'. Professor Sørensen suggests that this p.n. may contain ON híbýli 'a house, a home'.

JORDANGATE, *Jordanesgate* 1339, 1376 *AddCh*, 1379 *Mont, Jordanisgate* 1347 *Dow, Jordans-* 1451 *Chol, le Jordengate* 1513 Orm², *Jordaine Gate alias Jordaine Street* 1652 *ParlSurv, myll Streete alias Jorden Street* 1548 *Dav*, 'Jordan's street', named after *Jordan* de Macclesfield, d.1356, *v.* gata, cf. *Mill Street infra*. Orm² III 740n, cites without reference *portam Jordani de Macclesfeld*', a Latin translation of geat 'a gate', for gata 'a road', which recurs in *porta borialis de ville de Macclesfeld* 1410 *Mont* f.168d for 'the north road from the town of Macclesfield'. Macclesfield was not walled and had no town-gates.

MARKET PLACE, *locus mercati* 1347 *Dow, locus marcati* 1397 *Mont, le Market-place* 1471 *MinAcct, the merkett place* 1620 *Surv*, *v.* market, place. Here was *the Cross* 1611 *Din*, *v.* cros 'a cross'.

MILL LANE, *v.* Mill Green *infra*, *v.* lane.

MILL ST., named from the first silk-mill to be erected in Macclesfield, 1756, at the north end of Park Green (White 718), cf. Spital Field Houses *infra*.

MILL STREET (lost), 1652 *ParlSurv, via ducens ad le Mulneforde* 1312 Orm², *myll Streete alias Jorden Street* 1584 *Dav, the milnestreete* 1620 *Surv*, from the north end of Jordangate (*supra*) at *Hulleacre* (*infra*) to *le Mulneforde* 1312,

1388 Orm[2], 1359, 1361 *Dow*, *le Oldemulneforde* 1323 *ib*, on R. Bollin, about 110–918743, near Lower Heys Mill 215 *infra*, *v*. myln, strǣt, ald, ford.

PARK GREEN & LANE, *Park Green* 1652 *ParlSurv*, *Park Lane* 1831 Bry, named from Macclesfield Park *infra*, *v*. grēne[2], lane.

PEARLE ST., *Pearl Street* 1860 White, near the site of *Pyrlewalle* 1329 Orm[2], *the Pearlewell* (a close near Beech Lane) 1620 *Surv*, 'bubbling spring', from pyrl(e) and wella, wælla.

PINFOLD ST., 1860 White, *v*. pynd-fald.

THE SHAMBLES, 1860 White, *v*. sceamol.

SCHOOL BANK (lost), 1819 Orm[2], the original site of the grammar school at the east end of the church, cf. *le Scole House* 1552 Pat, *v*. scole-hous, scōl, banke.

SPITAL FIELD HOUSES (Roe Street), 1860 White, from the local industry of silk weaving. Spitalfields (Stepney Mx) was the centre of this trade from c.1685; the 'Spitalfields Act' of 1773 laid down the condition of work in the industry. The name refers either to the trade, to London weavers living in Macclesfield, or to statutory conditions under which the inmates worked, *v*. White 740, cf. Mill Street *supra*.

STANLEY ST., 1860 White, *Dogge Lone* 1350 Orm[2], *Doglane* 1584 *Dav*, 1611 *Din*, *Dog Lane* 1738 White, 'lane frequented by dogs', *v*. dogga, lane.

STEPHILL (local), a long flight of steps from Waters to the church, *v*. steppa, hyll.

WALLGATE (cf. Church St., *supra*), *le Wallegate* 1336 *Mont*, 1350 *Eyre et freq*, *Walgate* 1404 *Plea*, *Wallegatestrete* 1398 *Mont*, *Well Gate alias Well Gate Street* 1652 *ParlSurv*, *the Wallgate* 1611 *Din*, 'the road to the well', *v*. wælla, gata, alluding to the ancient town-well (Orm[2] III 740). The turn at the upper end of Church Street is *le Wynding' de Wallegate* 1370 *Mont*, *le Wending, -yng, de Wallegate* 1405, 1407 *ib*, *v*. wending 'a bend in a road'. Here also belongs *le Wallehull* 1343, 1415 Mont, *-hill* 1527 ChCert, 1584 Earw, *Walhill* 1441 ChRR (p), *Wall Hyll* 1549 ib, *the Wallhill* 1577 Orm[2], 'well hill', *v*. wælla, hyll.

WHALLEY HAYES, *the Walley Heys* 1819 Orm[2], cf. Whirleybarn *infra*, *v*. (ge)hæg.

WINDMILL ST., & *Brow* 1860 White, cf. *molendinum ventricitum de Macclesfeld* 1347 *Eyre*, *le Wyndemylneflat* E3, 1389 *AddCh*, *-flatte* 1414 *Mont*, *the Windmillfieldes, the great windmillfield* 1620 *Surv*, and *le mulneleg* c.1209 *Chol*, *le mulnefeld* E3 *Surv*, 1362 ChRR, *v*. wind-mylne, myln, lēah, feld, flat, brū, strǣt.

LOST STREET-NAMES: *viculus vocatur Botfysshlarder* 1396 *Mont*, *Botfis(s)hlarder* 1397 *ib* (from ME larder 'a larder', and the surname of William *Botfis* 1286 Court, John & William *Bottefissh*, *Bottesfisch* 1369 *Mont*, 1376 *Dow*, whose family had a house in Chestergate and this larder at the bottom of Wallgate. They were probably fishmongers; the surname means 'flat-fish', from OE *fisc* 'a fish' with ME *butte* 'a flat fish' (as in *halibut, turbot*), first recorded c.1280 NED, *butt* sb[1]); *Bullfield Lane, great & Little Bullfield* 1620 *Surv* (*v*. bula, feld, lane); *vicus vocatus le Cokschetlane* 1410 *Mont*, *Cockshute Lane* 1819 Orm[2] (off Jordangate, cf. Cockshead Fd *infra*, *v*. coccscyte, lane); *le Ded(e)strete* 1343 *Mont*, m14 *Dav*, 1439 Orm[2] ('dead street',

v. dēad, strǣt, perhaps near the churchyard); *þe Garrets* 1611 *Din* (*v.* garite);
Godiaflone 1337 *Mont, Godyaflone* 1353 *ib,* 1401 *AddCh, -lane* 1388 *Mont,
Godyaslone* 1375, 1397 *ib* (off Wallgate, 'Godiva's lane', from the OE fem.
pers.n. *Godgifu* and lane); *viculus vocatus Goselone* 1407 *ib, -lane* 1410 *ib* (off
Jordangate, 'goose lane', *v.* gōs, lane); *venella vocata Iaklane le Smyth* 1410 *ib*
('Jack the smith's lane', from the ME pers.n. *Jak(e),* a pet-form for *John*
(Reaney s.v. *Jack*), with smiδ, lane); *Kiln Street* 1611 *Din,* cf. *the Kiln in
Doglane* 1611 *ib, ortum toral'* 1379 *Mont,* tenement' *voc' Torral* (in *Jurdanes-
gate*) 1380 *Chol,* cf. *illud messuagium...cum torali meo ibidem* 1371 *Mont*
(from MedLat *toral(e)* 'a kiln', *v.* cyln); *placea Sancte Marie in Chastergate*
E1 *AddCh* ('St Mary's place in Chestergate', *v.* place); *Soutersgate* 1376
Mont, Souterslone 1376 *ib,* 1401 *AddCh, -lane, Sauterslane* 1401 *Mont,
Souterstrete* c.1414 *ib* ('cobbler's lane', *v.* sūtere, gata, lane, strǣt); *The
Townefield Lane, the Townefield* 1620 *Surv* (*v.* toun, feld, lane).

LOST BUILDINGS: *Bate Hall* 1819 Orm², 1860 White (lost by 1880 Orm² III
750; named from Humphrey *Bate,* mayor 1557, *v.* hall); *Macclesfield Castle*
(local) (*Buckyngeham howse or Buckyngeham Place* 1582 Earw, a mansion of
the dukes of Buckingham, 1446, built 1387–1410 by John de Macclesfeld,
not a castle though crenellated, *v.* Orm² III 747, Earw II 476, Sheaf³ 28 & 31
(6211, –15, 6991), cf. Castle Fd *infra*): *Gaol Tenement* 1819 Orm¹ (*geolaria*
1343 *Mont,* gaola (*de Macclesfeld*) 1350 Orm², *domibus et edificiis antiquitus
ordinatis pro Gaola de Macclesfeld* 1413 *Mont, þe Goal house* 1611 *Din,* cf. *le
Gealeberne* 1414 *Mont,* 'the gaol', 'the gaol barn', *v.* gaole, bere-ærn, *v.*
Orm² III 540, 741); *The Guildhall* 1682 Earw (*le Mothall* 1361 *Mont, the
Court-house* 1819 Orm², cf. *vi shoppae subtus Cameram aule placitorum* 1471
MinAcct, v. mothall; the moot-hall for the Halmote and Portmote courts of
Macclesfield manor and borough); *Heynhowsse* 1513 Orm² (a house in
Jordangate); *the King's Bake-house* 1819 Orm¹ (*furnus burgi* c.1260 Orm²,
crown property until 1818, still a bake-house 1819, Orm² III 365, *v.* bæc-
hūs); *Ogden Hall* 1611 *Din,* 1819 Orm¹ (a house in Chestergate, named from
Adam de *Okeden,* mayor 1428, Orm² III 750, cf. *Okedenskylne* 1513 Orm²,
v. cyln); *Pickford Hall* 1819 Orm¹ (from the family *Pickford* of Macclesfield,
Orm² III 742, *v.* hall); *Stapleton Hall* 1819 Orm¹, 1860 White (from the
family *Stapleton* of Upton, *v.* hall); *Town Well* 1819 Orm² II 741 (cf. Wallgate *supra, v.* toun, wella); *Worth Hall & Orchard* 1819 Orm¹, 1860 White
(probably from the surname from Worth 207 *infra* and hall, orceard).

BEECH BRIDGE & LANE (110–915745), 1860 White; *via que ducit ad
villam de Tydrinton* 1338 Orm², *Tytherington Road* 1860 White; (*the*)
Bach(e)lane 1620 *Surv,* cf. *le Bachebrok* E3 *AddCh, le Bache* 1337
Mont, 1373 *AddCh, -bank, -bonk* 1396, 1397 *Mont, le litil-, le lytul
Bache* 1405, 1412 *ib, le bagh'grene* 1507, 1515 *MinAcct, Baggrene* 1560
Sheaf, 'brook, bank, and green at a valley', *v.* bæce¹, brōc, banke,
grēne²: the valley and stream on the boundary of Macclesfield and
Tytherington, cf. Beech Hall 214 *infra*.

BOTHEGRENE (lost), 1503 *ChFor*, *le Bothegrene* E3 *Surv*, 1363 *ChFor et freq*, cf. (*le*) *Bothefeld* c.1301 *AddCh*, 1348 *MinAcct*, 1374 *AddCh*, *-fyld* (*lawne*) 1483 *Dow*, *le Bouthefeld* 1385 *Mont*, *le Bothesfeld* E3 *AddCh*, also *de Both, del-, de la Bo(u)the* 1286, 1287 *Eyre* (p) (at Macclesfield), 'field and green at the herdsmen's huts', *v.* bōth, grēne², feld, launde, cf. 215 *infra* and Boothgreen 181 *infra*.

BROKEN CROSS (110–893735), 1630 *AddCh, Brokencrosse* 1549 Pat, (*the*) 1573 *Surv, Brocken Crosse* 1602 *Dow*, cf. (*the*) *Brokencrosse lane, the cross lane* 1620 *Surv, v.* brocen, cros. This was at a meeting of medieval roads, cf. 45, 46, 47 *supra*.

THE FAIRESTEEDES, -STIDDES (lost), 1620 *Surv, le Fairestedes* 1360, 1414 *Mont, le Fairestudes* 1361 *Chol, le Fairesstyddes* 1462 *Dow*, 'the fair-grounds', *v.* feire, stede, styde. It was described in 1620 *Surv* as a fourteen-acre close on the west side of *the Backstreetes*. There was a pool here, *le mere super le Fairestedes* in 1360, 1361 and 1414, *v.* mere¹.

GALLOWS FIELD (lost)

> *le Galtreuehul* c.1300, *le Galtreuhull'* 1390, *le Galtrehul* 1331, *-hull* 1390, *le Galchtrehul* e14, *le galhtrehul(l)* 1312, *le Galghtreuhull'* 1371 all *Mont, Gallrey hill* 1620 *Surv*
> *le Galtreufeld* 1361 *Mont, le Galtrefeld* c.1414 *ib, Gawtry fielde(s)* 1584 *Dav*
> *Gal'tre-hey* 1555 *Orm², Gualtree hey* 1620 *Surv*
> *the Gallowes field* 1620 *Surv, Gallows Field* 1819 *Orm¹*, 1848 *TA*

'The gallows-tree hill, field and enclosure', *v.* galg-trēow, galga, hyll, feld, (ge)hæg; the place of execution of felons within the Hundred of Macclesfield.

GORSEYKNOLL (110–890735), *le Nol* 1337 *Eyre* (p), *le Gorstihull* E3 *Surv, -y-* 1384 *Rental, the Gorsty Knowle* 1620 *Surv*, 'the gorsy hillock', *v.* gorstig, hyll, cnoll.

HALLE FIELDS (lost), 1860 White, *Hallyfield* 1571 *Surv*, representing *le Hallelehe* 1240–57 *AddCh, Hallelegh* 1274 *Orm²*, (*le-*) 1384 *Rental*, (*le*) *Halleleg* c.1301 *AddCh*, Sheaf, *le Halleghe* 1355 *AddCh, le Hallegh* 1413 *Chol, le Hallee* 1369 *AddCh, le Halegh* 1487 *Chol, Hauley* 1508 *MinAcct*, 'glade at or belonging to a hall', *v.* hall, lēah, to which feld has been added. The p.n. also appears with ēg, feld, in *le Hallehee* 1356 Orm², *Halleyighfild* 1513 ib, 'the meadow-land of *Halle*'; with lēac-tūn 'an enclosed garden' in *le Hallelaghton* 1379 *Mont*; with orceard 'an orchard' in *le halle orchard* 1414 *Mont* (cf. *le ympeyorth infra*); with the form *Halegh* confused with a form of halh, halc, in the *Halecke fieldes* 1620 *Surv*. The *Halle Fields* lay between Jordangate and the R. Bollin, and belonged in part to Hurdsfield. White 1860 locates them near *Cuckstoolpit-Hill supra*.

HUNDREDFELDE (lost), 1560 Sheaf³ 24 (6463), probably the meeting-place of Macclesfield Hundred 51 *supra*, v. hundred, feld.

THE ISINGE (lost), 1620 *Surv*, *Esyng* 1274 Orm², 1467 *MinAcct*, *Hessyng'* 1467, 1471 *ib*, *Hesyng'*, *-inge* 1508 *ib*, 1560 Sheaf, *Eselyng* 1471 *MinAcct*, *Esynger* 1508 *ib*, *Esingar* 1560 Sheaf, cf. *Eyseruddynges* E3 *Surv*, *Esrudynges* 1341 *Eyre*, *Etsirudyng* 1384 *Rental*. This p.n. appears to be an -ing¹ formation upon an unidentified el., with kjarr 'marsh, brushwood', and ryding 'clearing'. The place was beside R. Bollin, adjoining *Halle Fields supra*, belonging in part to Hurds-field, at the end of a field called *Rowley* 109 *supra*, and was waste-land. The basis of the name might thus be hǣs 'brushwood'. However, Professor Löfvenberg suggests that *Esyng* 1274 may be from -ing¹ and efes, perhaps as an early instance of late-ME *ēsing* 'the eaves of a house' hence 'a roof, shelter, dwelling' (*v. easing, eavesing* NED). *Isinge* would then mean either 'the dwelling place' or, more likely, 'the place at the edge of a wood or hill'.

KNIGHT MOSSE (lost, about 110–908718), *a mosse sometyme called-* 1620 *Surv*, *Knuche* 1286 *Eyre* (Court 223 reads *Kunche* (?)), *parcum apud Knoche et Donnesmos* 1290 *ib*, *Knychmosse* 1337 *ib*, *Kneche Wode* 1347 *ib*, 'moss and wood at a hillock', v. cnwc, mos, wudu, cf. Danes Moss 67 *supra*, Moss Lane *infra*. However, Professor Löfvenberg suggests for the first el. an OE *cnycce* 'hillock' (a derivative of cnocc²), as suiting the spellings better than cnwc. This interpretation invites the withdrawal of this p.n. from the list of Celtic names in Ch in LCHS 119 (1967), 27.

LONGMOSS (110–887741), 1831 Bry, *le Snythelymor* E3 *Surv*, 1384 *Rental*, (*le Newefeld inter bundas foreste et le Park de Maclesfeld vocat'*) *Smetheleyemore* 1363 *ChFor*, *the longe mosse once called Smithley*

Moore 1620 *Surv, Long Mosse* 1652 *ParlSurv*, 'the moor at the cut-off clearing', from sniþ and lēah, with mōr[1], later 'the long moss', *v.* lang, mos. The place appears to have been a detached area outside the lands of the park but not in the surrounding Forest. The older name preserves an instance of the rare ME *sniþ* adj. 'cut off', from ME *sniðen* 'to cut' (*v. snithe* NED), cf. 'þat sniþ hill', *Alexander* 4095, a fifteenth-century text. This has been confused with the more common smēðe 'smooth'. Cf. Snidley Moor 334 *infra*.

MACCLESFIELD PARK (lost, 110–9072)

    (park and vivaries of Macclesfeld otherwise called) *Wilwhich* H3 Orm[2], (*boscus de*) *Wilwhik* 1217–32 ib, 1353 ib, *Wil(e)wic(h)* c.1217–32 ib, (1348) *MinAcct, Wyl(e)wick, -w(h)yk(e)* 13 Sheaf, 1358 *et freq MinAcct, Willewik'* 1348 *ib, Wilwick* 1353 Orm[2], *parcum de Whilwich* 1383 ib, *Wilwich Wood* n.d. Orm[2] III 63

    Weuerwick c.1217–29 (1499) Sheaf

    Fellewhycch 1384 *Rental*

    Welbecke 1560 Sheaf

    parcum de Makefeld, parcarius de Maclesfeld 1237 P *et freq* with spellings as for Macclesfield *supra, parcum de Macclesfelde Welbecke* 1560 Sheaf, *le Park de Maclesfeld* 1363 *ChFor, Macclesfields Parke* 1548 Sheaf, *Macclesf(i)eld-, Maxfeld Parck, -Parke* 1599 Orm[2], 1602 *Chol*, 1620 *Surv*

'Hamlet at a trap', *v.* wīl, wīc, later 'Macclesfield park', *v.* park. The royal park eventually included a large tract in the south-west of the township, cf. Ivyholme, Parkbrook, Park End, House, Mount, -side & -vale, and Parkett Heyes *infra*, Park Green & Lane *supra*. The location of *Wil(e)wic(h)* within it is not known. The place was imparked between 1217 and 1232, *v.* Orm[2] III 62, 742, Sheaf[3] 30 (6578). The *wīl* was probably a deer- or game trap, cf. Studies[2] 157, EPN II s.v. wīl, cf. also *Wileford* 328 *infra*.

ROEWOODS (110–887743), LOWER ROEWOOD, *le Rowode* (*de Macclesfeld*) E3 *Surv*, 1358 *MinAcct*, 1385 *Mont, Rowe Woods* 1578 Orm[2], *the (great) Roewoods, the Roewoode crofte* 1620 *Surv*, 'the rough wood(s)', *v.* rūh, wudu.

SWILLINDITCH (lost), 1848 *TA, le Swylcontdich* 1396 *Mont, Swylecunt dyche* 1397 *ib, Swilkontdyche* 1402 *ib, the Swilckhorne ditch* 1620 *Surv* (one acre arable near Broken Cross *supra*), from ME *swilen* (OE *swillan, swilian*) 'to wash, to swill' (cf. swiling WRY 7 254) and c(o)unte 'the female private parts', with dīc 'a ditch'. This was the name of a watercourse, probably part of the stream at Parkbrook *infra*. It is not clear whether the allusion is to custom or topography. Cf. *Shauecuntewelle* K 101, from ME *schaven* (OE *scafan*) 'to shave, to scrape', with wella 'a stream, a spring', where the allusion may be to the flinty bed of the stream. *Cuntelowe* Db 405 and Cunliffe La 73 are from c(o)unte and hlāw 'a mound, a hill', and clif 'a cliff', probably describing hills with clefts or caves in them, cf. *Cundeclif* 331 *infra*.

WATERS (GREEN), 1860 White, *Water* 1554 *Dow*, *(the) Waters* 1611 *Din*, 1614 *Dow*, from *aqua currens subtus villam de Macclesfeld* 1330 *Mont, torrens sub ecclesiam* 1363 *ib, aqua vocat' le Hee* 1359 *Dow, -le E siue Bolyne* 1414 *ib, Macclesfeldey* 1467 *MinAcct, aqua de Maccles-feld* 1508 *ib, the water (of Macclesfeld), Macclesfeld water* 1620 *Surv*, referring to R. Bollin 15 *supra*, v. wæter, grēne², ēa, cf. The Eyes 109 *supra*, Watercotes *infra*.

WHIRLEYBARN, WHIRLEY COTTAGES, GROVE & RD, *Whelley Com-(m)on(s)* 1620 *Surv*, 1652 *ParlSurv, Whelley Lane* 1620 *Surv*, cf. *Qwellegh* E3 *ib*, 1347 *Eyre, Welley* 1341 *ib, Whelley* 1415 Sheaf, 1417 ChRR *freq*, cf. Whalley Hayes st.n. *supra*, from hwēol 'a wheel', lēah 'a clearing', though the significance is not known, cf. Well-trough 89 *supra*. Whirleybarn was *Common Farm* 1831 Bry. Whirley Grove was *End of Whirley* 1831 ib. The modern forms arise from confusion with Whirley 101 *supra*.

BACKLANE HO, *Back Lane Farm* 1842 OS, from *Back Lane* 1831 Bry, now Birtles Road *infra*, cf. Fallibroome Rd, Westend Ho *infra*. The earlier name was *Saltpye House* 1831 ib, either from its having only one slope to its roof, or from its being a back-to-back structure, v. salt-pie, cf. Salt Pie 157 *infra*. BARRACKS LANE, cf. *Barracks* 1831 ib. BIRTLES RD, cf. Backlane Ho *supra*, Birtles 72 *supra*. BLACK SPRING, a well. BLAKELOW RD, LOWER BLAKELOW, v. Blakelow 153 *infra*. BOLLINGTON BARN, 1831 Bry, 'barn belonging to Bollington', cf. Bollington Ho 97 *supra*, Bollington 187 *infra*. BOSTOCK FM, 1831 ib. BOUGHEY LANE, 1831 ib. BOWDENDOWN, *Boden Hall* 1831 ib. BROADCAR RD, v. Broadcar

153 *infra*. BROOKSIDE, near a stream. BUXTON RD, 1860 White, leading to Buxton Db. CHANGING HO, *Toll Gate* 1842 OS. CHELFORD RD, *the lane leadinge to Henbury* 1620 *Surv*, cf. Chelford, Henbury 75, 78 *supra*. THE COTTAGE, 1831 Bry. CROMPTON BARRACKS & RD, *Crompton (Road)* 1860 White. CROOKEDYARD RD, cf. *Crooked Yard* 1848 *TA*, *v.* Crookedyard 127 *infra*. EDDIS-BURY FM, GATE & HALL, cf. *Eddisbury Close & Park* 1848 *ib*, *v.* Eddisbury Hill 139 *infra*. FALLIBROOME RD, *Back Lane* 1860 White, cf. Backlane Ho *supra*. FIELD BANK, 1831 Bry. FOREST RD, on the boundary with Macclesfield Forest 125 *infra*. GAWS-WORTH RD, from Broken Cross *supra* to Gawsworth, part of the perambulation of the Forest of Macclesfield 10 *supra*. HALFWAY HO, half-way to Broken Cross *supra*. HEYWOOD. HILL TOP. HOBSON'S POOL. HOLLYBANK FM. IVYBANK, *Potts Farm* 1842 OS, from the local surname *Pott*, cf. Pott Hall 130 *infra*. IVY COTTAGE FM, *Stacks Farm* 1842 ib. IVYHOLME, *Park Cottage* 1831 Bry, *Park Side Cottage* 1842 OS, from *Macclesfield Park supra*, cf, IVY HO, 1842 ib, IVY LANE & RD, IVYMEADE, all near Ivyholme within the old park. KNIGHT'S POOL, a mill-lodge. KNOWSLEY BOWER, *Knowsley Barn* 1831 Bry, *Knowsley Bank* 1842 OS, *v.* banke, bere-ærn, būr[1], perhaps named after Knowsley La 113, by connection with the earls of Derby. LARK HALL, 1831 Bry. LEAD-BEATERS COTTAGE & RESERVOIR, cf. *Leadbeater's Lane* 1860 White, from the surname *Leadbeater*. LIMEFIELD. LOWER HEYS MILL, cf. *the Lower Hayes* 1860 ib, partly in Tytherington 215 *infra*, cf. *Mill Street supra*. MACCLESFIELD COMMON, 1620 *Surv*. MEG LANE, near Broken Cross *supra*, *v.* meg, lane, cf. Fernlee 149 *infra*. MILE COTTAGE, one mile from the town. MILL GREEN & LANE, *Mill Green* 1860 White, from *Macclesfield Mills* 150 *infra*, *v.* myln, grēne[2], lane. MOSS LANE, cf. *le Littelmosse* E3 *AddCh*, *le Mos* 1373 ib, *la mosse de Macclesf'* 1351 *Eyre*, near Danes Moss 67 *supra* and *Knight Mosse supra*, *v.* lȳtel, mos. MOSS WELL, from Longmoss *supra*. THE MOUNT. PARKBROOK, 1831 Bry, near a stream running out of *Macclesfield Park supra*, cf. *Swillinditch supra*. PARK HO, 1831 ib, from Ryles Park *infra*. PARKEND (*v.* ende[1]), PARK MOUNT (1842 OS, *Mount Pleasant* 1831 Bry), PARKSIDE (COTTAGE) (1842 OS, *Sweetfield or Park Side* 1831 Bry, *v.* sīde), PARKVALE, and PARKETT HEYES (*le Park(e)hede* 1396 *Mont*, *the Parked Hey* 1620 *Surv*, '(the enclosure(s) at) the top end of the park', *v.* hēafod, (ge)hæg), are all named from *Macclesfield Park*

supra, *v.* park.   PEXHILL RD, from Broken Cross to Pexall 78
supra.   PIT HOUSES.   POT BROW (lost), 1831 Bry, *v.* brū.
PRESTBURY RD, 1860 White, *the lane goeinge to Vpton, Whitefield
Lane* 1620 *Surv*, cf. Upton, Whitfield 216 *infra*.   PUMP TREE,
Pump House 1831 Bry.   ROBINHOOD, 1842 OS.   RULOW KNOB,
1842 ib, *Rawley* 1560 Sheaf, *Ruley broocke(ford)*, *-Broucke* 1611
LRMB 200, *Rulie Brooke* 1620 *Surv*, 'the rough clearing', from rūh
and lēah, with brōc, ford, knob.   RYLES PARK (FM), RYLE'S POOL,
from the local surname *Ryle*.   SADDLER'S WAY, *Sadlers Lane* 1831
Bry, cf. *Sadlers Waye Heade* 1611 *LRMB*, 1620 *Surv*, 'the (top of
the) saddler's road', *v.* sadelere, weg, hēafod; perhaps an old pack-
horse road into Macclesfield Forest.   SALTBOX.   SANDY LANE.
SEPRAM, *v.* 128 *infra*.   SPRING COTTAGE, 1831 Bry.   SWINES-
PARK, cf. *Lower Swine Park* 1848 *TA*.   SYCAMOREHILL, *Tan Yard*
1831 Bry.   TEGGSNOSE FM, GATE & LANE, *Teggsnose Farm* 1842
OS, from Tegg's Nose 152 *infra*.   THORNLIEBANK.   UNS-
WORTH FOLD, from the surname *Unsworth* and fald.   WADWORTH'S
FM.   WATERCOTES, *the watercoates* 1620 *Surv*, *land in Macclesfeld
neghe to the runninge water there* 1571 (1620) *ib*, 'huts by the water',
v. wæter, cot, cf. Waters (Green) *supra*.   WESTBROOK HO, 1831
Bry, from Whitfield Brook *infra*.   WESTEND HO, *Back House* 1842
OS, cf. Back Lane Ho *supra*.   WHITFIELD BROOK, *v.* Whitfield 216
infra.   WINDYWAY HO (110–951733), 1831 Bry, cf. *the foote of the
Windiewaie* 1620 *Surv*, *v.* Windywayhead 145 *infra*.

FIELD-NAMES

The undated forms are 1848 *TA* 246. Of the others, 1286, 1290, 1350, 1361[1]
are *Eyre*, l13, c.1301, e14, E3[2], 1373 *AddCh*, 1322 (17), 1323[1], 1347, 1359,
1361[2], 1375, 1483, 1686 *Dow*, 1323[2], 1377, 1380, 1487, 1494 *Chol*, E3, 1620
Surv, 1217–32, 1338, 1430, 1555, 1565, 1819 *Orm*[2], 1349, 1358, 1467, 1471,
1507, 1508, 1515 *MinAcct*, 1357[2], 1363 *ChFor*, 1398, 1400, 1408, 1439, 1454
ChRR, 1453 (17), 1560 Sheaf, 1549 Pat, 1584 *Dav*, 1611 *LRMB* 200, and
the rest *Mont*.

(a) Ash Mdw; Big Brow (*v.* brū); Birtles Croft (cf. Birtles 72 *supra*);
Castle Fd 1819 (*Orm*[2] III 742, 'a place called the Castle Field, which was
probably the site of the local palace of the earls of Chester. In this a circular
mount or tumulus is still remaining', *v.* castel(l), cf. *Macclesfield Castle
supra*); Cockshead Fd (*le Cocsude* l13, *le Cokschete* c.1301, *the Coks(c)hute*
1322 (17), 1323, *-shote* E3, *the Cockshoot* 1611, *-shutt* 1620, *a field and lane
called Cockshute-lane* 1819, *v.* cocc-scyte, cf. *le Cokschetlane supra*); Far Fd
(1686); Fountain Dale; Frog Hill; Hollow Mdw; Horse Hey (*the horse haies*,

the horsehey crofte & head 1620); Jacket Heys; Ley Pasture; Lindop Fd; Muck Ridding (*Michel-, Muchelryding, -yng* 1363, *Michil Riddyng* 1430, *Mychell Ryddinges alias Calves Croftes* 1584, *Much Ridinges* 1620, cf. *les Rydinges, les Ryd(d)ynges* 1376, 1414, 'the (big) clearing(s)', *v.* micel, mycel, ryding); Rock Fd; Roe Fd; Rushy Fd; Tower Fd; Trinity Dole (*Trintie Dole* 1620, *le Trinite acre* 1414, probably associated with the chantry of Holy Trinity in Macclesfield church, Orm² III 752, first mentioned 1361 *Mont, v.* dāl, æcer).

(b) *Alysandrebanke* c.1330, *Alisandre(s)bonk* 1396, 1397, *Alysondresbonke* 1347, *Alissondurbank* 1359, *Alyson Durbank* 1361², *Alisondrebonk* 1397, *Alexander bancke* 1620 ('Alexander's hillside', from the ME pers.n. *Alexander* and banke, cf. *Sanderpingate* 109 *supra*); *Ashton Crofte* (*v. Hulleacre infra*); *Baillebut* 1471, *the Bayliffe buttes* 1620 ('the bailiff's strips of land', *v.* baillie, butte, perhaps identical with *terra Thome le Bailly* c.1330, named from Thomas de Macclesfield, clerk, bailiff of Macclesfield c.1280–1300 *Dow*, cf. Bailey Ridding 67 *supra*); *(the) Barkers Crofte & landes* 1620 ('the tanner's croft & plots', cf. *William le Barker de Macclesfield* 1323¹ and *unum Barkhous* 1350, 'a tan house', *v.* bark-hous); *the Barlie Crofte* 1620; *the Barnecrofte* 1620; *Birchfield* 1620; *Blagge Crofte* 1620 (from the surname *Blagg(e)*, common in Macclesfield, and croft, cf. *curtilagium Stephani Blagge* 1411); *le Blake Erthe* 1375 (*v.* blæc,erð or eorð); *Mosse Croft alias Blackleyes Croft alias Blacklach Croft alias Blackledge Croft* 1584, *Blacklach crofte, the Blacklech fieldes* 1620 ('the black bog', *v.* blæc, læc(c); near Longmoss *supra*); *Bukstall, -es* 1467, 1471, *Buckstall, Buckliffe alias-* 1620 ('(cliff at) the buck stall', *v.* buck-stall, clif, cf. Buxtorstoops 142 *infra*); *Cartelache* c.1301 ('boggy stream in stony ground', *v.* kartr, læc(c), cf. *Cartelache* 17 *supra*); *Clapam fields* 1620; *Cocke crofte* 1620 (*v.* cocc²); *the Crosse Crofte, the Crossefield* 1620 (cf. Broken Cross *supra, v.* cros); *le Daleacr(e)* 1357, 1361³, 1390, *Dale Aker, -Acre* 1611, 1620 (*v.* dæl¹, æcer); *le Dodeforde* 1286 (p) (Court 216 reads *-Rode-*), *Dotteford* 1467, 1471, *Datesford* 1560 ('Dodda's ford', from the OE pers.n. *Dodda* and ford, cf. Dodford Nth 20); *Edusecros* c.1301 ('Edus's cross', from cros and the eME fem. pers.n. *Edus*, a short form for an OE fem. pers.n. in *Ēad-*, cf. Reaney s.v. *Edis*); *the fower acre* 1620; *furbachcarr* 1620 (*v.* Thursbitch 141 *infra*); *Gee Crofte* 1620 (*v.* gee); *Gilburne crofte* 1620: *le Goselegh'* 1414 ('goose clearing', *v.* gōs, lēah); *Gorstie crofte & field* 1620 (*v.* gorstig); *greene boothes* 1620 (*v.* grēne¹, bōth); *le Hallclogh* E3 (*v.* hall, clōh); *Harpers Crofte* 1620; *Harrie-, the Harry crofte* 1611, 1620 (*v.* harwe 'a harrow'); *hefermidding* 1483 ('heifer midden', *v.* hēah-fore, midding); *Haydepole* 1467, *Hadepole* 1471, 1508, 1560, *-pule* 1560 (*v.* pōl¹ 'a pool'. The first el. may be hēafod but Professor Löfvenberg suggests OE *hegod*, pa. part. of *hegian* 'to fence in', cf. NED s.v. *hay, v.* 2); *le hengyngacre* E3, *the henging Acre* 1620 ('the hanging acre', *v.* hengjandi, æcer); *Hulleacre* 1338, *the Ashton Crofte bounding upon the Bach lane sometimes called the Hull Acre* 1620 ('hill acre', *v.* hyll, æcer; located, 1338, in the angle between Beech Lane *supra* and Mill Street *supra* about the top of Hibel Rd *supra*); *le hursted iuxta le ympʒort* 1414, *the Hursteed* 1620 (probably 'place at a wooded hill', from hyrst and stede); (*H*)*Ysebelesbathes*

1217–32, *Yssbellebothis* c.1301, *Isbellisbothis* e14 ('Isabella's booths', from bōth and the ME fem. pers.n. *Isabel(la)*); *Jackecroftes* 1620 ('little crofts', *v.* jack, croft); *Knoll copyes* 1565 (*v.* cnoll, copis); *le ladybryg* 1363 (*v.* hlǣfdige, brycg; a bound of Gawsworth, 71 *supra*); *Lethenardishustudes* 1290, *-hustes* 1347 ('Lethenhard's house-sites', from hūs-stede, -styde, with a pers.n. *Lethen(h)ard*, *v. Lethenhardesheye* 332 *infra*); *Le Longehalfacre* c.1301, *le longeacre* 1414, *the Longe Acre* 1620; *the Longelandes once Handfordes landes* 1620 (*v.* land); *the longeshutt* 1620 (*v.* scēat); *Margeriesmedewe* 1332, *-medowe* 1414, *Margerie meadowe* 1620 (from the ME (OFr) fem. pers.n. *Margerie* and mǣd); *the merled Crofte & earth* 1620 (*v.* marlede, croft, eorðe); *le mydulfeld* 1401 (*v.* middel, feld); *the Milne pipe* 1620 (a conduit, *v.* myln, pīpe); *a mosse sometyme called Millistons mosse* 1620 (*v.* mylen-stān, mos); *Nachomaresforlong* c.1312, *Naght(e)mar(e)furlonge*, *-forlong* 1393, 1397, 1402, *the Nightmare furlonge* 1620 (a troublesome or a haunted field, *v.* niht-mare (Angl. nǣht-), furlang); *le Newefeld* E3², *the Newfield* 1620; *the Oatefield* (*v. Vernon's ground infra*); *Off(e)nomes* 1358, 1414 (cf. *ofnome* 1323 *Dow* 37, *v.* af-nám); *the Owlers* 1620 (*v.* alor); *Pekokkes acre* 1414, *the Peacocke acre* 1620 (cf. Hugh *Pecok* 1286 Court, *v.* æcer); *Pecude-clyf* 1373, *le Pyckedhull* 1405, *le Pykkedhull* 1412, *le pycket-*, *pickethill* 1487, 1494, *greate pykehill*, *lyte pyckhill alias pyked hill croft* 1584, *the great Pickhead Hills*, *the little Pickhills*, *the Pickhead Croftes*, *the Picked Hole* 1620 ('the pointed cliff and hills', *v.* piked, clif, hyll; located 1412 *Mont* f.143d near Beech Lane *supra*); *Pilatecrofte* 1349 ('pill-oats croft', *v.* pīl-āte); *Pimlott Crofte* 1620; *the Plumme Crofte* 1620; *le Qu-*, *Whakandlowe* 1390 ('the quaking mound' *v.* cwakande, hlāw); *the Ramsell* 1620; *the Rough copyes* 1565 (*v.* copis); *the Sandy Crofte* 1620; *(le)Schelebrod(e)* 1359², 1362, *Scholebrode* 1414 ('the shovel's-breadth', *v.* scofl-brǣdu, cf. Db 717 and *Schowe Broade* 217 *infra*); *Stubbes bancke*, *Stubbses* 1620 (from stubb 'a stub, a tree-stump' and banke, cf. Stubs-End 68 *supra*); *The Tenter banke* 1549 (*v.* tentour, banke); *Thurbatchker* 1620 (*v.* Thursbitch 141 *infra*); *Tilacre* 1584, *Till Acre* 1620 (from dial. *till* 'poor soil, clay'); *le Turfmos* c.1300, *parcum vocat' turfmosse* 1357², *Turfmos* 1398 (p), ('peat moss', *v.* turf (cf. MedLat *turbaria* 'a peat cutting'), mos); *Vernon's ground* 1453 (17), *the Oatefield sometymes Vernons field* 1620 (from the surname *Vernon* and grund, also 'oat-field', *v.* āte); *the wall crofte* 1620 (from wall 'a wall' or wælla 'a well, a spring'); *the well hey* 1620 (*v.* (ge)hæg); *le Whetecroft* 1375 (*v.* hwǣte, croft); *Wofull Bower* 1620 ('cheerless shelter', *v.* woful, būr¹); *le ympeyorth* 1323, *-yord* 1400, *-e* 1439, *le ympȝort* 1414, *le yempeyorde* 1467, *-yerd* 1471 ('the nursery', *v.* impe-ȝard; alluding either to *le halle orchard* 1414 (*v. Halle Fields supra*), or to *pomerium quondam magistri Jordani de Macclesfeld'* 1379, 'the orchard which was formerly Mr Jordan de Maccles-field's').

4. MACCLESFIELD FOREST (110–9772)

    (la) Forest(a) de Macclesfeld, *-felt* 1337, 1345, 1347 *Eyre*, *Maccles-feld Forest* 1439 ChRR, *Maxfield Forest* 1656 Orm²

the severall Forrest 1611 *LRMB* 200, 1620 *Surv*
(*Macclesfield cum*) *le Forest* 1724 NotCestr, *Forest or Macclesfield le Forest* 1819 Orm²
Chapel in Forest 1724 NotCestr, (*Macclesfield*) *Forest Chapel* 1842 OS, 1848 *TA*

This township is the nucleus of the extensive Forest of Macclesfield 9 *supra*, cf. *Old Chamber infra*. The forms refer to the township as distinct from the forest, but some quoted under the forest-name may also refer to the township. The chapel became St Stephen's Church, *v.* ChetOS VIII 289, Orm² III 770.

ANKERS KNOWL (LANE) (110–975739), *Anchors* 1831 Bry, *Ankers Knoll* 1848 *TA*, cf. *del Ancres, -Hankeres, -Ankres* 1325, 1329 *Dow* (p), 'hermit's hillock', *v.* ancra, cnoll. There must have been a hermitage hereabouts, or land endowed, cf. Chantry Mdw *infra*.

BROOMYCROFTHEAD (110–985720), 1842 OS, (*le*) *Bromicroft* 1286 *Eyre*, (*in foresta*) 1347 *ib*, *le Bromycroft* 1357 ChFor, *Bromecroft* (*Water*) 1503 *ib*, *Broomy Croft* 1611 *LRMB* 200, '(hill and stream at) the broomy croft', from brōmig and croft, with hēafod, wæter. The water is Clough Brook 19 *supra*. The hill is Torgate Hill *infra*.

COOMBS (110–968707), 1842 OS, *cumbas foreste* 1291 Cl, *chacea del Combes in foreste de Macclesfeud* 1294 Ipm, *le Combes* 1355 *Eyre*, *haia del Coumbe(s)* 1303, 1304 Chamb, (*le*) *Coumbes* 1337 *Eyre*, (*les-*) 1388 ChRR, *la Coumbe* 1347 BPR, *lez Cowmbes* 1523 ChRR, 'the valleys', *v.* cumb, cf. (*le*) *Blak(e) Combes* 1503 ChFor, *the blacke-, the whyte Combs* 1611 *LRMB* 200, 'the dark (or fertile) and the white (or poor) parts of Coombs', *v.* blæc, hwīt.

DIMPLES, 1611 *LRMB* 200, *le(s) Dymples* 1357 ChFor, 1384 *Rental*, *Dimpus* 1831 Bry, 'the hollows', *v.* dimple.

HARDINGLAND (110–957725), *-s* 1831 Bry, *Ardingisbothe* 1286 *Eyre* (p), *Hard-, Herdyngesbothe(s)* 1357 ChFor (p), 1362 *Eyre* (p) 'Hearding's herdsman's-hut', from the OE pers.n. *Hearding* and bōth, cf. Hardings 154 *infra*.

OLD CHAMBER (lost, 110–973718), 1848 *TA*, *Chamber* 1831 Bry. This was *the newe Chamber* 1611 *LRMB* 200, *the Chamber in the Forest* c.1620 Orm², replacing *camera foreste infra Forestam de Macclesfeld* 1374 *MinAcct, le Chaumbre in Foresta* 1357 *ChFor, Oldechambre infra Forest'* 1503 *ib, the olde Chamber* 1611 *LRMB* 200, 'the little house, the lodging', *v.* chambre 'a room, an office' (MedLat *camera*), ald, nīwe, cf. Eddisbury 331 *infra*. This place was the chief hunting station of the forest, cf. the adjacent Toot Hill *infra*. Cf. Chamber Fm Db 159.

TOOT HILL (110–971718), 1831 Bry, 'look-out hill', *v.* tōt-hyll. Orm² III 770 refers to earthworks on top of it. The summit commands a view of the chief ranges of the forest hills, and it was probably used as a look-out by the foresters of Macclesfield at *Old Chamber supra*.

ASHTREETOP.   HIGHER & LOWER BALLGREAVE (110–9774), -*Baldgreave* 1831 Bry, *Ball Greave, Lower House* 1842 OS, perhaps 'beacon wood', from bēl¹ or ON bál and grǣfe.   BOTTOM OF THE OVEN, 1831 Bry, *v.* ofen 'an oven', the deep valley at 110–980725.   BRICKKILN WOOD, *Brick Kiln* 1848 *TA*.   BROCK LOW, *Brook Low, Brocklow Field* 1848 *ib*, 'badger hillock', *v.* brocc, hlāw.   BROOK BOTTOM (lost), & BROOKHOUSE, 1831 Bry, named from an affluent of Tor Brook *infra*, *v.* botm.   BUXTORS HILL, *Buxters* 1848 *TA*, probably 'buck-stall hill', *v.* buck-stall, cf. Buxtorstoops 142 *infra*.   CHAPEL HOUSE FM, cf. Macclesfield Forest *supra*.   CHARITY LANE, 1831 Bry.   CHEST HOLLOW (110–993720), *Holechestes* 1503 *ChFor*, adjoining *New & Old Chess* 1831 Bry, cf. *New Chess* 160 *infra*, 'disputed lands in a hollow' later '(hollow at) the disputed land' *v.* hol², ceast, holh. This is the boundary between Macclesfield Forest and Wildboarclough.   CLOUGH HO, 1848 *TA*, cf. *Cowclough(e) hedge* 1611 *LRMB* 200, 1620 *Surv*, '(hedge & house at) the cows' valley', *v.* cū, clōh, hecg, hūs.   CROOKEDYARD (110–953727), 1831 Bry, *le Crokedyorde* 1503 *ChFor, the Cro(o)ked yord* 1611 *LRMB* 200 (f.164, 'where a whicken tree did stand which was the ancient meere between Ranow and Sutton'), 'the crooked enclosure', *v.* croked, geard. This place is where Rainow, Macclesfield Forest and Sutton township used to meet.   DERBY ARMS (p.h.), *v.* Greenways *infra*.   DIRTY GATE, 1831 Bry, 'dirty road', *v*, gata.   FERRISER, 1831 *ib*, *Ferrisaw* 1848 *TA*.   FIELDHEAD, 1831 Bry, *Field House* 1842 OS, *v.* hēafod.   FOREST BARN (lost, 101–975750), 1831 Bry, on the Rainow boundary.   FOREST RD, on the Macclesfield boundary.   FOREST SMITHY, cf. *Smithy Field* 1848 *TA*.   FOX STAKE, 1848 *ib*.

GREENWAYS, 1842 OS, perhaps *the greene gate head* 1611 *LRMB* 200, and cf. *Grenewey* 1365 BPR (p), -*way* 1446 ChRR (p), *v.* grēne[1], weg, gata, hēafod. The place is mistakenly labelled *White Hill* by Bryant, presumably instead of *Isle of Man*, his name for Whitehills (*infra*). The *Isle of Man* would allude to the three-legs coat of arms of the earls of Derby, Lords of Man, principal lords here (cf. Derby Arms *supra*). The Downes family held lands in free forestership by service of holding their lord's (the earl of Derby's) stirrup and blowing a horn at Midsummer's Day at *the greene gate head* (*LRMB* 200). *Grenewey* would be the route from Macclesfield to Buxton Db, cf. 45 *supra*.   HACKED WAY LANE.   HAINCLOUGH, *Hinesclough* 1831 Bry, *v.* hine, clōh.   HIGHER & LOWER HOLLINTONGUE, *Hollin Tongue* 1831 ib, *Higher & Lower-* 1842 OS, 'tongue of land at a holly-tree', *v.* holegn, tunge.   HOOLEYHEY LANE, *Hooley Hey Pasture* 1842 ib, leading to Hooleyhey Fm 139 *infra*.   THE LACHES, LACHE GATE, BOTTOM OF THE LACHES, *Lache Gate, Bottom of the Leach* 1831 Bry, (*Bottom of*) *The Laches* 1842 OS, perhaps connected with *Lech* 1286 Court (p), *la Lache* 1287 *Eyre* (p), *Laches* 1339 Pat (p), *v.* læc(c) 'a boggy place', gata, botm.   LONG CLOUGH, 1783 Orm[2], *v.* clōh.   PARTING-GAP, 1831 Bry, perhaps the site of a deer-leap, or a sheep gate, *v.* gap.   PLATTING, 1831 ib, *v.* platting 'a foot-bridge'.   SEPRAM, 1842 OS, *Seprom* 1831 Bry, now Five Ashes (110–954729).   SHINING TOR, 1831 ib, 'bright rocks', *v.* scīnende, torr; cf. Tor Brook *infra*.   STAKE, 1831 ib, *v.* staca 'a stake', perhaps named from some post marking the Taxal boundary, cf. Stake Clough & Side 174 *infra*.   STANDING STONE (lost, 110–979715), 1842 OS, *Standingstone Side* 1831 Bry, cf. *Stondynstonsiche* 1357 ChFor, '(hill-side and water-course at) the standing-stone', *v.* standende, stān, sīde, sīc. The name was taken from a cross-slab standing-stone at 110–977713.   STONWAY (110–997726), -(*Toll Gate*) 1842 OS, *Stoneyway* 1831 Bry, *v.* stān(ig), weg. This is on the old Macclesfield–Buxton turnpike, and is a road-name for route XV 45 *supra*.   TOR BROOK, (Clough Brook 19 *supra*), cf. *Torbroc* 113 Dav (p), named from its source at Shining Tor *supra*, *v.* torr, brōc.   TORGATE (HILL), *Torgate* 1842 OS, 'cattle-walk at a rocky hill' *v.* torr, gata, cf. Broomycrofthead *supra*.   TRENTABANK (WOOD), *Tenter Bank (Lane)* 1831 Bry, *Trentabank* 1848 TA, 'drying-frame bank', *v.* tentour.   TUPCLOSE, 1831 Bry, *v.* tup, clos.   TURNSHAW FLAT, 1842 OS, *Turnshay Plat* 1831 Bry, *Turneshagh* 1503 ChFor, '(plot of land at) the round copse', *v.* trun,

sc(e)aga, plat², flat. TWELVEASHES, 1848 *TA*. WARRILOWHEAD,
1842 OS, *Werselowe* 1361 *Eyre, Warleighe* 1560 Sheaf³ 24 (5467),
perhaps 'felon's-, outlaw's mound', from wearg and hlāw, with
hēafod 'a hill, the head or top (end) of something'. WHITEHILLS
1842 OS, cf. Greenways *supra, v.* hwīt, hyll. WILDMOORBANK
HOLLOW, 1842 ib, *Wildmoorbank* 1831 Bry, -(*End*), *Wild Moss Bank*
1848 *TA, v.* wilde, mōr¹, mos, banke, holh, ende¹. WINCHALL-
TOP, *Starve House* 1831 Bry, *v.* topp, cf. foll. WHINSHAW, 1831
ib, 'gorse copse', *v.* whin, sceaga.

FIELD-NAMES

The undated forms are 1848 *TA* 247. Of the others, 1289 (17) is Court,
1318 City, 1357, 1503 *ChFor*, 1352, 1365 *Eyre*, 1384 *Rental*, 1487 Plea, 1528,
1542 ChRR, 1611 *LRMB* 200, 1831 Bry.

(a) The Acre, Acre Brow; Back Fd; Bailey Knoll (*v.* baillie, cnoll); Bank;
Bare Fd; Barley Croft & Knoll; Barn Fd; Bendiways Close; Bent (*v.*
beonet); Bolsters (cf. *del Bolastre* 1365, 'elder tree(s)', *v.* bolas, trēow);
Bottoms (*v.* botm); Brows (*v.* brū); Brushy Bank; Butts; Cadledock Fd
(*v.* keddle-dock); Calf Fd; Carthouse Mdw; Chantry Mdw (*v.* chaunterie 'a
chantry', cf. Ankers Knowl *supra*); Cockerill (perhaps 'cocker's hill', *v.*
cocker, hyll); Common Ling (*v.* lyng); Coney Greaves (*v.* coninger); Corn
Croft; Cote Fd and Mdw (*v.* cot); Crabtree Fd; Crook Fd (*v.* krókr); Day
Math ('a day's mowing', *v.* day-math); Dirty Fd & Place; Dog Kennels;
Door Croft (*v.* duru); Dry Knoll; Hollow Ellislack (*Elleslack* 1831, perhaps
Ellehale 1289 (17) (p), *-hale* 1318 (p), *Elhale* 1352, perhaps 'Ella's hollow',
from the OE pers.n. *Ella* (*Ælla*) and halh, slakki, with holh, but the first el.
may be elle 'elder-tree', cf. Ellis Bank 133 *infra*); Essmond Fd; Face Fd;
Fallow; Flat Haddon (perhaps 'heath-hill' with the adj. 'flat' affixed, *v.* hǣð,
dūn, flatr); Forest Side, Forests; Foster Butts ('the forester's strips',
v. forester, butte); Frank Fd; Gorsey Brow, Fd & Knoll; Gorseys (probably
'gorse enclosures', *v.* gorst, (ge)hæg); Grains (*v.* grein); Green Brow &
Knoll; Half Acre; Hambletons Torr or Fern Beds (*v.* torr, fearn, bedd, cf.
Hommerton 167 *infra*); Hang Fd; Harts Edge, Hartsfood Fd (these may
contain heorot 'a hart, a stag', with ecg, fōt); Hay Fd; Haywood Ground;
Heathy Torr (*v.* hǣðig, torr); Hole Fd; Holt Ley (*v.* holt, lēah); House Fd;
Intake; Jack Fd (*v.* jack); Knoll (*freq, v.* cnoll); Leys (*v.* lēah); Lime Close
& Fd; Long Butts; Marled Earth (*v.* marlede, eorðe); Mankin Croft,
Mawkin, -Holes (*v.* NED s.n. *malkin* 'a hare', *v.* hol¹); Milking Knoll
('hillock where cows are milked', *v.* milking, cnoll); New Fd, Ground, Mdw
& Piece; Old Close, Fd & Mdw; Oliver Piece; Orme Fd (from the east-
Cheshire surname *Orme*); Outlet (*v.* outlet); Park (*novum parcum (de foreste)
de Macclesfeld* 1487, 1528, 1542, *v.* nīwe, park, cf. *Macclesfield Park* 120
supra); Patch, -Brow; Pinfold (*v.* pynd-fald); Pingot (*v.* pingot); Pot Mdw;
Rainslow; Red Scarr ('red cliff', *v.* rēad, sker); Rough Fd 1831; Rushy Fd;

Saddle Cote ('hut in the dip in the ridge', *v.* sadol, cot); Seven Acres; Shaw Close (*v.* sceaga); Shop Fd; Small Dale ('little or narrow allotment', *v.* smæl; the final el., ModE *dale*, appears in several instances in Ch f.ns., and represents either, or both, deill ON or dǣl² OE, *v.* dale); Snield Banks; Spike Bank & Low ('brushwood bank and hillock', *v.* spic² (dial. *spike*), banke, hlāw); Spout Croft (*v.* spoute); Square End Fd; Stone Pit Fd; Stonistone (a reduplicating name, 'stony stony-field', *v.* stānig, stān); Stubble Fd; Tom Fd & Bank (*v.* toun); Tongue Sharp (*v.* tonge-sharp), cf. Tongue Sharp 162 *infra*); Triangle; Trueman Fd; Well Fd; Well Pool Mdw; White Fd & Ridge.

(*b*) *the backsides* 1611 (*v.* ba(c)ksyde); *Blaketonleyes* 1357 (*v.* blæc, tūn, lēah); *haya apud Bradeshagh* 1384 ('broad copse', *v.* brād, sceaga); *le holghlegh* 1384 (*v.* holh, lēah); *le lekbeddes* 1384 ('vegetable plots', *v.* lēac, bedd); *media haya* 1384 ('the middle enclosure', *v.* middel, (ge)hæg); *le Okencloghende* 1384 ('the end of Oaken Clough', *v.* ende¹, Oaken Clough 150 *infra*); *Pryndok Bonke in le Blake Combes* 1503 (perhaps '(hillside at) the pruned oak', from āc and the pa. part. of *prune* 'to lop, to trim a tree' (*v.* NED), with banke, cf. Coombs *supra*).

5. POTT SHRIGLEY (101–9479)

Shriggelepot 1348 *MinAcct*

Potte Shryggelegh 1354 *Eyre*, -*shrigley* 1420 *Dow et freq, passim* with spellings as for Pott and Shrigley *infra*

Potte et Schrygelegh 1357 *ChFor*, *Potte et Shriglegh* 1393 *Dow*, *vill' de Shrygelegh et Potte* 1358 *MinAcct*

The township is named from Pott Hall and Shrigley Park *infra*. Pott Shrigley is not a manorial name as stated in DEPN, cf. foll. and St Christopher's Church *infra*.

POTT HALL (101–946790)

Potte 1270 (17) Sheaf, *Pott* 13 (1611) *LRMB* 200, (*infra Pot-shrigley*) 1703 *Dow*, *Pot* 1286 *Eyre* (p)

Shriggelepot 1348 *MinAcct*

le Halle of Pott 1432 Orm², *Pot Kechyn olim vocat' Pot Hall* 1528 *Dow*, *Pott Hall* 1737 *ib*

From potte 'a deep hole', with hall, cycene. There is no pot-hole here. The name alludes to the dingle or deep clough at the head of which Pott lies. The hall was the seat of a family which adopted the local surname *Pott* (Orm² III 715), cf. DEPN s.v. *Shrigley, Pott*.

SHRIGLEY PARK formerly SHRIGLEY HALL (101–943797)

Sc(h)rigge-, Shriggeleg(h) 1285 Court (p), *Eyre*, 1286 *ib* (p), 1288 *ib*, c.1290 *Dow*, c.1301 *AddCh* and five examples with variant

spellings *Shrygge-, -ley(e)* to 1438 *Dow, Shrygglelegh* 1352 ChRR
(p), *Schriggrelegh* 1365 *Eyre*
Sherigg' 1285 *Eyre* (p), *Sherygley* 1503 Plea (p)
Sk(i)riggel' 1285 *Eyre* (p)
Scrygel(egh) 1285, 1290 *Eyre, Sc(h)-, Shrige-, Shrygelegh, -ley* 1342,
    1357 *Dow,* 1357 *ChFor,* 1359 Orm², 1384 *Dow,* Pat (p); *Srigeleg*
    l13 Seal (*Dow* 23)
Scriglegh e14 *AddCh,* 1313 *Dow, Shriglegh, -ley(e)* 1352 ChRR,
    1357 *ChFor et freq* with variant spellings *-le, Shrigg-, Shryg-;*
    Srigley 1375 *Eyre* (p)
Shreglegh 1357 *ChFor, -ley* 1492 *Dow* (p)
Shirgley 1368 *Eyre, Shirg(g)eley* 1383, 1388 Pat (p)
Shryghlegh, Shrighlygh 1547 Pat (p)
Shriley 1548 *Dow*
Shirlaghe, -leighe, -loghe 1560 Sheaf
The Hall of Shrigley 1545 *Dow,* (*capital messuage called Shrigley
    or-*) 1688, 1800 *ib, Shrigley Hall* 1611 *LRMB* 200, 1842 OS

'Glade frequented by missel-thrushes', *v.* scrīc, lēah, cf. Studies²
92. Here also may belong the surname of William de *Skyringel'* 1285
Eyre, if he is the same as William de *S(c)hriggel', Scriggeleg'* etc., *ib,*
v. ChetNS LXXXIV 286–7, s.v. *Shrigley, Skyringel'.* This would
produce another spelling showing *sk-* from Scandinavian influence,
with the addition of an unhistoric *-n-* by analogy with -ing(a)- place-
names. The later name of the hall is taken from *Shrigley Park* 1842
OS (1819 *Dow, the demeyne* 1545, *Shrigley Domaine* 1692, 1737 *ib*),
the site of *Shriggeleg' wode* 1288 Court, *boscus de Shriggeleg(h)* 1288
Eyre, 1357 *ChFor, Shriggeleyhey* 1357 *ib, v.* hall, park, demeyn,
wudu, (ge)hæg.

BAKESTONEDALE (FM), 1737 *Dow, Blakestonisdene* 1270 (17) Sheaf,
Bokestone Dene 13 (1611) *LRMB* 200, *Bakestondene* (*brok*) 1354 *Eyre,*
Baxtondene 1357 *ChFor, Baxendale* 1620 *Surv, Bakestonedale tenement* 1794 *Dow,* 'valley where baking-stones are got', from bæc-stān,
with dæl¹ or dalr replacing denu, cf. Longdendale 2 *supra.*

BERRISTALL DALE (101–947784), BERRISTALL HALL & WOOD (101–
950787)

(*le*) *By- Bistale* c.1270 (17) Sheaf, 13 (1611) *LRMB* 200
Berestowe 1347 *Eyre, -stow* 1505 *Dow, -stou* 1513 Plea

Berystowe 1357 ChFor, Beri- 1461 Dow, 1503 ChFor, Beri- 1819
  Dow
Barestow(e) hede 1467, 1471 MinAcct
Brastawold 1508 MinAcct, Brastwoode 1560 Sheaf
Beyrstowe 1528 Dow
Berystall 1567 Dow, Beri- 1611 LRMB 200, Ber(r)istal(l) 1737,
  1802, 1806 Dow
Birristall 1794 Dow
Berrestal c.1800 Dow

Probably 'place where berries grow', from berige-stall, -stōw,
beger-stōw, with mor[1], hall, hēafod, wudu and dæl[1]. The first forms
are from transcripts omitting an -er- contraction. This p.n. is of the
type discussed in WRY 2 243, 3 90, 141, 7 282, s.nn. Berristal Head,
Bairstow, where OE *berige-stall and *beger-stōw are adduced, cf.
Berrister 142 infra. The spellings of this Ch p.n. show that these
compounds are synonymous and interchangeable.

POTTMILL, 1737 Dow, Pottesmulne 1347 Eyre, Potte mylne 1589 Dow,
le Pott-Milne 1697 ib, cf. molendina de Shriggelegh 1352 ChRR,
-Potshrigley 1462 ib, Potshrigley Mylne 1547 Dow, v. myln, cf. Pott
Hall, Shrigley Park supra.

POTTS MOOR, Shriggel' mor 1357 ChFor, Shrigley Moore 1611
LRMB 200, 1620 Surv; Potteskerr 1393 Dow, Pot Ker c.1494 ib,
Pott(e)s Moore 1611 LRMB 200, Pott Moor 1737 Dow, Potmore 1806
ib, the moore 1717 ib, Great Bakestonedale Moor 1848 TA, v. mōr[1],
kjarr, cf. Bakestonedale supra.

REDACRE HALL & WOOD (101–945814)

  (le) Rud(d)yker, -car(re) 1347 Eyre, 1348 ChFor, Ruddingar 1589
    Dow
  Redeker 1412 Chol, Radker(e) 1467, 1471 MinAcct, Rydecer 1577
    Dow, Riddecar 1737 ib, Ridacar Farm c.1788 ib
  Ryddyngker, -carr(e) 1545 Dow, Ryddin(g)-, Ridding(e)carr(e) 1552
    ib, 1611 LRMB 200, the Ryddingar 1571 Dow, Riddy-, Ryddy-
    carre 1574, 1588 ib, Riddycar House 1692 ib
  (le) Ridacre 1503 ChFor, Ridacre Farm & Hall 1800 Dow
  Redacre Hall 1831 Bry

'Reedy marsh', from hrēodig and kjarr, with hūs, hall, wudu.

ANDREW'S KNOB, *Andrew's brow* 1794, 1816 *Dow*, cf. *Andrew Flash, Fould, Howse & Meadow* 1673, *The Flash Andrew's Fold* 1816, *Andrewes tenement* 1683, *Andrew's Ground* 1737, *Andrew's meadow* 1816 all *Dow*, named from the family of John *Andrew* 1495 *Dow*, v. brū, flasshe, fald, hūs, mǣd, knob, cf. Mottram St Andrew 202 *infra*. THE ARK HILL FIELD (lost), 1794, 1800 *Dow*, *Erkilhouse* 1492, *Erkylhowse* 1528, *Arkylle howse* c.1494 *ib*, *Arkhill* 1503 *ChFor*, (common called-) 1611 *LRMB* 200, 1620 *Surv*, *Arkhyll alias vocat' le Foxholes* 1554 *Dow*, cf. *Arkelesnotehurst* 1357 *ChFor*, perhaps 'Arnkell's house and nut-wood', from the ON pers.n. *Arnkell* (or ODan *Arnketil*), with hūs and hnutu, hyrst. BANFOLD FM, *Bamfold House* 1802 *Dow*, *Banfold* 1831 Bry, 'bean fold', v. bēan, fald. BIRCHENCLIFF, (-*e*) 1737 *Dow*, *Birchincliffe* 1611 *LRMB* 200, (-*knowle*) 1620 *Surv*, -*clife* 1650 *Dow*, 'hill side growing with birch-trees', v. bircen[2], clif, cnoll. BLAKEHEY WOOD, (*the*) 1819 *Dow*, (*le*) *blakehey* 1412 *Chol*, 1611 *LRMB* 200, *the Blakehay* 1748 *Dow*, 'the dark enclosure', v. blæc, (ge)hæg. BOWER CLOUGH, 1842 OS, is probably named after Jeremy *Bower* 1737 *Dow*, cf. *Jeremy Bower's Cliffs & Common* 1737 *ib*, *Jeremiah's Cliffs* 1806 *ib*, v. clōh, clif, commun. BRINK BROW, v. 142 *infra*. CASTLE FIELD COTTAGE (lost), 1848 *TA*, *the Castlefield* 1794 *Dow*, v. castel(l). CONEY GREEN HO (lost), 1802 *ib*, *Coney Green* 1737 *ib*, *Cuney Green* 1792 *ib*, v. coni, grēne[2], though the modern form may represent an older one from coninger. This place was included in Shrigley Park in 1795, v. *Dow* 444, and was the site of an inn from which the public road was diverted; it is not identical with *Coney Green* 1879 Sheaf[1] 1, 340, for which cf. *Higher Coney Green* 1848 *TA*. COPHURST KNOT, *le Coppethurst* 1384 *Rental*, (*the*) *Cophurst* 1611 *LRMB* 200, *Cophurst* (*Knott*) 1800 *Dow*, 'the pollarded wood', v. copped, hyrst, knǫttr. DALE TOP, the head of Bakestonedale *supra*. DEER CLOUGH. ELLIS BANK, 1848 *TA*, *the Elibank* 1658, *le Ellybank* 1703, -*s* 1794, *Ellibank* 1788 all *Dow*, possibly 'elder-tree bank(s)', from elle, ig[3], banke, cf. Elle Bank Db 115 (*Elibanke* Eliz), Ellislack 129 *supra*, Ely Brow, Ellabank, Ellybank 143, 201, 272 *infra*. ENGINE WOOD. GAUSIE BROW, v. gorstig, brū. GIBHILL, 1737 *Dow*, 'cat hill', v. gibbe[2], hyll. GREENCLOSE FM. HOLME WOOD, *the holmes* c.1494 *Dow*, *Holmes* 1748 *ib*, -*Wood* 1848 *TA*, *the hulmes* 1611 *LRMB* 200, -*Wood* 1794 *Dow*, land alternatively called *Pottesbancke* 1620 *Surv*, *Pottsbankes* 1683 *Dow*, *Pott Bank* 1753 *ib*, *Pot Bank* 1831 Bry, 'the damp ground', 'the bank opposite Pott', v. holmr, hulm, wudu, banke.   JACKSONBROW, v. brū.   JUMBER CLOUGH, *le Colclogh(e)* 1493, 1528 *Dow, the Jumble Clough* 1611 *LRMB* 200, *Cole Clough* or- 1673 *Dow*, 'coal valley', 'cluttered valley', v. col[1], clōh, jumble, cf. Coal Pit Fd *infra*.   LOWER HO (lost), 1819 *Dow*, 1611 *LRMB* 200.   MITCHELFOLD, *Gap House* 1831 Bry, v. gap, fald.   MOORSIDE, 1788 *Dow*; the place adjoins Park Moor 200 *infra*. The cottages here are also named *Mill Brow* 1890 *Deed* (H.A.T.), cf. *the Mill Brow* 1753 *Dow*, v. myln, brū, cf. Pottmill *supra*.   NAB WOOD, 1831 Bry, partly in Bollington, named from Nab Head 190 *infra*.   NEEDYGATE (101–948816), NEEDY GATE FM (101–947809, *High House* 1842 OS), half a mile apart but both on the same lane, and presumably named from it, v. nēdig, gata.   NORMANS HALL (101–937800), 1800, *Normansells tenement* 1683, *Normanshall Liuing* 1692, -*Farm* 1794 all *Dow*, the home of a family surnamed *Normonsell* 1461 ChRR, *Normansell* 1495 ib, *Normashall, Normanshyll* 1545 *Dow* (from sel 'a hut' and either norðmann 'a Norseman' or the OE pers.n. *Norðmann*), but it is not clear which name is original.   THE OAKRIDGE, *Okeridge* 1611 *LRMB* 200, *The Ocke ridge* 1683 *Dow*. OVERHEYES, *the overhey* 1611 *LRMB* 200, *the Over Hays* 1753 *Dow*, 'enclosures on a hill-side', v. ofer[2], (ge)hæg.   THE RAKES LANE (lost), c.1800 ib, *le Rakes* 1493 ib, *Rakes Lane* 1620 *Surv*, (*le-*) 1697 *Dow*, (*the*) 1711 ib, the name of the road 101–945785 to 952797, v. rake, lane.   ST CHRISTOPHER'S CHURCH formerly POTT CHAPEL, *Our lady of Dovnes Chapell in Pott* 1472 *Dow, the Chapell in Pot callyt Downes Chapell* 1492 ib, *the Chapell at Pott* c.1492 ib, *Potchapell* 1503 NewC, *Dounes Chaple alias Potte Chaple* 1566 Orm[2], *Pot-Chapel* 1656 ib, v. chapel(e); named after Geoffrey *Downes*, the founder, v. *The Library* 5th series, XV 47–53, cf. Pott Shrigley, Pott Hall *supra*. SHERROWBOOTH (101–959787), *the Sherowboothes* 1611 *LRMB* 200, *Sherra Booth* 1737 *Dow, Hardings* 1831 Bry, 'herdsmen's huts', from bōth. The first part of the name may be 'boundary ridge', from scearu and hōh, cf. Sharoe La 147, as the place stands on the end of a ridge on the Rainow boundary.   SIMPSON LANE, cf. *Simpson's Meadow* 1810 *Dow*, cf. William *Simson* 1692 ib.   SPULEY BRIDGE, v. 140 *infra*.   UNWINPOOL, 1819 ib, *Vnwin's house* 1611 *LRMB* 200, from John *Vnwyn* 1551 *Dow*.   WALKERSGREEN, *Walkers Bottoms* 1848 *TA*, from the occupational surname *Walker* (cf. walcere) with botm, grēne[2].   WEST PARK GATE, an entrance to Lyme Park, v. 200 *infra*.

FIELD-NAMES

The undated forms are 1848 *TA* 326. Of the others, 13 (1611), 1611 are *LRMB* 200, 1270 (17), 1560 Sheaf, 1344 Pat, 1347 *Eyre*, 1363, 1503 *ChFor*, 1384 *Rental*, 1467, 1471, 1508 *MinAcct*, 1620 *Surv*, 1819[2] Orm[2], and the rest *Dow*.

(*a*) Acre; Alcock Moor (cf. John *Allcock* 1800); Allens Nook 1811 (*the Nook* 1794); Alley mdw (*v.* aley); the Ashtree fd 1794; the Bank 1800; the Bard fd 1800; the barley croft 1806 (*-e* 1611); Barlow's Ground 1806 (1788, cf. Alexander *Barlow* 1495); Barn Fd (*the Barne feeld* 1673, *-Croft* 1794); Barn Mdw (1806); Bayleys 1800; the bent 1806 (1673, *v.* beonet); Bett mdw; Black Fd; the Bleaching Yard 1800; Blindmans Lane; the Boatfield 1800 (*v.* bōt); Boden Fd & Mdw (*Boden Ground* 1792, *Bowden Meadow* 1800, cf. *George Bowden's tenement* 1737); Bone Dust Fd (*the Bown field* 1800, 'field dressed with bone-dust', *v.* bone-dust); the Briary Fd 1800; Brick Kiln Fd; Broad Fd (1611); Brook Croft; the Brookhouse Croft 1800 (1611); the Broom Mdw 1800 (1794); the far & the near brow 1806 (*the (brown) brow* 1794, *v.* brūn[1], brū); the Bushy Fd 1800; the Calf Croft 1811 (*-e* 1611); Great Carr 1802 (*the Carr* 1611, *Carr Meads or Great Carr* 1788, *v.* kjarr); the Carthouse Croft 1800 (1794); the Cawdow 1811 (*v.* cū, dāl (ME *dole*), but the first el. may be calf 'a calf', as in Cawton NRY 52, Cawden WRY 6 135); Church Mdw (1794, *-s* 1819[1], cf. *le Chapel yerde* 1492, *-yarde* 1528, *the Church Field (Brow)* 1753, *v.* chapel(e), cirice, geard, brū, cf. St Christopher's Church *supra*); Close Wd; Clough (1800, *the Lower & Upper Clough field* 1794, *v.* clōh); Coal Pit Fd (1794, *le Coalefield* 1794, near Jumber Clough *supra*, *v.* col[1], pytt); Cockshutt mdw (*the Cockshutt meadowe* 1611, *v.* cocc-scyte); the Common Piece 1806; Corner Fd; the Cote Mdw 1800 (*the Cote Crofte* 1611, *v.* cot); Cow Pasture (1811); The Croft(s) 1800 (*the (Har) Crofte* 1611, *the Crofts* 1753); Crop Fd 1816; the Cross fd 1794; the Cut Croft 1800 (1528, *v.* cut); the Dam Mdw 1800 (1794, named from the artificial lake in Shrigley Park, *v.* damme); the Dirty Fd 1800 (1794); the Dock Ridding 1800 (*the Dock(e) Reading(e)* 1611, *v.* docce, ryding); the Dowd Fd 1800 (*Dodefeld* 1384, 1385, *the little-, the Rough Doodefield* 1611, *the Dew'dfield* 1794, perhaps 'endowed field' from ME *dowed*, pa.part. of *douen*, 'to endow', *v.* dow NED, cf. Doudfield 284 *infra*); Downes's Ground 1737 (*Downes meadow* 1611, from the name of the local family); the Dowry mdw 1806 (1800, *the Dowry* 1611, cf. *the Dowrie house* 1611, *v.* dowarie); Drain Mdw; Etchells Green 1788 (*the Etchus highfield* 1611, *Etchells* 1737, cf. Richard *Ecchuls* 1551, *v.* grēne[2]); Far Mdw (1794); Farm Yard Plantation; the Ferneyhole 1800 (*Fearney hole* 1653); Ferney knowl (*Fern(a)y knowl(e)* 1800); the Gorsty Brow 1800 (*v.* gorstig, brū); Great mdw (1794, *-e* 1611); Greave (*þe Greue* 1363, *the Grave* 1800, *v.* grǣfe); the Green fd 1806 (*Greenefield* 1611); the half acre 1800 (1694); Harrop Croft & Mdw (1800, *v.* Harrop 138 *infra*, cf. *Harrop's* 1737, *Harrop Brow* 1788, 1802, *v.* brū); the Hartsgreave 1806 (*the Hartes greave* 1611, 'the hart's wood', *v.* heorot, grǣfe); High Fd (1611); Higher Fd (1794); the Hill Mdw 1800 (*the Hill Meadowe otherwise called Wardes Meadowe* 1611, cf. Wards Mdws *infra*);

Hill Top (1692, v. *Hilltop* 190 *infra*, cf. *Hill Top Gate* 1795); the Hogue
Sherd 1816 (*Hauk-, Hawkesherd(e)* 1467, *Hawkyshert* 1492, *the Hawkesyard*
1611, *-yord* 1620, *-yoard* 1697, *the Hogshirt* 1711, *the Hougue Shird* 1794,
the Houge Sheird 1800, 'the hawk's gap', v. hafoc-scerde, cf. *The Hawkesyord*
166 *infra*); the Hole Ho 1816 (v. hol²); Hollow Mdw (1794); the hop pit mdw
1800; the horse pasture 1800; the hurst 1800 (v. hyrst); the Intake(s) 1806
(1794, v. inntak); the Jack Gate Mdw 1800 (1794); Jonas Bottoms (*Jonas's
Bottoms* 1788, cf. *Jonas Heywood's* 1737, *tenement called Jonas's* 1794,
v. botm); the Kiln Fd 1816 (*Kilne Crofte* 1611); the Kitchen Croft 1800 (*the
Kitchin Crofte* 1611); the near Knowle 1811; Lapwing Fd; the Larkfield
1794; the Lee (Mdw) 1800 (1794, *le lees* 1493, *the over & lower Lee* 1611,
v. lēah); the lined Ground 1800 (*the Lyme ground* 1611, *the Lymed Ground*
1735, v. līm); Little Mdw (*the litle meadowe* 1611); the long fd 1806 (*le
longefeld* 1508, *Longeffelde* 1560); the long lands 1800 (1735, *the longe loundes*
1611, v. land); the Long Mdw 1800 (1735, cf. *long meadow leys* 1611, v. lēah);
the Long Sides 1810 (*le Longeside* 1347, *le longside* 1467, *long Syde* 1503,
Longessyde(ridg) 1611, 'long hill-side' v. lang, sīde, hrycg); the lower fd 1806
(cf. *the lower Crofte* 1611); Marl Fd (cf. *the Marled Earth(s)* 1611, 1806, *the
new marled ground* 1611, *the marled ground* 1800, *Marl Pit(t) Brow* 1800);
the Meadow 1806 (*-e* 1611); Middle Fd (*the midle feild* 1611); the Mill Croft
1800 (1794, cf. *the Milne Meadowe* 1611, cf. Pottmill *supra*); Mobberley Wd
& Fd 1816 (probably from the surname from Mobberley 333 *infra*); the
Moss Pits 1806 (*the Mossepittes* 1611, *the Mosspit Meadow* 1794, 'turf pits',
v. mos, pytt); the Nicholls mdw 1800 (1794, *the Nickowe meadowe* 1611,
Nico Meadow 1673, *le Nicho meadow* 1697, perhaps 'nicker meadow', from
nicor 'a water-sprite'); Old Mdw (1810); the Old Woman's Mdw 1800
(1794); the Orchard Flatt 1800 (1611); the New & Old Paddock (*the Paddock
field* 1794, v. pearroc); the Patch 1806; Pingot (*the Pingott* 1611, cf. *The
Pingle* 1800, v. pingot, pingel); the higher, lower & middle pit 1806 (*Pitts*
1611); Poole Nook; Potatoe Bed; the Pott Fd 1800 (cf. *Pottesfeld* 1412,
v. Pott Hall *supra*); Pott Lane 1791; Potts Parts (*the parts* 1794, v. part);
Quarry Bank; the Race fd 1800; Redway Head; Ribbon Hills (1800, *the
Ribbow Hills* 1811); the Rough hay Carr 1800 (v. rūh, (ge)hæg, kjarr);
Rough Hill 1791; Rough Wd; the Round Mdw 1800 (*-e* 1611); the Rushy Fd
1811 (*the Rushiefield* 1611); School Ho (*the-* 1788, *the old School House Croft*
1794, cf. *the School field* 1788); Seven Day Work (*the Seavendaye(s) work(e)*
1611, cf. *the sixeday-work* 1611, 1800, v. day-work); Sheep Pasture (1794);
Shore mdw (1794, *the Shorefield* 1611, v. scor(a)); Six Acres (*Six Acre* 1673);
Smith's Croft 1795 (*Smythes Crofte* 1611, tenant John *Smythe*); the Smithy
Croft 1800 (*the Smythie Crofte* 1611, cf. *the Smithy Hill* 1819); Speck Mdw
(v. specke); the Spout Croft 1794 (v. spoute); Thorn Cliffe (v. þorn, clif);
Twenty Acres; the Wallet 1794 (v. walet); Wards Mdws 1802 (*Wardle
Meadows* 1800, cf. Hill Mdw *supra*); the Warwick Fd 1800 (*the Warrick Field
(Brow)* 1753); Well Croft & Mdw (cf. *the well field* 1794); the wheat croft
1806; Whistle Duck (perhaps the site of a decoy, but cf. dial. *Whistling-duck*,
EDD, 'the coot' or 'the pochard'); the White Gate Croft 1794; the White
hay booths 1806 (v. hwīt, (ge)hæg, bōth); Wood Fd; Woody (v. wudu,
(ge)hæg); the yeald 1800 (1794, *the heald* 1611, *Flatt Heald* 1794, v. flatr, helde).

(b) *Browneknowle* 1620 (*v.* brūn[1], cnoll); *the Cattcrofte* 1611 (*v.* catte, croft); *the Cauldwaye* 1611 (*v.* cald, weg); *the Claye Buttes* 1611 (*v.* butte); *the Clyffe* 1611, *Cliffe* 1620; *the Cocker meadowe* 1611, 1673; *Cowhey Woodes* 1611 (*v.* cū, (ge)hæg); *Culuercrofte* 1508, *Calvercrofte* 1560 ('*dove field*', *v.* culfre, croft); *les Culwacres* 1384, *Kil-*, *Kylvacres* 1467, 1471 (perhaps from cylfe 'a hill, an eminence' (cf. ON *kylfa* 'a club, the prow of a ship'), with æcer); *le Dodgreve*, *-greue* 1467, *Dedegreue*, *le Doggrave* 1471, *le Doggegraue* 1508, *the Doggraue* 1560 ('wood on a hill', *v.* dodde, grǣfe); *the Eyes* 1611 (*v.* ēg); *Foldsted* 1467, 1471, the same as *Oldefeld* 1508 ('the site of a fold', 'the old field', *v.* fald, stede); *the Hale house* 1611 (*v.* halh); *Haukesclog'* 13 (1611), *Hankislowe* 1270 (17), *Haukesclogh'* 1347, 1348 ('hawk's valley', *v.* hafoc, clōh, cf. Hogue Sherd *supra*); *Hayfield* 1494; *the Heath Croftes* 1611; *Hollinshurst* 1611 ('holly wood', *v.* holegn, hyrst); *Horebancke* 1611; *the leyfield* 1611 (*v.* lǣge); *Luysotesrudyng* 1384 ('Lisote's clearing', from a ME fem. pers.n. *Lisote*, 'probably a diminutive form of *Eliza(beth)*, and ryding); *the marryshfeld* 1611 ('marsh field', *v.* merisc); *the Higher Meadow heyes* 1660; *the Meadow-Plecke* 1611 ('meadow-plot', *v.* plek); *the Middlehey* 1611; *the Muckhill Crofte* 1611 (*v.* muk, hyll); *Oldefeld* (*v.* Foldsted *supra*); *Oxenforde Croft* 1344, *le Oxeforde* 1347, *-(in Shriggel'mor)* 1357, *-forth* 1494, *-(e)furth* 1528 (*v.* oxa, ford); *the great & litle Ridinge* 1611 (*v.* ryding); *Sawpitcroftes* 1611 (*v.* saw-pytt); *the Shrugges* 1611 ('the bushes', *v.* shrogge); *the lower Shutt* 1611 (*v.* scēat); *the Sprink* 1611 (*v.* spring); *the Stagge Crofte* 1611; *the Woe Crofte* 1611 (*v.* wōh); *Woodgrene* 1560 (*v.* wudu, grēne[2]); *Wooley* 1611 (*v.* lēah).

6. RAINOW (101–950760)

Rauenok' c.1270 (17) Sheaf, 1283 *Dow* (p), a.1303 *AddCh* (p), *-ock(e)* 13 (1611) *LRMB* 200, 1325 *Dow*

Rauenouh 1285 *Eyre*, *Raven(h)oh* 1287 *ib* (p), *Ravenowe* 1320 Plea, *Rauenowe* 1325 *Dow*, *-ow* 1357 *Eyre*, *-howe* 1347 *ib*, *Raven(s)-how(e)*, *-haw(e)* 1467, 1471 *MinAcct*, *-hall'* 1508 *ib*, *Rafnowe*, *-ou* 1345 *Eyre*, *Raunou* 1347 *ib*, *-ow*, 1508 *MinAcct*, *Rauennow* 1345 *Eyre*

Raneowe 1329 *Dow*, *Ranowe* 1357 *Eyre*, *-ow* 1445 *ib*, *Ranawe* (lit. *Raname*) 1462 ChRR, *Rano* 1503 Plea, *Rana* 1688 *Dow*

Raynow 1446 ChRR, *-e* 1490 *Dow*, *-noll* 1567 *ib*, *Rainow* 1724 NotCestr

'Raven's hill', *v.* hræfn, hōh; but the first el. might be the pers.n., OE *Hræfn*, ON *Hrafn*, although the lack of gen.sg. *-s-* tells against this. The village lies on the shoulder of a hill. *Ran(nes)woode* 1560 Sheaf[3] 23 (5414) appears to be a corrupt form of this p.n. The township consisted of three hamlets, Rainow, Harrop and Saltersford.

HARROP (101–9678)

> *Haroppe* 1337 *Eyre*, *-op* 1347 *ib*, (*haia de-*) 1467 *MinAcct*
> *Harrop* 1347 *Eyre et freq*, (*haya de-*) 1508 *MinAcct*, *Harrope*,
>   *Harropp infra Forest'* 1503 *ChFor*
> *Harap* 1349 *MinAcct*

Possibly 'hare valley', from **hara** and **hop**[1], with (ge)**hæg**. But the same p.n. appears in Ch at Harropgreen 183 *infra*, Haropgreen 90 *supra*, Harrop Edge 312 *infra*, five times in WRY (2 311, 3 249, 275, 6 123, 196), twice in Db (70, 121), and this repetition of 'hare valleys' may be suspicious. The first el. could be **hār** 'old, hoary, grey', perhaps here denoting valleys on boundaries. Professor Löfvenberg observes that this type of name may be a compound of **hær** 'a rock' and **hop**[1], meaning 'rocky valley' (cf. WRY 2 311). However, there are no early forms with *h-* in the second syllable. This feature, and the spelling *Harap*, suggest that the final el. could be **rāp** 'a rope, a measure of land, an extent of territory, a jurisdiction', cf. Rope 333 *infra*, and a series of p.ns. from **hār** and **rāp**, meaning 'old rope of land', or 'rope of land at a boundary', is feasible. Harrop in Rainow gives name to Harrop Brook 28 *supra*.

SALTERSFORD (HALL) (101–983763), *Salterford* 1409 *ChRR et freq* to 1611 *LRMB* 200, *-e* 1442 *ChRR*, *-forth* 1611 *LRMB* 200, *Saltford* 1452 *ChRR*, 1471 *MinAcct*, *-e* 1560 *Sheaf*, *Salteford* 1523 *ChRR*, *Saltersford(e)* 1503 *ChFor*, *Saltersford Hall* 1611 *LRMB* 200, 'salters' ford', *v.* **saltere** (gen.pl. **saltera**), **ford**, cf. *Salter's Close* 1848 *TA*. This place was on a saltway from Macclesfield to Buxton, cf. 49 *supra*.

BILLINGE HILL (101–9577), BILLINGE HEAD, SIDE & QUARRIES, [- indʒ], *le Bellyng'* 1503 *ChFor*, *Bellendge* (*Carr*), *Billinge(s) Carr(e)*, *Billinge* 1611 *LRMB* 200, 1620 *Surv*, *myne of stone called Billinge* 1620 *ib*, *Billinge Head & Side* 1831 Bry, from **hyll** 'a hill', **hēafod** 'the top end of-', **sīde** 'the side of', and either **sker** (cf. dial. *scar*) 'a rocky cliff', or **kjarr** 'brushwood, marsh', with a hill-name *Billinge*. Cf. Werneth Fm, Billinge Green, Billinge Meadow, High Billinge, The Billings 293, 329, 329, 332, 329 *infra*, Billing Hill WRY 4 153, Billinge La 66, 104. It is also possible that Billingshurst Sx 147, High Billinghurst Sr 235, Billings Hill ERY 78, Billington Bd 116, La 71, Bellington Hill Db 462, Billing Nth 132, Billingbank WRY 3 213 should be added to the list, *v.* BNF 2 (1967), 326–32. The La and Ch places, and many of the other examples, are upon or near prominent hills or well-marked relative elevations of the ground, and *Billinge* probably represents an -ing² derivative of OE bill 'a sword', figuratively 'a sharp ridge' (*v.* DEPN s.n. *Billinge*, and La 67) and alternatively of OE bile 'a beak, a bill', used in the topographical sense, 'a headland', as of a promontory, a ridge, or a hill-edge, cf. Bilham K 416. Cf. discussion in Löfvenberg 13. Barnes's deductions LCAS LXXI 45 are to be disregarded since *Billinge* is not an -ingas type of p.n., and *Bullingham* 1560 Sheaf³ 23 (5392) is probably a corrupt form for Bollington 187 *infra*, not evidence of an -ingahām p.n.

CALROFOLD (110–943747), possibly *Caluerhal* 1286 Court, *Callerhale* 1384 *Rental*, 'calves' corner', from calf (gen.pl. calfra) and halh, with fald, cf. *Cawrehey* 158 *infra*.

EDDISBURY HILL & HO, *campus vocat' Eddisbury* 1467 *MinAcct*, *Eddesbury* 1471 *ib*, *Edesbury* 1620 *Surv*, *Eas(e)bury*, *-berryes* 1611 *LRMB* 200, *Eddisbury Hill* 1831 Bry, cf. Eddisbury Fm, Gate & Hall 122 *supra*. 'Ēad's stronghold', perhaps from an OE pers.n. *Ēad* and burh, as in Eddisbury 331 *infra*, but the first el. could be the OE pers.n. *Eddi* as in Edingley Nt 160.

HOOLEYHEY LANE, UPPER & LOWER HOOLEYHEY FM (101–976754), *Holey(e)* 1282, 1285 *Eyre* (p), *Hoghlegh* 1342 Orm², *Holley* 14 Tab, *-ay* 1362 Cl, *Hulley* 1359 *Eyre* (p), *Hullegh'* in *Ravenshowe* 1467 *MinAcct*, *Hallegh'* 1471 *ib*, *the further & nearer Hooley hey* 1611 *LRMB* 200, 'clearing on a spur', *v.* hōh, lēah, (ge)hæg.

HORDERN FM (110–953745)

> *Horden* c.1280 *Dow*, *-ern* 1285 *For*, *-e* 1350 *Eyre* (p), *-irn(e)* 1290 *ib* (p), *-urn* 1347 *ib*, *-orne* 1620 *Surv*
> *Horthern(e)* 1287 *Eyre* (p)
> *Hordren* 1290 Court (p), *-e* 1316 *Fitt*, *-ron* 1290 *Eyre* (p), *-rom* 1357 *ChFor* (p), *Haurdrone* 1503 *ib* (p)
> *Horderon* 1467 *MinAcct*, *-eren* 1471 *ib*
> *Herden* 1508 *MinAcct*
> *Hurdron* 1528 *Dow*

'Store-house', *v.* hord-ærn. Cf. Back Edges *infra*.

INGERSLEY HALL, HIGHER INGERSLEY (101–946773)

> Ingaldeslegh' E3 Surv, Yngaldeslegh 1357 ChFor, Ingoldeslegh 1467
> MinAcct, Inglodeslegh 1508 ib, Inglidsleghe 1560 Sheaf
> Ingersley 1611 LRMB 200, Ingersly 1773 Dow, Little Ingersley
> 1799 ib
> le Over Ingarsley 1684 Dow

'Ingiald's clearing', from the ON pers.n. *Ingialdr* and lēah, with uferra, lȳtel. Cf. Waulkmill *infra*.

JENKIN CHAPEL (101–984765), 1819 Orm[1], erected c.1739 near *Jenkin's Cross* (Orm[2] III 771), *Jankynscros* 1364 *Eyre*, from which it was named, 'Jankin's, Jenkin's cross', from the ME pers.n. *Jenkin*, *Janekin*, diminutive of *John*, and cros, cf. *Jenkin's Clough* 1848 *TA*, *v.* clōh.

ONE HO (110–943741), 1831 Bry, -*Howse* 1490 Sheaf, *Anhus* c.1166 ib, *Onhuz* 1286 *Eyre* (p), -*hus* 1290 Court (p), -*hous* 1332 *Dav*, *Honhuss* e14 ib, -*house* 1347 ib, 'one house, house on its own', *v.* ān, hūs. This may even be an OE compound **ānhūs* analogous with OE ānseld 'lonely dwelling', ānsetl 'hermitage'.

RAINOWLOW (101–954772), 1831 Bry, *Ranowel(l)aue* 1467, 1471 *MinAcct*, *Ranow Lowe* 1611 *LRMB* 200, *v.* hlāw 'a mound'. Here are Big and Little Low *infra*.

REDMOOR BROW & FM, (*High*) *Red Moor* 1831 Bry, 1848 *TA*, cf. (*le*) *Red(e)mor* c.1283 Chest (p), 1286 *Eyre* (p), Court (p), cf. Redmoor Lane 273 *infra*, 'reed moor', *v.* hrēod, mōr[1].

SOWCAR FM (101–943779), *le Soweker* 1379 *Dow*, *le Souker* 1384 Rental, *le Sew(e)ker*, (*le*) *Soker* 1467, 1471 *MinAcct*, *Sowcarr* 1611 *LRMB* 200, 'sow's marsh', *v.* sugu, kjarr.

SPULEY (BRIDGE) (101–946784), *Spuleee, Speweleghforde* 1347 *Eyre*, *Spuelegh* 1384 *Rental*, *Spull(e)y* (*Sich(e)*) 1467, 1471 *MinAcct*, *Spilley* 1508 ib, 1560 Sheaf, *Spuley* 1611 Dow, *Spuley Bridge* 1794 ib, *Speulow* (lit. *Spen-*) 1831 Bry; upon Harrop Brook 28 *supra* and probably an older name for it meaning 'stream which spews forth', from spiwol and ēa. Dr von Feilitzen points out that the OE adj. *spiwol*, in addition to meaning 'emetic' as in the *Leechdoms*, could also mean 'liable to spew' and cites OE *līgspiwol* 'vomiting flame' (BT & BTSuppl). The adj. *spiwol* would be apt for a hill-side stream, subject to sudden flood. In *Spuleee*, *ēa* has been suffixed again to a form in which the final *-l* of the first el. has caused confusion with *lēah*. The bridge is *Rik-*, *Ricand(e)brigge* 1467, 1471 *MinAcct*, *Ricambridge* 1560 Sheaf, 'noisy, rumbling bridge', from ME *rykande*, cf. Sir Gawain 2337, ModEdial. *rick* 'to rattle, jingle, make a noise' (EDD), also *rickle* (EDD) 'to rattle, to jingle' recorded e15 NED. *v.* **brycg, ford.** *v.* Addenda.

THORNSET FM (101–953756)

> *Thorniside* c.1280 *Dow*, *Tornside* 1289 (17) Court (p), *Thornside* 1290 *Eyre* (p), *Thornesyde* E3 *Surv*
> *Thorncete* 1349 *MinAcct*, 1384 *Rental*
> (*le*) *Thorneshed* 1372 *Eyre*, (*-e*) 1428 ChRR, Earw, 1842 OS, *the Thorneshead* 1611 *LRMB* 200, *Thornshead* 1831 Bry
> *Thorncote* 1467 *MinAcct*, *Thornecotte* 1471 *ib*
> *Thornton* 1508 *MinAcct*, *Thorneton* 1560 Sheaf[3] 23 (5392)

'Thorny hill-side', *v.* **þornig, sīde.** The spellings show confusion with (ge)set 'a fold', **cot, hēafod** and **tūn**, cf. Hollinset 150 *infra*. The *-ton* forms are arbitrary substitutions by the clerks of *DuLa MinAcct*.

THURSBITCH (101–993751), *-batch* 1842 OS, *Thorsbreach* 1831 Bry, cf. *Thurbacheker* E3 *Surv*, *-batchker* 1620 *ib*, *Thurresbacheker* 1384 *Rental*, also *the farthinge or furbachcarr meadowe* 1620 *Surv*, '(brushwood, or marshy place at) the demon's valley', from **þyrs** 'a giant, a demon' and **bæce**[1], with **ker** (kjarr), **mǣd**. The second element is confused with **brēc** 'a breaking of land'. The alternative field name is from **fēorðung** 'a fourth part'.

TODS CLIFF (lost, 101–981783)

> *Toddisclif* 1285 *Eyre*, *Toddesclif* 1347 *ib*, *-cliff'* 1471 *MinAcct*, *-clyf* 1409 ChRR, *-e* 1462 *ib*, *-clyff* 1442 *ib*, *-e* 1523 *ib*
> *Todesclyf in foresta* 1348 *Eyre*, *-cliffe* 1620 *Surv*, *Tods Cliff* 1842 OS
> *Todeclyf* 1357 *ChFor*, *-cliffe* 1560 Sheaf, *Toddecliff'* 1471 *MinAcct*, *Todclyff* 1508 *ib*, *-cliffe* 1560 Sheaf

Tadeclyf' 1357 *ChFor*
Doddescliff 1452 ChRR

'Fox's bank', *v.* todd, clif, cf. Topcliff *infra*, Todd Brook 36 *supra*.

ANDREW'S EDGE, 1842 OS, *Anders Edge* 1831 Bry, *v.* ecg, cf. Mottram St Andrew 202 *infra*, Andrew's Knob 133 *supra*, Back Edges *infra*.
BACK-OF-THE-CROFTS, 1860 White, *Back o' th' Fold* 1831 Bry.
BACK EDGES (lost, 110–956744), 1831 ib, *Hordron Egge, Hordron lowe* 1503 *ChFor, Horderen Moore* 1611 *LRMB* 200, *Hordern Moor* 1684, 1711 *Dow*, cf. Hordern Fm *supra*, *v.* ecg, hlāw, mōr[1].   BANK CLOUGH & LANE, *Bank* 1688 *Dow*, cf. *the bancke Pingett, the lower & over bancke* 1611 *LRMB* 200, *v.* banke, clōh, pingot.   BAYTREE.
BENT END, cf. *the Bent Meadowe* 1611 *ib*, *v.* beonet, ende[1].   BERRISTALL DALE, *v.* 131 *supra*.   BERRISTER FM (101–952753), analogous with Berristall 131 *supra*, and probably the *Beristowe* 1503 *ChFor* mentioned in Lane-Ends Fm *infra*.   BIG LOW, *Great Lows* 1819 Orm[2], at Rainowlow *supra*, 'big mound', *v.* hlāw.   BLACK BROOK (BRIDGE), 1831 Bry, perhaps *le Bla(c)kwell* 1467, 1508 *MinAcct*, -*wall* 1508 *ib*, 1560 Sheaf, 'black stream', *v.* blæc, wella (wælla), mentioned 45 *supra* under route XIV.   BLACKROCK FM.   BLACKSHAW GAP (lost, 101–966774), 1842 OS, cf. *Blak(e)shae* 1285 *Eyre* (p), Court (p), -*shagh* 1355 *Eyre* (p), *Blacshawe* 1296 *Dav* (p), -*sha* 1549, -*shae* 1551 *Dow* (p), 'black copse', *v.* blæc, sceaga and gap, a passage through the boundary of Harrop *supra*.   BLAZE HILL, *v.* blesi.
BLUE BOAR FM, *Blue Boar* 1831 Bry.   BONNYCATTEY, *Bolt Field* 1831 ib.   BOWER CLOUGH, *v.* 133 *supra*.   BRINK (FM) (110–953741), *Brynkelowe et brynkewode iuxta le Wyndewayhed* 1503 *ChFor*, *the Brinck(e)* 1611 *LRMB* 200, *the brinke* 1620 Surv, *le Brink* 1703 *Dow*, *v.* brink, hlāw, wudu, cf. foll.   BRINK BROW (101–965790), 1848 *TA*, in Pott Shrigley and Rainow, near Brink Fm 199 *infra*, *v.* brink, brū, cf. prec.   BROAD MOSS, 1842 OS.   BROOK COTTAGES, near Millbrook *infra*.   BROOKHOUSE (FM, BRIDGE & CLOUGH), (*the Brookhouse* 1611 *LRMB* 200, near a tributary of R. Dean.   BROWN HOUSE, 1831 Bry.   HIGHER & LOWER BULLHILL, BULLHILL LANE, (*the*) *Bullhill* 1611 *LRMB* 200, 1831 Bry, *v.* bula, hyll.   BUMMER CLOSE, CLOSEBOTTOM, *Close* 1831 ib, *v.* clos, botm.   BURTON, *Burtons* 1842 OS, from the surname *Burton*.   BUXTORSTOOPS FM, *Buckstall* 1560 Sheaf, *Buckstostoope* 1611 *LRMB* 200, *Buxsters Stoop* 1831 Bry. This p.n., Buxtors Hill 127 *supra*, and *Bukstall* 124 *supra*, all within the old Forest of

Macclesfield, would be deer-traps, *v.* **buck-stall** (NED from 1503)
'a net for catching deer'. The 'stoop' (*v.* **stolpi**) would be a post for
securing the net.   CATS TOR, 1842 OS, *Catroche* 1503 *ChFor,*
Catstair piece 1848 *TA*, 'wild cat's rock', *v.* cat(t), roche[1], torr.
CHANT CLIFF FM.   CHAPEL LANE, is named from the old chapel
(101–952761) demolished 1844 (*v.* White 786), cf. *Chapel Field &*
Meadow 1848 *TA*.   CHARLES HEAD, *v.* 199 *infra*.   CLARKE HO,
Lark House 1831 Bry, cf. *Clarke Meadow, Clarke's Patch* 1848 *TA*,
from the surname *Clarke*.   CLEWSHEAD FM, *Clough Head* 1831 Bry,
at the head of Gin Clough *infra*, *v.* clōh, hēafod.   CLIFF HILL &
LANE, *v.* 107 *supra*, cf. *the two vnderclyfes* 1611 *LRMB* 200, *Cliffe,*
Far & Near Under Cliffe 1848 *TA*, *v.* under, clif.   CLOSEBOTTOM
v. Bummer Close *supra*.   CLOUGH HO & POOL, cf. *Clough Mill*
1842 OS, *v.* clōh.   COMMONBARN, *Charles Head Common* 1831
Bry, cf. Charles Head *supra*.   COOK HILL, 1848 *TA*.   COW
LANE, 1848 *ib*.   CRABTREE FM, *Crabtree Knowl* 1831 Bry, cf. *Crab-*
tree Slacke 1611 *LRMB* 200, *v.* cnoll, slakki.   CROOKEDYARD RD,
v. 127 *supra*.   CUTLER'S FM, cf. John *Coteler* 1492, William *Cutler*
1711 *Dow*.   DANEBENT FM, *Dane Bent* 1831 Bry, 'grassland by
R. Dean', *v.* beonet, R. Dean 20 *supra*.   DAWSONSBARN.
DRAGONS HOLE, a dingle in the course of Plunge Brook.   DUNGE
CLOUGH, *v.* 111 *supra*.   EAVES FM (101–981751), *Shepherds* 1831
Bry, cf. *del Euese* 1360 *Eyre* (p), *del Eves* 1438 ChRR (p), 'the edge
of a wood', *v.* efes; the place is on the boundary of Macclesfield
Forest.   ELY BROW, *El(l)ibank* 1848 *TA* (*freq*), cf. Ellis Bank 133
supra.   EWRIN LANE, 1842 OS.   FIRWOOD.   FOURLANE-
ENDS.   FOX HILL, 1848 *TA*.   GIN CLOUGH, 1842 OS.   GORSEY
BROW & KNOLL, cf. *the Gorse* 1611 *LRMB* 200.   GREAT LOWS
(lost, 101–979758), 1819 Orm[1], 1842 OS, 'big mounds', *v.* grēat,
hlāw.   GREEN BOOTH, *Greneboth(e)* 1467, 1471 *MinAcct*, *v.* 'green
out-pasture', *v.* grēne[1], bōth.   GREEN STACK, *Dixons* 1831 Bry,
v. stakkr.   GROVE.   GULSHAW HOLLOW.   HARROPFOLD (101–
966780), HARROP HO (101–973783) & WOOD, FURTHER HARROP
(101–966784), *Harrop Hall, Fold & Wood, Further Harrop* 1831 Bry,
v. Harrop *supra*.   HAWKINS LANE, 1831 *ib*.   HAYLES CLOUGH,
Hales- 1831 *ib*, cf. *Hayles Crofte* 1611 *LRMB* 200, *v.* halh, clōh.
HAZELTREE FM, *Asser Trees* 1831 Bry, *v.* hæsel, trēow.   HEDGE
Row, c.1546 Sheaf, (*the-*) 1806 *Dow, Edge Row* 1831 Bry.   HEYS-
HEAD (FM), 1831 *ib*, *v.* (ge)hæg, hēafod.   HIGH CLIFF, *The*
Highclyfe 1611 *LRMB* 200.   HIGHERLANE (FM), 1831 Bry, *Her*

Lane 1842 OS, *v.* hēarra. HOUGHGREEN, HOUGH-HOLE, *del Hogh* 1337 *Eyre* (p), *the holehouses* 1611 *LRMB* 200, *Hough Hole* 1831 Bry, '(green and hollow at) a hill', from hōh, with hōl[1] and grēne[2]. HOWLERSKNOWL, *Owlers Knowl* 1831 ib, 'alder hillock', *v.* alor, cnoll. INGERSLEY CLOUGH, 1831 ib. JOLLYCOCK FM, cf. *Jolly Cock Meadow* 1848 *TA*. KERRIDGE-END & SIDE, *Kerridge-End* 1750 Sheaf, 'the end and side of Kerridge', *v.* ende[1], sīde, Kerridge Hill 189 *infra*. KING'S CLOUGH, 1848 *TA*. KNOLLNOOK, *v.* cnoll, nōk. LAMALOAD, *Lo(w)melowe* 1479 ChRR, Orm[2], *Lomelode* 1503 *ChFor*, *Lamelode* 1519 ChRR, (*the*) 1611 *LRMB* 200, *Lamiload* 1620 *Surv*, *-lode* 1831 Bry, (*the*) *Lambie-*, *Lambye Loade* 1611 *LRMB* 200, 'loamy track or watercourse', *v.* lām, lāmig, (ge)lād, cf. Withinlow *infra*. LANE-ENDS FM (101–953751), *Hordern Lane End* 1831 Bry, cf. Hordern *supra*. This lane, 101–948757 to 110–957740, passing Berrister Fm *supra*, could be identified with *alta via ducens a Beristowe usque in forestam* 1503 *ChFor*, 'the highway from Berrister into the Forest of Macclesfield'. LANESIDE, 1831 Bry. LIMA FM & CLOUGH, *Lymewall* 1611 *LRMB* 200, *Lima* 1773 *Dow*, *Limewall alias-* 1791 ib, *Lima Clough* 1831 Bry, either 'lime spring', from līm and wælla, or 'spring in *The Lyme*', from *The Lyme* 2 *supra*, with clōh 'a dell'. LITTLE LOW, at Rainowlow *supra*, *v.* hlāw. LOWERBROOK FM, *Lowbrook* 1831 Bry, *Low(er) Brook* 1860 White. LOWERHILL FM. LOWER HO, cf. *Lowerhowse hey meadow* 1611 *LRMB* 200. LOWNDES FOLD, from fald and the surname *Lowndes* 1692 *Dow*, cf. *del Loundes* 1358, 1373 *Eyre*, *de Londes* 1378 *ib*, from land. MARKSEND QUARRIES, *Kerridge Quarry* 1842 OS, '*a stone-mine called Caridge*' 1508 *MinAcct*, cf. Kerridge *supra*. MARSH FM, cf. *The Marsh* 1831 Bry. MELLOW BROOK (Harrop Brook 28 *supra*) & CLOUGH. MILKINGSTEAD, *Milkingsteedes* 1611 *LRMB* 200, 'milking place(s)', *v.* milking, stede, cf. Milkingsteads 154 *infra*. MILLBROOK MILL, *Mill Brook* 1831 Bry. MILL LANE, named from Rainow Mill *infra*. MOSS BROOK, MOSS-SIDE BROOK, cf. *Moss (Butts)* 1848 *TA*, *v.* mos. NAB END, 1848 *ib*, 'hill end', *v.* nabbi, ende[1]. NEWBUILDINGS FM, *New Building* 1831 Bry. NEWHEY FM, *Newhey* 1831 ib, cf. *Old Hey (Lane)* 1848 *TA*, *v.* (ge)hæg. NEWINN, *New Inn* 1831 Bry. NORTH END. OAKENBANK, 1842 OS, *v.* ācen. THE OAKS, *del Okes* 1359 *Eyre* (p), *the O(a)kes* 1611 *LRMB* 200, *The Oaks*, *Oaks Wood* 1831 Bry, *v.* āc. OLDGATE NICK (101–995763), *v.* nick(e) 'a nick', the name of a gap in the Pym Chair scar, named from, and

probably a course of, the *Oldgate* road, *v.* 45 *supra*. ORMES
SMITHY, 1831 Bry, from the surname *Orme*, current in this district
from 1454 *Eyre*, ultimately the ON pers.n. *Ormr*, cf. *Ormesty* 271
infra. OX CLOSE, 1848 *TA*. PADDOCK-KNOLL, -*Knowl* 1831
Bry, *v.* pearroc. PATCH HO, *Patch or Blacksmith's Arms* 1831 ib.
PEDLEY FOLD & HO, from fald 'a fold' and a surname, cf. Pedley Hill
182 *infra*. PIKE LOW (101–967767), 1842 OS, 'pointed hill',
v. pīc[1], hlāw, cf. *Pykedelowe* 104 *supra*. PLUNGE BROOK, 1842 OS,
v. plunge. POTTS (lost), 1831 Bry, cf. John *Pott* (of Harrop) 1552
Dow. RAINOW MILL, *molendinum de Ranowe* 1471 *MinAcct*,
Ranow milne 1547 Pat. ROUNDKNOLL, -*Knowl* 1831 Bry. SADDLE
COTE, 'hut at the hill-saddle', *v.* sadol, cot. SILVER BANK,
-*bancke* 1611 *LRMB* 200, a figurative name, *v.* seolfor. SLACK I'
TH' MOOR, *Slack More* 1688 *Dow*, 'the hollow in the moor', *v.* slakki,
mōr[1]. SMITH LANE, *Smith's Lane* 1848 *TA*. SMITHYLANE FM.
SNIPE HO. SUGAR LANE (FM), *v.* Sugar Lane 184 *infra*. SWINDELS-
GATE FM, cf. Humphrey *Swindells* 1647 *Dow*, *v.* geat 'a gate'.
TAYLOR LANE. THE TORS, 1842 OS, *v.* torr. TOWER HILL
(FM), *The Towerhill* 1611 *LRMB* 200, probably 'tor hill', from torr
and hyll. VALEROYAL, 1831 Bry, named after Vale Royal 335
infra. WAGGONSHAW BROW & FM, *Wykynshawe* 1503 *ChFor*,
(*The*) *Wilkin-*, *Wilkenshawe* (*Lowe*) 1611 *LRMB* 200, *Waggonshaw*
1831 Bry, 'mountain-ash wood', *v.* cwicen, sceaga, brū, hlāw.
WALKER BARN, 1831 ib. WASHPOOL, cf. *Wash Pool Field* 1848 *TA*,
v. wæsce, pōl[1]. WAULKMILL, *Ingersley Mill* 1860 White, *v.* walke-
milne, cf. Ingersley *supra*. WHITELANDS, 1831 Bry. WHITESIDE
FM, *Whitesides* 1831 ib, either 'white hillside(s)', *v.* hwīt, sīde, or the
surname *Whiteside*. WIMBERRYMOSS FM, 'bog where whim-
berries grow'. WINDYWAYHEAD (110–953737), *le Wyndewayhed*
1503 *ChFor*, *Wynd-*, *Windaway Head* 1611 *LRMB* 200, '(the top of)
the windy-way', *v.* windig, weg, hēafod, cf. Windyway Ho 123 *supra*.
This is a road-name on the old Macclesfield–Buxton road, *v.* 45
supra. WINTER CLOSE (lost, 101–979785), 1831 Bry, 1848 *TA*,
'paddock used in winter', *v.* winter, clos, cf. foll. WINTERSIDE
(101–955780), 1831 Bry, 'hillside used for winter pasture', *v.* winter,
sīde, cf. prec. WITHINLOW, *the Wi-*, *Wythenload(e)* 1611 *LRMB*
200, 1620 *Surv*, 'track or watercourse growing with willows', *v.*
wiðigen, (ge)lād, cf. Lamaload *supra*. WOODEND FM, *Wood House*
1831 Bry, *Wood End* 1842 OS, named from Swanscoe Wood 108
supra. YEARNS LOW (FM) (101–962760, 966758), *Yeadsley* 1831

Bry, *Yanslow* 1842 OS, a hill and farm named from a tumulus at 101–964759, *v.* hlāw.

FIELD-NAMES

The undated forms are 1848 *TA* 335. Of the others 1286 is Court, 1337, 1347, 1364 *Eyre*, 1384 *Rental*, 1467, 1471, 1508 *MinAcct*, 1503 *ChFor*, 1560 Sheaf, 1611 *LRMB* 200, 1620 Surv, 1688, 1692, 1711, 1788 *Dow*, 1831 Bry, 1860 White.

(*a*) Alders (*v.* alor); Bar Fd (*the Barre field* 1611, cf. *Bar Crofte* 1611, *v.* barre); Barley Warth (*v.* waroð); Barn Fd & Mdw (*the Barnefield, -meadowe* 1611); Batterdock Fd (*v.* batter-dock 'the butter bur' or a similar plant); Bean Croft; Black Edge (*v.* ecg); Black Fd; Bollington Fd (from Bollington 187 *infra*); Bone Dust (Fd) (*v.* bone-dust); Bot mdw; The Bottoms (*v.* botm); Bow Ridding (*v.* ryding); Broadhurst (*v.* hyrst); Brow (*freq, v.* brū); Browside; Butts (Mdw) (*v.* butte); Butty Fd (*v.* butty); Calf Croft (*the Calfe Crofte* 1611); Carthouse Mdw; Church Fd (*the kirkefield* 1611, *v.* kirkja); Clayton Brow, Fd, Ground & Mdw (from clǣg and tūn, or the surname *Clayton*); Clod (*v.* clodd); Close Hill; Clough (*The Clough* 1611, *v.* clōh); Coalpit Bank; Cock Mdw; Cote Field & Mdw (*v.* cot); Cowlanes; Crowton Slack (*v.* slakki); Culvert Croft; Dirty Fd; Dowes (*the Dowes, the broad Dow, the Wall Dowes* 1611, *v.* dāl, wælla); Dry Earth; Ecton Hill 1831; Essey's mdw; Fat Fd (*v.* fǣtt 'rich'); Flake Pits (probably the same as 'gig-holes', i.e. holes in which a fire would be kindled, to dry flax laid upon hurdles across the top, *v.* fleke, pytt); Foothill; Forty Butts (*v.* butte); Frank Fd; Furze Bank; Gibraltar (*v.* 331 *infra*); Goore (*v.* gāra); Great Mdw (1688); The Green (*-e, Ranow Greene* 1611); Green Slack 1831 ('green hollow', *v.* slakki); Hall Mdw; Hastingshaw (*v.* sceaga, cf. *Astaneslegh* 51 *supra*); Higher Fd (*the Harfield* 1611, *v.* hēarra); Hill End; Hob Mdw (1860, *Hobbancke, Hobb meadow(e)* 1611, *v.* hobb(e)); Hog Brow (cf. *the Hogge Meadowe* 1611, *v.* hogg); Hollin Mdw (*v.* holegn); Hurst 1831 (*v.* hyrst); (The) Intake (*the Intacke* 1611, *v.* inntak); Jumper Lane Fd; Kiln Fd (cf. *the Kilne Crofte* 1611); Kiss Arse, Kiss Hill (probably 'hillock at or with a recess or hollow', from kjóss and ears, hyll, cf. *the Kisse Crofte* 1611, *v.* croft, and cf. Kishfield 112 *supra*, Kiss Wd 169 *infra*. Of course, names like Kiss Arse may be rude or ironic, but it is difficult to decide whether topography or manners is the criterion here); Knoll (*freq,* cf. *the Knowle* 1611); Lands Brow (*v.* land, brū); (Light) Lee(s) (*freq,* cf. *the (Heathy) Lee, the Leigh, the Ley Ridinge* 1611, *v.* lēoht, lēah); Ley Fd (*v.* lǣge); Lidia Fd, Lydiat's Brow (*v.* hlid-geat); Lime Fd & Piece (cf. *the Lymed Earth* 1611); Little Mdw (1688); Long Butts; Long Hey; Long Lee (*le Longlegh* 1364, *v.* lang, lēah); Low Edge; Marled Earth (*the-* 1611, *v.* marlede, eorðe); the Meadow (*-e* 1611); Middle Fd (1611); Middle Wood Fd; The Moor; New Lime, New Line England (i.e. 'liming land', land which needs a lime dressing); Nob (*v.* knob, cf. Nab *supra*); Old Garden (a meadow, *v.* ald, gardin); Old Lane; Old Man's Fd; Osbaldeston Croft (from the surname from Osbaldeston La); Palfrey Mdw; Park (*the little*

Park 1611); Pickhouse (*Piccles Meadowe* 1611, *v.* pigh(t)el); The Piece; Pincha Clough & Mdw (probably named from Pym Chair 174 *infra*, cf. Pym Chair Piece *infra*); Pingot (*v.* pingot); Plain; Pole Clough, Lane & Mdw (*Pole* 1620, *the Pole* 1711, 1788, *v.* pāl); Pym Chair Piece (*v.* Pym Chair 174 *infra*, cf. Pincha Clough *supra*); Ridge Mdw; Roe Fd; Rookery; Round Fd (cf. *The Round Meadowe* 1611); Rye Croft (*the Ry(e)crofte, Rycroft Wood* 1611); Sandhill; Shady Brow; Shay Clough (*v.* sc(e)aga); Shirt Brow (*v.* scerde, brū); Shoulder Hill Piece (*v.* shoulder); Smithy Carr & Croft (*Smithey Croft* 1688); Spout Fd (*v.* spoute); Square Fd; Stoney Croft (*Stony-, Stonicrofte* 1611, cf. *the Stanyflatt* 1611, *v.* stānig, croft, flat); Stubble Fd (*the Stubblefield* 1611); Sunny Brow; Sweet Fd; Switch Fd; Tanpit mdw (*v.* tan-pit); Little Tegnose 1831 (*v.* Tegg's Nose 152 *infra*); Three Nook; Tongue Shaft (a variant of tonge-sharp, *v.* Tongue Sharp 163 *infra*); Top o' th' Brow; Topcliff 1831 (at Tod's Cliff *supra*, *v.* topp, clif); (Little) Walls (*the Great* & *Little Walls* 1611, *v.* wælla); Warths (*v.* waroð); Wash Brow (*v.* wæsce, brū); Water Banks; Weatherlow Fd; Well Fd & Mdw (*the 'wellfield, willmeadowe* 1611); Wharf (*v.* waroð, cf. The Wharf 65 *supra*); White Fd (cf. (*the) Whyteflatt (End)* 1611, *v.* hwīt, flat, ende[1]); Wicken Fd (*v.* cwicen); Wilson Patch (*Wilsons Patch* 1611, from the surname *Wilson*); Windmill Fd; Wood Fd (cf. *the further-, the Highwood* 1611); Yell Brow (*v.* helde).

(b) *Ashencare* 1611 (p) (*v.* æscen, kjarr); *le Bykereslegh* 1384 ('bee-keeper's clearing', *v.* bīcere, lēah, cf. *le Bykersheye* 158 *infra*); *the Birchfield, Birchwood* 1611; *Blakeden(e)* 1347, *Blakdeyn* 1503 (*v.* blæc, denu); *Bossheadinge meadowe* 1611; *the bridgend* 1611; *broadhey* 1611 (*v.* brād, (ge)hæg); *Broomefield* 1611 (*v.* brōm); *Brushie lands* 1611 (*v.* brusshe, land); *Bryer paddock* 1611 (*v.* brēr, pearroc); *Burgas Hole* 1688; *Cheaswayes* 1611; *Christian house* & *Crofte* 1611, *Christian Croft* 1688, *Christians tenement* 1692 (from the surname *Christian*); *the Coppis* 1611 (*v.* copis); *Corner Crofte* 1611; *the (old) Cow(e)hey* 1611 (*v.* (ge)hæg); *the Darnall Eyes* 1611 (*v.* darnel, ēg); *Downes grounde* 1611 (from the family *Downes* of Shrigley); *the Eyes* 1611 (*v.* ēg); *Fittie Carr* 1611 (*v.* fit, kjarr); *Goodamfield* 1611; *Heath-Hayes* 1611; *Herrott Field* 1611 (probably land made over to meet a death-duty, *v.* heriot); *the How Meadowe* 1611 (*v.* hōh); *Hunbank* 1467, *Hanbanke* 1471, *Hundebank'* 1508, *-bancke* 1560 (perhaps 'hound's bank', *v.* hund, banke); (rivulum vocatum) *Hurdenbroke* 1467, *Hurdesbroke* 1508, *Hurdsbroke* 1560 (*v.* brōc, cf. 45 *supra*); *lamberhey* 1611 ('the lambs' enclosure', *v.* lamb (ge)hæg); *le Longelachemor* 1337, *Langelache-, Longbache More* 1503 ('(marsh at) the long boggy stream', *v.* lang, læc(c), mōr[1]); *Lowe Carre* 1611, 1620 (*v.* kjarr); *Lumhey, Lumsyde* 1611 (*v.* lum(m), (ge)hæg, sīde); *Masburnlach* 1611 (*v.* læc(c)); *Meghole* 1611 (*v.* myln); *Milne Crofte* 1611 (*v.* myln); *New Earth* 1611; *Oven Meadow* 1611 (*v.* ofen); *the Pearlefield* 1611 (*v.* pyrl(e)); *Rogers Knole* 1611 (*v.* cnoll); *the Rye Riddinge* (*v.* ryding); *the Sower Earth* 1611 (*v.* sūr, eorðe); *the Springe, the Sprinke* 1611 (*v.* spring); *The Trippett* 1611 (perhaps dial. *trippet* 'a three-legged trivet, a grid-iron'); *the Turnepies* 1611; *Wast Clough* 1611 (*v.* wēste, clōh); *Wydowes Crofte* 1611.

7. SUTTON DOWNES (110–9271), *vill' de Sutton et Dounes* 1494 ChRR, *Sutton Downes* 1710 Dow, *Sutton Higher or Downes* 1860 White. Part of this township is now included in Macclesfield 113 *supra*. The name is a composite one, like Pott Shrigley 130 *supra*, v. Sutton, *Downes infra*. The township is also referred to as *Sutton et Wynkyll* H8 Sheaf, *Sutton cum Winkle* 1724 NotCestr, cf. Wincle, Wincle Grange 164, 168 *infra*, from which it appears that Sutton included Wincle in the fifteenth century.

SUTTON (HALL) (110–925715)

> *Sutton* e13 (1608) ChRR, 1246 *Dow et freq*, *(in(fra) foresta(m) de Macclesfeld)* 1345 *Eyre*, 1352 BPR *et freq*, *(in hundred' de Macclesfeld)* 1378 ChRR, *(iuxta Macclesfeld)* 1379 *Dow*, *(iuxta Bolyngton)* 1467 *MinAcct et freq ib* to 1508, -a 1288 *Eyre*, -toun 1335 *Dow* (p), -tun 1379 *ib*, *Sutton Hall* 1611 *LRMB* 200
> *Sottona* l13 *Dav* (p), *Sotton* l13 *AddCh*, *Soton'* 1365 *Eyre*
> *Sunton* 1296 *Dav* (p)
> *Suton'* 1336, 1506 *Dow*

'South farm', v. sūð, tūn. It is south of Macclesfield. The reference to Bollington 187 *infra* is curious, as the townships do not adjoin. It may be a mistake for R. Bollin.

DOWNES (lost)

> *Dunes* e13 Dieul, 1238 P (p) *et freq* to 1286 *Eyre*, *le Dunis* 1285 *ib*
> *Dounis* c.1233 *Dow* (p), -es 1273 Ipm, 1285 *Eyre et freq* to 1494 ChRR, *(iuxta Macclesfeld)* c.1437 Orm², -us e14 *Dav* (p), -ez 1350 *Eyre* (p), *Douns* c.1320 *Dow* (p)
> *Doneys* 1240–57 *AddCh* (p)
> *Downys* c.1340 *Dow* (p), *(þe) Downes* c.1399 Sheaf, *(le-)* 1512 ChRR *et freq*, *(-in Sutton)* 1611 *LRMB* 200

'The hills', v. dūn; probably the upland part of the township. This place gave rise to *Downes*, the surname of an old Ch family. It gave name to Danes Moss 67 *supra* and also to *Dunneswode*(?) 1286 *Eyre* (Court 224 reads *Dimmeswode*), *Dunneswodhalg* 1384 *Rental*, 'Downeswood (nook)', v. wudu, halh.

STREET-NAMES: (OLD) MILL LANE, cf. Mill Green 122 *supra*, v. Macclesfield Mills *infra*; POOL ST., possibly the pool of the same mills; WATERSIDE, beside R. Bollin, cf. Waters 121 *supra*.

DANES TENEMENT (110–947703), *Mag Lane End* 1842 OS, cf. Fernlee *infra*, probably associated with *Dauenebonkes* c.1313 *Dow*, *Dane* 1503 *ChFor*, 1620 *Surv*, *Deane Eyes* 1611 *LRMB* 200, which refer to a stream near Nessit *infra*, presumably a tributary of R. Bollin with the same name as the R. Dane, cf. 20 *supra*, *v.* ēa, banke.

FERNLEE (110–9470)

> *Fernil(egh)*, *Fernileg(h)* 1283 *Dow* (p), 1286 *Eyre*, *-legh(e)* 1337 *ib*,
>   *Fernyle* 1286 *ib* (p), *-legh* 1305 Plea *et freq*, (*le-*) 1331 Plea
> *Firnil'* 1285 *Eyre* (p)
> *Ferneley* 1484 ChRR (p), *Fernelygh* 1611 *LRMB* 200
> *the Farni Legh* 1561 ChRR
> *the Fearnelie* 1611 *LRMB* 200
> *Meg Lone* 1831 Bry, *Mag Lane* 1842 OS

'The ferny clearing', *v.* fearnig, lēah. The 19th-century name means 'hoyden's, young woman's lane', from lane and dial. *meg*, from *Meg*, a pet-form of the common fem. pers.n. *Margaret*, cf. Meg Lane 122 *supra*, Meglane Wd 169 *infra*.

FOE LEE or FOXLEIGH (lost)

> *Foweleghe* 1337 *Eyre*, *le Foulegh* 1348 *ib*, (*le*) *Fogh(e)legh* 1355
>   *MinAcct*, 1363 BPR, 1384 *Rental*, 1397 Orm², *the Hyer & Lower*
>   *Foe Lee* 1611 *LRMB* 200
> *Foxlegh* 1362 Orm², 1437–8, 1524 ib, 1565 ChRR, (*le-*) 1440 ChRR,
>   1523 ib, *the-* 1564 Orm², *the Foxleigh* 1611 *LRMB* 200

'The bird-', 'the fox-glade', *v.* fugol, fox, lēah. These two names alternate in the description of a forest fee *terra del Fernileghe et Foweleghe* etc., cf. Fernlee *supra*. From the contexts, it could be supposed that *Foe Lee* was the older name of the place, surviving as the name of a plot of land, whilst *Foxleigh* replaced it as the p.n., and gave name to a dwelling here.

HIGH LEE (110–952687)

> *Heleg'* 1280 P (p), *-legh* 1290 *Eyre* (p) *et freq* to 1403 ChRR, *-leye*
>   1287 *Eyre* (p), *le Hele* 1288 *ib*
> *Heyelegh* 1285 *Eyre* (p), *Heghlegh* 1287 Orm² (p), (*le-*) 15 *Mont*,
>   (*-feld*) 1398 ChRR, *Heghelegh* 1341 *Eyre* (p)

le Hylye 1351 *Eyre, (le) High L(i)egh* 1437, 1439 Pat, *Highley field* 1611 *LRMB* 200

'(Open land at a) high clearing', *v.* hēah, lēah. Cf. (Low) Lee *infra.*

HOLLINSET (110–945685)

Holinsete 1285 *Eyre* (Court 212 reads *Holmesete*), *Holynset(e)* 1357 *ChFor* (p), 1364 *Eyre* (p), *Hollinset* 1831 Bry

Holyn(e)sheued 1337, 1366 *Eyre* (p), *-hed(e)* 1347 *ib et freq, Hollinshead* 1541 Earw, *Hollinshed, Hollyn-* 1560, 1561 Bardsley (p)

Holyngcete 1345 *Eyre* (p), *Holyncete* 1345 *ib* (p) *et freq* to 1384 *Rental, Holyncet* 1467 Bardsley (p)

Holyncoite 1467 *MinAcct*

Halyncote, -coȝte 1471 *MinAcct*

'Holly-tree fold', *v.* holegn, (ge)set, cf. Thornset 141 *supra.* The final el. has been confused with hēafod and cot. The latter is a spelling substitution of a kind frequently made by the scribes engrossing the *DuLa MinAcct* for Ch. Hollinset is the origin of the surname of the famous chronicler *Holinshed.*

KNOWLES HO, *le Nol* 1285 *Eyre* (p), *Nollefeld* 1345 *ib, le Nolle* 1362 *ib* (p), *The Know, The Knowes house* 1611 *LRMB* 200, *Nows House* 1831 Bry, 'the hillock', *v.* hnoll (replaced by cnoll), feld.

LANGLEY (110–9471), *Langel'* 1286 *Eyre, Langley* 1508 *MinAcct,* (*Litle-*), (*-Hale*) 1611 *LRMB* 200, *le longlegh* 1384 *Rental, Longley* 1467 *MinAcct,* 1611 *LRMB* 200, 'the long clearing', *v.* lang, lēah.

MACCLESFIELD MILLS (lost), *molendini de Makerfeld'* 1184 P, *molendinis de Macklesfeld'* 1252 Cl, *dua molendina de Mackelesfeld* 1353 BPR, *Macclesfield Mill* 1516 ChRR, *two watercorne Mills in Sutton commonly called Macklesfeild Mills* 1611 *LRMB* 200, cf. *þe Milnefield* 1611 *ib,* *v.* myln. These mills, both under one roof (Orm[2] III 744), belonged to the royal manor of Macclesfield but were situated in Sutton, beside the R. Bollin, near (Old) Mill Lane and Pool St. *supra,* Mill Green, 122 *supra.*

OAKEN CLOUGH, *le Okyneclogh* 1347 *Eyre, (le) Okenclogh* 1366 *ib,* 1503 *ChFor,* cf. *le Okencloghende* 150 *supra,* 'dell growing with oak-trees', *v.* ācen, clōh.

OLDFIELD, *del Oldefeld* 1357 *ChFor* (p), *Oldefeld* 1443 ChRR (p), *-filde* 1503 ib (p), *-felde* 1560 Sheaf, 'the old field', *v.* **ald, feld.**

RIDGE (HALL, HILL & GATE) (110–938708)

> *Rugge* 1353 ChRR (p), (*boscus del-*) 1359 *Eyre*, (*le-*) 1371 *Chol*, (*la-*) 1439 ChRR, *le Rudge* 1428 ib
> *le Ry(g)ges* 1428, 1429 ChRR, (*le*) *Rigges* 1503 ib, 1508 *MinAcct*
> (*le*) *Rigge* 1431 *Dow*, (*la-*, *le-*) *Rygge* 1434 ChRR, (*the*) *Ridge* 1543 Sheaf, (*-gate, -hill, -croft(es)*) 1611 *LRMB* 200, (*Hall*) 1710 *Dow*, *Rydge* c.1578 Orm²
> *Regges* 1560 Sheaf

'The ridge', *v.* **hrycg.**

ROSSEN CLOUGH (110–936695), (HILL OF) ROSSENCLOWES (110–935690), ROSSENDALE (BROOK & WOOD) (110–934704), *Rossendale Wood* 1831 Bry, *Rossen Clowes* 1842 OS, (*Big*) *Rosendale Wood* 1849 *TA*, probably associated with the local surname *de Rossyndale* 1360 *Eyre*, 1376 *Dow*, *Rosyndale* 1402 ChRR, *Rosendale* 1440 ib *et freq* in the Macclesfield district. The final el. is dæl¹ or clōh 'a valley', cf. Rossendale La 92 and Rams Clough 184 *infra*. The first syllable in these place-names and Rossington WRY 1 49 represents PrWelsh, OWelsh ros 'a moor, a heath'. The medial syllable in all these names, variously written *-in(e)-*, *-ing-*, *-en-*, *-un-*, may derive from the OE connective particle -ing-⁴, but may equally well be the OE noun-suffix -en¹ or the OE adj.-suffix -en². Professor Jackson rejects my suggestion (BNF 3 (1968), 186 of the OWelsh suffix *-inn*, *-enn* (Mod Welsh *-yn*, *-en*, cf. *Knukyn* 332 infra), from which I deduced an OWelsh form **rosinn*, *-enn* 'the little moor or heath', because he observes that the *-inn*, *-enn* suffix is not a diminutive but a singulative, and does not appear probable to him in this context. Nevertheless, such a form is defensible. The singulative effect would indicate some particularised aspect of a location—e.g. a particular piece of moorland in a general area of moors. Furthermore, Professor Richards observes that an OWelsh **rosinn* is quite possible as the origin of Welsh *Rhosyn* in Welsh place-names, although he has not noted any early examples (he points out *y Rhosin* 1694 in Llanfyllin, Montgomery-shire, *Rhosyn-goch* 1831 in Meidrim, Carmarthenshire, and the modern *Rhosyn y Mynydd* in Llanfechell, Anglesey).

SHADEYARD (110–917708)

(le) Schyde-, Scyd-, Schidyord 1283 Dow (p), 1285 Eyre (p), (le)
   S(c)hid(e)yord 1350, 1354, 1372 ib, -ʒort c.1414 Mont, le Shyde-
   yord(e) 1356 ChRR, Shydyort 1349 MinAcct (p), Schidyert 1350
   Eyre
Shyedyord 1285 Eyre (p) (Court 214 reads Shyedynd)
Schydworth 1316 ChRR (p), Shiddeworth 1358 MinAcct
Sydeyordelane 1503 ChFor
Shadeyard 1831 Bry

'Enclosure with a wooden fence', v. scīd-geard, scīd, worð.
Shedyard Db 152 is of this type, cf. Schidyord 109 supra, Shideyord
212 infra.

SYMONDLEY (110–930705), Si-, Symondesl' E3 Surv, 1384 Rental,
Simondley (-field), Symon(d)ley, Symentley(-knowle) 1611 LRMB 200,
Ley Farm 1831 Bry, 'Sigemund's clearing', from the OE pers.n.
Sigemund and lēah.

TEGG'S NOSE (-GATE, QUARRIES & WOOD) (110–9472), Teggesnase 1357
ChFor, Lit(t)le Teg(g)snose 1611 LRMB 200, 1620 Surv, (Greate)
Tegg(e)snose, (-Brouke) 1611 LRMB 200, Teg(ge)snose (-weare,
-brooke) 1620 Surv, Teggs Nose (Quarry) 1842 OS, cf. boscus voc'
Teggessenest(e), Liteltegessenest 1467, 1471 MinAcct, (Litel) Tegges-
nest(e) 1471, 1508 ib, and Luttegend' 1508 ib, the Tagg end 1611
LRMB 200, 'teg's nose and nest', v. tegga, nēs[1], nest, and lỹtel,
ende[1]. The 'nose' and the 'nest' are the names of a hill and a wood on
top of it. The weir (also called Longley Weare 1620 Surv) and the
brook were towards Langley supra, v. brōc, wer. The gate is an
entrance to the common here, v. geat. Cf. Teggsnose 123 supra.
Little Tegnose was in Rainow, v. 147 supra.

APPLETREE FM.   ARCHGREAVE, 1831 Bry, the Harts-, Harstgreave
meadowe 1611 LRMB 200, 'hart's copse', v. heorot, grǣfe.   BACK-
LANE HOUSE FM, 1842 OS, Bank Lane 1831 Bry, 'ridge lane', v.
bæc, banke, lane, the road running south-east past Ridge supra.
BACKRIDGES, 1831 ib, 'the back ridges', v. back, hrycg, cf. Ridge
supra.   BANKTOP, 1831 ib.   BARLEYFIELDS, 1842 OS, cf. the
Barleyfield 1611 LRMB 200.   THE BIRCHES.   BIRCH KNOWL,
1849 TA.   BISHOP'S CLOUGH, probably from the surname Bishop

and clōh, there being no recorded episcopal tenure here.   BLAKE-
LOW (FM, BANK & GATE), *le Blakelowell* 1471 *MinAcct*, *Blakelow*,
Blacklowe 1620 *Surv*, *Blakelow Stoop* 1842 OS, 'the black mound;
the hill, bank, post and gate there', *v.* blæc, hlāw. The gate is on the
boundary of Macclesfield Common 122 *supra*, cf. Blakelow Road
etc., 121 *supra*. The 'stoop' or pillar (*v.* stolpi) may have been a
landmark, a cross-shaft, or an old buck-stall post as at Buxtorstoops
142 *supra*.   LOWER BLAKELOW, *Bancroft* 1831 Bry, *Bankcroft* 1842
OS.   HIGHER BOARGREAVE.   BOLLINHEAD COTTAGE, 1842 ib,
v. foll.   BOLLINHEAD MILL, cf. prec, and *the Eye Head* 1611
LRMB 200, at the head of R. Bollin 15 *supra*, *v.* ēa, hēafod.   THE
BOTTOMS, *v.* botm.   BROADCAR, *Broad Carr Head* 1831 Bry,
'broad marsh', *v.* kjarr, hēafod.   BROADOAK, 1819 Orm[1].
BROOMS, *The* 1842 OS, *v.* brōm.   BROWNLOW, *Brownelowe* 1577
ChRR, (*Hill*) 1611 *LRMB* 200, *Brownlowe* 1620 *Surv*, 'the brown
hill', *v.* hlāw.   BRUNDHURST, 'burnt wood', *v.* brende[2], hyrst.
BYRON'S LANE & WOOD, *Byrons* 1831 Bry, (*Lane*) 1860 White, cf.
Byron Field 1703 (1860) White, and Henry *Biran*, *Byran* 113 *Dow*.
CESSBANK COMMON (110–958682), 1831 Bry, probably disputed
waste-land, on the Wincle boundary, *v.* cēast, banke.   CHURCH
HO, 1860 White.   CIVIT HILLS, 1842 OS, *v.* civet.   CLARKES
LANE.   COCKHALL, 1842 ib.   COPHURST (EDGE), *Cophursthall*
1561 Pat, *Cophurst* 1611 *LRMB* 200, 'bank wood', from copp and
hyrst, with ecg, hall.   CROKER (HILL), *Croker* 1831 Bry.   DAISY-
BANK.   (OLD) DOLLARDS. Dollards was *The Bank* 1842 OS.
LOWER DROVE HEY FM, cf. *the Higher Drovehey, Drovehey meadow*
1611 *LRMB* 200, 'drove enclosure', *v.* drāf, (ge)hæg.   FODEN
BANK (FM), 1789 Sheaf, cf. *Fodens (ground), the Fowdens Croftes, one
dwelling house called Fowden* 1611 *LRMB* 200 (tenanted by John
Fowden), from the surname *Foden* (*Fawdon* 1337 *Eyre, Fowdon* 1503
ChFor) probably from *Fodon* 331 *infra*, cf. Fodens 68 *supra*.
FOOLS NOOK, 1860 White.   FOX BANK, 1831 Bry.   GAWEND.
GOSLING GREEN.   GREENBANK, 1831 ib.   GREENBARN, 1831 ib.
GREEN BOWER (lost, 110–916715), 1831 ib, *v.* būr[1].   GREENWAY
BRIDGE (110–963687) & CROSS (110–956693), *Greenway Bridge* 1831
ib, *Greenway Cross or Cross o' th' Moor* 1880 Earw II 449, 'the green
road', from grēne[1] and weg; the road 110–953695 to 964685.
GURNETT, *Gurnet* 1842 OS, *Garnett Hall* 1849 *TA*.   HADDON,
1831 Bry, *Hatton Green* 1849 *TA*, cf. Haddon Croft 163 *infra*, 'heath
farm', *v.* hǣð, tūn, grēne[2].   HALLYCOMBS, *Holly Coombs* 1842 OS,

'holly valleys', *v.* **holegn, cumb.**   HANGING GATE (p.h.), 1860 White, *Gate Inn* 1831 Bry, not near foll.   HANGING-GATE FM (110–929687), 1842 OS.   HARDINGS, 1737 *Dow,* cf. Roger *Harding* 1611 *LRMB* 200, and Hardingland 126 *supra.*   HAWKSHEAD, *the Hawkesyord* 1620 *Surv, Hawkshead Wood* 1831 Bry, cf. Ratcliffe Wood *infra,* apparently 'hawk's enclosure', *v.* **hafoc, geard,** but probably 'hawk's gap', *v.* **hafoc-scerde,** cf. Hogsheads, *The Hawkesyord* 191, 166 *infra.*   HIGHLOW, 1831 ib, 'high hill', *v.* **hēah, hlāw.** HIGH MOOR, HIGHMOOR BROOK, *High Moor* 1831 ib. The brook joins Clough Brook 19 *supra.*   HOCKLEY, 1842 OS.   HOLLINHEY WOOD, *Holland Hey Wood* 1831 Bry, cf. *the long holland* 1611 *LRMB* 200, 'land in a hollow', *v.* **hol², land.**   HOLLIN LANE, *Hollins Lane* 1860 White, leads to Hollinset *supra, v.* **holegn** 'holly-tree', **lane.** THE HOLLINS, 1819 Orm², *del Holynes* 1348 *Eyre* (p), *The Hollyns* 1611 *LRMB* 200, *v.* **holegn.**   JARMIN, *Garmon* 1831 Bry, *Germans* 1842 OS, cf. Hugh *Germyn* 1551 *Dow,* John *Germayne* 1589 *ib.* (HIGHER) KINDERFIELDS, 1831 Bry, *the great & the litle Kinderfield* 1611 *LRMB* 200, possibly 'a tenement lately held by Margaret *Kyndur*' 1492 *Dow, Kyndur Howse* 1493 *ib,* an endowment of the chapel at Pott Shrigley, cf. *The Library* 5th ser., xv 48. The surname is probably from Kinder Db 114–15.   LEATHERS SMITHY, *Leather Smithy* 1842 OS. Probably like *Bullock Smithy* 256 *infra,* a smithy where drovers had their cattle shod in leather.   LEE, *The Leegh* 1611 *LRMB* 200, *v.* **lēah,** cf. foll.   HIGH & LOW LEE, *Ley House* 1831 Bry, *Lower Lee* 1842 OS, cf. prec. and High Lee *supra.* LINGERDS, *Linguards* 1831 Bry, from the family of William *Linghard* 1552 *Dow,* cf. Lingards 79 *supra.* The origin of the surname is probably 'heather enclosure', from **lyng** and **geard.**   LOWER HO, 1842 OS.   LYME GREEN, probably from the regional-name *The Lyme* 2 *supra,* and **grēne².**   MIDDLEHILLS GATE, cf. *Middle Hills* 1849 *TA, the Hills* 1611 *LRMB* 200.   MILKINGSTEADS, *the Milkensteades house* 1611 *LRMB* 200, 'the milking places' or 'places abounding in milk', from **milking** or **milken** and **stede,** cf. Milkingstead 144 *supra.*   MINNSIDE, *Minside* 1831 Bry, cf. Bosley Minn 55 *supra.*   MOSS COTTAGES (110–915714), cf. *Moss Farm* (110–913717) 1842 OS (*the Mossehowse* c.1600 Orm², *Moss House* 1831 Bry), *Moss Field Wood* (110–913709) 1849 *TA* (*le Mosse Feld* 1503 *ChFor,* (*the*) *Mosse field* 1611 *LRMB* 200), *Moss Pool* (110–917717) 1831 Bry, and *Sutton Mosse* 1503 *ChFor, Dindesmosse* 1611 *LRMB* 200, *Dinsmosse* 1620 *Surv, v.* **mos,** Danes Moss, Mosshead, Moss

Lane 67, 69, 122 *supra*. Mosslee, 1842 OS, cf. *Masseleybroke* 1467 *MinAcct* '(brook at) moss clearing', *v.* mos, lēah. Nabbs-End, *Nabs* 1831 Bry, *The Knabs* 1842 OS, 'the hill-tops (end)', *v.* knabbe, ende[1]. Nessit (Hill) (110–964705), (*l*)*e Nesset* 1384 *Rental*, the *Nesset* (-*hill*) 1611 *LRMB* 200, 'fold on a hill', from ness and (ge)set, with hyll. New Inn, 1831 Bry. The Oak, 1819 Orm[2], (*The*) *Great Oak* 1819 Orm[1], 1860 White, cf. Broadoak *supra*. Oakgrove, near Broadoak and The Oak *supra*, partly in Gawsworth 66 *supra*. Parrot Cottages. Parvey Cottage, Ho & Fm, *Parvey* 1831 Bry. Higher & Lower Pethills, *Pethills* 1831 Bry, *Higher & Lower Pettels* 1842 OS, perhaps from pightel 'a small enclosure'. Pot Lords, 1831 Bry, cf. *tenement in Sutton held by Lawrence Pott* 1551 *Dow*, also *Potts Meadow* 1849 *TA*. Lords is probably a short-form of lordes(c)hip 'a lordship, a domain'. Pyegreave, *Pyegreve* 1494 ChRR, -*s*, *Piegreve* 1561 ib, *Pygreave* 1620 *Surv*, 'magpie grove', *v.* pie[2], grǣfe. Rabb Clough, *Rap Clough* 1849 *TA*, *v.* clōh. Ratcliffe Bridge & Wood, *Ratcliff Bridge*, *Hawkshead Wood* 1831 Bry, *Ratcliff Wood* 1842 OS, cf. Hawkshead *supra*, 'red cliff', *v.* rēad, clif. Redhouses. Robinhood, *Moss End or Robin Hood* 1831 Bry, cf. Moss Cottages *supra*. Robin Wood. Rock Ho. Ryle's Arms Inn, *Ryles Arms* 1831 ib. Smallhurst, *Smalhurst lane* 1503 ChFor, *Smale(s)hurst, Smale-*, *Smallhurst Lane & Wood* 1611 *LRMB* 200, *Lone House* 1831 Bry, 'narrow copse', *v.* smæl, hyrst, lane. Spout Ho, 1831 ib, *v.* spoute. Sunny Bank. Sutton Common, 1611 *LRMB* 200, *pastura vocata le Mynne* 1516 ChRR, *common called the Mind, Mind lees* 1620 *Surv*, *v.* lǣs, cf. Bosley Minn 55 *supra*. Sutton End, *v.* ende[1]. Suttonsfold, *v.* fald. Sutton Lane Ends, Lane-Ends Fm, *Lane Ends* 1831 Bry, cf. *Sutton Lane* 1620 *Surv*. Sutton Oaks. Taylor Wood, *Taylors Wood* 1849 *TA*. Thick-withers, 1842 OS, *Thickwithens* 1831 Bry, 'thick willows', *v.* þicce[2], wīðign. Throstlenest, 1831 ib, 'thrush's nest', *v.* þrostle, nest. Tolletts Fm, *Tollits* 1831 ib. Turkshead Fm, *Turkshead* 1831 ib. Ward's Knob, from the surname *Ward* and knob 'a knoll'. Wettonway, -*Wey* 1831 ib, *v.* weg. The Wilderness, 1849 *TA*. Withenshaw, *Wi-*, *W*(*h*)*ythynsha* 1516 ChRR, 1519 Plea, *Nether Shaw* 1842 OS, 'willow copse', 'the lower copse', *v.* wīðigen, neoðera, sceaga. Wood Cottage, named from Robin Wood *supra*.

FIELD-NAMES

The undated forms are 1849 *TA* 377. Of the others, 1285 is Court, 1286, 1290, 1347, 1350, 1354, 1355, 1369, 1372 *Eyre*, 1332, 1336, 1351 (15), 1383, 1414 *Mont*, 1351, 1516[1], 1524 ChRR, 1357 *ChFor*, 1358, 1467, 1471, 1508 *MinAcct*, 1359 BPR, 1371[1] *Chol*, 1371[2], E3, 1620 *Surv*, 14 (1611), 1611 *LRMB* 200, 1384 *Rental*, 1399, 1578 Orm[2], 1393, 1414, 1528, 1602, 1716, 1722 *Dow*, 1516[2], 1519 *Plea*, 1560 Sheaf, 1611[2] *Din*, 1831 Bry.

(a) The Acre; Allers mdw (*v.* alor); Ashton Lane; Bank Fd (cf. *the (upper & lower) Bancke(s), banck meadowe & pasture* 1611)); Barker Fd (*Barkersfelde* 1524, *Barkers fieldes* 1611, 'tanner's field', *v.* barkere); Barn Croft & Mdw (*the barne crofte & meadow* 1611, cf. *the Barnefield* 1611); Bennetts Close Flatt (cf. Bennettshitch 160 *infra*, *v.* flat); Birchen Bank (*v.* bircen[2], banke); Birchen Ley (*Byrchunleigh* 1347 (p), *Birchunlegh* 1471, *Birchumlegh* 1467, *Brechehumlegh* 1508, 'clearing growing with birch-trees', *v.* bircen[2], lēah); Birchenough (cf. Birchenough Hill 160 *infra* and the local surname *del Byrchenhalgh* 1354, *Byrchynhalgh* 1528, *Berchin-*, *Birchenhough* 1716, 1722, 'corner growing with birch-trees', *v.* bircen[2], halh); Black Hill Fd, Blag Hill (*the Blaggehill* 1611, *v.* blæc, hyll); Bone Dust (*v.* bone-dust); Bottoms (*the Bothom* 1611, *v.* botm); Bower Leys (cf. *Boures-*, *Bowres Howse* 1516[1, 2], probably from the surname *Bower*, but cf. būr[1], *v.* lēah); Bowling Alley; Brickiln Fd; Briery Croft (*-e* 1611); Briery Field Clough (*v.* clōh); Brook Bottoms (*v.* botm); Broomy Shoot (*v.* brōmig, scēat); Buck Yard; Buckley Croft; Bull Park ('bull paddock', *v.* bula); Bullock(s) Fd & Mdw (cf. prec.); Burying Fd 1831 (the site is an old quarry at 110–964706 on Nessit Hill, cf. Burying Fd 87 *supra*); (Long & Lower) Butts (cf. *Blackbuttes*, *the longe butt* 1611, *v.* butte); Calf Hey (*the Calfe Hey(es)* 1611, cf. *Callerhay* 1467, *-haie* 1471, *v.* calf (gen.pl. calfra), (ge)hæg); Calve(s) Croft & Fd ((*the*) *Calf(e) Croft(e)* 1611, cf. *Caller Croft* 1524, *the Calver Croftes* 1611, cf. prec.); Cat Tail (*v.* cat(t), tægl); Cater Lane Plantation ('slanting lane', *v.* cater 'diagonal'); Church Fd; Clough (*the* 1611, *v.* clōh); Coal Pit Fd; Conney Gree (*v.* coninger); Coppice Bank & Mdw (*the Coppes* 1611, *v.* copis); Corbishley Mdw (from the surname from Corbishley 95 *supra*); Cote Mdw (1611, cf. *the Cotesfield, the Coat(e)field & -hey* 1611, *v.* cot); Large, Rough & Top Cow Hey (*the (greene, higher, little & middle) Cow(e)hey(s), the Cowhey Toppe* 1611 (*v.* cū, (ge)hæg); Cow Lane Mdw; Crab Tree Fd, Flatt & Wd (*the Crabtree Flatt* 1611, *v.* flat); Crompton Fd (cf. Crompton 122 *supra*); Dawson fd (*Dowsonsfield, Dawsonsclose* 1611, cf. John *Dowson* 1611); Day Croft (*v.* dey); Dirty mdw (cf. *the Dirrye Flatt* 1611, *v.* dyrty, flat); Dumble (cf. *Dumbellane pasture* 1611, *v.* dumbel, lane); Dunnocks Bank (*Dunnockes Bancke* 1611, 'hedge-sparrow's bank', *v.* dunnoc, banke); Ell Fd; Garner Croft; Higher & Lower George Croft, Georges Piece (*George Croftes* 1611); Gee Fd (*the Geefield* 1611, *v.* gee); Gladhurst (*v.* hyrst); Good Croft (*-e* 1611); Goose Mather (perhaps from mæddre); Gorse Fd (*the gorstie field* 1611, *v.* gorstig); Gorsey Knowl (*Gorstie Knolle* 1578, *v.* gorstig, cnoll); Green Croft (*the Greene Crofte* 1611, cf. *the greene flattes* 1611, *v.* flat); Guncar Lane (*v.* Gunco Lane 115 *supra*);

Hall Moss (*the How-mosse* 1611, *v.* mos); Hamilcotes (probably 'cottages at a scarred hill', from cot, with hamol, here used as a noun, cf. Hommerton 167 *infra*, but the first el. could be an OE pers.n. **Hamela*, or the ME pers. by-name *Hamel* (Reaney 153)); Hazel Bank; Hilty mdw; Hob Croft & Mdw (*the Hopp-, Hobb meadowe* 1611, *v.* hobb(e) 'a tussock, a hummock'); Hollin Hurst (*the hollenhurst* 1611, *v.* holegn, hyrst); Horse Close (1611); Hoskin (*the Hodgkin(s)field* 1611, from the ME pers.n. *Hodgekin*, a diminutive of *Hodge*, for *Roger*); Great & Little Hough, Hough Wd (*the great & little Haugh, the Hough meadowe* 1611, 'the nook, the corner', *v.* halh); Jennys Bank (cf. *Jenettes meade* 1611, from the ME fem. pers.n. *Jeanette*, with banke, mǣd); Johnsons Mdw (*-e* 1611); Kemp Croft (*Kembcrofte* 1611, probably a wool-combing place, cf. dial. *kemb* 'to comb', *v.* croft); Kiln Fd (cf. *the Kilne Crofte, the Kilncroftes* 1611); Kirk Fd (*v.* kirkja); Kitchen Bank (cf. *Kitchin croft* 1611); Lea Mdw (*Laye Meadowe, the Lee Meadowe* 1611, *v.* lǣge); (Great) Lee (*Great Ley* 1831, *v.* lǣge); Lee Fd (*the Layefield* 1611, *v.* lǣge); Less Bank; Lime Mdw (cf. *the Lyme Crofte* 1611, cf. *Lim-, Lymcroft* 1286, *Lyncroft* 1354 (p), *v.* lim 'lime', croft); Livesley Croft; Long Acre; Long Mdw (*-e* 1611); Long Slip (*v.* slipe 'a slip, a narrow strip of land'); Lynch Land (*v.* hlinc, land); Mares Hey (*the Mare-hey* 1611, 'mare's enclosure', *v.* mere², (ge)hæg); Meadow Bank; Meg Mdw (*Megge Meadowe* 1611, cf. Fernlee *supra*); Muck Fd (*v.* muk); Great & Little Nettlehurst (1611, le *Net(t)elhurst* 1371^[1,2], *Nettullhurst* 14 (1611), le *Nettlehurst* 1384, 'nettle wood', *v.* netel(e), hyrst); Old Wd (cf. *boscus de Sutton* 1357); Over Ridding (cf. (*Gleabe*) *Reading(es), Ryding(es), Riddinge* 1611, *v.* ryding); Patch; Picker (*-Eyes, Pickhowe* 1611, '(meadows at) a point', from pīc¹ and hōh, with ēg); Priest Fd (1611); Princes Hill; Rancied Meg Mdw (cf. Meg Mdw *supra*, also *the Ransett(es)* 1611, 'raven's fold', or 'Hræfn's fold', from hræfn or an OE pers.n. *Hræfn* and (ge)set, cf. Rainow 137 *supra*); Resting Clough (*the Rusting Clough meadowe* 1611, *v.* roosting, clōh); Rocklost (*trohelhurst, the Troughellhurste, Troughlust* (*Knowle*) 1611, 'trough hill wood', from trog and hyll, with hyrst); Rough Knowl(s); Salt Pie ('a lean-to shed', *v.* salt-pie, cf. Backlane Ho 121 *supra*); (Rough) Shays ('copses', *v.* rūh, sc(e)aga); Silters Bank; Slack Mdw (*v.* slakki); Slang (*v.* slang); Spout Mdw (cf. *Spout Crofte* 1611, *v.* spoute); Star Croft ('sedge croft', *v.* stǫrr²); Stone Stile Mdw; Stoney Wash Croft ('stony washing place', *v.* wæsce); Stubble Fd (cf. *Stubble Croft* 1611); Three Nook; Timber Hill (*Tymberhill* 1611, *v.* timber, hyll); Tom Pasture ('town- or common pasture', *v.* toun); Vetch Fd (*v.* fecche); Walkers mdw (*the Walker meadowe* 1611, from walcere 'a fuller' or the surname *Walker*); Warcock Hills (*v.* wer-cok); Water Bottoms (*v.* wæter, botm); Well Croft (*the well-, the wallcrofte* 1611, *v.* wella, wælla); Wheat Fd (*Weete-, Wheatefield & -flatt* 1611, *v.* flat); White Croft Fd; Windyway (*v.* 123 *supra*); Wood Fd & Mdw (cf. Old Wood *supra*, and *the (lower) wood, the wood(d) head & topp, vnderwood* 1611); Yew Tree Fd.

(*b*) *the Akers haugh* 1611 ('acre nook', *v.* æcer, halh); *Ball-, Bawe meadowes* 1611 (from ball 'a rounded hill'); *the Baresteades* 1611 ('bare places', *v.* bær¹, stede); *Batteslandes* 1467, *Baithlond* 1471, *pattelandes* 1508;

the Benty Croft 1611 (*v.* benty); *le Bykersheye* E3, *le Bikersegh'* 1371[1] ('bee-keeper's enclosure', *v.* bīcere, (ge)hæg, cf. *le Bykereslegh* 147 *supra*); *the Blacke Earthes* 1611 ('black ploughlands', *v.* erð); *the Blacke Loade* 1611 (*v.* (ge)lād; *Bireslescroft* 1467, *Borellescrofte* 1471, *Burrescroft* 1508, (lit. *Burrestrose*) 1560, (from croft and the surname *de*(*l*) *Burel*(*l*)*es* 1347, 1393, perhaps from byrgels 'a burial-place'); *le Brendmedo* 1351 (15) (*v.* brende[2], mæd); *le Brouncliff* 1336 (either 'brown cliff' or 'cliff at the edge of a hill', from clif with either brūn[1] or brún[2]); *Cawrehey, Cawro springe* 1611 (cf. Calrofold 139 *supra*, *v.* spring); *Crossebrooke* 1611; *Crowholt* 1611, *the Crawhoult* 1620 ('crow wood', *v.* holt); *Dayedoore* 1611 ('dairy door', *v.* dey, duru); *Eaton fielde* 1578; *the bare Eaves* 1611 (*v.* bær[1], efes); *Elcokesruddyng* E3, *Elkokesrudyng* 1383, *Elcokesrudyng'* 1384 ('Elcock's clearing', from the ME pers.n. *Elicok* and ryding); *the Flaggie Dole* 1611 ('allotment growing with flags', *v.* flagge, dāl); *foggy-, foggie field* 1611 (*v.* fogge); *Fokencrofte* 1611; *the furnifall hey* 1611 ('(enclosure at) the ferny clearing', *v.* fearnig, (ge)hæg); *the Gardenfield* 1611; *Halliwaye field* 1611 (*Halliwaye* is probably 'holy way', *v.* hālig, weg); *Hangman's Crofte* 1611; *le Haselynhurst* 1351 (15), *le Haslynhurst* 1383, *Haselenhurst* 1384, *Haslehurst* (*meadowe*) 1611 ('hazel wood', *v.* hæslen, hyrst); *le Haselyn*(*e*)*shagh* 1347, *Haselen*(*s*)*hagh'* 1357, *Haslenshawe* 1611 (*v.* hæslen, sceaga, cf. prec.); *le haystou* 1336 (perhaps 'fenced-in meeting-place', from (ge)hæg and stōw); *Henrie field* 1611; (*le*) *Herd*(*e*)*wyk*(*e*)*walle* 1369 (p), 1372 (p), 1384 (p) ('well-spring at a herd-farm', *v.* heorde-wīc, wælla); *Hiltington* 1611 (*v.* -ingtūn); *Hodg Croft* 1611 (the element *Hodge* in Ch p.ns. is not necessarily from the ME pers.n. *Hodge*, a pet-form of *Roger*, or from the derived surname, cf. NQ NS XIV, 2, 49. It probably also represents a dial. form of *hog* 'a hog'. The form *dodge* 1564–5 Morris 276 in the contexts 'dodge or byche', 'mastifes dodges', at Chester, stands for ME *dogge* < OE *docga*, *v.* dogga. This suggests the existence of alternative [-g-], [-dʒ-] pronunciations for the ME *dogge* which might well explain the origin of the vb. *dodge* (NED, cf. esp. senses 1 and 2, from the image of two dogs sparring for an opening, and 5, equivalent to the vb. *dog* 'to dog, to follow stealthily'). Similarly, OE *hocg* (*v.* hogg) > ME *hogg*(*e*) might represent alternative [hɔg], [hɔdʒ], i.e. *hog*, *hodge*. This would explain ModEdial. *hodge* 'a pig's belly or tripes' (EDD; the alternative *roger* would be a popular analogy with the pers.n. series). The pers.n. *Hodge* ('hog') for *Roger* would be a simple rhymed hypochorism, perhaps parallel with *Bill* for *Will*(*iam*). These alternative pronunciations also provide a feasible origin for the surname series *Dodge, Dodgson, Hodge, Hodgson*, etc. (ME *Doggeson, Hoggeson*). Analogous p.ns. in Ch are Hodge Croft, Fd, Hey, Mdw, Ridding (*freq* in f.ns.), Hodge 332 *infra*), Hodge-hill (86, 91 *supra*), Hodgefold (308 *infra*), Hodgel Brook (112 *supra*), Dodge-more Well (108 *supra*), Dodgsley (331 *infra*); hocg and hecg may be confused in the forms of *Hoggeryddyng* 332 *infra*); *the Hollinknowle, the Hollen-tongue & the Hollintrefield* 1611 ('holly knoll, tongue and tree', *v.* holegn, cnoll, tunge, trēow); *the pettie Hoyles* 1611 ('little hummocks', *v.* pety, hygel); *the Hustiddes* 1611 ('the house-steads', *v.* hūs-stede); *Hyde* 1611 (perhaps from hīd 'a hide of land'); *the Impyord* 1611 ('the nursery', *v.* impe-ȝard); *the Kimbols* 1611 (Professor Löfvenberg suggests that this may represent OE **cymbel*, a derivative of OE *cumb* 'a vessel', cf. ModEdial. *kimble* 'a washing-tub or tray' (EDD). The el. **cymbel* could denote a depression in the ground, cf. OE **cymbe*, another derivative of *cumb*, in Kyme L (DEPN), v. EPN s.vv. cumb, cymbe); *Kockersley* 1508, *Cokersley* 1560 ('cocker's clearing', v. cocker); *the marled Crofte, earthe & field* 1611 (v. marlede, eorðe); *the Orchard* 1524, 1611; *the Ovenhouse field* 1611 (v. ofen); *Owlerlee* 1611 ('alder glade', v. alor, lēah); *Oxfordcroft* 1399 (v. oxa, ford, croft); *Pilatescroft* 1371[1] (p) (v. pil-āte, croft); *the Pingow* 1611 (v. pingel, cf. pingot); *the Rishy Meadowe* 1611 (v. riscig); *the Ry(e)crofte* 1611; *Ryeroote* 1611 (v. ryge. The second el. is ModE dial. *root* (1846 NED) 'a grubbing-up, a rooting-out' from the vb. *(w)root* (NED) 'to root out, to grup up', (OE *wrōtan*, ON *róta*). This field would be one where swine were allowed to root about in rye stubble, cf. *Rye Route* 109 *supra*, Pye Root 186 *infra*, *the Swyne-Rootes* 193 *infra*, Roots 201 *infra*); *the Rymynge butt* 1611 (v. butte); *the Seaven Lowes* 1611 ('the seven mounds', v. seofon, hlāw); *the shortlandes* 1611 (v. sc(e)ort, land); *Shrogie field* 1611 (v. shrogge 'bush, brushwood'); *the Shuthorne* 1611 ('projecting corner', v. scēat, horn); *the Springe* 1611 (v. spring); *the Spurrefield* 1611; *Stackyord* 1611 (v. stak-ȝard); *Stanyfordlache* 1384, v. stānig, ford, læc(c)); *Stoken Bridge* 1611, *Stokenbridge* 1620 ('bridge made of logs', v. stoccen, brycg); *Stephale* 1414, *Stepull* 1602, *Stepall, the Stepole* 1611, *Steapoole* 1611[2] ('valley or hollow at a steep place', v. stēpe[1], halh); *Stockindole* 1611 ('allotment cleared of stumps', v. stoccing, dāl); *Stopinhul* 1285 (p), *-en-* 1350 (p), *Stopenhull* 1355 (p), 1357 (p), 1372 (p), *-on-* 1359 (p) (a surname derived from an unidentified p.n. 'Stoppa's hill', from an OE pers.n. *Stoppa* as in Stopham Sx 120, *Stoppingas* Wa xvii, Stopsley BdHu 163, v. hyll. The *-in-* could represent *-ing-*[4]); *Sutton Halk* 1611 (v. halc); *the Toddall* (*meadow*) 1611 (probably 'foxhole' from tod-hole); *the White Hill* 1611; *Wyncelfeld* 1467, 1471, 1508 (v. wincel, feld, cf. Wincle 164 *infra*); *(le)Wodal(e)rugg'* 1371[1], 1384 ('(ridge at) the wood nook', from wudu and halh, with hrycg); *Wolrichelegh* E3, *Wolrychelegh'* 1384 ('Wulfrīc's clearing', from the OE pers.n. *Wulfrīc* and lēah); *Wysshelegh'* 1336 ('marshy-meadow clearing', v. wisc, lēah, cf. John de *Whissheleg'* 1365 BPR III 482).

8. WILDBOARCLOUGH (110–9868)

Wildeborclogh' 1357 ChFor, *Wyld(e)-, Wild(e)bor(e)clogh* 1442 ChRR, *Wildebore(s)clough* 1611 LRMB 200, *Wildboar(s) Clough* 1724 NotCestr

Wylborclogh 1409 ChRR, *Wilberclogh* 1503 ChFor, *-bourglough* 1548 Sheaf

Wideborclogh 15 (1520) ChRR

Wildeberclogh 1467 MinAcct, *-bircheclogh* 1471 ib

Wudebor Cleyk 1508 MinAcct

Wisbersclough c.1639 Chol

'Wild boar's clough', *v.* wilde-bār, clōh. The clough is the long narrow valley of Clough Brook 19 *supra*, 110–978720 to 970663.

SHUTLINGSLOE (mountain 110–9769, farm 110–982695)

Shuclynglowebroc 1337 *Eyre*
Schutlynglowebrok 1337, 1350 *Eyre*, *Shutlynglowe* 1409 ChRR, *-ling-* 1452 ib, *Shutlynglos* 1461–83 (1520) ib
Shotlynglowebrok 1357 *ChFor*
Shitlynglowe 1358 *MinAcct*
Shuttinglowe 1459 ChRR, *-low* 1523 (1571) ib, *-ynglowe* 1467, 1471 *MinAcct*
Shultinglowe 1459 ChRR (Barnes[1] 878)
Shutlinghaw Hill c.1620 Orm[2]
Shutlingeslaw 1610 Speed, *Shutlingslaw* 1612 Polyolbion, *Shutlingslow Hill* 1656 Orm[2]

'Scyt(t)el's hill or mound', from an OE pers.n. *Scyt(t)el* and *-ing-*[4], hlāw, with brōc 'a brook'. The brook is Clough Brook 19 *supra*. The pers.n. is supposed also in Shitlington WRY, Nb, Shillington Bd, cf. WRY 2 206.

ALLGREAVE HILL, *Hallgreave Hill* 1848 *TA*, *v.* Allgreave 168 *infra*. HIGHER & LOWER BANGS, 1848 *ib*, *v.* banke.   BANKTOP, *Top of Bank* 1831 Bry.   HIGHER & LOWER BARN, 1842 OS, *High & Low-* 1831 Bry.   BENNETTSHITCH, *Bennets Itch* 1831 ib, *Bennet Sitch* 1842 OS, from the ME pers.n. *Benet* (OFr *Beneit*) and hiche 'an enclosure of hurdles', confused with sīc 'a small stream', cf. Bennetts Close Flatt 156 *supra*.   BERRYBANK (WOOD), UNDER BERRYBANK, *Berrybank* 1831 Bry, cf. Brookside Cottage *infra*.   BIRCHENOUGH HILL, cf. Birchenough 156 *supra*.   BLAZE, 1831 ib, *v.* blesi 'a bare spot on a hill-side'.   BLOSSOMS MEADOWS, *Blossoms Meadow* 1842 OS.   BRIDGE POOL, in R. Dane, near a footbridge.   BROOKSIDE COTTAGE, *Berry Bank End* 1831 Bry, named from Clough Brook 19 *supra*, Berrybank *supra*.   BROUGHSPLACE.   BURNTCLIFF TOP, *v.* brende[2], clif, cf. Stoneway Edge *infra*.   CHESHIRE KNOWL, *Low Bower Edge* 1831 Bry, *Low Boar Edge* 1848 *TA*, just in Ch against the Db boundary, cf. Dane Bower *infra*.   CHEST HOLLOW, cf. *New Chess* 1831 Bry, *v.* 127 *supra*.   CLOUGH BROOK, *v.* 19 *supra*, cf. Wildboarclough *supra*.   CLOUGH HO, 1831 Bry, *v.* clōh.   CORRECTION BROOK, named from *House of Correction* 1831 ib, a piece of

poor ground adjoining this stream.   CRAG COTTAGE, HALL &
WORKS, 1831 ib, v. cragge 'a crag, a rock', cf. Rottenstone *infra*.
CUCKOO ROCKS, *Bleak Knowl* 1842 OS, v. bleak 'cheerless, pale,
exposed'.   CUMBERLAND, 1831 Bry, 'encumbered land', from ME
cumber 'encumbrance' or 'stony land', from OFr *combre* 'a heap of
stones', v. WRY 7 173, *cumber* NED and land. The evidence is too
late for Cumbre (gen. Cumbra) 'Britons' .Similar are Cumberland
201 *infra*, *Comberwheyn* 211 *infra*.   CUT-THORN, 1831 ib, 'trimmed
or lopped-thorn', v. cut[2].   DAISYCLOUGH, *Daisey Clough* 1831 ib.
DANE BOWER (111–015700), *Dane Bower Bank* 1831 ib, *Boar Edge*
1848 *TA*, cf. *Dane hed'* 1503 ChFor, *The hedde off Dane* 1536 Leland,
Danehead 1619 Orm[1], *Davenhead* 1673 Sheaf, and *Dane Mosse* 1619
Orm[1], the source of R. Dane 20 *supra*, v. būr[1], hēafod, ecg, mos, cf.
Cheshire Knowl *supra*, Whetstone Ridge *infra*.   DANE COTTAGE,
The Cottage 1842 OS, named from R. Dane 20 *supra*.   DANE-
THORN, *Dane Thorn* 1842 ib, *Deane Thorne* 1848 *TA*, 'thorn-tree by
R. Dane', v. þorn, R. Dane 20 *supra*.   DINGERS HOLLOW, cf.
Dynges 1371 *Eyre* (p), v. dyngja, holh.   DRYKNOWL, 1831 Bry,
'dry hill', v. drȳge, cnoll.   DUBLIN (lost), 1831 ib, a house.
DUNKIRK (lost, 110–988664), 1831 ib, a house, v. 331 *infra*.   EDIN-
BURGH (lost), 1831 ib, a house.   THE FIRS (lost), 1831 ib, a house.
GALLOWAYKNOWL, 1831 ib, v. cnoll.   GLASGOW (lost), 1831 ib, a
house.   GOOSETREE, 1831 ib, 'gorse bush', v. gorst-trēow, cf.
Goosetrees 68 *supra*.   GREEN GUTTER, 1848 *TA*, a moor named
from the course of Yarnshaw Brook *infra*, 'green dingle', v. goter, cf.
ModEdial. *gutter* 'the bed of a mountain-side watercourse', cf.
Sheepclough-, Tinkerspit Gutter *infra*.   GREENWAY BRIDGE, v.
153 *supra*, cf. Piggford Moor *infra*.   HEILDEND, HEILD ROCKS &
WOOD, *Yeld-end* 1831 Bry, *Heild End & Rocks* 1842 OS, 'the hill-
side', v. helde, ende[1].   HELMESLEY (ROCKS & WOOD), *Helmsley*
1831 Bry, perhaps from helm 'a cattle-shelter' and lēah.   HIGH-
ASH, *High Ash* 1831 ib.   HILL END (lost), 1849 *TA*, 1842 OS,
Hill Farm 1831 Bry.   (FAR) HOLE-EDGE, (*Near*) *Hole Edge* 1831 ib,
Far Hole Edge 1842 OS, 'edge of the hollow', on the brink of the
Dane valley, v. hol[1], ecg.   HOLE HO (lost), 1831 Bry, v. hol[1], hūs.
HOLT, 1831 ib, 'the wood', v. holt.   KNAR, *The-* 1849 *TAMap*,
Nar 1831 Bry (lit. *Nan*), v. knar 'a rugged rock'.   LEECH WOOD,
Leach 1831 ib, cf. *Leech Hole* 1848 *TA*, 'the swamp', v. lece. *Leech
Hole* was a farm east of the wood.   LOVELANE BRIDGE (111–001664),
1842 OS, v. lufu, lane, alternatively *Quarnford Bridge* 1849 *TAMap*,

cf. *Cornford, Quornford* 1286 *Eyre, Quernesford* 1322 Cl, *le Quenesford*
1357 *ChFor, Querneford* 1445 *Eyre*, 'mill-ford' *v.* cweorn, ford,
whence Quarnford St.   LOWER HO, 1831 Bry.   LOWER KNOW
WOOD, *Lower Knoll* 1848 *TA, v.* cnoll.   MANCHESTER GARDENS
(lost), 1831 Bry, a homestead, *v. 333 infra.*   MIDGLEYGATE, 1831 ib,
-yate 1848 *TA, v.* geat 'a gate' and Midgley 167 *infra.*   MIDGLEY
HILL, 1848 *ib, Miggeleghlegh* 1357 *ChFor* 'clearing belonging to
Midgeley', *v.* lēah, cf. Midgley 167 *infra.*   MOUNT PLEASANT,
v. 333 infra.   MURRAY ROAD (lost, 111–002719 to 009700), 1831
Bry.   HIGHER & LOWER NABBS, *-Nabs* 1831 ib, *v.* knabbe 'hilltop'.   OWLER'S BRIDGE.   PANNIERS POOL (BRIDGE) (111–
001684), 1831 ib, on R. Dane, the St boundary, at Three Shire Heads
infra, v. pōl[1]. The name may refer to the panniers borne by pack-
horses watering here, cf. Panniers Pool Db 373.   PARKS, 1831 Bry.
PEARLS, 1831 ib, 'the springs', *v.* pyrl(e).   PIGGFORD MOOR
(110–965687), *Pickford Moor* 1831 ib, *Pigford Moor* 1848 *TA,*
perhaps named from an old ford at Greenway Bridge *supra* (110–
963687), '(moor at) the hill-ford', *v.* pīc[1], ford.   PINCHERS HOLE.
PLOUGH COTTAGE, *Plough Inn* 1831 Bry.   HIGHER & LOWER
RIDGE (lost), 1831 ib, hill-names.   ROBINS CLOUGH, 1831 ib, from
the ME pers.n. *Robin,* diminutive of *Robert,* and clōh 'a dell'.
ROTTENSTONE, *Nearer Crag* 1831 ib, *v.* cragge, cf. Crag *supra.* The
modern name is either 'crumbling rock' from rotinn and stān, or
ModE *rottenstone* (1677 NED) the term for a decomposed siliceous
limestone.   THE SCAURS, 'rocky cliffs', *v.* sker.   SHEEPCLOUGH
GUTTER, *v.* scēap, clōh, goter.   SPARBENT, 1842 OS, *Sparrow Bent*
1831 Bry, 'sparrow infested bentgrass', *v.* spearwa, beonet.   STONE-
WAY EDGE (lost, 110–991663), 1860 White, *Stony Way Head* 1842 OS,
the hamlet at Burntcliff Top *supra*, '(hill on) the stony road', *v.*
stānig, weg, ecg ,hēafod. This is a road-name on route XVIII 46
supra.   TAGSCLOUGH (HILL), *Taggeclogh* 1350 *Eyre, Yadsclough*
1831 Bry, *Tatch Cliffe Hill* 1848 *TA*, 'teg's valley', *v.* tagga, clōh.
THREE SHIRE HEADS, (111–009685), *the Three Sheres* 1533 Db 373,
the (three) shire stones c.1620 Orm[2], *The Three Shire Mears* 1656 ib,
'the three county-boundary stones', where Ch, Db and St meet,
v. þrēo, scīr[1], hēafod, stān, (ge)mǣre.   TINKERSPIT GUTTER
(111–015708 to 017704), 1831 Bry, cf. Tinker's Pit Db 374, *v.* goter.
This is the head-water of R. Dane, a boundary of the Forest of
Macclesfield *v.* 9 *supra.*   TONGUE SHARP WOOD (110–983679),
Tongue Sharp Clough 1848 *TA*, from wudu and clōh with ME *tonge-*

sharp (not in NED) 'a pointed thing like a tongue, the point of a tongue, a pointed tongue of land', from **tunge** and ME *scharp* 'a sharp edge, a point', (cf. scearp). The substantive use of *scharp* is first recorded l14 in *Sir Gawain* ll. 424, 1593, etc., *v*. NED *sharp* sb[1], 1, 2. The compound *tonge-sharp* is recorded early in *unum Tongesharp terre cum pertinenciis in Parva Barwe* ('a *tonge-sharp* of land...in Little Barrow') 1359 *Chol* G.36, *le tungesarp* 1281 335 *infra, Tungesharplond* c.1200 335 *infra*, and appears in Tongue Sharp 130 *supra*, 275, 316 *infra*. An analogous p.n. compound, from **tunge** and **sceaft**, seems to lie behind Tong(ue) Shaft 147 *supra*, 253, 335 *infra*. UNDERBANK, *Alders* 1842 OS. VICARAGE WOOD. WHETSTONE RIDGE, *High Bower Edge* 1831 Bry, *Higher Boar Edge* 1848 *TA*, cf. Dane Bower *supra, v*. hwet-stān, hrycg. WHITE COTTAGE. WILSHER PLACE (lost, 110–987717), 1849 *TAMap*, cf. *Walschawe* 1357 *ChFor* (p), *Willshaw meadow* 1848 *TA*, 'wood at a well-spring', *v*. wella, wælla, sceaga. WINDYHARBOUR (110–986672), 1831 Bry, 'windy shelter', at the summit of a pass on a track over Tagsclough Hill, *v*. windig, here-beorg. WOOD MOSS, 1831 ib. YARNSHAW BROOK & HILL, *Yarnshaw Brow, (Great) Yarnshaw* 1848 *TA*, probably 'eagle's wood', from **earn** and **sceaga**. The brook joins Clough Brook 19 *supra*.

FIELD-NAMES

The undated forms are 1848 *TA* 431, 1849 *TAMap* 431. Of the others 1337 is *Eyre*, 1611 *LRMB* 200, 1626 *Chol*, 1831 Bry.

(a) Acre; Back o' th' Hill; Backside (*pastur' vocat' Backsyde of Wyldboreclough* 1626, *v*. ba(c)ksyde); Bank Holme (*v*. banke, holmr); Bendways Moss (*Bendiway Moss* 1831, 'grassy road', *v*. benty, weg, mos); Bent (*v*. beonet); Black Knoll; Black Side; Boltshaw Piece (*v*. bolt, sceaga); Bottoms (*v*. botm); Brow; Browning Piece; Brunstone; Cinderhill (*v*. sinder, hyll); Clay Gutter (*v*. goter); Cliff Mdw; Coney Bank (*v*. coni); Cote Fd (*v*. cot); Counting Fd; Cow Hill 1831; Dearden; Dirty Fd; Downes piece (cf. *Downes* 148 *supra*); Finley Croft; Flasker Moor (1831, from flask 'a swamp', kjarr 'a marsh'); Flats (*v*. flat); Flax Close; Folly; Frost Cliff (1831, 'cliff at a ridge', *v*. forst[1], clif); Fuller's Mdw; Galle(y)wood (1831, at 111–007688, near Three Shire Heads *supra*, perhaps 'gallows wood' from galga and wudu); Glubbs; Green Dale; Green Hills; Green Slack (*v*. slakki); Haddon Croft (6x, cf. Haddon 153 *supra*); Haley Rushes; Harreds; Hazelbadge ('hazel valley', *v*. hæsel, bæce[1], cf. Hazlebadge Db 118); Hazling Shaw (*v*. hæslen, hæsling, sceaga); Hobhole ('goblin's hole', *v*. hob, hol[1]); Hollin Hey (*v*. holegn, (ge)hæg); Hollinbrook (*v*. holegn); Holme(s) (*v*. holmr); Hourush Mdw ((*the*) *Horeedge-, Horidge meadow(e)* 1611, *Here Edge Meadow* 1831, 'the grey edge', *v.* hār², ecg); Jointry ('held in jointure', *v.* jointure); Kirk Hill (*v.* kirkja); Knoll; Lark Park (1831, *v.* lāwerce, park); Lees (*v.* lǣs); Lewa(r); Lime Kiln Brow; Lockers Clough ('shepherd's dell', *v.* lōcere, clōh, cf. ME *lokere* 'a looker, one who looks after something, a keeper', Fransson 146); Long Butts (*v.* butte); Midding Croft (*v.* midding 'a midden'); Moor Fd; Moss (*v.* mos); Old man's croft; Old Park; Overhill (*v.* ofer², hyll); Ox Close; Pasture Heath; Pingot (*v.* pingot); Plat Gap Fd ('footbridge-gate', *v.* plat¹, gap); Rough Knoll; Row Hill (*v.* rūh); Saddlepit Fd; Sallen Green (*v.* salegn, grēne²); Sear; Shaw Croft & Green (*v.* sceaga); Shearing Fd; Sludder Hill ('slippery hill', *v.* sludder 'muddy, slippery'); Spout Bank (*v.* spoute 'a spring'); Stews (*v.* stuwe); Stones; Stoney Bank; Tenters Croft (*v.*tentour); Toothill ('look-out hill', *v.* tōt-hyll); Turf Moor ('peat moor', *v.* turf); Twitcha (*v.* twitchel 'a narrow passage'); Wall Nook ('a turning in a wall' *v.* wall, nōk); Wareing Mdw; Wash Croft (*v.* wǣsce 'a place for washing'); Wharf (*v.* waroð 'a meadow', cf 65 *supra*); White Fd; Wicken Stones 1831 (a line of outcrop boulders); Wildmoor Edge (1831, *v.* wilde, mōr¹).

(*b*) (*le*) *Southmosse* 1337 (*v.* sūð, mos).

9. WINCLE (110–958661) [winklə]

> *Winchul* c.1190 *AddCh*, *Winchull* 1237 P, *Wynchull* c.1190 (1285) ChRR, 1285 *ib*, 1357 *ChFor* (p), 1371 *Chol*, 1384 *Rental*, 1400 *Mont*, *Wynchul* 1349 *MinAcct*
> *Winkhull'* 1237 P, *Wynkhull* 1354 BPR, 1357 *ChFor*, 1358 *MinAcct*, 1370 *Eyre*, 1414 *Mont*, 1471 *MinAcct*
> *Wynkehull* 1291 Tax, 1379 *Eyre*, *-hill* 1467 *MinAcct*
> *Winkel* e14 ChRR (p), *Wynkell* 1357 *ChFor*, *Wincell* 1543 Orm², *Wynkull* 1499 Sheaf, *Wyncull* H8 *ib*, 1535 VE, c.1550 *Surv*, *-e* 1547 *MinAcct*, *Vincull(e)* 1554 *ib*, 1560 Sheaf, *Wynkyll* H8 *ib*, *Wynkall* 1554 *ib*
> *Wynhull* 1508 *MinAcct*, *Winhull* 1560 Sheaf, *Wynall* 1543 *ib*
> *Wincle* 1531 Sheaf, (*-Andrewe*) c.1602 *Chol*, *Wyncle* 1544 Plea, 1550 *Dow*, *Winkle* 1578 Earw, 1716 Wil, (*alias Winkhull*) 1710 *Dow*, (*Sutton cum-*) 1724 NotCestr, *Winckle* 1620 *Surv*, 1639 *Chol*, 1659 Earw

There are three possible derivations for this p.n. The first, and preferable, is from wincel 'a nook, a corner' (the final *-el* confused with ME *hull* from hyll 'a hill'), alluding to the hamlet's site in the bend of a valley, *Winchulcloch, Winchultlock* c.1190 *AddCh*, *Wynchul(l)clo(u)gh* c.1190 (1353) *ChFor* (inspex.), *the further & nearer Clough, Clough-head* 1611 *LRMB* 200, *v.* clōh, hēafod, cf. Winchcombe Gl 2 30, KPN 149, and the Danish p.n. *Vinkel* (DaSN IX 73, 168) alluding to a place at a river-bend (ex inf. Professor Sørensen).

The second, since the earlier references are to the site of Wincle Grange *infra*, is from wince 'a bend, a corner' and hyll 'a hill', meaning 'hill at, or in, a bend', alluding to the spur north of the Grange, which forms an elbow round the head of the valley in which the hamlet lies, cf. Winchhill Hrt 24. Dr von Feilitzen prefers this, and cf. DEPN. Professor Löfvenberg analyses the p.n. in accordance with his argument in Löfvenberg 232 (apparently rejected by Smith in EPN s.v. wince). He says that all the forms before 1300, including those cited for Wincle Grange *infra*, point to OE hyll as the second el.; that in these, *u* cannot possibly stand for an original *e* (from wincel), cf. Jordan §135 Anm.1; that Wincle cannot be compared with Winchcombe Gl, which shows OE forms with *Wincel-*; that the first el. is either an OE pers.n. **Wineca* as is suggested by DEPN, or the OE word *wince* 'winch, pulley', probably also 'well', i.e. 'well with a well-wheel turned by a crank', a sense which is evidenced in NED s.v. *winch* from c.1440 (cf. also dial. *wink* NED, EDD); and that it seems doubtful whether OE wince (EPN) was ever used in the sense 'angle, bend'.

Wincle has been suggested as the site of the lost *Hofinghel, Hofinchel* 1086 DB f. 264 which has been derived from hof 'a temple, a house' and wincel (Tait 115 and xii). The forms, however, suggest OE **hofincel*, from hof with the diminutive -incel 'a little house', and the place is associated in DB with Tintwistle, Hollingworth, Werneth, Romiley and *Laitone* 320, 309, 302, 292, 282 *infra*, at the other end of the Hundred. The suffix *-Andrewe* is an unsolved problem, cf. Mottram St Andrew 202 *infra*. Cf. *Wyncelfeld* 159 *supra*.

BUTTERLANDS (110–947671), *Botirlond* 1286 *Eyre*, *Buter-*, *Boterlondes* E3 *Surv*, *Butterlondesmede* 1371 *Chol*, *Butterlandes* 1602 *Dow*, 'rich pasture land (good for butter)', *v*. butere, land.

CLEULOW CROSS (CLOUGH & WOOD) (110–952674), *Clulow* E3 *Surv*, *-e* 1371 *Chol* (p), *Clulow Cross* 1538 Sheaf, *Clewlowe* 1352 *Eyre* (p), *Clewlow Cross* (*Farm*) 1831 Bry, *Clelowe* 1525 ChRR, 'the cross at Cleulow', the site of an Anglo-Saxon 'Mercian-style' cylindrical cross-shaft, illustrated Earw II 435, standing on a mound said to be artificial, in a prominent position at the head of a valley near the boundary of Sutton Downes 148 *supra* and a cross-roads, where the Congleton–Buxton road (route XVIII 46 *supra*) crosses the road from Macclesfield to Wincle (cf. route XVI *supra*). Cleulow is an unusual name. In the first draft of this work it had been noted that the first el. seemed to be ME *clywe*, *cle(o)we* (cf. OE *clīewen*, *clēowen*) 'a clew, a ball (of thread, yarn etc.)', which might be used here figuratively in the sense 'a clue, a guiding line (as through a labyrinth etc.)' to denote a mound serving as a landmark and road-marker on the wild moors. Professor Löfvenberg confirms that the first el. would seem to be an OE **clēo(w)* 'a clew, a ball' (PrGerm **klewa-*) cognate with OE *clīewen*. He suggests that Cleulow may mean 'ball-shaped mound' or 'round mound', and cites a possible analogy in Clee Hill Sa (DEPN).

DANE BRIDGE (110–965652), 1611 *LRMB* 200, *Dauenbrugge* 1357 *ChFor*, 'bridge over R. Dane', *v.* brycg, cf. R. Dane 20 *supra*. At or near this place was *scliderford* c.1190 *AddCh*, *Sclyderford* c.1190 (1353) *ChFor* (inspex.), *Sliderfordbrugge in Haukesyerd* 1347 *Eyre*, *Slyderford brugge* 1384 *Rental*, 'slippery ford', *v.* slidor, ford. Cf. *Hawkesyord infra*.

HIGHER & LOWER GREASLEY (110–9466), 1831 Bry, *Greselegh'* 1350 (p), 1355 *Eyre*, *Greasley* 1611 *LRMB* 200, *v.* lēah 'a clearing'. The first el. might be grǣg[2] 'a badger', but Professor Cameron observes that this p.n. may be analogous with Gresley Db 636, Greasley Nt 144, 'gravelly clearing', *v.* grēosn, cf. Studies[2] 175–6.

HAWKSLEE (110–938653), *Hauekeslee* 1286 *Eyre*, *(le) Haukeslegh-(clogh)* 1347, 1348 *ib*, -*ley*, *Hawkyslee* 1516 Sheaf, Orm[2], *Hawkeslegh*, -*ley* 1547, 1576 ChRR, *Hawksley* 1580 Orm[2], 'hawk's clearing', *v.* hafoc, lēah, cf. foll.

THE HAWKESYORD (lost), 1611 *LRMB* 200, *Hauek(i)sherd* 1285 *Eyre*, Court (p), *le Hawkesherd in Dauene Wode* 1347 *Eyre*, *Haukushert* 1530 *Plea*, 1561 ChRR, *(le) Haukeserd* 1337 *Eyre*, 1357 *ChFor*, *le Haukesert* 1352 *Eyre* (p), *le Haukesyerd iuxta Dauenbrugge* 1359 *ChFor*, cf. Daven Wood 55 *supra*, Dane Bridge *supra*. This name recurs in The Hogue Sherd, Hawkshead 136, 154 *supra*, Hogsheads, Hogshead Green, *Haukeshert*, *Haukesyerd*, 191, 231, 205, 276 *infra*, *Haukeserde*, Hawkers Head, *le Haukesherd* (twice), Hogshead (Lane), *Hawkeserte* 332 *infra*. It represents an OE **hafoc-scerde,-sceard* (*v.* hafoc, scerde, sceard), ME **hauekesherd*, -*shord*, 'a gap (e.g. in woodland), a cleft, in which a hawk may fly, or where hawking may be done'.

HOMMERTON (KNOWL (FM) & MOSS) (110–9667)

Hameldon 1347 *Eyre* (p), 1372 *ib* (p), *Hamildon* 1611 *LRMB* 200
Homeldon' E3 *Surv* (p), 1348 *Eyre* (p) *et freq* to 1384 *Rental*,
   (*boscus de-*, *Nether-*) 1357 *ChFor*, *-den* 1350 *Eyre* (p), *Homuldon'*
   1347 *ib*, 1359 BPR (p), *Homildon* 1364 *Eyre* (p)
Hamulton (*Mosse & Nase*), *Hannilton* (*Common*), *Hamalton or*
   Hamildon 1611 *LRMB* 200, *Hamelton Common* 1620 *Surv*
Hammerton Knowl, *Hammertons* 1831 Bry, *Hammerton formerly*
   called Hammelton, Hambleton or Hamilton 1880 Earw II 449
Homerton 1840 *TA*
Hambletons Torr 1848 *TA* 247

From **hamol, hamel** 'maimed, mutilated', and **dūn** 'a hill' (with
mos, nesu 'a nose', **cnoll, torr** 'a rock'), cf. **hamol** EPN for other
examples of this compound. Hommerton Knowl is the summit of a
ridge which rises gradually from the north-west and then falls away
steeply to the south-east, a profile which suggests that the ridge has
been cut off at the south-east end. Cf. Hamilcotes 157 *supra*, Hazels
infra.

MIDGLEY (WOOD) (110–9766)

Mugelegh' 1286 *Eyre*
Muggeleg', (*boscus de-*) 1286 *Eyre*, (*vaccaria de*) *Muggelegh'* E3 *Surv*,
   1347 *Eyre*, 1462 ChRR, (*molendinum de*) *Muggele* 1329 *MinAcct*
Myggelegh 1337 *Eyre*, 1359 Chamb, *-ley* 1409, 1523 ChRR,
   Miggele(e), (*boscus de*) *-legh* 1347 *Eyre*, *pastura de Miggele* 1353
   BPR, *Miggelegh Forde* 1357 *ChFor*, *Miggeley* 1413 *Mont*
Mogylegh 1366 *Eyre* (p)
Megerlegh' 1467, 1471 *MinAcct*, *Meggelegh* 1471 *ib*
Mydgeley 1503 *ChFor*, *Mydgley* c.1602 *Chol*, *Midgeley* 1611 *LRMB*
   200, *Midgesley* 1626 *Chol*
Magge legh 1508 *MinAcct*, *Maughley* 1560 Sheaf
(*North*) *Migley* 1547 *Chol*

'Midge clearing', *v.* **mycg, lēah**, cf. Midgleygate, Midgley Hill 162
supra.

SHELL BROOK (COPSE), *Schilbroke* n.d. (1611) *LRMB* 200, *Schup-*,
Schipbroc 1270 (17) Sheaf, *Shellbrook Coppy* 1842 OS, a name not
well recorded; alternatively 'sheep brook', *v.* **scēap, brōc** (cf. Ship-

brook 334 *infra*), and 'noisy brook', cf. ModEdial. *shill* 'shrill, loud, noisy' (cf. *shill* NED), which Professor Löfvenberg points out as from OE (WSax) **sciell*, **scyl*, (Angl) **scell*, (from PrGerm **skella-*), or OE (WSax, Angl) **scille* (PrGerm **skelliᵢa*).

WINCLE GRANGE (110–955654)

> *grangia de Winchul* 1252 (17) Dieul, *-Wynchull* 1285 ChRR, *-Wynkhull* 1354 BPR *et seq* with spellings as for Wincle *supra*, *grangia de Wynkehill* (*Wynkhull*) *in Sutton* 1467, 1471 *MinAcct* *Wyncle Grange* 1544 Plea, *Winkle Graunge* 1578 Earw, *Wincle Graunge Howse* c.1600 Orm²
>
> *Wyncull(e) Graunge* 1547 *MinAcct*, 1550 *Surv*, *Vincull(e) graunge* 1554 *MinAcct*, 1560 Sheaf
>
> *Wincell Grange* 1543 Orm², *Wyncell Grange* 1578 Earw
>
> *Wyncal Graunge* 1578 Orm²

'The grange', *v.* grange. This was a pasture estate granted to Combermere Abbey by the earl of Chester. It is first mentioned in *una carucata terre in foresta de Maclesfeld in loco qui vocatur Winchul ad grangiam faciendum* c.1190 *AddCh* 15771.

ALLGREAVE (BRIDGE & WOOD), 1831 Bry, *Awgreue* (lit. *-grene*) 1599 Orm², *Augreve* 1626 *Chol*, *-greave* c.1639 *ib*, *v.* græfe 'a grove'. The first el. may be hall 'a hall', cf. foll., and Allostock 329 *infra*.   ALL-MEADOWS, *Hall Meadows* 1842 OS, cf. prec.   BAGSTON (WOOD), *Bagstones Wood* 1842 ib, from bæc-stān 'a baking-stone'.   BARLEY-FORD (BRIDGE), *Barleyford* 1611 *LRMB* 200, *Barlyford* 1653 Earw, 'barley ford', probably a ford used for carting the harvest.   (LT) BARNFIELD WOOD, *Barfield Wood* 1842 OS, *Barn Field Plantation & Copy* 1850 *TA*.   BARTOMLEY (BOTTOMS) (110–965657), *Bartomley* 1831 Bry, either named after Barthomley 329 *infra*, or analogous with it and a further instance of the p.n. type 'wood of the men of *Barton*' from bere-tūn and hæme, with lēah, *v.* also botm and cf. Millhill 308 *infra*. In these late-recorded instances, the p.n. may be a straightforward compound of bere-tūn and lēah. Grave-goods from furnished burials have been found near Bartomley farm, *v.* Orm² III 769. BENNETTSHILL, *Bennet Hill* 1831 Bry, from the ME pers.n. *Benet*, perhaps a surname.   BRADDOCKS, 1860 White, probably from the surname *Braddock*.   BROOM BANK & WOOD, cf. *Broom* (*Field*) 1850 *TA*, *the broomefield* (*patch*) 1611 *LRMB* 200, *v.* brōm.

BROOMHILL COTTAGE, cf. *Broom Hill Bank* 1850 *TA*, perhaps *Brom(e)hul* 1286 *Eyre* (p), Court (p), *le Bromehull* 1354 *Eyre* (p), *v.* brōm, hyll. BROWN HILL. BURNTHOUSE, 1831 Bry. CESSBANK COMMON, *v.* 153 *supra.* DANEBRIDGE, 1860 White, *Golden Hill* 1831 Bry, a hamlet named from Dane Bridge *supra.* DUMKINS, 1831 ib, *Dunkins* 1842 OS, cf. dial. *dunnekin* 'a privy, a cesspool'. FEEDER COTTAGE, *Feeder* 1850 *TA*, near a watercourse feeding the Macclesfield Canal. FOLLY MILL, 1831 Bry, *Folly Grove Mill* 1842 OS, *v.* folie. GIBBONS CLIFF (WOOD) (110–973666), *Gibbins-Clyffe* 1611 *LRMB* 200, *v.* clif 'a cliff'. The first el. may be from gibbe 'a hump', for the place lies on a detached hill in a crook of the R. Dane, but it could be the surname *Gibben, Gibbin, Gibbon* (Reaney 134). GOLDEN SLACK, *Top o' th' Hill* 1831 Bry, *Higher Golden* 1842 OS, 'marigold valley', *v.* golde, denu, with slakki, cf. Golden Slack 56 *supra.* GRANGE COPSE, *Grange Plantation* 1850 *TA*, from Wincle Grange *supra.* HAMMOND'S HOLE, in R. Dane. HAZELS, *Hazells* 1831 Bry, *Hamulton Hassell, the further & narr Hassells* 1611 *LRMB* 200, 'the hazels', *v.* hæsel, cf. Hommerton *supra.* HERON COPSE, *Heron Copy* 1850 *TA*. HILL TOP, 1842 OS, *Bank Top* 1831 Bry. HOG CLOUGH, -*Wood* 1850 *TA*, *v.* hogg 'a hog'. HONEYFALL WELL, 'lucky well', from ModEdial. *honey-fall* (EDD) 'an unexpected stroke of good fortune'. KISS WOOD (110–946651), *Kiss Arse Wood* 1850 *TA*, 'hill and wood at a recess or hollow', *v.* kjóss, ears, cf. Kiss Arse 146 *supra.* LANEHEAD, 1831 Bry. LANEHOUSE (COPSE), *The Lanehouse* 1611 *LRMB* 200. LONGDALE, 1831 Bry, *v.* lang, dæl[1]. LONGGUTTER, 1831 ib, 'long watercourse', *v.* lang, goter. MARE-KNOWLES, *Mere Knowls* 1831 ib, *Mare Knowl* 1842 OS, 'boundary hillock(s)', *v.* (ge)mære, cnoll. MEGLANE WOOD, 1850 *TA*, *v.* meg and cf. Fernlee 149 *supra.* MELLORKNOLL(s), *Mellor Knoll* 1850 *TA*, *v.* cnoll, cf. Mellor Db 144. NABBS HILL, *v.* nabbi 'a projecting peak'. NETTLEBEDS, 1831 Bry, *v.* netel(e), bedd. OTTER'S POOL, in the R. Dane. OWLER'S BRIDGE, *v.* alor, brycg. OXCLOSE WOOD, (*Big*) *Ox Close Plantation* 1850 *TA*. PINGLE, -*Cottage* 1850 ib, *v.* pingel. RABB CLOUGH, *v.* 155 *supra.* ROOKERY WOOD, 1842 OS. ST MICHAEL'S CHURCH, *Winckle Chappell* 1665 *Dow.* SANDYWAY (110–954672), 1831 Bry, *v.* sandig, weg, a road-name on route XVIII 46 *supra.* SCAR POOL, in R. Dane, 'pool at a cliff', *v.* sker. SPARROWGREAVE, 1831 ib, *v.* spearwa, græfe. TIMBERHURST WOOD, *Tymberhurstes* 1611 *LRMB* 200, 'timber wood', *v.* timber, hyrst. TOLLS, *-Intake* 1850 *TA*, *Towle* 1860 White, perhaps from **toln** 'a toll', but the significance is not clear. TOP House. WHITELEE (CLOUGH & WOOD), *White Lee or Whytlegh* Eliz Orm², *White Lee Paper Mills* 1860 White, cf. *Paper Mill Copy* 1850 *TA*, 'white clearing', *v.* hwīt, lēah. WHITE RIDGES (WOOD), *White Ridges* 1850 *ib.* WINCLE MINN, *the minde lees, Wincle Comon*, (common called) *The Mindes* 1611 *LRMB* 200, *v.* Bosley Minn 55 *supra.*

FIELD-NAMES

The undated forms are 1850 *TA* 438. Of the others 1190 is *AddCh*, 1190 (1353), 1357, 1503 *ChFor*, 1286, 1287 Court, 1347 *Eyre*, 1611 *LRMB* 200, 1620 *Surv.*

(*a*) Adder Fd; Alum Fd; Bailey Bank; Bank (cf. *the Bancke meadowe* 1611); Barlow (Lane); Barn Fd (*the Barnefield (Banckes)* 1611); Bent (cf. *the Bentclose, Bent Meadow, the Bent Heyes* 1611, *v.* beonet): Big Hay (*v.* (ge)hæg); Birchen Bank (*the Birchenbancke* 1611, *v.* bircen²); Black Earth (1611, *v.* eorðe); Blakelow ('black mound', *v.* blæc, hlāw); Blow Bank (*the bloehill* 1611, 'blue hill', *v.* blā(w)); Bottoms (*v.* botm); Brickiln fd; Bridge Heys ('enclosures at a bridge', near Dane Bridge *supra*); Bull Stone ('rock where a bull stands', *v.* bula, stān, cf. Deer Stones WRY 3 147); Butty Mdw (*v.* butty); Bye Flat(t) (*the Byeflatt(es), the By(e)flettes devyded with the water, -which is parted with a Ryver* 1611, 'the flats of land in the bend of a river', *v.* byge¹, flat, cf. Bye Flatt 330 *infra*); Cale Mdw (*v.* cāl); Calf Croft (*the Calfecrofte* 1611); Cane; Cart House Bank; Coal Pit Fd; Cold Hey; Cote Mdw (cf. *Cotefield leyes, the Coteclose meadowe* 1611, *v.* cot, feld, lēah); Cow Heads ('head-lands where cows are pastured', *v.* cū, hēafod, cf. Horse Heads *infra*); Cow Hey (cf. *the Cowhey Flashe* 1611, *v.* flasshe); Cressett (probably a field with a brazier, *v.* cresset); Daisey Flat(t); Dale (*v.* dæl¹); Dane Green (from grēne² and R. Dane 20 *supra*); Dawson Fd & Mdw (*Dosons meadowe* 1611, held by Edward *Doson*); Dublin Bank; Eyes (Bank) (*the great, little & longe Eyes, Ferne Eyes, Eyes Heat* 1611, 'the water meadows', *v.* ēg, fearn, hǣð): Little Fall (*v.* (ge)fall 'a felling-place'); False Fd; Ferney Heys; Flash Croft (*Flashie Crofte* 1611, 'swampy croft', *v.* flasshe, -ig³); Garden End (*the* 1611); Glade End (*the Gleade* 1611, 'end of the glade', *v.* glæd³, ende¹); Gold Placks (*the Gowplecke* 1611, 'small plot(s) by a drain', *v.* goule, plek); Gorsefield, Gorsey mdw & piece (cf. *the lower & over Grostie field* 1611, *v.* gorstig); Green Fd; Green Way (*v.* grēne¹, weg); Grub Hole; Hazel Bank; Holly Bank; The (Long) Holme (cf. *the Lymiholme, Martinshoume* 1611, from holmr, with lang, līm, -ig³, and the ME pers.n. *Martin*); Horse Heads (*v.* hors, hēafod, cf. Cow Heads *supra*); Intake (*the Intack* 1611, *v.* inntak); Junction of Waters; Kiln Croft (*the Kilne Crofte* 1611); Kitchen(s) Bank; Lane Croft (cf. *the Lanesyde* 1611); Lea-, Ley Fd (*the laye-, the leyfield* 1611, *v.* lēah, feld); Lead Grains ('watercourse gulleys', *v.* lǣd, grein); Lees (*v.* lǣs); Lime Bank Wd, Lime Fd (*lymefield* 1611, *v.* līm); Loam Close (*v.* lām); Long Dole Fd & Slang ('long allotment', *v.* lang, dāl, with slang); Lower Croft (*-e* 1611); Lower Fd (*the-* 1611); Lower Heys (cf. *the middle & nearer Hey* 1611, *v.* (ge)hæg); Macclesfield (Fd & Mdw) (named after Macclesfield 113 *supra*); The Mallion; Marl Croft & Fd; Meg Dale (*v.* dæl[1] and Meglane *supra*); Mill Mdw (cf. *the Milne Feild* 1611); The Moss; Nuttery Old Mdw; Old Town House; Orchard Piece; Ox Hey; Paddock (*the Paddocke* 1611, *v.* pearroc); Peas Butts (*v.* pise, butte); Pingot (*v.* pingot); Pit Fd; Pool Bank (cf. *blacke poole Bancke* 1611, *v.* blæc, pōl[1]); Pugh mdw; Rabbit Bank; Ridding(s) (*v.* ryding); Riddington Wd (perhaps 'enclosure at a cleared place', from ryding and tūn); Rye Croft mdw (*the Rycrofte* 1611); Six Day Math ('six days' mowing', *v.* day-math); Slang (*v.* slang); Spink (*Sprinke wood* 1611, *v.* spring 'a young plantation'); Spout Croft (*v.* spoute); Stair Fd (*Starefield* (*Clough*) 1611, 'steep field', *v,* stæger[2], feld, clōh); Stocken Flatt (*Stokenflatt* 1611, 'flat ground cleared of stumps', *v.* stoccing, flat); Stocks Green (*v.* stocc, grēne[2]); Stone Hey (*the-* 1611); Stone Pit Fd; Stubble Fd (cf. *the Rystubble* 1611, *v.* ryge, stubbil); Sutton Fd (named after Sutton 148 *supra*); Swindells (Copy) (*the Swin(e)-, Swynehills* (*Wood*) 1611, 1620, 'swine hills', *v.* swīn[1], hyll); Sych (*v.* sīc 'a drain'); Toad Hole Mdw ('fox-hole meadow', *v.* tod-hole); Wath ('water meadow, ford', *v.* vaðr); Well Bank & Fd; White Fd; Will Hill (*Willhill* 1611, *v.* wella); Wood Fd; Woodwards Mdw (*Wooddars meadowe* 1611, 'the wood-ward's meadow', *v.* wodere, wodeward, mǣd).

(b) *The Aker* 1611 (*v.* æcer); *Archenhurste* 1611 (*v.* hyrst); *the Bentiefield & -head* 1611 (*v.* benty, feld, hēafod); *the Blakamore* 1611 (*v.* blæc, mōr[1]); *Castell Clyff, -Cliff* 1503, *the Castle Cliffe* 1611 (*v.* ceastel 'a heap of stones', clif, cf. Castle Cliff Rocks in Leek Frith parish St, across R. Dane at 110–986658); *Cornford* 1286, *-forde, Cormesforde* 1287 (p), ('ford where corn is carried', *v.* corn, ford); *the Edoe field* 1611; *the Frame* 1611; *furnus comitis qui est iuxta viam que venit de scliderford* c.1190 ('the earl's oven which is next the way coming from *Scliderford*', cf. Dane Bridge *supra*); *Furrowmend Heys* 1611; *gorsthul* c.1190, *-hull* c.1190 (1353), *Goster hill* 1611 ('gorse hill', *v.* gorst, gorst-trēow, hyll); *grenelache* c.1190, *-lach* c.1190 (1353) ('the green bog', *v.* grēne[1], læc(c)); *Hangmans Crofte* 1611; *the Heyclough pasture* 1611 ('hay dell', *v.* hēg, clōh); *the Hillockes* 1611 (*v.* hylloc); *the hollenfield* 1611 ('holly-tree field', *v.* holegn); *le Holmelegh* 1347 ('wood or clearing at a marsh', *v.* holmr, lēah); *Hormesestrete* 1357 ('Ormr's main road', from strǣt and the ON, ODan pers.n. *Ormr*, cf. *Ormesty* 271 *infra*); *the houstiddes, the House Steddes or Croft* 1611 ('the croft the house stands in', *v.* hūsstede); *the Howknowle* 1611 ('the promontory hill', *v.* hōh or haugr, cnoll); *the Impyords* 1611 ('the nurseries', *v.* impe-ʒard); *the Marrysh-, Marrishfield* 1611 ('marsh field', *v.* merisc, mareis, feld); *the Marstables* 1611 (perhaps 'boundary-posts' from (ge)mǣre and stapol); *Mildomeadowe* 1611; *the Parke* 1611; *the Pictor Meadowe* 1611 ('pointed tor' *v.* pīc[1], torr); *querstan(e)sich* c.1190, *querastanesich* 1190 (1353) ('mill-stone stream', *v.* cweorn, stān, sīc); *Ratunesclogh* 1347 (from clōh 'a deep valley', with a p.n. *Ratun*, perhaps 'roe-deer enclosure', from rā[1] and tūn); *the Rie Pingle* 1611 (*v.* ryge, pingel); *the shawe* 1611 (*v.* sceaga); *the Trough Meadowes* 1611 (*v.* trog); *the wall crofte & meadow, the Wale meadowe* 1611; *the Weete Flatt, the Wheetough* 1611 ('wheat plot', 'wheat corner', *v.* hwǣte, flat, halh); *the Wickenfield* 1611 ('mountain-ash field', *v.* cwicen); *Withienlache* c.1190, *Wy-*c.1190 (1353) ('boggy stream growing with willows', *v.* wiðigen, lǣc(c), cf. Withinleach 175 *infra*); *Wycleyord* 1347, *the yordes* 1611 ('the enclosure(s)', *v.* geard, cf. Wincle *supra*).

viii. Taxal

Taxal parish was a chapelry of Prestbury parish 181 *infra* until 1377, Orm²
III 782. Taxal township was transferred to Db in 1936, and is now in
Hartington Upper Quarter c.p. and Fernilee c.p. Yeardsley cum Whaley
township was transferred to Db in 1936, and is now included with Chapel
in le Frith Db, in Whaley Bridge c.p., named from Whaley Bridge 178 *infra*.

1. TAXAL (111–7901)

> *Tackeshale* c.1251 *For*, *-hal'* 1285 *Eyre* (Court 213 reads *Tatkeshal*),
> *Tackishalch* 1273 Ipm, *Takes-* 1273 Orm², *Takis-* 1273 IpmR,
> *Tacheshale* 1345 *Eyre*, *Takkeshall* 1527 Earw
> *Taxhale* 1274 Pat, Fine, *-hall* ll3 Tab, 1512 *ChEx*, ChRR, Orm²,
> *-hal* 1690 Sheaf
> *Tackesal'* 1285 *Eyre*, *-e* 1335 *Dow*, *Ta(c)kessale* 1344 Pat, 1357
> *ChFor*, *-all* 1547 Orm², *Takkessale* 1451 Pat
> *Tacsal* 1288, 1348 *Eyre*, *-e* 1357 *ChFor*, *Tacsall* (*infra forestam de Macclesfeld*) 1445 *Eyre*, *Thacsale* 1378 *ib*, *Tacksall* 1328 (1724)
> NotCestr, *-e* 1493 *Dow*, *Taksale* 1347 *Eyre*, c.1420 Orm², *-all* 1451 Pat
> *Taxsale* 1376 Orm², *Tacsal(l)* 1497 ChRR
> *Taxall* 1502 ChRR

The final el. is halh (dat.sg. hale) 'a nook'. The first el. is unidentified. It is inflected in the gen.sg. *-es*. It may be a pers.n. The
unrecorded OE pers.n. *Tatuc* proposed in DEPN depends upon the
erroneous *Tatkes-* spelling for *Tackes-* (cf. Stretton 335 *infra* and
DEPN for a similar *c, t* confusion). Taxal may contain the ODan
by-name *Taki* ('surety, bailsman'; ModDan pers.n. *Tage*) with an
analogical anglicised strong-declension gen.sg. in *-s*. The OScand
pers.n. would give significance to Normanwood *infra*. However, Dr
von Feilitzen informs me that ODan *Taki* is an exclusively Danish
name, not to be looked for in this English context. Perhaps it would
be preferable on formal grounds to reject the re-modelled ODan
pers.n. and to read Taxal as a genitival-composition of an early
instance of ME *tak* 'a lease, a tenure, a revenue' (a.1300, *tack* sb²

NED; cf. ON *tak* 'a taking hold of'), and to interpret the p.n. as meaning 'valley at-, -of-, -belonging to-, a land-holding or an acquired estate'.

NORMANWOOD (111–009783), *-wod* 1337 *Eyre*, *-wode in Taksale* 1347 *ib*, *Normanneswode super vast' de Tacsale* 1357 *ChFor*, 'the north-man's or Northmann's wood', *v.* Norðmann, wudu, cf. Normans Hall, *Normonwode* 134 113, *supra*, Taxal *supra*.

OVERTON (111–006786), 1301 *Pat et freq*, (*in Taxhale*) 1530 Orm², (*the Hall of-*) 1613 *ib*, *-toun* 1493 *Dow*, *-tone* 1565 *ib*, *Ouerton* 1496 *ib*, 'farm on a hill', *v.* ofer², tūn.

BLACKHILLGATE, 1831 Bry, *v.* geat. BOTANY BLEACH WORKS, *Botany Mill* 1831 *ib*, *Bleach Works* 1842 OS. CASTEDGE, *the Castid* 1629 Orm², *Castids* 1665 Earw, *Castage* 1831 Bry, perhaps 'place haunted by jackdaws' from cā and stede. The pl. form [-dz] has been confused with [-dʒ], hence *-edge*. CAT & FIDDLE INN (111–002719), 1831 *ib*, an important inn on the highest point on the Macclesfield–Buxton turnpike. CATS TOR, 1842 OS, *v.* cat(t), torr. COOPERS NOSE, 1842 *ib*, cf. *Cowper house* 1611 *LRMB* 200, from the surname *Cooper*, with nōs(e) 'a headland, a promontory'. CROWHILL, 1831 Bry. DALE OF GOYT, *v.* dæl¹ or dalr, cf. Goyt's Bridge *infra*. DEEP CLOUGH (111–013767), *le Depeclogh'* 1335 *Dow*, *v.* dēop, clōh. DEEP CLOUGH (111–010725), *Mill Clough* 1842 OS, *v.* clōh, cf. Goytsclough Mill *infra*. DERBYSHIRE BRIDGE (111–016719), 'bridge into Derbyshire', on the county boundary at the head of R. Goyt, cf. *Chastreschireforde* 1337 *Eyre*, 'ford into Cheshire', from ford, cf. Cheshire 1 *supra*, which may in fact have been here. DOWRY, *Dowery* 1831 Bry, 'the dower place', *v.* dowarie. EMBRIDGE CAUSEWAY, 1819 Orm², 'even or level causeway', from emn and brycg, with caucie; a road-name on route XIV 45 *supra*, cf. The Street *infra*. ERRWOOD, 1693 Earw. FOXHOLE HOLLOW. FOXLOW EDGE, 1842 OS, cf. *Foxlowe* 1286 *Eyre* (p), *-lawe* 1290 *ib* (p), 'fox-hill', *v.* fox, hlāw and ecg. GOYT'S BRIDGE & MOSS, GOYTS CLOUGH (MILL), (cf. Db 373), *ad quosdam mosses jacentes inter aquam de Guyte et aquam de Dane mosse* 1619 Orm², *Goyte Bridge* 1621 Sheaf, *Goyt Bridge*, *Goyts Clough*, *Goyt's Moss* 1831 Bry, named from R. Goyt 27 *supra*, *v.* brycg, mos, clōh, cf. *Head of the Goyt* 1831 *ib* (*v.* hēafod 'source', Goytshead Db 373),

Dale of Goyt *supra*. Goyt's Moss is a bound of the Forest of Maccles-field, cf. 9 *supra*. The mill (111–013734, *Polishing Mill* 1831 ib, *Scouring Mill* 1842 OS) gave name to Deep Clough *supra*.   HILL-BRIDGE WOOD, perhaps 'intake on a hill', from brēc 'a breaking of land'.   HOO MOOR, 1831 Bry, *Hulmor*' 1335 *Dow*, v. hyll, mōr[1]. INTAKE, *Intakes* 1831 Bry v. inntak.   ISSUE TORR, 1831 ib, v. torr. JACOB'S CABIN.   JEP CLOUGH, cf. *Jep Croft* 1844 *TA*, v. clōh, croft. The first el. may be the ME pers.n. *Jep*, *Geppe*, a pet-form of *Geoffrey* (Reaney 133), but dēop or djúpr 'deep' is possible, cf. Deep Clough (2x) *supra*.   KNIPE, 1842 OS, *The Nipe* 1611 *LRMB* 200, 'steep rock', v. gnípa.   LADBITCH WOOD, *Ladbitch(mouth)* 1738 *Dow*, *Ladbatch Plantation* 1842 OS, 'lad's valley', v. ladda, bece[1]. This is the upper part of Mill Clough *infra*, to which the form *-mouth* probably refers, v. mūða.   LANEHEAD.   LODGE COTTAGES & WOOD, v. Taxal Lodge *infra*.   MACCLESFIELD RD, leading to Macclesfield 113 *supra*.   MADSCAR, cf. *Madscarr Close* 1844 *TA*, and Park Wood *infra*, v. sker 'a rock, a rocky cliff'.   MARCHING-TON FM, either from Marchington St, or the derived surname. MASTERS (111–013772), 1831 Bry.   MILL CLOUGH, cf. Ladbitch *supra*.   MOSS HO (111–015715), *Moss Houses* 1831 Bry, named from Goyt's Moss *supra*.   OAKEND, 1831 ib.   OLDFIELD, 1831 ib.   OLDGATE NICK, v. 114 *supra*, cf. The Street *infra*.   OX-BENT, 1844 *TA*, 'ox bent-grass', v. oxa, beonet.   PARK WOOD, *Madscar Park Wood* 1831 Bry, cf. Madscar *supra*.   PYM CHAIR (101–995767), *Pim's chayre* 1611 *LRMB* 200, *Pim Chair*, *-Cheare* 1738 *Dow*, from the ME pers.n. *Pimme* (OE *Pymma*, v. Reaney s.v. *Pim*) and chai(e)re 'a chair', (cf. cadeir), referring to the rocks of Taxal Edge, v. 112 *supra*.   QUARRY BANK.   REDDISH, 1831 Bry, probably like Reddish La 30, from hrēod 'a reed' and dīc 'a ditch'. SHINING TOR, v. 128 *supra*.   SHOOTER'S CLOUGH, 1842 OS, v. scēotere, clōh.   SITCH HOUSES, *Sitch House* 1831 Bry, v. sīc 'a watercourse'.   STAKE CLOUGH & SIDE, 1842 OS, cf. Middle Moss *infra*, Stake 128 *supra*, v. staca.   THE STREET, a road-name on route XIV, 45 *supra*, cf. Oldgate Nick *supra*, v. strǣt.   STUBBIN, *Stubbins* 1831 Bry, v. stubbing 'a place where trees have been stubbed'.   SUNNYBANK.   SUNNYSIDE.   TAXAL EDGE, *Taxall-* 1620 *Surv*, *Great Edge* 1844 *TA*, an escarpment on the Kettleshulme boundary, v. ecg.   TAXAL LODGE, *The Lodge* 1831 Bry.   TAXAL WOOD.   TODDBROOK RESERVOIR, fills the valley of *Tinkers Brook* 1831 ib, the lower reach of Todd Brook 36 *supra*, cf. *the Tynkars*

Bancke 181 *infra*, *v.* tink(l)ere.   THE TORS, 1842 OS, *v.* torr.
WINDGATHER ROCKS, *v.* 111 *supra*.   WITHINLEACH MOOR, named
from *Withinleach* 1831 Bry, *v.* wīðigen, læc(c), mōr^1, cf. *Withienlache*
172 *supra*.

FIELD-NAMES

The undated forms are 1844 *TA* 387. Of the others 1335 is *Dow*, 1337, 1356
Eyre, 1344 Pat, 1357 *ChFor*, 1358 *MinAcct*, 1498 ChRR, 1611 *LRMB* 200,
1620 *Surv*, 1631, 1676, 1720 Earw, c.1720 Orm^2, 1842 OS, 1860 White.

(a) Andrew Mdw; Ashton Croft; Aspin Croft (*v.* æspen); Back o' th'
Edge (*the backside of Taxall Edge* 1611, 1620, cf. Taxal Edge *supra*); Back
Pearl Brows ('the farther-off slopes at a rill', *v.* back, pyrl(e), brū); Bent
(*v.* beonet); Birches Wd (*Birch Plantation* 1842); Bracken Bank 1831; Bridge
Ends, Fd & Wath (*v.* waroð, cf. Waths 113 *supra*); Brow; Bullen Fd; Calf
Croft; Church Mdw; Clarkes Mdw & Nook; Clay acre; Clough (*v.* clōh);
Collin Mdw; Common Land; Coneygrey (*v.* coninger); Cow Hey; Dirty
Mdw; Eight Day Work (*v.* day-work); Eyes (*v.* ēg); Fearney Hey (*v.* fearnig,
(ge)hæg); Field Ends & Heads (*v.* hēafod); Flower Fd; The Gallows Yard
c.1720 (*v.* galga, geard, the supposed place of execution in which the Downes
family of Taxal exercised the right of hanging within their bailiwick of the
Forest of Macclesfield, *v.* Orm^2 III 779n); Garden Wath (*v.* vað); Geldee
Piece; Great Brow; Hem Paddock (*v.* hemm 'a border', pearroc); Hey
Bottom (*v.* hēg 'hay', botm 'bottom land'); Hog Mdw; Hollow Fd; House-
wife; Hulme Bottom (*v.* hulm, botm); Hungart; Joife; Jordan Croft; Kirk
Bank Wath (*v.* kirkja, banke, vað); Knowl Piece; Lee, Long Lees (*v.* lēah);
Lightbirch 1702 ('pale birch-tree', probably 'silver birch', *v.* lēoht, birce, cf.
Birch Db 60); Lilly Mdw; Lime Piece; Long Lands; Longshut (*v.* scēat);
Lovely Croft; Middle Moss (1831, cf. Stake Clough *supra*, *v.* middel, mos);
Moor Fd; Mosseley Bottom (*Mosely* 1498, 'moss clearing', *v.* mos, lēah,
botm): Old Alice Piece; Oldham Fd (perhaps 'old marsh', from ald and
hulm, as in Oldham La 50, but the basis may be the surname derived from
it); Paddy Croft; Park (End); Redfern Wd ('red fern wood', *v.* rēad, fearn,
wudu); Redmoor Wath ('water-meadow or ford at reed-moor', from hrēod
and mōr^1, with vað or waroð); Rick Slick Mdw ('smooth meadow where a
rick stands', from slike and mǣd, with hrēac); Rid(s), Rid Ends (cf. *New
Ridd* 1611, *v.* ryde 'a clearing', cf. New Rid 180 *infra*); Round Croft; Rushy
Fd; Rye Croft; Saw Pit Brow & Wath (*v.* saw-pytt, brū); Six Day Work
(*v.* day-work); Spout Croft (*v.* spoute 'a spring'); Square Croft & Mdw;
Stoney Fd; Swaine Flatt (*v.* sveinn 'a young man, a swain', flat); Swan
Piece; Swine Park (*the Swyne Park* 1611, 'swine inclosure', *v.* swīn^1, park);
Tenter Close (*v.* tentour); Three Nook Mdw; Wain House Fd; Wains Mdw
(*Wains Pasture* 1831, from the surname *Wain*); Wall Mdw (*v.* wælla);
Warth Bottom (*v.* waroð, botm); Water Gate ('gateway to the water',
v. wæter, geat); Wath ('ford, water-meadow', *v.* vað); Well Croft & Fd
(cf. Wall Mdw *supra*); Whaley Wath ('meadow belonging to Whaley' (176
infra), *v.* vað); White Lee (Mdw & Wd) (*v.* hwīt, lēah); Wickin Style ('stile

at a mountain-ash', *v.* cwicen, stigel); Winterfold ('fold used in winter', *v.* winter, fald).

(*b*) *Brekwellehurst* (*v.* 180 *infra*); *Cowparkehouse* 1631 (*v.* cū, park, hūs); *Euerholtclogh'* 1335, *Euerholt* 1337, (*boscus de*) 1357, *Heuereholt*, *Euerisholt* 1337, *Eruesholt*(*brok*) 1356, 1358 ('wild boar's wood', *v.* eofor, holt, with brōc, clōh, cf. Harrol Edge 331 *infra*); *le Heghasels* 1335 ('the high hazels', *v.* hēah, hæsel); *Holbrokheghes* 1335 (*v.* hōl², brōc, (ge)hæg).

2. YEARDSLEY CUM WHALEY (111–0082), *Hirdeslewaylie* 1348 *MinAcct*, (*vill' de*) *Urdeslegh Waylegh* 1358 *ib et freq* to *Yerdesley Wayley* 1620 *Surv*, *Hurdesle-*, *Yurdesle et Wayley* 1400 *JRC*, Sheaf *et freq*, with other spellings as for Whaley, Yeardsley *infra*.

WHALEY (HALL) (111–0081) [¹weili]

> *Wal'* c.1211–25 Facs (p), *Walegh* 1290 *Eyre* (p), *-ley* 1411 Orm², 1453 ChRR, *Wallegh'*, *-ley* 1508 *MinAcct*, *Waleys* 1548 Earw
>
> *Weile* H3 *JRC*, c.1250 Sheaf, *Weyeleye* 1284 Ipm, *-legh* 1288 *Eyre*, *Weyleg'* 1285, *-le* 1383, *Wayle* 1288, *-ley* 1337, *-legh* 1347 *ib et freq*, *-lie* 1348 *MinAcct*
>
> *Veley* m13 *SocAnt* (p), *Weleye* 1286 *Eyre*, *Weley* 1523 ChRR, *-s* 1548 Orm², *Wely* 17 *Chol*
>
> *Woley* m13 *SocAnt* (p), *-leg'* l13 *AddCh* (p), *-legh* 1345 *Eyre*, *-lee* 1494 *SocAnt* (p)
>
> *Wheleie* 1304 Chamb (p), *-ley* 1690 Sheaf
>
> *Whaley* 1399 ChRR, *Whalley* 1547 Pat
>
> *Wealey* 1620 *Surv*

'Clearing at a road', *v.* weg, lēah. The early *Wa-* spellings apparently derive from the Merc form wæg (Campbell §328).

YEARDSLEY (HALL) (111–0083)

> *Erdesl'* 1285 *Eyre* (p), *-ley*(*e*) 1327, 1330 Pat (p), *-lee* 1347 *Eyre*, *-legh* 1401 Sheaf, *-le* 1402 *JRC*, *Erdesslegh' iuxta Walley* 1471 *MinAcct*, *Erdisley* 1522 MidCh (p)
>
> *Urdesle* 1285 For (p), *-legh* 14 *JRC*, *Surv*, 1347 *Eyre*, *-ley* 1337 *ib*, *Urdisl'* 1285 *ib*, *-legh* 1357 *ChFor*, *-ley* 1442 Tab (p), *Urdusley* 1425 *ib*
>
> *Hurthesle* 1288 *Eyre*, *Hurdyslegh* 1370 *ib*
>
> *Hirdesle*(*gh*) 1348 *MinAcct*, 1349 *Eyre*, *Irdeslegh* 1390 Tab (p), *-le* 1408 *JRC*, *Yrdesle* 1408 Sheaf
>
> *Yurdesle* 1400 Sheaf

Yerdsley 1401 Sheaf, *Yerdysley* 1500 Orm², *Yerdes-* 1522 Tab (p)
Hurdlegh 1467 *MinAcct*, *Hurde-* 1471, 1508 *ib*, *-ley* 1560 Sheaf
Edirslegh iuxta Waley 1467 *MinAcct*
Yordesley 1553 Pat
Y(e)ardes-, *Yardisley (Greene)* 1611 *LRMB* 200, *Yeardsley* 1631
Orm²
Earsley 1673 Sheaf
Erdley Hall 1690 Sheaf
Yeardley 1799 ChRR

Perhaps as suggested in DEPN, 'Ēorēd's wood or clearing', from
the OE pers.n. *Ēorēd* and *lēah*. But similar forms occur in Eardswick,
Erdeshurstes, Earnshaw 331 *infra*, and in *Erdeswyk* 53 *supra* a lost place
in this Hundred, which can hardly be all derived from this pers.n.
The common first el. in these p.ns. is probably **hirde, hyrde, heorde**
'a herdsman'. The persistent loss of *H-* is parallel to that in the prefixed *Hall-* of Allostock, *Allom* 329 *infra*, with stress-shift in the
diphthong of **heorde**.

HAWKHURST (HEAD) (101–998814), *Haukeshurst (Moor)* 1347 *Eyre*,
Hawkeshurst 1399 *JRC*, *-hirste* 1500 Orm², *Hawkshurst* 1500 Earw,
Hawkehurst 1400 *JRC*, 'the hawk's wooded-hill', *v.* **hafoc, hyrst.**

HOCKERLEY (LANE) (111–007821), *Hokerlegh* 1285 *Eyre*, *-ley* c.1490
Surv, *Hockerl(e)y (Stones)* 1611 *LRMB* 200, 1620 *Surv*, 'clearing at a
hill', *v.* **hocer, lēah**, cf. Stoneheads *infra*, Occerly, Hockley 275, 300
infra.

LIGHTHASSELLS (lost), 1611 *LRMB* 200, *Lytth-*, *Lyttehaseles* 1288
Eyre, *Lythaseles* (lit. *Lych-*) 1289 Court (p), *Lyghthaseles* 1350 *Eyre*
(p), *Leghthasell* 1370 *ib* (p), *le lighthasull* 1467, 1471 *MinAcct*,
Lichasell 1508 *ib*, 'the light hazels', *v.* **lēoht** 'light (-coloured)', **hæsel.**

RINGSTONE (CLOUGH) (111–005825, –007824), *Ryngstones*, *-stanes*
1285 *Eyre* (p), *Ry-*, *Ringestone(s)* 1550 *MinAcct*, Earw, 1580 *Dep*,
Ringstones 1604 Earw, 1611 *LRMB* 200, cf. *le Rynge* 1357 *ChFor*,
'ring of stones, stone-ring', *v.* **hring-stān.**

STONEHEADS (111–003817), *Stone Head* 1831 Bry, *de(l) Stones* 1348
ChFor (p), 1384 *Rental* (p), *Hockerl(e)y Stones* 1611 *LRMB* 200, 1620
Surv, 'headland at the stones', *v.* **stān, hēafod**, cf. Hockerley *supra*.

WHALEY BRIDGE (111–010815), (-*a small village on the Manchester Road*) 1860 White, *Whaley* 1842 OS, named from a bridge over R. Goyt, cf. *a new bridge at Waylie* 1611 *LRMB* 200, *Whaley-bridge* c.1620 Orm², *Wely Bridge* 17 *Chol*, *v.* brycg, cf. Whaley, Yeardsley cum Whaley *supra.*

BANKSIDE.   BLACK HILL, *Blacke hill end(e)* 1611 *LRMB* 200, *Blackheath End* 1620 *Surv*, 'black hill or heath', cf. 271 *infra*, Longside *infra.*   BOTHOMES HALL, *Bothoms Hall* 1831 Bry, *Bottoms Hall* 1724 NotCestr, 1845 ChetOS VIII, 'hall in valley bottoms', *v.* botm.   BROOK HO, 1860 White.   BROOKFIELD HO.   BROWNOUGH, *the browne haugh* 1611 *LRMB* 200, *Brounough* 1620 *Surv*, *the Brow(e)hough* (*meadow*), *Bromoughe, Brannoughe* 1611 *LRMB* 200, 'brown hollow', *v.* brūn¹, halh.   DEANE COTTAGE.   DIGLEE, *Dig(g)leigh* 1611 *LRMB* 200, -*lee* 1620 *Surv*, 'ditch clearing', *v.* dīc, lēah. DEPN s.v. *Disley* (269 *infra*) adduces Diglee in the form *Digley* and cites for it a spelling *Dyghleg'* which belongs to Ditchley 331 *infra.*   FALLHEY, *the falehey* 1620 *Surv*, cf. *del Falle* 1380 *Eyre* (p), 'the tree-felling enclosure', *v.* (ge)fall, (ge)hæg.   FURNESS CLOUGH, FURNESS VALE, from Furness 272 *infra.*   GOYT MILL, possibly the site of *Whaley Mill infra*, named from R. Goyt.   GREENS CLOUGH. HADFIELD FOLD, from fald 'a fold, a farmstead' and the p.n. Hadfield Db 103, or the derived surname.   JOULE BRIDGE, cf. Gowhole Db 153 (*Jawhill* 1587, *Jowhole* 1767). Db 153 relates these with a Db surname *Joule.* These names may also be related to the f.n. Jowl Hole 186 *infra.* It is possible that the el. in common is ModE *jowl* 'a jaw' (NED *jowl¹*), used in a topographical sense 'ravine', cf. OE ceafl in Charlesworth Db 68.   KISHFIELD BRIDGE, *v.* 112 *supra.* HURST CLOUGH, cf. *The Hurst* 1611 *LRMB* 200, '(valley at) the wooded hill', *v.* hyrst, clōh.   LONGSIDE PLANTATION, *Blackmoor Plantation* 1831 Bry, cf. *Long Side* 1842 OS (a ridge extending north into Disley, *v.* Longside 273 *infra*), *the Longesydewaie, -waye* 1611 *LRMB* 200, 1620 *Surv*, 'the long hillside', *v.* lang, sīde, with weg, cf. Black Hill *supra.*   NEW HOUSE FM, *Pingot* 1831 Bry, *v.* pingot. NOOK COTTAGE, *Nook* 1831 ib.   PENNANT END & KNOB, *The Pennant, great & litle pendent* 1611 *LRMB* 200, *Pendant End* 1831 Bry, 'cnoll at-, end of-, a declivity', *v.* pendaunte, ende¹, knob. PLAGUE STONE (101–995816), 1″ OS, *Standing Stone* 6″ OS, *Stone* 1842 OS, cf. *del Horeston'* 1348 *ChFor* (p), 'the hoar stone', *v.* hār², stān. The modern name doubtless derives from the suitability of this place, a standing stone near the Lyme Handley boundary, for use as a quarantined rendezvous in times of epidemic sickness. SCAR WOOD, 1831 Bry, *v.* sker 'a rocky cliff'. SLATERSBANK (WOOD), *Slaters Bancke Wood* 1611 *LRMB* 200, from the surname *Slater* (ME *sclater* 'slate layer'). START, 1831 Bry, *v.* steort 'a tail, a projecting piece of land'. STICKING MIRES, *the Stickethmire, the Stickinmyer* 1611 *LRMB* 200, *Sticking Mire* 1831 Bry, the modern form is rationalised to 'clinging mire' from ModE *sticking*, adj. 'adhering', and mýrr 'a mire, a bog, mud', but the earlier form is an adverbial nickname, 'stick in the mud'. TODDBROOK RESERVOIR, *v.* 174 *supra*. WATERSIDE BRIDGE, cf. *the litle meadowe at the Waterside* 1611 *LRMB* 200, and Waterside Db 78, *v.* wæter 'water' (R. Goyt), sīde. WHALEY LANE, *Wheley lane Head* 1690 Sheaf, cf. Whaley *supra*. WHALEY MILL (lost), *molendinum de Waylegh'* 1347 *Eyre et freq, molendinum de Waley alias Wayleymylne* 1453 ChRR, *Walmylne* 1508 *MinAcct, Wall Miln* 1547 Pat, cf. Whaley, Goyt Mill *supra*. WHALEY MOOR, 1819 Orm², cf. Whaley *supra*.

FIELD-NAMES

The undated forms are 1844 *TA* 423. Of the others 1287 is Court, 1354, 1361, 1367, 1372, 1380, 1381, 1445 *Eyre*, 1335 *Dow*, 1348, 1503 *ChFor*, 1408 *JRC*, 1595, 1611 *LRMB* 200, 1620 *Surv*.

(*a*) Bank(s) (*the Bancke(s)* 1611); Barren Fd (*v.* bareine); Higher & Lower Bent (*the over & the lower Bent* 1611, *v.* beonet); Birch Hay; Brickiln Fd; Broadhurst ('broad wood', *v.* hyrst); Browne's Croft (*the Brownes Crofte* 1611); Calf Croft & Hey (*the Calfecroft, the Calfehey* 1611); Clay Acre; Coal Bank (*v.* col¹); Cow Hey (*the-* 1611); Cross (*v.* cros); Crow Flatt (*the Crowe Flatt* 1611, *v.* flat); Dirty Mdw; Great, Higher, Little & Lower Flatt (*the Flattes, Hall Flattes, the Nearer & the Sandieflatt, the flatt meadowe* 1611, *v.* flat); Higher & Lower Galley Acre (*the garlicke Akers* 1611 *v.* gārlēac, æcer); Great Hole; Great Hurst (*v.* hyrst); Great Mdw (*the-* 1611); Green (*v.* grēne²); Green Mdw; Half Acre; Half Day Math ('half a day's mowing', *v.* day-math); Harry Mdw (*the Harrie meadowe* 1611); Hem Mdw (*v.* hemm); Higher Fall (cf. *the faule, the Falls* 1611, (*lane*) 1620, *v.* (ge)fall, cf. Fallhey *supra*); Higher Hey; Higher Mdw (*the over meadowe* 1611, *v.* uferra); Higher Piece; Hollin Hey ('holly enclosure'); Hollin Hurst (*the Hollinhusrt* 1611, 'the holly wood', *v.* holegn, hyrst); Hollow Mdw (*v.* holh); Horse Ridding (*the horse-Ryding, the horseridinges wood* 1611, *v.* ryding); Hulme (*v.* hulm, cf. *The Hulme* 1611, probably in Disley, 276 *infra*); Imbrows (*the Ymbulls* (*meadowe*) 1611, from brū 'a brow, a hill' and hyll 'a hill', perhaps with imbe 'a swarm of bees' as first el.); Ironstones Holes; Laining Butts (*the leaninge butts* 1611, *v.* butte); Ley Fd (*the-* 1611, *v.* lǣge, cf. Lower Fd *infra*); Little Heys; Long Cut; Long Hurst (*Longhurst* 1503, 1611, 1620, *a bancke comonlie called Longhurst or Brockholes* 1611, 'long wooded-hill', otherwise 'badger-holes', v. lang, hyrst, brocc-hol); Long Lands (v. lang, land); Lower Fd (*the two layefieldes* 1595 (1611), *lower & overfield* 1611, cf. *the neatherfield* 1611, v. lǣge, neoðera, cf. Ley Fd *supra*, Over Fd *infra*); Lower Mdw (-*e* 1611); Marl Churl (v. marlede, ear[2]. For the second el. v. Blackeyer 265 *infra*); Meadow Head ('top of the meadow', v. hēafod); Megs Yard (v. meg, geard); Milking Fd (v. milking); Moor Fd (*the Moorefield* 1611); Muck Mdw (v. muk); New Patch; New Rid (*the new Ridd* 1611, v. ryde, cf. Rid(s) 175 *supra*); Nib Carr (*the-* 1611, v. hnybba, 'a promontory', kjarr); Oakes Fd; Old Mdw; Olliwell's Piece; Orchard Fd; Over Field (v. Lower Fd *supra*); Ox Hey & Pasture (*the Oxehey, the Oxe Pasture* 1611); Park (*one peece of ympalled ground called the Parke* 1611); Rough (Mdw) (cf. *the Rughfield* 1611); Round Croft (*the Round Crifte* 1611); Rye Croft (*the Ryecrofte* 1611); Rye Flatt; Saw Pit Fd (v. saw-pytt); Share Mdw (v. scearu 'a share'); Sitch Fd (v. sīc); Smithurst Fd; Stone Croft & Fd (*the Stonecroft, the Stonefield* 1611); Stoney Bank; Stubble Fd; Sunday Flatt (v. Sunnan-dæg 'Sunday', flat); Tan Bar Hole 1831 (probably a hole for steeping tan-bark, v. *tan-bark* NED); Tan Yard (v. tan-yard); Top o' th' Hill (*Topp of the Hill* 1611); Trusty Carr (*the Thrustercarr* 1611, v. kjarr); Turner Hey (*the Turner(s) Hey, Turnar hay wood* 1611); Wath (v. vað 'a ford'); Well Croft; Wet Fd (*the two Wett fieldes* 1611); Whaley Pasture; Wheat Fd (*the Wheatfield* 1611, cf. *the Wheatclose* 1611); Wilkin Bottom (*the Wilkinbothom* 1611, from botm 'bottom', with the ME pers.n. *Wilkin*, diminutive of *William*); Will Grass.

(b) *the Bareast meadowe* 1611 (perhaps 'bare-arse meadow', a bare hill, from bær[1] and ears); *Birch-field* 1611; *the Birchin know(l)e* 1611, *the Birchenknowe* 1620 ('knoll growing with birch-trees', v. bircen[2], cnoll); *Brekwellehurst* 1287 (p), *Brokwalhurst* 1354 (p), 1367 (p), 1387 (p), -*walle-* 1354, *Brocwalhurst* 1361 (p), *Brocholehurst* 1372 (p), *Brokhalhurst* 1380, *Brokealhurst* 1445 (p) (*freq* as a surname in this part of Macclesfield Hundred, cf. 113, 176 *supra*; location unknown, but cf. Brocklehurst 330 *infra*; '(wooded-hill at) the brook-spring' from brōc and wella (wælla), with hyrst, the second el. replaced by halh, hol[1]. Had it survived, the modern form would be *Brocklehurst*, cf. George *Brocklehurst*, aged native of Kettleshulme 1783 *Dow*, John *Brocklehurst* of Macclesfield 1791 *Dow*, cf. also Wych Fm in Adlington 185 *infra*); *the Carrfieldes* 1611 (v. kjarr); *Cliffehey* 1620 (v. clif, (ge)hæg); *the Cote meadow* 1611 (v. cot); *the Flashcarr(e)* 1611, 1620 (v. flasshe, kjarr); *the flaxeyord* 1611 ('enclosure where flax is grown', v. fleax, geard); *the Hagh patch* 1611 (v. halh); *the Hall Clough* 1611; *the Hawkeshutt bancke* 1611 ('hawk's-corner bank', v. hafoc, scēat); *the Hedgrowes* 1611 ('the hedge-rows'); *Horse Crofte, the Horse close* 1611; *le Kerkehous in Irdesle* 1408 ('the church house', v. kirkja, hūs); *the Kerrie meadow* 1611 ('marshy meadow', v. kjarr, -ig[3]); *the Kilne Crofte* 1611; *the morebancke* 1611; *Nixon meadowe* 1611 (from Richard *Nixon*, tenant); *the nether Ollers* 1611 (v. neoðera, alor); *the Paddocke meadowe* 1611 (v. pearroc); *the Phillipp Crofte* 1611 (cf. Philip's Mdw 275 *infra*); *Pounosehurst Wood* 1611; *le Roker* 1348 (p), *Roe Carr, Roecarre-wood, the Rocarrs* 1611 ('rough marsh', v. rūh, kjarr); *Sharle meadowe* 1611; *the Sluce Earth* 1611 (*v.* scluse, erð); *the Smythie field* 1611; *one peece of ympalled ground called the Swyne Parke* 1611 (cf. Swine Park 175 *supra*); *the Tynkar's bancke* 1611 (*v.* tink(l)ere, cf. Toddbrook Reservoir *supra*); *the Warth* 1611 (*v.* waroð 'water-meadow'); *Wayley-, Waylye Slacke* 1611, *Wealey Slacke* 1620 (*v.* slakki 'a hollow', cf. Whaley *supra*); (*the*) *Weeteshawe* 1611, 1620 ('wet copse', *v.* wēt, sceaga); *the Wyllgreafe, the Wilgrave Wood* 1611 ('wild grove', *v.* wilde, grǣfe); *Woodruffe meadowe, the Woodruffes fieldes, Woodrooffe, Woodroofe Clough* 1611, *Woodrooffclough* 1620, *v.* wudu-rofe, clōh); *the Wyrebothom* 1611 (*v.* wīr 'bog-myrtle', botm).

ix. Prestbury

The ancient parish of Prestbury originally included the parishes of Alderley, Gawsworth and Taxal 94, 66, 172 *supra*, and the Chapelry of Macclesfield 106 *supra*, *v.* Orm² III 646, Renaud 1–20, ChetOS VIII 283n. These divisions isolate the townships 1. Bosley, 2. North Rode 54 *supra*, and 3. Birtles, 4. Capesthorne, 5. Chelford, 6. Henbury cum Pexall, 7. Marton, 8. Siddington, 9. Lower Withington, 10. Old Withington 72 *supra*. The rest of the parish contained 11. Adlington, 12. Bollington, 13. Butley (*v.* Prestbury *infra*), 14. Fallibroome (*v.* Prestbury *infra*), 15. Lyme Handley, 16. Mottram St Andrew (now a c.p. including Newton *infra*), 17. Newton (*v.* prec.), 18. Poynton with Worth, 19. Prestbury (now a c.p. including Butley and Fallibroome *supra*), 20. Tytherington (now included in Macclesfield c.p. 113 *supra*), 21. Upton (now included in Macclesfield c.p. 113 *supra*), 22. Woodford (now included in Hazelgrove cum Bramhall c.p.).

11. ADLINGTON (101–9180)

    Eduluintune 1086 DB, *Adelvinton* 1248 Ipm
    Adelinton(e), -yn- 1252 RBE, c.1270 Adl, c.1280 Dow, *-ing-, -yng-*
      c.1270 Adl, 1287 *Eyre* (p)
    Adlinton, -yn- 1286 *Eyre*, 1316 Orm² *et freq, -ing-, -yng-* 1337 *Eyre*,
      1362 BPR *et freq*
    Aldelyn(g)ton 1352 BPR

'Ēadwulf's farm', from the OE pers.n. *Ēadwulf* and -ingtūn.

BOOTH GREEN (FM) (101–925810), *le Herlesbothe* c.1270 (1611) LRMB 200, *le Erlesbothe* (*holyn*) 1384 *Rental, le Bothegrene* 1349 *MinAcct*, 'the earl's booth', 'the green at the booth', *v.* eorl, bōth, grēne². This place may be the lost *Bothegrene* referred to under Macclesfield 118 *supra*, cf. also 215 *infra*; the *holyn* (*v.* holegn 'a holly tree') is probably associated with Hollingsworth Smithy *infra*. Adlington was a manor of the Earl of Chester.

HOLLINGSWORTH SMITHY (101–913804), *forgea apud Holynwrth* 1285 *For*, *Hollinworth Smithie* 1663 *Dow*, 'the holly enclosure', *v.* holegn, worŏ, with smiŏŏe 'a smithy' added, cf. *forgea de-*, *forgea apud le Bothegrene* 1349 *MinAcct*, and *le Erlesbothe holyn* 1384 *Rental*, *v.* Booth Green *supra*.

HOPE GREEN (FM) & LANE (FM) (101–914822), *Hope* c.1250 Chest, 1286 *Eyre*, (*le-*) c.1270 Adl, c.1280 *Dow*, *Hope Hall* 1560 Sheaf, *Hope Green* 1751 ib, *Hope Lane* 1831 Bry, cf. *le Furhope* 1521 *Dow*, 'the valley', *v.* hop[1], and also grēne[2].

PEDLEY HILL (FM) & Ho (101–927812), *Peddeleg, -legh(e)* 1248 Ipm, 1249 IpmR, (*-broke*) 13 (1611) *LRMB* 200, (*grangia Johannis de*) *Peddeley* 1441 *Eyre*, *Pedeleg(broc)* 1270 (17) Sheaf, *-legh* 1359 *Dow* (p), *-ley(e)*, (*-feld, -heth*) 1363 *ChFor*, *Peddisle* 1285 *Eyre* (p), *Pyddelegh'* 1287 Court (p), *Pedlegh* 1361 *Dow*, *Padeleygrene* 1363 *ChFor*, *Higher & Lower Pedley Hill* 1831 Bry, from lēah and an OE pers.n. *Pēoda* as in Pedwardine He, Pedwell So (DEPN), or an OE pers.n. *Pedda, Pædda*, a derivative of OE *Pad(d)a*, with grēne[2], brōc, hyll, feld, hǣŏ. Cf. 99, 105, 145 *supra*, also Pedley Brook 32 *supra*.

SHIRDFOLD (101–906823), 1842 OS, *Shert* 1395 Orm[2], *le Shert* 1440 *Eyre*, *le Sherde* 1438 Earw, '(fold at) the gap', *v.* scerde, fald, cf. Fulshaw Hall 228 *infra*, Shert Hall 271 *infra*, and Orm[2] III 664.

WHITELEY GREEN & HEYS (101–920787), *Wyteleg'* 1286 *Eyre*, *Whetelegh* 1354 *ib* (p), *le Qwytelegh'heye* 1363 *ChFor*, *Whitelighey* 1403 CRC, *Whyteleghgrene, Whytelyghhey* 1462 Ch (Orm[2] III 657 reads *-greve, -hay*, Earw II 237 reads *-greene*), *Whitelegh Grene* 1499 Sheaf, *Wheteley* 1555 ib, 'white clearing or wood', *v.* hwīt, lēah, with grēne[2], (ge)hæg, cf. Whiteleyhey Fm 195 *infra*.

(EAST) WOODEND FM, WOOD FM, WOOD HO & LANE (END) (101–9381, 9482), *Woodends, Wood Lane* 1831 Bry, *Wood Farm* 1842 OS, named from *boscus de Adelinton* 1286 *Eyre*, *boscus de Adelynton Wodehouses* 1363 *ChFor*, *Adlyngton Wode* 1403 CRC, 1462 Ch, *common or waste called Adlington Wood* 1680 *Dow*, *v.* wudu, ende[1], hūs.

ADLINGTON HALL & MILL, 1842 OS, *the hall of Adlyngton* 1549 ChRR. ASHLEY FM. BARTON'S CLOUGH, cf. *Barton Croft* 1848

TA, from the surname *Barton* and clōh.   BRECK QUARRIES, *Breck*
1831 Bry, *v.* brekka 'a slope'.   BRICKYARD FM.   BRIDGE FM,
named from a railway bridge.   BROOK HO, 1831 Bry, named from
R. Dean.   BROOKLEDGE FM & LANE, cf. *Brookledge (Croft)* 1848
TA, 'brook bog', *v.* brōc, læc(c).   BUTLEY BRIDGE, leading to
Butley 193 *infra*.   BYE PIT (lost), 1831 Bry, a coal-pit, *v.* byge[1] 'a
bend, a corner'.   CLARK GREEN (FM), *Clarke* 1560 Sheaf, *Clarks
Green* 1831 Bry, *v.* grēne[2]; the first el. is probably a surname, but it
could be dial. *clart* 'mud, clay'.   CLAYTONGREAVES, 1860 White, cf.
Clayton Croft & Green 1848 *TA*, from the surname *Clayton* and
græfe, cf. Robert *Cleaton* tenant in 1582 *Dow*.   DAIRYHOUSE
WOOD, 1848 *TA*, cf. Dairy Ho 195 *infra*.   DANGEROUS CORNER,
Corner 1831 Bry.   HIGHER & LOWER DOLES FM, *Higher & Lower
Long Dows* 1831 ib, *Long Doles* 1842 OS, 'long allotments', *v.* dāl.
FOUR-LANE-ENDS.   GEE PARTS, 1848 *TA*, cf. *Gee Corn Field*, *Gee
Meadow* 1848 *ib*, 'crooked divisions of land', from gee in ModEdial.
'crooked', also 'turning aside (to the left)'.   GIBSON WOOD, 1831
Bry, cf. John *Gibson* 1773 *Dow*.   GORSE WOOD (FM).   GREEN
FM, named from Whiteley Green *supra*.   HARROPGREEN FM,
HARROP LANE, *Harrop Green* 1831 Bry, cf. Haropgreen 90 *supra*,
v. Harrop 138 *supra*.   HIBBERTBROW FM & WOOD, *Hibbert Brow*
1807 *Dow*, *v.* brū and cf. John & Thomas *Hebbert*, tenants in 1634
Dow.   THE HOLE, 1842 OS.   HOLEHOUSE LANE, 1831 Bry,
Owlers Lane 1842 OS, *v.* alor.   HOLLING BUSH (lost), 1831 Bry,
'holly bush', *v.* holegn, busc.   ISLES WOOD, *The-* 1831 ib, *the
Holes* 1842 OS, cf. *the Gorsty-*, *the Mottram Hyles* 1680 *Dow*, *v.*
hygel 'a hillock', cf. Reginald *Mottram* 1634 *Dow*.   ISSUES WOOD.
JEPSON CLOUGH, 1831 Bry, cf. Raynolde *Gep-*, *Jepson*, tenant in 1551
Dow, *v.* clōh 'a dell'.   LANEHEAD FM, *Lanehead* 1842 OS.
LOCKGATE FM, *Lockgate* 1831 Bry, 'a gate with a lock on it', *v.* loc,
geat.   LODGE BROW & FM, *Lodge* 1831 ib, *v.* loge, brū.   LONDON
RD, the Stockport–Macclesfield turnpike.   LONG LANE.   MARL-
FIELDS FM & HO, *Marlsfield* 1831 Bry, *Marlfields* 1842 OS, *v.* marle,
feld.   MAUBERN HALL.   MILL HO (BRIDGE), *the Millhouse*
c.1620 Orm[2], *the Milnehouse* 1696 Earw, *Davenport Bridge* 1831 Bry.
NOGGIN FM, *v.* nogging.   OAK FM.   PARK CORNER, 1860 White
(a gamekeeper's cottage), *Adlington Park* 1848 *TA*.   PEGGIE'S
LANE, cf. *Peggy Green Field* 1848 *ib*, from dial. *peggy* (EDD) 'the
game of hockey played with a wooden ball, or *piggy*'.   POLE FM,
Poole House 1831 Bry, *v.* pōl[1] 'a pool'.   POYNTON BRIDGE, on the

Poynton boundary.   RAMS CLOUGH (101–943820), 1842 OS, *v.* ramm, clōh, the same place as *Rosineclough* 13 (1611) *LRMB* 200, *Rosunclowe* 1270 (17) Sheaf, on the north-east boundary of Adlington, cf. Rossen Clough 151 *supra.*   REDBROOK BRIDGE, COTTAGE & FM, cf. Red Brook[2] 34 *supra.*   RODDICK-KNOLL.   ROUNDY-LANE FM, *Roundy Lane* 1831 Bry, *Roundhill Lane* 1842 OS, possibly from roundy 'lumpy' with lane.   RUSHLEYWALLS, *Rushley Wall* 1831 Bry, cf. *Le Rushiley* 1567 ChRR, 'the rush-grown clearing', from riscig and lēah, with wælla 'a well, a spring'.   RYLES WOOD, cf. *Royles Green* 1848 *TA*, from the surname from Royle 237 *infra.* SANDHOLES FM & MOSS, *Sandhole(s)* 1831 Bry, 1848 *TA*, cf. *Sandhole Isles* 1848 *ib*, 'sand-pit(s)', cf. Isles Wood *supra.*   SCHOOLFOLD, *Woodend* 1831 Bry, cf. *School Field* 1848 *TA*, 'fold and field belonging to a school', *v.* fald, cf. Woodend *supra.*   SKELLORN GREEN (FM), *Skellow Green* 1831 Bry, *Skelhorn Green* 1842 OS, cf. *Skillon Croft* 1848 *TA*, *v.* grēne[2] 'a green', cf. Peter *Skelhorne* of Adlington 1574 *Dow*, John *Scalehorne* (at Macclesfield) 1467 *MinAcct*. The surname is probably toponymic, 'a horn-shaped piece of land at a shieling', from skáli and horn, cf. *Skeylhornrudyng* 334 *infra.*   SMITHYMEADOW PITS, cf. *Smithy Meadow & Field* 1848 *TA*.   SNAPES (lost), 1831 Bry, the home of John *Snape* 1800 *Dow*. SPRINGBANK, 1842 OS.   STARKIE HO, *Starkey House* 1842 ib, cf. William *Starky* 1555 Sheaf.   STAR PIT (lost), 1831 Bry, a coal-pit. STREET LANE (FM & LODGE) (101–920818), *Street Lane* 1842 OS, a road-name in route XIV 45 *supra.*   STYPERSON PARK & POOL, *Styperson lane* 1689 *Dow*, *Styparson Park Corner* 1794 *Dow*, *a park call'd Stiperly* 1700 Earw. *Styperson* probably represents *Styperston*, from tūn 'a farmyard, a farm' (cf. Snelson 93 *supra* for -ston > -son) and stīpere 'a post, a prop'.   SUGAR LANE (FM). This may be from sugre 'sugar', alluding either to an Ascension- or Easter-Day sugar-drinking custom (EDD, s.v. *sugar*) or to 'sweet land', cf. Sugar Lane 145 *supra*, WRY 2 109.   SWINEROOD WOOD, *Swine Roods (Wood)*, *-Roads-* 1848 *TA*, 'swine clearings', *v.* swīn[1], rod[1].   TAN-YARD FM, *Tan Yard House* 1848 *ib*, *v.* tan-yard.   TRUGS I' TH' HOLE, 'troughs in the hollow', *v.* trog, hol[1], cf. Trugs i' th' Hole 102 *supra.*   WALNUT-TREE FM.   WARDSEND (BRIDGE & FM) (101–9382), *Wards End* 1842 OS (lit. *Wands*), *Coal Office* 1831 Bry (near Bye Pit *supra*), *v.* ende[1] 'the end of a town', cf. Thomas *Ward* 1521 *Dow*.   WATERMEETINGS, *Water Meeting* 1831 Bry, a confluence. WELL FM, 1842 OS.   WHITE HALL.   THE WILDERNESS, 1842 ib,

Hermitage 1831 Bry. WINDMILL INN, 1831 ib. WINTERFOLD, *Wintersfold* 1831 ib, 'fold used in winter', *v.* winter, fald. WYCH COTTAGE & WOOD, *Vetch House & Woods* 1831 ib, *Wych* 1842 OS, *Wych Wood* 1848 *TA*, probably from wice 'a wych-elm or -hazel'. WYCH FM, *Brocklehurst* 1831 Bry, from the local surname *Brocklehurst*, cf. prec., and *Brekwellehurst* 180 *supra*. YEWTREE FM.

FIELD-NAMES

The undated forms are 1848 *TA* 4. Of the others, 13 (1611) is *LRMB* 200, 1270 (17), 1560, 1751 Sheaf, 1280, 1384, 1521, 1551, 1553, 1581, 1619, 1634, 1679, 1680, 1689, 1736, 1766, 1807, 1810 *Dow*, 1345, 1350, 1354, 1360, 1441 *Eyre*, 1363 *ChFor*, 1412 *Chol*, 1467, 1471, 1508 *MinAcct*, 1549 ChRR.

(a) The Acre (1810); Adams Fd; Adlant Fd (*v.* hēafod-land); Allen Wd; Aspin Wd; Aspin Hurst ('aspen wood', *v.* æspen, hyrst); Back Croft; (The) Backside; Bank(s), Bank Top; Barbers Wd (cf. George *Barber* 1679); Barn Field Bottom (*v.* botm); Bean Flatt (*v.* flat); The Bent, Bent Heys ('grassland', 'grassy enclosures', *v.* beonet, (ge)hæg); Bings Mdw (*The benges* 1345, *del Benges* 1350 (p), *del Bynges* 1360 (p), 'the hollows', *v.* bing); Black Hey; Black Leach ('black bog', *v.* blæc, læc(c)); Bliss Fd; Bonis Hall Park (named from Bonis Hall 194 *infra*); The Bottoms (*v.* botm); Bradley Fd (cf. Thomas *Bradley* 1736); Briary-, Briery Fd; Brickiln Fd & Mdw; Bridge Wd; Briley Fd; Brinks (*v.* brink); Brook Fd; Brooms Croft, Broomy Fd (*v.* brōm(ig)); The Brow(s), Brow Fd (*v.* brū); Brue Flit ('tethering-ground at a brow', from brū and dial. *flit* 'to shift, a shift', referring to moveable tethers), Buckleys Fd; Bungal Croft; Butt Field Lane (*v.* butte); Butty Fd (*v.* butty); Buxton Croft (either from dial. *buck-stone* 'a stone on which linen is beaten' (cf. *buck* sb.[2] EDD), or from the surname from Buxton Db); Calf Croft; Carr Man; The Carrs (*v.* kjarr); Chapel Fd; Chumtree Croft (from chump 'a log of wood' and trēow); Clay Flatt; (The) Clough(s) (*v.* clōh); Coal Pit; Coat Mdw (*v.* cot); Great & Little Cockshead(s) (*v.* cocc-scyte); the Collins Croft 1807, 1810; Colt Fd (*v.* colt); Colters Eye ('colt-herd's meadow', *v.* coltere, ēg); Coppy Mdw & Wood Fd (*v.* copis); Cote Brow (*v.* cot, brū); Cow Hey; Crab Tree Flat (*the Crabtryeflatt(e)*, *-tr(i)e-* 1551, 1553, 1581, *v.* flat); Crossledge ('marshy stream running athwart a field', *v.* cros, læc(c), cf. Brookledge *supra*); The Cunnacre (*v.* coninger 'a rabbit warren'); Daft Fd (*v.* 331 *infra*); Dale Eye Fd (*v.* dæl[1], ēg); Dare Pit Fd; Nine Daymath ('nine days' mowing', *v.* day-math); Four & Little Day Work ('four and one days' work', *v.* day-work); Little Demain (*v.* demeyn); Dick Fd; Downe's Fd (from the *Downes* family of Pott Shrigley); Driving Road; Dry Hill; The Farthing (*v.* fēorðung); Ferney Mdw; Fleam Hurst ('wooded-hill at a mill-fleam', *v.* flēama, hyrst); Fold Fd; The Folly; Forty Acres; Great & Little Four Acres; The Furlongs (*v.* furlang); Further Mdw (*-medowe* 1581); Gad Hole ('gad-fly hollow', *v.* gad); Gaskells (cf. William *Gaskell* 1634); Girk Croft; The Gladdin(g) ('the glade', *v.* glad(d)en, cf. Gladding Hurst 201 *infra*); Goody Flatt; Great Charles's Hey; Great Ridding (*v.* ryding); The

Greaves (*v.* grǣfe); Green Brow (*v.* brū); Grinkall; Guady Brows; Haddy-hough; Hadfield Mdw; Hall Croft; Hen Croft; Henshaws Nook (from the surname *Henshaw*); Hide croft; The Hills; Hill Head; Hoe Mdw (*v.* hōh); Hollow Fd; Holt Fd & Wd (*v.* holt, cf. *the wheate Houte* 1581, *v.* hwǣte 'wheat'); The Homestall ('stall near a house', *v.* home 'near home', stall); Hooley Parts (cf. Thomas *Hooley*, tenant in 1807); Horse Grass(es) (*le horse gresse* 1521, *the laugher* (*logher*) & *over horse gresse* 1551, *the horse grasses* 1766, 'grazing for horses', *v.* hors, gærs); The Horsteads (*v.* hors, stede); Humphrey Fd; Little Hurst (*v.* hyrst); Huspush ('a hustle, a busy time', from dial. *huspush*); Island Croft; (The) Jack Croft & Gate 1807, 1810 (probably from dial. jack 'unused' (EDD s.v. *jack*), cf. Jack Fields Fm 62 *supra*); Jig Platt (*the Gigg platt* 1807, 1810, *v.* gigge, plat²); Johns Fd (*Johanesfeld, campus Johannis Elene* 1363, named after *John* (c.1354) son of Elena de Legh, lady of Adlington (c.1324)); Jowl Hole (perhaps 'hollow at a ravine', from ceafl and hol¹, *v.* Joule Bridge 178 *supra*); Kiln Croft (*the Kylnecroft* 1551, *the Kilnecroft*(*e*) 1553, 1619); Kitchen Hey & Mdw; The Knowl; Lady Hole ('lady's hollow', *v.* hlǣfdige, hōl¹, cf. *le lauedyredyng* 1363, 'the lady's clearing', *v.* ryding, assarted c.1351 by Elena de Legh); Lawn Mdw (*v.* launde); The Lease (*v.* lǣs); Lime Fd (1810); Long Acres; Long Butts (*v.* butte); Low Fd, Lowermost Fd; Marl Earth ('marl ground', *v.* eorðe); Marl Pit Fd & Piece; Marshland Fd (cf. John & Robert *de Mershelond* 1384, 1406, Rauf *Merchland, Marsheland* 1551, *v.* mersc, land); Martha Mdw; Mathews Fd; The Menerith ('common stream', *v.* (ge)mǣne, rið); Middle Cale (*v.* cauel, cf. Middlecale 200 *infra*); Milking Croft & Fd; The Mossley ('moss clearing', *v.* mos, lēah, cf. *de Mosselegh* 1376 (p)); Mottershead Mdw & Parts (named after the *Mottershead* family, tenants here 1773, *v. Dow* 438, cf. *Mottershead* 203 *infra*); Nether Fd; Nut Hey (*v.* hnutu, (ge)hæg); Oat Fd; Old Masters Mdw; Olivers Fd; The Oulest ('owl wood', *v.* ūle, hyrst); Out Fd; The Outlett (*v.* outlet); Oven Fd; Owler Fd ('alder field', *v.* alor); The Paddock (*v.* pearroc); Park Wd; (Further & Nearer) Parts (*v.* part); Pasture Fd (*the higher & lower pasture field* 1810); The Patch(es); Pearce's Little Fd (from *Piers*, a ME (OFr) form of *Peter*, cf. *Peter* de Legh of Adlington 1385, 1412, 1460, 1495, four generations); Pim(b)lott Croft (from the pers.n. or surname *Pimblett* from eModE *Pymlot*, Reaney 252); Pinfold Croft (*v.* pynd-fald); The Pingot (*v.* pingot); Pitstead ('site of a pit', *v.* pytt, stede); The Plain; Pollitt Fd; Big & Little Pool, (Long) Poolsteads (*v.* pōl¹, pōl-stede, cf. Pitstead *supra*); Potatoe Bed & Fd; Pott Fd, Potts Barn Fd (from Thomas *Pott* 1634, cf. Pott Hall 130 *supra*); Pottle Hurst (*v.* hyrst 'wooded-hill'; the first el. is obscure); Priest Fd; Pye Root (from pie² 'a magpie', and root, cf. *Ryeroote* 159 *supra*); Reddish Mdw (named after Thomas *Reddich*, Elizabeth *Reddish* 1680); Great & Little Ring (*v.* hring); Roodle(d)ge (*v.* lǣc(c), cf. Brookledge *supra*); Rough(s); Round Croft & Mdw; Roundy Hey ('rounded enclosure', *v.* rond, (ge)hæg); Rushy Fd & Mdw (cf. *le Rushihey* 1549, *v.* riscig, (ge)hæg, cf. Rushleywalls *supra*); Rye Hill; Saw Pit Fd (*v.* saw-pytt); School Fd; The Seminary; Sheet Croft; Ship Croft (*v.* scēap); The Shute ('steep slope', *v.* dial. *shute* (EDD), cf. scēot³); Little Simpson Fd (cf. William *Sympson* 1589); Siss Croft; The Slack (*v.* slakki); Soft Mdw; Spout

Fd (*v.* spoute); Stack Croft & Yard (*v.* stakkr, stak-ʒard); Lower Stones; Stone Ponds; Swine Croft; Thistle(y) Fd; Toad Carr Mdw (cf. *terra vocata Todelache* c.1280, 'toad marsh', *v.* tāde, læc(c), kjarr); Toe Fd; Turn & Rails; Wall Croft, Fd & Mdw (*v.* wælla); Wall(ed) Fd (*v.* wall); Walters Fd (cf. *campus Thomae Wulder* 1363); Great & Long Waters; The Waste; Well Fd & Mdw; Wet Fd; Wheat Croft & Fd; White Fd (*the-* 1807); Withering Fd (*v.* withering); Great Woodford Eyes (*v.* ēg, cf. Woodford 217 *infra*); Worth Fd (*v.* worð).

(*b*) *Adekyneschar*' 1363 ('Adekin's marsh', from the ME pers.n. *Adekin*, a pet-form of *Adam*, and kjarr, cf. Adams Fd *supra*, 192 *infra*); *cald(e)wall(e) siche* 13 (1611) ('the cold-spring stream', from cald and wælla, with sīc; it ran into *Peddeleg' broke* and formed the boundary between the wood of Adlington and the Forest of Macclesfield, *v.* Pedley, Woodend *supra*, *Merebroc infra*); *Cornesfeld* 1363 ('crane's field', *v.* corn², feld); *Le Merchaces* 13 (1611), *Meroke* 1270 (17) ('the boundary oak(s), *v.* (ge)mǣre, mearc, āc; a point on the boundary between the wood of Adlington and the Forest of Macclesfield, cf. foll. and Woodend *supra*); *Merebroc* 1270 (17) ('boundary brook', *v.* (ge)mǣre, brōc, cf. prec., *cald(e)wall(e) siche supra* and *Holybroke* 29 *supra*); *le Outewode* 1441 ('the outlying part of the woodland', *v.* ūt, wudu, cf. Woodend etc., *supra*); *Pecokfeld* 1363 ('field of a man called Peacock (a by-name)', *v.* feld, cf. Hudde *Pecok*, *Pecoc* 1285 Court); *Procktes Greene* 1689; *Williamesfeld Champayne* 1363 ('William Champayne's field', *v.* feld, cf. Robert *Chaumpeyn* 1288 ChetNS LXXXIV, xlix); *Wyrecotesfeld* 1363 ('field at *Wyrecote*', from feld and a lost p.n. from wir 'bog-myrtle' and cot 'a cote, a cottage').

12. BOLLINGTON (101–9276)

> *Bolynton* 1270 (17) Sheaf, 1288 *Eyre et freq*, (*-in foresta de Maclisfeld*) 1325 Dow, (*-iuxta Tideryngton*) 1373 *ib*, (*-iuxta Macclesfeld*') 1454 *Eyre*, *Bolinton* 1285 *ib*, 1320 *Dow*
> *Bolington(e)*, *-yng-* 1285, 1287, 1290 *Eyre et freq*, *Bollyngton*, *-ing-* 1559 Pat
> *Bulyngton* 1365 Pat (p), *Bullington* 1560 Sheaf
> *Balington* 1526 ChRR

'Farm on R. Bollin', from tūn and the r.n. *Bollin*, cf. R. Bollin 15 *supra*, Bollington 330 *infra*. Ekwall RN 40 observes that this place is on a stream now called R. Dean (cf. 20 *supra*) a principal tributary of R. Bollin, which must formerly have shared the name of the main stream. Webb's *Itinerary*, c.1620 (Orm² III 546) has 'and so to Bollington situate on the Bollin'.

STREET-NAMES: CHURCH ST., 1860 White; HIGH ST., 1860 *ib*; INGERSLEY RD, *Sowcar Lane* 1860 *ib*, cf. Sowcar, Ingersley 140 *supra*; WATER ST., 1860 *ib*, backing upon R. Dean, *v.* wæter.

BEESTON BROW, 1860 White, *Beestall-bancke* 1611 *LRMB* 200, *-Bank* 1686 *Dow*, *-Brow* 1688 *ib*, 'hillside where a bee-hive stands', *v*. bee-stall, brū, banke.

BONNYBANKS PARK, *Bolywode* c.1320 *Dow* (p), 1357 *ChFor* (p), *Boliwode* 1370 *Eyre* (p), *Bolly Woodes* 1611 *LRMB* 200, *Boniwood*, *-y-* 1686, 1688 *Dow*, probably 'wood where logs are got' from a ME adj. *bolig* (bolr, bola 'a log, a tree trunk', with -ig³) and wudu.

KERRIDGE (hamlet 101–935765), KERRIDGE HILL (110–942760, also in Rainow, cf. KERRIDGE END & SIDE 144 *supra*) [kerid3]

> (*le topp de*) *Caryge* 13 (1611) *LRMB* 200, *Carigge* 1467, 1471 *MinAcct*
> (*le Cop de*) *Kayrug*, *-Cairug* 1270 (17) Sheaf³ 18, *Cayrugh* 1286 Court (p), *Cayrug(ge)* 1341, 1350, 1355 *Eyre* (p), (*boscus de*) *Kayruge* 1357 *ChFor*
> *Kerug* 1286 Court (p)
> *Kayryche* 1363 *Eyre* (p), (*hill called*) *Kayridge*, *-rydge* 1611 *LRMB* 200, 1620 *Surv*
> *S(t)ar(r)igge* 1471, 1508 *MinAcct*, *Starnige* 1560 Sheaf³ 24 (6463)
> *Cayregge*, *-edge*, *Careegge* 1503 *ChFor*
> *Cargag'* 1508 *MinAcct*, *Cariage or Carage* 1620 *Surv*
> (*houses on*) *Kearitch* 1620 *Surv*
> *Kerich* 1686 *Dow*, *Cher(r)idge* 1716 *ib*, *Kerridge* 1842 OS

'Boulder ridge', *v*. cæg, hrycg, the latter el. confused with ecg 'the edge of a hill'. The first el., OE **cæg* 'a stone, a boulder' (corresponding to MDu kei, kay '(block of) stone', EFris kei 'stone') is discussed by M. Löfvenberg EStud 43, 41, who introduces it to replace OE *cæg* 'a key' in EPN. An analogous p.n. is Cabus La 165, from cæg 'a boulder' and ball 'a rounded hill', for which La 165 and DEPN adduce OE *cæg* 'a key' in some sense such as 'a peg'.

OWL-HURST LANE (lost), 1819 *Dow*, *Holehurstishende* 13 (1611) *LRMB* 200, *the Holehursthrinde* 1270 (17) Sheaf, (*a common called*) *Holehurst* 1611 *LRMB* 200, 1620 *Surv*, *the Oule-hurst* 1611 *LRMB* 200, *a messuage known by the names of the Owzle Hole and Owlhurst* 1791, 1797 *Dow*, 'wooded hill with a hollow in it, or overlooking a hollow', *v*. hol¹, hyrst. The first el. was confused with ūle 'an owl', and a later name contains ōsle 'blackbird'. The thirteenth-century forms, from late copies, contain either hēafod 'head', or ende[1] 'end', referring to a boundary-point between the woods of Bollington and the Forest of Macclesfield.

SHATWELL FOLD, 1791 *Dow*, *Shatwele fold* 1788 *ib*, *Shadwell fold* 1791 *ib*, from a family surnamed *Shotwall* holding land here 1495 ChRR, cf. *Shotsall* 258 *infra*, and fald 'a fold'.

SHEEPING STEAD (lost), 1848 *TA*, *le Hepynstydes*, *les Shupenstydes* 1397 *Dow* (103, 104), *Shepynstedes* 115 *ib*, *the Shippen-stiddes* 1611 *LRMB* 200, 'brambly places', from a ME adj. hēopen (*v*. hēope, hēopa, -en[2]) and stede. For the development of *Sh-* from *H-* before a stress-shifted diphthong, cf. Shap We 2 165, Shoop Tree Nook We 2 54.

ADSHEAD BARN (lost), 1860 White, cf. Adshead Green 100 *supra*. BARLEYGRANGE.   BEECH HO.   BLEAK HO.   BOLLINGTON CROSS, 1750 Sheaf.   BOLLINGTONHALL FM, *Hall* 1842 OS, cf. *del Halle* 1339 *Dow* (p), *v*. hall.   BOLLINGTON LANE (lost), 1860 White, *þe lane of Bollington* 1501 Earw.   BOLLINGTON MILL, *molendinum aquaticum de Bolynton* 1347 *Eyre*.   BRACEY GREEN (lost), 1831 Bry, cf. John *Bredset* 1366 *Dow* 86, *v*. grēne[2].   BRADSHAW HALL (lost), 1831 Bry, probably from the surname *Bradshaw*.   BRIDGEND, 1860 White.   CHANCERY LANE.   CLARKE LANE (FM), 1848 *TA*, *Clacke Lane* 1831 Bry, cf. Lawrence *Clerke* 1545 *Dow*.   CLOUGH BANK.   COCKSHEADHEY FM, *Cockshutt Hey* 1611 *LRMB* 200, (*Farm*) 1819 *Dow*, *-Hay* 1791 *ib*, cf. *Cockshoot Close* 1611 *LRMB* 200, *Cocksheads* 1844 *TA*, 'cock-shoot enclosure', *v*. cocc-scyte, (ge)hæg.   COW LANE.   DAWSON FM, cf. *John Dosons Lands* 1686 *Dow* 374.   ENDON HALL (FM), *Whitthill* 1501 Earw, *Whithill* 1503 ChFor, *Whyt Hill*, *Whittell* 1611 *LRMB* 200, *Whitel*, *Whitle* 1686, 1688 *Dow*, *Whiteleys Farm* 1831 Bry, *Endon House* 1842 OS, 'white hill', *v*. hwīt, hyll. The origin of the modern name is not known. It may be 'end on', alluding to the layout of the house.   FIVEASHES COTTAGES, *Fiveashes* 1831 Bry.   FLASH LANE, leading to Flash Fm 195 *infra*. GAG QUARRY.   GARRET HOUSES.   GATLEY GREEN (lost), 1831 Bry, cf. Francis *Gatley* c.1722 *Dow*, *v*. grēne[2].   GNAT HOLE, 1842 OS, a midge-infested hollow beside R. Dean, *v*. gnætt, hol[1], cf. Gnathole 199 *infra*.   GREENFIELD, 1860 White.   GREEN LANE (FM).   GRIMSHAW LANE, 1860 *ib*, probably from the surname

Grimshaw, cf. Grimshaw La 76, 84. HALL HILL, *(the) Hale hill* 1611 *LRMB* 200, 'hill at a nook', *v.* halh. HIGHER LANE. HILLTOP (lost), 1831 Bry, *Hilltopp Tenement* 1692 *Dow*, *Hill Top (Gate)* 1795 *ib*. HOLLINHALL FM, *Hollynghall* 1550 *MinAcct*, *Hollin Hall* 1611 *LRMB* 200, 'holly-tree hall', *v.* holegn. HURST BROW, HO & LANE, *(the) Hurst* 1611 *LRMB* 200, 1620 *Surv*, *v.* hyrst. IVY HO, 1831 Bry. JACKSON LANE, cf. Lawrence *Jackson* 1545 *Dow*. LIMEFIELD HO, 1860 White. LONG LANE (FM), *(the) Long Lane* 1791 *Dow*. LONG ROW COTTAGES (lost), 1848 *TA*, *v.* rāw. LOWERHOUSE, 1831 Bry. LOWER MILL, downstream from Rainow Mill 145 *supra*. MILL LANE, *the Milne-lane* 1611 *LRMB* 200, leading to Rainow Mill 145 *supra*. MODE HILL (FM), *Modehill* 1686 *Dow*, *Maud Hill* 1860 White, *v.* hyll. MOSS FM, cf. *the Mosse*, *Bollington Mosse* 1611 *LRMB* 200, *v.* mos. (THE) MOUNT (FM), *The Mount* 1831 Bry, *(Farm)* 1860 White, *v.* mont. NAB FM, HEAD & WOOD, *the Nabb* (a winter pasture) 1736 *Dow*, (a messuage) 1791 *ib*, *(Wood)* 1831 Bry, 'the hill', *v.* nabbi, hēafod, cf. Nab Wood 134 *supra*. NORTHEND QUARRIES, at the north end of Kerridge Hill. OAK BANK, FOLD & LANE. OVEN HO, 1831 Bry, cf. *Oven House lands* 1686 *Dow*, 'bakehouse', *v.* ofen, hūs. POOL BANK. REDWAY LANE. THE ROOKERY (a house), *Crow Nest* 1831 Bry, *Rookery* 1842 OS. SADDLE OF KERRIDGE, a dip in the ridge of Kerridge Hill *supra*, *v.* sadol. SHRIGLEY RD, 1860 White, leading to Pott Shrigley 130 *supra*. SOWCAR, *v.* Sowcar Fm 140 *supra*. STAKEHOUSE END (lost), 1860 ib, *the Steakulls* 1611 *LRMB* 200, *Stekulls* 1611 *ib*, 1620 *Surv*, *Stakers End* 1831 Bry, probably from staca 'a stake' and hyll 'a hill', with ende[1]; the name of the area at the junction of High St., Lord St., Cow Lane & Chancery Lane. TINKERS CLOUGH, *(The)* 1611 *LRMB* 200, cf. *þe Tynkers Hill* 1611 *LRMB* 200, 'tinker's dell and hill', *v.* tink(l)ere, clōh, hyll, cf. Tinkerspit Gutter, Todbrook Reservoir 162, 174 *supra*. TURNERHEATH, 1831 Bry, *the heath*, *Tiderington Heath* 1611 *LRMB* 200, cf. *þe land of Thomas Turnor* 1501 Earw, *v.* hǣð, cf. Tytherington 214 *infra*. WATER HOUSE (MILLS), *Waterhouse* 1842 OS, *(Mills)* 1860 White, 'house by the water', *v.* wæter. WHITE NANCY, *(an ornamental summer house called-)* 1860 ib, *Summer House* 1831 Bry, *Northern Nancy* 1842 OS, a whitewashed tower at the northern end of Kerridge Hill, its conical shape resembling a woman in a bell-shaped cloak. OLD WINDMILL, WINDMILL LANE.

FIELD-NAMES

The undated forms in (a) are 1848 *TA* 60, and in (b) 1611 *LRMB*. Of the others 1270 (17) is Sheaf, 13 (1611), 1611 *LRMB* 200, 1363, 1503 *ChFor*, 1384 *Rental*, 1467, 1471, 1508 *MinAcct*, 1501 Earw, 1620 *Surv*, and the rest *Dow*.

(a) Asps (1686, *The Aspe Crofte* 1611, 'the aspens', v. æspe); Bailey Fd (v. baillie 'a bailiff'); the Barly Croft 1736 (1611, v. bærlic); Barn Croft & Fd (*the Barne Crofte* 1611, *The Barn Field* 1736); Beaster Fd, Brow Bestre; Great & Little Bent 1686, 1688 (*the Little Bent* 1611, 'grassland', v. beonet); Bilberry Brow; Black Butts (*The Blackbutes* 1611, v. butte); Black Mdw (*the blacke meadowe* 1611); Blue Shead; Bolton (v. bōōl-tūn); Bottom Mdw (*the Bothom* 1611, v. botm); Bridge Flatt (1611, v. flat); Far & Nar Broom(e)-field 1688 (*the lower & over Broomefield* 1611, cf. *Broomecroftes* 1611, v. brōm); Brow (Fd & Side) (v. brū, sīde); Buglaw (*Buglow* 1501, *the (little) Buglow(e)* 1611, 'the sprite-haunted mound', v. bugge, hlāw, cf. Buglawton 330 *infra*); Carr Mdw (cf. *the Midle Carr* 1611, v. kjarr); Close (Mdw) (cf. *the great Close* 1657, v. clos); The Clover Fd 1736; Coal Pit Bank (cf. *Coalpit Croft & Fields* 1802); Crooked Banks (*the crooked Buttes* 1611, v. croked, butte, banke); Cross Fd (v. cros); Crow Butts (*Crowbuttes* 1611, v. crāwe, butte); Demath 1688 (*Daymath* 1686, 'one day's mowing', v. day-math); Elmtree Close; Engine Fd; Fox Holes (*the Foxeholes* 1611); Gang Mdw (*the Gange Meadowe* 1611, 'meadow at a track', v. gang); Garden Croft; Golden Green 1819 (cf. *the Gold Crofte* 1611, v. golde 'marigold'); Higher & Lower Greene 1686, 1688 (*the Har- & Lowergreene* 1611); Hanging Brow (v. hangende, brū); Hard Acre 1686, 1688; Lower Hew Mdw; High Fd(s) (*the Highfield* 1611); High Hey (cf. *the Hey, Neather Hey* 1611, *Nether Hey* 1688, v. neoðera, (ge)hæg); Great & High Hill(s) (cf. *the hill* 1611); High Wood Plantation; Higher Acre; Higher Fd & Mdw (*the Harfield, the Har-meadowe* 1611, v. hēarra 'higher'); Hogsheads (*the Hawkes Yord* 1611, *Great & Little Haukshut* 1686, apparently 'hawk's yard', v. hafoc, geard, but cf. Hogshead Green 231 *infra*, *The Hawkesyord* 166 *supra*, with which this is probably analogous, v. hafoc-scerde); Horse Pasture (cf. *the Horseclose* 1611); Horse Race ('race-track for horses', v. ras); Hunger Hill 1688 (þe *Hungerhill* 1611, -hil 1686, 'barren hill', v. hungor); Hyson Croft (cf. Hyson Green Nt 151); Intake (*the Intacke* 1611, (*Higher & Lower*) *Intack* 1688, v. inntak); þe Kelts land c.1728; Kiln Croft (*the Kilne Croft(e)* 1611, *Kilcroft* 1686, *Great & Little Killne Croft* 1688); Kirkhough 1686 ((*The*) *Kirkall, Kirkeh(a)ugh, Kirkowe field, Litle Kirkhough* 1611, 'nook of land belonging to a church', v. kirkja, halh. There is no ancient church in Bollington, but lands here belonged to Downes Chapel at Pott Shrigley from 1493 *Dow* 165); Knowl Fd (v. cnoll); Lay Pool Mdw; Lees Lands 1686; Lime Croft; Little Mdw (1688); Lower Fd & Mdw (*the Lowerfield & meadowe* 1611); Marl'd Fd (cf. *the Marled field, Earth & Knowle* 1611, v. marlede, feld, eorðe, cnoll); Marl Pit Fd; Meadow Stead ('meadow place', v. mǣd, stede); Middle Piece; Mill Fd, Hollow, Mdw & Pool; Motrams Meadow 1688 (from the surname *Mottram*, cf. Mottram 202, 313 *infra*); (Further & Nearer) New Hey (*the*

Higher & Lower New-hey 1611); New Meadow & Part 1686 (*v.* part); Oak Fd (cf. *Okenfield* 1611, *Oke(n)flatt* 1686, 1688, *v.* ācen, feld, flat); Old Fd (*Oldfield* 1686); Old Moor; Old Stubble; Page Lands 1686 (*Page Croft & -field* 1611); (Far) Piggotts Part (cf. Henry *Pygot* 1366 *Dow, v.* part); Pingot (*þe Pingott* 1611, *v.* pingot); Little & Long Pit Fd; Pool Hey (*the Poolehey* 1611); Pot Fd; Potatoe Fd; Further & Near Riddings (*The Riddinges* 1611, *v.* ryding); Road Bit; Rope Walk; Rough (cf. *Rough Meads* 1686, *-meadow* 1688, *v.* rūh, mǣd); Rush Mdw (cf. *the Rushie Crofte & Hey* 1611); Sandy Butts (*Soundibootes, Sandybuttes* 1611, *Soundey Buts* 1686, *Saunderbutts* 1688, 'sandy selions', *v.* sandig, butte); Shaloone Croft 1688 (*Shallon-, Shawlane Croft* 1611, *Shalone Croft* 1686, 'the copse lane', *v.* sceaga, lane, cf. *le Shalone* 206 *infra*); Shrigley Brow & Mdw (*v.* Shrigley 130 *supra*); Shude Hill (probably from dial. *shood* 'husks, chaff', *v.* scēod, hyll, cf. WRY 7 241); Sich House Lands 1686 (*Sitch House* 1611, *v.* sīc 'a little stream'); Smithy Fd (*the Smythfield, the Smythye Crofte*, 1611); Spout Mdw (*v.* spoute); Stafford (a pasture, cf. Thomas *Stafford* 1684 *Dow*); Stephen Mdw; Stew (*v.* stuwe); Stone Bank & Fd (cf. *The Staneridge* 1611, *Stoney ridge* 1688, and *Stone-stidd* 1611, *v.* stān, stānig, banke, hrycg, stede); Sumerhill Dole 1688 (*the Somer Dole* 1611, *Sumerhill* 1686, *v.* sumor, dāl, hyll); Thern Lett ('thorn-tree allotment', *v.* þyrne, hlēt); Town Croft (cf. *The Townefield* 1611, 1686, 1688, 'the common field of the town'); Transport; Tunstidd 1686, 1688 (*the-* 1611, *v.* tūn-stede); le Twisting Alley 1687; Wath (*v.* vað); Well Fd; White Mdw (*the-* 1611); Wild Youth (probably 'uncultivated ground', *v.* wilde, eorðe).

(b) *Adams field* (*v. Adekyneschar* 187 *supra*); *The Aker* (*v.* æcer); *the Asshen Crofte* (*v.* æscen); *Assheinholmes* 1453, *Axenholmes* 1492, *Asshenholmes* 1528 ('ashen water-meadows', *v.* æscen, holmr); *Ballesperth* 1384 (*v. Sparth infra*); *the bancke*; *þe Beaue Laughen* ('fair glade', *v.* bel[2], launde); *the Birchencrofte* (*v.* bircen[2]); *the black Earth* ('black ploughland'); *the blanch field* ('white field', *v.* blanche); *the blunt hey*; *Bowstrake* (*v.* straca 'a strip of land'); *the Bridlecrofte* (*v.* brigdels); *the Brookelandes* '(selions by a brook', *v.* brōc, land); *the Browne Leigh & Ryding* (*v.* brūn[1], lēah, ryding); *the Bustacke*; *le Byrchineschagh* c.1325 (p) (*v.* bircen[2], sceaga); *the Calfehey Greaves* ('copses at *Calfehey* ("the calf enclosure")', *v.* calf, (ge)hæg, grǣfe); *the Churchway, the (litle) Kirkewayefield* (*v.* cirice, kirkja, weg); *the Clayridge(s)* (*v.* clǣg, hrycg); *le Clif* 1270 (17), *le Clyfe* 13 (1611) (*v.* clif; this is the steep south-east end of Nab Head *supra*); *the Clough meadowe* (*v.* clōh); *the Coppice: the Coweford meadow* (*v.* cū, ford); *the Crofthill*; *Dernehurst* 1503 ('secluded wood', *v.* derne, hyrst); *the Dole Meadow, Kilne Dole, Longe & Pottes Dole* (*v.* dāl 'a share', cf. the surname *Pott* from Pott Hall 130 *supra*); *the broad, Kilne & long Downes* (from the surname *Downes* (of Shrigley 130 *supra*) from *Downes* 148 *supra*); *Edmundshawe* ('Edmund's copse', from the OE pers.n. *Ēadmund* and sceaga); *the Ellmichers* (probably 'brushwood, or marsh, growing with elms', *v.* elmen, kjarr, cf. foll.); *Elmenewalle* 1270 (17), *le Holimme walle* (?*for Helmine-*) 13 (1611), *Elmingshall* 1611 ('elm spring', *v.* elmen, wælla, cf. prec.); *The Fall(e)* (*v.* (ge)fall); *Greneleghholme* 1508 ('(water-meadow at) the green glade', *v.* grēne[1], lēah, holmr; cf. *Grenelache-*

hous(e) 1467, 1471, referring to the same place, '(house at) the green bog', *v.* læc(c)); *þe Haddinges*; *Harders* (*v.* heard, ersc); *the Herry meadowes*; *the Heylde* (*v.* helde); *the Hick Crofte*; *the Hollinhey* (*v.* holegn, (ge)hæg); *Hondekynryding* 1363, *Atkin Ryding* 1611 (from the ME pers.n. *Hondekin, Handekin*, a diminutive of *Hand, Hond(e)*, (cf. *Handekyn* Starky 1287 Court 232) with ryding. It was an assart c.1347, cf. *Adekyneschar* 187 *supra*); *The Hustides Carre* (*v.* hūs-stede, kjarr; partly in Hurdsfield, cf. *The Houstides* 109 *supra*); *Jankynescroft* 1348 ('from the ME pers.n. *Janekin*, diminutive of *John*, and croft); *The Laycrofte* (*v.* lǣge); *the Lidyate croft* (*v.* hlid-geat); *le longecroft* c.1320, *Longe Crofte* 1611; *the Longe Wood*; *the March Meadow* (probably from mersc 'a marsh'); *the meane meadowe* ('the common meadow', *v.* (ge)mǣne); *Mokes Crofte* (probably 'donkey's croft' from dial. *moke*); *Oate Crofte*; *the Okencliffe* (*v.* ācen, clif); *The Ollers* (*v.* alor); *the Orchard Croft*; *Ordeshill* 1503, *Ordsell, Ardes-Hall* 1611, *Ordsell* 1620 (*v.* hyll; the first el. may be an OE pers.n. *Ord* (a short form of names in *Ord-*) as in Ordsall La 32, Nt 90, but O. von Feilitzen SNPh 40, 10 notes the possibility of OE *ord* 'point, spear-point, spear' in such p.ns. analogous with the type of p.n. containing lūtegār, cf. ord); *le Outlane* 1503 ('outlying lane', or 'lane to the outlying parts', *v.* ūt, lane); *Overthwart buttes* ('strips of land lying athwart', *v.* ofer-þwart, butte, cf. The Sikes ERY 131); *Pingle* (*v.* pingel); *Pitt Banck*; *The Pludge* (cf. dial. *plodge* (EDD) 'to wade, a splash', and plodde, pludde); *the poolefield*; *the Ridground* ('cleared ground', *v.* (ge)ryd(d)); *the Ry(e)crofte & -field*; *rivulus vocat' Setlowbroke* 1503 ('brook at *Setlow* ("the flat-topped hillock")', *v.* (ge)set, hlāw, brōc; a stream towards Adlington); *the Shawe meadow* (*v.* sceaga); *le Sidewaye* 1270 (17), *Le Syddeway* 13 (1611) ('the hill-side way', *v.* sīde, weg; a boundary line down the side of Kerridge Hill *supra*); *The Slacc, The Slacke* (*v.* slakki); *Sparth* ('place full of sheep-muck', from ON sparð (pl. *spörð*) 'sheep droppings'. With this goes *Ballesperth* 1348, either 'sheep-muck midden like a hillock' or 'place full of sheep-droppings at a hillock', from sparð and ME balle (OE *ball or ON bǫllr). The el. sparð is probably in the forms quoted in Db 749 s.v. sporðr. Cf. Sparth WRY 2 281); *Stayre Croft, Stayrefield* (probably 'steep croft & field', *v.* stæger² (ModE dial. *stair*, adj.) 'steep'); *the Swyne-Rootes* ('rooting-places for swine' *v.* swīn¹, root, cf. *Ryeroote* 159 *supra*); *the Turfe Pittes* ('peat diggings', *v.* turf, pytt); *Turne Meadowe* ('round meadow', *v.* trun); *the Warth* (*v.* waroð); *the Weete Crofte, Wheat Croft* (*v.* hwǣte); *the Wett Field & Meadow* (*v.* wēt).

13. BUTLEY (101–9077)

Butelege 1086 DB, *-le* 1345 Eyre, *-leye* 1363 ChFor
Botelege 1086 DB, *-leg'* 1286 Eyre (p), *-ley* 1536 ChRR
Butteleg(h) 1268 (14) Chest, 1269 Adl *et freq* to 1513 ChRR, *-leye* 1288 Court, *-le* 1290 ib (p), *-ley* 1377 Orm², *Buttilegh* 1341 Eyre, *-y-* 1345 Plea
Botteleg' 1286 Eyre, *-legh* 1320 Plea
Butleghe 1288 Court, *-legh* 1364 Eyre, *-lay* 1411 Chol, *-leyea* 1431

Adl, *-ley* 1561 *Cross*, ChRR *et freq*, (*cum Newton*) 1819 Orm[1],
-leigh 1560 *Cross*, *-leye* 1569 ChRR, *Buttley* 1409 *Chol*, *-legh*
1490 Adl

'Butta's clearing', from an OE pers.n. *Butta* and lēah, (cf. DEPN,
s.v.). The *Bo-* spellings are most probably due to AN orthography.
The two DB entries are taken by Tait, 213n., to be moieties of the
one manor. Earw II 254 suggests that one or the other represents
Newton 205 *infra*.

FOXTWIST (101–896797)

> *Foxwist, -wyst* c. 1238 Adl, (1623) ChRR, Orm[2] (p), (*-hegh*) 1345
> *Eyre*, (*O(u)ld(e)-*) 1427 Earw, 1428 ChRR, 1431 Adl, (*Butteley-*)
> 1462 ib, (*-Heith*) 1501 *Dav*, (*the Hall of*) 1611 *LRMB* 200
> *Foxwisp* 1285 *Eyre*, *-es* (lands called) 1400 ChRR
> *Foxquist, Foxquyst* 1287 *Eyre*
> *Foxwychȝ* 1337 *Eyre*
> *Foxwest* 1535 Sheaf
> *Old & Netherfoxwixt* 1536 ChRR
> *Foxwyse* 1560 *Cross*
> *Foxtwist* 1831 Bry

'Fox-earth', *v.* fox, wist; the final el. is replaced by wisp 'a wisp'
in two instances, probably with a topographical extension of meaning,
e.g. 'covert'. The prefixes *Old* and *Nether* refer to a removal of the
original house in 1359 (Chamb 251–2). Cf. Foxwist Green 331 *infra*,
Disley 269 *infra*.

BONIS HALL, 1764 Orm[2], *Bonardishall* 113 Tab, *Bonisal* e14 Orm[2],
Bonnisall 1559, *Bonisall* c.1630 ib, 'Bonard's hall', from the OG
pers.n. *Bonard* and hall.

HEYBRIDGE LANE (FM), *Heyebirches* m13 Chest, *Heubyrches* 1347
Eyre (p), *Hewbirches* 1428 ChRR, *Hewebirche* 1536 ib, le *Heybriche*,
-brych 1448, 1450 Adl, *He(y)bridge Lane* 1831 Bry, 'high birches' *v.*
hēah, birce, with later metathesis, and confusion with brycg 'a bridge'.

BALL LANE, 1831 Bry, *v.* ball.   BLAZEHILL FM, cf. *Blaze Hill Field*
1848 *TA*, *v.* blesi 'a bare spot'.   BOLLINGTONFIELD Ho, named
from Bollington 187 *supra*.   BONIS WOOD, *Bonishall Plantation*
1848 *ib*, *Pitstead* 1842 OS, 'site of a pit', *v.* pytt, stede, cf. Bonis Hall

supra. BRADLEY MOUNT, 1860 White, cf. *Bradley Brow* (*Field*)
1848 *TA*, *v*. mont, brū, cf. Thomas *Bradley* of Adlington 1736 *Dow*.
BRIDGE-END, at the Butley end of Prestbury Bridge.   BULLSHEAD
FM.   BUTLEY ASH, BRIDGE, HALL & TOWN, *Butley Hall* 1574
Earw, *the Hall of Butley* 1611 Orm², *Butley Ash & Town* 1831 Bry.
Butley Ash is a p.h. named after an ash-tree, *v*. æsc. The bridge spans
R. Dean. Butley Town (*v*. toun) is the hamlet of Butley, so distin-
guished from the manor-house (*v*. hall), cf. Fittontown, Vardentown
101, 102 *supra*.   CARR HO, *Buteleyecarr* 1363 *ChFor*, *The
Carr* 1848 *TA*, 'the marsh', *v*. kjarr.   COLLINS WOOD, *Collin
Plantation & Dam Field* 1848 *TA*, perhaps from dial. *collin* 'burnt-off
furze stump' (EDD s.v. *colon*), but the first el. may be the surname
Collin(s) (Reaney 74), *v* .damme.   DAIRY HO, 1831 Bry, cf. Dairyhouse Wood 183 *supra*.   DANDY FM, *Dandy Hall* 1831 ib, cf.
Hugh *Dondy* c.1330 *Dow*.   DEER PARK, *Adlington Park* 1831 Bry,
cf. Adlington 181 *supra*.   DOD'S MARSH.   DUMBAH FM &
HOLLOW, DUMBER LANE, *Dumber Lane* 1831 ib, from dumbel 'a
wooded dingle'.   FLASH FM, cf. *Flash Field* 1848 *TA*, Flash Lane
189 *supra*, Orangetree *infra*, *v*. flasshe.   FOLDARBOUR.   FOREIGN
HEY, 'enclosure outside a boundary', *v*. forein, (ge)hæg. The significance of this name is not known.   HAWTHORN FM.   HILLTOP
FM, *Hilltop* 1831 Bry.   HOWLANEHEAD, *Trugs i' th' Hole* 1831 ib,
cf. Trugs i' th' Hole 102 *supra*. The modern name may be connected
with *Urlane Moor* 1238 (1621) ChRR.   LANE-END FM.   LONDON
RD, the Stockport–Macclesfield road.   MOTTRAM BRIDGE, *v*. 204
infra.   OAK FM.   ORANGETREE INN, 1860 White, *Flash Inn*
1831 Bry, *The Flash* 1882 EDD s.v. *flash*, *v*. Flash Fm *supra*.
PARK HO, *Parck House* 1584 Earw, (*the*) *Parkehouse* 1644 ib.
PARKSIDE, *Pinfold House* 1831 Bry, *v*. pynd-fald. The modern name is
from Deer Park *supra*.   PARK WOOD, 1848 *TA*.   PLANT HO,
1831 Bry.   PRESTBURY LANE, leading to Prestbury 212 *infra*.
SANDYHEAD FM, *Sandholes* 1842 OS.   TOP O' TH' HILL.   WALNUT-
TREE.   WHITELEYHEY FM, *v*. hwīt, lēah, (ge)hæg, cf. Whiteley
182 *supra*.   WILLOT HALL, 1678 Orm², from the family of
Wil(l)ot de Foxwist 1286 *Eyre*, cf. Orm² III 668.   WOODSIDE FM.
HIGHER YEWARDS (101–897787), *Butley Lodge* 1842 OS, *Yemonds*
1602 Orm² III 666 (an unreliable form), *Higher & Lower Yowards*
1831 Bry, *The Yewards, Yewards Meadow* 1848 *TA*, 'the river mea-
dows', *v*. ēa, waroð (in the form *warod* discussed in Löfvenberg 220).
Lower Yowards became a sewage works 101–895786.   YEWTREE FM.

FIELD-NAMES

The undated forms are 1848 *TA* 88. Of the others, 1238 is Orm², 1238 (1621), 1238 (1623), 1399, 1426, 1428 ChRR, c.1268 Chest, 1287, 1345 *Eyre*, 1363 *ChFor*, 1423 Plea, 1467, 1480, 1490, 1495 Adl, 1501 *Dav*, 1773, 1795 *Dow*, 1831 Bry.

(*a*) Ackers Croft (*v.* æcer); The Acre; Alley Cock Hill (cf. Richard *Alicok* 1393 *Dow*, tenant in Bollington); The Bank; Bare Arse (*v.* bær¹, ears); Barley Knowl; Black Marsh; Blake Hey (*v.* blæc, (ge)hæg); Blakelett ('black allotment', *v.* blæc, hlēt); The Blakeyers (cf. Blackeyer 265 *infra*): Boat Fd (*v.* bōt); Bold Fd (*v.* bold); Bottoms (*v.* botm); Briary Fd; Brickiln Fd; Bridge Wd 1831 (from Butley Bridge *supra*); Brook Croft & Fd; Brookshot ('corner of land by a brook', *v.* brōc, scēat); Broomy Knowl; Great & Rough Brundley ('burnt clearing', *v.* brende², lēah); Budge Croft; The Bungs ('the banks', *v.* banke, ME *bonk*); Calf Croft; Cart House Croft; Cash Fd; Church Fd & Mdw; Clover Patches; Clump; The Cob, Great & Little Cobley (*v.* cobb(e) 'a round hill, a tump', lēah); Colley Fd (*v.* colig); Cow Hey & Lane; Crooked Mdw; Cross Shute (*v.* cros, scēat); The Docks (*v.* docce); Dogdains Croft; The Dothering (probably from dial. *dother* 'the yarrel or corn-spurrey', *v.* doder, -ing²); Dye Bank (probably 'milking bank', *v.* dey); Far-, Further-, Great-, Higher-, Little-, Long-, Lower-, Middle- & Near(er) Eyes (*Netherhees* 1490, *The Eyes* 1795, cf. *totas illas insulas iuxta Bolyn versus Mottrom* c.1268, 'the water-meadows', *v.* ēg); The Fall (*v.* (ge)fall); Four Day Math ('four days' mowing', *v.* day-math); Fox Bank & Holes (cf. Foxtwist *supra*); Garden Fd; Gee Croft ('crooked croft', *v.* gee); Gerry Fd; Golden Flatt; Gorsey Holes; Gramage; The Green; Grey Marsh; Hack Carr ('wicket-gate marsh', *v.* hæc(c), kjarr); Half Day Work ('half a day's work', *v.* day-work); Hard Fd; Hazel Bank; the Hease (*v.* hǣs 'brushwood'); Far & Near High Breeches (*v.* brēc); Hill Croft & Flatt; Hob Fd (from either hob 'a hobgoblin', or hobb(e) 'a tussock'); Hold Tree Fd; Hollands Fd; Great & Little Hollinhurst ('holly wood', *v.* holegn, hyrst); Hollow Fd; Homestead (*v.* home, stēde); Horse Croft; Hot Hill (*v.* hāt); House Croft; Hulme Fd (*v.* hulm); Further & Nearer Hurst (*v.* hyrst); The Intake (*v.* inntak); Great & Little Isabel Fd; Kingshaw; Kitchen Croft; The Knott (*v.* cnotta, knottr); Knowl Hey (*v.* cnoll, (ge)hæg); Latch Croft (cf. *Le Lache* 1238 (1621), 1287 (p), *v.* læc(c) 'a bog'); Ley Fd (*v.* lēah or lǣge); The Light Oaks ('the light oaks', *v.* lēoht, āc); Lime Croft; Long Butts (*v.* lang, butte); Long Shute (*v.* lang, scēat); Macclesfield Heys (cf. Macclesfield 113 *supra*, *v.* (ge)hæg); Mare Sittings (from mere² and dial. *sitting* 'a resting place'); Marl Fd; Marl'd Carr (*v.* marlede, kjarr); The Moss; Mothers Croft; Mount Mdw (*v.* mont); Nether Hey; New Mdw; Oak Fd; Oakenshaw Fd ('oaken copse', *v.* ācen, sceaga); Oatley ('oat clearing', *v.* āte, lēah); Old Mdw; Old Woman's Fd; Oralds Fd; Ornal Fd; Outlett (*v.* outlet); Oven Fd; Owlar Fd, Owler Head Fd, Light Owlars (*v.* alor 'alder tree', lēoht, hēafod, cf. Light Oaks *supra*); Owlhurst ('owl wood', *v.* ūle, hyrst, cf. Owl-Hurst Lane 188 *supra*); Ox Hey; Parsons Mdw (*v.* persone); Pass Mdw; The Patch; Pea Croft; Pell Well (perhaps 'spring

where hides are washed', from pel and wælla, cf. *Pellewell* WRY 7 230);
Pickfords Mdw (cf. John *Pickford* 1773); the Pickhurst ('wood at a hill',
v. pīc[1], hyrst, cf. *Koppedehurste infra*); Pinfold Croft (cf. Parkside *supra*);
Little Pingot (*v.* pingot); Pit Fd & Holes: The Plunge (*v.* plunge); Push
Plough Mdw (*v.* push-plough); Pyegrave ('magpie grove', *v.* pīe[2], græfe);
Rails Fd (*v.* rail(e)); Rashy Croft (from dial. *rash* 'a rush', cf. riscig); Reads-,
Reeds Mdw (perhaps from hrēod 'a reed'); Big & Little Rhodes (*v.* rod[1],
'cleared land'); Ridding (*v.* ryding); River Wash (*v.* (ge)wæsc); Rood Land
(*v.* rōd[2], land); The Rough (*v.* rūh); Round Croft; Row Hurst (*le Rohehurst*
c.1238 (1621), 'the rough wooded-hill', *v.* rūh, hyrst); Rushy Fd (cf. Rashy
Croft *supra*); Rye ,Croft & Fd: The Rye List ('the rye-sown border of a
field', *v.* ryge, list); Shay Fd (*le Shagh* 1428, 'the copse', *v.* sceaga); Slutch
(*v.* slutch); Smithy Croft; South Fd; Great & Little Spars (*v.* spart);
Springy Hill; Spur Croft (from spora, dial. *spur* 'a tree stump'); Stud Croft
(*v.* stōd); Three Corner'd & Three Nook'd Mdw; The Toad Hill; Town
Hey(s) (*v.* toun, (ge)hæg); Turney Eyes (*v.* ēg, cf. The Eyes *supra*); Wall Fd
(*v.* wælla); Watsons Carr (cf. Carr Ho *supra*); Well Croft, Fd & Mdw
(*v.* wella); Wet Croft & Fd; Wethers Fd (*v.* weðer); Wheat Bank, Croft &
Fd; Wheat Eyes (*v.* ēg); Wheel Fd (*v.* hwēol 'a wheel, something round, or
circular'); White Mdw; Wood Fd.

(*b*) *Butteleyeheth* 1363 (*v.* hǣð); *Daydrddyng* (lit. *Dadrydayng*) 1495
(*v.* ryding); *le Hok* 1238 (1621) (*v.* hōc 'a hook (of land)'); *le Koppede-,
Keppedehurste* 1238 (1621), (1623) ('the peaked wooded-hill' or 'the lopped
wood', *v.* copped, hyrst, cf. Pickhurst *supra*); *Roley* 1428 (*v.* rūh, lēah);
Thornicroft 1467 (*v.* þornig, croft); *Usulwell* 1480 ('ousel spring', *v.* ōsle,
wella).

14. FALLIBROOME (101–8975), FALLIBROOME FM

Falingbrome 1153–1181 (17) Orm[2], *-brom* 1232 (1580) Sheaf,
   Fal(l)ingbrom,-yng- 1290 *Eyre*, 1337 Plea, 1345 *Eyre*, 1401 *AddCh*,
   -e 1408 Earw, *-browne* 1467 Adl, *Fallinge Broome* 1477 Orm[2],
   a messuage in Falyngbrome called le Falyngbrome 1477 ChRR
Fal(l)inbrome 1246 Orm[2], Earw, *-br'm* 1285 *Eyre* (Court 208 reads
   -brum), *-brom* c.1330 Fitt, *-yn-* 1345 *Eyre*, *-e* 1358 *MinAcct* (p),
   Falymbrome 1370 *Eyre*
Fal(l)inisbrom 1248 Ipm, 13 IpmR
Falibrom 1274 Orm[2], *-y-* 1328 Fitt, *-e* 1373 Plea (p), *-bro(o)me*
   1433 ChRR (p), 1436 Earw (p), *Fallibro(o)me, -y-* 1438, 1455
   Earw, *-bro(m)* 1560 Sheaf
Falkynbrom 1290 *Eyre* (p)

'Broom at the fallow land', *v.* fælging, brōm, cf. Broome Fd *infra*.
Galingbrom, Lingbrom 1290 Court 247 are erroneous forms of
Falingbrom.

DUMBER WOOD, cf. *Dumble Meadow* 1849 *TA*, 'the hollow', *v.* dumbel.   FLEETS FM.   LANE ENDS FM, *Lane End* 1860 White. MANOR HO, 1860 ib.   SPENCER BROOK, *v.* 35 *supra*.   WALNUT TREE FM, 1860 ib.

FIELD-NAMES

The forms are from 1849 *TA* 168.

(*a*) Barn Fd; Brickiln Fd; Broome Fd (cf. Fallibroome *supra*); Calves Fall (*v.* calf, (ge)fall); Clough Fd; Cross Fd (*v.* cros); Foden (probably 'colourful hollow', *v.* fāg, denu, cf. *Fodon* 331 *infra*); Gravel Hole Fd; Hall Mdw; Hollow Mdw; Hunger knowl ('hunger hill', *v.* hungor, cnoll); Kiln Fd; Long Short; Moss; Newport; Pingot (*v.* pingot); Thieves Hole (*v.* þēof, hol¹); Thistley Fd.

15. LYME HANDLEY (101–9682), *Lyme Hanley* 1478 Orm², cf. *Handley*, Lyme Hall *infra*.

HANDLEY (lost), HANDLEYBARN, HANDLEY CLOUGH & FOOT

> *Hanley* 1269 Adl (p), 1328 ChRR *et freq*, *-e*, *-lee* 1285 Court, *-legh* 1286 Eyre *et freq* to 1358 *MinAcct*
> *Hannelegh* 1337 Eyre (p), 1348 *MinAcct*
> *Haunley* c.1515 Orm²
> *Handley* 1542 ChRR, (*-barn*) 1848 *TA*

'At the high clearing', from hēah (hēan wk.dat.) and lēah, with bere-ærn 'a barn', and clōh 'a dell'. Handley Foot, so named 1831 Bry, 1848 *TA*, was *Nether Hanley* 1466 Earw, *Handley Fold* 1842 OS, 1848 *TA* (*v.* neoðera 'lower', fōt 'foot, bottom of', fald 'a fold, a farmstead'). Higher & Lower Cliff Fm *infra* were *Over Hanley* 1466 Earw, *Handley Head, Top of Handley* 1831 Bry, 1848 *TA* (*v.* uferra 'higher', hēafod 'head, top end of', topp 'top'.)

LYME HALL & PARK

> *Lyme* 1312 Ipm *et freq*, (*-in foresta de Macclesfeld*) 1337 Eyre *et freq*, (*boscus de-*) 1347 *ib et freq*, (*foresta de-*) 1357 ChFor, 1359 BPR, (*manerium et parcum*) 1466 Earw, *Lyme in Hanley* c.1527 ib, (*mansion house in*) 1611 LRMB 200, *Lyme Hall & Park* 1831 Bry
> (*boscus de*) Lym 1354 BPR *et freq* ib to 1363
> *Lime* (*Hall*) 1690 Sheaf, 1693 Dow, 1724 NotCestr

This is the regional name The *Lyme* 2 *supra* with hall 'a hall', and park 'a park'.

BAILEY'S FM, *The Bailey's House* 1848 *TA*, referred to from 1466 Orm², Earw, *v.* baillie 'a steward, a bailiff'. BOLLINHUSRT (BRIDGE & WOOD), *Bollinhurst (Gate)* 1831 Bry, *Bollin Hurst Wood* 1842 OS, 'pollard wood', *v.* bolling, hyrst, cf. East Lodge *infra*, Bollinhurst Brook 16 *supra*. BOW STONES (101-973813), BOW-STONEGATE, *Bowstoneyate* 17 Earw, *-gate* 1831 Bry, (*The*) *Bow Stones* 1819 Orm¹, cf. *two ancient pillars* 1809 *Dow* 534, *v.* boga 'a bow', stān 'stone', geat 'a gate'. The name *Bow Stones* may have arisen from the convenience of this monument as a fulcrum for bending a bow. The stones are the cylindrical shafts of a twin cross of the pre-Conquest 'Mercian' type like Cleulow Cross 165 *supra*, standing beside a ridgeway, cf. *Antiquity* XI 296. Near Bowstonegate are the graves of a number of victims of the plague, buried here 1646 (*v.* Earw II 314), hence *Plague Corner 1646* 1831 Bry, *Grave 6″* OS. BRINK FM, (*The*) *Brink* 1816 *Dow*, 'the brink' *v.* brink, cf. Brink Brow 142 *supra*. BROOKSIDE, 1831 Bry, named from Bollinhurst Brook 16 *supra*. BROWSIDE CLOUGH & FM, *Browside* 1831 ib, *v.* brū, sīde, clōh. CAGE HILL, 1848 *TA*, named from *Lyme Cage* 1831 Bry, *v.* cage 'a cage'. CHARLES HEAD, 1842 OS, *Churleshead* 1611 *LRMB* 200, 1831 Bry, cf. *Charles Head Foot* 1831 ib, Charles Head, Commonbarn 143 *supra*, 'peasant's hill', *v.* ceorl, hēafod, fōt 'the foot of-'. CLIFF (CLOUGH), *Higher & Lower Cliff* 1831 Bry, *v.* clif, clōh, cf. foll. and *Handley supra*. HIGHER & LOWER CLIFF FM, *v. Handley supra*, cf. prec. CLUSE HAY, *Cloughs Hey* 1842 OS, 'enclosure in a dell', *v.* clōh, (ge)hæg. COALPIT CLOUGH, 1848 *TA*, *v.* clōh. COPPICESIDE, 1848 *ib*, *Coppice* 1831 Bry. CORNFIELD FM, 1831 ib, *v.* corn¹. CORNHILL FM, *-House* 1848 *TA*, *v.* corn¹, cf. prec. CROW WOOD, cf. *Crow Croft* 1848 *ib*. DEERFOLD. EAST LODGE, *Bollinhurst Gate* 1831 Bry, an entrance to Lyme Park *supra*, cf. Bollinhurst *supra*. ELMERHURST, *Elmer Hurst* 1842 OS, probably a corruption of *Elmenhurst*, 'wooded-hill growing with elms', from elmen and hyrst. FLAT CLOUGH, cf. *The Flat* 1848 *TA*, *v.* flat 'a level piece of ground', clōh. GNAT-HOLE (BROOK), 1842 OS, *Knathole* 1831 Bry, 'gnat hollow', *v.* gnætt, hol¹, cf. Gnat Hole 189 *supra*. The brook joins Todd Brook 36 *supra*. GREEN FM, *Greens Farm* 1831 ib. GRIFFINS COTTAGE, *Hurst* 1831 ib, *The Hurst House* 1848 *TA*, 'wooded-hill' *v.* hyrst. HAGG FM, *The Hag* 1831 Bry, *v.* hogg 'wood marked off for felling; a wood, a copse'. HAMPERS WOOD, *Hamper's (Plantation)* 1848 *TA*. HASE BANK (WOOD), 1848 *ib*, *v.* banke. HIGHER MOOR, (&

Lower-) 1848 *ib.*   HILLTOP FM, *Hilltop* 1842 OS.   HOLE HO, 1848 *TA, v.* hol[1].   HOLLINCROFT BROW, *Hollincroft* (*Wood*) 1848 *ib,* 'holly-tree croft', *v.* holegn, croft.   HOLME WOOD, 1831 Bry, *v.* holmr.   KENNEL WOOD, from Lyme Hall dog-kennels. KNIGHTS LOW, 1842 OS, 'young man's hill or mound', *v.* cniht, hlāw.   KNOTT, *The Knot* 1848 *TA, v.* cnotta, knǫttr 'a hillock'. LANTERN WOOD, 1842 OS, *Lanthorn Wood* 1831 Bry, the site of an old lantern turret removed from Lyme Hall.   MATHER CLOUGH, 1831 ib, from clōh 'a valley', with maðra 'madder', or eModE *mather* 'the stinking camomile'.   MIDDLECALE FM, *Rowbothams* 1831 ib, *Rowbottom* 1842 OS, *late Rowbottoms House* 1848 *TA,* from the surname *Rowbotham* [roubɔtəm], cf. foll.   MIDDLECALE PIT & WOOD, *Cale Wood, Middle Cale* 1831 Bry, *The Middle Cale Colliery* 1860 White, from ME **cauel** 'a division or share of land, an allotment of land', cf. Db 675, New Mills Db 150, Middle Cale 186 *supra,* Cale Green 297 *infra.*   NEWHAY, *New Hey* (*Brow*) 1848 *TA, v.* nīwe, (ge)hæg.   PADDOCK, 1842 OS, (*Lodge*)1831 Bry, *v.* pearroc, loge. PARKGATE, 1831 ib, cf. Lyme Park *supra.*   PARK MOOR, 1842 OS, cf. prec.   PLATT WOOD (FM), 1842 ib, *Plats Wood* (*Farm*) 1831 Bry, *v.* plat[2] 'a plot'.   PURSEFIELD (WOOD), *Purse Fields Plantation* 1848 *TA,* cf. *le Purs* 1347 *Eyre,* from OE, ME **purs** 'a purse', probably a place with only one extrance or exit.   REED BRIDGE, HILL & FM, *Reeds Farm* 1831 Bry, *Reed's Farm House* 1848 *TA,* from the surname *Reed;* cf. Reed Bridge 112 *supra.*   RICHARDSON'S FM, *Bens Wood* 1842 OS, *late Richardson's House* 1848 *TA,* from the pers.n. *Ben,* a shortened form of Benjamin.   RYLES WOOD, 1831 Bry, *Royal Wood* 1842 OS, '(a wood at) the rye hill', *v.* ryge, hyll. SESTER BRIDGE, cf. *Chesterbreades* 1611 *LRMB* 200, 'plank-bridge on the way to Chester', from the p.n. Chester and **bred** 'a plank, a board'. The bridge carries the Macclesfield–Kettleshulme road over Gnathole Brook.   SPONDS (HILL), BACK & HOLLOW SPONDS, *The Sponds* 1816 *Dow,* (*Hill*) 1842 OS, cf. Spondsbottom 112 *supra,* from **spann**[1] 'a span'; this moorland tract represents an interval between the cultivated lands of the townships to east and west, Pott Shrigley & Kettleshulme 130, 110 *supra* (cf. **spenne**). A similar situation exists at *Sponneheth* 334 *infra,* Span 325 *infra.*   SWEET HILL (CLOUGH), *Sweet Hill* (*Brow*) 1848 *TA, v.* swēte, hyll, clōh, brū.   THROSTLE-NEST FM, 1831 Bry.   WEST PARKGATE, *Parkgate Farm* 1831 ib, cf. Lyme Park, Parkgate *supra.*

FIELD-NAMES

The undated forms are 1848 *TA* 244, 1850 *TAMap* 244. Of the others 1347 is *Eyre*, 1349 *MinAcct*, 1831 Bry.

(*a*) Back o' th' Hedge; Bank End & Top; Barley Croft; Barn Fd; Bean Croft; Beehive Brow (*v*. brū); Bent (*v*. beonet); Brick Hill Fd (*v*. brykekyl); The Brow (*freq*, *v*. brū); Bull Close; Cabbage Ground; Calf Croft; Carr Mdw (*v*. kjarr); Cater Slack (*v*. cater 'diagonal, slanting, out of the square', slakki 'a hollow'); Cloudy Fd ('rocky, lumpy field', *v*. clūdig); Clough (*v*. clōh); Coal Wd; Corner Bit & Piece; Cote Fd; Cowlane; Crooked Mdw; Cross Fd (*v*. cros); Cumberland (cf. Cumberland 161 *supra*); Dewsbury Banks 1831; Doles (*v*. dāl); Drake Carr (*v*. Drakecar 272 *infra*); Drinkwater Mdw; Dry Croft; Dysop Head Fd (*v*. Dissop Head 272 *infra*); The Elbows (land in the meanders of a brook which form 'elbows' in it, *v*. elbowe); Ellabank (perhaps 'elder-tree bank', *v*. elle, banke, cf. Ellis Bank 133 *supra*); Ellerstyle ('stile at an elder-tree', *v*. ellern, stigel); Fair Hairstead; Flax Yard (*v*. geard); Fore Door ('in front of the door', a field in front of Hole Ho *supra*, *v*. fore); Fur Brow ('further brow'); Garden Acre; Gaskell Brow & Fd; Gladding Hurst ('wooded-hill with a glade', *v*. glad(d)en, hyrst, cf. The Gladdin(g) 185 *supra*); Glead Acre (probably 'kite field', *v*. gleoda); Grimshaw Fd; Gun-hole; Hazlehurst (*v*. hæsel, hyrst); Hey Fd; Hilley Fd; Hollin Knowl & Wd (*v*. holegn 'holly-tree); The Hollows; Hongs: Little & New Isles (*v*. hygel); Kiln Fd; Kith Hill; The Knoll; Lady Croft (*v*. hlǣfdige); Laidlow; Lands End; Lime Fd; Long Mead; Long Pingot (*v*. pingot); Lyme Croft, Fd & Pasture (cf. Lyme Hall *supra*); Main Mdw ('demesne meadow', *v*. main); Mare Coppice (*v*. mere[2] 'a mare'); Marl Croft & Fd; Meg Wiggin (*v*. meg, cwicen 'a mountain ash', cf. Fernlee 149 *supra*); Milking Fd (*v*. milking); Newfoundland England; Nigh Mdw (*v*. nēah); Oakshaw (*v*. āc, sceaga); Old Liking; Old Warren; Orchard Fd; Outlet (*v*. outlet); Pale Fd (near the boundary of Lyme Park *supra*, *v*. pale); Park Croft & Side (cf. Lyme Park *supra*); The Patch; Pit Croft; Plain Fd; Plater Smithy; Plunge Croft (*v*. plunge); Raily Fd; Red Piece; The Ridge; Rookery; Roots (*v*. root); The Rough(s), Rough Bank & Brow (*v*. rūh); The Round; Rushy Carr Wd, Rushy Fd, Piece & Wash (*v*. riscig, kjarr, wæsce); Sheep Wash (*v*. scēap-wæsce); Shirt Close (from scerde 'a cleft, a gap', cf. Shert Hall 271 *infra*); The (Lower) Shut (*v*. scēat); Spout Croft (*v*. spoute); Spring Wd (*v*. spring); Square Brow (*v*. squar(e), brū); Stepheads; Stepping Stone Hurst (*v*. stepping-stone, hyrst); Stubbins (*v*. stubbing); Swine Park (*v*. swin[1], park); The Tang (*v*. tangi 'a tang', the field is pan-handle shaped); Tanpit Hole; Yan Tard Mdw (*v*. tan-yard); Three Cornered Fd; Three Nook Fd; Three Nooked Pingot (*v*. pingot); Top Fd; Top o' th' Hill; Turf House Mdw ('meadow at a house built of, or roofed with turf', *v*. turf); (The) Wath(s) ('water-meadows', *v*. vað); Well Croft, Fd & Mdw; Wheat Fd; Whimsey; White Smyth; Wibbersley Shay (*v*. sceaga, scaga, cf. Wybersley 282 *infra*); Wood Bottom, Brow, Ends & Fd (*v*. botm, brū).

(*b*) *una forgea in foresta de Macclesf' apud-, una forgea leuata in bosco de*

Lyme apud (*le*) *Haselyneshaghe, Haselenschawe* 1349 ('copse growing with hazels' *v.* hæslen, sceaga. The wood of *Lyme* referred to may, of course, be *The Lyme* 2 *supra* as an alternative name of the Forest of Macclesfield, not alluding specifically to Lyme Handley, *v.* 4 *supra*, cf. foll.); *le Haukesclogh in bosco de Lyme* 1347 ('hawk's valley', *v.* hafoc, clōh, cf. prec., and *Hawkescloughe* 58 *supra*); *le Midde*(*l*)*wode* 1347 (*v.* middel, wudu).

16. MOTTRAM ST ANDREW (101–8878)

> *Motre* 1086 DB
>
> *Motterom* 1240 Adl (p), 1349 JRL (p), *-um* c.1280 *Fitt* (p), c.1310 Chest, *-am* 1651 *Dow*, *Mottorum* 1357 BPR
>
> *Mottrom* m13 Chest *et freq*, (*-iuxta Prestebur'*) 1313 Plea, (*Andrew*(*e*) *Andreu*) 1362 *Dav*, 1365 BPR, 1379 IpmR, *-e* 1329 Pat (p), *Mottram* m13 Chest (p) *et freq*, (*Andrewe*) 1408 ChRR, (*St. Andrew*) 1848 *TA*, *Mottrum* 1285 Court, *Dow*, Chest *et freq*, (*-iuxta Prestebur'*) 1309 Plea, (*Andreu, Andrew*(*e*)) 1350, 1369 Eyre, 1387 Adl, *Mottroum* 1357 BPR (p)
>
> *Motrum* 1285 Court (p), *-om* 1288 ib, (*-andreus*) 1351 BPR, *-am*, *-em*, (*-andrew*(*e*)) 1408 Adl
>
> *Moterum* 1286 Court (p), (*Andreu*) 1381 *Eyre*
>
> *Motern* 1304 Chamb (p)
>
> *Mottrun* c.1330 *Fitt*, *-on* 1333 Misc, 1347 *Eyre* (p), 1355 BPR (p)
>
> *Mortrome* 1552 Pat
>
> *Motterham* 1692 Sheaf

This difficult place-name appears again in Mottram in Longdendale 313 *infra*. It may be '(at) the assembly trees', from (ge)mōt 'a meeting, an assembly' and trēo(w) (nom.pl. *trēo*(*w*), dat.pl. *trēowum, trēum*) 'a tree, a pillar, a cross', the DB form representing the nom.-pl., and the later ones the dat.pl. Alternatively, Professor Smith suggested OE *(*ge*)*mōt-rūm*, 'meeting-space', *v.* (ge)mōt, rūm, which requires the DB form to be corrupt. The second of the two explanations given in DEPN is based on a spelling for *Mottershead infra*, which is not supported by the original MS. The first (OE (*ge*)*mōt-ærn* 'council-house', *v.* (ge)mōt, ærn) depends much upon the local-surname form *Motern* 1304 Chamb 64, *v.* ES 64, 223. It would reconcile the *Motern, Mo*(*t*)*t*(*e*)*rum* forms if the basis of *Mottram* were OE mōtere 'a councillor, a speech-maker', (cf. *Mottershead infra*) in the dat.pl. form mōterum, meaning 'at the speakers'. Cf. Knight's Grange 332 *infra* for a personal designation used as a simplex p.n. For the apparently sg. form in DB, the result of a reduction *-um* > *-en* > *-e* in the inflexional ending, cf. Studies³ 29-34.

The suffix *St Andrew* has not been explained, save that 'up to that century (i.e. the eighteenth) this township was always called Mottram Andrew, the Saint being a modern addition', Earw II 347. For a spurious *Saint* introduced before the personal element of a manorial p.n., cf. Cotton Edmunds, Lach Dennis 331, 332 *infra*. It is suggested in Orm² III 692, that the old suffix *Andrew* was 'perhaps derived from the patron saint of some long forgotten domestic chapel' (cf. Chapel Fd *infra*), but it also appears with Wincle 164 *supra* in a late example, and the same word may occur in Andrew's Edge 142 *supra*. An unimportant family surnamed *Andrew* was in the area late in the fifteenth century, cf. Andrew's Knob 133 *supra*, but there is no evidence of a manorial connection with Mottram or Wincle.

In the earliest instance, *Motromandreus* 1351, the affix appears to be disguised as Latin, and it may well be a Latinisation of some form like *-andre* or *-andreu(s)*. Such a form could easily have been taken as the gen.sg. of the pers.n. *Andrew*, or as the nom.sg. of the pers.n. *Andreas*. If the affix were a significant expression *-andreus* or *-andre*, it might represent ON *anddyri* 'a porch', with hūs or ON hús, i.e. 'house with a porch', alluding to some such structure at Mottram.

MOTTERSHEAD (lost)

> *Mottersheved* li2 (17th) Orm², *-hede* 1432 Sheaf (p), *-hed* 1586
>   *Dow* (p), *-hedde* 1587 *Cross* (p), *-head* 1611 Orm² (p), *Mottersched*
>   1550 *Dow* (p), *Motturshed* 1482 Adl (p)
> *Mottresheued* 1287 *Eyre* (p) (Court 231 reads *Moctresheved*), 1303
>   ChF (p) *et freq*, *-heuyd*, (*-us-*) 1370, 1371 *Eyre* (p), (*-is-*), *-hed*
>   1349, 1357 *ib* (p), (apud Mottram Andrewe in quodam loco
>   vocato) *Mottreshede* 1369 *Eyre*
> *Moterusheved* E2 Orm² (p), 1337 ib (p), *-hede* 1407, 1417 ib
> *Motresheved* 1308 Cl (p)
> *Moutresheved* 1337 Plea (p), *-hed* 1337 (17) Orm²
> *Mottromsheued* 1349 Orm² (p)
> *Motturushede* 1373 *Eyre* (p)
> *Muttreshedde* 1513 ChEx (p)

'Speaker's hill', *v.* mōtere, cf. Mottistone Wt 164. The DEPN explanation depends upon the *Moct-* spelling 1287 Court 231, which seems to be an error for MS. *Mott-*. Cf. Mottram St Andrew *supra*, DEPN s.n. *Mottram*. This lost place gave surname to a family whose seats were Higher & Lower Ho *infra*, v. Orm² III 697. Halewysa *de Mottromsheued*, prioress of the nuns of Chester 1349 (Orm² I 347) is otherwise called *de Mottersheved*. The form was influenced by Mottram *supra*.

LEE HALL, 1560 *Cross*, *Le(z) Legh(es)* 1387, 1393, 1395 Adl, *Legh Hall* 1480 ib, *Lyehall* 1536 ChRR, *Leigh Hall* 1569 ib, 'the woodland glade(s)', v. lēah, hall.

ALLEN'S FM, *Allens* 1831 Bry.   BLACKERSHALL FM, BLACKHURST BROW, probably 'black wooded-hill', v. blæc, hyrst.   BROOK COTTAGE, *-House* 1831 ib.   BROOK HO, *Rowbothams* 1831 ib, 1848 *TA*, either 'rough bottom-lands' v. rūh, botm, or named from the derived surname *Rowbotham*.   CHERRYORCHARD.   THE CLOUGH, v. clōh.   COMMONEND, cf. Kirkleyditch Common *infra*.   DEAN, *-Farm* 1831 Bry, *(le) Deyne* 1519 *Dav*, 1520 ChRR, *Deane* 1664 Sheaf, 'the valley', v. denu.   LOWER & UPPER GADHOLE, *Gadhole* 1831 Bry, 'gad-fly hollow', v. gad.   GOOSEGREEN, *Free School Farm* 1831 ib.   GREENBANK.   GREENDALE, 1831 ib.   HIGHER FM.   HIGHER & LOWER HO, *(Lower) House* 1831 ib, cf. *two messuages called le Halle howzes* 1433 Orm², v. hall, hūs, cf. *Mottershead supra*.   HUNTER'S POOL (FM), 1848 *TA*.   KIRKLEYDITCH (COMMON), *Ketley Ditch* 1831 Bry, *Kitley Ditch Common* 1842 OS, *Gatley Ditch Common* 1848 *TA*.   MILL FM & LANE, *Mill Lane* 1831 Bry, *le lane yate* 1519 *Dav*, v. geat.   MOTTRAM BRIDGE 1831 Bry.   MOTTRAM CROSS, 1831 ib, v. cros.   MOTTRAM (OLD) HALL, 1831 ib, *manerium de Mottrum Andrewe* 1433 Earw, *Mottram Hall* 1645 ib.   MOTTRAM WOOD, *boscus de Mottram* 1286 *Eyre*, *Hall Wood* 1831 Bry.   OAK HO, 1831 ib.   PARKSIDE.   PRESTBURY LANE (lost), 1860 White, cf. Prestbury 212 *infra*.   PRIEST LANE.   READ'S WOOD.   STANYEACOP, probably 'bank at a stony enclosure', v. stānig, (ge)hæg, copp.   TOMGREEN FM, *Tomgreen* 1831 Bry, perhaps 'town's green', v. toun, grēne².   TURNER'S HO.   WITHENLEE, 1842 OS, *Within Ley Common* 1831 Bry, 'willow clearing', v. wīðign, lēah.   WOODSIDE (COTTAGE), *Woodside Cottage* 1831 ib, named from Mottram Wood *supra*.

FIELD-NAMES

The undated forms are 1848 *TA* 278. Of the others 1831 is Bry, 1842 OS, 1860 White, 1880 Earw, l13 (17), 1504, 1519[1] *Dav*, 1285 Court, c.1288 (14) Chest, c.1414 Mont, 1519[2] *NewC*.

(a) The Acre; Bank; Bent (*v.* beonet); Birchfield; Broad Mdw; Brook Fd; Broom Fd (cf. *Bromecrofte* 1519[1], *Rydingkerre infra*, *v.* brōm, croft); Chapel Fd 1880 (the supposed site of an ancient chapel, *v.* Earw ii 352, cf. *the fild wherin the Chapell of Mottrom stondez* 1504, *the feild wherein the chappell of Mottram standeth* 1519[2]. The dedication may have been to St Andrew, cf. Mottram St Andrew *supra*); Churley (perhaps connected with John de *Chorlegh'*, a tenant in Mottram l12 Orm[2] iii 697, *v.* ceorl, lēah); Cinder Croft (*v.* sinder); Clod (*v.* clodd); Cote Fd; Givers Green; Hare House Green (*Arras Green* 1831); Healey Hill Common (*Heley Hill* 1842, probably 'high clearing', *v.* hēah, lēah); Hollin Croft (*v.* holegn); Hollow Mdw; Horse Pasture; Lime Croft; Little Brook 1831 (the stream on the Prestbury boundary); Little Hey; Long Fd; Mare Fd (*v.* mere[2]); Marl Fd; May Croft; Mean Hay ('common inclosure', *v.* (ge)mǣne, (ge)hæg); Middle Mdw; Nicholson's Fd; Outlet (*v.* outlet); Owler Mdw (*v.* alor); Pingot (*v.* pingot); Pool Fd; Rough Fd; Rushy Mdw; Shippon Flat (*v.* scypen, flat); the Smithy Fd 1860; Spittle Field (from spitel 'a hospital', perhaps the site of an infirmary, cf. *Cecilia quondam uxor' Jordani le Leper*, 1376 Orm[2] iii 693); Turnay Hills Common (*Turney Hills* 1831, probably 'hills at a round enclosure', *v.* trun, (ge)hæg); Weir Holes Wd 1842 (*v.* wer, hol[1]); Well Croft.

(b) Haukeshert c.1288 (14) ('hawk's gap', *v.* hafoc-scerde, cf. *The Hawkesyord* 166 *supra*); *Low(e) Fild(e)* 1519[1] (*v.* lágr 'low'); *Oldefild* 1519[1] (*v.* ald, feld); *le Redbroke* c.1414 (*v.* Red Brook 34 *supra*); *Rydingkerre, le Kerre iuxta hoke* l13(17), *quadam quercus iuxta Bromecrofte in le Ryddeker claus' vocat' Ryddiker* 1519[1] (probably 'reedy marsh', from hrēodig and kjarr, as Redacre 132 *supra*, though the first el. could be ryding 'a clearing', or an -ing[2] formation from hrēod. The contexts allude to an oak near *Bromecrofte*, cf. Broom Fd *supra*).

17. NEWTON (101–8881), NEWTON HALL

Neutun e13 Orm[2], 13 *Fitt*, *-tona* 13 *Dav*, *-ton* 1285 Court *et freq*, (*-iuxta Wydeford*) 1335 Plea, (*in Buttylegh*) 1428 ChRR, (*-iuxta Foxwist*) 1503 *NewC*
Newton l13 (17) *Dav*, 1488 ChRR (p), (*-juxta Butley*) 1819 Orm[1], *Newton Hall* 1831 Bry

'New farm', *v.* nīwe, tūn. Cf. Woodford 217 *infra*, Foxtwist 194 *supra*, Butley 193 *supra*.

BENT FM, *Bent Medowe* 1437 *NewC*, *-Medowe* 1500 *Dav*, *The Bent* 1505 *NewC*, *v.* beonet 'bent-grass'. BOUNDARY FM, on the boundary with Butley 193 *supra*. LEES LANE, *Less Lane* 1842 OS, *v.* læs. NEWTON CHAPEL (site of, 101–883808), *Newton Chapel(l)* 1536 Earw, cf. *Chapel Yard* 1848 *TA* (a meadow), *v.* chapel(e), geard. NEWTON HEATH, *bruer' de Newton* 113 (17) *Dav*, *Neuton-*, *Foxwist Heath* 1437 *NewC*, *Neuton heith aliter vocat' Foxwist heith* 1500 *Dav*, *v.* hæð. It is near Foxtwist 194 *supra*. PITLANE FM, cf. *(lez) mospittes* 1501 *ib*, *les Mossepittes* 1511 *NewC*, *þe old mosse pittes* 1531 *Dav*, 'peat-diggings', *v.* mos, pytt.

FIELD-NAMES

The undated forms are 1848 *TA* 292. Of the others, 1286 is *Eyre*, 1505, 1511 *NewC*, and the rest *Dav*.

(a) Bank (cf. *the bonkes* 1505, *v.* banke); Barn Fd; Bean Fd; Bridge Fd (cf. *le Brugehuses iuxta Newton'* 1286, *The brig House* 1505, 'houses at the bridge', *v.* brycg, hūs, named from Mottram Bridge 204 *supra*); Calf Croft; The Carrs (*the Kerr* 1505, *v.* kjarr); Clover Fd; Cockshead (*the Cokshote*, *-shete* 1505, *v.* cocc-scyte); Common Fd & Piece; Corode Mdw (from cor(r)odie 'a pension, an annuity, an ecclesiastical stipend', probably connected with Newton Chapel *supra*); Daisy Croft; Eyes ('water-meadows', *v.* ēg); Great Mdw (cf. *Medoofild* 1500, *v.* mǣd, feld); Half Acre; Horse Hey (*the Horshey* 1505); The Intake (*v.* inntak); Long Croft; Marl Fd (cf. *the marled earth & yords* 1505, *v.* marlede, geard, eorðe); Mobberley Croft; New Mdw; Pasture Fd; The Pool (Fd & Mdw) (cf. *The Pole dame* 1505, *v.* pōl[1], damme); River Wash (land beside the R. Bollin, *v.* wæsce); Skelhorn Croft (cf. Skellorn Green 184 *supra*); Stock Fd; Stone Fd (*The Stonfild* 1505, *v.* stān, feld); Sun Fd; Tilly Fd (this recurs 213 *infra*); Wet Fd; White Fd; Yew Tree Croft.

(b) *le Blakerth, le black earth* (or *blak akre*) 1505, 1511 (*v.* blæc, erð, æcer); *Bothefildez* 1500 (*v.* bōth 'herdsman's hut', feld); *the chokchurld, Chokecherle* 1505 (apparently a field which made a farm-hand choke, from ME *cheoken* 'to choke' and ceorl); *Coldwall mosse* 113 (17) ('(moss at) the cold spring', *v.* cald, wælla, mos); *the Coningree* (*v.* coningre); *le Coppedhurst* 113 (17) ('the polled wood', *v.* copped, hyrst); *Foxhurst* 113 (17) ('fox wood', *v.* fox, hyrst); *The Furrow Furlong* 1505 (*v.* furh, furlang); *boscus de Harpercroft* 1501, *the Harpcrofte* 1505, *þe Harpercroft wode* 1531 ('harper's field', *v.* hearpere, croft, wudu); *The Hendhey* 1505 (perhaps 'end enclosure', *v.* ende[1], (ge)hæg, but the first el. may be (ge)hende 'near, to hand, serviceable'); *Katherin Eyes* 1505 ('Katherine's meadows', from the ME fem. pers.n. Katherine and ēg); *the Milne of Neuton* 1505 (*v.* myln); *le Shalone* 113(17) ('the copse lane', *v.* sceaga, lane); the lane forming part of the east boundary of the township, cf. Shaloone Croft 192 *supra*).

18. POYNTON WITH WORTH (101–9183)

POYNTON

Poninton 1248 Ipm *et freq* to 1349 Earw, (*-a*) c.1280 *Dow*, *-yn*(*g*)-
  1270 ChF *et freq* to 1501 *Dow*, 1530 ChRR, (*-a*) c.1310 Chest,
  -ing- 1285 Eyre, *Ponintun* c.1280 *Dow*
Povinton 1249 IpmR, 1292 ib, Ipm, *-yn-* 1411 *Mont*, 1412 *Chol*,
  1519 ChRR, *-yng-* 1467 *MinAcct*, 1519 ChRR
Pouindon c.1280 *Dow*, *-ton* c.1280 *ib*, 1286 *Eyre*, *-yn*(*g*)- 1289 *ChFine*
Poynton 1325 Pat (p) *et freq*, (*Poinington or*) c.1620 Orm², *-e* 1565
  Dow, *Pointon* 1536 Leland, *Poynynton* 1423 Orm², *Poyngton*
  1530 *Dow*, *Poyington* 1559 Pat
Powynton 1357 *ChFor*, *Pownton* 1551 *Dow*

'Farm called after Pofa', from an OE pers.n. *Pofa* with -ing-⁴, tūn.
The pers.n. appears as **Pofa*, **Pufa*, in Pooley Wa 22, Punish Wood
PNK 151, *Povenden* PNK 407. On the basis of the *Pon-* spellings,
Poynton has been derived from an OE pers.n. *Pūn*(*a*), as in Poynings
Sx 286, *v.* DEPN s.v., but the form of the name has been confused
by orthography. The evidence of the *Pov-*, *Pow-* spellings, taken
with the few orthographically clear *Pou-* spellings, suggests that the
numerous readings *Pon-* represent *Pou-*, mistaken through the
similarity of *n* and *u* in MSS. The village was *The Greene* 1743 *Dow*,
Poynton Green 1831 Bry, 1842 OS, *v.* grēne².

WORTH HALL FM (101–936838)

Wirth 1161–1182 Dieul (p), *Wyrhte* 1345 *Eyre*
Worthe c.1200 Orm² (p), 1484 ChRR (p), *Worth* c.1233 *Dow* (p) *et
  freq*, (*aula de-*) 1350 *Eyre*, (*the-*) 1553 *Dow*, (*-or the Hall of
  Worth*) 1619 *ib*, (*-Hall*)) 1693 *ib*, *Woorth infra Poynton* 1551 *ib*,
  Wourth(*e*) 1589, 1621 *ib*, *W*(*o*)*roth* 1467, 1471 *MinAcct*
Wrth c.1210 Dieul, m13 *Dav* (p), *Wrtht* c.1270 Adl (p), *Wrht* l13
  AddCh (p)
Wurth e13 Dieul, 1297 *Werb* (p), 1462 *Dow*, (*-in Poynton*) 1548 *ib*,
  -e 1472 *ib*, *Wurh* e13 Dieul, *Wurht* e13 Facs (p), c.1232 *Fitt* (p)

'The curtilage', *v.* worð, wyrð. Cf. Park Fm *infra*.

DOGHILLGREEN (101–910845), *Doggehul* c.1280 *Dow*, *Doghull* 1357
Eyre (p), *-hill* 1642 Earw, (*Moor*(*e*)) 1720, 1728 *Dav*, *Dog-hill Green*
1766 *Dow*, 'dog hill', *v.* dogga, hyll.

HEPPLEY (101–932833), *Heppeleg'* c.1280, *-legh* c.1320, 1327, *Hepley* 1490, (*molendinum de-*) 1521 all *Dow*, 'bramble clearing', *v.* hēopa, lēah, cf. Hockley *infra*.

LOSTOCKHALL FM (101–905829), *Lostok* 1285 *Eyre*, (*hamlet' de-*), (*-in Wideford*) 1289 *ChFine*, *Lostock* 1286 *Eyre* (p), (*maner' de-*) 1522 Plea, *Lostocc* 1551 *Dow*, *Lockstocke heath* 1615 *ChCert*, 'pig-sty hamlet', *v.* hlōse, stoc, cf. Lostock Gralam 332 *infra*, Woodford 217 *infra*.

PYKFORD (lost), 1357 *Eyre*, *Pikeford* c.1280 *Dow* 11, 1286 *Eyre* (p), *Pyke-* 1288 Court (p), *-e* 1351 *Eyre*, *Picford* 1352 *ib*, *Pyk-* 1357 *ib*, *Pikkeford* 1460 *Dow* (p), 'pike ford', *v.* pīc[1] 'the pike (a fish)', ford. *Dow* 11 is a grant of Doghillgreen *supra* to Richard de Worth (Bryant shows Doghillgreen as a detached part of Worth hamlet), with 'a portion of heath lying between *Doggehul* (Doghillgreen *supra*) and the fields of *Pikeford* and the boundary of *Bromhale* (Bramhall)'. The ford was probably near Mill Hill Bridge *infra*, 101–916853. A local surname, *de Pyc-*, *Pykford*, (later *Pickford*), is common about Macclesfield 1337 *Eyre*, probably from this place, but perhaps from Piggford Moor 162 *supra*, cf. Ladythorn 260 *infra*.

ACCOMMODATION, H.A.T. identifies with *Pointon Lane End(s)* 1738, 1766 *Dow*.   ANSON PIT & RD, *High Meadow Pit* 1831 Bry, *Anson Fields* (local, H.A.T.), a colliery.   BARLOW FOLD & HO, 1831 Bry, probably from the family *Barlow* of Fallibroome (Earw II 347), *v.* fald.   BEECHFIELD.   BEN'S WOOD.   BLACK HOLE.   BRICK-FIELD.   BROOK COTTAGE, named from Norbury Brook 32 *supra*. CARRWOOD, cf. Thomas de *Kere* 1357 *ChFor*, *v.* kjarr 'brushwood', 'marsh'.   CAWLEY LODGE & NURSERY, *le Cowhey* 1530 ChRR, *Cow Hey Wood* 1831 Bry, *Corley* 1635 *Dow*, *v.* cū, (ge)hæg, lēah. CHESTER RD, *Chapel Lane* 1857 *Map* (H.A.T.), from the old chapel of Poynton which preceded the present church, cf. *Poynton Chapel infra*. CLAYTONFOLD, cf. William *Clayton* 1766 *Dow*, tenant of Hockley *infra*, *v.* fald.   CLUMBER COTTAGE, HO & RD, *v.* clympre (dial. *clumper*) 'a lump, a clod'.   COPPICE SIDE, 1831 Bry, cf. Poynton Coppice *infra*.   CORRECTION BROW & FM, *House of Correction* 1831 ib.   CRESCENT, *Crescent Inn* 1831 ib.   DALEHOUSEFOLD, 1831 ib, *Dales tenement* 1711 *Dow*, *Dale House* 1743 *ib*, from the surname *Dale*, *v.* fald.   DICKENS LANE, 1842 OS.   ELMBEDS

(Fм), 1842 ib, *Elmbed* 1831 Bry, *v.* foll.   Elm Wood, *Elmbed Wood* 1831 ib, *v.* elm, bedd.   Fleetbank Fm, *Dig Green* 1831 ib, cf. *le-, la Dich(e), -Dych(e)* c.1280 *Dow* (p), 1286, 1288 Court (p), 1349 *MinAcct* (p), 'the ditch', *v.* dīc. The origin of the modern name is unknown.   German Lodge & Pool, *German Pool* 1831 Bry, originally *Richardsons Meadow* after James *Richardson* 1766 *Dow* 434, later named after a coal-pit, *Garman Pit*, sunk there c.1845 (H.A.T.). Green Lane.   Hazelbadge Bridge, *v.* hæsel 'a hazel', bæce[1] 'a stream, a valley'.   Higherbarn, *High Barn* 1831 Bry, cf. *Lower Barn* (lost) also called *Gramophone Terrace* (local, H.A.T.).   High-field, cf. *the Heighe fielde* 1581, *the hye Feild* 1619, *the Highfield* 1743 all *Dow.*   Higlane, 1766 *ib*, *High Lane* 1842 OS.   Hilltop, 1831 Bry.   Hockley (101–932833), 1711 *Dow*, (a tenement) 1766 *ib*, cf. *the Hockley Higher Croft* 1743 *ib*, now the name of a district near Hepley *supra*, cf. Claytonfold *supra*, and sometimes used as an alternative name for Hepley (H.A.T.). The name recurs 154 *supra.* Perhaps these p.n.'s are from hocc 'a hock, a mallow', and lēah 'a clearing', but the material is too late and scanty.   The Homestead.   Horse-Pasture Pit, *Poynton Pits* 1831 Bry, from *Upper & Bottom Horse Pasture* (local), fields where pit-haulage horses were grazed (H.A.T.).   Lady's Incline & Wood.   Lawrance Pit. London Rd.   Long Chimney.   Long Plantation.   Lostock Terrace, *v.* Lostockhall *supra.*   Lowerpark (Fm & Rd), *Lower Park, Back Lane* 1831 Bry, cf. Park Pit, Poynton Park *infra.* Marlfield Cottages, cf. *le Marlde Crofte* 1521 *Dow*, *le Marle-croght* 1530 ChRR, now called *Waterloo Meadow* (H.A.T.), cf. Waterloo *infra*, *v.* marlede, croft, cf. Marljurr *infra.*   Middlewood Rd, leading to Middle Wood 283 *infra.*   Midway (Fm), 1842 OS, *Bridge Street* 1831 Bry, a hamlet at Poynton Bridge *infra*, half-way from Poynton to Adlington.   Millhill Bridge & Fm, *Poynton Mill*, and *a messuage and a mill called the Mill Hill Tenement*, and *Poynton Bridge* 1714 *Dow*, cf. *Pykford supra.*   Mount Vernon, from the *Vernon* family, landowners here.   Nelson Pit, a colliery. New House Fm, *New House* 1831 Bry.   Newtown.   Norbury Hollow Bridge, *v.* holh, cf. Norbury 287 *infra.*   North Lodge. Oak Bank & Field.   The Paddock.   Park Fm (101–925834), *Old Worths* 1831 Bry, *Lagherworth* 1490 *Dow*, *the Laugher worth* 1551, *(logher)* 1553, *(lower)* 1581, 1766 *ib*, probably the location of the eight acres in Poynton enclosed with a hedge by Richard de Worth (1285 Court 212), *v.* lagher (cf. lágr), worð, cf. Worth *supra.*   Parkgate,

PARK HOUSE FM, PARK LANE & LODGE, cf. Poynton Park *infra*. PARK PIT (PLANTATION), the location of *Upper Park* 1831 Bry, cf. Lowerpark *supra*, Poynton Park *infra*. PETRE BANK, *the Helde* 1551 *Dow, the heild* 1553 *ib, the Heald* 1619 *ib, the Pear Tree Bank* (*part of the Heald*) 1743 *ib*, Peartree Bank 1857 H.A.T., *v.* helde 'a slope, a declivity'. PHILLIP'S BRIDGE. PINFOLD, *-House* 1831 Bry. POOL HOUSE, 1831 ib. POTTERS CLOUGH. POYNTON BIRCHES, *Birches* 1842 OS. POYNTON BRIDGE, crossing Poynton Brook into Adlington, cf. Millhill Bridge *supra*. POYNTON CHAPEL (lost), *cappella de Ponynton* 1312 Orm², *ecclesia beate Marie de Poynton* 1464 ib, cf. Chester Rd *supra*. POYNTON COPPICE, 1831 Bry, cf. Coppice Side *supra*. POYNTON LAKE. POYNTON PARK, 1705 Orm², *Povynton hey infra forestam de Macclesfeld* 1412 *Chol, parcum Johannis Warren' in Poynton* 1490 *Dow, at Poynton is a parke* 1536 Leland, *parcum de Pownton* 1551 *Dow, v.* park, (ge)hæg, cf. Lowerpark, Park Pit *supra*. POYNTON TOWERS, 1860 White, a residence with turrets, replacing *Poynton Hall* 1831 Bry, 1860 White, *maner' de Pou- Povyn(g)ton* 1358, 1471 *Minacct*. PRINCE'S INCLINE & WOOD, named from a coal pit (disused) called after the Prince Consort, (H.A.T.). SHADYOAK, 1842 OS. SERPENTINE WOOD. SHRIGLEY RD, named from Shrigley 130 *supra*. SMITHFIELD. SPRINK FM, SPRINGBANK COTTAGE, *Sprink* 1831 Bry, *Spring Farm* 1842 OS, *v.* spring 'a spring'. TOWERS FM, cf. Poynton Towers *supra*. VERNON PIT, a coal-pit belonging to the Vernon family. WALKER PIT, a coal-pit in *Walker Field* (H.A.T.), cf. *The Walkers folde, felde* 1551, *The Three Walkers-fields* 1619 *Dow, v.* fald, feld. WARDSEND BRIDGE, cf. Wardsend 184 *supra*. WATERLOO (RD), cf. Marlfields *supra*. WESTFIELD. WIGWAM WOOD (101–910833), *Poynton Moor* 1842 OS. WOODFORD RD, *a Lane neare Poynton Mill in Poynton called Stanley Lane* 1714 *Dow*, cf. *Stanley House* 1621 Orm², probably from the surname *Stanley*. WOODHOUSE FM, 1842 OS, *Wood End* 1831 Bry, cf. *boscus de Ponyngton* 1363 ChFor, *v.* wudu, hūs, ende[1]. WOODSIDE, named from Lady's Wood *supra*. WORTH CLOUGH, cf. *Lower Clough Pit* 1831 Bry, *v.* clōh. YEWTREE FM.

FIELD-NAMES

There is no *TA* for Poynton with Worth. Of the forms listed, c.1280, c.1320, 1327, 1464, 1490, 1551, 1553, 1581, 1586, 1599, 1619, 1743, 1748, 1766 are

Dow, 1354, 1355 *Eyre*, 1363, 1503 *ChFor*, 1411, 1414 *Mont*, 1495, 1530 ChRR, 1831 Bry, 1842 OS, and the undated forms and those marked 1913 and (H.A.T.) are supplied from documents and information by Mr H. A. Trippier.

(a) Barn Mdw; Bid Mdw; Big Hay Mdw; Bills Mdw; Bower Stump(s) 1831, 1842 (*v.* stump); Bradley Mdw (cf. *de Bradelegh'* 1354 (p), 'broad clearing', *v.* brād, lēah); Far & New Broard Fd (*v.* brād); Brook Fd; Calf Croft; Castle Fd (*the castell felde* 1551, 1581, -*fyld* 1553, *The Castle-Feilds* 1619, *the Castle Hill Field alias the Castle Field* 1743, perhaps a field with supposed earthworks in it, *v.* castel(l)); Gees Pit 1831; Grimshaw Fd; Harley Bridge; the Harrop Croft 1743 (if not from the derived surname, perhaps another instance of the p.n. type *Harrop*, *v.* 138 *supra*); Big & Little Hopes, Far Hope Mdw (*v.* hop[1]); Kings Fd, King William Fd (named after a coal-pit, *King William pit*, closed down last century, H.A.T.); Long Mdw; Marljurr (*Marletyourth* 1490, *Greatt marledyearth of Hepley* 1551, *Ould merled Earth* 1599, *the Marled Earth* 1619, 1743, 'marled ground', *v.* marlede, eorðe, cf. Marl Jurr 267 *infra*); New Ground; the Pool tail 1743; Roughs 1831; Rushey Fd; Speedwells 1831 (a lost house-name, in Norbury Hollow, on Middlewood Rd); Stones Green 1842; Wheat Fd; (Little) White Croft; Wood's o' th' Lane 1748, 1766 (from Mary *Wood*, tenant).

(b) *Adredeleg'* c.1280, *Alderleyhurst* 1363 (apparently 'Aldŏryŏ's wood or clearing', from the OE fem. pers.n. *Aldŏryŏ* and lēah, like Alderley 94 *supra*, with hyrst 'a wooded-hill'. The place is described c.1280 *Dow* 13, as next to Hepley *supra*, on the north side); *Le Berecroftes* c.1280 ('the barley crofts', *v.* bere, croft); *Boterhale* 1354 (p) (*v.* butere 'butter', halh 'a nook', cf. Butterhouse Green 263 *infra*); *Brendhurst* 1530 ('burnt wood', *v.* brende[2], hyrst); *Briddesruding'* c.1280 ('bird's clearing', *v.* bridd, ryding; *Dow* 13 places it on the south side of Hepley *supra*); *le Callerleys* 1530 (probably 'calves' clearings', from calf (gen.pl. calfra) and lēah); *le Cartegate* c.1320, 1327 ('the cart road', *v.* cræt, gata); *Cartelachehurst* 1363 (*v.* hyrst, *Cartelache* 17 *supra*); *Cokeshote heye* 1464, *Cokshote Hey* 1495 ('cock-shoot enclosure', *v.* cocc-scyte, (ge)hæg); *the Comberwheyn medow* 1551, *the Cumberwyne Medowe* 1553 (from winn[1], wynn 'a pasture', cf. Witherwin, the Whayne 336, 335 *infra*. The material is too late to prove the first el. Cumbre (gen. Cumbra) 'Britons', so the p.n. may well be analogous with Cumberland 161, 201 *supra*, from cumber 'an encumbrance', or combre 'a heap of stones', cf. WRY 7 173); *le Dene* 1411, 1414 (*v.* denu); *Fernleghker* c.1320, 1327, *le Fernyleghcar* 1363, cf. John *Ferneleghes* 1503 ('(the marsh at) the ferny clearings', *v.* fearnig, lēah, kjarr; this place was on the east side of Hepley *supra*); *the Gorstye feld* 1551, -*Feylde* 1586, *the Gorstie felde* 1581, *the gorstiffeilde* 1619 (*v.* gorstig); *Gorstye knoll* 1551 (*v.* gorstig, cnoll); *le grenecroft* c.1280 (*v.* grēne[1] 'green', croft); *the grett & the litle Heisberne* 1551, -*heysborne*, -*heysboure* 1553, *the litle & the longe Hays Barne* 1581, *the Litlecasbarne* 1619; *le Heweruding* c.1280, *Heagh ryding* 1490, *the High-ridding(e)* 1551, 1553 ('high clearing', *v.* hēah, ryding); *le Holynkastel* c.1320, 1327 ('holly-tree bank', *v.* holegn, ceastel); *le Middilschawe* c.1320, 1327, *Midulschag'* c.1320 ('the middle copse', *v.* middel, sceaga, cf. Middle Wood

283 *infra*); *the Palefeld & -medow* 1551, (*meydowe*) 1553, *the Paled Field* 1599 (within the pale of Poynton Park *supra, v.* pale); *Rydd-, Ridding, -yng* 1551, (*the*) *Rydding(e)s* 1599, 1619 (*v.* ryding); *the Rye Croft(e)* 1551, 1619, *the Roye Croft* 1553 (*v.* ryge, croft); *le Shideyord* (lit. *le Shiderord*) 1530 ('(enclosure with) a wooden fence', *v.* scīd-geard); *the Shippon Hill Croftes* 1551, *the shippenhylles crofte* 1553 (*v.* scypen, hyll); *Skynner(s)fylde* 1490 ('skinner's field', from skinnari or the surname *Skinner* and feld); *Wardes Meadow* 1599 (cf. Wardsend 183 *supra*); *Lyttle Wheate Croft* 1599; *le gret Wodhey* 1530, *lowerwodhey* 1551 ('wood enclosure', *v.* wudu, (ge)hæg); *the Mylne of (the) Worth(e)* 1551, 1553 (*v.* myln, cf. Worth Hall *supra*); *le Wycttebrokes, le quitebrock* c.1320, *le Wyttebrok* 1327 (*v.* hwīt, brōc); *Wythenchawebrok'* c.1280 ('(brook at) the willow-copse', *v.* wiðign, sceaga, brōc).

19. PRESTBURY (101–8976)

> *Prest(e)bur'* c.1170–1182, m13 Chest, *-bury* 1215 Facs, 1237 (17), c.1240 Chest, (*-e*) c.1540 Dugd, *-buria* c.1220, c.1310 Chest, *-buri* 1221 (17) ib, (*-e*) 1539 *Dow, -bure* 1363 *Eyre*
> *Prest(e)bire* l12 (1285) Ch, Adl, *-bir'* 1267 Cl (p), (*-y*) 1279 Pat, *-byri* 1536 Leland
> *Presteberi* 1181 Facs, *Prestbere* l15 *Dow, -bery* 1505 *ib*
> *Presbury* 1428 ChRR, *-burie* 1557 Sheaf, *-by* 1536 Leland

'Priests' manor', *v.* prēost (gen.pl. prēosta), burh. This was a manor belonging to the abbots of Chester, cf. Spittle Ho, Abbot's Hay *infra*. By people in Bollington, this village is sometimes called *Mansionville*, an allusion to the more pretentious style of the place.

BROOKFIELD HO, named from Spencer Brook 35 supra.   BRUNDRED FM, *Brundritt House* 1692 *Dow, Brundreth House* 1831 Bry, from the family of Robert *Brundrett* 1602, John *Brundreth* 1686 *Dow*, of Bollington.   CASTLE LANE, probably from some supposed earthwork, *v.* castel(l).   COCKSHEAD (WOOD), *Cockshead* 1831 Bry, 'a cock-shoot', *v.* cocc-scyte.   COLLAR HO, 1831 ib.   CRABTREE FM.   DALEBROW, 1831 ib, *v.* dæl[1], brū.   FIELD'S FM.   GREENBANK.   HILL TOP.   HOLLYBANK FM.   MILL FM, named from *Prestbury Mill* 1831 Bry.   NEW LANE FM, *New Lane* 1831 ib.   NORMAN'S HALL, *Norman Chair Hall* 1831 ib, *Norman Hall* 1842 OS, a modern name, re-modelled after Normans Hall 134 *supra*. Perhaps the house got its name from an odd piece of furniture.   OAKTREE FM.   PRESTBURY BRIDGE.   PRESTBURY HALL, 1831 Bry, *the mancion house* 16 Earw.   SPITTLE HO, 1831 Bry, *Le Spittle* (*Spittal*) *howse* 1624 Earw, Orm², cf. Spittle Fd 205 *supra, v.* spitel 'a hospital', perhaps connected with the abbot of Chester's manor of Prestbury, cf. Abbot's Hay *infra*. WITHENLEE FM, cf. *Within Lee Field & Patch* 1848 *TA*, 'willow glade', *v*. wīðign, lēah.

FIELD-NAMES

The undated forms are 1848 *TA* 329. Of the others c.1220, c.1250, c.1270 are Chest, 1362, 1364 *Eyre*, 1363 *ChFor*, 1430 Orm², 1448, 1480 Adl, 17 *Harl* 2151, 1724 NotCestr, 1880 Earw.

(a) Abbot's Hay 1880 (*& Bank* 1724, *the Abbott's Hay (Bank)* 17, *v.* (ge)hæg; associated with the abbots of Chester, lords of the manor. This was near Spittle Ho *supra*); Acre; Asp Fd (*v.* æspe 'an aspen-tree'); Bank Mdw; Barbers Fd; Barn Fd; Black Fd; Blackwell Mdw (*v.* blæc, wella); Brickiln Fd; Brook Mdw; Broom Fd (*v.* brōm); Broomy Knowl (*v.* brōmig, cnoll); Brow(y) Fd (*v.* brū, -ig³); Bye Flatt (*v.* byge¹, flat); Cap Fd; Clarkes Patch; Clough (Hey *& Mdw*) (*v.* clōh); Clover Fd; Common Fd; Cote Mdw; Cow Lane; Little Day Work (*v.* day-work); Dick Fd; Door Flatt (*v.* duru, flat); Edgerow Croft (*v.* hecg-ræw); (The) Eyes (*v.* ēg 'a water meadow'); Fox Holes; Gorsey Croft *& Fd*; Green Fd; Greety Hey ('gritty or sandy enclosure', *v.* grēot (dial. *greet*), -ig³); Grey Shoot ('badger's corner', *v.* græg², scēat, but scēot³ 'a steep slope' is possible); Half Acre; Hanging Bank *& Mdw* (*v.* hangende); Harbour Fd (*v.* here-beorg); Hen Croft; High Fd *& Knoll*; Horse Pasture; House Mdw; Kid Fd (*v.* kide 'a kid'); Knoll Fd; Lady Knowl (*v.* hlǣfdige, cnoll); Lee (*v.* lēah); Lime Fd; Long Butts (*v.* butte); Marl Fd; The Marleach, Morleach mdw (*v.* marr, mōr¹, læc(c)); Little Maw; Milking Fold (*v.* milking); Moneys Croft; Moss Mdw; Newton's Knowl; Old Hock (Clough) (*v.* āc, clōh); Old Mdw; Outlet (*v.* outlet); Owler Fd (cf. *Olres* c.1250, *v.* alor); Pack Saddle Fd (*v.* pakke-sadil); Pasture Fd; Peas Fd; Pit Fd; Plainers Wd; Powell's Clough; The Rough; Rye Croft; Sankey Croft; Saw Pit Fd; Schofield (*v.* skáli 'a temporary hut or shed', feld); Shippon Fd; Shipton Fd ('sheeppen field', *v.* scēap, tūn); Six Acre; Spencer Fd *& Mdw* (probably from the surname *Spencer*, cf. Spencer Brook 35 *supra*); Spring Fd (*v.* spring 'a well-spring'); Stable Fd; Stony Croft, Fd *& Flatt*; Sweet Fd; Tan Yard Fd *& Mdw*; Three Corner Bit; Tilly Fd (cf. 206 *supra*); Vicar's Harbour (*v.* here-beorg 'shelter'); Wall Mdw (*v.* wælla 'a well, a spring'); Wetstone Fd (*v.* hwet-stān 'a whetstone'); White Fd; Willow Croft; Wilshaws Clough (*v.* clōh); Womans Fd; Wood Fd.

(b) le Baches 1430 (*v.* bæce¹ 'a stream, a valley'; from a deed endorsed *Bothes lands* t.Eliz, which may refer to foll.); *Bothes* c.1220 (*v.* bōth 'a booth, a herdsman's hut', a district in the western part of the township, towards Harebarrow 101 *supra*, *v*. ChetNS LXXXII 786); *Cokemonscloht* c.1220 (from the ME surname *Cokeman* 'cook's man' (Reaney s.v. *Cockman*) and clōh 'a dell'); *Echeleshull* 1363, 1364 (land assarted c.1359, *v.* ēcels 'an addition, land added to an estate', hyll, cf. Etchells 239 *infra*); *Ewode* 1448 ('yew wood' or 'wood by a river', *v.* īw or ēa, wudu, cf. How Day Head 327 *infra*); *Frewineslache* c.1270 ('Frēowine's boggy stream', from the OE pers.n. *Frēowine* and *læc*(c)); *Marythorn* 1480 ('Mary's thorn' from the ME fem. pers.n. *Mary* and þorn); *Presteslache, Preisteslache* (lit. *Freisteslache*) c.1220 ('priest's boggy stream', *v.* prēost, læc(c)); *Spelenford* c.1220 (*v.* ford. The form may contain a misreading for *Swelen-*, cf. **swelgend** 'a deep place').

20. TYTHERINGTON (101–9175)

> *Tidderington* c.1245 Chest, 1573 Orm², *Tydderynton* 1379 *Dow*, *-yng-* 1521 *ib*, *Ti-*, *Tyderinton* 1249 Earw (p), c.1260 *Dav* (p), *-a* l13 *Dow*, *-yn-* 1329 Cl (p), *Thi-*, *Thyderinton(e)* 1252 RBE (p), 1254 P (p), *Tid-*, *Tyderington* 1258 Earw, *-yng-* 1287 Court, (*-e*) 1565 *Dow*, *Tydiryngton* 1287 *Eyre*, *Tidirinton* e14 Orm²
> *Tydernthon* 1240–57 *AddCh* (p)
> *Tederinton* 1246–58 (14) Chest (p), *-ing-* 1328 Cl (p), *-yng-* l15 *Dow*
> *Tuderinton* 13 Orm², *-yng-* 1288 Court (p), 1514 *ChEx*, *-ing-* 1517 Earw
> *Tider-*, *Tudirton* c.1250–88 Chest, *Thidirton* 1277 P (p), *Tidderton* c.1620 Orm²
> *Tridinton* c.1270 Adl (p)
> *Tidrinton(a)* c.1280 *Dow*, *-yn-* 1499 ChRR, *Tydrinton* 1316 Plea, *-yn-* 1357 *Mont*, (*-e*) 1371 AD, *Tyddrinton* 1397 Sheaf, *Ti-*, *Tydrington* 1307 Fine (p), *-yng-* 1354 BPR (p)
> *Tirdirington* 1288 Court (p)
> *Todryngton* 1301 (1344) Pat
> *Tedrynton* 1400 JRL, *-yng-* 1512 *ChEx*
> *Tythrenton* 1480 Adl, *Ti-*, *Tytherington* 1620 Earw, 1622 *Cross*, 1860 White
> *Tetrynton* 1499 Orm², *Teterington* 1560 *Cross*
> *Tyttryngton* H8 Sheaf, *Tyteryngton* 1545 *Dow*
> *Tyddyngton* 1521 *Dow*
> *Tegrington* 1560 Sheaf

'Tȳdre's farm', from an OE pers. by-name *Tȳdre* and -ing-[4], tūn. For the pers.n. see Tytherington Gl 3 xi, 19–20, W 168, Tytherton W 91–2, and DEPN s.nn. Tytherington may be meant by the form *Cudynton iuxta Macclesfield* 52 *supra*.

BEECH BRIDGE (FM), BEECH HALL, LOWER BEECH, *le Bache* c.1425 Orm², (*the*) 1501 Earw, (*Hall*)1573 Orm², *The Bach Hall* 1611 LRMB 200, *Bach Bridge* 1621 Sheaf, cf. Beech Lane 117 *supra*, *v.*

bece[1] 'a stream, a valley'. The name is taken from the valley of R. Bollin between Macclesfield and Tytherington.

ALLEN COTTAGE, 1860 White.   BALL LANE.   (OLD) BLUE BELL FM, *Blue Bell* (*Inn*) 1842 OS, 1860 White.   COLD ARBOUR, *Colde Harbor* 1573 Earw, 'cold shelter', *v.* cald, here-beorg.   HOBSON HO, 1831 Bry.   LONDON RD.   LOWER HEYS MILL, *Lower Heys* 1842 OS, cf. 122 *supra*.   MANOR FM & HO.   MOATHALL FM, *the Moat* 1611 Orm[2], *Moat House* 1831 Bry, *v.* mote 'a moat'. OLDHAM'S HOLLOW (FM), *v.* holh 'a hollow', cf. John *Ouldham* 1697 *Dow* and also Oldham's Wood 102 *supra*.   POOL END, 1842 OS. PRESTBURY WOOD, 1848 *TA*, on the boundary of Prestbury 212 *supra*. TYTHERINGTON COTTAGE FM, TYTHERINGTON (OLD) HALL, TY-THERINGTON LANE & WOOD, *Big Wood, Tytherington Hall, Tytherington House* 1831 Bry, *The Cottage* 1860 White.   WOODLAND COTTAGE, near Prestbury Wood *supra*.

FIELD-NAMES

The undated forms are 1848 *TA* 398. Of the others 1250–88 is Chest, 1403 *Dow*, 1404 Plea, 1501 Earw, 1611 *LRMB* 200.

(*a*) Ash Knowl; Bancroft Fd (*v.* bēan, croft); Banky Fd; Barley Fd; Barn Fd; Birch Fd (*the birchfield* 1501); Black Moss (cf. *the black lach* 1501, 'black bog' *v.* læc(c)); Boundary Fd; Braddock; Brick Fd; Brook Mdw; Brow; Buggler; Bull Fd; Bye Flatt (*v.* byge[1], flat); Calf Hey; Clothes Yard; Clover Fd; Cockshut (*v.* cocc-scyte); Crown Mdw; Daisey Mdw; Dumble (*v.* dumbel); Fern Hill; Glen Fd (*v.* glenn); Greet Fd (*v.* grēot 'gravel', cf. dial. *greet*); Hardings Mdw; Heald (*v.* helde); Heliot (perhaps *heriot* 'a death duty', *v.* heriot); Hollow Fd; Leighton mdw (*v.* lēac-tūn); Lime Fd; Long Butts; Marl Pit Fd; Middle Fd; Mill Fd; Old Mdw; Ox Hey; Pingot (*v.* pingot); Poor Fd; Prestbury Mdw (cf. Prestbury 212 *supra*); Pretty Fd; Pump Fd; Rushy Fd; Rye Croft; Sheep Hill; Slang (*v.* slang); South Fd; Sprink(s) (*v.* spring 'a young wood'); Stack Yard; Sun Bank; Titherington Fd; Toll Bar Ho, Croft & Fd (cf. *Toll Gate* 1842, a turnpike gate); Well Mdw; Wilsons Mdw.

(*b*) *le Bothegrene* 1403 ('the green at the herdsman's hut', *v.* bōth, grēne[2]); *Le Bradall* 1404; *le Brownefield Brooke* 1611 (*v.* brūn[1], feld); *Le Cooker* 1404 (*le nether cocker meadowe* 1611, *v.* cocker); *le Eyes* 1611 (cf. *insulas iuxta Bolyn versus Mottrom* c.1250–88, *v.* ēg 'a water-meadow', cf. 196 *supra*); *Heyeleyes* c.1250–88 ('high clearings', *v.* hēah, lēah; also called *Heyebirches* (ib), cf. Heybridge Lane 194 *supra*); *Nouthereuse* c.1250–88 ('the lower edge (of a wood)', *v.* neoðera, efes); *Tiderington Heath* 1611 (*v.* hǣð; on the Bollington boundary, cf. Turnerheath 190 *supra*).

21. UPTON (110–9074)

> Upton e13 Orm², 1286 *Eyre et freq*, (*-Superior*) 1315 *AddCh*,
> (*Ouer(e)-*) 1366 *Dow, Plea*, (*-Falebrome*) 1384 (1528) *Dow*,
> (*-iuxta Maclesfeldiam*) 1545 *ib*, *-ia* e13 (1608) ChRR, *-e* (*superior*)
> 1315 *Dow, -tune* 1232 Orm² (p), *-toun* 1361 *Dow*
> *Hup(e)ton* c.1233 *Dow*, Orm²
> *Opton* 1285 *Eyre*, E2 *JRC*, 1348 *Mont, Hoptona* l13 *Dow*

'High farm', *v.* upp, tūn. Presumably the village had a higher and
a lower part, *v.* uferra, superior. Cf. Fallibroome, Macclesfield 197,
113 *supra*.

WHITFIELD BROOK & MOUNT

> *Ratonfeld* 1288 Court, (*the*), *-es* 1497 *Dow, Ratounesfeld* 1331 *ib*,
> *Ratonesmosse* 1347 *Eyre, -feld* 1365 *Dow*, (*the*) 1460 Orm², ChRR,
> *Ratonsfeld* 1495 ib, *-tunes-* 1341 *Eyre, -tuns-* 1495 (1528) *Dow*,
> *Ratunfeld* 1553 *ib*, *Rotten feilde* 1602 ib, *-fieldes* 1611 *LRMB*
> 200, (*the*), *-Feildes or the Whytfeildes* 1625 *Dow*
> *Whitfeld* 1495 ChRR, (*le-*) 1545 *Dow, -e, -fyld* 1551 *ib, -field* 1589 *ib*,
> (*Great*) 1637 ChRR, *-feild* 1596 *Dow, Whytfeld* 1551, *-e* 1585 *ib*,
> *-feild* 1611 *LRMB* 200, *-feildes* 1625 *Dow, Whitefeld* 1528,
> *-field(e, -s)* 1596 *ib*, (*Brooke & Lane*) 1620 *Surv, Whytefylde* 1582
> *Dow, the Whyttelfeld* 1553 *ib*

'The rat-infested-, the rat's field', 'the white field', *v.* raton, hwīt,
feld, mos, cf. Prestbury Rd 123 *supra*. The place is described as *terra
quae fuit Orme Rata'ii* c.1288 Orm², (*Ratarii*) Earw, (*Raton'*) *Mont*,
(cf. Earw II 7), 'the land which belonged to Orme the rat-catcher',
from the pers.n. ON *Ormr*, ODan *Orm* and MedLat *ratonarius* 'a
rat-catcher'. The brook joins R Bollin 15 *supra*.

ASHFIELD.   BACKLANE FM, *Back Lane Cottage* 1842 OS, *Hammon
Shaw* 1831 Bry, cf. Backlane Ho 121 *supra*. The earlier name is from
sceaga 'a wood', with an unid. first el.   BOLLIN BROOK FM, named
from R. Bollin, *v.* 16 supra.   BROOKSIDE, near Whitfield Brook
supra.   HALFMILE HO, 1831 Bry.   HIGHFIELD HO.   MOUNT
PLEASANT.   RYELANDS, *v.* rye-land.   SWISS COTTAGE.   SYCA-
MORE.   UPTON COTTAGE, GRANGE, HALL, PRIORY & WOOD, *the
hall of Upton* 1624 Orm², *Upton Hall* 1632 Earw, *The Priory* 1831 Bry,
Upton Cottage & Priory 1842 OS, *The Grange* 1860 White.   The

Grange and the *Priory* are modern residences. WESTBANK HO, 1842 OS. YEW TREE FM.

FIELD-NAMES

The undated forms are 1848 *TA* 406. Of the others 1315 is *Dow* and *AddCh*, 1384 *Rental*, 1611 *LRMB* 200, 1689 Rich, 1831 Bry.

(a) Barn Fd (cf. *the barne crofte* 1611); Clay Holes; Fosters Barn 1831; Frog Mdw; Garden Fd; Gather Wind (cf. Windgather 111 *supra*); Hough Wd (v. hōh); Hunger Knowl (v. hungor, cnoll); Kershut ('marsh-corner', v. kjarr, scēat); Long Butts; Ox Hey; Sweet Fd; Thistley Fd; Upton Pit; Well Croft (*the walle crofte* 1611, v. wælla); Windmill Fd; Wood Mdw.

(b) *Le Bircheneflattes* 1315 ('flats growing with birches', v. bircen[2], flat); *Le Coldewalle* 1315 (v. cald 'cold', wælla 'a spring'); *le Firr(e) Croslondes*, *-landes* 1315 (v. feor, comp. firra (Angl, cf. fierra WSax) 'further', cros 'cross', land 'a strip of land'); *the Kilne crofte* 1611; *the long meadow* 1611; *the long Shoote* 1611 (v. scēat); *lytelcrofte* 1384 (v. lȳtel, croft); *Le Marlput(es)* 1315 (v. marle-pytt); *the mossefieldes* 1611, *Mosse fields* 1689 (v. mos, cf. *Ratonesmosse* 1347 *Eyre* under Whitfield *supra*); *the new Close* 1611; *the great & little Poole field* 1611 (v. pōl[1]); *the Schowe Broade* 1611 (cf. *le Schelebrode* 125 *supra*, v. scofl-brǣdu).

22. WOODFORD (101–8882)

Wid(e)ford(e) 1248 Ipm, 1249 IpmR *et freq*, (*in Ponyngton*) 113 ChF, *-fort(he)* 1455 MidCh, 1481 *Dav*, *Wyd(e)ford* 1276 Cl, 1348 *Eyre et freq*, (-*in villa de Ponynton*) 1369 *Eyre*, *-e* 1350 *ib*, *-fort* 1521 *Dow*, *Wydyforde* 1350 *Eyre*
Wodeford 1296 *Dav*, 1376 *Eyre*, *Wodford* 1419 JRL (p), *-e* 1498 ChRR, *Woddefort* 1480 Adl, *Wood(e)ford(e)* 1430 MidCh (p), 1488 ChRR, 1536 Leland
Wedeford 1349, 1417 Orm[2], 1437 *Dav*

'Ford at a wood', from wudu (earlier OE widu), and ford. The name is probably that of a crossing of R. Dean at Deanwater Bridge (101–877818).

BACK LANE (FM), *Back Lane* 1842 OS, cf. 254 *infra*. BRICKYARD PLANTATION, cf. *Brick Croft* 1848 *TA*. THE CROFT. DEAN-WATER BRIDGE & HO, *Deyne Water infra Wydford* 1552 *Dav*, *Dean-water* 1632 Earw, v. wæter, cf. R. Dean 20 *supra*, Woodford *supra*. FODEN FIELD. HAWTHORN FM. HILLTOP FM, 1842 OS. KINGSTREET (now DEAN FM, 1″ O.S., 101–877823), origin and age

unknown. The approach road was *Jack Lane* 1831 Bry, *v.* jack.
LUMB FM, *v.* Lumb Brook[1] 30 *supra.*   MOOREND FM, 1831 ib.
MOOR FM, cf. *Far & Near Moor, Moor Field* 1848 *TA.*   MOSS
WOOD, *Wydefordmosse* 1341 Eyre, *Wydford Mosse* 1500 Dav, 1521
Dow, *v.* mos.   NEW HALL FM, *Newhall* c.1620 Orm[2], *Woodford
Hall* 1724 NotCestr, cf. Old Hall *infra.*   OLDFOLD, 1848 *TA*, *v.*
ald, fald.   OLD HALL FM, *the Hall of Woodford* 1593 Earw,
Woodford Old Hall 1831 Bry, cf. *Hall Lane* 1831 ib, New Hall *supra.*
PUMP FM.   SCHOOLHOUSE FM.   SQUAREFIELD TERRACE, *Wrights*
1831 ib, cf. *Square Field* 1848 *TA.*   LOWER & UPPER SWINESEYE,
Swineseye 1831 Bry, *Swines Hey* 1842 OS, 'swine's enclosure',
v. swīn[1], (ge)hæg.   YEWTREE FM, 1842 ib.

FIELD-NAMES

The undated forms are 1848 *TA* 447. Of the others 1831 is Bry, 1842 OS,
1289 *ChFine*, 1348 *Eyre*, 1521, 1552 Dav, 1766 *Dow.*

(*a*) Acre; Bailey Croft (*v.* baillie); Barber Mdw; Barkers Croft; Barley
Croft; Barn Fd; Barratt's Croft, Barretts; Bean Croft; Billy Moor; Blackears
(cf. Blackeyer 265 *infra*); Blake Fd (*v.* blæc); Bog Moss; Bottoms (*v.* botm);
Brisk Fd; Broad Fd; Brook Fd; Broom; Bubotham Fd (perhaps 'booth
bottom; the hollow at a herdsman's shelter', *v.* bōth, botm); Burn Mdw;
Burnt Stack; Burton Fd (*v.* burh-tūn); Butty (*v.* butty); Calf Croft; Carr
(Mdw) (*Wydfford Kerr alias Kerr Medowez* 1552, *v.* kjarr, mǣd); Cart
House Croft; Chantley Fd; Clark Fd; Cliff Hey; Clover Moss; Coffin Croft;
Cranberry Beds 1842; Croft; Davenport's Croft; Dry Fd; Echop (*v.* hop[1]);
Ellyew Fd; Fallow Fd; Ferishaw Croft; Flash Fd (*v.* flasshe); Folly (*v.*
folie); Gosty Croft (*v.* gorstig); Grammums Croft (cf. *Grandmother's Croft*
1766, probably dower-land); Green Hill; Great & Little Heath; Herry Hay;
Hey Fd (*v.* (ge)hæg); Hill Fd; Hollow Fd; Homestead Croft; Horse
Pasture; Hoycome Flat; Hudstead (probably 'site of a shelter', from hōd
and stede, but cf. Hutstead 227 *infra*); Hunt Fd; Intake (*v.* inntak); Isles
('hillocks' *v.* hygel); Jack Croft (*v.* jack, cf. Kingstreet *supra*); Jenny Hey;
Jenny Lane End; Kitchen Mdw, Kitchenend Fd; Knole, Knowles (*v.* cnoll);
Lime Fd; Long Butts; Long Flatts; Long Lane 1831; Lostock (*v.* Lostock-
hall 208 *supra*); Lout; Marl Fans, Fd & Heys; Mead (*v.* mǣd); Meadow
Blows; Meadow Spot (*v.* spot 'a small piece'); Mill Fd; Moat Fd; Morgans
Croft; Nankeen Fd; Old Croft; Old Woman's Mdw (cf. Grammums Croft
supra); Orchard Croft; Parrott Croft; Pig Fd; Pingot (*v.* pingot); Plough
Piece; Priest Fd; Push Ploughed Fd (*v.* push-plough); Rough; Round Croft;
Royal, Royle Fd ('rye-hill', *v.* ryge, hyll); Rushy Fd; Sandhole Fd; Shaw
Shette ('copse corner', *v.* sceaga, scēat); Sheep Cote & Hey; Long Sheete
(*v.* scēat); Shipponing Fd (*v.* scypen); Shirt Croft (*v.* scerde); Six Acre(s);
Slate Mdw & Moor (*v.* slæget); Sludge Fd (*v.* sludge); Soond Fd (*v.* sand);

Stack Croft; Stackyard; Stock Fd; Sutton Mdw (v. sūð, tūn); Tan Yard; Tenter Croft (v. tentour); Warren Fd (v. wareine); Wash Fd (v. wæsce); Water Croft; Well Mdw; White Fd; Whitley Carr ('(marsh at) the white wood', v. hwīt, lēah, kjarr); Will Croft; William Fd; Big & Little Within Fd (v. wiðign); Worthington Fd; Wrenshaw Mdw (cf. 227 infra); Yarwood Mdw; Yolk of the Egg (v. 336 infra).

(b) alta strata and Derlingesyate 1289 ('the high street' and 'Darling's gate', from OE dēorling 'darling' (perhaps as a pers.n.) and geat 'a gate', referring to the supposedly Roman road along Bramhall Lane, Pepper Street & Street Fields 259, 260 infra, v. Oldgate 45 supra); del Eyes 1348 (p), the ees 1521 ('water-meadows', v. ēg); la Lydyate 1289, (v. hlid-geat); les Neweputtes 1289 ('the new pits', v. nīwe, pytt); la Russhylach(e) 1289 ('the rushy bog', v. riscig, læc(c)); les Turfputtes 1289 ('the turf pits, the peat diggings', v. turf, pytt).

x. Wilmslow

The ancient parish consisted of 1. Wilmslow (the church and churchyard), 2. Bollin Fee (including the hamlet of Hough), 3. Chorley (including the now separate c.p. of Alderley Edge), 4. Fulshaw, 5. Pownall Fee (including the hamlets of Morley and Styal, the latter of which had a brief existence as a c.p. in the nineteenth century). This survey follows the boundaries drawn in Bryant's map of 1831.

1. WILMSLOW (101–8481)

Bolyn ecclesia 13 IpmR 1 46

Wilmesloe m13 Fitt (p), *Wil-*, *Wylmeslowe* 1287 Eyre, l13 Fitt et freq, *-low* 1330, 1354 ib, *-louwe* 1348 Eyre, *-lawe* 1286, 1287 Court, *-ley* 1629 Sheaf, *Willmeslawe* 1513 Plea, *Wilmislawe*, *-lowe* 1260 ib, *Wyl-* 1289 Court (p), *Wylmyslow* 1552 Dav, *Willmislowe* 1317 Fitt, *Wil-*, *Wylmuslo(u)we* 1331 ib, 1341 Eyre, 1411 Chol

Wimmislowe 1286 Court, *Wymmeslow* 1469 AD, *Wymslowe* 1498 ChRR, *Wym(e)slow(e)*, *-is-*, *-ys-* 1533 Earw, 1535 VE, Sheaf, *Wimslow* 1696 ib

Wilmslowe 1286 AddCh (church of), 1288 Court (p), *-lo* 1653 Sheaf, *-low* c.1620 Orm², 1724 NotCestr, *-ley* 1629 Sheaf, *Wylmslow* 1513 Earw

Wyneslowe 1341 Eyre (p), *Wyn(n)slowe* 1535 Sheaf

Welmeslowe 1352 Eyre (p), 1348 Sheaf, *Wemslow* 1521 ib

Windesloo 1480 Earw

Wymbslow 1535 Sheaf

Wylnslawe 1550 MinAcct

'Wīghelm's mound', from the OE pers.n. *Wīghelm* and hlāw. In the first form, the church is 'the church of Bollin', cf. Bollin Fee *infra*, to which the advowson belonged. This p.n. is confused with that of Wimboldsley 335 *infra*, in *Wynbaldeleg* c.1230 Orm² III 587n., and *Wimboldsley or Wilmslow* c.1620 ib 545. Wilmslow is the name of the church and churchyard, extended to the old village which lay in the townships of Bollin Fee and Pownall Fee (Orm² III 586). The street-names of this village, and unidentified f.ns. and minor-names for the parish as a whole, are grouped for convenience.

STREET-NAMES

CHANCEL LANE, running past the chancel end of Wilmslow Church; CLAY LANE, *v.* clǣg; CLIFF ROAD, cf. *The Cliff* 1860 White, *v.* clif; DUNGEON WALK, a narrow footpath; GREEN LANE, 1860 ib, *Parsonage Green* 1831 Bry, cf. Green 222 Hall *infra*; GROVE AVE. & ST., cf. *Grove Cottage* 1860 White, Grove Fel 233 *infra*; HALL RD, HAWTHORN GROVE, LANE & WALK, cf. Hawthorn Hall 229 *infra*; HAWTHORN ST., *Pepper Street* 1842 OS, cf. prec. and Pepper Street (Chester) 333 *infra*; LADYFIELD ST., cf. Ladyfield 223 *infra*; MACCLESFIELD RD, *Macclesfield Lane* 1840 *TA*, cf. Macclesfield 113 *supra*; MILL LANE & RD, cf. Corn Mill 222 *infra*; NEWTOWN; OLD BROW, *v.* brū; WATER LANE, R. Bollin, *v.* wæter.

FIELD-NAMES

For modern names cf. the several townships. The sources of the following unidentified names are 13¹ Cre 353, 13², c.1280, c.1330 *Fitt*, 1287 Court, 1337 *Eyre*, 1348, 1595, 1609 Earw.

(b) *le*, *la Bache* 13² ('the valley-stream', *v.* bæce¹); *Bulegrene* 1595 ('bull green', *v.* bula, grēne²); *Impeyord* 13² ('nursery', *v.* impe-ȝard); *Scharechale* 13¹, *Scharshal* 1287 (p), *-e*, *Charshale* c. 1330 (p), *Sharshale* 1337 (p), *Sharshall* 1348 (*v.* halh. The first el. is obscure. Professor Löfvenberg suggests an OE pers.n. **Scear*, corresponding to ODan *Skar* as in Scarisbrick La 124); *the Toade Lane* 1609 (*v.* tāde); *Vinnecrumbe* 13¹, *Winetrumbe* c.1280 (p) ('pasture bend', *v.* winn¹, crumbe).

2. BOLLIN FEE

> *dominium de Bolyn* c.1237 Earw, 1329 *Fitt*, *-Bollen* 1666 *ChCert*
> *villa de bolin* m13 *Dav*, *-e* 1286 *Eyre*
> *Bollen Fee* 1626 Earw, *Bollin-Fee* 1724 NotCestr, *township of Bollinfee* 1819 Earw

'The lordship of Bollin', from the river-name Bollin (15 *supra*), and ME feo (OFr *feu*, MedLat *feudum*), cf. Bollin Hall *infra*, Wilmslow 219 *supra*.

Bollin Hall (101-8581)

(manerium de) *Bolinn* e13 MidCh, *-ynne* 1286 *Eyre*, *-enne* 1289
Court, *-yn* c.1220 Tab, c.1237 Orm[1], Earw *et freq*, (a messuage
called the manor of) 1477 ChRR, *-in* m13 *Dav*, 1317 *Fitt*, *-yne*
c.1280 *ib*, 1285 *Eyre*, *-ine* 1286 *ib*, *-en* 1523 ChRR
Bollin 1314 Plea *et freq*, (*Park*(*e*)) c.1620 Orm[2], 1633, 1682 Earw,
(*Hall*) 1724 NotCestr, *-yn* 1428 (1551) ChRR, 1634 JRL, *-en*
1536 ChRR

'Place on R. Bollin', named from the R. Bollin 15 *supra*, v. hall,
park. Cf. Bollin Fee *supra*, Bollington 187 *supra*, 330 *infra*.

Hough (Green & Lane), locally The Hough [t'ʌf] (101-8679), *le Hogh* 1289 (17) Court, 1324 *Fitt*, *le Houggh* 1329 *ib*, *the Houghe House* 1610 Earw, *Hough* 1601 *Traff*, (*in Wilmslow*) 1740 *JRC*, v. hōh 'a ridge'. The place lies under Alderley Edge 95 *supra*. Cf. Mains Fm *infra*. The form *Hoh'* 1176-1208 Chest, ascribed by DEPN to 'Hough near Knutsford', refers to Hoo Green in Mere 332 *infra*. Cf. Hough 332 *infra*.

Colshaw (101-8582)

Collesawe c.1280 *Fitt*, *-schagh* 1341 *Eyre*
Colsahe c.1280 *Fitt*, *-sache* l13 Earw, *-sagh* 1345 ib, *-shaw* 1320
Plea (p), *-e* 1609 Earw, *-schagh* 1336 *Mass* (p), *-shagh* 1341
Plea (p)
Cholsahe e14 *Fitt*
Astles Farm 1831 Bry

'Charcoal copse', c. col[1], sceaga. *Astle* is the surname from Astle
76 *supra*.

Dean Row (101-8681)

le Dene 1286, 1290 Court (p), *Eyre* (p), 1336 *Mass*, 1357 *Eyre* (p),
Dene 1371 ib
Denerawe, *-rowe* 1477 ChRR, Orm[1], *-row* 1512 Earw, *Deynerowe*
1477 ChRR, *-Row* 1552 *Dav*, (*the*) *Deynrowe* 1529 Earw, *-Roe*
1531 ib, *Deaneroe* 1580 Orm[2], *-rowe* 1624, *Dean Rowe* 1628 Earw,
-Row 1724 NotCestr, *Dane Row* 1840 *TA* 327

'Row (of houses) at a valley', v. denu, rǣw. This hamlet lies
between the valleys of the rivers Bollin and Dean 15, 20 *supra*. The

r.n. Dean may be taken from this place. The first record is the surname of Heyne *del Dene* of *Bolynne* (Bollin Fee), Court 217. But the valley in question may be that at Bollington 187 *supra*, in which case Dean Row is named after the river.

FINNEY GREEN (101–8582)

> *Wyctunstall* 1286 *Eyre* (lit. *Wyotunstall* Court 220), *Wyktonstal(l)* 1347, 1368 *ib*, *Wykedonstall* 1370 *ib* (p)
> *Wygetunstal'* 1286 *Eyre* (p), *Wigtonstalle* 1355 BPR (p)
> *Wictetunstal* 13 Cre (p)
> *Wittonstall* 1302 Earw, *Wytonestal* 1354 *Eyre* (p), *Wydonstall* 1370 *ib* (p), *Wyttonnstall* 1378 *ib* (p), *Wyttynstall* 1453 ChRR (p)
> *Wytstonstal* 1341 *Eyre*, *Wykstonstall* 1357 *ib*
> *Finney Green* 1831 Bry

'The site of the enclosure with a dwelling in it', *v.* wīc-tūn, stall. The modern name is taken from the family of John *Finney* who married the heiress of the *Wittonstall* family in 1608 (Earw I 149), *v.* grēne² 'a green', cf. *Finney Field* 1840 *TA*, Finney Lee 226 *infra*.

THE HEYES, HEYES LANE, *le Hegh* 1336 *Fitt* (p), (two places called) *Heyis* 1343 *ib*, *Far, Near & Chorley Heys, Big & Lt. Jenny Heys* 1840 *TA*, *Jenneyshey Lane* 1831 Bry, *Janesheys Lane* 1842 OS, 'the enclosures', *v.* (ge)hæg, with the fem. pers.n. *Jane* and lane 'a lane'. These extend into Chorley 225 *infra*.

ASHFIELD.   BEECH.   BODEN HO, 1831 Bry, *John Bodens House* 1628 Earw.   BOLLINFEE BRIDGE, crossing R. Dean into Handforth, *v.* 254 *infra*.   BIG & LITTLE BRICK HILL FM, *v.* bryke-kyl 'a brick-kiln'.   BROOK FM.   BROWN'S FM.   CASTLE ROCK, on Alderley Edge, probably a figurative name, there being no castle here, *v.* castel(l).   CHONAR, -*House* 1842 OS.   CLAYTON'S FM, cf. *Clayton Field* 1840 *TA*.   CORN MILL, 1831 Bry, *unum molendinum* 1246 Earw, *molendinum de Bolyne* 13 Fitt, -*Bolyn* c.1330 *ib*, *v.* myln, cf. Bollin Fee & Hall *supra*.   THE CROFT.   DEANBANK, cf. Dean Row *supra*.   DEANWATER BRIDGE, *v.* 217 *supra*.   FAULKNER'S FM, cf. *Falkners Field* 1840 *TA*.   GREEN END, *Dean Row Green* 1831 Bry, cf. Dean Row *supra*, *v.* grēne², ende¹.   GREEN HALL, named from *Parsonage Green* 1831 Bry, cf. Green Lane 220 *supra*.   HANDFORTH BRIDGE, crosses R. Dean into Handforth 254

infra. HILLSIDE.   HILLTOP, 1831 ib.   THE HOLE.   THE
HOLLIES, *Adsheads* 1831 ib, from the surname from Adshead 100
supra. THE HOMESTEAD.   HUNTERS CLOSE.   LADYFIELD, 1840
TA, cf. Ladyfield St. 220 *supra.*   LAND LANE.   LEES LANE, *v.*
206 *supra.*   MAINS FM, or HOUGH HALL FM, *Mears Farm* 1831
Bry, cf. *Great, Little, Higher & Middle Main(s)* 1840 *TA,* and Hough
supra, v. main 'demesne land, home farm'.   MALTKIN FM.
MANOR HO.   THE MEADOW.   MOSS TERRACE, cf. *Moss (Croft,
Field, Intake, Lane, Meadow & Piece)* 1840 *TA.*   NEW INN, 1840
ib.   OLD BRIDGE, crossing R. Bollin near Wilmslow Church, cf.
Wilmslow Bridge *infra.*   ROSEVALE FM.   SANDHOLE FM (lost),
1831 Bry, cf. *Sandhole Field* 1840 *TA.*   SOUTH LODGE, cf. *Lodge
Field Wood* 1831 Bry, *v.* loge. This is at Bollin Hall *supra.*   SWISS
VILLA, *Swiss Cottage* 1860 White, cf. Swiss Hill 225 *infra.*   THORN-
GROVE, 1860 ib.   THORN HO.   UNICORN (p.h.), 1831 Bry.
UPTON HO, 1831 ib.   VERDON BRIDGE & HO, *Vardon House in
Hough* 1616 Earw, part of *dominium de Verdone in Com. Cestriae* 1434
Dugd, named after the family of Geoffrey or Edmund *le Verdon* 1339,
1387 Earw 1 151, cf. Vardentown 102 *supra.*   WHARTON (lost),
1831 Bry.   WHITE HALL (BRIDGE), *the Whyte Haule* 1587 Earw,
-Hall 1596 ib, *v.* hwīt, hall.   WILMSLOW BRIDGE, crossing R.
Bollin at Wilmslow, cf. Old Bridge *supra.*   WILMSLOW PARK,
parcum Ricardi (de Fyton) 13 Fitt, *a fair house and park called Bollin
Park* c.1620 Orm², *Bollin parke* 1633 Earw, *v.* park, cf. Bollin Hall
supra.   WIZARD'S WELL, *Holly Well* 1831 Bry, *Holy Well* 1842 OS,
cf. The Wizard of the Edge (p.h.) 98 *supra, v.* hālig, wella.   WOOD-
BANK, a house, on the site of Bent Wood *infra.*   YEWS FM.
YEWTREE.

FIELD-NAMES

The undated forms are 1840 *TA* 57. Of the others, e14 is *Fitt,* c.1300, 1437¹,
1447, 1463, 1609, 1610, 1616, 1628 Earw, 1361 *Eyre,* 1428 (1551), 1437²,
1472 ChRR, 1437³ Orm², 1628 JRL 32, 1724 NotCestr, 1831 Bry. For (*b*)
cf. also 220 *supra.*

(*a*) Aarons Acre; Alders Croft; Ashwood 1831; Badder Croft; Bailey
Moss (*v.* baillie); Barley Fd; Barn Fd; Barratt mdw (probably from ME
baret 'strife, trouble, dispute', referring to land of disputed ownership, cf.
Barettfelde 239 *infra*); Barrow Croft (*v.* bearg); Bate Mdw; Bean Fd; Bear
Wood Mdw; Ben Acre (*v.* bēan); Bend Mdw; Bent; Bent Wd 1831 (*v.*
beonet); Birch Mdw; Black Croft & Fd; Blake Earth (*v.* blæc, eorðe); Booth's
Acre; Bottoms (cf. *Bothumlondes* e14, *-landes* c.1300, *del Bothum de Bolyn*

1361 (p), from botm, boðm 'a valley bottom', and land 'a strip of land'); Brady Croft; Brick Kiln Fd; Britters Mdw; Broad Fd & Hey; Brook Mdw; Broom Hill; Brow Fd & Side; Browy Fd; Bunk Mdw; Burgess Croft; Burton Croft; Buxton Mdw; Carr (v. kjarr); Carrott Fd; Cash Fd; Castle Fd (v. castel(l)); Chamber End; Chapel Park; Chorley Croft & Moss (cf. Moss Lane, Chorley 225 infra); Clay Croft & Flat; Big Cloose (v. clos); Clough Fd; Clover Croft & Fd; Coll(e)y Fd (v. colig); Coppy Mdw (v. copis); Corn Fd; Cote Fd & Mdw; Cow Hey; Crabtree Fd; Craggs Mdw; Cranberry Moss; Croft Green; Daisey Fd; Down below field; Dob's Croft; Door Fd (v. duru); Dove Lands; Duckers Orchard; Fallow (v. falh); Ferry Fd; First Fd; Five Acre; Flax Butts (v. fleax, butte); Fulshaw Moss Pitt (cf. Fulshaw 227 infra); Garden Fd; Gee Croft (v. gee); Glade Fd; Gold Fd (v. golde); Gorsty Fd; Grandmother Mdw; Green Croft; Greets Croft, Greety Croft (v. grēot 'gravel', -ig³); Hackney Hey (cf. Hackney Lane 1831, v. hakenai); Half Corner; Halilands 1724; Hallow Mdw; Hard Fd; Hare Hole; Harry Lane; Hawk (v. halc); Hazle Fd; Heath Park; Hedge Croft; Henshaw Bank ('hen wood', v. henn, sceaga); Hey Croft (v. (ge)hæg); High Butts (v. hēah, butte); High Heath; Hob Mdw (v. hobb(e)); Hollow Lane Fd; Horse Mdw & Pasture; House Fd & Mdw; Hungerhill (v. hungor); Intake (v. inntak); Jack Fd (v. jack); John's Croft; Kelsall Fd (cf. Kelsall House 1616, probably from the surname from Kelsall 332 infra); Kiln Fd & Hill; Knowl (v. cnoll); Lane Croft & Fd; Lapwing Fd; Lawton Mdw; Lee Mdw (v. lēah); Lifeless Moss 1831 (v. līf-lēas); Lime Croft; Lions Mdw; Little Moss; Long Butts & Shoots (v. butte, scēat); Loon Fd (v. land 'a strip of land'); Macclesfield Mdw (cf. Macclesfield 113 supra); Marl Fd; Mary's Hill (cf. St Mary's Cliff 226 infra); Meadow Brow; Middle Fd; Mill Bottom & Fd (v. botm); Muttons Fd; Narrow Slip (v. slipe); New Acre; Nine Acre(s) (cf. Nine Acre Wood 1831); Nut Woods (v. hnutu); Old Mdw; Oven Back (v. ofen, bæc); Over Acre & Croft (v. uferra); Ox Hey; Park Fd; Pigeon Hill; Pingot (v. pingot); Pit Fd; Potatoe Moss; Railway Piece; Recabuck; Road Fd (v. rād); Roast Meads; Rood Acre (probably land dedicated to a rood-cross, v. rōd²); Rough; Round Croft, Fd, Flat & Hey; Rushy Bent (v. beonet); Rye Croft & Fd; Saddle Brow (v. sadol, brū, cf. Saddlebole 102 supra); Sandy Thart; Sawpit Croft (v. saw-pytt); School Fd; Little Schoolmaster, Schoolmaster's Mdw; Short Butts (v. sc(e)ort, butte); Siddall Croft; Side Slip (v. sīde, slipe); Slack Leech ('boggy stream at a hollow', v. slakki, læc(c)); Sludge Mdw (v. sludge); Smith(y) Fd; Soon Fd (v. sand); Spiggot; Spout Mdw (v. spoute); Square Croft & Fd; Stable Fd & Mdw; Stack Fd; Stocking Mdw (v. stoccing); Summer Work Fd (a field left fallow in summer, v. summer-work NED); Swells Fd; Tan Fd; Thistley Fd; Three Corner'd Croft, Three Nook'd Mdw; Toll Barr Fd; Trench Fd; Trough Fd & Mdw (v. trog); Trout Pits; Walk Mill Heys (v. walke-milne, (ge)hæg); Wall Mdw (v. wælla 'a well, a spring'); Walter Fd; Wantons Fd; Wash Fd (v. wæsce); Watches; Water Pipe Fd; Weir Course; Well Croft, Fd & Mdw; Wheat Fd, Hey & Stubble; White Heads (v. hēafod); White Hey; Great & Little White Leech (Mdw) (Whitelach, -lage 1463, -lache 1472, 'white bog', v. hwīt, læc(c)); White Leys (v. lēah); Wilkin Fd; Wood Fd; Woodwards Mdw; Yellow Croft & Mdw.

(b) *Bolyn Home* 1428 (1551), 1437, (*le-*) 1447, *-holme* 1437, *Holmes Lane* 1628 (*v.* holmr 'water-meadow', cf. Bollin Fee & Hall *supra*); *The Killcarrs* 1609, 1620, 1628 ('kiln marsh', *v.* cyln, kjarr, cf. Carr *supra*); *Stanyfurlong* c.1300 (*v.* stǎnig, furlang).

3. CHORLEY (101–8378)

Cheorleia 12 Earw

Chorlegh c.1200 *Fitt et freq*, (*-iuxta Werford*) 1364 *Eyre*, *-leg* c.1330 *Fitt*, *-lei* 13 Cre, *-leya* 13 *Fitt*, *-ley* 1357 ChRR (p) *et freq*, *-lee* 1285 *Eyre*, *-lay* 1411 *Chol*

Cherleg' 1286 *Eyre*, c.1313 *SocAnt* (p), c.1330 *Fitt*, *-legh* E2 Orm², 1329 *Fitt* (p), 1341 *Eyre*, *-le* 1310 Cl, *-leigh* 1313 *SocAnt* (p)

Charlegh 1393 Adl (p)

Jorle 1420 *JRC* (p)

'Peasants' clearing', *v.* ceorl, lēah. For *Jorle*, *v.* 332 *infra*.

ALDERLEY EDGE, 1860 White, now a distinct c.p. formed from the eastern half of Chorley township with parts of the hamlet of Hough in Bollin Fee 221 *supra*, named after the hill Alderley Edge 95 *supra*, and, until 1779 'a dreary common containing nothing but a goodly number of Scotch firs' (cf. White 883, Orm² III 567).

STREET-NAMES

ALDERLEY RD & LONDON RD, *v. Street Lane* 98 *supra*; HEYES LANE, *v.* The Heyes 222 *supra*; LONDON RD, *v.* Alderley Road *supra*; LYDIATE LANE, *Lidyate in Chorley* 1610 Earw, 'a swing gate', *v.* hlid-geat, cf. Trafford Fm *infra*; MOSS LANE, cf. Chorley Moss 224 *supra*; SWISS HILL, a road of villas supposedly in a Swiss style, cf. Swiss Villa 223 *supra*; TRAFFORD RD, cf. Trafford Fm *infra*.

THE RYLEYS (FM), RYLEYS LANE, *Ruylegh* 1304 Chamb (p), 1309 Plea, *-leg'* c.1320 *Fitt* (p), *Ryley* 1399 ChRR (p), (*Great & Little*) 1645 Cre, 'rye clearing', *v.* ryge, lēah.

BROOK COTTAGE & HO, 1860 White, named from Preston Brook *infra*, cf. foll. BROOK LANE, *Preston Lane* 1842 OS, cf. prec. and *Preston House infra*. BROOMFIELD HO, cf. *Broom Field* 1840 *TA*. CHORLEY HALL (LANE), *Chorlegh Hall* 1640 Earw; now in Alderley Edge c.p. COMMON CARR, *The Carr* 1831 Bry, *Common Cars* 1842 OS, *v.* kjarr. DAVENPORT HO, 1831 Bry, named after the *Daven-*

port family, cf. Davenport Green 231 *infra*.   FIELD'S FM, *Bowers
Farm* 1831 Bry.   FODEN LANE (lost), 1842 OS, *Fodens Lane* 1831
Bry, probably from the surname *Foden*, as in Foden Bank 153 *supra*.
GORSE HO, *Gorsty House* 1831 ib, *Gorses* 1609 Earw, *v.* gorst, gorstig.
GRANGE HO, *The Grange* 1831 Bry, *v.* grange.   THE KNOLL, *-s*
1860 White.   LINDOW (END), *Lindow End* 1831 Bry, cf. Lindow
Moss 230 *infra*.   LINGARDS, from the surname *Lingard*.   MEADOW
BROW.   THE MOSS, LITTLE MOSSES, *Little Moss* 1842 OS.   THE
OAK (lost), 1874 Earw, *The Oake* 1609 ib, *v.* āc.   ORRELLS WELL,
Orrels Well 1831 ib. Orrell is a surname.   OSWALD COTTAGE &
FM.   POOL FIELD (lost), 1860 White.   PRESTON BROOK (> Swim
Brook 36 *supra*), 1882 Orm² III 602, cf. foll. and Brook Lane *supra*.
PRESTON HO, (lost, 101–836790), 1616 Earw, 1860 White, *Homfrey
Preston's House* 1596 Earw, cf. prec. and Brook Lane *supra*. Humfrey
Preston lived here 1590 Earw. His family appears to have given name
to the place, which in turn gave name to the stream.   ROW OF
TREES, 1831 Bry, from a row of lime-trees (Earw I 167).   ST
MARY'S CLIFF (lost), 1860 White, a house, cf. Mary's Hill 224 *supra*.
STONE HO (lost), 1831 Bry, (*the-*) 1679 Earw.   STREET LANE ENDS
(lost, 101–843782), 1831 Bry, cf. *Street Lane Field* 1840 *TA*, *Street
Lane* 98 *supra*.   TANYARD FM, 1842 OS, *Chorley Brook Tan-Yard*
1831 Bry, but not on a stream, *v.* tan-yard.   TRAFFORD FM, cf.
Trafford Villa 1860 White, *Lydiate Homestead* 1840 *TA*, *a fair old
house belonging to the Traffords* c.1620 Orm² III 545, cf. Lydiate Lane
supra. The *de Trafford* family were landlords here.

FIELD-NAMES

The undated forms are 1840 *TA* 108. Of the others 113, 1324, c.1330, 1336
are *Fitt*, e14 Earw, 1831 Bry. For (*b*) cf. also 220 *supra*.

(*a*) The Acre; Alder Fd; Bank; Barley Fd; Barn Fd; Barr Fd (*v.* barre);
Bean Croft; Black Fd; Booths Croft; Bottoms (*v.* botm); Boozy Fd ('field
near the cattle shed', from ModE dial. *boosy, boozy* 'a cow-stall', *v.* bōsig,
bōs); Bradshaw Fd; Brickiln Fd; Bridge Hurst (Lane & Mdw) (*Bruggehursd*
113, *-hurst* e14, 'wood near a bridge', *v.* brycg, hyrst); Broad Oak; Brook
Croft & Fd; Brookes Copy (*v.* copis); Broom Croft; Buxton; Calves Croft;
Chorley Green (Fd); Cinderhill (*v.* sinder); Clough; Clover Fd; Coblers
Acre; Cockshutt (*v.* cocc-scyte); Colt Heys; Crowley (*v.* crāwe, lēah); Day
Fd (*v.* dey); Day Math (*v.* day-math); Day Work Fd (*v.* day-work); Dead
Lane (*v.* dēad); Dear Bought (*v.* 329 *infra*); Dicken Wd; Dingway Brow &
Croft ('way to a muck-heap', *v.* dyngja, weg, cf. 228 *infra*); Dodge; Finney
Lee (*v.* lēah, cf. Finney Green 222 *supra*); Flash Mdw (*v.* flasshe); Garden

Mdw; Garner Fd (*v.* garner); Glade; Golden Croft; Gravel Hole; Green Fd; Greety Croft (*v.* grēot, -ig³); Hazel Croft; Hemp Butt, Mdw & Ridding; Hill Fd; Home Croft; Hoozley (probably 'blackbird glade', *v.* ōsle, lēah); Horse Hey, -Hay; House Fd, Leasow & Mdw (*v.* lǣs); Hungerhill (*v.* hungor); Hutstead (probably 'hut site', from ModE *hut* 'a shed' and stede, but cf. Hudstead 218 *supra*); Intake (*v.* inntak); John's Mdw; Keepers Cockshutt ('gamekeeper's cock-shoot', *v.* cocc-scyte); Kiln Fd; Kitchen Mdw; Lambs Croft; Lions Croft; Lousey Mdw; Main Hays, Heys (*v.* main, cf. Mains Fm 223 *supra*); Marl('d) Fd; Middle Fd & Piece; Moss Croft, Fd, Mdw, Nook & Piece, Long & Middle Moss; Nans Croft (cf. Nansmoss 232 *infra*); Narrow Moss; Nats Croft; New Fd; Nine Acres (*Nine Acre Wood* 1831); Oldham (perhaps 'old enclosure', from ald, hamm, but the final el. may be hulm); Orchard Mdw; Out Fd; Outlet (*v.* outlet); Palisade; Pingot (*v.* pingot); Pit Croft & Fd; Pool Mdw; Poolstead (*v.* pōl-stede); Ridding (*v.* ryding); Road Piece; Robins Croft; Rough Lane, Fd & Moss; Round Mdw & Moss; Rushey Fd & Mdw; Rye Fd; Sandhole Fd; Shade Mdw (perhaps dial. *shade* 'a shed'); Shippon Croft; Slackley Hey(s) ('enclosures at a glade in a hollow', *v.* slakki, lēah); Small Mdw (*v.* smæl); Smith Fd; Spring Pit Carr (*v.* spring 'a well-spring', pytt, kjarr); Square Croft; Sun Fd; Tan Pit Fd; Three Cornered Mdw & Piece; Toad Hole (*v.* tāde, hol¹); Tom Croft (*v.* toun); Top Fd, Piece (*freq*) & Rough; Turnip Croft; Two Brows (*v.* brū); Vetch Fd; Wall Croft (*v.* wælla 'a well, a spring'); Waltons Ground, Far Waltons; Warford Croft (cf. Gt. Warford 104 *supra*); Watch; Well Fd & Mdw; Wheat Fd; Wiery Croft (cf. dial. *wire* 'a plant-stem or tendril, a briar'); Wood Heys (cf. *boscum de Cherleg* c.1330 *v.* wudu, (ge)hæg); Wrenshaw Mdw (perhaps 'wren copse', from wrenna and sceaga. The f.n. also occurs in Woodford 219 *supra*).

(*b*) *le Heth* 1324 (p) (*v.* hæð); *Rohelowe* 113, *Rohalowe* e14 ('rough mound', *v.* rūh, hlāw); *Wetschaus* 1336 ('damp copses' *v.* wēt, sceaga).

4. FULSHAW (101–8480)

Fuleschahe m12 Tab, *-shae* 13 Cre (p), *-schawe* 1252 RBE, 1338 Pat
Fulshea H2 Orm², *Fulschae* c.1200 *Fitt*, *-sh-* 1260 Orm² (p), 1285 Court, *-scha* c.1200 Earw, *-sh-* 1479 ChRR, *-shagh* 1277 Earw, *-sch-* e14 *Fitt* (p), *-e* 1349 *MinAcct*, *-shawe* 1288 *Eyre*, *-sch-* 1349 *ib*, *-shaw* 1521 Sheaf, *-schage* 1317 *Fitt* (p), *-sahe* 13 *ib* (p), *-sawa*, *-sawe* 1260 Plea, Court, *Fulchauue* 1287 ib, *Fullshagh'* 1467 *MinAcct*, *-shage* 1560 Sheaf
Folsaga 12 Earw (p)
Foylsahe 1286 *Eyre* (p)
Foleghshawe 1287 Court (p), *Folischae* 1288 ib
Foulschaye 1317 *Fitt*, *-shawe* 1353 BPR

'Foul copse', *v.* fūl, sc(e)aga, but the spellings *Foyl-* 1286, *Folegh-*

1287 (metathesised), indicate an alternative name 'fowl copse', *v.* fugol, cf. Fullhurst 331 *infra*, Fulshaw Mdw 77 *supra*.

FULSHAW HALL, *Fulshawe Haule* 1587 Earw, (*le*) *Scherd* l13 *Fitt* (p), 1285 Court, *le Shert* 1277 Earw, (p), *le Sherd* 1361 *Eyre* (p), *Scherd in Fulshaw* 1507 Earw, *v.* scerde 'a gap'. The present Fulshaw Hall, on the site of a house called *Sherd* (cf. the family surname *Sherd* in Shirdfold, *Shert Hall* 182 *supra*, 271 *infra*), succeeds an earlier house *the Hall of Fulshaw* 1413 Earw, which stood in a field called *the Blackfield* (Earw I 151, 157), cf. Black Fd, Old Hall Crofts *infra*.

ALCOCK GREEN (local), 1860 White, 1880 Earw, named after the family of Edward *Alcock* 1613 Earw I 154n.   BLACKBROOK COTTAGE.   BROOKFIELD.   BROOKFIELD BRIDGE, crossing Preston Brook, cf. Brook Lane 225 *supra*.   BROOK LANE, 1860 White, cf. Brook Lane prec.   CHORLTON HO, cf. *Chorlton's Croft* 1840 *TA*. FULSHAW BANK, CROSS & HO, *v.* banke, cros.   FULSHAW PARK, *Hawkers Green* 1831 Bry.   HAREFIELD (FM).   PUMP HO (lost), 1860 White.   STOCKTON FM.

FIELD-NAMES

The undated forms are 1840 *TA* 174. The others are 1393, 1413, 1880 Earw. For (*b*) cf. 220 *supra*.

(*a*) Aspen Fd (*v.* æspen); Barrow Croft (*v.* bearg); Barton Croft (*v.* beretūn); Bent (*v.* beonet); Black Acre; Black Fd (*the Blackfield* 1413, *v.* blæc, feld, cf. Fulshaw Hall *supra*, Old Hall Crofts *infra*); The Bottoms (*v.* botm); Brick Kiln Fd; Brook Mdw; Broom Fd; Butterfly Bank; Dark Heys (*v.* deorc, (ge)hæg); Dingway Croft & Mdw (*v.* 226 *supra*); Goodman's Acre 1880 (cf. *Gudamons* 1393, probably from gōd-mann or the ME pers. byname *Good-*, *God-*, *Gudman* (Reaney 137)); Half Kernel; Hardhill Brow (*v.* heard, hyll, brū); Hare Mdw (*v.* hara); Hawthorn Croft; Hollands Croft, Little Holland Mdw; Honest Mdw; Lancashire Acre; Loon Fd (*v.* land); Massey Croft (from the family *Massey*, landowners here); Old Hall Crofts 1880 (*v.* ald, hall, cf. Fulshaw Hall *supra*); Peas Hill (*v.* pise); Pingot (*v.* pingot); Poor Fd; Round Heys; Rush Fd; Sand Fd; Shippon Fd; Singa Moor; Smithy Fd; Three Nook Fd; White Knowl; Windmill Fd.

5. POWNALL FEE, 1634 JRL, *feodum de Pownehale* 1290 Ipm *et freq* with spellings as for Pownall Hall *infra*, from which it is named, with ME feo 'a fee, a lordship', cf. Bollin Fee 220 *supra*.

MORLEY (GREEN) (101–8282)

> *Morlegh* c.1200 *Fitt et freq*, (*in Pounale*) 1328 *ib*, (*parcum de*) 1358
> *MinAcct, -leg'* 13 *Fitt*, (*le-*) c.1320 *ib*, -*ley*(*e*) 1330 Pat (p), 1332
> Ipm (p), *Morely* 1655 Sheaf
> *Morlengis* 1286 *Eyre* (p)
> *Morlees* 1329 *Mass*
> *The Green* 1831 Bry

'Woodland glade at a moor', *v.* mōr[1], lēah.

POWNALL HALL (101–8381) & FM

> *Pohenhale* c.1166 Chest, *Pokenhal* 1286 Pat, *Pownehale* 1290 Ipm,
> *Pwenale* 1408 ChRR, *Pouenall* 1460 Rich
> *Pounale* c. 1200 *Fitt et freq, -hal* 1287 Court, *Pounal* 1357 Chamb (p),
> -*all* 1388 ChRR *et freq*, (*Hall*) 1536 ib, *Pownall* 1397 ib *et freq*, (*the*
> *Hall of*) 1598 Earw, (*Halle*) 1616 ib, *Pownhall* c.1620 Orm[2]
> *Hye Punal* 13 Earw, *Hee Punale* m13 ib, Orm[2], *Punhal*(*e*) 1287
> Court
> *Penyale* e14 *Fitt, Pennale* 1378 Plea, 1394 ChRR, -*all* 1490 Adl,
> *Pevnall* (lit. *Pebnall*) 1495 ib
> *Ponal* 1348, 1382 *Eyre, Ponnale* 1382 ib

'Pohha's nook', from the OE pers.n. *Pohha* (cf. **pohha** 'a pouch,
a bag') and halh. Cf. Pownall Bridge 105 *supra*.

STYAL (GREEN) (101–8383)

> *Styhale* c.1200 Orm[2], c.1320, 1337 *Fitt, -hal* 1286 *Eyre, Stihall*
> 1356 *ib*
> *Stiale* (*in Pounale*) 1331 *Fitt*, 1337 *Eyre, Styale* 1352, 1381 *ib*,
> *Styall* 1364 *ib*, 1513 Plea, *Styal* (*Green*) 1842 OS, *Stiall* 1477
> ChRR *et freq*
> *The Green* 1831 Bry

'Corner of land with a sty or pen', *v.* stigu, halh. Smith preferred
this (EPN II 153), but an alternative first el. is stīg 'a path' (DEPN).

HAWTHORN HALL, *Har*(*e*)*thorn*(*e*) c.1200, c.1320, 1337 *Fitt, Haythorn*(*e*)
1512, 1532, 1688 Earw, *Hathorne* 1562 ib, (*the*) *Hawthorn*(*e*) 1655 ib,
1661 Sheaf, 'the hoar thorn', *v.* hār[2], þorn, with later spellings from
hæg-þorn, hagu-þorn 'the hawthorn'.

LINDOW MOSS (101–8281, but formerly 816785 to 830817), an extensive bog giving name to LINDOW COMMON, 1831 Bry, LINDOW COTTAGE, GROVE & Ho and Davenport Green (*infra*) in this township, Lindow Fm in Mobberley 333 *infra*, Lindow (End) in Chorley 226 *supra*, and Lindow End in Great Warford 105 *supra*. The earlier forms are *Lyndowe More* 1421 AddCh, *Great & Little Lindoe* (in Wilmslow and Mobberley parishes respectively) 1608 Sheaf. This is probably 'lime-tree hill', from lind and hōh.

NORCLIFFE FM & HALL (101–8283)

Norheclof c.1200 Fitt
Northcliffe c.1200 (17) Orm², *-cliff* 1276 Cl, *-clyff* 1276 Ipm, *-clif* 1260 Court, *-clyf* 1307 Plea, (vill' de) *-clyve* m13 Earw, (*in Pounale*) 1397 Plea, *Nord(e)-, Nort-, -clyffe, -clif* 1270 Earw, 1276 Ipm, IpmR
(*Le*) *Norclif* 1276 Earw, *-clyf(f)* 1378, 1387 Plea, *-clyffe* (*Mylne*) 1612 Earw, *-cliff* 1427 ChRR, *-e* (*heth*) 1335 Fitt

'North cliff', *v.* norð, clif, with hall, myln, hǣð. It is named from the steep north bank of R. Bollin.

OVERSLEY BANK, COTTAGES, FM, FORD (BRIDGE) & LODGE (FM) (101–824829, 822838, 816835, 814832, 816829 & 824837 respectively), *Vulverichelei* 13 Cre 353, *Ulresford* 13? Orm², *Vulriswode* (lit. *Bulriswode*) c.1320 Fitt, *Oulersleyford* 1674 Mere, *Oversley fourd* 1660 Earw, *-ford* 1831 Bry, *Oversley Bank* 1860 White, *Overley Ford* 1842 OS, '(ford at) Wulfrīc's wood', from the OE pers.n. *Wulfrīc* and lēah, with ford. The ford was at the southern limit of *Ullerwood* 335 *infra*, to part of which, near Hooksbank Wood (101–813826) *infra*, the *Fitt* reference alludes. One *Wulfrīc* held Butley 193 *supra*, and possibly Wilmslow, TRW and TRE, *v.* Tait 213, n. 232.

RYLANCE (lost), 1634 JRL 32, *riheland* 13 Cre (p), *Rylondis* c.1200, c.1320 Fitt, *-land-* c.1200 (17) Orm², *Ruylondis* c.1310 Earw, c.1320 Fitt, *-es* E2 Orm², c.1320 Fitt, 1354 Eyre, *-londs* 1337 Fitt, *-lond* 1349 Eyre, 'rye selions', *v.* ryge, land. The place gave rise to a surname *Rylands, -lance*, which appears in *Croft at Back of Roylance's* 1840 TA 57 (Bollin Fee).

STANEYLAND (101–8482)

Stanilondis c.1200 *Fitt*, *-es* 13 *Dav* (p), 1285 Court (p), *-y-* c.1300
JRL 32 *et freq, Stanilandis* 1336 *Mass* (p), 1345 *Fitt, Stanelands*
1458 ChRR (p)
Stanylond 1285 Court (p), *-i-* l13 *Fitt* (p), *-land* 1288 Court (p)
Sanilondis 1286 Court 216 (p)
Stalilance House, Stalilandes-green 1616 Earw

'Stony selions', *v.* stānig, land.

APPRENTICE'S HOUSE (lost), 1840 *TA, Prentice House* 1831 Bry.
BANK HO, *Quarry Bank Farm* 1831 ib, cf. Quarry Bank *infra.*
BEECH FM.   BLACK LAKE, *v.* lake 'a lake'.   BOLLINHEY, 1831
Bry, *Bollen Hey* 1666 ChCert, 'enclosure belonging to Bollin Fee',
v. (ge)hæg, Bollin Fee *supra.*   BOUNDARY LODGE, on the boundary
of Lindow Moss *supra* and Mobberley 333 *infra.*   BURLEYHURST
BRIDGE & WOOD, *v.* 330 *infra.*   BURNED HEY WOOD, *Brindey Heys
Wood* 1831 Bry, *Burnt Hey Wood* 1842 OS, 'burnt enclosure(s)',
v. brende[2], (ge)hæg.   CARR WOOD, cf. *Carr Meadow* 1840 *TA,*
v. kjarr 'brushwood, marsh'.   CROSS FM, *-House* 1831 Bry, cf.
Styal Cross *infra.*   DAVENPORT GREEN, *Lindow Side* 1831 ib, 1842
OS, cf. Davenport Ho 225 *supra,* Lindow Moss *supra.*   DEAD-
MAN'S CLOUGH, 1840 *TA,* perhaps named from the discovery of a
corpse, *v.* dede-man, clōh.   FARMFOLD.   GIANT'S CASTLE, a
figurative name for rocks on the bluff bank of R. Bollin.   GRAVEL
LANE.   GREEN LAKE *v.* lake 'a lake' cf. Black Lake *supra.*
HEALD HO (lost), 1860 White.   HIGHFIELD.   HOGSHEAD GREEN,
1831 Bry, *Haukesharte* 1610 Earw, 'hawk's gap', *v.* hafoc-scerde, cf.
Hogsheads 191 *supra, Hawkesyord* 166 *supra.*   HOLE FM, *Old Farm*
1831 Bry, *v.* ald.   HOLLINLANE, *Holly Lane* 1860 White, *v.*
holegn.   HOOKSBANK WOOD, *Hooks Banks* 1842 OS, *le hokysklif*
c.1320 *Fitt,* 'hook bank', *v.* hōc 'a hook, a bend in a river', banke,
clif, cf. Oversley *supra.*   HOPE LANE (lost), 1831 Bry, running into
Handforth near Grange Fm 254 *infra, v.* hop[1].   LACY GREEN,
1578 Earw, cf. *Lacey Meadow* 1840 *TA,* supposedly named after the
de Lacey family, *v.* Earw 1 134.   LINNEY'S BRIDGE, *Linny Bridge*
1831 Bry, cf. *Lyney* 1520 ChRR, probably 'flax water-meadow',
v. līn, ēg.   LODE HILL (FM), *Load Hill, Old Squires* 1831 Bry, cf.
Lodehill Field 1840 *TA,* at the head of a watercourse running down to
R. Bollin east of Norcliffe Hall, *v.* (ge)lād 'a watercourse'.   MOOR

LANE (HO).   MOSSBROW, near Nansmoss *infra*, *v.* brū.   MOSS
FM & LANE, 1842 OS, *Moss Side* 1831 Bry, from Shadow Moss 242
infra, which extends into Styal hamlet.   NANSMOSS, 1831 ib, cf.
Nan Croft, Nanny's-, Nans Hole 1840 *TA*, from *Nan*, a pet-form of
the fem. pers.n. *Ann(e)*, with mos 'a moss', cf. Moss Brow *supra*.
NEWGATE (HO), a house on the Mobberley boundary, at the west end
of a road across Lindow Moss, 'new road', *v.* nīwe, gata.   OAK
BROW, COTTAGES & FM, *The Oak* 1831 Bry.   OAKWOOD FM, 1860
White, *The Manse* 1831 Bry.   PARKFIELD, *-Pasture* 1840 *TA*.
PIGGINSHAW (BROOK), perhaps from sceaga 'a wood' with an un-
identified first el. The brook joins R. Dean.   PLATT COTTAGE,
v. plat[1].   QUARRY BANK, (*House*) 1831 Bry, *Quarrell Bank* 1710
Earw, *the Quarrell Hole* 1784 ib, *v.* quarrelle, cf. Bank Ho *supra*.
SMALLWOOD HO (lost), 1788 ib, cf. Thomas *Smallwood* 1664 ib 1 167.
SOUTHFIELD, *Clattering Gate* 1831 Bry.   STAMFORD LODGE, 1842
OS.   STONE HO.   STRAWBERRY LANE.   STYAL CROSS, an
ancient cross removed from its original site near Cross Fm *supra*.
THREETHORNE COTTAGE, cf. *the Three Thorns* 1608 Sheaf, a boundary
of Lindow Moss.   TOP O' TH' GREEN (lost), 1831 Bry, cf. Styal
Green *supra*.   TIMPERLEY HO (lost), 1842 OS, *Timporley Fold*
1831 Bry, *v.* fald, cf. Timperley 335 *infra*.   TWINNIES BRIDGE,
Pownall Bridge 1831 ib, *Twinneys Bridge* 1842 OS, cf. *Big, Long &
Corner Twinnies* 1840 *TA*, crossing R. Dean between Styal and
Pownall.   VALLEY HO.   WHITAKER'S FM (lost), 1860 White.
WILMSLOW CROSS, 1842 OS, *Cross* 1831 Bry, *v.* cros.   WOODEND.
WOOD FM, 1842 OS.   WORMS HILL, *Worm Hill Brow* 1831 Bry,
Wirmhill 1840 *TA*, *v.* wyrm, hyll, brū.   YEWTREE FM.

FIELD-NAMES

The undated forms are 1840 *TA* 327. Of the others e13, c.1260, 1616, c.1787
are Earw, c.1200 (17), m13 Orm², 1320, 1330, 1343 *Fitt*, 1328 *Traff*, 1831
Bry, 1842 OS.

(*a*) The Acre; Alder Fd & Hill; Apple Tree Fd; Baguley Wd (a
meadow, cf. Baguley 329 *infra*); Bailey Brow, Croft & Heys (*v.* baillie);
Barley Fd; Barn Fd & Mdw; Barrow Flat(s) (*v.* bearg 'a castrated boar',
flat); Bean Butts; Beesley Mdw; Bell Fd (perhaps land endowing a church-
bell, *v.* belle); Ben Back; Bent (*v.* beonet); Birch Flatt; Birchalls; Black
Croft; Black-, Blake Fd (*v.* blæc, cf. dial. *blake* 'black, dark-coloured');
Blakeley Fd (*v.* blæc, lēah); Bottoms (*v.* botm); Bought Ridding (*v.* ryding);
Briary Croft; Brick (Kiln) Fd; Bridge Eye(s) (*v.* ēg); Broad Buttes; Brook

Fd; Broomy Knowl & Patch; Brow Edge Lunt (*v.* land); Brow Side;
Buggart Fd ('hobgoblin's field', *v.* boggard); Butt Mdw (*v.* butte); Calf
Croft; Carrot Ground; Carrow Fd; Carrs (*v.* kjarr); Cattail Fd (*v.* cat(t),
tægl); Chapel Fd & Mdw; Chapmans Croft; Cherry Barrow (*Chiribarwe*
m13, 'cherry-tree grove', *v.* chiri, bearu, cf. 82 *supra*); C(h)rimes (*v. le
Crymbe* 331 *infra*); Clay Acre, Fd & Mdw; Cliffe Head (*v.* clif, hēafod, cf.
Cliff Rd 220 *supra*); Clover Fd; Cockshut (*v.* cocc-scyte); Colt Heys; Cop Fd
(*v.* copp); Copper Fd; Cote Fd & Mdw; Cow Hey, Lane, Mdw & Pasture;
Crabtree Fd; Cromlocks Bottoms; Cross Shoots ('transverse strips of land',
v. cros, scēat); Dane Fd (*v.* denu, cf. Dean Row *supra*); Dear Bought; Dick
Ridding (*v.* ryding); Dig Flat (*v.* dīc, flat); Disley Kirk c.1787 (a cavern once
inhabited by a man named *Disley* (Earw II 142), *v.* kirkja 'a church'); Dole
(*v.* dāl); Double Banks 1842; Downes Fd (from the surname *Downes*); Dry
Croft, Hurst & Knowl (*v.* hyrst); Dunsfield Mdw; Far Land; Ferny Brow
Mill; Ferry Fd; Filnut Lane; Fogg Croft (*v.* fogge); Fox Hole; Garden Mdw;
Gibbs Mdw; Goer (not from gāra, for the shape is not right; perhaps gor);
Golden's Fd; Goose Croft; Gorsey Bank, Fd & Knowl; Green Fd & Piece;
Greety Croft (*v.* grēot, -ig³); Grove Mdw (cf. Grove Avenue 220 *supra*);
Guide Post Fd; Half Kernal; Harehill Mdw (*v.* hara, hyll); Hawk (*v.* halc);
Hawthorn Fd & Mdw; Heys; Hield Fd (*v.* helde); Hills; Hob(b) Fd (*v.*
hobbe); Hodge Croft (*v.* hocg); Holm (*v.* holmr); Hollins (*v.* holegn); Holt
(*v.* holt); Hooks (*v.* hōc); Horse Pasture; House Bank; Intake (*v.* inntak);
Iron Fd, Little Iron (*v.* hyrne, cf. Heronbridge 332 *infra*); Jack Ridding
(*v.* jack, ryding); Jenkin Fd (from *Jenkin*, diminutive of *John*); Jenny's
Mdw, Jenny Tray; Kelsall Fd (cf. *Kelsall House* 1616, from the surname from
Kelsall 332 *infra*); Kiln Fd & Hill; Kings Picker (*v.* pichel); Knowl; Land-
mans Fd (cf. *landman* NED sb. 2, 4); Lane Fd & Piece; Lawton Fd; Ley
Patch (*v.* lǣge); Lime Fd; Little Fd (*freq, v.* lȳtel 'little', in one instance
contrasted with Broad Fd, with the meaning 'narrow'); Long Butts, Close,
Croft, Fd, Hurst, Moss, Shoot & Stone (*v.* butte, hyrst, scēat, stān); Lords
Acre (*v.* hlāford); Lowndes (*v.* land); Mab Croft; Main Mdw (*v.* main, cf.
Mains Fm 223 *supra*); Maize Acre; Mare Heys (*v.* mere²); Marl('d) Fd
& Heath; Massey Fd (from the *Massey* family, landowners here); Matthers
Fd; Meadow Bank; Meetinghouse Fd; Meg Croft (*v.* meg); Mickle Fd
(*v.* micel, mikill); Mill Fd, Mdw, & Wd; Millington Bank; Moss Fd &
Mdw; Munday Corn (perhaps named after some service done here on a
Monday, *v.* Mōnandæg); Myddyhurst (*v.* middel, hyrst); Nether Fd; New
Building Bank; Nibb Croft; Nick Fd; Nields Mdw; Nook; Little Nursery;
Oak Croft, Oaks Fd & Mdw; Oat Croft & Fd; Old Fd, Lane, Mdw, Moss
& Wd; Oliver's Fd; Orchard Mdw; Osier Ground; Outwood Mdw ('out-
lying wood', *v.* ūt, wudu); Ox Hey; Paddock (*v.* pearroc); Parkers Moor;
Peartree Knowl; Perch Croft; Pern; Pet Fd; Pig Cote Croft & Fd; Pingot
(*v.* pingot); Pipers Acre; Pit Fd; Play Ground (*v.* plega); Quarry Head
(*v.* hēafod, cf. Quarry Bank *supra*); Reddyshaw (perhaps *le Rudeschawe* 1285
Court 213 (p), *Rudyshagh* 1349 *MinAcct* (p), 'rue copse', from rūde and
sceaga); Red Leach (*v.* rēad, lǣc(c)); Ridding (*v.* ryding); Ringway Wd
(cf. Ringway 333 *infra*); Road Fd; Rood Land (*v.* rōd³); Rough Bank,
Bottom, Hey & Moss; Round Bent, Croft & Top; Rushy Fd; Ryles Head

(probably '(the head of) the rye hill', v. ryge, hyll, hēafod); Sand Bank &
Fd; Sawpit Fd (v. saw-pytt); Seven Days Work (v. day-work); Severing;
Sheep Pasture; Shippon Fd & Flat; Shoot (v. scēat); Short Butts (v.
sc(e)ort, butte); Shut Fd (v. scēat); Slitch Croft (v. slicche); Smithy Fd;
Soon Fd & Mdw (v. sand); Sour Dale (v. sūr, dæl²); Stable Fd; Stack Yard;
Standon; Stock Fd; Stondry Lunt (v. land); Stocking Bridge (perhaps
'bridge of logs', v. stoccen, brycg); Ston(e)y Flat; Straight Fd; Stubbs (cf.
del Stubbes 1328 (p), v. stubb 'a tree-stump'); Styall Leets (v. (ge)lǣt 'a
meeting of roads'); Sun Croft & Fd; Sussgreaves (v. grǣfe 'a grove'; the
first el. may be as in Sossmoss 97 supra); Swimbrooke ('stream with a
swim in it', v. swim, brōc, cf. Swim Brook 36 supra); Tan Yard Fd (cf.
Tan Yard 1831, v. tan-yard); Tetlocks; Thistle Eye (v. ēg); Three Cornered
Croft; Tibb Hill; Tile Yard; Top Rough; Town Fd; Trefoil; Vetch Butts;
Wall Fd, Walley Mdw (v. wælla 'a well, a spring'); Water Mdw, Waters
Head (v. wæter, hēafod); Weir Eyes (v. ēg); Well Fd; Wheat Fd; Will Croft
& Eye; Wind Gap (v. wind, gap); Wind Mill Fd; Witch Grass ('quitch,
couch-grass', v. cwice); Workhouse Fd; Wood Fd & Mdw (cf. Styal Wood
1842); Wood Park 1831; Yard Mdw (v. geard).

(b) le Batzelettlog 1343 ('(dell at) the junction of the valley-streams',
v. bæce¹, (ge)lǣt, clōh); le Blake lache de Shadoke mosse c.1200 (17) ('the
black boggy stream', v. blæc, læc(c), on the north-west boundary of Styal,
near Shadow Moss 242 infra); Helimgreuis m13, c.1260 (the second el. is
grǣfe 'a grove, a copse'); le Herdemonis-croft c.1320 ('the herdsman's croft',
v. hirde-mann, croft); le Klocys c.1320 ('the valleys', v. clōh, cf. foll.);
le Lyndeneclotz 1343 ('the clough(s) growing with lime-trees', v. linden,
clōh); le Mosegrene e13 (v. mos, grēne²); le Siche c.1200 (17) (v. sīc; the
north-west and west boundary of Styal, from Shadow Moss to R. Bollin);
boscus de Pounale c.1330 ('Pownall wood').

xi. Northenden

Transferred to the County Borough of Manchester La, in 1931. The ancient
parish included Northern Etchells 240 infra, and a few fields in Baguley
township.

NORTHENDEN (101–8389) [ˈnɔːrðəndən, older ˈnourðin, -ən]

Norwordine 1086 DB, -wordeyn 1398 Add, -wrdinam (acc.) 1119
(1150) Chest, -wurding, -warding c.1270 Earw

Northwrthinam (acc.) 1119 (1280) Chest, Norwrthyn c.1220 ib,
-in l13 ib (p), Nort(h)wrthin, -yn 1285, 1286 Eyre, 1297 Pat, l13
Chest, Nor(t)(h)worthin, -yn c.1250 Earw, 1286, 1287, 1290
Court, l13 Chest, 1333 ChRR, (Norht-) c.1310 ib, Nor(th)-
werthin, -yn, -ver- 1287 Eyre, 1344 ChRR (p), 1370 Earw,
-wurthyn 1297 CRV, c.1310 Tab, Norworhyn c.1290 Orm²,

Norhtwor'yn c.1320 ib, *Nortwourthin* 1335 *JRC*, *Northwarthyne* 17 *Harl.* 1994

Norirdene 1280 Earw

Norworthei 1287 Court

Northworth'm 1291 Tax, *-wortham* 1350 Chamb (p)

Northurthin c.1310 Tab, ?*-yne* (lit. *Northurwyne*) 1335 *JRC* 814, *-urdene* 1346 Bark (p), *-erden(e)* 1345 *Eyre*, 1360 ChRR *et freq* to *Northerden* 1831 Bry, *Northerdern* 1458 ChRR, *-don* 1535 VE, *-orden* 1408 MidCh, *-irden* 1437 Plea

Northden 1350 ChRR (p), *Norden* 1357 ib (p), *-e* 1445 Orm²

Northwynden 1366 *Eyre*, *Northenden* 1439, 1477 ChRR, (*or Norden*) c.1620 Orm², *-don alias Northenkenworthe* 1550 ChRR

Northyn 1379 *Eyre*, *Northen* 1527 Earw, 1656 Orm²

Northerleydene 1395 Orm²

Netherdene 1404 ChRR, *Netherden* 1568 ib

Northoden 1513 ChRR

Northernden 1514 Orm¹

Northern 1841 *TA*

'North enclosure', 'worðign in the north', *v.* norð, worðign, cf. Kenworthy *infra*.

STREET NAME: BOAT LANE, leading to a ferry called *Northen Boat* Orm² III 612, over R. Mersey, *v.* bāt, lane.

HAZELHURST (101–806903), *Hasulhurst* 1260 Court (p), 1376 *Eyre*, *Hasel-* 1336 ChRR (p), 1562 ib, (*the*) *-e* 1568 Earw, *Hasle-* 1635 ib, *Hasil-* 1460 ChRR (p), *Hahilhurst* 13 Earw, c.1290 Orm², *Asilhurst* c.1310 Tab, (*Grete*) *Hassilhurst* 1494 Orm², Earw, (*Huchyn*)*hasselhurst* 1494, *-e* 1568 ib, 'hazel wood', *v.* hæsel, hyrst. The manorial prefixes are grēat 'great, big', and the ME (OFr) pers.n. *Huchon*, diminutive of *Hugh* (OFr *Hue*).

KENWORTHY (101–8290) [ˈkenədi, ˈkenəːði]

Kenworthin 13 Tab, 1286 *Eyre* (p)

Kenworthey 1276 Earw (p), 1371 Orm², *-e* 1310 *Dav* (p), *-worthy* 113 (18) Sheaf, 1316 Plea, *-worthay* 1370 *Eyre*, *-e*, *-worthai* 1420 *JRC*, Sheaf, *-worthee* 1539 Earw, *-worthei* 1550 Pat

Keneworthei, *-wro-* 1287 Court (p), *-wourthey* 1335 *JRC*, *-ay* 1358 *Eyre*, 1377 *CoLegh*

Kennerhey 1288 Court (p), *Kenworhay* 1373 *Dav* (p)

Kenorthey E1 JRL, *Kennerthey* 1296 Plea, *Kennerdy* 1841 *TA*
Kenuerthey 1296 Orm², *Kenver(d)hee* c.1310 Tab
Kynworthey 1425 Plea, *-worthe* 1553 Pat (p)
Northendon alias Northenkenworthe 1550 ChRR
Kenerdley alias Kenworthey 1602 Orm²
Kenerden 1644 Earw
Canada 1831 Bry, *Kennedy* 1842 OS

'Cēna's curtilage or enclosure', from the OE pers.n. *Cēna*
(< *Cǣna*), v. worðign, worðig.

SAXFIELD (101–825900), *Saxefeld* 13 Earw, c.1290 Orm², *the Higher*
& Lower Saxe Felde 1578, *Saxefielde pitte* 1586 ib, *Great & Higher*
Sak Field 1841 *TA*, cf. *Saxbroke* 1494 Earw I 269 (i.e. Baguley Brook
329 *infra*, a boundary of Hazelhurst *supra*), 'Saxons' open country',
v. Seaxe, feld. The name belonged in 6″ OS to a house erected on
land which bore it; in the thirteenth century the area so called
extended to the southern boundary of Northenden, to Hazelhurst
supra, and included part of Wythenshaw *infra*. In the construction
of the house 'some much decayed weapons etc., were found there
buried', which led Earwaker to derive the name from OE seax 'a
knife, a short sword', v. Earw I 269, 270, cf. Orm² III 611. It is to be
presumed that there was a settlement of Saxons among the Anglian
population of north-east Ch.

WYTHENSHAWE (101–8189)

  (*le hay de*) *Witenscawe* 13th Earw, c.1290 Orm², *Wythensache* l13
    (18) Sheaf³ 20, *W(h)ythenschagh, -schawe* 1306 Plea (p), 1316
    Orm², Earw, 1370 ib, *Wythenshagh* 1351 *Eyre* (p), 1354 *ib*,
    -shawe 1548 Sheaf³ 45, *Withenshawe* 1607 Earw, *-shaw* 1724
    NotCestr
  Wythynshagh 1348 *Eyre*, 1364 *ib*, 1409 *JRC*, *Withynshagh* 1348
    Earw, 1427 ChRR, *Wythinshagh* 1370 Orm², Earw, *-ynshaw*
    1417 ChRR, 1423 Plea (p), *Withinshaw(e)* 1547, 1553 Pat *et freq*
    Withanshaw 1656 Earw

  'Willow copse', v. wiðign, sceaga.

BEECH HO, *Lane End* (*Farm*) 1831 Bry, 1842 OS, at the end of
Yewtree Lane *infra*.   THE BIG ROUND, cf. *Round Hay* 1841 *TA*,
v. rond, (ge)hæg; a wood in Wythenshawe park.   BRADLEYGATE,

1831 Bry, *Broadley Gate* 1842 OS, cf. *Bradles* 1578 Earw, '(the gate at) the broad clearing', *v.* brād, lēah, geat.   BUTTON LANE (101–810905), *Button Lane, Button Demath & Shutts* 1841 *TA*, from lane, day-math, scēat, with a p.n. or el. *Button* which also gives name to Button Brook 17 *supra* which rises hereabouts. *Button* may be an old p.n. in tūn.   CLEVELAND LODGE, *Myrtle Grove* 1831 Bry. CRINGLEWOOD, 'circular, or winding, wood', *v.* kringla, cf. ModE dial. *cringel* 'a twist', cf. also Cringle Ho 244 *infra*.   FORD COTTAGE & LANE, named from Northenden Ford, on R. Mersey in Didsbury La.   GIB LANE, 1841 *TA*, *Gilbert Lane* 1842 OS, *v.* gibbe[2].   HILLEND, 1842 ib.   KENWORTHY HALL, HO & LANE, *the plase of Kenworthaye, -worthai* 1420 *JRC*, Sheaf, *Kennerdy Road* 1841 *TA*, *Kenworthy House* 1860 White, *v.* place.   LAWTON HO (101–807901) & MOOR (101–808903), *Loyton Moor* 1831 Bry, *Lawton Eye, Lowton Park* 1841 *TA*, perhaps an old p.n. in tūn, *v.* mōr[1], ēg, park.   LONGLEY LANE, *Langlye* 1578 Earw, *Langley* 1841 *TA*, 'long woodland glade', *v.* lang, lēah.   MERE WOOD, there is a pool in it, *v.* mere[1].   MOOR END, FM & LANE, *Moor-syde* 1602 Orm[2], Earw, *(the) -side* 1644 ib, *Morside* 1646 ib, *Moorend* 1831 Bry, *Northen Moor* 1860 White, *v.* mōr[1], sīde, cf. Northenden *supra*.   THE MOUNT, 1831 Bry.   NAN NOOK WOOD, *Nan Nook Plantation* 1842 OS.   NORTHENDEN BRIDGE.   NORTHENDEN MILL, 1831 Bry, cf. Mill Hill *infra*.   OAK HO, *The Oak* 1831 ib.   PIPERHILL, 1499 *JRC*, *le Pyperhill* 1476 Earw, *-hyll* 1477 Orm[2], 'piper's hill', *v.* pīpere 'a piper', hyll, but cf. Pepper Street (Chester) 333 *infra*.   RACK HO, 1831 Bry.   ROYLE GREEN, 1831 ib, '(green at) the rye-hill', *v.* ryge, hyll, grēne[2], cf. Royalthorn 241 *infra*.   SALE ROAD, leading to Sale 334 *infra*.   STENNER.   WYTHENSHAWE BRIDGE, HALL & RD, *Withenshawe Hall* 1607 Earw.   YEWTREE HO & LANE, *Yewtree* 1831 Bry.

FIELD-NAMES

The undated forms are 1841 *TA* 299. Of the others, 13, 1316[1], 1396, 1476, 1494[1], 1539, 1578, 1579, 1586 are Earw, m13, 1310 *Dav*, 1287, 1288 Court, c.1290, 1316[2], c.1320, 1468, 1477, 1481, 1494[2], 1508 Orm[2], 1296 Plea, c.1310 Tab, 1335, 1420, 1486, 1499, 1501 *JRC* 814–31, 1341, 1345, 1348, 1351, 1358 *Eyre*, 1408 ChRR, 1831 Bry.

(a) (The) Acre; Ardens Fd; Austin Croft; Bank; Barn Croft, Fd & Mdw; Bell Croft (*v.* belle); Birch Dole (*v.* dāl); Black Fd; Bleak Fd (*v.* blāc); Bradshaw (*v.* brād, sceaga, cf. Broad Shay Mdw *infra*); Broadhurst (*v.* brād,

hyrst); Broad Shay Mdw (v. brād, sc(e)aga, cf. Bradshaw *supra*); Brook Fd;
Broom Fd (v. brōm); Brownhill (*le Brounehull* 1288 (p), *-hul* 1341, *la-* 1351,
Brounhul c.1290 (p), *-hull* c.1320 (p), *le Brounhyll* 1468, *Brounhill* 1508,
'brown hill', v. brūn[1], hyll); Burgess Croft; Burnt Croft (v. brende[2]); Carr
(Brow, Mdw & Wd) (v. kjarr); Chadwick Mdw; Chandlers Hey; Cherry
Tree Croft (cf. a parcel of land called *Cheretre* 1494[2], 'the cherry-tree',
v. chiri, trēow); Church Croft; Clay Acre; Clover Fd; Cock Pitt (v. cockpit);
Cookson's Eye (v. ēg 'a water-meadow'); Little Coppice; Cow Falls (v.
(ge)fall); Crimbucks (*the Crymbalt3* 1481, probably from halc 'a nook,
a corner' and the el. discussed at *le Crymbe* 331 *infra*, cf. Crimbabent 245
infra); Didsbury Mdw (on the La bank of R. Mersey, adjoining Didsbury
La); Dig Leech ('ditched bog', v. dīc, lece); Dob Rudding (v. ryding);
Dole(s) (v. dāl); Eatsey, Eatsey Bottom (*Estey* c.1290, c.1320, 'east island or
water-meadow', v. ēast, ēg, botm 'bottom-land'); Falls Fd & Mdw, Farther
Falls (*the fall* 1481, v. (ge)fall); Flithill (probably from (ge)flit 'strife,
dispute' and hyll); Grass Hey; Greece Bridge (apparently 'bridge with
steps', from grese 'a flight of steps'); Green; Hardings Loont (v. land);
Hemp Croft; Hen Butts; Hey; Hey Head (v. hēafod, cf. Heyhead 242 *infra*);
High Fd; Hole; Holt (v. holt); Hoo (v. hōh 'a projecting piece of land in the
bend of a river'); Hooley (v. hōh, lēah); Horse Croft & Hey; Hough (v. hōh
'the end of a ridge'); House Fd & Mdw; Intack (v. inntak); Island (v. ēg-
land 'an island'); Keckers Croft; Kiln Croft (*The Kylne Croft* 1481); Lamb
Pitts ('loam pits', v. lām, pytt); Leasow Pits (v. lǣs); Lees Mdw (v. lǣs);
Leesing Pits; Lime Grove 1831; Little Eye (v. ēg); Little Hey; Long Fd;
Loont (v. land); Lower Park; Maggots Croft & Fd; Marl(ed) Fd (v. marle,
marlede); Marledge; Massey Fd; Mean Croft ('common croft', v. (ge)mǣne);
Middup (perhaps 'middle enclosure' from middel and hop[1], but cf. Middop
WRY 6 171, Midhope WRY 1 225 'land between valleys', v. mid, hop[1]);
Midley (*le middel eye* 1316, *Middeleye* 1316[2], 'the middle water-meadow',
v. middel, ēg); Milking Fd (v. milking); Mill Hill (*le Mylle Hylle* 1539,
v. myln, hyll); New Fd; New Street (v. strǣt); Nick Fd; North Acre;
Northern Eye ('Northenden water-meadow', v. ēg); Old Mdw; Old Wills
Md; Oven Croft; Great & Little Park; Pears Lane Croft; Peas Croft (v.
pise); Pingot (v. pingot); Pithan; Platt Bridge (cf. *de(l) Plat* 1287 (p), 1296,
del Platte 1408 (p), v. plat[1]); Poor House Fd; Rabbit Warren; Rawsons Hey,
Rowsons Mdw; Reaps (perhaps 'brushwood', from ModEdial. *reap*); Rye
Fd; Safe Long (v. furlang); Sally's Mdw; Salters Hey (cf. *Salteres hull* 1335,
Saltershill 1499, *le Salterhyll* 1476, 1477, v. saltere, hyll, (ge)hæg; this
would be associated with the salt-way across Northenden Ford, v. Crump
102–3, cf. 49 *supra*); Sharson Fd (cf. Sharston Green 242 *infra*); Shawcross
Fd; Sibley; Slack Fd (v. slakki); Slope (v. slope); Smethill ('smooth hill',
v. smēðe, hyll, but cf. *Smethelegh'* 1337 *Eyre* (p), v. smēðe, lēah); Smithy
Fd; Square Fd; Stack Croft & Yard; Stockin Bridge (probably 'bridge built
of stocks', v. stoccen, brycg); Strange Mdw; Street Lane Croft (v. strǣt);
Sun Earth (v. sunne, erð or eorðe); Sunacres (v. sunne); Sunderland (v.
sundor-land); Thistley Fd; Tom Bank Lane & Mdw (v. toun); Triangle;
Twin Ridding (v. twinn, ryding); Union; Urchin Park (v. urchon, park);
Vaudreys Loont & Shutts (from the surname *Vaudrey*, a local family,

v. land, scēat); Ward Langton; Water Hey (*v.* wæter, ēg); Watershead (*v.* wæter, scēad); Well Croft; West Fd; Wharf Hey (*v.* waroð, ēg; cf. Wharf 65 *supra*); Wheat Croft & Fd; Willow Hall ('spring or stream at a willow', *v.* wilig, wælla); Withen Fd (*v.* wiðign, feld).

(b) *Audisay* 1485; *Barettfelde* 1476, *Barettsfelde* 1477, *Barettȝ fyld* 1481, *Baretteȝ fildeȝ* 1499 ('disputed field', or 'field where quarrels take place', from baret and feld, cf. Barratt Mdw 223 *supra*); *le botehey* 1501 ('enclosure in which somebody has rights and privileges', *v.* bōt, (ge)hæg); *the Calfe Croft* 1578; *Chantry Lands* 1579 (from the endowment of a chantry in the parish church (Earw 1 309), *v.* chaunterie); *Elescawe* c.1290 (perhaps 'Ella's wood', from the OE pers.n. *Ella* and sceaga, but the first el. may be elle, ellern 'an elder tree'); *Emots Eie* 1578 (perhaps 'Emma's water-meadow', from the ME fem. pers.n. *Emmot*, a pet-form of *Emma*, and ēg, but the first el. might be eā-mōt, 'a confluence'); *The Hall Felde* 1578 (*v.* hall, feld); *Hesteyrwode* c.1310 (17) (*v.* wudu); *Issherbyght, Ussherbught* 1396, *Yscherbyȝthe* 1420 (the name of land on both sides of a bend of R. Mersey between Kenworthy *supra* and Barlow La, *v.* byht 'a bight, a river bend'. The first el. is obscure. It may be the word which appears in the mysterious La surname *Isherwood, Usherwood* (Bardsley 421, 778)); *Longacre* 1494 (*v.* lang, æcer); *the Long Eie* 1578 (*v.* lang, ēg); *Mollacre* 1494 (perhaps from molle 'a mole', and æcer); *Newhay* 1494 (*v.* nīwe, (ge)hæg); *Northwode* c.1310 (17) (*v.* norð, wudu); *Salehey* 1494[1] (*v.* (ge)hæg, cf. Sale 334 *infra*); *the Swyne Park* 1578 (*v.* swīn[1], park); *Symacresse* 1494[1]; *Thornefeld* 1494[1] ('thorn-tree field', *v.* þorn, feld); *le Waisse* c.1320 ('marsh', *v.* wesse); *le Welfehay* 1494[1] (probably *Wolfe-*, 'wolves' enclosure', *v.* wulf, (ge)hæg); *Kegwrthe* m13 (p), *-worth* 1310 (p), *Keggeworth* 1348, *Kegwood* 13 (p) (either a surname from Kegworth Lei, or a lost place near Northenden, *v.* worð, cf DEPN s.v. Kegworth).

xii. Northenden & Stockport

ETCHELLS. A township in moieties, originally manorial (Orm[2] III 619), in Northenden and Stockport parishes. Northenden Etchells was transferred to Manchester La, with Northenden 234 *supra*. Stockport Etchells is now included in Cheadle cum Gatley Urban District c.p., *v.* Gatley 244 *infra*, Cheadle 246 *infra*.

Hecheles 1154–89 Orm[2], (*le*) *Echeles* 1272 Cl (p), 1281 AD *et freq*, (*-eȝ*) 1489 ChRR, (*-is*) 1248 Ipm, *Esch-* 1348 BPR, *Etch-* 1408 Orm[2], *Ecch-* 1446 ChRR, *Echels* 1404 ib, *Ecch-* 1517 ChEx, *Etch-* 1688 Sheaf

Ochel' 1286 Court, *Eyre* (? for *Echel'*)

Eccles 1289 (17) Court (p), 1408 Orm[1], *Echlis* c.1290 Orm[2], *-es* 1371 *Eyre*

Etchells 1302 Tab, *Ech-*, *-(e)s* 1397 ChRR, 1504 Plea, 1568 ChRR, *Ecch-* 1517 ChEx, *Ettch-* 1636 Sheaf, *Etchwells* 1322, 1340 Orm[2],

Etchulls 1527 ib, E(c)chilles 1441 Eyre (p), 1452 SocAnt, 1454
Eyre, Echill'y 1527 ChRR (? for Echillis)
Acholles 1431 Cl
Eychells c.1602 Chol

'Land added to an estate', v. ēcels. Some spellings show the
second syllable interpreted as hyll 'a hill', or wella 'a well'. If Agnes
de Nechel H3 Orm² III 622n. belongs here, the form derives from
atten (OE æt þǣm) 'at the-'.

FIELD-NAMES

The following unidentified minor-names cannot be allocated to their part of
the township.

(b) le Bakhous 1354 Eyre ('the bake-house', v. bæc-hūs); le Clay 1354
Eyre (p), (v. clǣg 'clay'); le Loue 1346 BPR (p) (v. hlāw 'a mound or hill');
Smalwode 1290 Court (p) ('narrow wood', v. smæl, wudu); Swaynescroft
1290 Court (p) (from croft, with either sveinn 'a young man, a servant' or
the ON pers.n. Sveinn).

1. NORTHERN ETCHELLS (101–8285), 1860 White, Northerden
Etchells 1831 Bry, cf. Northenden 234 supra, v. Etchells 239 supra.

BENCHILL (101–8288)

Baginchul 13 Tab, Bangengehull 1289 Court (p), Baginghull 1302
Tab, Baghinghalle c.1310 ib
Baynchull 1302, 1326 Tab, Baunchull 1370 Earw
Benshall 1669 Earw, 1831 Bry, Benchall Field 1841 TA, Bench Hall
1843 TAMap
Benchill 1842 OS

'Hill called after Bēage or Bǣga', from hyll with an OE -ing-
suffix formation upon the OE fem. pers.n. Bēage, or the OE masc.
pers.n. Bǣga (Bǣgia BCS 139, cf. Baywell Wo 121, Bayworth Brk
DEPN). The -ing formation may be -ing-⁴, but the assibilation
indicates -ing².

BROWNLEY GREEN (101–8286)

Brumleg' 1260 Court (p), -legh 1290, 1295 ib (p), Bromeley 1417
Plea, -Greene 1634 Sheaf

Broundle Green 1600 Sheaf, *Brounley-*, *Browneley Greene* 1658 ib, *Brownley-* 1711 ib
Brownlow (Green) 1831 Bry, 1860 White

'Broom clearing', v. brōm, lēah, with grēne[2] 'a green'. Later spellings show *-low* (hlāw 'a mound') substituted for unstressed *-ley*.

CROSSACRES GREEN (101–8387), *Crosacres* 1290 *Eyre*, *Crossacres* 1614 Earw, *Crosackers* 1658 Sheaf, *Cross Acre Green* 1842 OS, 'plough-lands near a cross', v. cros, æcer.

(LOWER) HAVELEYHEY (101–8287), *Alveleyhey* 1318 Earw, *Alynghey* 1369 (17) Orm[2], *Alvyleghey* 1370 Earw, *Alvenley-*, *Alvanley Hey* 1417 ChRR, Plea, *Alvenley* 1597 Earw, *Alvandeley* 1507 *MinAcct*, *Overley Hey* 17 Orm[2], *Haveley Hey* 1842 OS, '(enclosure at) Ælfa's clearing', from the OE pers.n. *Ælfa* (v. Redin s.nn. *Ælf*, *Æ(l)ffa*, representing pers.ns. in OE *Ælf-*), v. lēah, (ge)hæg.

PEEL HALL (RD) (101–8386), *the Pele of Echellys* 1519 Orm[2], *(the) Peele* 1578 Earw, 1613, 1633 Orm[2], *the Parke of Peele* 1602 Orm[2], *Peel Hall & Lane* 1831 Bry, v. pēl 'a palisade', cf. NED s.v. *peel* 'a stockaded or palisaded (and moated) enclosure' (1596). This is the ancient, moated, manor-house of Etchells. Cf. Peel 333 *infra*.

POUNDSWICK (LANE) (101–8287), 1843 *TAMap*, *Pundesok'* 1280 P (p), *Poundseck* 1712 Sheaf, *-ack* 1831 Bry, *Pounsacke* 1568 Earw, 1602 Orm[2], *Powns-* 1661 Sheaf, *-wick* 1860 White, cf. *Poundsack*, *Pownsack Patch* 1838 TA 34 (333 *infra*), 'oak at a pound', v. pund, -es[2], āc.

ROYALTHORN WOOD (101–8289)
    (?*Ra*)*gel(l)* 1248, 1249 Ipm, IpmR
    Ryale 1260 Plea
    Ruyel' 1285 Court (p), *Ruyl* 1295 Sheaf (p), (*in Ecchels*) 1370 Earw,   *-e* 1377 *Eyre*, (*in Echeles*) 1417 ChRR, *Ruyhul(l)* 1318 Earw,   1354 *Eyre* (p), *Ruyll* 1417 ChRR, Plea
    Ryehull 1287 Court (p), 1289 (17) Orm[2] (p), *Ryll* 1369 (17) ib,   *Ryle* 1520 ChRR
    Roille 1290 Court (p), *Royl(l)e* 1380, 1382 *Eyre*
    Rile Thorn in Ecchils 1536 Earw
    Royalthorn 1831 Bry

'(Thorn at) the rye-hill', from ryge and hyll, with þorn. The earliest spelling is dubious, v. Ipm 1 31. The 1260 Plea form appears to contain hale, dat.sg. of halh, 'a corner'. Cf. Royle Green 237 *supra*, which is probably connected with this place.

SHADOW MOSS (101–8385), 1831 Bry, *Shaddows Moss* 1842 OS, *Shadoke mosse* 1190–1280 (17) Orm², Earw, (Orm¹ reads *Shaders Moss*), cf. Shadow Moss in Hale 334 *infra* (*le Shadmosse* 1481 ChRR), and Mossbrow and Nansmoss in Pownall 232 *supra* and Moss-Side *infra*. The p.n. is 'moss, or bog, at a boundary or a boundary-oak', from scēad, āc and mos. Shadow Moss is near the boundary between Macclesfield and Bucklow Hundreds. Cf. Sharston Green *infra*.

SHARSTON GREEN & HALL (101–8388), *Sharston* 1248 Ipm *et freq*, *Sch-* 1285 *Eyre* (p), *Ch-* 1602 Earw, Orm², *Sharstone* 1661 Sheaf, *Shareston* 1598 ChRR, 1662 Sheaf, *Sharson* 1636 ib, (*-Green(e)*) 1644 Earw, (*& Hall*) 1831 Bry, from stān 'a stone', and either sceard 'notched, mutilated' or scearu 'a boundary', cf. Shadow Moss *supra*.

ASH WOOD, *Big, Little, Middle & Kitchin's Wood* 1831 Bry, *Peel Wood* 1842 OS, v. cycene 'a kitchen', cf. Peel Hall *supra*.   BAGULEY BOTTOMS, v. botm 'a hollow', cf. Baguley 329 *infra*.   BAILEY LANE, cf. Baileys Croft 245 *infra*, 'bailiff's lane', v. baillie.   CHAMBER HALL, 1831 Bry, v. chambre.   COXTON HALL, *Cookstone Hall* 1831 ib, *Cockson Hall & Meadow* 1841 *TA*.   DARK LANE.   GREEN BANK.   HATCHETT'S WOOD, *Two Acre Wood* 1831 Bry.   HEY-HEAD, 1831 ib, 'the top end of an enclosure', v. (ge)hæg, hēafod, cf. Hey Head 238 *supra*.   HOLLYHEDGE, 1842 OS, *Hollin Head* 1831 Bry, v. holegn 'a holly tree', hecg 'a hedge', hēafod 'head, top end of'.   LONGLEY LANE, v. 237 *supra*.   MOSS NOOK, 1841 *TA*.   MOSS-SIDE, 1831 Bry, named from Shadow Moss *supra*.   OUT-WOOD LANE, 'lane to an outlying wood', v. ūt, wudu; on the boundary with Ringway 333 *infra*.   PARK WOOD, *Park Plantation* 1831 ib, 1842 OS, cf. *Peele Park* 1578 Earw, *the parke of Peele* 1602 ib, v. park, cf. Peel Hall *supra*.   ROSEHILL.   ROUND WOOD.   SHARSTON HO, 1842 OS.   SHARSTON MOUNT, *The Mount* 1831 Bry.   STONE HALL (lost), 1831 ib.   STONEPAIL, 'stone fence', v, stān, pale.   WIGANSHILL, 1831 ib, *Wigon-, Wiggins Hill* 1841 *TA*, 'mountain-ash hill', v. cwicen (dial. *wiggen*), hyll.   THE WOOD, *Smalls* 1831 Bry, cf. Bolshaw Outwood 244 *infra*.   WOODHOUSE

LANE & PARK, *the woodhouse lane* 1675, 1694 Earw, *Wood House* (*Lane*) 1831 Bry, 'house at a wood', *v.* wudu, hūs.

FIELD-NAMES

The principal forms in (*a*) are 1841 *TA* 166. 1842 is OS.

(*a*) Alders, Alder(y) Croft (*v.* alor); Bare Croft (*v.* bær[1]); Barn Acre; Bean Mdw; Bell Croft (*v.* belle); Black Field Wd; Black Hey & Shutt (*v.* scēat); Bolshaw (cf. Bolshaw Outwood 244 *infra*); Bone Dust Fd (*v.* bonedust); Booth Fd & Mdw (*v.* bōth); Borrow Fd; Bradley (cf. Bradleygate 236 *supra*); Brickiln Fd; Brinkshaw Fd (*v.* Brinkshaws Fd 245 *infra*); Broad Oak; Big & Little Brook, Brook Shut(t) (*v.* brōc, scēat, cf. 245 *infra*); Brown Fd; Brundage; Butley Woods; Buttermilk Fd; Cank ('a round hill,' *v.* canc); Churn Milk; Clover Croft; Cobbs (*v.* cobb(e) 'a round lump, a cobb'); Cock Fd; Colt Fd; Coppy Fd (*v.* copis); Court Fd; Cow Acre & Lane; Cowslip Croft; Cross Fd & Shutts (*v.* cros, scēat); Crow Fall Mdw (*v.* crāwe, (ge)fall); Doctors Mdw; Doles (*v.* dāl); Dove House Mdw; Driving Lane; Duck Park (*v.* dūce, park); Etchells Fd; Little & Middle Eye (*v.* ēg); Far Moss; Flax Croft; Garner Fd; Gatley Acre & Croft (*v.* Gatley 244 *infra*); Good Mans Hey (*v.* gōd-man, (ge)hæg); Goose Croft; Gors(e)y Fd & Mdw; Greenwood Side; Gritley Fd (*v.* grēot, lēah); The Halves (*v.* half); Ham Brook (*v.* hamm, brōc, cf. Ham Hey 245 *infra*); Hamnett(s) Croft & Hey; Hansen Wd; Hardey Croft (*v.* St Ann's Rd 245 *infra*); Hash Mdw; Hazel Lane 1842; Heald Green Mdw (*v.* Heald Green 244 *infra*); Henhurst (*v.* henn, hyrst); Heys Mdw (*v.* (ge)hæg); Hollin Croft, Hollins (*v.* holegn); Hollow Croft & Mdw; Hough Mdw (*v.* hōh); House Fd; Intack (*v.* inntak); Jack Fd (*v.* jack); Janet Acre; Jonathans Croft; Kel(l)sall(s) Mdw & Intack (cf. Kelsall Croft 246 *infra*; from the family *Kelsall* of Bradshaw Hall 248 *infra*); Knott Lane (*v.* cnotta 'a hillock'); Ley Fd (*v.* lǣge); Light Wood Heys (*v.* lēoht); Maker Fd (*v.* Makers Moor 246 *infra*); Marley Hey (*v.* marle, -ig[3], (ge)hæg); Meggs Hey (*v.* meg); Mersey Fd (near R. Mersey); Mill Acre; Millers Mdw; Moss Mdw; Mossack(s); Mount Car or Fd (from Sharston Mount *supra*, *v.* kjarr); Netherhurst (*v.* hyrst); Oat Greaves (*v.* āte, grǣfe, cf. Wood Greaves *infra*); Old Hey Wd; Old Ley (*v.* lēah); Partridge Fd; Picca (perhaps from pightel 'a small enclosure', cf. Picka Fd 246 *infra*); Pingot (*v.* pingot); Pirtles Croft; Pit Fd; Pooles Intack (*v.* inntak); Poor's Ho; Preston Croft; Round Mdw; Over Rudding (*v.* uferra, ryding); Rush(e)y Fd, Hay, Hey & Mdw; Salt Rushes (*v.* salt[2], risc); Sand Hill; Shay Fd (*Saghffeld* c.1290 Orm[2], 'field at a wood', *v.* sc(e)aga, feld); Sheeps Hey; Shippon Croft & Fd; Shoe Broad (*v.* 334 *infra*); Slip Wd (*v.* slipe); Slothers Mdw (from dial. *slother* 'to slip, to slide, mud', or *slother* 'a sluggard'); Slutch Close, Croft & Mdw; Smithy Croft; Stable Croft & Mdw; Stathe Fd (*v.* stæð); Stoney Butts & Knoll; Street Fd (*v.* strǣt); Stumps (*v.* stump); Summer Fd (*v.* sumor); Swine Cote Mdw; Tan Croft; Tankards Hey; Thistley Croft & Fd; Toad Hole; Trout Mdw; Truck Lane Croft; Trunk Lane Fd; Turn Rudding ('round clearing', *v.* trun, ryding); Vetch Fd; Wall Flatt (*v.* wælla, flat); Walton Fd; White Fd; Wighurst (*v.* hyrst); Withenshaw Rooms 'allotments belonging to Wythenshawe', *v.* rūm[1], cf. Wythenshawe 236 *supra*); Wood Greaves (*v.* grǣfe; this and Oat Greaves *supra* are two parts of a tract of land probably originally called *Greaves*); Worthington Croft.

2. STOCKPORT ETCHELLS (101–8485), 1860 White, cf. Stockport 257 *infra, v.* Etchells 239 *supra*.

BOLSHAW OUTWOOD, OUTWOOD FM & RD (101–8485), *Bolshagh'* 1380 *Eyre, -shaw or Bolshaw Wood* 1578 Earw, *Bolshaw Outwood* 1812 *EnclA* (Cheadle), *þe Outwood* 1586 Earw (Cheadle), cf. *Bolshawecroft* 1288 *Eyre* (p) (Court 236 reads *-shave-*), and *Bollens(c)hawehefed* 1291 Earw (255 *infra*), 'tree-trunk copse', or 'pollard copse', *v.* bola or bolling, sceaga, croft, hēafod: 'the outlying wood', *v.* ūt, wudu. The original woodland extended into several townships, cf. Bolshaw 243 *supra*, Outwood Fm and Hall 255, 250 *supra*.

GATLEY (101–8488)

> *Gatescliue* 12 (17) *Chol*
> *Gateclyue* 1290 *Eyre, -clyf(fe)* 1381, 1383 *ib, Gaticlyue* 1290 *ib,*
>   *Gatlyff* 1427 *Dav* (p), *Gaddecliffe* 1453 *CoLegh*
> *Gatley* 1602 Earw, Orm[2], (*Green*) 1831 Bry, *Gattley* 1704 Sheaf

'Goats' bank', *v.* gāt, clif, cf. Gatley Acre 243 *supra*.

HIGH GROVE, 1831 Bry, *Heegrove* R1 Earw (p), *Hegrave* 1285 Court, 1334 ChRR (p) (?), *-greue* 1290 *Eyre* (Court 245 reads *-greve*), *Heghegreve* 1348 Chamb (p), *þe High Greeve* 1579, 1609 Earw, 'high copse', *v.* hēah, grǣfe.

BEECH HO, *Tan Yard* 1831 Bry, *v.* tan-yard.   BROOKFIELD. BROOKSIDE.   BROWN LANE.   CHASELEY.   CRINGLE HO, *Daisey Bank* 1831 *ib, v.* kringla, cf. Cringlewood 237 *supra*. The house is in a nook of the township boundary.   DARK LANE BRIDGE.   FINNEY LANE, perhaps 'grassy enclosure', *v.* finn, (ge)hæg.   GATLEY BROOK (R. Mersey).   GATLEY HILL (BRIDGE), *Holt Farm* 1831 Bry, *v.* holt.   GATLEY OLD HALL, 1860 White, *Gatley Hall* 1831 Bry. GATLEY RD, *Gatley Lane* 1839 *TA*.   GREENBANK.   GREENHALL BRIDGE, cf. *Green Hall* 1831 Bry.   GRIFFIN FM, *Griffin Inn* 1831 *ib.* HEALD GREEN, 1841 *TA* 166 (243 *supra*), cf. *Heald House* 1860 White, perhaps associated with David son of Leuk *del Helde* 1289 Court 132, *v.* helde 'a slope', grēne[2] 'a green'.   HIGHFIELD HO, *Highfield (Farm)* 1860 White. HOPE FM (lost), 1831 Bry, *v.* hop[1]. HORSING STOCK (lost, 101–857862), 1831 ib, the name of a hamlet at a smithy on the Cheadle boundary, presumably from a mounting-block there. LOWER HO, 1831 ib.   LUM HEAD FM & WOOD, *the Lumme* 1578 Earw, *Lumm* 1831 Bry, *Lum Head (Wood)* 1839 *TA*, '(the top end of) the pool', *v.* lum(m), hēafod.   THE MEADOWS.   OLDHALL FM, near Bolshaw Outwood, not Gatley Old Hall.   OUTWOOD FM & RD, *v.* Bolshaw Outwood *supra*.   PYM GATE, *Pimgate* 1722 Sheaf, *Pymm Gate* 1831 Bry, cf. *Pim Field* 1839 *TA*, *Pym Cottage* 1860 White, either from **geat** 'gate' or **gata** 'a road', with an unidentified first el., cf. Pym Chair 174 *supra*.   ST ANN'S RD, *Hardy Field Lane* 1831 Bry, cf. Hardey Croft 243 *supra*. The old name is probably 'hard enclosure', *v.* heard, (ge)hæg. The later one is from the modern St Ann's Hospital here.   TORKINGTON LODGE, cf. *Torkington Meadow* 1839 *TA*, named from Torkington 299 *infra* or the derived surname. TURNFIELD HO.   WATERFALL.   WILMSLOW RD, from Wilmslow 219 *supra*.   YEWTREE COTTAGE.

FIELD-NAMES

The undated forms are 1839 *TA* 165. Of the others 1346 is BPR, 1354, 1359 *Eyre*, 1369 Orm[1], 1527 Earw, 1831 Bry, 1860 White.

(a) Aspen ('growing with aspens', *v.* æspen); Baby Croft; Backside; Baileys Croft & Mdw (cf. Bailey Lane 242 *supra*); Bark Mill (*v.* bark(e), myln); Barn End & Fd; Barlow Fold (*v.* fald); Beaten-, Beaton Ridding (*v.* ryding); Bens Mdw; Birchen-, Birchin Acre (*v.* bircen[2]); Black Croft; Bleak Croft, Flatt & Mdw (*v.* blāc); Blue Cap (ModE dial. *bluecap* is a name for the blue titmouse or various kinds of wild flower such as the cornflower, *v.* EDD); Brandley Croft; Brinkshaws Fd (*Brynkeswas* 1354, cf. Brinkshaw Fd 243 *supra*) Bruckshaws Brow *infra*, Brancha Fd 330 *infra*. The later forms suggest 'copse(s) at a brink', *v.* brink, sceaga; but the one early form is 'marsh at a brink', *v.* wæsse); Brook Fd; Brookshutt (*v.* 243 *supra*); Broom Croft; Brown Hedge; Bruckshaws Brow (cf. Brinkshaws Fd *supra*, *v.* brū); Budgers Croft; Bulkeley Brow (*v.* brū, cf. Cheadle Bulkeley 246 *infra*); Bung Croft; Butty Mdw (*v.* butty); Call Hey; Bailey & Little Carr, Carr Mdw (*v.* kjarr, cf. Baileys Croft *supra*); Cawdon; Chapel Fd; Cheadle Fd (cf. Cheadle 246 *infra*); Clay Fd; Clayton Hey (*Clayton* 1359, 'clay enclosure', *v.* clæg, tūn); Coal Croft (*v.* col[1]); Cocker Hill (*v.* cocker); Cote Fd; Cow Hill Lane; Crimbabent (from beonet 'bent-grass', with the el. which appears in Crimbucks 238 *supra*); Dove House Croft; Dunnister; Ellens (*v.* ellern); Flash (*v.* flasshe); Front Croft; George or Calf Croft; Gilley Hey; Goer (cf. 233 *supra*); Great Mdw; Green Acre; Grieves Mdw; Ham Hey (cf. Ham Brook 243 *supra*, *v.* hamm); Hawkes Flight; Hay Croft (*v.* hēg); Heywoods Fd; Hill Head (*v.* hēafod); Hob Croft (*v.* hobbe); Hollow Croft & Fd; Holly Bank 1860; Holts Mdw (cf. Gatley Hill *supra*); Hurst Green(cf. Adam *del Hurst* 1346, *v.* hyrst); Joan's Hey; Jowetts; Kelsall Croft (cf. Kel(l)sal(l)s 243 *supra*); Kiln Fd; Lady Knoll (*v.* hlǣfdige, cnoll); Long Flatt; Long Fold 1831; Long Lane Fd (cf. *Long Lane* 1860); Longshaw (*v.* lang, sceaga); Long Shutt (*v.* scēat); Long Tom Fd (probably 'long town-field', *v.* toun); Makers Moor, Sweet Maker (cf. *Maker Field* 1841 *TA* 166, 243 *supra*. These may contain kjarr 'brushwood, marsh', and an unidentified first el. However, they may be analogous with Makerfield La 93, *the two Makerfields* ib 94); Mare Hay; Marl Mdw; Match Croft; Mill Hough (*v.* hōh); Moors Croft; Nag Hey (*v.* nagge, (ge)hæg); Nan Fd; Odd Flatt & Hey (*v.* odde, flat, (ge)hæg); Old Mdw; Old Womans Fd; Ox Hey; Passage Mdw; Pear Tree Orchard; Peas Fd; Peers Fd; Picka Fd (cf. Picca 243 *supra*); Pitstead (*v.* pytt, stede); Potatoe Fd; Road Mdw; Round Shaw (*v.* sceaga); Sapper Crofts; Shippon Croft & Yard; Slack (*v.* slakki); Smethurst Croft & Fd (*v.* smēðe, hyrst); Smithy Croft; Sown Wd; Stable Croft; Stile Fd; Stony Butts; Swan Bear Slip (*v.* slipe); Tan Yard (*v.* tanyard); Thistle Croft; Tolly; Turnpike Road Fd; Twin Fd (*v.* twinn); Vetch Hey; Water Fd; Well Croft Ho; Wellens Mdw; Wharf (*v.* waroð, cf. Wharf 65 *supra*); Whinberry Bank; Withins (*v.* wiðign); Wood Head (*v.* hēafod.)

(*b*) *le Hethes* 1527 (*v.* hǣð 'heath'; Orm² 1 714 reads *le Nethes*).

xiii. Cheadle

The ancient parish consisted of 1. Cheadle (now included in Cheadle cum Gatley c.p., except Cheadle Heath, Edgeley and part of Adswood, now in Stockport county borough c.p.), 2. Handforth cum Bosden (Handforth now included in Wilmslow c.p., and Bosden, a detached part of the township five miles to the north-east surrounded by Stockport parish (*v.* note, 253 *infra*), now divided between Stockport county borough and Hazel Grove cum Bramhall c.ps).

1. CHEADLE (-BULKELEY & -MOSELEY) (101–8588) ['tʃiːdəl, older local 'tʃedəl]

Cedde 1086 DB

Chedle 1153–1180 Orm² (p), m13 *Fitt* (p) *et freq*, *-legh* 1286 Court (p), (-*e*) 1518 Plea, *-lee* 1315 ib (p), 1326 Ipm, *Chedll'* 1379 *Eyre*

Chelle c.1185–1200 Facs, H3 Orm² (p), c.1292 CAS NS 10, *AddCh*, *Chelleia* c.1225 CAS NS 10, *Chel'* c.1185–1200 Facs, *-e* c.1280 *Dav* (p)

Cheddle e13 *AddCh*, c.1287 *ib*, 13 AD, e14 Mere (p), *Cheddel'* 1289 Cl, *-e* 1318 Pat (p), 1326 Fine

Sheddeleye 1291 Tax

Chelde 1252 RBE, 1338 Pat

Schedlea c.1270 Adl, *-le(e)* c.1280 *Dow*

Shedele c.1270 Adl (p)

Chedele c.1275 *Chol*, 1283 Cl (p), 1287 *Dow* (p), 1294 IpmR, e14
 AD (p), 1315 *Chol* (p), 1349 *Eyre*, *-lee* c.1280 *Dow* (p), *Chedule*
 1359 BPR (p), *Chedale* 1559 Orm²

Chedel 1281 AD (p), 1318 Pat (p) *et freq*, *-ell* 1377 ChRR (p),
 -yll l13 (15) *Chol* (p), 1419 MidCh, *-il(l)* 1391 Orm², 1394 Pap,
 ChRR, *-hill* 1527 ib, *-ul* c.1313 *Dow* (p), *-ull* 1379 *Eyre*, *Chedehull*
 1434 BM

Cheadle 1294 AD, 1296 Plea *et freq*, *-Buckley* 1724 NotCestr,
 -Bulkeley 1812 *EnclA*, 1831 Bry, *-Moseley* 1724 NotCestr,
 -Mosley 1730 *Dep*

Gedelegh 1297 *Fitt*

Chadlee 1326 InqAqd, *-le(y)* 1468 *MinAcct*

Chydull 1420 MidCh

Cheidill 1527 Orm²

'*Ched* wood', from PrWelsh **cę̄d* (Brit cę̄to-, Welsh coed) 'a wood',
to which lēah has been added. Cf. Cheadle St, *v.* Jackson 327. On the
identification of the DB p.n. with Cheadle, *v.* Tait 213n., and
Gomellehs infra. The manorial suffixes derive from Richard de
Bulkelegh 1326 Earw I 170, from Bulkeley 330 *infra*, who held a
moiety of Cheadle (cf. *Bulkeley Field* 1844 *TA* 97), and Sir Nicholas
Moseley c.1599 Orm² III 634, who bought the manor of Cheadle
Hulme *infra* (cf. *Moseley Field* 1844 *TA* 96, and Moseley Fm etc.,
infra).

CHEADLE HULME, HOLME BANK & HALL (101–8785)

 Hulm l12 Facs (p), 1285 *Eyre* (p), (*le-*) 1290 ib, 1362 BPR, (*in
 vill' de Chedle*) 1388 Orm², *-e* 1379 *Eyre*, 1384 *Dow* (p), (*and
 Chedulhulme*) 1496 Earw

 Holme 1337 *Eyre* (p), 1373 Pat (p), 1585 Earw, (*and Chedulholme*)
 1527 ChRR, *Holm* 1345 *Eyre*

 Chedle Hulm 1345 *Eyre et freq*, with spellings as for Cheadle *supra*
 and Hulme; *Chedyll-Hulme, Chedulhulme* 1527 ChRR, *Cheadle
 Hulme* 1669 Orm², (*alias Cheadle Moseley*) 1810 Orm²

 Cheadle Holme 1572 *Chol*

'The water-meadow', *v.* hulm. Cheadle Hulme is 'the hulm of
Cheadle', cf. Cheadle Moseley *supra*.

ADSWOOD (FM, HALL, & MILL) (101–8887), *boscus de Addiswode* m13 *Chol*, *Addeswodde* c.1513 Orm², *-wood(e)* 1572 *Chol*, 1599 Earw, *Adswood* 1663 Sheaf, *(in Cheadle)* 1681 ib, *(Hall & Mill)* 1831 Bry, '*Ǣddi's wood*', from the OE pers.n. *Ǣddi* and **wudu**. Adswood Hall is now in Stockport c.p. Another house of the name appears in Cheadle, 6″ OS, but it was *Downs's* 1831 Bry, cf. Downs Bridge *infra*.

CHEADLE HEATH (101–8789), 1831 Bry, *brueria* l12 Facs, *Schedleheth* 1367 Eyre, *v.* hǣð 'heath', cf. Cheadle *supra*. This place is now included in Stockport.

EDGELEY (HO) (101–8889)

   Edisseleg(a) m13 *Dav* (p), l13 *Dow*, AD, *-lee* 1294 ib (p), *Eddisslegh* 1249 Earw (p), *Edisgeleye* 1285 *For*, *Edis(s)heleg(h)*, *-ysshe-* 1287 Court (p), 1301 ChF (p), Orm², 1304 Chamb (p), 1361 Orm², 1374 *Eyre*, 1535 Plea, *-ley* 1404 *LRO* Dx 15, *-ysh-* 1377 *Eyre*
   Hedihslethe l12 Facs
   Hedislethe l12 Facs, *-leth* l13 Tab (p)
   Edislee l12 *Chol* (p), (*H-*), *-ley* m13 *ib*, *-(e)leg'* 1276 Earw (p), 1287 Court, *-legh* 1379 *Eyre*, *Edysley* 1384 *ib*
   Hedesleh' l12 Facs (p), *Edeslegh* 1305 ChF (p), 1348 *Eyre* (p), *Eddesley* 1394 Earw, 1436 *Chol* (p), 1512 *ChEx*
   Eggesley 1428 *Dav*
   Eggeley 1423 ChRR (p), 1527 Plea, 1549 ChRR, *Egele* 1516 Sheaf, *Edgeley* 1550 Pat, (*House*) 1831 Bry, *Edgley* 1724 NotCestr

'Clearing at an enclosed park', *v.* edisc, lēah. Cf. Edgeley Lodge 331 *infra*.

STREET-NAMES: EDGELEY FOLD, *v.* fald, cf. Edgeley *supra*; FORD ST., leading to R. Mersey, *v.* ford; HEATH ST., *v.* hǣð, cf. Cheadle Heath *supra*; LARK HILL, 1860 White, *v.* lāwerce, hyll; STOPFORD ST., cf. Stockport 294 *infra*.

BRADSHAW HALL (LANE), *Bradschawe* 1357 *ChFor* (p), *Bradshaw* 1550 Orm¹, (*-e*) 1637 ib, (*Hall*) 1831 Bry, (*Gate*) 1844 *TA* 97, 'broad copse', *v.* brād, sceaga, gata.

ABNEY HALL, the site of *Chedelgrove* 1372 AD, *Grove* 1831 Bry, 1842 OS, (*House*) c.1855 Orm², *v.* grāf 'a grove', cf. Cheadle *supra*. The modern name appears to be from Abney Db 25, or the derived

surname. ACK LANE, *Hack Lane* 1812 *EnclA*, 1842 OS, *v.* haca.
ACRE LANE, cf. *Acre Field* 1844 *TA* 97. APPLETREE FM. BAM-
FORD GRANGE, cf. *Bamfords Field* 1844 *ib* 96. BATES LEY, -*Lay*
1845 *TAMap* 97, partly in Bramhall township, *v.* Bates Lay 259 *infra*.
BELMONT, *Bellevue* 1831 Bry. HIGHER & LOWER BENT FM, cf.
The Far & Near Great Bent, Bent Croft, Field & Ley, -*Lay* 1844 *TA*
96, 97, *v.* beonet. BIRD HALL, cf. *Bird Acre & Hill* 1844 *ib* 97,
v. bridd. BOLSHAW RD, cf. Bolshaw Outwood 244 *supra*. BRIDGE
HALL, from the family of John fil. Robert *del Brugge* of Stockport
1348 Orm² III 629, cf. William *Bridge* of *Bridge Hall* c.1540 Earw.
BRIDGE HO. BRINKSWAY, 1844 *TA*, 'road at a brink', *v.* brink,
weg. It runs along the south edge of the Mersey valley. BROOK-
FIELD, 1842 OS. BROOKHEAD, 1842 ib, 'source of a brook',
v. hēafod. BROOK LODGE, 1831 Bry. BROOKSIDE, 1831 ib.
BRUNTWOOD HALL, now the Town Hall of Cheadle cum Gatley,
adjoined a hamlet called *Marl Hey* 1831 Bry, *Windy Arbour* 1842 OS,
v. brende², wudu, marle, (ge)hæg, windig, here-beorg. CARFIELD
HO (lost), 1860 White, *v.* kjarr. CHAPEL WALKS, a path leading to
a chapel near Gillbent, *v.* walk. CHEADLE BRIDGE, 1842 OS, site
of *Chedleford* 1580 ChRR, *v.* ford. CHEADLE GREEN (local), *The
Green* 1844 *TA* 96, *the land in front of the dwelling-house of Robert
Harrison, Esq.* 1810 Earw I 184. CHEADLEHALL, *Chedull Halle*
1510 Chol, the manor-house of Cheadle Bulkeley *supra*. CHEADLE
LANE BRIDGE, on Manchester Rd, whose former name it may pre-
serve. CHEADLE ROAD, *Street Lane* 1831 Bry, 1844 *TAMap* 96,
v. strǣt, lane. CHEADLE OLD ROAD. CHEADLEWOOD, *Wood
Farm* 1842 OS, cf. *nemus de Chedell'* 113 (15) Chol, cf. Cheadle *supra*.
CHORLTON BROOK. CHURCHLEY (ROAD), *Chircheleye*, -*leys* 1460
ChRR, probably 'clearing(s) belonging to a church', *v.* cirice, lēah.
COOPERS FOLD. COUNCILLOR LANE. DEMMINGS, cf. *Great &
Little Demmings, Demmings Meadow* 1844 *TA* 96, 97, *v.* demming 'a
dam'. DEPLEACH HALL, *Deep Leach* 1844 *TA*, cf. *Depelache* 1366
Eyre (p), 'deep boggy-stream', *v.* dēop, lǣc(c), lece. DOWNS
BRIDGE, cf. Adswood Hall *supra*, perhaps from a branch of the family
of *Downes, v.* Downes 148 *supra*. GILLBENT (101–865847), 1812
EnclA, Gilbent 1661 Sheaf, *v.* beonet 'bent-grass'. This p.n. means
'grassland at *Gill*'. With it go *Gill Lane* 1831 Bry (101–863857 to
865847), *Gill Bent Bridge* 1842 OS carrying *Gill Lane* over a railway,
and the f.ns. *Gill Croft, Field, Meadow & Body Patch* 1844 *TA* 96, 97.
Body is obscure, as is *Gill*. Topography rules out gil 'a ravine'.

There is no evidence to support ModEdial. *gill* 'a female ferret', or 'the ground ivy *nepeta glechoma*', (EDD). If the historical pronunciation were [dʒil], however, this p.n. might be associated with *le Chill* 1286 Court 228 (p), *Chilley* 1347 *Eyre*. Both these forms occur under Macclesfield Hundred, and probably refer to one place. *Chilley* may represent OE *cilda-lēa*, 'woodland glade belonging to young men', from cild and lēah, for Gillbent was an ancient common down to 1812.   GORSEYBANK MILL, cf. *Gorsey Bank* 1844 *TA* 96.   GREEN-HALL BRIDGE, *v.* 244 *supra*.   HALLCROFT, *Moorpan* 1831 Bry, cf. *Hall Croft* 1844 *TA* 97, *v.* mōr¹, panne.   HEATH BANK (Ho) (101–267895), 1831 Bry, cf. Cheadle Heath *supra*.   HEATHBANK (Rd) (101–872861).   HEATHSIDE, cf. Cheadle Heath *supra*.   HIGHFIELD COTTAGE & Ho, cf. *High Field* 1844 *TA* 96, 97.   HILL-TOP, 1659 Earw.   HOLLY BANK, 1860 White.   HOLLYWOOD PARK, *Holly Wood* & *Vale* 1831 Bry.   HURLBOTE GREEN (lost, 101–855846), *v.* Hurlbote Grange 254 *infra*.   HURSTHEAD, *Hirst-head* 1831 Bry, *Hursterds* 1842 OS, *v.* hyrst, hēafod.   IVY HOUSE FM, 1831 Bry.   LADY BRIDGE (FM), 1831 Bry, *þe Ladie Bridge* 1587 Earw, *Ladies Bridge* 1671 ib, 'lady's bridge', *v.* hlǣfdige, brycg, cf. Lady Brook 30 *supra*.   LANE END FM, *The Lane End* 1730 *Dep*.   LARK HILL (FM), cf. *Lark Hill Road* 1812 *EnclA*, *Moultons* 1831 Bry, *v.* lāwerce, hyll. *Moulton* is a surname.   LONG-SIGHT LANE (101–869844). This is a straight stretch of road 300 yards in length, providing a long 'sight' or view, in the sense used in surveying etc., *v.* lang and NED s.v. *sight* sb. 6 b, d. There is a suburb of Manchester La, called Longsight, which may be of similar origin.   MANCHESTER RD, *v.* Cheadle Lane Bridge *supra*.   MIDDLETON COTTAGE, cf. *Middleton's Road* 1812 *EnclA*.   HIGHER & LOWER MILL, 1831 Bry; the lower mill at 101–855889 was 'one water mill' 1349 Earw; the higher, at 101–855882, is the likely site for the *molendinum* 112 Facs 14, which must have been between Cheadle and Edgeley.   MOSELEY FM, GRANGE, HALL, HO & RD, *Moseley Hall* & *Park* 1860 White, named from the manorial affix *Moseley* being taken as a p.n. analogous with the *Hulme* in Cheadle Hulme.   MOSS LANE, leading to Kitts Moss 260 *infra*.   ORRISH-MERE FM, *Hollins Mere* 1831 Bry, *Hollin Mere Farm* 1842 OS, *Orange Mere* 1844 *TA* 97, *v.* holegn 'holly-tree', mere¹ 'a pool'.   OUT-WOOD HALL & HO, cf. *þe Outwood* 1586 Earw, *Bolshaw Outwood* 1812 *EnclA*, *v.* Bolshaw Outwood 244 *supra*.   PARKGATES, PARK RD, named from Bramhall Park 259 *infra*.   PEAR TREE FM (lost),

1860 White, was in Adswood. Pinfold Fm, cf. *Pinfold* (*Fold*) *Field* 1844 *TA* 96, 97, *v.* pynd-fald. Pingate Lane, cf. *Pingot* (*Meadow*) 1844 *ib*, *v.* pingot. Pump Ho (lost, 101–878856), 1845 *TAMap* 97, 1812 *EnclA*, *Pump Farm* 1842 OS, *v.* pumpe. The Ramillies, *Further & Nearer Ramilies* 1844 *TA* 96, 97. Round-thorne Fm (lost), 1860 White, in Cheadle Heath, *v.* rond, þorn. Schools Hill, *Scowes Hill* 1591 Earw, *Schools Hill* 1842 OS, cf. *Schoolesis within Chedle* ('a dangerous passage, when the water is up, in London Way') 1621 Sheaf, perhaps associated with Henry *del Scoles* 1374 AD IV 183, *v.* skáli 'a hut, a shed', hyll. The 1621 form is apparently the genitive of the surname *Scho(o)les*, which appears in this Hundred as *de Scolis* 1286 Eyre, *del Scoles* 1356, 1369 *ib*, 1429 Plea. Slain, perhaps slinu 'a slope', if this is an old p.n. This would suit the topography, but no early form has been found. Smithy Green, 1844 *TAMap* 96. Spath Lane, cf. *Spath Intake* 1844 *TA* 97, *v.* 255 *infra*. Springfield Ho, cf. *Spring Field* 1844 *ib* 96, 'well-spring field', *v.* spring. Stanley Green, 1831 Bry, after the family *Stanley* of Handforth. Stanley Ho (lost), 1860 White, in Edgeley. Stockport Rd, the main road to Stockport. Tan Pits Fm, *Tan Pits* 1842 OS, *v.* tan-pit. Tenements Lane, *v.* tenement. Turves Rd, *Turf Lane* 1831 Bry, cf. *Turves* 1844 *TA* 97, *v.* turf. Wallnut-Tree Fm (lost), 1860 White. Wilmslow Rd, *London Way* 1621 Sheaf, the road to London, *v.* weg, cf. Wilmslow 219 *supra*. Woodland Fm.

FIELD-NAMES

The undated forms are 1844 *TA* 96 (Cheadle Bulkeley) and 97 (Cheadle Moseley), with 1812 *EnclA*, 1845 *TAMap* 97. Of the others l12 is Facs 14, (a grant of lands between Cheadle and Edgeley, about Cheadle Heath; the forms are taken from the facsimile), m13 *Chol*, 1364 *Eyre*, 1431 AD, 1588 Earw, 1812 *EnclA*.

(a) Acorn Hill (*v.* æcern); Ainsworth Croft; Alder Fd, The Alders (*v.* alor); The Asps, Asp Pits (*v.* æspe); Astle (cf. Astles Croft 255 *infra*); Back Fd & Mdw; Bancroft Mdw (cf. *Bancroft's Road* 1812); Bang Croft, Bank Fd (*v.* banke); Barn Fd, Hill & Mdw; Barrow Fd & Mdw (*v.* bearg 'a castrated boar'); Bean Croft, Mdw & Fd; Birch Bank, Birches; Black Acre & Mdw; Blake Hey (*v.* blæc, (ge)hæg); Bleaching Croft; Bloom Fd, Bloomley Croft, Bloomy Croft; Blossoms Hey; Blue Button Fd (*v.* dial. *blue-buttons* '*Scabiosa succisa*, devil's bit'); Boat Mdw (*v.* bōt); Bottom Fd & Mdw; Bow Bent; Brick Kiln Fd & Mdw; Bridge Fd; Broad Fd & Mdw; Brook Croft, Mdw & Shut (*v.* scēat); Great & Little Broster, Broster Hill

& Wd; Brow Mdw; Brown Fd (v. brun[1]); Browne's Croft (cf. *Brown's Road* 1812); Bruckshaw's Rd 1812 (cf. Bruckshaw's Brow 245 *supra*); Bullock Hey; Burlows Heys; Butty Fd, Mdw & Wharf (v. butty, waroð); Calf Croft; Calver; Canks (v. canc); The Carr, Carr Bank & Mdw (v. kjarr); Carrot Croft; Castle Fd (v. castel); Cauliflower; Cheadle Fd & Nook (v. nōk, cf. Cheadle *supra*); Chiphill Croft & Fd (v. Chip Hill Fm 259 *infra*); Church Fd; Clay Acre & Fd; The Closes; Clover Fd & Ley; Coal(y) Croft (v. cōl, cōlig); Cockshuts (v. cocc-scyte); Common Croft, Fd, Mdw & Piece (cf. *Cheadle Hulme Common Road* 1812); Coolton Leece; Coppice; Corn Fd; Great, Little, Far & Near Cowhey; Cow Lane Croft; Crab Ley, Crabtree Flat (v. crabbe, lēah, flat); The Crew (v. crew); (Little) Crooks (v. krókr); Cross Lane Mdw (cf. *þe Crosse* 1588, v. cros); Crowhill; Cuny(g) Greaves (v. coninger); Daisy Hill; Dale Fd (v. dæl[2]); Dam Flat (v. damme, flat); Dip Ho; Ditch Croft; Docky Hulme (v. docce, hulm); Dole, Dole Butt (v. dāl, butte); Duffy Lane fd; Long & Short Ears (cf. Pease- & Robin Ears *infra*, v. Blackeyer 265 *infra*); Earth Fd (v. erð); Fallow Mdw; Fern Croft; Ferry Fd; Filmot Croft ('polecat croft', from ModE dial. *filmot*, v. fulmart); First Fd; Fisher Croft; Fish Pool; Fitchy Fd (v. ficche); The Flash (v. flasshe); Flat Fd & Hey (v. flatr); Fodens Platt 1845 (cf. *Fowden's Road* 1812, v. plat[2]); Fold Fd; Ford Mdw; Gathill Fd (v. gāt, hyll); Gibbin Heys; Gilts Fd; Glade Fd; Goodall Hurst (v. hyrst); Goose Hey; Gorsey Croft & Knowl; Green Fd & Croft; Gull(e)y Close (v. gully); Hall Acres, Croft & Mdw; Hawking Hey; Hay Croft (v. hēg); Hay Green Mdw; Hayshed (v. (ge)hæg, hēafod); Heath Fd & Mdw; Hemp Fd; Hills Mdw; Hob Hill (v. hobbe, hyll); The Hole; Hollins (v. holegn); Horse Coppice & Pasture; Horse Stones; The Hough, Hough Hey (v. hōh); House Fd & Mdw; Hull Croft (v. hyll); Hunger Hill (v. hungor); Hutton Fd; Intake; Iron Acre (v. hyrne); The Island (v. ēg-land); Ivy Bank; Jack Hey (v. jack); Kelsall Fd & Mdw (from the family *Kelsall* of Bradshaw Hall *supra*); Kensall; Kid Croft (v. kide); Kiln Fd & Hey; Kitchen Fd & Mdw; Great & Little Knoll, Knoll Hey; Lapwing Croft; Ledge Ley; The Lee(s) (v. lēah); Lickers; Lime Fd; Lindow Fd (probably has the same origin as Lindow Moss 230 *supra*); Littlewood Mdw; Lodge Top; Long Croft, Fd, Ley, Mdw, Shut & Wd (v. lēah, scēat); The Louke (v. lowk); Madge Fd; Major Croft & Fd; Mare Croft; Marl Acre & Fd; Marl'd Churl (v. 180 *supra*, Blackeyer 265 *infra*); Marsh Acre; Meal Acre; Mile Stone Fd; Milking Bank (v. milking); Mill Fd & Mdw; Millington Fd; Moor Fd; Moss Croft Fd, Mdw & Room (v. rūm[1]); Mottram Acre; Mouse Croft, Mouse Trap; Neds Croft; Nell Fd, Nelly Mdw; Nether Fd; New Fd & Hey; Newton Croft; North Croft; Little Oake, Oaks, Oaks Hill (v. āc); Orchard Croft, Fd & Mdw; Oven Croft, Oven Back Mdw (v. ofen, bæc); Paddock (v. pearroc); Park Shut (v. park, scēat); Pasture Fd; Pease Croft; Pease Ears (cf. Long & Short Ears *supra*); Pickshaw; Pigcote Croft & Mdw; Pillow Croft (Dole) (v. dāl); Pit Croft; Pitstead Croft (v. pytt, stede); Plat Mdw (v. plat[2]); Pool Croft; Pownall Croft & Mdw (cf. Pownall Fee 228 *supra*); Pump Croft; Push Plough (v. push-plough); Rabbit Fd; Rectors Mdw (from the rector of Cheadle); Red Shrubs (v. rēad, scrubb); Redrose; Red Shutts (v. rēad, scēat); Ridings (v. ryding); Robin Ears (v. Long & Short Ears *supra*);

Roger Hey; Rogues Lane; Rough Fd & Shaw (v. rūh, sceaga); Roundabout (v. 333 infra); Round Shut & Wd (v. rond, scēat); Royott; Rushes; Rushy Fd & Mdw; Rye Croft & Fd; Salter Ridings (v. saltere, ryding, cf. 49 supra); Sand (Hole) Fd; Sandy Heys; School Mdw; Scruting; Higher & Lower Shaw (v. sceaga); Sheep Croft & Walk (v. scēap, walk); Shippon Croft & Fd; Shut (v. scēat); Sidebottom Mdw (v. sīd 'wide', botm 'bottomland'); Slack Fd & Mdw (v. slakki); Slutch Fd; Smale Croft (v. smæl 'narrow'); Smith Croft & Fd; Smithy Fd; Soss (cf. Sossmoss 97 supra); Sough Fd & Mdw (v. sogh 'a bog, a swamp'); the South Fd; Sow Acre (v. sugu); Spring; Sprink Mdw (v. spring); Square Fd; Stable Croft & Fd; Stack Croft, Mdw & Yard; Steracks; Stoney Bank; Stringers Croft (cf. Stringer's Road 1812); Stubble Heys; Swallownest; Swindellents (the last el. is obscure, the first part of the name appears to be the same as in Swindells 256 infra); Tan Croft (v. tan); Thicket Fd; Thistley Fd; Thorn Fd; Three Nooked Fd; Timperley Croft; Tongue Shaft (cf. Tongue Sharp 162 supra); Tot Hills (v. tōt-hyll); Turnpike Fd; Upton Croft; Vetch Fd; Water Pit Fd; Weir Croft & Fd; Well Fd & Mdw; West Fd; Wet Edge; The Wharf (v. waroð); Wheat Croft, Fd & Ridge; White Bread (v. hwīt, brǣdu); White Fd; Wildgoose Hay; Wilkin Croft, Wilkins Croft; Wilmer Shut (v. scēat); Withinshaw Fd (v. wīðign, sceaga); The Wood, Wood Heyes & Hill; Worthings Croft (from ModE dial. worthing 'manuring').

(b) (rivulus qui dicitur) blakeleybroc m13 ('brook at the black clearing', v. blæc, lēah, brōc); Durandescrout, Durandeshalht l12 ('Durand's croft and nook', from the OG pers.n. Durand with croft, halh); Godinesker l12 ('Godwine's marsh', from the OE pers.n. Godwine and kjarr); Gomellehs l12 ('Gamel's clearings', from the ODan pers.n. Gamal and lēah; this may well refer to the Gamel who held Cedde DB and corroborate its identification with Cheadle supra); Hetunesti l12 (probably 'the path to Heaton', v. stīg, cf. Heaton Norris La 30, across R. Mersey); Kingessuire l12 ('the king's neck of land', v. cyning, svíri); le Lambreheye 1364 ('the lambs' enclosure', v. lamb (gen.pl. lambra), (ge)hæg); moara l12 (v. mōr¹); le Overparke 1431 ('the higher park', v. uferra, park, cf. Chedelpark (lit. Cledel-) 1345 Eyre); Sandigate l12 (v. sandig, gata); Shidgateswra l12 ('nook, corner of land, at Shidgate', v. vrá. The older name is either 'gates made of palings', or 'road along which billets are borne', from scīd 'a split piece of wood' (cf. NED s.v. shide) and geat (nom.pl. gatu) 'a gate' or gata 'a road'); Stenris(h)iche l12 ('watercourse in stony shrubland' from steinn and hrís, v. sīc); Wulfphut, -puht l12 ('wolf pit or trap' v. wulf-pytt).

2. HANDFORTH CUM BOSDEN. This township was composed of the detached moieties of a double manor. Bosden, part of the territory of Stockport parish (v. note 246 supra) was granted by Robert de Stokeport (Stockport) to Harry de Honefort (Handforth) c. 1233–6, and thenceforth was part of the manor of Handforth cum Bosden, a township of Cheadle parish (Earw 1 238).

HANDFORTH (101–8583)

> *Haneford* c. 1153–81 (1285) Ch (p), Chest (p)
> *Hannford* 1331 *Chol* (p), *Han-* 1394 ChRR (p), c. 1536 Leland (p), 1548 Pat, (*alias Handfurth*) 1576 ChRR
> *Honeford* l12 Facs (p) *et freq* to 1335 *Fitt*, *-e* c.1320 *ib*, *-fort* c.1200 Orm², *Honneford* 1286 Court
> *Honford* 1249 Earw (p), c.1270 Orm², 1287 *Dow* (p) *et freq*, (*in villa de Chedle*) 1372 *Eyre*, (*nigh Wimslawe*) 1669 Orm¹, *-forte* 1338 Orm²
> *Hondford* 1238 (1623) ChRR (p), 1371 *Dav* (p) *et freq*, *Honde-* 1354 BPR (p), *-e* 1498 ChRR (p), *Hontfort* 1455 MidCh (p), *Hondsford* 1547 *Dow*
> *Hangford* 1383 Cl (p)
> *Henforth* 1440 *Hesk* (p)
> *Handforde* c. 1536 Leland, *-ford* 1576 ChRR, *-fort* 1551 Orm², *-forth*, *-furth* 1576 ChRR, *Handeforde* 1565 *Dow*

DEPN proposes 'Hana's ford' or 'cock's ford', from the OE pers.n. *Hana* or hana 'a cock' and ford. Also possible is 'the ford at the stone(s)', from hān, (gen.sg. *hāne*, gen.pl. *hāna*) and ford, which might refer to markers placed at the ford, cf. Stapleford, *Honeford*, *Handforth* 334, 332, 331 *infra*. The confusion with OE, ME *hand*, *hond* 'a hand', is paralleled in Handbridge 331 *infra*. The ford was probably across R. Dean at either Handforth Bridge *infra*, or Bollin-fee Bridge 222 *supra*.

ASH FM (lost), 1844 *TAMap*. BACK LANE, 1842 OS, *v.* 217 *supra*. BLOSSOMS FM (lost), 1844 *TAMap*. BEECH FM, this is in a hollow, perhaps bece¹ 'a valley-stream'. BOLSHAW ROAD, *v.* Bolshaw Outwood 244 *supra*, Outwood Fm *infra*. BROOK FM, *Brook House* 1842 OS. BULL'S HEAD (p.h.), 1831 Bry. DAIRY HO, 1831 ib. THE GRANGE, GRANGE FM, *Clay House* 1831 ib, *Hope Lane Farm* 1842 OS, cf. *Hope Lane* 1831 Bry, leading from Styal to Handforth, cf. 231 *supra*, *v.* clǣg, hop¹. GROVE-END, (*Lane*) 1831 ib. HALLMOSS, HALL WOOD, *Hall Moss* 1831 ib, cf. Handforth Hall *infra*. HANDFORTH BRIDGE, *v.* Handforth *supra*. HANDFORTH HALL, *the hall of Hanford* 1631 Earw. HURLBOTE GRANGE (101–855846), with *Hurlbote Green* 250 *supra*, *Hurlbote Green* 1831 Bry, *Holbert Farm & Green* 1844 *TA* 96, 186, probably named from the family of William *Horlebot* 1260 Court, with grēne². *Grange* is modern. For the

surname, *v.* Reaney s.v. *Hurlbatt.* LANE SIDE FM, *Laneside* 1844
TAMap. MERRITH'S FM, *Merricks* 1831 Bry, 1844 *TAMap.*
MILL DAMS (101–863828), at Handforth Print Works (101–860828),
1842 OS, probably the site of *the weyre of the mill of Hondfort* 1543
Earw, built c.1291 ib I 263, *v.* myln, damme, wer. OUTWOOD FM
(101–852847), 1844 *TAMap*, probably near the site of *Bollens(c)-
hawehefed* 1291 Earw, 'the head of Bolshaw', *v.* hēafod, cf. Bolshaw
Outwood 244 *supra.* PARSONAGE, *The-* 1831 Bry. SAGARS
ROAD. SPATH GATE & LANE, *Spath Lane* 1842 OS, *Spaths, Spath
Gate* 1844 TA, *TAMap*, cf. 251 *supra*, perhaps for *sparth-* from sparð
'sheep droppings' with geat, lane. Cf. also The Spath Db 582.
SPOUT, cf. *Spout Brow* 1844 *TA*, *v.* spoute, brū. WILLOW FM.
WILMSLOW RD, cf. 251 *supra.* WREN'S NEST.

FIELD-NAMES

The undated forms are 1844 *TA* 186.

(*a*) Acre; Astles Croft (*v.* 251 *supra*); Back Croft; Barley Croft; Barn
Croft & Fd(s); Barrow Croft (*v.* bearg); Beech Fd (*v.* bece[1]); Bent (*v.*
beonet); Bentley Mdw; Bitter Sweet Mdw; Black Fd & Mdw; Great, Little
& Round Bosden Thorn (*v.* þorn 'a thorn-tree', cf. Bosden 256 *infra*, the
detached part of the manor and township, to which this land probably
belonged); Bottoms (*v.* botm); Bowling Green; Brick Kiln Fd; Briery Bank;
Broad Fd; Brook Fd & Mdw; Brown's Fd & Mdw; Butty Lane (*v.* butty);
Cart House Fd; Chesnut Fd; Clay Lane; Clough (*v.* clōh); Clover Fd;
Common Croft & Mdw; Coppice; Corner; Cow Hey; Cranberry Moss;
Croft Moor Loons (*v.* croft, mōr[1], land); Crooked Fd; Crow Hill; Daisy Fd;
Dobbin Fd, Dobbins Brow (*v.* brū, cf. Dobbin Brook 22 *supra*); Door Fd
(*v.* duru); Eddish Croft (*v.* edisc); Fallows (*v.* falh); Fender Mdw (doubtless
from fender 'a ditch, a watercourse', cf. The Fender 23 *supra*); Gate Way;
Goit (*v.* gote, dial. goit 'a watercourse'); Gooseberry Fd; Green Fd;
Handkerchief (*v.* 331 *infra*); Hay Shade Croft; Henshaw Croft; Hodge Hey
(*v.* hocg); Hollow Gardens & Mdw; Horse Close, Hey & Pasture; House
Close & Fd; Hulme Fd (*v.* hulm); Hursteads (cf. Hursthead 250 *supra*);
Intake; Isle of Man (a three-pointed star-shaped field, *v.* 332 *infra*); Jack
Ridding (*v.* jack, ryding); Jeremy Hey; Kiln Croft & Fd; Kitchen Croft &
Fd; Lady Knowles (*v.* hlǣfdige, cnoll); Lee Bank (*v.* lēah); Long Fd; The
Loons (*v.* land); Marl Croft, Great Marl, Marl Fd, Marl; Marsland Fd;
Masters Fd; Meadow Bottoms (*v.* botm); Mellows Croft; Mickley Ditch
(probably 'big enclosure', from micel and edisc); Middle Hey; Middleton
Croft; Mill Fd; Moor Fd & Mdw; Moss, -Croft, Fd & Mdw; Mothers Fd;
Muck Mdw (*v.* muk); New House Fd; Oat Fd; Oates Flatt (*v.* āte, flat);
Old House Mdw; Ormes Croft (from the surname *Orme*); Oven Fd; Ox
Hey; Paddle Fd; Park; Pegs Croft; Pinfold Fd & Mdw (cf. *Pynfold Haye*

1548 Pat, *v.* pynd-fald); Pingot (*freq, v.* pingot); Pit Croft, Pitstead Mdw, Pitts (*v.* pytt, stede); Platting Mdw ('footbridge meadow', *v.* platting); Poor Fd; Priest Fd; Rough Fd; Round Mdw; Rushy Fd; Rye Croft; Sand Hole Croft & Fd; Saw Pit Croft (*v.* saw-pit); Shippon Mdw; Shuttelworth Fd; Stable Mdw; Stack Yard; Stapleton(s) Fd & Mdw; Summerwork Fd (*v. summerwork* (NED) 'land left fallow in summer'); Sun Fd (*v.* sunne); Thistle(y) Fd; Turnpike Croft; Vetch Fd; Water Croft, -field & Mdw; Well Fd; Wet Mdw; Wheat Fd; White Croft; Wood Fd.

BOSDEN (101–9287, 88)

> *Bosedun* c.1233–6 Earw, *-don* 1248 Ipm, 1321 *AddCh* (p), *-den* l13
>   (1577) ChRR, 1360 BPR (p), *Bosseden* c.1270 (17) Sheaf
> *Bosdon* 1249 IpmR, 1286 Court (p) *et freq*, (*in villa de Chedel*) 1337
>   *Eyre*, (*Boson alias*) 1576 ChRR, *-den* 1286 Court (p), (Boson
>   alias) 1575 Orm², *-doun* 1361, 1366 *Dow* (p)
> *Bostone* 1287 Court (p), *Boston* 1366 *Dow* (p)
> *Bosendon* 1296 Plea (p)
> *Boson alias Bosden, -don* 1575 Orm², 1576 ChRR, *Bossen* 1662
>   (1724) NotCestr, 1680 Orm²

'Bōsa's hill', from the OE pers.n. *Bōsa*, and dūn.

BEANLEACH (RD) (101–927884), *Benelache* 1364 *Eyre*, *Beanleach* 1831

Bry, *New Lane* 1831 ib, 'boggy stream at a place where beans are grown', *v.* bēan, læc(c). Near this place was *Saltersbrugge* 292 *infra*. Beanleach was probably a tributary of Poise Brook 33 *supra*.

HAZEL GROVE (101–920870), 1842 OS, *domus vocatus Bullock-Smythy*

1619 Orm¹, *Bullock Smith(e)y* 1592 Earw, 1760 Sheaf, *Hesselgrove* 1690 ib, *-grave* 1775 ib, *Hazle Grove, formerly Bullock Smithy* 1860 White, *v.* bulluc, smiðð̄e, hesel, hæsel, grāf, græfe. This hamlet, in the several townships of Bramhall, Norbury, Bosden and Torkington, now gives its name to Hazel Grove cum Bramhall c.p. (Hazel Grove and Bramhall U.D.). It was a boundary point of the Forest of Macclesfield 10 *supra*. At this place, and probably also at Leathers Smithy 154 *supra*, drovers had their cattle shod with leather shoes (information of the Rev. Mr Hankinson).

SWINDELLS ORCHARD 1844 *TA*, *Swynesdeluis* 1286 *Eyre*, *Swyndelues*

1368 *ib*, E3 Orm², 1379 Earw, *Swyndelfs* 1519 ChRR, *Swyndells* 1563 ib, *Swindels* 1602 Orm², 'swine('s) diggings', *v.* swīn¹, (ge)delf. This p.n. gives rise to a surname often found in NE Cheshire.

Bosden Cottages, Fm, Fold, Hall & Ho, *Bosden House* 1831 Bry, *Bosden Fold* 1842 OS. Bosden Hall appears to be 'the house of Robert Handford' which is a bound of the Forest of Macclesfield, *v.* 10 *supra*. Brook Vale, *Brandy Row* 1831 Bry, *Brandy Brow* 1844 *TAMap*, *v.* rāw 'a row of houses', brū. Brook Ho (2x), from Poise Brook 33 *supra*. Cow Lane. Offerton Rd, leading to Offerton 290 *infra*, forming the boundary of Bosden and Torkington 299 *infra*. Old Fold, 1844 *TAMap*, *v.* ald, fald. Poise Ho (101–932873), 1831 Bry, cf. foll., *Poise Brook, Meadow & Mill* 1844 *TA*, Poise Brook 33 *supra*, *v.* Poise Bridge 300 *infra*. Wellington Mill, 1860 White, *Poise Mill* 1844 *TA*, *v.* myln, cf. prec.

FIELD-NAMES

The principal forms in (a) are 1844 *TA* 186.

(a) America (*v.* 329 *infra*); Back o' th' Ox House; Bank Fd; Barn Fd; Botany Bay (*v.* 330 *infra*); Bridge Fd; Brown Heath; Browy Fd; Bull Park; Butty Mdw (*v.* butty); Clover Fd; Colly Thorn; Corn Hill; Cow Hey (Knowle); Crow Bitch Hill (cf. *the Crowbitch meadow* 302 *infra*, possibly 'crow beech-tree', from crāwe and bēce[2]); Daisy Fd; Dam Mdw (*v.* damme); Day Pit Fd (*v.* dey); Dole (*v.* dāl); Dry Lands; Engine Mdw; Front Croft; Gorsey Bank; The Greave (*v.* grǣfe); Hopwood Fd; Horse Close; House Mdw; Intake (*v.* inntak); Jesse Mdw (cf. Jessiefield 291 *infra*); Kiln Knowle (*v.* cyln, cnoll); Kilverton Mdw; Long Brook Fd; Long Lands; Marled Earth; Meadow Brow; Middle Fd; Mill Hey; Moor Fd & Piece; New Mdw; Old Mdw; Great & Little Orchard; Over Croft; Ox Hey; Great & Little Pasture; Pit Fd; Potatoe Fd; Proxies (this land may have been held by a delegated manorial service rendered by proxy; or it may have produced a rent to pay an ecclesiastical *proxy*, a commutation of an incumbent's obligation to procure lodging for a bishop during visitations, *v. proxy* NED); Rough Fd; Rye Croft Fd; Scholes (*the Schoales* 1697 JRL, 'the sheds', *v.* skáli, cf. *Aschuluescoles infra*); Sew Fd (*v.* sugu); Spring Mdw (*v.* spring); Stack Croft; Stone Croft; Swine Cote Mdw; Wallnut Fd; Well Mdw; Wheat Fd; Willstead (probably from wella 'a well, a spring', and stede 'a place, a site').

(v) *Aschuluescoles* 1322 *Mont* ('Æscwulf's sheds', from the OE pers.n. Æscwulf and skáli, cf. Scholes *supra*).

xiv. Stockport

The ancient parish contained fourteen townships. Etchells, a detached township, is dealt with at 239 *supra*. The others were 1. Bramhall (part now included in Hazel Grove cum Bramhall c.p. and part in Stockport county borough c.p. The former includes Woodford 217 *supra*, Norbury and

Torkington *infra*, and part (formerly all) of Bosden 256 *supra*, and formerly included Offerton *infra*, cf. Hazel Grove 256 *supra*), 2. Bredbury (now part of Bredbury and Romiley c.p., which with Romiley *infra* includes Compstall, formerly a c.p. formed out of parts of Werneth, Brinnington *infra*), 3. Brinnington (*v.* Bredbury *supra*, Stockport *infra*), 4. Disley Stanley (from which Newtown was transferred to Db in 1894, *v.* Db 155), 5. Dukinfield (a detached township, made a municipal borough 1899, part now included in Stalybridge c.p. 305 *infra*, but now including parts of Matley 312 *infra* and of Newton 316 *infra*), 6. Hyde (made a municipal borough 1881, now including Godley 306 *infra*, Newton 316 *infra*, and parts of Werneth *infra*, of Hattersley 307 *infra*, and of Matley 312 *infra*), 7. Marple (now a c.p. including Mellor and Ludworth from Db), 8. Norbury (*v.* Bramhall *supra*), 9. Offerton (*v.* Bramhall *supra*, Stockport *infra*), 10. Romiley (*v.* Bredbury *supra*), 11. Stockport (an ancient borough (1220), a county borough (1835), and a c.p. now including Offerton *supra*, and part of Bosden 256 *supra*, from Hazel Grove cum Bramhall c.p., and parts of Brinnington *supra*, cf. Cheadle 246 *supra*, and of Bramhall *supra*, as well as Heaton, Reddish and Sandfold in La), 12. Torkington (*v.* Bramhall *supra*), 13. Werneth (dismembered in the nineteenth century, part included in Hyde *supra*, the remainder, formerly Compstall c.p., is now included in Bredbury and Romiley c.p., *v.* Bredbury *supra*). In this or Mottram in Longdendale parish was probably the site of the lost place *Hofinchel, Hofinghel* DB, *v.* 165 *supra*.

1. BRAMHALL (101–8986)

Bramale 1086 DB, *-hal* e14 *Chol* (p), *-hall* 1612 Earw, *Bramall* 1578 ChRR, 1831 Bry

Brom(h)ale H2 (17) Orm², 1181 P (p), m13 *Fitt* (p), c.1280 *Dow* (p) *et freq*, *-hal* l12 Sheaf, *-halgh* 1337 *Eyre* (p)

Brumhale 1287 Court

Bromehale 1426 Plea, 1433 ChRR

Brom(m)all, Brom(e)hall 1446, 1448 ChRR, *Chol, Bromehaule* 1536 Leland, *Bromhell* 1545 Plea,

Bromeholme 1551 Fine

Bramhull alias Bromham 1559 Pat

'Broom-nook', *v.* brōm, halh (dat.sg. hale).

SHOTSALL or SHOTSTALL (lost, 101–8988)

Shotiswall 1288 Court (p), *-wall* 1355 *Eyre* (p), (*in Bromale*) 1358 *ib*, *Sch-* 1445 Earw, *Shottiswall* 1541 ib, *-wall, anciently a hamlet here* 1882 Orm² III 829

Shoteswell 1352 Orm² (p), *Shottes-* 1345 *Eyre* (p), 1355 BPR, *Shots-* 1352 Earw (p)

Shetewall 1345 *ChFine* (p), *Sheteswall* 1347 *Eyre* (p)
le Shot(te)walles 1541 *Dav*, ChRR
Shotsall, Shotstall 1849 *TA*

'Scēot's spring', from an OE pers.n. *Scēot* and wælla 'a spring, a well, a stream'. The *TA* fields became Davenport Golf Course (cf. Davenport *infra*) where not built over, and here arose a small stream running westward into Adswood 248 *supra*.

ACK LANE, *Hack Lane* 1842 OS, cf. 249 *supra*. ARDEN GRANGE. BARLOW'S LANE, from the surname *de Barlowe* 1364 *Eyre*. BARN-FIELD RD. BATES LAY, *-Ley* 1831 Bry, from the surname *Bate(s)* and lēah, cf. Bates Ley 249 *supra*. BIRCH HALL, 1831 ib. BIRKLANDS. BRAMHALL BRIDGE. BRAMHALL GRANGE, *Olivers* 1831 ib. BRAMHALL GREEN, 1831 ib. BRAMHALL HALL, *le manoir de Bromhale* 1371 *Dav*, *Bramhall Hall* 1831 Bry, *v.* maner. BRAMHALL LANE (101-893852 to 899890), 1849 *TA*, marked as a Roman Road 6″ OS, *v. Street Fields infra*. BRAMHALL LODGE & PARK. BRAMHALL MOOR, 1831 Bry, *Snybbismore* 1541 Earw, *Snybes More or Stockport More* 1614 ib, *Stopport Moore* 1644 ib, cf. Moorfield *infra*, 'the moor toward Stockport', *v.* mōr[1]; the origin of *Snybbis-, Snybes-* is not known. BREWHOUSE GREEN (lost), 1831 Bry, *Brewers Green* 1690 Sheaf, at Hazel Grove 256 *supra* or Stepping Hill 298 *infra*. BRIDGE LANE, cf. Womanscroft Bridge *infra*. CARR WOOD, *Car* 1842 OS, (*Mistress*) *Carrwood* 1849 *TA*, 'brushwood, marsh', *v.* kjarr. CHARLESTOWN HO, *Charlestown* 1831 Bry. CHIP HILL FM, *Chiphill* 1642 Earw, 1831 Bry, perhaps 'market-place hill', from cēap and hyll, cf. Chiphill Croft & Field 252 *supra*. DAIRYGROUND, 1831 ib, cf. foll. FURTHER DAIRYGROUND, *Dairy House* 1831 ib, cf. prec., *v.* deierie. DAMERY, *Damary or Damery-hey* 1877 Earw, *Dummarys* 1849 *TA*, apparently from the surname *Damary* (ME *Daumary*); here lived the family *Seel*, cf. *Seel's Lane* 1877 Earw I 455, and 'a farm called *Liels* (? Seel's) *farm*' 1684 ib I 378. DAVENPORT (PARK & RD), cf. *Davenport Field* 1849 *TA*, from the *Davenport* family, lords of Bramhall. DISTAFF FM, *Discheifes* (*alias Distaves*), *Dischieves Tenement, the three Great Discheifs, one Less Discheife* 1726, 1728, 1729 *Dav*, *Discheif* 1841 *TAMap*, *-chief* 1842 OS, also called *Roades, Rhodes Tenement* 1726, 1728 *Dav*, from the *Rhodes* family living here, cf. *Rhodes Meadow* 1849 *TA*. The origin of *Dischief* is not known. GREAT OAK (lost), 1831 Bry, cf. *Broad*

Oak 1849 *TA.*   GRUNDY FOLD, from the surname *Grundy*, and **fald.**   HARDY FM, cf. the surname *Hardy*, cf. *de Harday* 1354 *Eyre* (p).   HATHERLOW (LANE) (101–917867), *Hatherlow* 1831 Bry, (*-Farm*) 1842 OS, *Hetherlow* 1849 *TA*, cf. Hatherlow Pasture & Lane, Heatherlow Meadow, 289 *infra*, 'heather hill', *v.* hǣddre, hlāw, cf. Norbury Low 288 *infra*.   HAZEL GROVE, *v.* 256 *supra*.   HILL HO.   KENNERLEY ROAD, *v.* 296 *infra*.   KITT'S MOSS, *Kits Moss* 1831 Bry, *Kitts-* 1842 OS, *v.* mos.   LADYBROOK RD, *v.* Lady Brook 30 *supra*.   LADYTHORN, *Pickfords* 1831 Bry, from a surname derived from *Pykford* 208 *supra*.   LEADBEATERS (lost), 1831 ib, cf. *Leadbeater Field* 1849 *TA*, from the surname *Leadbeater*. LINNEY'S TENEMENT, *Le Rylandes or Lynneys tenement* 1634 JRL, *Faulkners* 1831 Bry, *v.* rye-land, tenement. *Linney* is a surname. LODGE FM, *Lodge* 1831 ib, *v.* loge.   LONDON RD.   LONG PITS (lost), 1842 OS, *Armitage's* 1831 Bry.   LUMB, *The-* 1831 ib, *v.* lum(m) 'a pool'.   LUMB LANE, *Hand Lane* 1842 OS, cf. *Handlane* (*Meadow*) 1849 *TA*, renamed from prec., the southern part of Hand Lane, towards the Woodford boundary, marked *Roman Road* 6" and 1842 OS, *v. Street Fields infra*.   MILE END, *v.* 297 *infra*.   MOOR- FIELD HO, cf. Bramhall Moor *supra*, *Moor Field* (*freq*) 1849 *TA*. MOORLAND ROAD.   MOSCOW HALL, *Moscow* 1831 Bry, perhaps named from its lonely situation.   MOSS LANE, cf. *Moss Meadow* 1849 *TA*.   NEW BARN (lost), 1831 Bry, 1860 White.   NEW HO, 1831 Bry, *New Farm* 1842 OS, *v.* nīwe, the house was built 1668, Earw I 455.   PATCH, *-Farm* 1831 Bry, *v.* pacche.   PEPPER STREET FM (101–905864), *Bramhall Pepper Street* 1649 Earw, *Pepper Street* 1819 Orm² III 536, *an old road called 'Pepper Street'* 1882 Orm², extending northward from Lady Brook at 101–903859 to 905867, conjectured to be a Roman road (Orm² III 536n., Earw I 455n.) cf. Lumb Lane *supra, Street Fields infra*, Pepper St. (Chester) 333 *infra*, *v.* 45 *supra*.   POWNALL GREEN & HALL, *Pownall Green* 1831 Bry, perhaps connected with Pownall 229 *supra*.   GREAT REDDISH WOOD, 1842 OS, perhaps 'rye enclosure', from ryge and edisc. RUTTERS LANE.   STEPPING HILL, 'hill with a stepped or paved road', from ModE *stepping* 'a set of steps, stone(s) to step on' and **hyll**, perhaps the location of Brewhouse Green *supra*.   STREET FIELDS (lost), 1842 OS, *Street Field* 1849 *TA* (2x), *v.* strǣt 'a street, a paved or main road', fields at 101–897854 lying in line with Pepper Street and Lumb Lane *supra*, cf. Bramhall Lane *supra, v.* 45 *supra*. SYDDAL HO & RD, *Siddall* 1726 Dav, *-Houses* 1831 Bry, cf. Thomas

Sydall 1598 Earw.   TENEMENT LANE, passing Linneys Tenement
supra.   WALLBANK, *Wallbank Hill* 1609 Earw, *Wal-* 1666 ib, 1726
Dav, Warbank Hill 1831 Bry, 'well-spring bank', *v.* wælla, banke,
hyll; on the north bank of Lady Brook 30 *supra,* cf. Pepper Street
supra.   WOMANSCROFT BRIDGE, 1831 ib.   WOODS MOOR (LANE),
Woods Moor 1831 ib, cf. *Woods Moor Piece* 1849 *TA,* cf. Bramhall
Moor *supra.*

FIELD-NAMES

The undated forms are 1849 *TA* 67. Of the others 1361 is *Eyre,* 1541, 1612
Earw, c.1728 *Dav,* 1831 Bry.

(a) Acre Fd; Addshill; Ash Croft; Backside; Bark (a meadow); Barley Fd
(*Þe barlie feld* 1541, *v.* bærlic); Barn Croft, Fd & Mdw; Bently (*v.* beonet,
lēah); Birch Hey Fd (cf. Birch Hall *supra*); Birchill Fd (*v.* birce, hyll);
Blackley (*v.* blæc, lēah); Blungarr; Bong Acre, Bongs (*v.* banke); Bow
Greave (*v.* grǣfe); Bradshaws Rough (cf. Bradshaw Hall 248 *supra*); Brick
Hey Mdw; Brick Kiln Croft & Mdw; Bridge Croft; Brieley Fd (*v.* brēr,
lēah); Brook Fd; Broom Mdw; Broom(e)y Flat(t); Brow Fd; Browns
Barrow; Bullock Wife Mdw; Bushy Bing Mdw ('bushy hollow', *v.* busc,
-ig³, bing); Buttery Mdw; Butty Patch(es) (*v.* butty); Calf Croft; Carr Fd
(*v.* kjarr); Cart House Fd; Carter Fd (c.1728); Cash Croft (-*field* c.1728);
Cat Tail Fd (*v.* cat(t), tægl); Catty's Clough; Chaplet Mdw; Cheadle Nook
(cf. Cheadle 246 *supra*); Clay Croft; Coat Mdw (*v.* cot); Coppy Fd (*v.* copis);
Corn Fd; Corner Fd; Court Mdw; Cow Fd, Hey & Holt (*v.* (ge)hæg, holt);
Cross Furlong (*v.* cros, furlang); Daisey Fd (*Dazy fields* c.1728); Dakinfield;
Dan Fd; Great Darlingshaw (101–899838, *v.* sceaga, cf. *Derlingesyate* 219
supra); Disnick; Ditch Croft; Door Fd (*v.* duru); Great Duly Fd; Flake;
Flat Gate 1831 ('gate at a flat', *v.* flat, geat); Forty Acre; Garnett; George
Fd; Gorsey Fd & Lane; Great Field (Clough) (*v.* clōh); Great Mdw (c.1728);
Gritley Fd (*v.* grēot, lēah); Handkerchief Croft (*v.* 331 *infra*); Hanks; Healey
(*v.* hēah, lēah); Hemp(s) Clough (*v.* hænep, clōh); Hey Croft; Hick Fd;
Great & Green Holes; Horse Close; Hough Mdw (*v.* hōh); Hunt Ground;
Intack (*freq, v.* inntak); Jefferns Croft; Jennetts Croft; Johnney Heys;
Katt Croft; Kiln Croft; Kitchen Mdw; Lane Croft; Great & Little Leys
(*v.* lēah); Lime Fd (c.1728); Little Hey; Lomper Patch (*v.* lumber); Long
Acre; Longton (*v.* lang, tūn); Lyes Mdw; Madge Fd; March Fd; Marl
Churl (*v.* Blackeyer 265 *infra*); Marl(ed) Earth & Fd; Melton Fd;
Milking Brow Fd, Milkybrow (*v.* milken, milking, brū); Mill Mdw & Wd;
Norbury Mdw (cf. Norbury 287 *infra*); Number Two; Old Woman's
Fd; Old Wd (cf. Wood Bottom *infra*); One Dole (*v.* dāl); Out Fd
(*v.* ūt); Outlet (*v.* outlet); Parks, Parks Wd (*v.* park); Peter Fd (c.1728);
Pinfallow Fd; Pinfold Mdw (*v.* pynd-fald); Pingott (*v.* pingot); Pit Fd &
Stead, (*v.* pytt, stede, cf. Pool Fd *infra*); Pongs (probably for Bongs *supra*);
Pool Fd & Stead (*v.* pōl-stede, cf. Pit Fd *supra*); Prickley Fd; Priest Fd
(Ash), Priest Mdw; Push Plough Fd (*v.* push-plough); Riddings (*v.* ryding);
Robert o' Barley Fd; Round Fd & Mdw; Rough Fd; Roy(e) Fd; Rush(e)y

Croft & Riddings (*v.* riscig, ryding); Schofield Mdw (from the surname *Schofield*); Shew Bread (*v.* Shoe Broad 243 *supra*); Shippon Mdw; Shot Pit Fd; Slate Land; Snape ('boggy piece of land', *v.* snæp); Soothole; Spath (*v.* sparð); Spring Croft & Fd; Stack Croft; Sun Flat (*v.* sunne); Swine Coat Fd (*v.* swin[1], cot); Thistley Croft; Towns Mdw (*v.* toun); Turf Room (*v.* turf 'turf, peat', rūm[1] 'room, space'); an allotment of land in which turf could be cut); Wall(s) Mdw (*v.* wælla); Wan Wood (Brow); Waste Pit Mdw; Well Croft & Fd; Wheat Fd; White Fd, Furlong & Leack (*v.* hwīt, lǣkr); Within Croft (*v.* wiðign); Wood Bottom Pasture, Wood Fd, Woodrough Fd (cf. *Bramhall Wood* 1612, Old Wd *supra*, *v.* botm, rūh); Yard Croft Wd.

(*b*) *le Marihalle* 1361 (a messuage, probably 'Mary's hall', from the ME fem. pers.n. *Mary* and hall).

2. BREDBURY & LOWER BREDBURY (101–9291)

Bretberie 1086 DB

Bredburi(e) H2 (17) Orm[2] (p), *-buri* c.1190, e13 Facs (p), *-bury* 1249 Ipm *et freq*, *-e* 1551 *Dow*, *-bur(e)* c.1280 *ib* (p), 1304 Chamb (p), *-biri* e13 (1608) ChRR (p), 1287 *Eyre* (p), *-b(er)i(a)* 1238 (1623), c.1240 (1619) ChRR (p)

Bradbur(y) c.1270 Adl (p), 1287 Court (p), *-e* 1565 *Dow*, *-burie* 1638 Earw, *-buru'* 1425 Tab (p)

Brebburi 1271 *AddCh*

Bredebyr' 1285 For (p), *-buri, -bury* 1288 Court, 1292 Ipm, *Breddebury* 1327 Earw

Predbury 1358 *Eyre*

Bretlebury 1422 Plea

'Stronghold or manor-house built of planks', *v.* bred, burh (dat.sg. byrig).

ARDEN HALL, MILL & WOOD (101–9293)

Hawardene 1286 Court (p), *-den* 1355 Earw, Orm[2], (*Hall*) 1672 ib, *Har-* 1597 Earw, *Hauwardynheye* 1348 *Eyre*

Haurthin, -yn 1337, 1350 *Eyre* (p)

Harden 1500 Earw *et freq*, *-yn* 1539 Orm[1]

Arden 1601 Sheaf, (*Hall & Wood*) 1831 Bry, (*Mill*) 1841 *TAMap*

Harderne 1648 ChRR

Ardene in Bredbury 1611 Sheaf, *Ardern Hall* 1860 White

'The high enclosure', *v.* hēah (wk. hēa), worðign, (ge)hæg, cf. Hawarden Fl (NCPN 215) and Harden St (DEPN). The earliest reference cited is to Thomas *de Hawardene*, arraigned with Elcocy the butcher of Werneth (302 *infra*), *v.* Court 216; but an earlier one is possible in Alexander *de Auirdene* 1285 *Eyre* (Court 209 reads *Anir-*).

The p.n. has been confused with the surname of the family *de Arderne, de Arden*, of Alvanley (329 *infra*). The family came from Nth or Wa and acquired this estate by marriage c. 1330 (cf. Wa 11, 209, *v.* Orm² II 75–82). The surname takes the forms *de Harderna* 1153–81 Orm², *Hardern* 1274 Cl, *Erdern* e13 Dieul, *Ardern(e)* e13 VR, Whall, Dieul, *et freq, -a* 1245 Chest, *de Ardena* 1244 ib, *-e* 1252 RBE *et freq, de Ardenn* 1275 Cl, *de Ardein* 1387 ChRR, *Ardren* 1288 Court, *Darderen* 1364 BPR, *Arderen* 1545 *Dow, -on* 1528 *ib*, *Ardran* 1545 *ib*; and *Hordron* 1550 *ib* which is confused with Hordern 139 *supra*. DEPN and EPN are misled by the confusion of surname and p.n.

BUTTERHOUSE GREEN, 1831 Bry, cf. (*Near*) *Butterhouse, Butterhouse Field* 1842 *TA*, probably the same as *Botera(y)les* 1348, 1354 *Eyre* (p), 'the rich-pasture nooks', *v.* butere 'butter', halh, cf. *Boterhale* 211 *supra*.

CROOKILLEY (WOOD) (101–9191), *Crokingles* 13 Tab, *Crokuill'* 1259 Sheaf, *-uile* 1289 (17) Court (p), *Crokeley* 1514 *ChEx*, *Crukilly* 1831 Bry, *Cruickley* 1841 *TAMap*, *Crookhilly* (*Wood*) 1842 *TA*, perhaps 'a clearing called after Crōc', from the OE by-name *Crōc* (from ON *Krókr*, cf. crōc 'crook') with -ing-⁴, lēah.

OTTERSPOOL BRIDGE (101–937895), 1831 Bry, *Rughondisbrugge* c.1270 (17) Sheaf³ 18, Orm² III 539, *a certaine Bridge nowe called Awterspoole bridg and of auncient tyme called Rohehendisbridge* 1611 *LRMB* 200 f.180, *ad quendam pontem modo vocatum Otterspoole Bridge et anti-quitus vocatum Rohehoundesbrigg* 1619 Orm², *Otterscole* (a horse bridge) 1621 Sheaf, *Otterscoe Bridge* 1841 *TAMap*; a bridge with three names, *v.* brycg. The earliest appears to be from rūh 'rough', and hund 'a dog, a hound', but might be from a ME pers. by-name *Rugh-hond*, 'rough-handed', while the later names are from oter 'an otter' with pōl¹ 'a pool' and skógr 'a wood'. This bridge was on the boundary of the Forest of Macclesfield, cf. 9 *supra*.

WOODLEY (101–9492), *Wod(e)ley, -legh* 1326 Orm², 1354 *Eyre*, 1392 Orm², *Wodeley iuxta Stokport* 1513 ib, *Wodlegh* 1344 ChRR, *Woodley* 1615 Orm² *et freq*, 'clearing in a wood', *v.* wudu, lēah.

ALVANLEY HO, commemorates the Arderne family's connection with Alvanley 329 *infra*. APETHORNE JUNCTION, a railway-name, cf. Apethornfold 303 *infra*. ARDEN ARMS (p.h.), 1831 Bry, from the Arderne family of Harden *supra*. BACK LANE (Woodley), 1842 *TA*. BANKFIELD, cf. *Bank Field* 1842 *ib*. BARRACK HILL (FM & LANE), *Barrack Hill* 1780 Earw, possibly from barrāco- 'hilly' and hyll, but in view of the late record, barrack 'a temporary shelter, a hutment', is preferable. BEIGHT BRIDGE, *Bight Bridge* 1621 Sheaf, cf. *le By-*, *Bight milne* 1419 ib, *Beet Wood* 1842 *TA*, *Beet Fields* 1860 White, also Beet Bank in Denton La, on the opposite side of R. Tame, '(bridge, mill etc., at) the bight', *v*. byht 'a river bend', brycg, myln. The river makes a great loop here. BENTS LANE (FM), *Bent's Lane* 1860 ib, *Bench Lane* 1842 *TA*, from benc 'a bench, a shelf' or beonet 'bent grass'. BERRYCROFT LANE, *Berry Croft* 1842 *ib*, *v*. berige, croft. BOGGART HO (lost), 1842 *ib*, *Bogherd House* 1831 Bry, *v*. boggard 'a hobgoblin, a ghost'. BREDBURY BAR, 1860 White, a turnpike gate, *v*. barre. BREDBURY GREEN, HALL & HO, *Bradburie Hall* 1638 Earw, *Bredbury Green* c.1770 ib, *Bredbury House* 1860 White. BROOKFOLD FM, *v*. brōc, fald. BUNKERS HILL, 1831 Bry. CASTLE HILL, 1805 (1877) Earw. There is no record of a castle, although Earw I 478 records *Battle Lane* & *Field* and *Bloody Pits* in the vicinity towards Harden Hall. The significance of these is not evident, *v*. castel(1). CHARLTONFOLD, 1842 OS, *v*. fald. CLAP GATE FM, *Clap Gate* 1842 *TA*, *v*. clap-gate 'a self-closing gate, a kissing-gate'. DARK LANE, 1842 OS. FURTHER HEY, 1842 *TA*. GEORGE LANE, *George's Lane* 1860 White. GILBERTBANK (COTTAGE). GOITE HALL, *the Goit* 1590, 1619 Earw, (house called) *Goit* 1634 ib, 1819 Orm², *Goit-hall* c.1623 ib, *Goyte Hall* 1643 ib, *Goyt Hall* 1672 ib, 'hall at R. Goyt', from R. Goyt 27 supra and hall, cf. Harrison Brow, Goite Wood *infra*. GORSEY BROW. GRAVELBANK, cf. *Gravel* 1842 *TA* (*freq*). HALL LANE (Woodley), leading to Manor Ho *infra*. HARRISON BROW, cf. Roger *Harrison* of *Gytehouses* 1441 ChRR, 'houses by R. Goyt', *v*. hūs, brū, cf. Goite Hall *supra*. HARRYTOWN HALL, *the Harrye Town in Bradbury* 1740 Earw, *Harrytown* 1831 Bry, *Harryton Hall* 1860 White, perhaps from OE hēarra, comp. of hēah 'high' with toun, cf. Harry Croft *infra*. (HIGH & LOW) HATHERLOW, *Hatherlow* 1769 Earw, (*Higher* & *Lower*) 1842 *TA*, 'heather hill', *v*. hæddre, hlāw. HIGHFIELD (HALL & LANE), *Highfield* 1831 Bry. HIGH LANE (FM). HOLLY BANK (lost), 1842 OS.

THE HOMESTEAD.   HORSFIELD'S ARMS (p.h.), the location of
Midway House 1842 ib.   LINGARD (LANE), *Lingards Lane* 1831 Bry,
from the surname *Lingard* (cf. Robert *Lyngard* 1287 Court 231).
LONGACRE FM.   MANOR HO, 1860 White, cf. *maner' de Wodeley*
1422 Plea, and Hall Lane *supra*, *v.* maner.   MIDDLE FM, 1831 Bry.
MIDDLE MILL.   MILL HILL, 1831 ib.   MILL LANE (1) (101–
935893), from Offerton 290 *infra* to Otterspool Bridge near which was
Old Mill 1831 ib, (2) from Arden Mill *supra* southward to Woodley
supra, *Mill Lane & Coal Pit Lane* 1842 OS, the latter referring to the
south end of it.   MOUNT PLEASANT.   PEAR TREE FM, 1831 Bry.
POLEACRE FM & LANE, *Poleacre* 1831 ib, 'field at a pool', *v.* pōl[1],
æcer.   There is a stream between this and Polebank 304 *infra*, cf.
Bowlacre 303 *infra*.   REDHOUSE LANE, 1842 OS.   RHODES'S
(lost), 1831 Bry, a farm on Turner Lane *infra*, from the surname
Rhodes.   SALTERSLANE, a house on Werneth Rd, *v.* saltere 'a
salter', lane, cf. *Saltersfield* 1842 *TA*, and Salter's Lane, *Saltersbridge*
294, 292 *infra*, Werneth Rd *infra*; perhaps associated with Crump's
'Saltway F' (LCAS LIV 130–4), *v.* 50 *supra*.   SCHOOL BROW.
SMITHY GREEN (lost), 1831 Bry, at the smithy (6″ OS) in Woodley.
SPRINGBANK FM & HO, *Spring Bank* 1860 White.   STOCKPORT RD,
the way to Stockport 294 *infra*; a turnpike, also marked as a Roman
road 6″ OS.   STRINGERS WEIR.   TIMPERLEY FM, *Timperl(e)y*
1831 Bry, 1841 *TAMap*, cf. Timperley 335 *infra*.   TOP MILL, cf.
Middle Mill *supra*.   TURNER LANE, 1860 White.   HIGHER &
LOWER WATERSIDE, *Waterside (Farm)* 1831 Bry, beside R. Goyt,
v. wæter, sīde.   WERNETH RD, leading to Werneth 302 *infra*, cf.
Salterslane *supra*.   WOOD BANK 1831 ib, now in Stockport c.p.
THE WOODLANDS.   WOOD MILL, 1860 White.   WOODSIDE.
YEW TREE FM, 1842 OS, *Yew Tree* c.1590 Earw, *v.* īw, trēow.

FIELD-NAMES

The undated forms are 1842 *TA* 68. Of the others, E3 is *Surv*, 1355, 1366
Eyre, 1419 Sheaf, 1831 Bry, 1842 OS.

(*a*) Annis Croft; The Bank; Barley Croft & Mdw; Barn Croft; Bean
Mdw; Beet Croft; Ben Hey (perhaps 'bean enclosure', *v.* bēan, (ge)hæg);
Bent (Fd), Bentley (*v.* beonet, lēah); Black Croft; Blackeyer (*v.* blæc, cf.
Blakeyers, Blackears, Old Years, Long & Short Ears, Pease & Robin
Ears 196, 218, 88, 252 *supra*, and Little Yerr, Stone heyer and perhaps
Mayers 294, 317, 327 *infra*, Goodiere Fd 331 *infra*. All seem to contain an el.
in common, represented by -(*h*)*eyer*(*s*), -*yerr*, -(*y*)*ears*, which also appears as

-jurr after *-(e)d* in Hard & Red Jurr *infra* and Marl Jurr *infra*, 211 *supra*, and Malljurs 332 *infra*, Mawgers 333 *infra*, from which the pa.part. marlede 'having been dressed with marl' is inferred, as in Marl'd Jurr 289 *infra*, contrasting with Marleyer *infra*. Marl Churl 180, 252, 261, *supra* 305 *infra*, Marl Churls 333 *infra*, and Marl(ed) Julls 333 *infra*, probably represent the same, with final *-r(r)* > *-rl* through the influence of the preceding *-rl-* in *marl(ed)-*, and with an assimilation of *-rl* to *-ll*, cf. Marl Chur(r) 287 *infra*. Runjoe 333 *infra* may belong here, first el. rond 'round'. For the common el., eyrr 'a gravel-bank', has been suggested (Db 424, *Lyttell Ayer* 1557, *Littleare* 1737), but this does not suit all these places. OE ēar 'mud' is too archaic, nor does it suit the places. The occurrence of both sg. and pl. forms with a variable y- spelling, suggests a specific substantive with a diphthong subject to stress-shifting. It is probably eModE *ear* '(the action of) ploughing', (from *ear* (OE *erian*) 'to plough, to till', NED), with a transferred meaning, 'land for ploughing, a piece of arable', cf. erð, ere³. The el. eorðe 'earth, ground', becomes *Year* in New Years Eye 333 *infra*); The Bottoms; Braddock (perhaps 'broad oak', v. brād, āc); Breedy Fd ('field full of ridges and reans', v. brǣdu 'a strip, a breadth of land', -ig³); Brick Croft & Flat; Brick Kiln Fd; Bridge Mdw; Brierley (Wd) (1842, 'brier clearing', v. brēr, lēah); Broad Fd; Brook Fd; Brow (Fd); Bull Croft; Butty Rd (v. butty, rod¹, 'clearing divided into butts'); Calf Hey; Catterfall ('diagonal felling', from dial. cater 'diagonal, rhomboidal', (ge)fall); Charles Croft; Cheetham Fds & Mdw; Clegg's Gate (*Clegs yate* 1831, from the surname *Clegg* and geat 'a gateway'); Clod Fd; Clough; Clover Fd; Coal Pit Fd; Coats Lane & Mdw (v. cot); Cockshut(e) (v. cocc-scyte); Colliers Warth (v. colȝere, waroð); Coppice Croft; Cow Hey; Crab Tree Fd; Croft Bank; Dace Pound Fd ('pond with dace in it', v. pund); Dark Hey; Dawson Croft; Door Fd (v. duru); Elder croft; Fair Platt (v. fæger, plat²); Fat Hey ('rich, fertile enclosure', v. fǣtt, (ge)hæg); Finney Fd (v. finn, ēg); Fitch Fds ('vetch fields', v. ficche); Garden Croft; Gee Bank Wd, Gee Hill (v. gee, cf. Gee Parts 183 *supra*); Goite Wd (cf. Goite Hall *supra*); Gors(t)ey Close, Croft, Fd, Hey & Wd (v. gorstig); Grampus; Gwen Accum; The Handley, Denton Hanley (perhaps 'at the high clearing', from hēah, (wk. dat.sg. hēan), and lēah, cf. Denton La); Hard Jurr (v. Blackeyer *supra*); Harry Croft (Bottom) (v. botm, cf. Harryton *supra*); Henshaw ('hen copse', v. henn, sceaga); Higginbotham (v. Higgenholes Db 33 (where this name is cited as a surname), Reaney s.v. *Higginbotham* (citing Oakenbottom La 46), Bardsley 382 (who finds the surname frequent in Stockport & Marple). The principal spellings of it are *Higgyn-*, *Higginbothom*, *-am* 1522, 1542 Earw, *-bottom* 1645 ib *et freq*, with variants *Hyggyn-* 1563 Bardsley, *Heken-* 1578 Earw, *Hichin-* 1579 ib, *Heggin-*, *Hegen-* 1620, 1621 Dow, *Hegin-* 1639, 1672 Earw, *Heghin-* 1694 Dow, *Hicka-* 1695 Reaney, *Higen-* 1762 Bardsley, with *-bothome*, *-botom*. The final el. is botm 'a valley bottom'. Reaney derives the first el. from æcen 'growing with oaks' influenced by ON eik (cf. eiki). This is unconvincing, since it does not account for *H-*. His other suggestion, a La and Ch dialect word *hickin, higgin* 'a mountain ash', would be most attractive if these forms were known or recorded (not in EDD). The La and Ch dialect words for a mountain ash are *quicken, wicken, wiggen* (v. cwicen)

which would have produced a surname *Wigginbotham*. Db proposes the ME pers.n. *Higgin, Hickin*, diminutive for *Hick*, a pet form of *Richard*, as also does Bardsley. This is quite possible. But the form *Higgin-* reappears in Higgin's Clough 272 *infra*, Higginbotham Mdw 289 *infra*, Higginslane 332 *infra*; in the first two, like the Db instance, with a word for a valley or hollow, and in the last with a definite article, circumstances suggesting that the first el. may well be a significant word rather than a pers.n. It is possible that the *Higgin-* form in these names represents an *-ing*[1] formation upon OE hec the Merc. form of hæc(c) 'a wicket-gate', cf. *heck* NED. An OE *hecing 'a wicket-gated place' perhaps 'a hurdle fold' would lead to ME **hek(k)in(g)-*, *heckin(g)-* > *he(g)gin(g)-*, *hig(g)in(g)-*)-); High Earth (*v.* eorðe); Hipley ('hip clearing', *v.* hēope, lēah); Horse Close, Fd & Pasture; House Croft, Fd & Mdw; Intake; Kiln Croft & Fd; Knowle (*v.* cnoll); Lime Fd; Little Hey; Long Fd & Hill; Longstead Wd ('wood occupying a long site', *v.* lang, stede); Low Croft (*v.* lágr); Lowe Croft (perhaps 'mound croft', from hlāw, but cf. prec.); Marl Fd & Jurr, Marl'd Earth, Marleyer (*v.* marle, marlede, eorðe, cf. Blackeyer *supra*); Mill Fd; Moor Croft & Fd; Needhams; Nether Fd; New Bridge Plantation (cf. New Bridge 297 *infra*); New Close & Mdw; Nicklebottom (from botm, with either nicor 'a water sprite', or dial. *nicker*, *nickle* 'a woodpecker, a goldfinch'); Nickolas; Old Mdw, Moor & Pasture; Orchard Fd; Orster Croft (*v.* oxter); Outlet (Wd) (*v.* outlet); Oven Croft; Owlers (*v.* alor); Ox Hey; Park Fd, Mdw & Wd, North & East Park (*The Park* 1842; near Arden Hall & Wood *supra*); Pavement Head ('the top end of a pavement', *v.* pavement, hēafod); Pigeon Croft; Poolstead Croft, Pool Steads ('place where a pool is', *v.* pōl-stede); Potter; Quarry Bank Wd; Rangett; Red Hill; Red Jurr (cf. Blackeyer *supra*); Rick Yard; Riddings (*v.* ryding); Ridge; Rigging Mdw; Road Mdw; Robins Croft; Rough, *freq*; Rough Fd, Mdw & Moor; Round; Round Fd & Mdw; Roundabout Warths (*v.* waroð and 333 *infra*); Royle Hey, Royley Gill Wd, Royley Mdw & Wd (*v.* ryge, lēah, (ge)hæg, gil); Rushey Fd; Rye Croft; Sand Bank; Sand Pit Fd; School Fd; Sedge Mdw (*v.* secg[1]); Sharples (*v.* scearpol, cf. Sharples La 47); Shaw Wd (*v.* sceaga); Shootleys Pool; Short Acre; Slack, Slack Acre & Mdw (*v.* slakki); Slang (*v.* slang); Sling (*v.* sling, cf. prec.); Slope ('a slope', *v.* slope); Small Croft; Smithy Fd & Mdw; Sour Fd; Spoil Bank (*freq*, from coal mining and quarrying, *v.* spoil-bank); Spout Fd (*v.* spoute); Stable Fd; Stateley Mdw; Stone(y) Croft & Fd; Store Mdw; Swan Pool (*v.* swan[1], pōl[1]); Tailor Croft; Tame Wd (from R. Tame 36 *supra*); Tang (*v.* tang); Tenters (*v.* tentour); Thatchers Wd (1831, now in Stockport c.p.); Thistley Croft, Fd (Wd) & Gill (Wd) (*v.* gil); Town Croft & Fd; Warrity; Warths (*the Werths* 1419, cf. Colliers- & Roundabout Warth *supra*, *v.* waroð); Way Fd (*v.* weg); Well Croft, Fd & Mdw; Wheat Fd & Tops (*v.* topp); White Bear Mdw; The Wood, Wood Acre, Wood Gate Croft.

(b) *Blakeacre* E3 ('black ploughland', *v.* blæc, æcer); *Kyrkemedewe* 1355 (p) (*v.* kirkja, mǣd); *le Style* E3 (*v.* stigel); *del Wyndybonke* 1366 (p) ('windy hillside', *v.* windig, banke).

3. BRINNINGTON (101–9192)

Brinintona H2 (17) Orm², Bry-, Brinyn(g)ton, -in(g)- 1308 ib (p),
1327 Plea, 1337 Eyre, 1338 AD, 1348 Eyre, Brinnin(g)ton 1285
Court (p) (lit. Brimin-), 1290 ib (p), -yng- 1378 Eyre, Brynnyngton
(lit. Brymyng-) 1287 Court (p), Brynnyn(g)ton (alias Portwodde)
1549 ChRR
Bruninton c.1200, e13 Orm² (p), 1248 Ipm, -yn(g)- 1304 ChF (p),
1321 Plea, E3 Surv, 1341 Eyre
Brenyn(g)ton 1378 Eyre, 1386 Plea, 1443 ChRR, Brennyngton
(alias Portewood) 1550 Pat

'Farm called after Brȳni', from the OE pers.n. Brȳni and -ing-⁴,
tūn.

PORTWOOD (101–9091), boscus de Stokeport R1 Orm², Portwode 1337
Eyre, -wood 1510 MidCh, (Brynington alias) 1622 Orm², -woode 1630
ib, -wodde, (Brynnyngton alias) 1549 ChRR, Portewood 1550 Pat,
'wood belonging to the port, (Stockport 294 infra)', v. port², wudu.
There was a hall here, Portwood Hall c.1620 Orm², Portwood Old Hall
1860 White, now lost, the site being the south side of Great Portwood
St. west of Carrington Rd.

STREET-NAMES: CARRINGTON RD, cf. Carrington Bridge 297 infra; POOL
LANE, Poole Lane 1860 White, v. pōl¹ 'a pool'; GREAT PORTWOOD ST.,
1860 ib, cf. Portwood supra; (BACK) WATER ST., 1860 ib, v. wæter; WITHEN'S
Row, 1860 ib, v. wiðign 'a willow', rāw.

ASHERBOTTOM FM, Asher Bottom 1842 TA, 'bottom-land growing
with ashes', v. æscen, botm.   BLACKBERRY LANE.   BRINNINGTON
HALL & MOOR, 1842 OS.   BRINNINGTON MOUNT, 1831 Bry.
HOLLOW, Wood Houses 1831 ib, 1842 OS, 'houses at a wood', v.
wudu, hūs, holh.   MANOR FM.   MANOR HO, 1860 White.
MAYCROFT, 1842 TA.   MEADOW MILL.   MOORFIELD COTTAGE,
cf. Moor Field 1842 ib and Brinnington Moor supra.   PARK
BRIDGE, Portwood Bridge 1831 Bry, cf. Portwood supra, v. 298 infra.
POLLETT, Pollitts Farm 1842 OS, from the surname Pollitt.   POTT.
STRINES, 1842 ib, beside R. Tame, 'the channels', v. strind.
THORNHILL FM.   WARTH MEADOW, Wharf Meadow 1831 Bry,
1842 TA, v. waroð 'a meadow by a stream'.   WHITE BANK HO,
1860 White.

FIELD-NAMES

The undated forms are 1842 *TA* 74. Of the others, 1360, 1362 are *Eyre*, 1831 Bry.

(*a*) Antic; Barley Croft; Barn Fd & Mdw; Black Croft; Broad Fd & Mdw; (The) Brow (cf. *Brow Wood* 1831 Bry, *v.* brū); Brown Croft; Burnt Earth (*v.* brende², eorðe); Carr Bank Wd (*v.* kjarr); Clapper Mdw (*v.* clapper); Clay Croft; Cockshot, Cockshot Heaviley (*v.* cocc-scyte, cf. Heaviley *infra*); Corbel Fd; Cote Fd (*v.* cot); Cow Brow; Crow Park; Flake Fd (*v.* fleke); Foot Gate Heaviley ('foot-way', *v.* fōt, gata, cf. Heaviley *infra*); Forty Acre; Gladden (*v.* glad(d)en); Goit (*v.* gote); Goose Hey (perhaps 'goose enclosure' but probably 'gorse enclosure', *v.* gōs, gorst, (ge)hæg, cf. Goosetrees 68 *supra*); Hag Wd 1831 ('haw, hawthorn wood', *v.* hagga); Half Acre; Hard Croft Wd; (Cockshot-, Foot Gate-, Slutch Gate-) Heaviley (probably associated with Heaviley 296 *infra*); High Fd; Hill(s), Hill Fd; Hole Wood Land (*v.* hol¹); Horse Brow & Hey; House Fd; Intack (*v.* inntak); Island (*v.* ēg-land); Kiln Croft Wood Brow; Kiln Fd; Knowle; Great, Lesser & Little Lands; Lane Fd; Long Croft, Hey & Mdw; Marled Earth, Fd & Hey; Mill Wharf (*v.* hwearf or waroð; cf. Wharf 65 *supra*); Mine Hey; New Fd; Paddock; Palmer Bottom (*v.* botm); Pasture Fd; Pitsteads (*v.* pytt, stede); Pound (*v.* pund); Pugsley Bank (*v.* banke); Pump Mdw; Red Heath; Ridded Earth (from *ridded*, pa.part. of *rid* (ME *rydde*) 'to clear woodland', and eorðe or erð); Royal Mdw (probably 'rye-hill meadow', *v.* ryge, hyll, with mæd); Rushy Fd; Side Brow (*v.* sīd 'long, large', brū); Slutch Gate Heaviley ('slutch way', *v.* slutch, gata, cf. Heaviley, *supra*); Throstle Bank; Twitchell (*v.* twitchel 'a narrow passage', cf. twicen(e)); Well Fd (cf. *Well Wood* 1831); Wet Fd; Wheat Fd; White Field Bank; Wood Mdw.

(*b*) *del Ol(e)res* 1360, 1362 (p) ('the alders', *v.* alor).

4. DISLEY-STANLEY, *Disteley Stanley* 1453 ChRR *et freq*, with spellings as for Disley, and Stanley Hall *infra*.

DISLEY (101–9784) [dizli]

> *Destesleg'* c.1251 *For* (p), *Destlegh* 1394 Orm², *Destellegh* 1471 *MinAcct*
>
> *Distislegh* 1274 Orm² (p), *-leye* 1285 *Eyre* (p), *Di-*, *Dysteslegh* 1308 Ipm, 1354 *Dow et freq* to 1495 ChRR, *-ley* 1337 *Eyre*, *-le(e)* 1345, 1347 *ib*, *Dystysleg* 1337 *ib*
>
> *Di-*, *Dysteleg(h)*, *-le(e)*, *-ley(e)* 1286, 1288, 1289 (17) Court, Orm² *et freq* to 1533 ChRR, *Distelishethe* 1316 Pat, *Distell'* 1288 Orm², *Distellegh* 1467 *MinAcct*, *Distilegh* 1495 Orm², *Distilleighe*, *-aghe*, *-eithe* 1560 Sheaf
>
> *Distley* 15 ChRR, 1487 Plea, (*-legh*) 1503 *ChFor*, 1535 VE

Disley 15, 1542 ChRR *et freq*, (*alias Deane*) 1580 *Dep*, *Dysley* 1590, 1690 Sheaf
Disseley 1447 *Eyre*, *Dy-*, *Disceley* 1547 *Chol*, 1553 Pat, *Dy-*, *Dis(c)heley* 1561 ChRR, *Dishley* 1582 Orm², c.1639 *Chol*
Desley 1528 ChRR

The final el. of Disley is lēah 'a clearing, a wood, a woodland glade'. The first el. has not been defined. DEPN is irrelevant, cf. Diglee 178 *supra*. EPN s.v. suggests dȳstig 'dusty', but the forms with an apparently gen.sg. inflexion, *Destes-*, *Distes-*, *-is-* etc., are against this unless the second *-s-* is intrusive, or unless dȳstig is used as an OE pers. by-name *Dȳstig 'Dusty', cf. *Dūst* (Tengvik 311).

The first el. of Disley probably recurs, with hop¹ 'a valley', in Dissop Head *infra*. It may be an unidentified compound containing OE wist (gen.sg. *-e* fem; *-es* masc. in some compounds) 'being, existence; home; food, sustenance', *v.* BT & BTSuppl s.v. *wist* (and compounds cited there), also EPN s.v. In Sx the word denotes a tract or measure of land (Sx 452, 562, NED s.v.), and in Foxtwist, Foxwist 194 *supra*, 331 *infra*, it must mean 'fox's home', i.e. 'place supporting a fox, a fox's living'. OE dæg-wist 'food, a meal', i.e. 'the day's provision or sustenance', could be the word required here, Disley and Dissop then being 'woodland glade' and 'valley, at a place to which the day's provisions must be taken', or 'at a place where meals are eaten', or 'at a place where a living is had from day to day'. But *dæg-wist* has not yet been found in other p.ns., and the picnic connotation does not seem acceptable. A preferable alternative would be to suppose an analogy with Fox(t)wist, an OE compound *dæge-wist* 'dairy-maid's living' (*v.* dæge). Disley and Dissop would then be 'at a place where the dairy-maid makes a living', possibly lēah and hop¹ suffixed to the gen.sg. form of an older p.n. from *dæge-wist*.

The village of Disley was also known as DISLEY DENE (*Disteslegh-dene* 1341 *Eyre*, *Destlegh Deyne* 1394 Orm², *Distley Deyn* 1535 VE, *Disteley Dean* 1548 Earw, Orm², *Disley alias Deane* 1580 *Dep*, *Disley Deane* 1611 *LRMB* 200, *-Dene* 1724 NotCestr) from its situation in a valley, *v.* denu, cf. *Deane lache* 1503 ChFor, (*the*) 1550 *MinAcct*, (*v.* læc(c)), *the Deane House* 1550 Earw, (*v.* hūs).

STANLEY HALL (101–9785)

Stanlega c.1200 Orm² (p), *-le* c.1210 Dieul, *-leg'* 1281 Plea, *Dow* (p), *-l'* 1285 *Eyre*, *-leye* 1285 *Court*, *-lye* 1288 ib (p), *-legh* 1302

Orm², 1341 *Eyre et freq*, *-ley* 1301 Sheaf, 1389 ChRR *et freq*, (*oon chefe place called*) 1515 Earw, (*Hall(e)*) 1549 ib, 1550 *MinAcct*, *-leighe* 1560 Sheaf, *-leigh* 1616 *LRMB* 200, *-ligh* 1620 *Surv*

Staneleye 1296 Pat, *-legh* 1312 Plea *et freq*, *-ley* 1414 ChRR (p), *-leighe* 1611 *LRMB* 200

Standeley 1536 Leland

'Woodland glade at a stone or rock', *v.* stān, lēah.

NEWTOWN (101–9984), 1860 White, a modern name; part of Disley transferred to Db, *v.* 258 *supra*.

ORMESTY (lost, a tenement in Disley), 1286, 1337 *Eyre* (p), 1384 *Rental*, 1416 *JRC* 806, *Ormisty* 1286 *Eyre*, 'Orm's path', from the ON, ODan pers.n. *Ormr* and stīg, cf. *Hormesestrete* 171 *supra*. The same pers.n., and the derived surname *Orme*, still current in east Ch, appear in Ormes Smithy 145 *supra*, Ormes Moor 325 *infra*, and the lost *Ormelegh* 53 *supra*.

SHERT HALL (lost), 1860 White, *Sherde* (*in villa de Distellegh*) 1467, 1471 *MinAcct*, *Shirt* 1664 *Dow*, cf. the surname *de Sherde* 1342 Orm², *del S(c)herd* (of Stanley) 1384 *Rental*, 1389 ChRR, 1393 *Dow*, *Sherte* 1503 *ChFor*, *v.* scerde 'a gap, a cleft, a pass', which would exactly suit the location of Disley Dene *supra*. The family surname is also associated with Fulshaw Hall 228 *supra* (the earliest record) and Shirdfold 182 *supra*.

ASPS, 1842 OS, *Asp's Meadow* 1849 *TA*, *v.* æspe 'aspen tree, white popular'. BADGERSCLOUGH, 1831 Bry, 'badger's valley', from ModE *badger* (cf. bagga), and clōh. BANKEND, *the Banck end* 1611 *LRMB* 200. BENT COTTAGE, BENTSIDE, cf. *Further & Middle Bent* 1849 *TA*, *v.* beonet 'bent-grass'. BLACK HILL, the location of *a hill called Hitchin Lowe*, *Hitckin Low* 1611 *LRMB* 200, *Hichinlowe* 1620 *Surv*, *v.* hlāw, cf. 178 *supra*, Longside *infra*. BOLDER HALL. BOLLINHURST BRIDGE, *v.* 199 *supra*. BRINES. BROADHEY (HILL), *the Narrbrodhey*, *the Broad hey* (*field*) 1611 *LRMB* 200, *Broadhey* 1831 Bry, 'the broad enclosure', *v.* brād, (ge)hæg, nēarra 'nearer'. BROADS, cf. *Broad's Field & Meadow* 1849 *TA*. BURYMEWICK WOOD. 'Bury me wick!' is an ejaculation meaning

'Bury me alive!', i.e. 'May I be buried alive if...unless...'. Cf. Burymewick 293 *infra*, Bury me Wick Mill 313 *infra*.   CARR, *The Carr* 1611 *LRMB* 200, *v.* kjarr 'brushwood, marsh'.   CART HO, *v.* carte-hows.   CLOUGH, *The Clough* 1611 ib, *Clough House* 1831 Bry, *v.* clōh 'a dell, a valley'.   CLOUGHSIDE, *v.* clōh, sīde. COCKHEAD, *Cocks Head* 1831 ib, *Higher & Lower Cockshead* 1849 *TA*, *v.* cocc-scyte 'a cock-shoot'.   COCK-KNOLL, 1849 *ib*, *Cock Knowl* 1831 Bry, *v.* cocc[1] 'a hillock, a cock', cnoll.   CORKS (LANE), cf. *Cork's Meadow* 1849 *TA*.   DANEBANK, on a bank overlooking Disley Dene *supra*, *v.* denu.   HIGHER DISLEY, *Lanehead* 1660 Earw, 1842 OS, 'the top end of a lane', *v.* lane, hēafod.   DISLEY-BANK WOOD, *Bank Plantation* 1842 ib.   DISLEY HALL, 1831 Bry. DISSOP HEAD (101–980819), *Dis(s)op(p)head, Dis(s)op(e)* 1611 *LRMB* 200, 1620 *Surv*, *Dysop Head* 1831 Bry, cf. *Dysop Head Field* 1848 *TA* 244 (201 *supra*), 'the top end of *Dissop*', *v.* hēafod. *Dissop* is the name of a saddle at the head of two valleys on the boundary between Lyme Handley, Disley Stanley and Yeardsley cum Whaley, a topography suggesting hop[1] 'a small valley'. The first el. is discussed under Disley *supra*.   DRAKECAR, *le Drakeker* E3 *Surv*, 1384 *Rental*, *Drake Carr (Meadow)* 1848 *TA* 244 (cf. 201 *supra*), *Drakes Carr* 1831 Bry, 'the dragon's marsh', *v.* draca, kjarr; doubtless drawn from folklore.   DRYHURST (WOOD), *Dryhurst* 1503 *ChFor*, 'dry wooded-hill', *v.* drȳge, hyrst.   ELLYBANK, (*a hill called*) *Ellybancke, the Ellibancke* 1611 *LRMB* 200, (common called) *Ellebanke* 1620 *Surv*, *Elliebancke* 1660 Earw, *Ellibank* 1684 Sheaf, perhaps 'elder-tree bank', from elle, -ig[3], and banke, cf. Ellis Bank 133 *supra*.   FIRWOOD HILL.   FURNESS HO, ROW, VALE & WORKS, *Furnace* 1831 Bry, (*Works*) 1860 White, *v.* forneis 'a furnace'.   GREEN LANE.   GREENS CLOUGH, 1849 *TA*. GREENSHALL *Greeneshall* 1564 Orm[2] (*the*) 1611 *LRMB* 200 *v.* hall 'a hall'; perhaps manorial.   GROVE MILL, 1831 Bry.   HAGBANK, 1831 ib, 'haw bank', *v.* hagga.   HAREWOOD, *Dam Side* 1831 ib, named from a mill-dam here.   HIGGIN'S CLOUGH, 1849 *TA*, *v.* clōh 'a dell'; for the first component cf. Higginbotham 266 *supra*. HIGHFIELD, cf. *High Field (Meadow)* 1849 *ib*.   HILLSIDE, 1849 *ib*. HOLLINWOOD COTTAGES.   INGLEWOOD.   JACKSONSEDGE, *Top of Jacksons* 1831 Bry, cf. *Jaxon Sprynges* 1550 *MinAcct*, *Jackson tenement* 1611 *LRMB* 200, *Jackson's Meadow & Croft* 1849 *TA*, from the surname *Jackson*, *v.* ecg 'an escarpment', spring 'a young copse', cf. also Edge Piece, Stanley Hall Edge, *Wharnedge infra*, referring to the ridge running north to south through the western part of the township. KILN HO & KNOLL, *Hill Knoll* 1842 OS, *Kiln Knoll(s) & Meadow* 1849 *TA*, cf. *the Kilnecrofte* 1611 *LRMB* 200, *v.* cyln, cnoll. KNATHOLE (WOOD), *Potter Hey Wood* 1842 OS, *Potta Hey Wood, Knat Hole* 1849 *TA*, 'gnat hollow', *v.* gnætt, hol[1], cf. Pottershey *infra*. LANE ENDS, *Lane End* 1831 Bry, cf. Higher Disley *supra*. LEATHERS, 1831 ib. LIGHTALDERS, 1831 ib, *the light ollers* 1550 *MinAcct*, 'the light alders', *v.* lēoht, alor. LILLIECROFT. LODGE ROW. LONG LANE. LONGSIDE, *Longside House* 1831 Bry, named from *le longsyde* 1384 *Rental, Longside* 1611 *LRMB* 200, (*Hill*) 1690 Sheaf, a hill extending into Yeardsley cum Whaley, cf. 178 *supra*, Black Hill *supra*, *v.* lang, sīde. MEADOW BANK. MOOR-FIELD, -SIDE & -WOOD, *Moorside, Moorwood(s)* 1831 Bry, 1842 OS. MOWHOLE, 1849 *TA*. MUDHOUSE LANE. MUSLIN ROW. PARK HILL. PLATTS (lost), 1831 Bry. POTTERSHEY (CLOUGH), *the Pottwaye hey, Pottwell hay* 1611 *LRMB* 200, *Potta Hey Shut & Wood* 1849 *TA*, *Potter Hey Wood* 1842 OS, cf. Knathole Wood *supra*, *v.* (ge)hæg, clōh. The origin of *Pottwell-, Potter-* is probably *Potte-, Puttewalker de Distellegh'* 1467, 1471 *MinAcct, Potteswaller* 1508 *ib*, '(brushwood at) the spring or stream at a deep hole', *v.* potte 'a deep hole', wella (Merc wælla), kjarr. REDHOUSE LANE. REDMOOR LANE, 1831 Bry, cf. Redmoor 140 *supra*. ROACH-HEY WOOD, *Ritch-Hey* 1611 *LRMB* 200, *Upper & Woody Roach Hey* 1849 *TA*, 'enclosure at a rock', *v.* roche, (ge)hæg. The location is a steep bluff over R. Goyt. For the modern form, cf. The Roaches St. ROCKS, 1831 Bry, *v.* roke 'a rock'. SCHOLES FOLD, cf. *Scholes's Field* 1849 *TA*, from the surname *Scholes* and fald 'a fold'. SHADY OAK. SHRIGLEY POTTERSHEY (2x), cf. Pottershey *supra*. The prefix may be manorial, or a recurrence of the place-name Shrigley (130 *supra*). SPENCER HALL. SPRINGFIELD VILLA, cf. *Spring Field* 1849 *TA*; there is a spring nearby, *v.* spring. STANLEYHALL WOOD, 1849 *ib*, cf. Stanley Hall *supra*, *v.* 283 *infra*. STONERIDGE (HIGHER & LOWER), *Stan-, Stoneridge* 1611 *LRMB* 200, 1620 *Surv, Upper Stoneridge* 1831 Bry, *v.* stān, hrycg. STRAFFORD HO. TORVALE, the valley of R. Goyt under Torr Top in New Mills Db, *v.* torr, val, cf. Warkmoor Rd *infra*. WARD LANE. WARKMOOR RD (101–997851), named from *le Werkesmor* (*boscus*) E3 *Surv*, 1347 *Eyre*, 1384 *Rental*, -*moor* 1347 *Eyre*, (*the*) *Warkes Mo(o)re* (*Wood*) 1611 *LRMB* 200, *Warksmoor* (*Wood*) 1849 *TA*, *Works Moor* 1831 Bry, 'Weorc's moor', from an OE pers.n. *Weorc*, and mōr[1], cf.

Wirksworth Db 413. *Warksmoor* became Torvale *supra*.   WATER-
SIDE (UPPER- & MILL), *Watersyde* 1660 Earw, *Waterside House &
Mill* 1831 Bry, beside R. Goyt, *v.* wæter.   WIDOWHURST, (*House*)
1849 *TA*, *Widows Hurst* 1831 Bry, *v.* hyrst.   WILLOW HO.
WOODBANK HO.   (LITTLE) WOODEND, WOODEND HO & MILL,
(*Little*) *Woodend* 1831 ib, 'the locality where the wood was', *v.* wudu,
ende[1], cf. *boscus de Stanlegh* 1364 Eyre, *Stanley-, -legh Wodde* 1503
ChFor. Woodend was *Middle Wood* 1831 Bry. It was not at the *end*
of the wood.   WOODGRANGE, near Disleybank Wood *supra*.
WOODSIDE MILL, near a wood at Newtown *supra*.

FIELD-NAMES

The undated forms are 1849 *TA* 144. Of the others, 1286 is Court, 1316 Pat,
E3 *Surv*, 1347, 1361 *Eyre*, 1348, 1357, 1503 *ChFor*, 1384 *Rental*, 1467, 1471,
1508, 1550 *MinAcct*, 1560 Sheaf, 1611 *LRMB* 200, 1620 *Surv*, 1660 Earw,
and 1831 Bry.

(*a*) Abraham Fd; Acre Fd; Adam's Croft; Ash Fd; Back o' th' Hill;
Backlane Head Fd (*v.* hēafod); Bagshaw Mdw; Balgie; The Bank (*-e* 1611);
Barley Croft; Barn Fd (*freq*, cf. *the Barnefield* 1611); Big Ley; Birchen Hey
(*v.* bircen[2], (ge)hæg); Black Acre (*blacke acre* 1611); Black Fd & Heath (cf.
the Blacke Yarthe 1550, *v.* blæc, eorðe); Blackmoor (*v.* blæc, mōr[1]); Bonny
Flats; Bottom Clough; Briary Fd; Bridge Brow Wd; Broad Fd (*the broad-
field* 1611); Broadricks; The Brow; Burnt Stile (*v.* brende[2], stigel); Butcher's
Ground; Calf Fd (cf. *the Calfe Croft* 1611); Cato Fd & Mdw; Church Fd
(cf. *the Church crofte* 1611); Clayton Croft & Hey; Clough Head ('top of the
dell', *v.* clōh, hēafod); Coalpit Fd; Colchut Hill; Common Piece (cf. (*the*)
Com(m)on wood 1611); Cooper's Croft; Cop Thorn (probably 'pollarded
thorn' from copped, þorn); Coppice; Corner Bit; Cow Fd & Hey; Crack-
Hurst (*v.* kráka, hyrst); Cripple Knoll ('hill with a burrow in it', *v.* crypel,
cnoll); Cumberland (*v.* cumber, combre, land); Dale Piece (*v.* dæl[1]); Day-
hurst ('dairy wood', *v.* dey, hyrst); Deep Wd; Dig Nest; Disley Wd (*Dysteley-
wod* 1357, *v.* wudu); Dole (*v.* dāl); Dower Fd (*the Dowry*, 1611, *v.* dowarie);
Dry Fd; Edge Piece (cf. *le Edge* 1550, also Jacksonsedge *supra*, *v.* ecg); Great
& Little Eyes (*The Lower & Over Eyes* 1611, *v.* ēg 'water-meadow');
Flash Fd (cf. *Flashcarre* 180 *supra*, *v.* flasshe 'a shallow water'); Flowery
Croft (*the Flowry Crofte* 1611); Lower, Middle & Top Frank; Further Mdw
(*-e* 1611); Gorsey Brow & Fd, Gorsty Fd (*v.* gorstig, brū, feld); Gravel Bed;
Great Fd & Mdw; The Green; Half Acre; Hall Croft; Hamper Mdw &
Piece; Hard Head (*v.* heard, hēafod); Harry Riding (*the Henry Rydinge
Meadowe, the two Henry Rydinges* 1611, *v.* ryding); Heathy Piece; High Hey
(cf. *the Hey* 1611, *v.* (ge)hæg); Higher Row; The Hill; Hodge Hey (*the
Hodghey meadowes* 1611, from either hocg 'a hog', or the pers.n. *Hodge*,
a pet-form of *Roger*, cf. Rocher Hey *infra* and (ge)hæg); Hole Mdw; Hollow
Mdw; Home Croft, Fd, Mdw, Pasture & Wd; Horse Coppice, Fd &

Pasture; House Fd & Mdw; Intake; Higher, Little & Lower Jenkin Croft
(*Jankyns Croftes* 1550, from the ME pers.n. *Jankin*, diminutive of *John*, with
croft); Kettledock Fd (*v.* keddle-dock); The Knoll, Knoll Pasture (cf.
del Knolles de Dystelegh 1361 Eyre (p), *v.* cnoll 'a hillock'); Lady Croft (*v.*
hlǣfdige); Long & Short Lands; Level Fd; Lime Fd; Locker Fd (*v.* loca,
cf. Reaney s.n. *Locker*); Lodge Fd & Mdw; Long Croft (*Lancroft* 1550,
v. lang, croft); Longshut (*v.* scēat); Lower Fd (*the-* 1611); Marled Fd (*the
Marle(d) field* 1611); Marsland Croft (perhaps 'marsh land', *v.* mersc, land);
Mellor Mdw (cf. Mellor Db); Middle Fd; Middle Row; Miller's Piece;
Near(er) Mdw (*the Nar(r)meadow(e)* 1611, 'the nearer meadow', *v.* nēarra);
Nell Nook; New Mdw (1611); Nurse Croft; Occerly (cf. Hockerley 177
supra, Hockley 300 *infra*); Old Earth (*v.* eorðe or erð); Old Warren; Orchard
Fd; Outlet; The Park; Pea Hey; Peck Croft; Philip's Mdw (cf. *the Phillipp
Crofte* 1611, 180 *supra*); Pin Croft; Pingot (*v.* pingot); Pit Hack (perhaps
'wicket-gate at a pit', *v.* pytt, hæc(c);) Plot (*v.* plot); Pole-, Pool Bank
(*v.* pōl[1]); Poor Ground; Poor's Land; Ring Mdw (*the Ringe meadow* 1611,
v. hring 'a ring'); Rocher Hey (perhaps associated with (*le*) *Roger(e)sbothum*
E3, 1357, 1384, 'Roger's valley-bottom', from the ME (OFr) pers.n. *Roger*
and botm, cf. Hodge Hey *supra*); Rock Fd, Rocky Piece (cf. Rocks *supra*);
Rough; Rushy Field; Higher & Lower Shoot (cf. *Further & Nearer Shutt*
1611, *v.* scēat); Slids (*Slidd* 1831, perhaps *slid* (EDD), a dial. form of ModE
slade, *v.* slæd, cf. Slid Mdw 287 *infra*); Slipe (*v.* slipe 'a narrow strip of
land'); Smithy Fd; Spinney; Spite Fd (perhaps one hard to work); Spring,
Sprink (*the Springe* 1611, 'young wood', *v.* spring, cf. Jacksonsedge *supra*);
Square Fd; Squirrel Style; Stable Mdw; Stackyard; Higher & Lower
Standlow (*the Neather & the Overstanlow* 1611, 'stone-hill', *v.* stān, hlāw,
neoðera, uferra); Stanley Bank, Stanley Hall Edge, Stanley Mdw (*Stanley
Edge* 1831, *v.* ecg and cf. Stanley Hall, Jacksonsedge *supra*); Stonepit Fd;
Stoney Fd; Stubble Fd; Tanners Mdw; Tenter Bank, Croft & Fd (*v.*
tentour); Thistley Fd & Piece; Three Cornered Piece; Three Nooked Bant
(*v.* beonet); Three Quarters; Tinker Riding, Tinker's Flat (*The Tymker flatt*
1611, *v.* tink(l)ere, ryding, flat); Tit Croft; Tongue Sharp (*v.* tonge-s(c)harp,
cf. Tongue Sharp 162 *supra*); Top Clough; Torr (*v.* torr); Training Knolls;
Tum Croft; Turnep Croft; The Warth (1611, *v.* waroð); Webster Hey
(Wd) (*Webster Hey, Webstarr hay wood* 1611, from the occupational surname
Webster and (ge)hæg); Well Croft & Fd; Wet Earth, Mdw & Piece;
Whitehead Fd; Wood Fd, Mdw & Piece.

(b) Beryhouskechyn 1467, 1471, *Predehawes kethyn* 1508, *Predicanskyne*
1560 ('the manor-house kitchen', *v.* burh, hūs, cycene, with scribal errors in
the two later spellings); *the Highe, Midle & Jumble Bleckett(es)* 1611 (*v.*
jumble); *the broken bancke* 1611 (*v.* brocen, banke); *the Castell* 1560 (*v.*
castel(l), but there is no castle here); *Coras banck* 1611, *Cowralls Ban(c)ke*
1611, 1620 (*v.* banke; the first el. is the Ch surname Calrall); *Crosseley
hurst(e)* 1503, (*the*) *Crosseleigh(e)* 1611, -*legh* 1620 ('cross clearing', *v.*
cros, lēah, hyrst); *le Grenehurst* 1384 ('green hill', *v.* grēne[1], hyrst); *Greis*
1467, *Greys* 1471, *Gyres* 1508 ('stairs', *v.* grese); *the hangingflatt* 1611 ('flat
plot of ground on the edge of a hill', *v.* hangende, flat); *the Hassell Rowe* 1611

('row of hazels', *v.* hæsel, rāw); *Haukesyerd, le Haukesherd* 1347 ('hawk's gap', *v.* hafoc-scerde, cf. *Hawkesyord* 166 *supra*); *Hawybridg* 1611 (*v.* brycg); *The Heathfield* 1611 (cf. *Distelishethe* 1316, *v.* hǣð, cf. Disley *supra*); *Heghlegh*' 1384 ('high clearing', *v.* hēah, lēah); *Hermytesbothum* 1384 ('hermit's valley-bottom', *v.* ermite, botm); *Hibbart Wood & Meadow* 1611 (cf. Hibbert Lane 284 *infra*); *the Hive Field* 1611 ('bee-hive field', *v.* hȳf); *the Hulme* 1611 (*v.* hulm, cf. Hulme 179 *supra*); (rivulum vocatum) *Hardelsbroke* 1467, 1471, *Hurdenbroke* 1471, *Hurdeswallesbroke* 1508, *Hurdswell* 1560 (the evidence is not good, the spellings being from *MinAcct*, but perhaps the 1508 form is the true one, from brōc added to a p.n. from wella (Merc wælla) 'a stream'. The first el. could be the OE pers.n. *Hygerēd*, or the OE *Ēorēd* found in the nearby Yeardsley 176 *supra*); *Knapwarth* 1611 ('young man's meadow', *v* cnapa, waroð); *Lyme Parke syde* 1611, 1620 (*v.* sīde, cf. Lyme Park 198 *supra*); *Morleyhorthe* 1550 ('tilled land at moor clearing', *v.* mōr[1], lēah, eorðe); *Parua Mosley* 1503, *Moselegh* 1357 (*v.* 283 *infra*); *Olrennshawe* 1348 (p) ('copse growing with alder-trees', *v.* alren, sceaga); *the Overfield* 1611 (*v.* uferra); *the Pichowe* 1611 (*v.* pīc[1], hōh); *the Pygreave (Croftes)*, *Pigrave wood* 1611 ('magpie copse', *v.* pīe[2], grǣfe); *the Rondwardhurst* 1611 (probably rond 'round', prefixed to a p.n. *Wardhurst*, 'watchman's woodedhill', *v.* weard, hyrst); *the Stebinges* 1611 (*v.* stybbing 'a place with treestumps'); *Stonybothome* 1660 ('stony valley-bottom', *v.* stānig, botm); *Wharnedg(e)* 1611, 1620 ('mill-stone edge', *v.* cweorn, ecg, cf. Jacksonsedge *supra*); *Wodewalhurst* 1384 ('wooded-hill at a deep pool in a wood', from wudu and wēl[2], with hyrst, cf. *Wodewal(-e-, -es-)croft* 1288, 1289 Court (p), not located, *v.* croft); *Wytehalh* 1286 (p) ('white valley', *v.* hwīt, halh).

5. DUKINFIELD (101–9497)

Dokenfeld H2 (17) Orm[2], 1297 Plea (p), *Dokinfeld* 1285 *Eyre et freq* with variant spellings *Doken-* (to 1620 *Dow*), *Dokin(g)-, Dokyn(g)-Dokun-, Docun-, Docken-, -feld(e), -feeld, -feild, -field, -felt* to *Dokenfeild* 1620 *Dow, Dockenfield* 1620 Orm[2]

Dukenfeld H2 (17) Orm[1], 1285, 1337 *Eyre, -felt* m13 *Fitt* (p), *-field* 1819 Orm[2], *Ducinfilde* l13 *SocAnt* (p), *Duckenfyld, -felde* 1550 Pat, *-field* 1724 NotCestr, *Duckingfield* 1646 Earw

Dokenefeld 1285 *For*
Dunkenefeld 1321 Plea
Doukinfeld 1337 *Eyre*
Dukefeld 1345 *Eyre*
Dekenfeld 1348 *Eyre*

'Ducks' open-land', *v.* dūce (gen.pl. dūcena), feld.

STREET-NAMES: ASTLEY ST., 1850 *TAMap*, *Dog Lane* 1831 Bry, cf. *Dog Lane Colliery* 1850 *TAMap*, 'dog lane', *v.* dogga, later named after the *Astley* family of Dukinfield Hall; CHAPEL HILL, 1860 White, from a non-conformist chapel built 1707; FURNACE ST., *Furniss Hill & Street* 1860 White, from

furneis 'a furnace'; GATE ST., the location of *Southgate House* 1831 Bry,
v. geat 'a gate'; HIGHFIELD ST., cf. *High Field* 1849 *TA, Highfield Buildings*
1860 White; MEADOW LANE, 1860 ib, *v.* mǣd, lane; OLD HALL ST., leading
to *Hall Green* 1707 Earw, 1860 White, cf. Dukinfield Hall *infra*; HOLLINS
ST., *Hollin Street* 1860 ib, cf. Hollin's Lane *infra*.

DEWSNAP FM & LANE (101–944968)

> le *Dewis(c)nape* l13 *AddCh*, -*snape* 1290 *Eyre* (p), *Dewysnape* 1285
> *ib* (p), 1304 Chamb (p) (lit. *de Wysnape*), 1312 Plea (p), 1321
> *AddCh* (p), (*le-*) 1361 *Eyre* (p), -*snap(pe)* 1285, 1286 *ib*,-*scnap*
> 1494 *SocAnt* (p), *Deuysnape* 1285 *Eyre* (p), *Deuyssnape* 1340
> BPR (p)
> *Deusnape* 1287 *Eyre* (p), 1294 Earw (p), le *Dewsnape* 1404 *LRO*
> Dx15 (p) *Dewsnap* 1831 Bry, *Dewsnop* 1842 OS

'Dewy bogland', *v.* dēawig, snæp, cf. Dewsnip 310 *infra*, and
Dewsnaps 327 *infra*, Db 77.

BANKWOOD MILLS, 1860 White, 'wood at a hill-side', *v.* banke,
wudu.   BANNS, -*Farm* 1850 *TAMap*.   BARLOW WOOD (lost),
1842 OS, cf. Plantation Fm *infra*.   BARNMEADOW WORKS, *Barn
Meadow Mills* 1860 White.   BAZIER.   BIRCH LANE, 1860 ib.
BRADLEYHURST FM, '(wooded-hill) at the broad clearing', *v.* brād,
lēah, hyrst.   BROADBENT FOLD, *Hough Hill* 1831 Bry, 1842 OS,
cf. Hough Hill *infra*, *v.* fald. *Broadbent* is a surname.   CASTLE
IRON WORKS & MILL, CASTLE ST, cf. *Castle Hall House* 1850
TAMap, probably a building with mock crenellation, there being no
castle here, *v.* castel(l).   CHEETHAM HILL RD, *Hyde New Road*
1860 White, in which Mr Edward *Cheetham* was resident, *v.* Hyde
279 *infra*.   DUKINFIELD HALL, *house called Dokenfield* 1622 Earw,
Dukenfield Hall 1819 Orm².   DUKINFIELD LODGE, *Dukenfield-* 1819
ib.   EARLY BANK WOOD, 1842 OS.   EASTWOOD, -*House* 1842 ib.
FIR TREES, 1831 Bry.   (OLD) GORSE HALL, *Gorse Hall* 1831 ib,
house called Gorses 1622 Earw, *v.* gorst 'gorse'.   HALL QUARRY,
named from Old Gorse Hall *supra*.   HOLLIN'S LANE, leading to the
site of *Hollins* 1831 Bry, 1850 *TAMap*, cf. *Hollins Meadow* 1849 *TA*,
Hollins St. *supra*, *v.* holegn 'holly'.   (NEAR) HOUGH HILL, HOUGH
HILL RD, (*Nigher*) *Hough Hill* 1831 Bry, *Lower-* 1850 *TAMap*,
'prominent hill', *v.* hōh, hyll, cf. Broadbent Fold *supra*.   HUNTERS-
TOWER, 1831 Bry, a folly built 1807 by Francis Dukinfield Astley,
v. Earw II 23.   JOHNSON BROOK (R. Tame), JOHNSONBROOK RD,

Johnson Brook 1842 OS, from the surname *Johnson*.   KENYONS (lost, 101–953971), 1850 *TAMap*, *Kenyon* 1842 OS, from the surname *Kenyon*.   KNIGHTS HOUSES, *Knights Farm* 1850 *TAMap*. LAKES, 1842 OS, *Lakes Cottage* 1831 Bry, v. lacu.   LODGE FM, *Old Lodge* 1831 ib.   LYNE EDGE (101–960970 to 963978), 1842 OS, *Line Edge* 1831 Bry, from ecg 'an edge, a ridge', and the old region-name *The Lyme*, v. 3 *supra*, cf. Ashton under Lyne La 29, two miles north of this.   NEWTON WOOD, 1860 White, a hamlet named after Newton Wood 317 *infra*.   OAKFIELD HALL, *Oakfield* 1860 ib. OLD HALL MILL, cf. Dukinfield Hall *supra*.   OLD MILL (lost), 1850 *TAMap*.   PARK FM (lost), 1860 White.   PETERSBURGH FURNACE (lost), 1831 Bry, an iron-works, v. furneis.   PICKFORD LANE, (& *Street*) 1860 White.   PLANTATION FM, -*House* 1850 *TAMap*, *Wood Ends* 1831 Bry, at the west end of Barlow Wood *supra*.   QUARRY STREET MILLS, *Quarry Mills* 1860 White, from an old quarry approached by Quarry St.   RANGE COTTAGES & RD, v. dial. *range* 'a strip of land'. Here it refers to a row or range of cottages built in a strip of land.   SANDY LANE, cf. *Sandy Vale* 1850 *TAMap*, 1860 White, *Sandiway Vale* 1860 White.   SCHORAH WOOD (lost, 101–945980), 1842 OS, now a cemetery. This looks like an old name, but no early forms are available.   TOWN LANE, 1860 White.   WATERHOUSE BRIDGE & WOOD (lost, 101–936968), 1831 Bry.   WINDYHARBOUR, *Cold Horbor* 1831 ib, 'cold, windy shelter', v. windig, cald, here-beorg.   YEWTREE (LANE) 1831 ib.

FIELD-NAMES

The undated forms are 1849 *TA* 148.

(*a*) Bank Bottom & Mdw; Big Mdw; Bottoms (v. botm); Brick Kiln Mdw; Dry Earth; Great Field Top; Marled Earth; Pasture Fd; Pingle (v. pingel); Primrose Field Whath (v. vað 'a ford' or waroð 'a meadow'); Round Mdw; Tenter Croft (v. tentour); Titherington Mdw; Top Mdw; Tower Fd (cf. Hunterstower *supra*); Wet Hole.

(*b*) *Rasseboth*' 1286 *Eyre* (p) (Court 221 reads -*both*), -*boutham* 1428 ChRR, *Rasshebotham* 1480 Adl (perhaps 'level valley-bottom', from boðm and ME (NWMidl) *rasse*, as in 'a rasse bi a rokke' *Sir Gawayn* 1570, and 'a rasse of a rock' *Cleanness* 446, for 'a level space beside a rock' and 'a level part, or top, of a rock'; but Professor Löfvenberg suggests that the first el. may be OE (Nb) ræsc (WRY 7 234), ModEdial. *rash*, the NCy variant of OE risc, ModE *rush*, 'a rush, a rush-bed', as in Thickrush, Rash, WRY 6 238, 258, cf. Cu 489 s.v. rysc, and Rash, Wellrash, Cu 270. A surname formed from this p.n. appears in Rassbotham St. in Stalybridge La); *Wodanclogh* c.1380–1415

Bowman, Barnes[2] (probably 'crooked valley', from wōh and denu, with clōh. Dr Barnes in LCAS lxxi 48 suggests the god-name Wōden as first el., but this usually appears with gen.sg. inflexion, and often in a mutated form, i.e. *Wōdnes-*, *Wēdnes-*, and it would be rash to insist upon so important an etymology on the evidence of the recorded form. Cf. Wedneshough Green 309 *infra*).

6. HYDE (101–9595)

> *Hida* e13 Dieul, m13 *Dav* (p), *Hide* 1240 Adl (p), 1249 Earw *et freq* to 1596 ChRR
> *Hyde* e13 Orm[2], c.1233 *Dow* (p) *et freq*, *la-* 1282 Court (p), *Hyda* 1286 *Eyre*
> *Huyde* 1403 CRC, and eight examples, ChRR, Adl, Ch to 1519 ChRR

'The hide of land', v. hīd. This may be *terra del Hoyth* l13 (18) Sheaf[3] 20 (4788).

STREET-NAMES: BROOK ST., cf. Godley Brook 306 *infra*, v. brōc; LUMN HOLLOW, 1860 White, cf. *The Lumm* 1831 Bry, v. lum(m) 'a pool', holh; MILK ST., GREAT NORBURY ST., 1839 *TA*, perhaps named from the *Hyde* family's connection with Norbury 287 *infra*; SHEPLEY ST., TOM SHEPLEY ST., cf. *Shepleys* (*Tenement*) 1839 *TA*, and Richard *Shepley* of Hyde 1627 Earw, surnamed from Shepley La; THROSTLE BANK ST., v. Throstle Bank Mill *infra*; TINKERS PASSAGE, cf. *Tinker Road & Street* 1860 White, after Francis William *Tinker*, a mill-master then; WATER ST.; WELL MEADOW, cf. *Well Meadow* 1839 *TA*, v. wella 'a well', mǣd.

BACKBOWER (LANE), 1839 *TA*, *Bower Fold* 1831 Bry, *Bank Bower* 1842 OS, from būr[1] 'a cottage, a dwelling', and fald 'a fold', with bakke 'a back, a ridge' and banke 'a bank' (cf. bakki), from its situation on a hillside. BACK LANE, 1860 White. BAYLEY FIELD MILL, cf. *Bailey Field* 1839 *TA*, v. baillie 'a bailiff'. BROOMSTAIR BRIDGE, cf. Broomstair Mills in Haughton La, across R. Tame. CARRFIELD MILL, -s 1831 Bry, cf. *Carr* (*Field*) 1839 *TA*, 'marsh field', v. kjarr. CLOUGHFOLD FM, 'fold in a dell', v. clōh, fald. FLOWERY FIELD HO, cf. *Flowery Field* 1839 *TA* and Flowery Fd 316 *infra*. FOXHOLES, 1839 *ib*, v. fox-hol. GEE CROSS, v. 303 *infra*. GOWER HEY BROOK, HO & WOOD, *Gore Hey Wood* 1831 Bry, cf. *Far & Near Goer Hey* 1839 *TA*, 'enclosure at a gore', v. gāra, (ge)hæg. The gore is a peninsula of higher ground formed by the valley of the brook. HOVILEY (BROW), *Hoviley-*, *Overley Brow & Lane* 1860 White, cf. *le Ouerlybonk* 1341 *Eyre*, 'clearing at the edge of a hill', *v.* ōfer[1], lēah, banke, brū.   HYDE CHAPEL, HALL & LANE, *Hyde Hall* 1819 Orm[2], *Hyde Chapel* 1831 Bry, *Hyde Lane* 1839 *TA*. Hyde Chapel was an early Unitarian chapel at Gee Cross, *infra*, founded 1708. Hyde Hall, demolished 1857, was 'generally called Hyde Mill from an ancient mill near the mansion' 1819 Orm[1], *Hyde Mill* 1860 White.   KINGSTON (BRIDGE, HO & MILLS), *Kingstone House* 1831 Bry, *Kingston (House)* 1839 *TA*, *Kingston Mill* 1860 White.   KNOTT-FOLD, KNOTT LANE, *Knot Fold* 1831 Bry, *v.* knot, fald, lane.   LONG MEADOW MILLS (lost), 1860 White.   MANCHESTER RD, 1860 ib, from Manchester La.   MILL LANE, cf. Hyde Hall *supra*.   MOT-TRAM RD, *Mottram (New) Road* 1860 ib, cf. Mottram in Longdendale 313 *infra*.   RALPHFOLD, 1839 *TA*, *v.* fald.   RIDLING LANE.   SILVER HILL RD, *Silver Hill*, 1831 Bry.   SLACK MILLS, 1831 ib, 'mills in a hollow', *v.* slakki.   SMITHY FOLD, 1831 Bry, 1839 *TA*, cf. *Smithy Lane* 1860 White, *v.* smið ðe, fald.   STOCKPORT RD, 1860 ib, cf. Stockport 294 *infra*.   THROSTLE BANK MILL, cf. Throstle Bank St. *supra*, *v.* þrostle, banke.   WALKERFOLD, WALKER LANE, *Walker Fold* 1831 Bry, *Walker Lane* 1860 White, from the occupational surname *Walker* ('a fuller') and fald, lane.   WILSON BROOK (R. Tame 36 *supra*), the culverted lower reach of Godley Brook 306 *infra*, cf. *Wilson Field* 1839 *TA*, from the surname *Wilson*.   WOOD-END HO & LANE, *Woodend* 1842 OS, cf. *boscus de Hyde* 1285 *Eyre*, *v.* wudu, ende[1].

FIELD-NAMES

The undated forms are 1839 *TA* 217.

(*a*) Banky Fd & Mdw; Barn Fd; Bear Hurst (*v.* bær[1] or beger, hyrst); Beggers Well (*v.* beggere, wella); Ben Croft & Mdw (*v.* bēan); Black Croft; Brick Kiln Fd (*v.* bryke-kyl); Bridge Fd & Hey; Broad Fd; Burgess Wifes Mdw; Butty Mdw (*v.* butty); Charles Croft; Cheethams Croft (cf. Cheetham Fd & Fold 303 *infra*); Cinders Croft (*v.* sinder); Clothes Hedge Fd (alluding to the country practice of drying laundry upon hedgerows); Dad Mdw; Dais(e)y Fd; Dig Fd (*v.* dík 'a dyke, a ditch'); Dobhill ('daub hill', *v.* daube, hyll); Dry Croft; Duffas ('dove-house', *v.* dove-house); Eals; England Mdw; Fat Hey (*v.* fætt); Fern Hill; Fine Fd; Fleet Fd (*v.* flēot); Great Gee Fd (*v.* gee, cf. Gee Cross 303 *infra*); Geranium Fd & Mdw; Greave(s) (*v.* grǣfe 'a grove'); Greens; Handford Fd; Haymakers Mdw; High Trees; Holts (*v.* holt); Hopper Croft; Hopwood Little Fd; Hyde Lanes (cf. Hyde Lane *supra*, but perhaps from leyne 'a tract of arable land'); Kettle Dock (*v.* keddle-dock); Knowls (*v.* cnoll); Lady Hey(s) (*v.* hlǣfdige, (ge)hæg); Lilly Gardens; Lower Moor; Mickle Fd (*v.* mikill); Mill Wd; Moor Hey; Old Isaacs; Ouche (*v.* ouche); Owen Fd; Paradise (*v.* paradis); Pear Tree Fd;

HYDE, MARPLE —

Piddall Croft; Pin Croft; Pingle (v. pingel); Red Wd; Rushy Fd; Scotch Holes; Seeded Fd; Shaw Mdw (v. sceaga); Slate Croft (v. slate); Sloping Banks; Solomons Barn; Springs ('well-springs', v. spring); Stone Pit Fd; Stoney Croft; Stubble Fd; Summer Bank (v. sumor); Taylor Fd; Thomas Croft; Three Pound Mdw; Twitcher Mdw (v. twitchel 'the fork of a road; a narrow passage'); Worm Hole (v. wyrm, hol[1]).

(b) *la Lone* 1287 Court (p) (v. lane); here may belong *Wetfelde* 1285 Court 210 ('wet field', v. wēt, feld).

7. MARPLE (101–9588)

Merpille e13 (1287) *Eyre*, 1287 *ib*, *Merpil* e13 (1288) *ib*, 1288 *ib*, 1289 (17) Court, *Merpill* 1290 *Eyre*
Mercholl e13 (1288) *Eyre*
Merpull e13 (1353–7) *ChFor*, 1286 *Eyre* (p), 1287 Court, 1354 *Eyre*, 1357 *ChFor*, 1358 Plea, 1380 ChRR and seven examples ib, *Dow*, JRL 32, *MinAcct* to 1492 *Dow* (p), *Merpul* 1301 ChF, 1322 *Mont*
Merpel e13 (1608) ChRR, 1248 Ipm, c.1251 *ChFor*, 1308 Cl, 1398 Orm[2] (p)
Merple e13 (1608) ChRR, 1356 BPR
Marpell e13 (1611) *LRMB* 200
Merphull 1283 Ipm, 1285 Court (p), 1337, 1364 *Eyre*, 1355 *MinAcct*, 15 *Mont*, *Merphulle* 1309 Plea, *Merphul* 1351 *Eyre*
Marpil 1285 Court
Marple 1355 BPR, 1602 Sheaf, 1619 ChRR *et freq*
Marpull 1376 Orm[2], 1401 ib
Merpoll 1431 *Dow* (p)
Merpole 1454 *Eyre*, *Merpool* c.1620 Orm[2] III 546
Marple is a difficult p.n.

The township occupies a prominent hill (Marple Ridge, Hilltop *infra*) overlooking the valley of R. Goyt, here the county boundary. Ekwall (DEPN), relying upon the *Merphull* form, supposes *Marple* a hill-name, with hyll (MEdial. *hull*) added to a compound *mǣr-hop* 'boundary valley', from (ge)mǣre and hop[1], i.e. 'hill at a boundary-valley', which exactly describes the topography here. But there are no forms with a vowel between *r* and *p* such as might be expected to represent the reduction of *hop* in the compound; there is no record of the original p.n. *Merhop(e)* from unmodified *mǣr-hop*, and further, OE hyll is unlikely to be represented by ME *hill(e)* in this position, in this dialect, at these dates, in these records. It would be reasonable to suppose the *Merphull* form to be the result of a confusion of some other final el. with **hyll** through metanalysis (*Mer-pill, -pull > Merp-(h)ill, -(h)ull*) and by association with the hill at Marple Ridge. The preferable etymology is that offered in Sx 386, from (ge)mǣre and **pyll**. The location of Marple at the county boundary on R. Goyt, and the similarity of the second-syllable forms, *-pill(e), -pil, -pull, -pel(l), -ple, -phul(l)* to those in Crimple WRY 7 124, RN 104 (add *Crimpel* 1213 Cur) confirm the first el. as (ge)mǣre 'a boundary', and the second el. as OE **pyll, pull, pōl**[1], probably Welsh **pwll** originally. Marple is '(at) the stream at the boundary', perhaps originally a r.n. for R. Goyt; cf. R. Mersey 31 *supra*, of which Goyt is a head-stream.

WYBERSLEY HALL, LANE & RD (101–9685)

> *Wybir(i)sleg'* e13 (1287) *Eyre, Wy-, Wibirsleg'* 1287, 1288 *ib, Wibereslee* e13 (1608) ChRR, (1611) *LRMB* 200, *Wyberesleg'* 1290 Court, *-lee* 1308 Cl, *-legh'* 1357 *ChFor, -is-* 1289 (17) Court (p), *Wibreslega* e13 (1608) ChRR, *-ley* 1249 IpmR, *Wy-* 1403 ChRR
> *Wyberlegh* e13 (1357), 1357 *ChFor, -le* 1288 Court, *-bur-* e13 (1357) *ChFor, -ley* l14, 1403 ChRR, *Wybberlegh* 1390 ib, 15 *Mont*
> *Wilbrislegh* e13 (1288) *Eyre, Wilb(e)rislegh* 1285 *ib*
> *Wilberlegh* e13 (1288) *Eyre*
> *Werbirl'* e13 (1288) *Eyre, Wir-* 1288 *ib*
> *Wibbersleg(h)* 1248 Ipm, Orm[2], *-ley (Hall)* 1831 Bry, 1849 *TA, Wibberislegh* 1288 Court, *Wibbresl'* 1301 Orm[2], *-ley* 1380 ChRR
> *Webbersley Hall* 1849 *TA*

'Wīgbeorht's wood', from the OE pers.n. *Wīgbeorht* and **lēah**. Cf. Stanley Hall Wood *infra*. The *Wilb-* spellings represent *Wibb-*; and *Werb-, Wirb* contain intrusive *-r-* from the following syllable.

LOW & OLD LEIGHTON (f.ns., 101–955873), 1849 *TA*, cf. *Laitone* 1086 DB f.264, 'farm at the clearing or wood', *v.* **lēah, tūn**. *Laitone* could have been in this district. It was in the demesne of Earl Hugh as a waste estate of only one virgate DB, appearing in a list with *Hofinchel* 165 *supra*, Tintwistle, Hollingworth, Werneth and Romiley 320, 309, 302, 292 *infra*. Marple and Wybersley were in the earl's demesne down to e13 when they were granted to the Vernon family, but are not named in DB.

MARPLE WOOD, 1842 OS, with Torkington Brook & Wood 36 *supra*, 300 *infra*, the location of *Hi(n)derleklow* (lit. *-klop*) e13 (1608) ChRR, *Hinderleklow(th)* (lit. *-klop(p)*) e13 (1611) *LRMB* 200, *Hunderleyclogh* e13 (18) Earw, *Henderleghesclogh* 1348 ChFor, *Hynderleghclogh* c.1350 JRL, '(valley at) the hind's glade', from ON hind, (gen.sg. hindar) and lēah, with clōh.

MIDDLE WOOD, 1831 Bry, *Midlewood* 1611 *LRMB* 200, probably *Cartelachehurst* 1363 ChFor, from the lost stream-name *Cartelache* 17 *supra* with hyrst 'a hill, a wood'. The later name is 'wood in the middle', *v.* middel, because it is in or adjoins the three townships Poynton, Norbury and Marple, cf. Middlewood Rd, *Middilschawe* 209, 211 *supra*. Middlewood and Mossley *infra*, (*the district of Mossley and Middlewood* 1849 *TA*), may represent the district known as (*pastura de*) *Bluntebroc* e13 (1287) Court, *Blentebrok* e13 (1288) *Eyre*, *Bluntesbroch* e13 (1357) ChFor, *-brok* 1357 *ib*, (*infra forestam de Maccl'*) 1366 *Eyre*, from the old name of Bollinhurst & Norbury Brooks, *v.* 16 *supra*. The southern boundary of Marple & Wybersley ran along High Lane *infra* in e13, but now it follows Bollinhurst Brook.

MOSSLEY (lost), 1849 *TA*, *Moselegh* 1357 ChFor (under Disley 269 *supra*), (*-in villa de Merpull*) 1358 *Eyre*, *Parua Mosley* 1503 ChFor (under Disley 269 *supra*), (close called) *Little Moseley* 1579 *Dep*, *Little Mosseley* 1611 *LRMB* 200, 'moss clearing', *v.* mos, lēah, cf. Middle Wood *supra*.

STANLEYHALL WOOD, 1831 Bry, 1849 *TA*, cf. 273 *supra*, *Wibberleklow* (lit. *-klop*) e13 (1608) ChRR, *Wiberleklow(th?)* (lit. *-klop(p)*) e13 (1611) *LRMB* 200, *Wybrysleg' cloyes* (lit. *-beg'*) 13 (1611) *ib*; *Wibbersleyclogh* e13 (18) Earw, from Wybersley *supra* and clōh 'a dell'. This clough is the south-east boundary between Marple and Disley townships.

ANDREW FM & LANE, *Andrew's Lane* (*Meadow*) 1849 *TA*, 1850 *TAMap*. AQUEDUCT HO, *Watch House* 1831 Bry, at the aqueduct carrying Peak Forest Canal across Marple Dale. BARLOW WOOD. BARNFOLD, 1778 Earw, *Barnsfold* 1831 Bry. BEAMSMOOR, 1831 ib, *v.* bēam 'a tree, the trunk of a tree squared for use', mōr[1]. BEECH-WOOD. BOOTH COTE, 1831 ib, cf. *Booth Croft & Field* 1849 *TA*,

v. bōth, cot.   BOTTOM BRIDGE.   BOTTOMLOCK HO, from a lock
on Peak Forest Canal.   BOWDEN (LANE), *Boden Farm* 1831 Bry,
Bowden Farm 1842 OS, cf. Thomas *Bowden* of Marple 1678 Earw.
BRABYNS BROW, COTTAGE & HALL, *Brabins Hall* 1831 Bry, built
c.1750 by Henry *Brabin*.   BRENTWOOD.   BRICK BRIDGE (RD),
from a bridge over Peak Forest Canal.   BROOKBANK COTTAGES, at
the head of Torkington Brook.   BRYDGES FM, from the family
Bridge of Marple.   CARR BROW, 1831 Bry, cf. *Lower & White
Carr Knoll, Middle Carr* 1849 *TA*, and Thomas *del Ker* 1290 Court,
v. kjarr 'brushwood, marsh', brū, cnoll.   CARRINGTON BARN,
1831 Bry.   CAWKWELL FIELD'S FM.   CHAPEL HO, *-Fold* 1849
TA, *v.* fald.   CHURCHGATE LODGE, near a footpath leading to the
parish church.   CHURCH LANE.   COTEFIELD, cf. *Cote Field &
Meadows* 1849 *ib*, *v.* cot.   THE COTTAGE.   CROCKSONHALL.
CROSS LANE, 1831 Bry.   (HIGHER & LOWER) DANBANK, (BRIDGE),
Danbank 1831 ib, *Danbank* (*Bar, Homesites, House & Wood*),
Dunbank Toll House 1849 *TA*, *Higher & Lower Dam Bank* 1860
White, cf. *Higher Dan's Bottoms & Meadow, Dan's Croft & Bridge,
Lower Dan(e)s Bottoms* (*House*), *Danes Bottom, Croft & Carr* 1849
TA, perhaps 'valley bank', from denu and banke, with barre 'a
barrier' (from a turnpike here), botm 'valley-bottom', brycg, kjarr.
This is the name of a district at the lower end of the valley of
Torkington Brook.   DARK LANE.   DOLEFIELD, cf. *Great Doles*
1849 *TA*, *v.* dāl.   DOOLEYLANE, 1849 *ib*, cf. *Doe Leys* 1849 *ib*,
perhaps from dial. *dow* 'to thrive to prosper', or dā 'a doe', with
lēah or lǣge.   DOUDFIELD, *Dodfield* 1831 Bry, *Dood Field* 1849 *TA*,
cf. Dowd Fd 135 *supra*.   DOVE HO, *The-* 1732 *Dep*, (*-Green*) 1849
TA, *v.* dove-house.   ECCLES BRIDGE, cf. *Further & Nearer Eccles
Field* 1849 *ib*.   FIELD HO, *The Field* 1860 White.   FOXLOW,
cf. *Foxlowe meadow* 1849 *TA*, 'fox hill', *v.* fox, hlāw, perhaps the
origin of the surname *Foxelowe, -lawe* c.1233 Dow, 1290 Court *et
freq.*   GARDEN HO.   GOYTCLIFFE, *Goit Cliffe Torr House &
Clough* 1849 *TA*, cf. Adam *del Clef* 1290 *Eyre*, *v.* clif, torr, clōh and
R. Goyt 27 *supra*.   GOYT COTTAGE, cf. prec.   GREENBANK.
HARTLEY.   HAWK GREEN, 1842 OS, *Half Green* 1831 Bry, prob-
ably for 'hough green', *v.* hōh 'a ridge', grēne[2].   HAZELBANK.
HIBBERT LANE, 1850 *TAMap*, *Hibberts Lane, Hibbert Croft, Field &
Piece* 1849 *TA*, from the family *Hibbert* of Marple, cf. *Hibbart Wood
& Meadow* 276 *supra*.   HIGH LANE, 1842 OS, *Ho Lane* 1690 Sheaf,
'lane leading to a hill', 'high-lane', *v.* hōh, hēah; the *magnum*

cheminum e13 (1611) *LRMB* 200, which forms the southern boundary of the original Marple & Wybersley, *v.* Middle Wood *supra*, cf. Buxton Rd 288 *infra*.   HILLTOP, 1831 Bry, cf. *del Hull de Merphull* 1364 *Eyre* (p), and Marple *supra*.   (THE) HOLLIES.   HOLLINS FOLD, GREEN, HO & MILL, *Hollin* 1831 Bry, *Hollins* 1842 OS, (*Croft, Farm, House*) 1849 *TA*, *v.* holegn 'a holly tree', fald, grēne[2], myln, hūs.   HOLLINWOOD PLACE, *Hollin Wood* 1849 *ib*, *v.* holegn. THE HOMESTEAD.   IVY HO, 1831 Bry.   LARCHFIELD.   LEECOT. LEY HEY PARK & WOOD, *Ley Hey* 1831 ib, (*House & Wood*) 1849 *TA*, *Lee Hey* 1842 OS, 'pasture enclosure', *v.* lēah, (ge)hæg.   LOMBER HEY HO, *Lumberhey* 1831 Bry, (*House*) 1849 *TA*, from (ge)hæg 'an enclosure' with either lumber 'lumber', or lambra gen.pl. of lamb 'a lamb'.   LUMM HO, *Lumb House* 1831 Bry, *v.* lum(m) 'a pool'. LYME VIEW.   LOWER MARPLE, *Low Marple* (*House*) 1849 *TA*. MARPLE BRIDGE, 1621 Sheaf, whence the hamlet-name of Marple Bridge Db 143.   MARPLE BROOK (Torkington Brook).   MARPLE DALE (FM), *Marple Dale* 1831 Bry, (*House, Wood*) 1849 *TA*, *v.* dæl[1]. MARPLE HALL, 1831 Bry, *the Plase* 1606 Orm[2], *the Greater-house* c.1690 ib, *v.* place.   MARPLE MILL, *molendinum de Merpull* 1354 *Eyre*.   MARPLE RIDGE (2x), *The Ridge, Little Ridge* 1849 *TA*, (*Marple*) *Ridge* 1860 White, the northern hamlet being *Mount House* 1842 OS, 'the ridge', *v.* hrycg, cf. 282 *supra*, Marple *supra*, and Lower Ridge, Ridge-end *infra*.   MARSLAND FOLD, -*House* 1849 *TA*, from the local surname *Marsland* and fald.   HIGHER MOSS-ACRE, *v.* mos, æcer.   MOULT WOOD.   THE MOUNT.   NABTOP (HO & LANE), *Nab Top* 1831 Bry, *Nab Cop* 1860 White, cf. *Nab Croft* 1849 *TA*, *v.* nabbi 'a knoll, a hill', topp 'summit'.   NEEDHAMS (lost), 1850 *TAMap*, -*Fold* 1849 *TA*, *Needham* 1831 Bry, probably from the surname *Needham*, with fald.   NORBURY SMITHY (lost), 1850 *TAMap*, 1842 OS, perhaps connected with the Hyde family of Norbury 287 *infra*.   OLDCLOUGH, 1842 ib, *Owlclough* 1831 Bry, 'owl dell', *v.* ūle, clōh.   OLDKNOW RD, after Samuel *Oldknow* of Mellor Db, d.1828, *v.* Earw II 55–6.   OTTERSPOOL BRIDGE, 1849 *TA*, *v.* 263 *supra*.   PEACEFIELD.   PEERES.   POSSET BRIDGE, a canal bridge.   PRIESTFIELD, *Priest('s) Field* (*House*) 1849 *TA*, *v.* prēost, feld.   RHODE HO & MILL, *Road House* 1831 Bry, -*s* 1850 *TAMap*, probably from rod[1] 'a clearing'.   LOWER RIDGE, RIDGE-END (FOLD), *Ridge End* 1831 Bry, (-*Fold & House*) 1849 *TA*, *v.* hrycg, ende[1], fald, cf. Marple Ridge supra.   RIVINGTON, perhaps named after Rivington La 48.   ROMAN BRIDGE, *Windy-*

bottom Bridge 1831 Bry, 'windy valley-bottom', *v.* windig, botm, cf. Windybottom Farm Db 146. ROSEHILL HO, *Rosehill* 1831 ib SARAJEVO, a house-name. SARANAC, cf. prec. SCHOOL HOUSE FM, SCHOOL LANE. SLACK HALL, *Slack* 1831 ib, cf. *del Slakkes* 1361 *Eyre* (p), 'the hollow', *v.* slakki. SPOUT HOUSE(S), *Spout House* 1831 Bry, 'house at a spring', *v.* spoute. SPRINGFIELD. SPRINGWATER MILL, 1860 White, *Bone Mill* 1831 Bry, at *Clough Bottom* 1842 OS, *v.* clōh, botm. STOCKPORT RD, leading to Stockport 294 *infra.* STOKE LACY. STONEHURST. STRINES RD, cf. *The Strines Bridge* 1849 *TA*, named from Strines Db 152. THROSTLEGROVE, *Throstle Grove Homesites* 1849 *ib*, *v.* þrostle, grāf. TORKINGTON LANE, leading to Torkington 299 *infra.* TURFLEE, 1849 *ib*, *Tufleys* 1831 Bry, 'turf clearing', *v.* turf, lēah. TURN-CLIFF WOOD, *Turncliffe-* 1842 OS, 'turning cliff', *v.* trun, clif, a bank over a bend of R. Goyt. WATERSIDE, beside a canal. WEST TOWER. WHITECROFT, *Bottom of the Trough* 1831 Bry, *No Mans Land* 1842 OS, in the bottom of the valley of R. Goyt, near the county boundary. WINDLEHURST (-FOLD, HO & RD), *Windle-hurst* 1759 Earw, *-Fold* 1842 OS, *-lane* 1849 *TA* 297, *Windlehirst* 1831 Bry, 'grassy hill', *v.* windle, hyrst, fald. WITHINGTON HILL FM. WOOD FM, WOODFIELD, *Wood Farm* 1842 OS, (*Homesites*), *Wood Field* 1849 *TA*, from Marple Wood *supra*, *v.* 336 *infra.* YEWTREE COTTAGE.

FIELD-NAMES

The undated forms are 1849 *TA* 254, 1850 *TAMap* 254.

(*a*) Acre; Allat; Amen Corner (*v.* 329 *infra*); Barley Earth (*v.* eorðe); Barn Fd & Mdw; Bean Croft; Bee Croft (*v.* bēo 'a bee'); Bent, Bents Wd (*v.* beonet); Birches; Black Earth (*v.* eorðe); Blacksmith's fd; Bramhall (cf. John *de Bromhal* 1290 Court, 'broomy nook', *v.* brōm, halh, cf. Bramhall 258 *supra*); Breeches (*v.* brēc 'breaking, land newly broken for cultivation'); Brick-kiln Fd; Bridge Fd; Broad Fd; Brook Croft; Browy Fd; Bull's Close; Butty Croft (*v.* butty); Calf Croft (Knoll); Calf Hey; Cart Leach (four fields so named, *v. Cartelache* 17 *supra*, Cartledge 289 *infra*); Chapel Acre, Croft & Fd (cf. Chapel Ho *supra*); Clay Fd; Clayton Croft; Clod Bridge Acre (*v.* clodd 'a clod', brycg; perhaps from a plat made of clods); Clough (*freq*, *v.* clōh); Clover Fd; Coalpit Croft, Fd, Hill & Wd; Coe Fd; Colliers Acre & Lake (*v.* colȝere); Common Piece & Ridge (cf. Marple Ridge *supra*); Corn Fd; Cow Lane; Dairy Slack (*v.* slakki); Daisy Fd; Dale Croft (*v.* dæl[1], cf. Marple Dale *supra*); Drake Hill (*v.* draca 'a dragon'); Dry Fd; Erkin-sough Fd & Mdw; The Eyes (*v.* ēg); Fearing Croft; Ferny Hey; Finch; Flash Mdw (*v.* flasshe 'a swamp'); Flat Fd; Footway Fd; Fox Holes

(v. fox-hol); Gladden (v. gladden); Golden Croft & Mdw; Gold Hole;
Goose Carr (v. kjarr); Gorsey Croft; Great Fd, -Wd; Haddon Fd (perhaps
'heath hill', v. hǣð, dūn); Hall Wd; Hard Croft; Hawthorn; Great & Little
Hay, Hey; Hay Shade Fd ('hay-shelter field', from hēg 'hay', and dial.
shade 'a shelter'); Heater Croft; Hell Heys Mdw, Pasture & Wd (v. hell or
helde); Hollow Fd; Homesites (v. 332 infra); Honey Croft; Horse Pasture;
Iron Bridge ('bridge at a corner', v. hyrne, brycg, cf. Heronbridge 332 infra);
Jack Bank (v. jack); Jud Croft & Fd; Killey Knoll; Kiln Croft & Fd;
Knoll; Knot (v. knǫttr); Lee (v. lēah); Ligginhurst; Lime Fd; Lin(n)s Row
(v. rāw 'a row of houses'); Long Fd; Long Row (1831 Bry, 'long row of
houses', v. lang, rāw); Lucerne Fd (v. 332 infra); Madge Fd; Mading Hole;
Mare Knoll (v. mere²); Mare's Nest (v. mere², nest); Marl; Marl Chur(r) &
Fd; Marled Earth (v. marlede, eorðe, cf. Blackeyer 265 supra); Meadow
Wd; Mean Fd (v. (ge)mǣne); Mill Fd, Goit & Wd (v. gote, cf. Marple Mill
supra); Mires ('miry places', v. mȳrr, ME mire 'a mire'); Moor Piece;
Mossy Fd; Novel Rough; Old Lane; Old Woman's Croft & Mdw; Orchard
Fd; Orken Fd; Owl Wd; Ozier Holt (v. osier, holt); Patch; Pease Croft;
Pedmores Croft; Pickee; Pickstones Ho; Pidgeon Croft; Pingle (v. pingel);
Pingot (v. pingot); Plain; Plumley (v. plūme 'a plum-tree', lēah); Potatoe
Fd; Pott Lane; Pye Greave ('magpie wood', v. pie², grǣfe); Little & Long
Ridge (cf. Marple Ridge supra); Rose Acre; Rough Fd, Hey & Piece; Round
Hill; Routing Walls ('roaring springs', v. hrūtende, wælla, cf. Db 736 s.v.
hrūtende); Rush Hey; Rye Fd; Sandhole Fd; Sawpit Fd, Hill & Knoll
(v. saw-pytt); Sharm Hill; Little & Long Shut (v. scēat); Slab Hole; Slid
Mdw (v. Slids 275 supra); Smithy Fd & Mdw; Spooner; Spring Mount Ho;
Sprink (v. spring); Square Fd; Stable Fd & Mdw; Stag Fd; Stair Fd &
Wd (from stǣger¹ 'a stair', or stǣger² 'steep', probably the latter, cf.
Broomstair 279 supra); Stoney Acre, Bank, Croft & Fd; Sutton Patch (v.
pacche); Swan Fd; Tang (v. tang); Tanyard Fd & Mdw (v. tan-yard);
Threaphurst ('disputed wood', v. þrēap, hyrst, cf. 288 infra); Tootings Hill
('hill at a look-out place', v. tōt, -ing¹ or -ing², hyll); Top o' th' Wood;
Torr Barn Fd, Torr Wd (v. torr 'a rocky outcrop'); Town Fd; Triangle Fd;
Tup Croft; Underhill (v. under); Walve Hill; Warth (v. waroð); Well Fd;
Wet Earth (v. wēt 'wet', eorðe); Wheat Acre Clough, Wheat Croft & Fd;
White Carr (v. kjarr); Wood Mdw & Piece; Wothman's Hay; Wych Fd &
Mdw (cf. Ralph Wyche 1522 Earw).

(b) Hendenethebothum 1290 Court (p) (perhaps 'bottom land at the near
heath', v. (ge)hende 'near at hand', hǣð, botm).

8. NORBURY (101–9185)

Nordberie 1086 DB, *Northbury* 1248 Ipm *et freq* to 1359 Pat, *-bur'*
1285 Eyre, 1363 ChFor, *-b'* 1354 Eyre, Northbur' 1285, 1286 ib
(Court reads *-bury*), *-bury* 1363 ChFor
Norburi H2 (17) Orm², *-bury* 1354, 1370 Eyre, 1435 Chol, 1503
Plea *et freq*, *-burie* 1676 Earw, *-berie* e13 Orm², 1577 Dow, *-bery*

e13 Earw (p), 1492 *Dow, -beri* c.1240 (1619) ChRR (p), *-bere* 1311 *Eyre, -bir'* e14 *Chol* (p)

'At the north manor-house or stronghold', v. norð, burh (dat.sg. byr(i)g). The archæological significance is not known, nor do we know whether this place was 'north' in relation to some particular place or from its location in the north part of the hundred. It was at the north-western extremity of the Forest of Macclesfield.

BUXTON RD, *High Lane* 1831 Bry, leading to Buxton Db, cf. High Lane 284 *supra.*   CHESTER RD.   DEAN LANE, cf. *Dean Eye Brow & Field* 1849 *TA*, 'valley water-meadow', v. denu, ēg.   FIRTREE COTTAGE, *Firtree House* 1842 OS.   FORD COTTAGE, v. ford. HAZEL GROVE, v. 256 *supra.*   HIGHER FM, *High Farm* 1842 ib. JACKSON'S LANE, 1831 Bry.   LONDON RD, the main road from Stockport at Hazel Grove.   MACCLESFIELD RD, the *strata via* of the bounds of the forest of Macclesfield between Prestbury 212 *supra* and *Norbury Low infra*, v. 10 *supra* and Orm² III 539.   MARSDEN HO, 1831 Bry.   MILLBANK, 1842 OS, cf. Millhill 209 *supra.* MILL FM & LANE, *Mill Lane* 1849 *TA*, cf. Norbury Mill *infra.* NORBURY BRIDGE, crosses Norbury Brook 16 *supra.*   NORBURY CHAPEL, *Norburie Chappell* 1676 Earw.   NORBURY HALL.   NORBURY HOLLOW, *Northburyhalgh* 1363 ChFor, *Norbury Clough* 1849 *TA*, *Mill Clough* 1850 *TAMap*, v. halh, holh, clōh, myln, cf. Norbury Mill *infra.*   NORBURY LOW (lost), *Northb'yclowe* (lit. *Northby-clowe*) 13 (17) Orm², *Northb'yelowe, -bury-* c.1270 (17) Sheaf, *Norburie Lowe* 1611 LRMB 200, *ad quendam collem antiquitus vocatum Norbury Low jacentem ultra domum vocatum Bullock-Smythy* 1619 Orm², 'the hill at Norbury', v. hlāw, a boundary of the Forest of Macclesfield (cf. 10 *supra*) located near Hazel Grove (101–921869) 256 *supra*, probably near Hatherlow (101–917867) 260 *supra.* NORBURY MILL, 1831 Bry, cf. Mill Fm & Lane, Norbury Hollow *supra*, *Mill Croft & Field* 1849 *TA.*   NORBURY MOOR, 1831 Bry. NORBURY MOOR FM, *Moss Pits* 1831 Bry, v. mos, pytt.   OX HEY (FM), 1849 *TA*, *Hawks Hey* 1842 OS, v. oxa, (ge)hæg.   ROBIN-HOOD POOL, named from the adjacent *Robin Hood*, 1849 *TA*, an inn. SHEPLEY HO, *Shepleys* 1831 Bry, from the surname Shepley, cf. 279 *supra.*   SHORES.   THREAPHURST (LANE), *le Threpehurst* 1337 *Eyre*, (-e) 1528, 1542 ChRR, *le Threphurst* 1348 ChFor, *Threaphurst* 1831 Bry, (*House & Crofts*), *Hough Threaphurst* 1849 *TA*, 'disputed wood; wooded hill which is the site of a dispute', *v.* þrēap, hyrst, hōh 'a spur, a heel of land'. This place is near the boundary of Torkington 299 *infra*, and was presumably disputed territory. WINDLEHURST RD, *Windlehurst Lane* 1849 *TA*, *v.* 286 *supra*. YEWTREE FM.

FIELD-NAMES

The undated forms are 1849 *TA* 297. Of the others 1290, 1348 are *Eyre*, 1357, 1363 *ChFor*, 1831 Bry, 1842 OS.

(a) Acre Mdw; Alder Croft; Arse Butts (*v.* ears 'an arse, a buttock', butte); Barley Croft & Stubble; Barn Fd; Beaton Fd (1842 OS); Bent (*v.* beonet); Blake Shoot (*v.* blæc, scēat); Brick Kiln Fd; Brierly Hill (*v.* brēr, lēah); Brook Eye, Fd & Mdw (*v.* brōc, ēg); Broom Fd & Shoot (*v.* brōm, scēat); Browy Fd (*v.* brū); Calf Croft; Cartledge (cf. Cart Leach 286 *supra*, *v.* Cartelache 17 *supra*); Chapel Fd & Mdw, Church Fd (cf. Norbury Chapel *supra*); Coalpit Fd (there were collieries in this township in 19); Cock Fd; Cold Harbour ('cold shelter', *v.* cald, here-beorg); Dam Mdw (*v.* damme); Door Fd (*v.* duru); Eccles Pasture; Eyes Mdw (*v.* ēg); Farrington Fd; Fold Fd; Forty Acre; Four Fd; Gladden (*v.* gladden); Goose Croft; Gravel Fd; Great Fd; Ground Fennel (probably from the plant-name); Hanging Dole ('allotment on a brow', *v.* hangende, dāl); Hatherlow (Pasture & Lane), Heatherlow Mdw (*v.* Hatherlow 260 *supra*, *Norbury Low supra*); Hawken Fd; Heir Fd; Hemp Yard; Hey Norbury (cf. *Hey Lane* 1831, passing Higher Fm *supra*, 'the part of Norbury at the Hey', *v.* (ge)hæg); Higginbotham Mdw (either from the surname *Higginbotham*, or another example of the p.n. type Higginbotham 266 *supra*); Home Mdw; Horse Croft Pasture; Hough Mdw (*v.* hōh, cf. Threaphurst *supra*); Intake (*v.* inntak); Kiln Croft & Fd; Lady Greave Fd ('lady's grove', *v.* hlǣfdige, grǣfe); Lime Brow & Fd (*v.* līm, brū); Lime Kiln Bank; Little Heath; Long Fd(s); Madge Croft (*v.* madge); Mare Fd & Flat (*v.* mere²); Marl'd Jurr (*v.* Blackeyer 265 *supra*); Masters Mdw; Meg's Lane; Merryhill (*v.* myrge, hyll); Middle Fd; Middlewood Mdw (near Middle Wood 283 *supra*); Muck Earth (*v.* muk, eorðe); New Close; Nuncle Fd (from ModE *nuncle*, a side-form of *uncle*, 'an uncle'); Old Mdw; Orchard Corner, Fd & Mdw; Paradise (*v.* paradis); Pinfold Fd (*v.* pynd-fald); Priest Hey (*v.* prēost, (ge)hæg); Raileys; Rough Fd & Heath; Round Fd; Rye Croft; Sawney Croft; School Fd; Sheep Hay, -Hey; Slack (*v.* slakki); Smithy Croft; Sour Fd; Spout Mdw (*v.* spoute); Spring Croft ('well-spring', *v.* spring); Stack Croft; Stew Mdw (*v.* stuwe); Stoney Mdw; Tan Yard Croft (*v.* tan-yard); Thistley Fd; Thorn Fd; Vetch Croft; Wall Fd (*v.* wælla); Well Croft & Mdw; Wheat Croft; White Fd; Willcroft (*v.* wella); Willow Mdw; Windmill Fd; Wood Fd; Wormstow Greave ('wood in which cattle shelter to avoid flies', *v.* wyrm-stall, grǣfe).

(b) *Bluntesbroke* (*v.* Bollinhurst Brook 16 *supra*); *Caldewalerydyng* 1363, and *Caldewalsiche* 1357 ('(clearing and watercourse at) the cold spring', from cald and wælla, with ryding, sīc); *del Clyf* 1348 (p) (*v.* clif 'a bank'); *del Gore*

D P N

1348 (p) (*v.* gāra 'a gore, a triangular plot of ground'); *le lane* 1363 (*v.* lane); *Renuenlegh* 1363 (a dubious reading, *v.* lēah 'a clearing', cf. *Ranelegh-ruydynges* 302 *infra*).

9. OFFERTON (101–9288)

Offirtun John Orm^2 (p)
Offurton John, 1226 Orm^2 (p), *-thon* 1378 *Eyre*
Offerton 1248 Ipm *et freq*
Offreton E1 Orm^2 (p), 1337 *Eyre*, 1363 *ChFor*
Offrington c.1295 Orm^2, *Offrynton* 1454 *Eyre*, 1540 *AddCh*
Offorton 1351 *Eyre*
Affreton 1439 ChRR

Offerton is a difficult p.n., which must be taken with Offerton Db 155, although the latter has no *ington* forms. The two places, however, occupy similar sites, close to a river and on a route-way. DEPN and Db 155 discuss various possibilities for the first el. The base is obviously a pers.n., but the form is elusive. Db 155 suggests an OE pers.n. *Offhere*, though OE pers.ns. in *Off*- are not recorded. DEPN suggests the OE pers.ns. *Oftfōr*, *Ōsfrið* as alternatives to a p.n. in ford, such as *Offan-ford* 'Offa's ford', from the OE pers.n. *Offa*. The recorded forms suggest that the first el. could be either the OE pers.n. *Oftfōr*, or the pers.n. *Odfrid*, *Oudfride* (either the OG *Odfrid* or OScand **Auð-frið*) discussed by Bjorkman NP 106. But, on balance I agree with Professor Cameron, who now thinks that both names represent an **Offan-ford-tūn* '(the farmstead at) Offa's ford', *v.* tūn. The Ch p.n., however, has an alternative formation, representing **Offanford-ing-tūn* 'the farmstead called after *Offanford*', *v.* -ing-^{4}, or **Offanfordinga-tūn* 'the farmstead of the folk of *Offanford*', *v.* -ingas.

Tait rejects the identification of Offerton with the lost *Alretune* DB 267b ('farm at the alder-tree', *v.* alor, tūn), which was in *Hamestan* (Macclesfield) Hundred, but points out that Ollerton 333 *infra*, with which the DB form has been identified, is in a different hundred, *v.* Chet NS LXXV 215n.

BONGS, 1831 Bry, 'the banks', *v.* banke.   BROOKDALE COTTAGES. BROWN HO, 1831 Bry, *Browen House Meadow* 1849 *TA*, cf. foll. BROWN HOUSE FOLD BROOK, from prec., cf. 297 *infra*, *v.* fald, brōc. It becomes Hempshaw Brook 297 *infra*.   DAISY BANK.   DAN-

BANK BRIDGE, *v.* 284 *supra*. DODGE FOLD (lost), 1831 Bry, 1882 Orm², a hamlet named after the *Dodge* family, cf. Orm² III 838, *v.* fald 'a fold'. FIVE HOUSES, 1831 Bry. FOGGBROOK (BRIDGE), *Fog Brook* 1849 *TA*, a hamlet and bridge on Poise Brook 33 *supra*, 'grassy stream', *v.* fogge, brōc. GILDEDHOLLIES. GIPSY LANE. HIGHFIELD. HOLIDAYHILL, 1849 *ib*, *Holliday Hill* 1882 Orm². THE HOLLIES. JESSIEFIELD, *Jessie's Meadow* 1849 *TA*, cf. Jesse Meadow 257 *supra*. LISBURNE LANE, *v.* 297 *infra*. LYMEFIELD. MOUNT COTTAGE. MOUNT PLEASANT. NAB, *The* 1860 White, *v.* nabbi 'a knoll, a hill'. OFFERTON FOLD, *Hempshaw Lane End* 1860 White, cf. Hempshaw Lane 297 *infra*, *v.* fald. OFFERTON GREEN & HALL, 1831 Bry, 1842 OS. OFFERTON LANE. OFFERTON MOUNT. OLD FM. RIDGE, *v.* hrycg. SHADYOAK, 1831 Bry. SUNDIAL, 1848 *TAMap*, cf. *Dial Field* 1849 *TA*, *v.* dial. SYCAMORE VILLA. TOP O' TH' GREEN FM, *Top o' th' Green* 1849 *ib*, cf. Offerton Green *supra*. WARREN WOOD, 1831 Bry, *v.* wareine. WOOD COTTAGE. WOODLANDS.

FIELD-NAMES

The undated forms are 1849 *TA* 304. Of the others 13 (17), 1619 are Orm² III 539, c.1270 (17) Sheaf, 1363 *ChFor*, 1364 *Eyre*, 1611 *LRMB* 200, 1831 Bry, 1848 *TAMap*.

(a) Acre; Airy Fd; Ass Pasture; Back Fd; Barley Mdw (*Barlie Meadow* 1619, *v.* bærlic, mǣd; at 101–926885, on the north bank of Poise Brook 33 *supra*, adjoining the site of *Saltersbrugge infra*); Barn Croft, Fd & Mdw; Beanleach (*v.* 256 *supra*); Bottom Fd; Boundary Fd; Brierley (*v.* brēr, lēah); Broad Fd; Broad Stone 1848 (*v.* brād, stān); Brook Bottom (*v.* botm); Brow (*v.* brū); Brown Hill (*v.* brūn¹); Carr Mdw (*v.* kjarr); Chantry (*v.* chaunterie); Coblers; Corner Mdw; Cow Lane Bottom (*v.* botm); Croft Hill; Cuts Clough (*v.* cutte, clōh, cf. dial. *cut* in Cutts Mdw 331 *infra*); Dam Mdw & Side; Dog Kennel Mdw; Dry Knoll; Elbow (*v.* elbowe); End o' th' lane; Flat Fd; Flax Croft; Foot Road Fd; Garden Mdw; Grove; Hall Croft & Pool (from Offerton Hall *supra*); Hanging Brow ('overhanging hillside', *v.* hangende, brū); Hard Croft & Fd; Harrop Roughs 1831 (from rūh 'rough ground', with either a surname, or a p.n. like Harrop 138 *supra*); Hazel Bank; Hill Top; Home Pasture; House Mdw (*v.* hūs); Intake (*v.* inntak); Kiln Fd; Lappage; Level Fd; Long Fd & Side; Low Mdw; Marl Fd; Middle Acre; Moor Fd, Little Moor (cf. *vastum de Offreton* 1363, *v.* mōr¹); Mouse Hole; North Brow; Off Mdw; Offerton Mdw; Old Mdw; Oldhams Tenement 1848 (from the surname *Oldham* and tenement); Orchard; Pigot's Fd; Pingot (*v.* pingot); Pit Fd, Pit Head Fd; Riding (*v.* ryding); Road Mdw; Rough Fd & Piece; Round Mdw; Rowbothams 1848 (either 'rough bottom-land', from rūh and botm, or the related surname

Rowbotham); Rye Croft; Shoulder of Mutton (*v.* 329 *infra*); Skirts (*v.* skirt); Smithy Croft; South Brow; Spar Croft; Spring Wood Mead (*v.* spring); Stony Fd; Three Corner(s); Top Croft; Vine Yard (*v.* vinȝerd); Well Croft & Fd; Wilderness; Wood Mdw & Top.

(*b*) *Alaynesfeld* 1364 (from the ME (OFr) pers.n. *Alain* and feld); *Reddish Meadow* 1619 (at or near Beanleach 256 *supra*, probably 'reed-ditch', from hrēod and dīc, cf. Reddish La 30, *v.* foll.); *Saltersbrugge* 13 (17), *Saltersisbrugge* c.1270 (17), *Saltersbridge* 1611, *ad quendam ponticulum vocatum a Platt antiquitus vocatum Saltersbrigge et jacentem inter pratum vocatum Barlie Meadow* (*v.* Barley Mdw *supra*) *et quoddam pratum vocatum Reddish Meadow* (*v.* prec.) 1619 ('salter's bridge', *v.* saltere, brycg, plat[1]; a point on the boundary of the Forest of Macclesfield, near Beanleach 256 *supra*, at 101–927884 where Poise Brook leaves Beanleach Rd, a site not noted by Crump but perhaps connected with his 'Saltway F', *v.* LCAS LIV, 130–4, cf. Salterslane 265 *supra*).

10. ROMILEY (101–9490)

> *Rumelie* 1086 DB, *Rumilegh* 1321 Plea
> *Rumley* R1 Orm[2]
> *Romileg* 13 Tab, *-lee* 1285 Court (p), *-ley* 1512 Orm[2], (*or Chadkirk Chapelry*) 1860 White, *Romylegh* 1332 Plea *et freq*, *-ley* 1372 Orm[2], 1519 ChRR, *Romel'* 1293 Plea, *-legh* 1315 ib, *-le* 1345 Eyre (p), *-ley* 1417 ChRR, Plea, 1596 ChRR
> *Romesl'* 1254 P
> *Ramylegh* 1369 (17) Orm[2]
> *Romley* c.1620 Orm[2]

'Roomy clearing', *v.* rūm[2], lēah, cf. Romeley Db 238, Rumleigh D 223.

CHADKIRK CHAPEL & HO

> *Chaddekirke* c.1306 JRL (p), *-kyrke* 1345 Dow (p), (*cantaria de*) *Chadkirke*, *-kyrke* 1535 VE, (*the Chapel of-* & *a messuage called-*) 1544 Orm[2], (*-Chappell*) 1642 ib, *-kyrk* 1551 Dow, *-kirk* 1660 (1845) ChetOS VIII, (*chapel of-*) 1724 NotCestr, *Chadekyrke* 1548 Earw, *-kerke* c.1662 Surv
> *Shadkirke* 1368 Dow (p), (*canteria de*) *-kyrk* 1550 MinAcct
> *Chad Chapel* 1621 Orm[2], 1724 NotCestr, *Chadchapell* 1621 Earw

'Chad's church', from the OE pers.n. *Ceadda* and kirkja, chapel(e). The dedication is to Ceadda (St Chad), bishop of Lichfield 669–72. Orm[2] III 849, which mistakenly identifies Chadkirk with *Cedde* DB (cf. Cheadle 246 *supra*), observes the lack of evidence about the age of this chantry chapel.

RIDGWAY (f.n.), 1849 *TA*, (*le*) *Rugwey* 1286 Court (p), *-e* 1289 (17) ib (p), *-way* 1294 Earw (p), *Ruggewey* 1290 Court (p), 1341, 1380 *Eyre*, *-way* 1341 *ib*, (*le-*) 1350 *ib* (p), þe *Riggewey* 1345 *ib*, *-e*, *-waye* 1408 Orm[2] (p), ChRR (p) (lit. *Bigge-*), *le Ryggeway* 1382 *Eyre* (p), 'the ridge-way', *v.* hrycg, weg; alluding to a road over Werneth Low 304 *infra*.

BARLOWFOLD, 1849 *TA*, *v.* fald. BEECH FM & LANE. BEECH-FIELD. BENFIELD CLOUGH, NEAR BENFIELD, *Banfield* 1831 Bry, *Benfield* 1842 OS, cf. Far Benfield 303 *infra*, 'bean field', *v.* bēan, feld, clōh. BIRCHVALE FM & HO, *Birchvale* 1842 ib. BURY-MEWICK, cf. Burymewick Wood 271 *supra*. CHURCH LANE. CROSS MOOR (lost, 101–942907), 1831 Bry, 1849 *TA*, 'moor at a cross', *v.* cros, mōr[1]. DINGLEHOLLOW, cf. *Dingle Meadow* 1849 *ib*, 'deep hollow', *v.* dingle. DYE LANE. GOTHIC, *-Farm* 1860 White, *Five Houses* 1831 Bry. GOOSEHOUSEGREEN, 1849 *TAMap*, *v.* gōs, hūs, grēne.[2] GREAVEFOLD, 1831 Bry, 'fold at a grove'. *v.* grǣfe, fald. GREENHILL HALL, *Greenhill* 1831 ib. GREEN LANE, *-House* 1849 *TA*. GUYWOOD (COTTAGES & LANE), 1842 OS. HEALD, (*The*) 1831 Bry, *Hield* (*House*) 1849 *TA*, *TAMap*, *v.* helde 'a slope'. HEALD WOOD (HO), *Doctors Brow* 1831 Bry, *v.* brū, cf. prec. HERMITAGE. HEYES, *Broad, Highmost & Long Heys* 1848 *TA*, *v.* (ge)hæg. HIGH LANE. HILL-END. HYDE-BANK, 1842 OS, *v.* banke, cf. Hyde 279 *supra*. LANE-ENDS, 1831 Bry. LONGSIGHT COTTAGE, *v.* lang, sight. MOSSACRE, 1831 ib, *v.* mos, æcer. NEW HO. OAKHURST. OAKWOOD HALL & MILL, *Oakwood Garden, Hall, Mill & Round* 1849 *TA*. OLD HOUSE FOLD, *v.* fald. ORANGETREE FM & HO, *Orange Tree* 1849 *ib*. REDBROW WOOD, cf. Springwood Hall *infra*. RYDEACRE, *Ride Acre* 1849 *ib*. SANDY LANE. SPRINGWOOD HALL, 1842 OS, *Redbrow Fold* 1831 Bry, 'young coppice', *v.* spring; formerly '(farm at) the red hill', *v.* rēad, brū, fald, cf. Redbrow Wood *supra*. STERNDALE. STOCK DOVE INN, 1849 *TA*, *New Inn* 1831 Bry. TOP-O'-TH'-HILL, 1849 *TA*. WATERFALL COTTAGES. WATER-LOO, 1831 Bry. WATERMEETINGS, 1849 *TA*, *Water Meeting* (*Farm*) 1831 Bry, 1842 OS, at the confluence of R. Etherow and R. Goyt, cf. Watermeetings Cottage (Werneth). WERNETH FM & HO (101–942913), *Werneth* 1849 *TA*, *Billings Green* 1831 Bry, cf.

Werneth 302 *infra*. The place is near Top o' th' Hill *supra*, at the south-west spur of Werneth Low, so the older name is taken to be another example of the p.n. type *Billing(e)*, *v.* Billinge Hill 138 *supra*.

FIELD-NAMES

The undated forms are 1849 *TA* 337 and *TAMap* 337. Of the others 1337, 1345, 1348, 1349 are *Eyre*, 1510 Orm², 1381 Bry, 1842 OS.

(a) Barn Fd; Batty Yard (*v.* geard); Bear Hurst (*v.* beger or bær¹, hyrst); Bennisons; Bent Hey (*v.* beonet); Blackcroft; Blake Butts (*v.* blæc, butte); Bony Field Mdw; Bottoms (*v.* botm); Bradshaws Fd; Brick Kiln Fd; Canal Side; Carna Fd; Chapel Mdw (cf. Chadkirk *supra*); Great Cimshaw; Clayton Lane (*v.* clǣg, tūn); Clough Mdw (*v.* clōh); Cockshutts (*v.* cocc-scyte); Copper House Fd; Cow Heys; Crabtree Croft; Dale Fd, Deal Orchard (*v.* deill, dǣl²); Dirty Leach ('dirty bog', *v.* dyrty, læc(c)); Dody Fd; Drained Mdw; Dry End; Elm Bank Wds; Eyes (*v.* ēg); Gallows Bottom (*v.* galga, botm); Gladder Hurst (*v.* hyrst); Godridge; Gorsey Fd; Hanover; Hard Fd; Higinbothom's Enclosure (cf. probably from the surname *Higginbotham*, cf. Higginbotham 266 *supra*); Holehouse Fold (*v.* hol¹, hūs, fald); Hoo Riding (*v.* hōh, ryding); Horse Heys; Hurst Heads (*v.* hyrst, hēafod); Kirkwood Fd (*v.* kirkja, wudu, cf. Chadkirk *supra*); Longmost Acre; Lucern Croft (*v.* 332 *infra*); Mad lock; Mancum Croft; Mayor Fd; Middup (*v.* mid, hop¹, cf. Middup 238 *supra*); Mocus; Owl Holes (*v.* Rough End *infra*); Paunge; Peel Mdw, Little Peel (*v.* pēl); Pinfold Mdw (*v.* pynd-fald); Pingot Mdw (*v.* pingot); New Printshop Fd (after a printing works here, 6″ and 1842 OS); Riding (*v.* ryding); Rough End Owl Holes (*v.* ūle, hol¹); Round Croft; Rushy Fd & Wd; Salter's Lane (*v.* saltere, lane, cf. Salterslane 265 *supra*); Sandhole Fd; Smithy Fd; Stone Pit Croft, Fd & Plantation; Stonery ('place where stone is got', *v.* stonery); Stoney Croft; Swallow Croft; Tang, Tang Shuts (*v.* tang, scēat); Top o' th' Wood; Union Fd; Wartle Mdw; Warth (*v.* waroð); Well Mdw; Wet Fd; Willow Hall Ho; Wise Fd; Withoms Croft; Little Yerr (cf. Blackeyer 265 *supra*).

(b) *le Coldharbor* 1510 ('cold shelter', *v.* cald, here-beorg); *Karlcotes* 1345, *Carlecote* 1348 (p), *Carlecotes* 1349 ('peasants' huts', *v.* karl (perhaps replacing ceorl), cot, cf. *Carlisboth* 52 *supra*); *Woddhous* 1337 (p), *þe Wodehous* 1345 ('house at a wood', *v.* wudu, hūs).

11. STOCKPORT (101–8990)

Stokeport 1154–89 (1318) Pat (p), 1188 P, *-porta* 1173 Earw, *-porte* 1190 LaCh, *Stokeport* e13 Fitt, Facs *et freq* with variant spellings *-porte*, *-pord*, *-part* to *Stokeporte* 1550 Dow
Stokporte 1249 IpmR, *-port* 1269 (1292) Ch (p), *Stocport* 1272 Chest, *Stockport* c.1274 ib *et freq* with variant spellings *Stok-*, *Stoc-*, *-port(e)*, *-pord*

Stockeport(e) 1276 Cl (p), 1501 *Dow*
Stoppord 13 (17) Sheaf (p), 1337 *Eyre*, 1432 *AddCh*, 1437 *NewC*,
 (*-e*), (*apon Mersey*) 1536 Leland, *Stopport* 1348 *Eyre*, 1372
 AddCh, *-e* 1565 *Dow*, (*alias Stockeporte*) 1576 ChRR, *-porth(e)*
 1541 Sheaf, *Stoport* 1341 *Eyre*, *-perd* 1687 Sheaf
Stockford 1288 (17) Chest, *Stokfort* 1357 BPR (p), (*alias Stopford*)
 1690 Sheaf
Stopford 1347 *Eyre*, *-e* 1400–5 PremIt, 1488 (18), 1506 Earw,
 -fort 1357 *ChFor*, *-forth* 1589 *Dow*, *-Stoppeford* 1365 BPR,
 Stoppford 1616 Earw, *Stopfford alias Stokport* 1527 Orm²
Stockeniport 1551 *Dow* 232
Stapporte 1583 ChRR
Stopwurthe c.1543 Orm² III 849, *-worth* 1644 Earw

'Market-place at a hamlet', *v.* stoc 'a secondary settlement', port².
The town was made a borough by charter in 1220. The late and unique
spelling *Stockeniport* may suggest a popular etymology 'market-place
constructed of, or enclosed with, logs' (i.e. 'stockaded') from stoccen
(cf. stocc). In DEPN Ekwall derives the p.n. from stocc and port and
suggests that the original final el. may have been ford. The *Stoke*-
spellings are against stocc. The variant forms of the p.n. could have
arisen from the assimilation *kp* > *pp*, and from the coincidence of
final *-t* as in *port* and unvoiced final *-d* as in *ford* > (*fort(h)*) which
led to the substitution of *-ford* for *-port*.

STREET-NAMES

Of the spellings, 1351 is *Eyre*, 1541² Sheaf, 1680 Atlas, 1714 *Dep*, 1742, 1759,
1769, 1777 JRL, 1831 Bry, 1849 *TA* 369, 1860 White and the rest Earw.

ARDERN FIELD ST., *Ardern Field* 1860, from the surname *Arderne*, cf. Arden
262 *supra*.
BRIDGE ST., 1849, leading to Lancashire Bridge *infra*.
UPPER BROOK ST., 1860, *Brook Street* 1849, cf. Hempshaw Brook, *Broke-
house infra*.
CALE ST., cf. Cale Green *infra*.
CARRINGTON FIELD ST., *Carrington Field* 1860, cf. Carrington Bridge *infra*.
CHESTERGATE, 1849, *-otherwise the Petty Carr* 1769, *the Petty Carr* 1759,
Petty Carr 1680, 'the little marsh', later 'the road to Chester', *v.* pety,
kjarr, gata, cf. Chester 330 *infra*, Chestergate 115 *supra*.
CHURCHGATE, 1680, *the-* 1541², 'the way to the church', *v.* cirice, gata.
DAW BANK, (*House*) 1860, 'jackdaw bank', *v.* daw(e), banke.
GORSEY BROW, *v.* gorstig, brū.
GREAT MOOR ST., cf. Stockport Great Moor *infra*.

HEAPRIDING ST., *Heap Rydeings* 1712, *v.* hēap, ryding.
HEATHFIELD RD, cf. *Heathfield House* 1860.
HIGH ST., 1860, cf. *Top of the Hill Houses infra, v.* hēah.
HILLGATE, *the Hilgate* 1423, *the Hillgate* 1549, *Hilgate Street* 1577, 'road up a hill', *v.* hyll, gata.
HOPES CARR, *Hope Cars, Hope's Carr* 1860, *v.* kjarr 'brushwood, marsh'.
KENNERLEY RD, *Kenworthy's Grave* 1831, *Kennedy Grove* 1860, from a surname derived from Kenworthy 235 *supra* and grǣfe.
LONGSHUT LANE, 1849, cf. *Longshut Field* 1860, *Longshote* 1438, *the Longe Shitte* 1549, *the Long Shutt* 1742, *-shoot, -shut(t)* 1777, 'the long corner of land', *v.* lang, scēat.
MARKET PLACE, *the-* 1541[1], *the Market Sted* 1537, *Market Seyd* 1549, *v.* market, stede, sīde, place.
MERSEY ST., 1849, cf. R. Mersey 31 *supra*.
MILLGATE, *the-* 1457, 1557, *the Mylne-, Milnegat(e)* 1541[2], 1626, (*Street*) 1577, *Millgate Street, Mill Hill* 1680, 'the road to the mill', *v.* myln, gata, hyll.
PARK ST., cf. *way to mills and parks* 1680, and Park Bridge *infra*.
TOLLBAR ST., 1860, cf. *Bar House* 1849, *v.* toll-bar.
UNDERBANK, *under the Bonck* 1454, *-banke* 1549, *the underbancke* 1577, *-bank* 1714, cf. *Merseybonke* Rl, *le Bonk* 1351 (p), 'under the bank', *v.* under, banke.

Lost Street-names are *Rosen Banke* 1680 (*v.* banke); *Shyre Lane* 1636 (*v.* scīr[1] 'a shire, a district'); (a lane called) *Shokswall* 1577 (cf. *Shotsall* 258 *supra*); *Stokport Lane* 1423 (Dr Barnes identifies it with Stockport Road); *Winn Banke* 1680 (*v.* banke).

LOST BUILDINGS: *le Brokehouse* 1283 Orm[2], Earw, 1438 ib, ('house at a brook', *v.* brōc, hūs; a burgage near 'the rivulet of Stokeport', i.e. Hempshaw Brook *infra*); *the Market Cross* 1656 Earw, *Market House & Cross* 1680 Atlas (cf. Market Place *supra*); *Millgate House* 1680 ib (cf. Millgate *supra*); *Petty Carr House* 1680 ib (cf. Chestergate *supra*); *Top of the Hill Houses* 1680 ib ('houses on top of a hill'; the site is now High St. *supra*); *Town End House* 1860 White, *Towns End* 1775 Earw (*v.* toun, ende[1]); *Woodhall* 1643 ib ('wooden mansion', *v.* wudu, hall; but perhaps this is Portwood Hall, in which case 'hall at a wood').

CASTLE HILL (local), *castellum de Stokeporta* 1173 Earw, *del Castelhull* 1355 *Eyre* (p), the site of a castle held against Henry II, cf. Earw 1 330–1, *v.* castel(l), hyll.

HEAVILEY, c.1636 Sheaf, *Hethy-, Hethileg(h)* 1283 Earw, 1286, 1290 Court (p), 1360 *Eyre* (p), *Heuileye* 1285 *ib*, (*le*) *Heuylegh* 1354, 1372 *ib*, *Heveley* 1423 Earw (p), *Heaveley Lane* 1577 ib, 'heathy wood or clearing', *v.* hǣðig, lēah.

NANGREAVE FM & LANE

Knavenegreue (lit. *-grene*) 1281 Plea (p), 1282 Court (p), *Knauen-*,
  Knaungreue 1364, 1366 *Eyre* (p)
Cnaugreue 1361 *Eyre* (p), *Cnafgref, Knafgreue* 1369 *ib* (p), *Knavgreue*
  (lit. *-grene*) 1391 ChRR (p), *Knawe-, Knauy-, Knauegreue* 1364,
  1373, 1376 *Eyre* (p)
(*le*) *Knangre*(*a*)*ve* 1392 Earw, 1399 Sheaf (p), *Nangreave* 1576
  ChRR, *-greave* 1831 Bry

'The servants' or young men's wood', *v.* cnafa (gen.pl. cnafena),
græfe.

BANKS LANE, *Bank Lane* 1849 *TA, v.* banke.   BROOKFIELD HO,
1860 White, cf. foll. and Hempshaw Brook *infra*.   BROWN HOUSE
FOLD BROOK (> Hempshaw Brook), *v.* 290 *supra*, cf. prec.   CALE
GREEN, 1831 Bry, *Kale Green* 1844 *TA, v.* cauel 'an allotment of
land', cf. Middlecale 200 *supra*.   CARRINGTON BRIDGE MILL, cf.
Carrington Field St. *supra*, Carrington Rd 268 *supra*, all containing a
surname derived from Carrington 330 *infra*.   CASTLE (FARM
LANE).   COW LANE.   DIAL HO, 1860 White, from next.
DIALSTONE LANE (FM), *Dial Stone Lane* 1849 *TA*, 'lane near a sun-
dial stone', *v.* dial, cf. prec.   HALL ST., 1849 *ib*, the main road
leading to Offerton and Marple 290, 281 *supra*.   HAWFIELD
GARDENS.   HEMPSHAW BROOK (R. Goyt), *Stok*(*e*)*port Broke*,
-Brook 1419 Orm², Earw, *rivulus de Stokeport* 1438 *ib, v.* brōc, cf.
foll. and Stockport *supra*.   HEMPSHAW LANE, HEMPSHAWGATE FM,
Impeshagh 1362 Orm², Earw, *the Empshaw yate* 1595 *ib, Hempshaw
Lane* 1842 OS, '(road to) the sapling-copse', *v.* impa, sceaga, gata,
cf. prec. and Offerton Fold 291 *supra*.   LANCASHIRE BRIDGE, 1831
Bry, *apud novem pontem* 1377 *Eyre, a great stone-bridge which divides
them from Lancashire* 1656 Earw, giving rise to a surname *de Ponte*
1282–3 Orm², *del Brugge* 1316 Plea, *del Brigge, Bruge* 1391 ChRR,
v. brycg, cf. Bridge Hall 249 *supra*.   LAWRENCE BARN'S FM,
Lowndes Barn 1842 OS, *v.* bere-ærn, cf. Lowndes Lane *infra*.
LISBURNE HO & LANE, *Lisbon House* 1842 *ib*.   LOCKWOOD FOLD,
v. fald.   LOWNDES LANE, from the local surname *Lowndes*, cf.
Lawrence Barn's Fm *supra*.   MILE END (HALL & LANE), *Myle
End* 1614 Earw, (*a fair house at-*) 1621 *ib, Mile End Hall* 1617 *ib*,
Miles End Hall 1690 Sheaf, a mile from the town, *v.* mīl, ende[1].
MILLGATE BRIDGE, cf. Millgate *supra*.   MOORFIELD.   NEW

BRIDGE (LANE), *the new bridge beyond Stockport* c.1620 Orm², *New Bridge* 1831 Bry, (*Lane*) 1849 *TA*.   NEW ZEALAND RD, *New Zealand* (*Road*) 1849 *ib*.   OFFERTON FOLD, *v.* 291 *supra*.   PARK BRIDGE, *Portwood Bridge* 1831 Bry, cf. *parcum de Stokeport* R1 Orm², *le Parke* 1345 ib, *The Park* 1537 Earw, *the Litle & the Meyne Parke* 1541 Sheaf, *the two Parks* 1680 Atlas, *a field below the Castle, called the Park* 1860 White, cf. also *The Park Mills* 1860 ib, Park St. *supra*, *v.* park.   PARK LANE, 1849 *TA*, named from the park at Wood Bank 265 *supra*.   ROWCROFT SMITHY (lost), 1860 White, *Rocroft Smithers* 1818 Sheaf, *Rowcross Smithy* 1831 Bry, *Roucroft* 1349 *Eyre* (p), *Rowecrofte* 1354 *ib* (p), *del Roycroft* 1384 *ib* (p), 'rough croft', *v.* rūh, croft.   SHAW HEATH, 1711 (1860) White, 1712 Earw, 'copse heath', *v.* sceaga, hǣð.   STEPPING HILL, *v.* 260 *supra*. STOCKPORT GREAT & LITTLE MOOR, 1860 White, *del Mor* 1348 *Eyre* (p), *-e* 1390 ChRR (p), *Stockport Moor* 1712 Earw, (*-& Little Moor*) 1831 Bry, *v.* mōr¹.   STRINGER'S WEIR.   TURNCROFT LANE, 1511 Earw, *Turne-* 1577 ib, *-crofte* 1626 ib, 'round croft', *v.* trun, croft. WELLINGTON BRIDGE & RD (SOUTH), 1849 *TA*, after the first Duke of Wellington.   WOOD COTTAGE.

FIELD-NAMES

The undated forms are 1849 *TA* 369. Of the others 1283², 1428, 1609¹ are Orm², 1285 Court, 1351 *Eyre*, 1439, 1481, 1609² ChRR, 1480 Adl, 1501 *Dow*, 1541, 1690, 1819 Sheaf, 1831 Bry, 1860 White, and the rest Earw.

(a) Bank Top 1831 (cf. Wood Bank 265 *supra*); Black Fd; Boundary Lane; Brook Cottage (cf. *Brooke Villa* 1860 White); East Bank 1860; Garden Fd & Mdw; Gibbet Lane (*v.* gibet); Goit Mdw (cf. R. Goyt 27 *supra*); Green Lane; Greenside 1740 (*v.* grēne²); Intake; Lane End; Moor Stripe (*v.* mōr¹, strīp); Mottram Moor 1860; New Piece; Old Lay (*v.* lēah); Pinfold Lane (*v.* pynd-fald); Pit Fd; Royal Lane; Stripe (*v.* strīp).

(b) *the Bastile Room or place* 1537 (a parcel of land in the Market Place *supra*, from ME *bastile* 'tower of a castle', and rūm¹ 'a space', alluding to the site of the castle at Castle Hill *supra*); *the Bothum*(e) 1609 (cf. Hobbekin *de Bothum* R1, *v.* boðm 'a valley-bottom'); *Cyslyfield* 1438 (probably near Longshut Lane *supra*, and named from *Cicely* wife of Richard de Stokeport c.1300, or *Cicely* de Eton her grand-daughter c.1332, cf. Earw 1 343, 349); *the Crokidde Close* 1541 (*v.* croked, clos); *Hakebrugg'* 1285 (p) ('bridge at a corner' *v.* haca, brycg, cf. Hackbridge Sr 41); *Horrock Lee* 1554 (*v.* lēah); *Le Kidfyld* 1439, *-feld* 1481, (*the*) *Kyd*(*de*)*feld* 1541 (perhaps from kide 'a kid'); *Medowcroft* 1351 (p) (*v.* mǣd, croft); *the morehouse or the Whole Crofte* 1501; *the Padockarre* 1549 ('frog marsh', *v.* paddok, kjarr); *Walterruding* R1 ('Walter's clearing', from the ME (OG) pers.n. *Walter* and ryding).

12. TORKINGTON (101–9387)

> *Torkinton(eia)* 1181, 1183 P (p) *et freq, Torkington* 1249 Earw (p)
> *et freq* with variant spellings -*in(g)*-, -*yn(g)*-, -*tone*; *Thorkynton*
> 1365 BPR (p), *Torkynson* 1512 *ChEx* (p), *Tortinton* 1527 (1581)
> ChRR, *Torkenton* 1582 *Dow,* 1692 Sheaf
> *Turkynton* l13 (15) *Chol* (p), -*ington* 1286 Court (p)
> *Terkynton* 1432 Sheaf

Perhaps 'farm called after Turec', from an OE pers.n. *Turec,* and
-*ingtūn.* No such pers.n. is recorded, but it is suggested in DEPN for
this p.n. and Torksey L.

BROADOAK (101–939875), *The* 1819 Orm², *Hopwoods* 1831 Bry, cf.
Hopwoods Mdw *infra,* probably from a surname *Hopwood.* Adjacent
is a moated site (*Moat* 1842 OS, *site of Roman Camp* 1849 *TAMap*),
probably *citum manerii de Torkyngton aqua circumclusum cum pomeriis
et gardinis ibidem* 1465 JRL, Orm², also called 'a certain manor house
inclosed with great ditches and water, built by John de Legh' 1384
ChFor, and *le Legh hous* c.1350 JRL, 'the house of the Legh family'
(*v.* hūs), at *le Graeureeslond*' 1363 *ChFor* ('the digger's land', from the
ME occupational surname *Grauer* 'one who digs' and land) where
John de Legh is reported to have taken in and cleared sixty acres of
royal woodland and built a hall of two chambers and a kitchen, moated,
and outside the moat a barn, stables, wards etc., c.1354, cf. Etchells
infra.

HEPPALES (lost)

> *Hep-, Hophal'*, -*hales,* -*halis* 1285, 1287 *Eyre,* Court, 1355 Orm²,
> *Hephals* 1369 *Mont* (p), -*hale* 1375 *Eyre* (p)
> *Heppalis* 1315 JRL, -*es* 1348 *ChFor,* 1545 Orm², (-*iuxta Torkyn-*
> *ton*) 1349 JRL, (*le*) -*ez* 1377 *Eyre, Heppal'* 1349 *MinAcct,* -*all'*
> 1372 *Mont,* -*als* c.1394 Orm², -*alles* 1458 JRL, *Hoppales* 1322
> *Mont*
> *Heppe-, Hoppehals* 1365 *Mont, Heppehales* 1369 *Eyre* (p), *Hepehale*
> 1467 *MinAcct*
> *Hepwales* 1379 *Eyre*
> *Hopehall* 1471 *MinAcct*
> *Hepples* 1485 Orm², (-*in villa de Torkynton*) 1489 ChRR
> *Hopedale* 1508 *MinAcct*

'Wild-rose nooks', *v.* hēope, halh, cf. Heppley 208 *supra.*

POISE BRIDGE (101–933874), *Poice Bridge (Pingot)* 1849 *TA*, v. **brycg, pingot**, cf. Poise Brook 33 *supra*, Poise Ho, Wellington Mill, 257 *supra*. The earliest references for this series of names appear as f.ns. in Torkington township, *le Puysclogh'* c.1350 JRL, *The Poyce* 1579 ib, *The Poices* 1849 *TA*, referring to the little valley running north through the hamlet, 101–933869 to 933874. The later names appear to be taken from the stream-name. This is a back-formation from the first el. of *Puysclogh'* which must have been seen as a r.n. with **clōh** 'a dell' added. *Puysclogh'* is 'pease valley', a place where pease grew, from **peosu**, the back-mutated form of **pisu**, 'pease', represented by ME *puys* with the AN *-ui-* orthography.

BROOKSIDE FM, near Ochreley Brook *infra*.   CLOUGH HO, v. **clōh**. ETCHELLS, v. **ēcels** 'an addition, land added to an estate'; perhaps part of the incroachment referred to at Broadoak *supra*, cf. Etchells 239 *supra*.   GREENCLOUGH 1849 *TAMap*, v. **clōh**.   HAZEL GROVE, v. 256 *supra*.   HOCKLEY HALL, OCHRELEY BROOK (> Poise Brook 33 *supra*), cf. *Hockley Field or Wharmby's Meadow* 1849 *TA*; perhaps analogous with Hockerley and Occerly 177, 275 *supra*. The surname *Wharmby* appears in this part of Ch from c.1578 (Thomas *Wharmby* Earw II 61). It derives from Quarmby WRY 2 301, or from some identical lost Ch p.n., 'farmstead at a mill', v. **kvern, bý**. MOULT WOOD.   OFFERTON RD, v. 257 *supra*.   TORKINGTON BROOK, v. 36 *supra*.   TORKINGTON HALL & LODGE, 1819 Orm². TORKINGTON HOUSES, LANE & RD.   TORKINGTON WOOD, cf. *Netherwod* 1377 *Eyre, the Wood, the little Woodfield* 1697 JRL, v. **neoðera, wudu**, cf. Marple Wood 283 *supra*.

FIELD-NAMES

The undated forms are 1849 *TA* 402. Of the others 1348 is *ChFor*, 1514 Plea, 1842 OS, and the rest JRL.

(a) The Acres (v. Hole Mdw *infra*); Ass Green; Back Fd (v. Great Riddings *infra*); The Bank (v. Little Knoll *infra*); Barn Fd (*the Barnefield* 1697, cf. Bean Fd *infra*); Barn Field Nook; Battledores (*the Battle Doales* 1697, from batail 'battle, judicial battle' and **dāl** 'a share of land'; but the significance is not clear); Bean Fd or Barn Fd (cf. Barn Fd *supra*); Blake Croft (*the-* 1697, v. **blæc**); Bore Ho; Brick Kiln Fd or Clay Shut (v. **bryke-kyl, clæg, scēat**); Broad Croft or Great Mdw (*the Broodcroft* 1556, *the Broad Crofts* 1697, v. **brād, croft**); Broad Fd (v. Daisy Fd, Flat Fd *infra*); Brook Fd (2x), Brook Fd or Nearer Great Hey (cf. Great Hey *infra*); Broomy Fd

(cf. *The Brooms* 1697, *v.* brōm); Brown Hills; (Long) Calf Croft, Calves
Croft (cf. Torn Lee *infra*); Chip Fd (*the Chippefilde* 1465, *v.* chippe, feld);
Cinder Fd (*v.* sinder); Clay Shut (*v.* Brick Kiln Fd *supra*); Clayton Piece;
Clover Fd (cf. Rid(d)ings *infra*); Coal Oaks (*v.* Little Scholes *infra*); Cock-
shutt Hey (*the Cockshuthay* 1697, *v.* cocc-scyte, (ge)hæg); The Common Fd,
Lower & Middle Common (cf. *Torkynton Comyn* 1556, *v.* commun, cf.
Sawpit Fd *infra*); Cote Fd (*v.* cot); Cotter Lands (*the Cotter lains* 1697, 'the
cottar's plots of land', *v.* cottere, leyne, land); Crab Orchard (*v.* Marl Fd
infra); Daffodil Croft; Daisy Fd or Great Broad Fd (cf. Flat Fd *infra*); Dirt
Fd or Lower Door Fd, Little Dirt Fd (*v.* drit, duru, cf. Martins Mdw *infra*);
Dry Knoll or Rye Knoll (*v.* drȳge, ryge); Ferny Hey; Finchey (*Fyncheley*
1579, *the Finch ley* 1637, 1697, *v.* finc, lēah); Flat Fd or Little Broad Fd
(*v.* flatr, cf. Daisy Fd *supra*); Furlongs (*the Furlong* 1697, *v.* furlang);
Gorsey Knoll; Great Hey (cf. Brook Fd *supra*); Great Mdw (*v.* Broad Croft
supra); The Green (*Torkynton Grene* 1466, *alias vocat'* the Lagher Grene 1556,
Torkington Greene 1637, *v.* grēne[2]); Grindle Hill (1697, cf. *Grenlowemedewe*
1347, 'green mound meadow', *v.* grēne[1], hlāw, mǣd); Hall Croft (*v.* Lane
Side Fd *infra*); Healer Croft or Further Hey; Hilly Lea (*the Hillylee* 1697,
v. hyll, -ig[3], lēah); The Hole Mdw or the Acres (*v.* hol[2]); Hollow Fd or
Long Mdw; Hollow Mdw or Rushy Mdw; Horse Croft or Smiths Fd;
Hwist; Jack Croft (*the-* 1697, *v.* jack); Little Knoll or the Bank, Pit Fd or
Kiln Knolls, Spout Mdw or Knoll, Wood Fd or Round Knoll (*v.* cnoll,
spoute, cf. Dry Knoll *supra*); Lane Side Fd or Hall Croft; Lime Fd or
Sheepers Mdw (*Sheephouse meadow* 1697, *v.* scēp, hūs); Little Fd or Little
Ridings (*v.* Rid(d)ings *infra*); Little Mdw or House Croft; Long Lee (*the-*
1465, *v.* lang, lēah); Long Mdw (*v.* Hollow Mdw *supra*); Long Shutt (*the*
long shoote 1692, *v.* lang, scēat); Lower Fd (cf. Meg Fd *infra*); Maper Fd
(cf. Meg Field *infra*); Marl Fd or Crab Orchard (cf. *the Marlet Erthe* 1465,
v. marlede, eorðe); Martins Mdw or Higher Door Fd (*v.* duru); Meg Fd or
Lower Fd, -Maper Fd, -Middle Fd; Merry Hills (*the-* 1697, *the Merry Hill*
1637, *v.* myrge, hyll); Middle Fd (cf. Meg Fd *supra*, Mill Fd *infra*); Mill Fd
or Middle Fd; Old Mdw; Orchard Fd (cf. *le Orchard Flatte* 1465, 1697,
v. orceard, flat); Parnell Fd or Further Piece; Pearsons Croft (*v.* Roadside
Fd *infra*); Lower & Top Pinfold or (Higher) Tut Doors (*v.* pynd-fald, cf.
Tut Zow 305 *infra*); Pingot (*v.* pingot); Pit Bank; Pit Fd (*v.* Kiln Knolls
supra); Pitstead Fd (*v.* pytt, stede); Pool Fd; Reddish Croft, Great & Little
Redditch (cf. *Reddish Mdw* 292 *supra*); Rhodes Wd 1842; Dry-, Further-,
Great-, Horse- & Little Rid(d)ings (cf. *le Ruydynghed* c.1350, (*the Nether*)
Rydynges 1465, 1466, *Rye Ridinges* 1579, *v.* ryding, hēafod, ryge, and Back
Fd, Clover Fd, Broadoak, Little Fd *supra*); Roadside Fd or Pearsons Croft
(*the Pearson Croft* 1697); Rushy Mdw (*v.* Hollow Mdw *supra*); Rye Knoll
(*v.* Dry Knoll *supra*); Sawpit Fd or Common Fd (*v.* saw-pytt, cf. The
Common Fd *supra*); Little Scholes or Coal Oaks (*v.* lȳtel, skáli, cf. *Cowduck*
infra); Sheepers Mdw (*v.* Lime Fd *supra*); Sign Post Fd; Smiths Fd (*v.*
Horse Croft *supra*); Spout Mdw or Knoll (*v.* spoute, cf. Knoll *supra*); Stack
Fd; Tan Yard (*v.* tan-yard); Torn Lee or Long Calf Croft (*the Calfe Croft*
1697, *v.* calf, croft, þorn, lēah); Tut Doors (*v.* Pinfold *supra*); Wharmbys
Mdw (*v.* Hockley Hall *supra*); Will Fd.

(b) *Adsheads Tenement* 1697 (from the surname *de Addeshede* 1440, cf. Adshead Green 100 *supra*, *v.* tenement); *the Cowduck* 1697 (perhaps 'cold corner', *v.* cald, hōc, cf. Coal Oaks *supra*); *the Crowbitch meadow* 1697 (*v.* Crow Bitch Hill 257 *supra*); *Dame Isabell' Acre* 1465 (probably called after *Isabel* wife of John de Legh, 1349 Orm² iii 835, cf. Broadoak *supra*, near which this field lay, *v.* æcer); *Edmond Knoll* 1579 (from the pers.n. *Edmund* (OE *Éadmund*) and cnoll); *le Gatelker* 1348 (probably '(brushwood at) the goat hill', *v.* gāt, hyll, kjarr); *the Hollins Croft* 1697 (*v.* holegn); *le Hurstes* 1440 (p) (*v.* hyrst 'a wood, a hill'); *the Higher & Lower Juddole* 1697; *the Kerre Medowe* 1465 ('the marsh meadow', *v.* kjarr, mǣd); *le Lehe* (*inter Torkynton et Heppalis*) 1315 (from lēah 'a clearing', perhaps with ēa, 'a stream'); *Torkynton Mershe* 1514 (*v.* mersc); *the Meane Heyes* 1556 (*v.* (ge)mǣne, (ge)hæg); *Nelhous* c.1350; *the Oldfild* 1556 (*v.* ald, feld); *le Pament* 1465 ('the pavement', *v.* pavement); *the Pickford Croft* 1697; *Pye Wood* 1697 (*v.* pīe² 'a magpie'); *Raneleghruydynges* 1347 ('(clearings at) the raven-wood', *v.* hræfn, lēah, ryding, cf. Rid(d)ings *supra* and *Renuenlegh* (?) 290 *supra*); *the Shagh' Greve* 1465 (cf. *Ralph del Shagh'* 1398, *v.* sceaga 'a copse', grǣfe 'a grove'); *the Shepon Flatte, le Chapon Flatte* 1465 (*v.* scypen, flat); *le Stanyelessiche* c.1350 ('(watercourse at) the stony meadow', *v.* stānig, lǣs, sīc).

13. WERNETH (101–9592)

> *Warnet* 1086 DB
> *Wernyt* 1285 *For, Wernitum* 1304 City (p), *Wernith'* 1286 *Eyre*, 1819 Orm², *-yth* 1370 ib, (*-e*) 1508 ChRR, *-eth* 1415 Orm²
> *Weranith* c.1300 Tab, *Werenyt* 1378 *Eyre*, (?) *Werinith* 1321 Plea (lit. *Wermuth*), *-yth* 1382 ib (lit. *Wermyth*)
> *Werniht* 1304 AddCh
> *Wi-, Wyrnith, -yth* 1315 Plea, 1337, 1349 *Eyre*, *-e* 1536 Plea, *Wyrneth* 1616 Orm²
> *Wurnyth* 1368 *Eyre*

'Place growing with alders, an alder swamp', from Brit verno- 'alders', with a suffix -eto-, as in Gaul *Vernetum*, cf. Werneth La 51, Warren Burn Nb (DEPN s.n.), and Jackson 555. Cf. Long Alders Wood *infra*.

BEACOM FOLD (101–967911), HOUSES (969921) & WOOD (972918), *Bekum* 1292 Ipm, *Beacom Houses* 1795 Barnes¹ 766, *Beacom* (*Houses & Wood*) 1839 *TA*, 1842 OS, *Backum Houses* 1831 Bry, 'bee-valley', *v.* bēo, cumb.

HIGHER & LOWER HIGHAM, HIGHAM LANE, *Hegham* c.1330 *Fitt* (p), 1406 ChRR (p), *Higham* 1609 Earw, (*in Werneth*) 1642 ib, (*Higher &*

Lower) 1842 OS, (*Lane*) 1839 *TAMap*, cf. John *Higham* of Werneth 1540 Earw, 'high homestead', *v.* hēah, hām.

Apethornfold & Lane, *Apethorn* 1831 Bry, *-Farm* 1839 *TA*, 'the wild-rose tree', from eModE *hep-thorne* (1513 NED, cf. hēopa, hēope, þorn), *v.* fald, cf. Gibraltar Ho, Linnet Mill *infra*.   Arnold Hill, 1839 *ib.*   Ash Tree.   Back o' th' Hill, 1831 Bry. Bardsleyknowl, *Prentice House* 1831 ib, *v.* cnoll; *Bardsley* is a surname.   Far Benfield, *Ben Field* 1839 *TA*, *Bentfield* 1860 White, cf. Benfield Clough, Near Benfield 293 *supra*.   Birches, 1839 *TA*.   Bowlacre (Fm & Rd), *Boleacre* 1831 Bry, *Bowl Acre* 1839 *TAMap*, cf. Poleacre 265 *supra*, Polebank *infra*.   Broad-meadow, 1839 *TA*.   Chapels, *Chapel* 1839 *ib.*   Cheetham Field & Fold, *Cheetham's Fold* 1839 *ib*, cf. *Cheetham's Croft* 1839 *ib* 217, *Cheetham's Smithy* 1839 *TAMap*, from the surname *Cheetham*, *v.* fald.   Far Clough Fm, Near Cloughside, (*Far*) *Clough Side* 1831 Bry, *Far & Near Clough Side* 1842 OS, *v.* clōh 'a valley, a dell'. Compstall (Bridge & Mills), *Compstall Bridge* 1608 Earw, (& *Mills*) 1831 Bry, *Compstall* 1842 OS, *Compstall Bridge* ('a populous village') 1860 White 872, giving its name to a nineteenth-century c.p. formed out of Werneth, *v.* 258 *supra*. No early material has been found, but the p.n. could be from cumb 'a valley' and stall 'a place, a site' or 'a fishery', since it lies beside R. Etherow under Beacom *supra*.   Cowlishaw Cottages, *Collishaw* (*Plantation*) 1839 *TA*, 'charcoal wood', *v.* colig, sceaga.   The Croft. Edmund's Fm, *Edmund's* 1839 *ib.*   Ferndale.   Gee Cross (Fold), *Gee Cross* 1831 Bry, *-e* 1629 Earw, the site of a stone cross at a cross-roads, associated with the family of Dicon *Gee* 1494 Earw, Robert *Gee* of *Gee Crosse* 1629 ib, *v.* cros 'a cross', cf. White 871. The Gerrards, Gerrardswood, *Gerards* 1831 Bry, cf. Stockport Road *infra*.   Gibraltar Bridge, Ho & Mill, *Apethorne House*, *Gibraltar Mill* 1831 Bry, cf. Gibraltar Wood in Denton La, and Apethornfold *supra*, *v.* 331 *infra*.   Gin Well.   Hackingknife (101–964935), *Hacking Knife* 1839 *TA*, an 800 ft. promontory probably named from its sharp profile.   Hillside (101–947919), 1842 OS, *Mockbeggar Hall* 1831 Bry, *v.* mock-beggar.   Holly-well Cottages.   Hyde's Fm, *Hydes Place* 1831 ib, *Hyde's* 1839 *TAMap*, from the surname *Hyde* and place.   Joel Lane, cf. *Joel Brows* 1839 *TA*, *v.* brū.   Keg, *Keg Barn* 1831 Bry.   Linnet Mill, *Apethorn Mill* 1839 *TAMap*, *-s* 1860 White, cf. Apethornfold *supra*.   LOFTYTOP, *Low* 1831 Bry, from its position on Werneth Low *infra*, v. hlāw.   LONG ALDERS WOOD, 1839 *TA*, v. lang, alor, cf. Werneth *supra*.   LOWBANK, *Bank Farm* 1839 *TAMap*, *The Bank* 1842 OS, v. hlāw, banke 'a bank, a hill', cf. Werneth Low *infra*.   LOWTOP, 1831 Bry, 'top of the Low', cf. Werneth Low *infra*.   MORTIN CLOUGH & FOLD, *Mortin Clough* 1839 *TA*, *Martin Fold* 1831 Bry, from the surname *Martin* and clōh, fald. MOTTRAM OLD RD.   THE MOUNT, *Werneth Low* 1842 OS, cf. Werneth Low *infra*.   MOUNT PLEASANT (HO), 1831 Bry.   NEEDHAM'S FM, *Needham's* 1839 *TAMap*, *Flank Hall* 1831 Bry, on the flank of a hill, v. flank. The later name derives from the surname *Needham*.   NETHER HEY, (*Great & Little*) 1839 *TA*, v. neoðera, (ge)hæg.   PINFOLD (*Field*) 1839 *ib*, v. pynd-fald.   PIPER'S CLOUGH, (*Field*) 1839 *ib*, v. pīpere, clōh.   POLEBANK COTTAGES & HALL, *Pole Bank* 1831 Bry, 'pool bank', v. pōl[1], banke; near a stream running into R. Tame past Bowlacre *supra*.   RADCLIFF-FOLD, 1831 *ib*, *Ratcliffe Fold* 1839 *TAMap*, v. fald.   RIDD WOOD, *Ridd* 1839 *TA*, *Slade Wood* 1831 Bry, v. ryde 'cleared land', slæd 'a valley'. RUSHFIELD COTTAGE, cf. *Rushy Field* 1839 *TA*.   SCHOOL LANE (FM), cf. *School* 1839 *TAMap*.   SILVER SPRING, *Trough Houses* 1831 Bry, *Watering Trough* 1842 OS, from a wayside horse-trough. SPOUT, *Spout House* 1839 *TA*, v. spoute.   SPRINKS WOOD, *Spring Wood, Further & Nearer Springs* 1839 *ib*, v. spring 'a young wood'. STOCKPORT RD, 1860 White, *Gerards Brow* 1831 Bry, cf. The Gerrards *supra*.   THISTLYFIELD, 1831 *ib*.   UPPER CASTLE. WERNETH BROOK (Godley Brook 306 *infra*).   WERNETH-HALL, *Wernith Hall* 1819 Orm[2].   WERNETH LODGE.   WERNETH LOW (a hill, 101–9592), c.1620 Orm[2], *Wernith Low* 1621 Earw, 1819 Orm[1], v. hlāw 'a hill', cf. Loftytop, Lowbank, Lowtop *supra*.   WHITE GATES, 1860 White.   WICKEN, *The Firs* 1842 OS, cf. *Great & Little Wicker* 1839 *TA*, from dial. *wicken* 'mountain ash', cf. cwicen. WOODFIELD, 1839 *TA*, *Long Field* 1842 OS.

FIELD-NAMES

The undated forms are 1839 *TA* 418, the others are 1540 ChRR, 1615 Earw, 1831 Bry, 1842 OS.

(a) Acorn Croft; Acres; Ash House Fd (cf. *High Ash* 1831, *Ash* 1842); Aspen Clough (v. æspen, clōh); Backside Fd; Bait Mdw (v. beit); Bank; Barley Fd; Barn Fd & Mdw; Bent (v. beonet); Birchen Flat; Bone Dust Fd (v. bone-dust); Bredbury Fd (cf. Bredbury 262 *supra*); Bretland Fd & Wd (named from the *Bretland* family of Thorncliff 309 *infra*); Briarley (*v.* brēr, lēah); Brick Kiln Fd; Bridge Fd; Broad Hey; Brow Fd; Brow(s); Bull Fd; Calf Hey; Callor Fox Wd (perhaps from colefox 'a colefox'); Carns ('cairns', *v.* carn); Carr (*v.* kjarr); Clay Acre; Clothes Hedge Mdw (alluding to the drying of laundry on hedgerows); Clough (*v.* clōh); Clover Fd; Coal Mdw; Coal Pit Fd; Cockshut (*v.* cocc-scyte); The Common Fd; Corn Fd; Cow Hey; Cowhill; Crab Mdw (*v.* crabbe); Cut Tor Top (from torr, topp, with ME cutte (adj.) 'cut off, truncated, slashed'); Dab Acre; Dam Fd (*v.* damme); Dingle Fd (*v.* dingle); Dry Knowl; Elmhurst (*v.* elm, hyrst); Ferny Shaw (*v.* fearnig, sceaga); Flat Hey; Frame; Gee Mdw (cf. Gee Cross *supra*); Gig Fd (*v.* gigge); Gorsey Fd; Greenslip (*v.* grēne[1], slipe); Hanging Bank (*v.* hangende); Hesker, Hesketh Mdw (perhaps 'horse track', *v.* hestr, skeið); High Lane (along the ridge of Werneth Low *supra*, *v.* hēah, lane); Hills; Hollin Croft & Hurst, Hollins Row (*v.* holegn, hyrst, rāw); Hoo Riding (*v.* hōh, ryding); Houghton Fd; House Fd; Kiln Croft & Fd; Knowls; Land Rood Top & Wd (*v.* land, rod[1]); Lime Fd; Long Acre; Long Hill & Hurst (*v.* hyrst); Lousy Thorn (*v.* lūs-þorn); Marl Churl & Knowl (*v.* Blackeyer 265 *supra*); Marled Earth & Hey; Marlpit Mdw; Mean Wood Fd (*v.* (ge)mǣne); Middle Fd; Mill Hill; Mottram Croft (cf. Mottram in Longdendale 313 *infra*); Mouse Fd; Old Lowke ('old weedy field', *v.* lowk); Paradise (*v.* paradis); Park; Patch; Pease Fd & Mdw; Peet Hey (*v.* pete); Picker; Pingot (*v.* pingot); Pitstead (*v.* pytt, stede); Poor Fd; Ridings (*v.* ryding); Rig Fd ('ridge field', *v.* hrycg); Rough Fd; Round Brows; Rush(e)y Fd; Rye Fd; Sheep Hay; Slate Acre (*v.* slæget); Smithy Fd; Snape (*v.* snap); Sour Butts; Stansfield Mdw (*v.* stān, feld); Stone Low (*v.* stān, hlāw); Sugar Fd (perhaps from sugre, cf. Sugar Lane 184 *supra*); Swine Hill; Tut Zow (cf. Tut Doors 301 *supra*); Twitches (dial. twitch 'couch grass' (EDD)); Underbank (*v.* under, banke); Well Fd; Wheat Croft; White Hill & Lands; Wood Fd & Mdw.

(*b*) *Ceall fields* 1615 (probably a bad form of *Cecillfeld* 1540, 'Cecil's field', from the ME pers.n. and surname *Cecil*, from Welsh *Seisill*).

xv. Mottram in Longdendale

The ancient parish now forms three c.ps., Tintwistle, Stalybridge and Longdendale. It comprised 1. Godley (now included in Hyde c.p. 258 *supra*), 2. Hattersley (now included in Hyde and Longdendale c.ps.), 3. Hollingworth (part now included in Mossley La, and the remainder in Longdendale c.p.), 4. Matley (now included in Dukinfield, Hyde, Staly-bridge & Longdendale c.ps., cf. 258 *supra*), 5. Mottram in Longdendale (now included in Longdendale c.p.), 6. Newton (now included in Hyde and Dukinfield c.ps. 258 *supra*), 7. Stayley (now included, with Stalybridge La, and part of Matley *supra*, in the c.p. of Stalybridge Ch), 8. Tintwistle (of which the hamlet of Micklehurst is now included in Mossley La, and the rest is a c.p. in Ch). In this or Stockport parish was probably the lost place *Hofinchel, Hofinghel* DB, *v.* 165 *supra*.

1. GODLEY (101–9695)

   Godel' 1211–25 Facs (p), 13 *SocAnt*, 1285 Court (p), *Godele, -lay*
   13 *SocAnt, -leg(h), -lee, -ley(e), -lei* 1285, 1286, 1287 Eyre, l13
   SocAnt, AddCh, 1316 *SocAnt, -leygh'* 1360 *MinAcct, Godelegh
   in Longdendale* 1361 BPR, *Godilegh* 1321 Plea
   Goddeley c.1220 *AddCh* (p), *-legh* 1386 Plea, *-ligh* 1397 ChRR
   Godley 1364 Mere *et freq, (-in Longdendale)* 1448 ChRR, *(Hall)*
   1590 Earw, *-legh'* 1318 *SocAnt, -ly* 1419 *ib,* 1540 ChRR
   Gadlegh 1394 *CoLegh*

   'God(d)a's clearing', from the OE pers.n. *God(d)a* and lēah.

BONEMILL DAM.   BONNYFIELDS, cf. *Bonny Field* 1845 *TA* (*freq*),
'fair fields', from ModEdial. bonny.   BOSTON MILL (local), 1831
Bry.   BROOKFOLD, BROOK HO & SIDE, *Brook Side* 1831 ib, *Brookfold* 1842 OS, *v.* sīde, fald, cf. Godley Brook *infra.*   DOVE HO,
1831 Bry.   GODLEY BROOK (> Wilson Brook 280 *infra*), *torrens de
Godele* m13 *SocAct, v.* brōc. This is also *Wardle Brook, v.* Wardlebrook Fm 313 *infra.*   GODLEY GREEN, 1831 Bry, *v.* grēne[2].
GODLEYHILL, 1842 OS, *The Hill* 1831 Bry.   GODLEY VALE HO,
1860 White.   GREEN BANK, 1860 ib.   GREEN FM & LANE,
named from Godley Green *supra.*   GREEN HILL HO.   HIGH
BANK MILLS.   HIGH ST., 1860 ib, 'the main street', *v.* hēah.
HOVILEY BRIDGE, *v.* 279 *supra.*   IDDESLEIGH.   LONGLANDS (2x),
'long fields', *v.* lang, land.   MOTTRAM (NEW) RD, cf. Mottram
Old Rd 280 *supra.*   MOUNT PLEASANT.   THE OAKLANDS,
OAKLANDS COTTAGE, *Oaklands Hall* 1842 OS, *v.* āc, land.   PUDDING
LANE, 1845 *TA, v.* pudding, cf. Db 757, StNLn 102.   BOTTOM &
TOP ROW, *v.* rāw 'a row of houses'.   SUNDIAL, 1845 *TA, Pit House*
1831 Bry.   SWINDELLS FOLD, 1831 ib, from the surname *Swindells,*
cf. Swindells Orchard 256 *supra, v.* fald.   TETLOWFOLD, 1831 ib,
Tetley Fold 1842 OS, cf. Edmund *Tetlowe* 1554 Earw, Reginald
Tetlawe 1649 ib, *v.* fald. The surname *de Tettelowe,* probably from
Tetlow La 33, appears in the Longdendale district 1377 *Eyre.*
THE THORNS.   WOODSIDE, 1846 *TAMap, Wood Bottom Side* 1831
Bry, named from Wood Bottom 313 *infra, v.* sīde.

FIELD-NAMES

The undated forms are 1845 *TA* 176, 1846 *TAMap.* The others are 13,
c.1300, 1316 *SocAnt,* 1379, 1380 *Eyre,* 1831 Bry, 1860 White.

(a) Acre Head (v. hēafod); Andrew Fd; Back Saddle (v. back, sadol); Banky Fd; Barn Flatt; Bottoms (v. botm); Brick Kiln Fd; Broad Hey; Brushwood; Calf Croft; Close Brows (v. clos, brū); Clough (v. clōh); Crab Fd; Crooked Shutt (v. croked, scēat); Hare Hill Mdw (v. hara, hyll); Hole Fd; Homescites; Kiln Hey; Knott Fd (v. knottr); Lenten Fd (v. lencten); Long Shut (v. scēat); Lower Hills; Marled Earth (v. marlede, eorðe); Mean Mdw (v. (ge)mǣne); Oliver Fd (1831); Pingle (v. pingel); Rushy Fd; Sand Hole Fd; Sheep Hey; Shut (v. scēat); Shuttleworth Fd (cf. Shotelworth 1379, Shotelesworth 1380 (p), 'bolted enclosure', v. scyttels, worð, cf. Shuttleworth La 63); Spout Mdw (v. spoute); Tang (v. tang); Well Fd; White Lands ('poor fields', v. hwīt, land); Winter Pasture.

(b) Baldewinleie 13 ('Baldwin's clearing', from the ME (OG) pers.n. Baldwin and lēah); le Brendherthe 1316 ('the burnt ploughland', v. brende[2], erð); Simunddele c.1300 ('Simond's clearing', from the ME pers.n. Simond (cf. ON Sigmundr, OE, OG Sigemund) and lēah).

2. HATTERSLEY (101–9792)

> Hattresl(ey), -is- e13 Facs (p), AddCh (p), 1249 IpmR (lit. Haccres-), -legh l13 AddCh, -lay m13 SocAnt (p), -le 1359 Eyre (p), Hatresleye 1285 For, -legh 1362 Earw
> Hattersley 13 (17) Tab, 1621 Sheaf et freq, -leigh 1246 (18) Orm[2], -leg' 1255 Plea, -le 1288 Eyre (p), -legh 1290 Court, Hattirsleg' 1248 Ipm
> Hatteresl(e), -leg(h) 1286, 1288, 1290 Eyre, 1293 Plea, Hatereslegh 1360 MinAcct
> Hatterlegh 1286 Court (p)
> Hatteslee 1345 Eyre (p)
> Hastreslegh 1357 Eyre

The final el. is lēah 'a clearing'. For the first, Ekwall (DEPN and Studies[2] 81) suggests a reduced form of hēah-dēor 'a stag, a deer'. Cf. the f.n. Hatter Shoot infra.

BOTTOMS HALL, 1724 NotCestr, Bothum 1359 Eyre (p), Bothoms 1461 Earw, (-hall) 1625 Sheaf, Bothams Hall c.1620 Orm[2], Bothums Hall 1621 Sheaf, 'valley bottom', v. boðm. v. Addenda.

APPLE ST. BACK WOOD, 1842 OS. BUNKERS HILL. LOWER CLIFF, Cliff 1831 Bry, cf. Higher Cliff(e) 1840 TAMap, 1842 OS, v. clif. CLOUGH, 1840 TAMap, v. clōh, cf. next. CLOUGH-BOTTOM, v. clōh, botm, cf. prec., and Hurstclough 314 infra. COCK BROW, v. cocc[2], brū. COURT HO, 1840 TAMap, 1842 OS.

FIELDS, 1840 *TAMap*, -*Farm* 1831 Bry. FURTHER LANE, 1860
White. GREAT WOOD, *Bottoms Hall Wood* 1831 Bry, cf. Bottoms
Hall *supra*. GREENSIDE, 1831 ib, 'at the side of a green', *v.* grēne²,
sīde. HARTLEYFOLD, 1831 ib, *v.* fald 'a fold, a homestead or
farmyard'; probably with a surname, cf. next. HODGEFOLD, cf.
prec. and 314 *infra*. IDLE HILL, 'barren, useless hill', *v.* īdel.
INTAKE, *v.* inntak. JOBS. LEYLANDS, 1840 *TAMap*, *v.* lǣge,
land. LOWEND, 1831 Bry. LUMM, *Lumb* 1831 ib, *Lumm* 1839
TA, 'deep hollow', *v.* lum(m). MILLHILL, the site of *Brittomley
Mill* 1831 Bry, cf. *Brittomley Field* 1839 *TA*. The origin of *Brittomley*
is not clear. If not a surname, it may be analogous with Bartomley 168
supra, Barthomley 329 *infra*. MOTTRAM NEW RD. NEW HO,
1840 *TAMap*. NIMBLENOOK, 1831 Bry. OLIVERSWELL, cf.
Oliver Fd 307 *supra*. PINFOLD (LANE), *Pinfold House* 1831 ib,
v. pynd-fald. PINGOT, -*t* 1839 *TA*, 'a little field', *v.* pingot.
RHODESFOLD, 1831 Bry, *v.* fald, cf. Hartleyfold *supra*. SPRING-
BANK. TOR (WOOD), *Torr House & Wood* 1831 ib, (*Hopwood*)
Tor 1842 OS, *v.* torr 'a rock'. UNDERWOOD COTTAGES, under
Great Wood *supra*. WINDY HARBOUR, 1840 *TAMap*, 'windy
shelter', *v.* windig, here-beorg.

FIELD-NAMES

The undated forms are 1839 *TA* 195, of the others e13, c.1287 are *AddCh*,
1288 Court, 1360 *MinAcct*, 1842 OS.

(*a*) Bass Lot (*v.* báss, hlot); Bent (*v.* beonet); Birchin Row ('row of birch
trees', *v.* bircen², rāw); Black Fd; Bone Dust Fd (*v.* bone-dust); Bredust
Mdw; Brick Croft; Brierly Doll ('(allotment at) the briery clearing', *v.* brēr,
lēah, dāl); Bull Stake (either the stake at which bulls were baited, or at which
cows were served, *v.* bula, staca); Calf Hey; Captain Fd; Craddock;
Didsbury Fd; Elmost; Footgate Fd ('footpath field', *v.* gata); Gird Croft;
Hack Stock Fd; Hanging Bank (*v.* hangende); Hatter Shoot (from the ME
occupation-name, *hattere* 'a hatter' or the same first el. as Hattersley *supra*,
v. scēat); Higher Brow; Higher Holme (*v.* holmr); Horn Stead Mdw (cf.
John *de Hornstede* 1287 Court 231, 'place at a horn of land', *v.* horn, stede);
Horse Steads (*v.* hors, stede); Jud Croft; Kiln Fd; Knowfield (*v.* cnoll);
Lawkers; Lime Fd; Mean Mdw (*v.* (ge)mǣne); Mears Mdw & Stalls
(*v.* (ge)mǣre, stall); Miles Mdw; Milking Fds (*v.* milking); Overhey (*v.*
uferra, (ge)hæg); Park; Peacock; Potter Fd (*v.* pottere); Push; Pye Hey
(*v.* pie², (ge)hæg); Rannat Hole; Rough Heys, Lee & Mires (*v.* mýrr);
Roy Fd (*v.* ryge); Rushy Fd; Shirt Cliff (Wd) & Fds (*v.* scerde, clif, cf.
Shert Hall 271 *supra*); Soot Fd (*v.* sōt); Sour Butts (*v.* butte); Square Fd;
Squire Mdw; Steel 1842 (probably from stigel 'a stile'); Tauldley (perhaps

'the old clearing', v. ald, lēah, with the def. art. prefixed); Tenerfields (perhaps for Tenter-, v. tentour); Thieves Hole (v. þēof, hol[1]); Three Nook Croft; Tinker Road (v. tink(l)ere, rād); Tollbar Croft; Turf pits (v. turf); Vetch Fd; Warth (v. waroð); Well Fd.

(b) le Blackottthecroft c.1287 ('black-oath croft', from blæc and ME othe (OE āð) 'an oath', with croft, perhaps a piece of poor land which gave rise to the imprecation, or the scene of some other kind of dire swearing); Crounebroc 1288 ('crane brook', v. cron, brōc; Croune- is due to over-rounding of cron); le hallecroftis broc e13 (v. hall, croft, brōc); le russilache e13 ('rushy boggy-stream', v. riscig, læc(c)).

3. HOLLINGWORTH (102–0096)

Holisurde 1086 DB

Holinewurth' e13 Facs (p), *Holneworhht* 1287 Court (p), *Huline-worth* 1286 Eyre (p)

Holinwrd, -w(o)rth(e) 13 SocAnt (p), 1285, 1286 Court, l13 AddCh (p), *-yn-* l13 SocAnt (p) *et freq*, (*Magna, Parua*) 1358, 1360 MinAcct, (*in Longdendale*) 1419 SocAnt, 1860 White, *Hollin-worth, -yn-* 1318, 1359 (17) Sheaf, (*Nearer*) 1645 Earw

Holingworth 1286 Court (p), *-yng-* 1354, 1359 BPR (p), *Holling-worth* c.1621 Orm[2]

'Holly enclosure', v. holegn, worð. Cf. Longdendale 2 *supra.*

STREET NAMES: MARKET ST.; MOORFIELD ST., cf. Moorfield *infra;* WATER LANE, v. wæter; WOOD ST., named from Thorncliffwood *infra.*

THORNCLIFF HALL, THORNCLIFFBARN, -VALE & -WOOD

Thorntelegh 1360 Rental, (*le*) 1451 Earw, *Thronkley* 1408 (17) ib, *le Thornelegh* 1409 ib

Thornecliff 1617 Earw, *-e Hall* 1699 ib, *Thorncliffe* 1636 ib, *-cliff* (*Hall*) 1724 NotCestr

'Clearing at a thorn-copse', v. þorniht, lēah, cf. Little Thorncliff 313 *infra*, Thorncliff WRY 2 246. This was the home of the *Bretland* family, surnamed from Britland Edge 321 *infra.*

WEDNESHOUGH GREEN (102–003960) [ˈwensuf], *Wedenscough* 1795 Barnes[1] 808, *Wednescough Green* 1795 Earw, *Wedensough Green* 1795 Barnes[1] 808, 1831 Bry, 1846 *TA, Wednessough Lane* 1842 OS, *Wednesoff Croft & Field* 1845 TA 277, v. grēne[2], croft, lane, feld. The final el. of Wedneshough appears to be ON skógr 'a wood', confused, through metanalysis, with OE hōh 'a spur, a promontory', cf. Myerscough La 148. Dr Barnes (Barnes[2] 48) is almost certain the first el. is the god-name **Wōden** (cf. *Wodanclogh* 278 *supra*). If the first el. be taken as *Wedens-* the forms certainly resemble those of other **Wōden** place-names, but the ON el. skógr would be an unlikely second el. in an OE pagan p.n. unless it were to replace OE **sceaga**. The first el. should be taken as *Weden-*. This could be a form of OE **wīðign** 'a willow', **wīðigen** 'growing with willows', and the p.n. would then be analogous with Wythenshawe 236 *supra*, save for the substitution of skógr for sceaga. However, it would well be that *Weden-* here represents an OE **wēoden* 'covered with-, growing with weeds' (*v.* **wēod, -en**[2]), cf. *weeden* NED. The forms are too late for any definite etymology; they should certainly not be used to support a hypothesis so historically important as that the first el. is the name of an A.S. pagan god.

WOOLLEY (BRIDGE & LANE)

> *Woleg'* 1286 Court (p), *-legh* 1330 *Woll et freq*, *-leye* 1286 Court (p), *-ley* 1339 *Woll*, 1421 Plea, (*-medowe*) 1394 Orm[2], *Wole*(*medow*, *-oue*) 1394, 1395 *CoLegh*
> *Wollay* 1360 *MinAcct*, *-ey* 1400 ChRR
> *Wooley* 1737 Earw, (*-Bridge*) 1842 OS, *Woolley* 1831 Bry

'Wolves' clearing', *v.* **wulf** (gen.pl. *wulfa*), **lēah, mǣd**. Part of the hamlet is in Db, *v.* Db 105, cf. Woolley Mill & Lane 326 *infra*.

ARROWSCROFT HO & MILL, *H-* 1831 Bry. HIGHER, LOWER & MIDDLE BANK, 1842 OS, *the Bancke* 1645 Earw, *v.* **banke**. BENT MILL, cf. *Bent House* 1831 Bry, **beonet**. BOAR FLAT, 1842 OS, *Bowyers Flat* 1831 Bry, *Boor Flat* 1845 *TA*, from the occupational surname *Bowyer* and **flat**. BRUSHES RESERVOIR & QUARRY, cf. Brushes 318 *infra*. COCK KNARR, 'rugged rock at a hill', *v.* **cocc**[1] 'a heap, a hill', **cnearr**. DEVIL'S BRIDGE. DEWSNIP FM, cf. *Dewsnaps Croft* 1845 *TA*, 'dewy bog', *v.* **dēaw, snæp**, cf. Dewsnap 277 *supra*. DIAL HO, *v.* **dial**. ETHEROW BLEACH WORKS, the site of *Hollingworth Mill* 1831 Bry. ETHEROW HO, 1842 OS, named from R. Etherow 23 *supra*. FIELDS, *Feilds* 1645 Earw, *v.* **feld**. GALLOWS CLOUGH, 1842 OS, *v.* 312 *infra*. GREEN LANE. GREEN SPOT SPRING, *Grey Springs* 1831 Bry, 'spring at a green piece of ground', *v.* **grēne**[1], **spot**; the earlier name is probably from the nearby *Grey Stones* 1831 ib, *v.* **græg**[1] 'grey'. HALL FM, near Hollingworth Hall *infra*. HARDTIMES, 1831 ib, a derogatory name for a poor place. HARRIDGE, *v.* 319 *infra*. HOBSON MOOR, 1831 ib, *v.* mōr[1]. HOLLINGWORTH BROOK (R. Etherow), 1842 OS, also *Mill Brook* 1842 ib, cf. Millbrook *infra*. HOLLINGWORTH HALL, 1831 Bry. HOLLINGWORTHHALL MOOR, *v.* mōr[1], cf. prec. HOLLY GROVE, 1842 OS. IRON TONGUE (HILL). LANDSLOW GREEN (FM), *v.* grēne[2]. Landslow may contain hlāw 'a hill, a mound'. LEES HILL. LONGDENDALE, *v.* 2 *supra*. LUMB, 1842 ib, *Lumm* 1831 Bry, *v.* lum(m). MEADOWBANK. MILLBROOK (BRIDGE), *Mill Brook* 1842 OS, (*Bridge & Mills*) 1831 Bry, cf. Hollingworth Brook *supra*, Woolley Mill, Millbrook Ho 326, 324 *infra*. MOORFIELD TERRACE, cf. *Moor Field* 1845 *TA*, (*House*) 1860 White. MOORSIDE, 1842 OS, near Hollingworthhall Moor *supra*. MOUNT PLEASANT. NETTLE HALL, *v.* netel(e). NORTH BRITAIN, *-Brittain* 1846 *TA*, so-named from its remote position in the north part of the township. OGDEN CLOUGH, *v.* 325 *infra*. MOTTRAM OLD HALL, (*The*) *Old Hall* 1724 NotCestr, (*-anciently Nether Hall*) 1845 ChetOS VIII. OLD RD. PACK SADDLE, the name of a pass on the ridge west of Middle Bank *supra*, *v.* pakkesadil. RABBIT LANE. RED HO. ROE CROSS, 1842 OS, cf. Lower Roe Cross 315 *infra*. SLATEPIT MOOR, 1842 ib, *v.* slate, pytt. SPOUTGREEN, 'green at a spring', *v.* spoute, grēne[2]. SWINESHAW BROOK & MOOR, 1842 ib, *Swineshaw Brook* 1831 Bry, probably 'swine wood', *v.* swīn[1], sceaga. VALE FM. WASTELODGE RESERVOIR. WICKEN SPRING (CLOUGH), '(valley of the) spring at a mountain-ash', *v.* cwicen, spring, clōh. WIDOWSCROFT, *v.* widuwe.

FIELD-NAMES

The undated forms are 1845 *TA* 204. Of the others 1360 is *Rental*, 1377, 1395 Orm[2], 1394 *CoLegh*, 1665, 1738 Earw, 1831 Bry, 1842 OS.

(*a*) Bankers Hill; Besso' Cotton's Parlour 1831 (a secluded place at the head of Ogden Clough *supra* apparently named after one Elizabethan Cotton, *v.* parlur); Black Pit Fd; Bone Dust Fd (*v.* bone-dust); Bretland Mdw (from the family *Bretland* of Thorncliff Hall *supra*); Brows Wd (*v.* brū); Calf Hey Mdw; Carr Brows (cf. *Carr Wood* 1842, Carr Brook 17 *supra*, *v.* kjarr, brū); Catley Intake 1831 (*v.* inntak); Cellar Ho 1783; Claylands; Cote Hurst Wd (*Cote* 1831, *v.* cot, hyrst); Crow Hill; Flatts (*v.* flat); Gibralter Pasture (*v.* 331 *infra*); Gorses; The Heald (*v.* helde); Hilbert Rood; Hilkley; Hills Clough 1842 (*v.* clōh); Hob Fd (*v.* hobbe); Hollin Hey & Wd (*v.* holegn); Hough (*v.* hōh); Jockey Fd; Kite Fd (*v.* cȳta); Knowe Croft (*v.* cnoll); Long Loont (*v.* land); Marld Fd (*v.* marlede); Meg(g) Fd;

Midons Croft; Plumbtons; Pricket Fd; Ralph Hill; Riggs Fd (v. hryggr);
Rye Croft; Sheep Wash Fd (v. scēap-wæsce); Spout Croft (v. spoute);
Staley Wd 1842 (cf. Stayley 317 infra); Stoney Dole (v. dāl); Top of the
Moor 1831; Vineyard Mdw (v. vinȝerd); Warren Intake (v. wareine, inntak);
Wear Brows, Weir Fd (v. wer); Wharth (v. waroð); White Fd; Will Hey
(v. wella); Wood Fd.

(b) (le) Oldefeld 1360, (-en Holynworth) 1394, the Oldfield 1665 (v. ald,
feld).

4. MATLEY (101–9795)

Mattel' 1211–25 Facs (p), Mat(t)ele(y) 13 SocAnt (p), 1337 Eyre,
    Matteleg(h) 1285, 1287 Court (p), -lei 1330 Earw, Mattileg' 1286
    Court (p)
Mattlegh 13 Earw (p), -ley 1724 NotCestr, Matley l13 SocAnt (p),
    1831 Bry, -legh 1394 CoLegh

'Matta's clearing', from an OE pers.n. Matta and lēah. For the
pers.n., cf. DEPN s.nn. Martinhoe D, Matfen Nb, Mattingley Ha.

ALDERS, v. alor.   BARDSLEY GATE, 1842 TAMap, from the surname
Bardsley from Bardsley La 29 and geat 'a gate'.   BATES.
BLUNDERING LANE, cf. Blundering Mill 1831 Bry, Blundrat Mill 1842
TAMap, perhaps a corruption of branderith 'a grating, a grid-iron,
a brazier'.   CHEETHAMS, Cheetham 1842 OS, from the surname
from Cheetham La 33.   CLOSE, -s 1842 TAMap, v. clos.   GALLOWS
CLOUGH, 1842 OS, the boundary of Matley, Stalybridge and Holling-
worth, perhaps a place of execution, v. galga, clōh.   GOLDEN
SPRING, a well-spring, cf. Silver Spring infra, v. spring.   HARROP
EDGE (HO), Harop 1360 Rental, Harroppe Edge 1613 Earw, Harrop
Edge 1831 Bry, perhaps '(ridge at) the hare's valley', v. hara, hop¹,
ecg, but cf. Harrop 138 supra.   LONGLANDS, 1840 TA, 'long
selions', v. land.   MARL VILLA.   HIGHER & LOWER MATLEY
HALL, Parua-, Magna Mattelegh 1360 MinAcct, Matley Hall 1831
Bry, Lower Matley Hall 1842 TAMap, v. parua, magna.   MATLEY
LANE (FM).   MATLEYMOOR, Matley Moor 1831 Bry.   MINIA-
TURE CASTLE.   MOTTRAM (NEW) RD, cf. Mottram in Longdendale.
NEW INN 1″ OS, 1842 TAMap.   OAK, -House 1842 OS, Far Fold
1831 Bry, v. fald.   POTHOUSES, Pottery 1842 TAMap.   PUDDING
LANE, boundary with Godley 306 supra, v. pudding.   RAGLANDS,
1831 Bry, Rag Land 1842 TAMap.   SHOPWELLS, Shop Wells 1831
Bry, v. wella 'a well, a spring'. The first el. may be sc(e)oppa 'a shop,

a shed'. Cf. Wardlebrook Fm *infra*.   SILVER SPRING, 1842 OS, cf.
Golden Spring *supra*, *v.* spring 'a well-spring'.   TAYLORFOLD,
1842 *TAMap*, cf. *Taylor Field* 1840 *TA*, from the surname *Taylor*
with fald.   LITTLE THORNCLIFF (lost), 1842 *TAMap*, cf. Thorncliff 309 *supra*.   TONGE HO, *Lower Tonge* 1840 *TA*, *v.* Tonge Fold
320 *infra*.   WARDLEBROOK FM 1" OS (101–97895, at Shopwells
supra), *Wardle Brook* 1842 *TAMap*, a stream 101–982955 to 974944
becoming Godley Brook 306 *supra*, from a lost p.n. *Wardle*, probably
the home of Dikon de *Wordhull* 1286 Court 216, 'watch hill', *v.*
weard, hyll, cf. Wardle 335 *infra*.   WESTWOOD (CLOUGH), *High &*
Low Westwood 1831 Bry, 'the west wood', *v.* clōh.   WINTER
BOTTOM, 'a valley bottom which can be used in winter', *v.* winter,
botm, cf. Summerbottom 315 *infra*.   WOODSIDE, 1831 ib.
WRIGLEYFOLD, 1831 ib, *v.* fald.

FIELD-NAMES

The undated forms are 1840 *TA* 260. The others are 1842 OS and 1831 Bry.

(a) Bent, Bent Brown *&* Wd (*v.* beonet, brún[2]); Bleak Earth (*v.* blāc,
bleikr, eorðe); Bottom (*v.* botm); Bowlers Fd; Briddy-, Bridley Acre (perhaps
'young birds' clearing', *v.* bridd, lēah); Brow Hey (*v.* brū, (ge)hæg); Buckley
Wd 1842 (*Woolley's Wood* 1831, named from the *Bulkeley* family, landowners
here, cf. Wholley Fd *infra*); Bury me wick Mill (cf. Burymewick Wood 271
supra); Button Fd; Carr Mdw (*v.* kjarr); Chip Croft (*v.* chippe); Church
Fd; Ciceley Fd; Clough (*v.* clōh); Cote Edge (*v.* cot, ecg); Cow Lane (cf;
Cow Lane 331 *infra*); Dead Lane ('a lane leading nowhere', *v.* dēad);
Dirty Fd; Edge(s) (*v.* ecg); Fat Hey (*v.* fætt, (ge)hæg); Gorsy Fd; Granny
Fd; Greenings; Gutter Fd (*v.* goter); Hard Earth *&* Fd (*v.* heard, eorðe);
Hole; Hollingwood (*v.* holegn, wudu); Jenkin Croft; Lane Clough; Lough
Hey; Mare Hey; Marled Earth (*v.* marlede, eorðe); Marsland Mdw; Moor
Croft; Neat Fd (*v.* nēat); Nurse Mdw; Old Rakes ('old paths', *v.* rake);
Patch; Pets Croft; Pingot (*v.* pingot); Rough Hay; Round Edge (cf. *Round*
Hill 1831, *v.* rond, ecg); Rye Croft; Shippon Croft; Snapes (*v.* snæp);
Sour Dock (the common sorrel *rumex acetosa*); Swindle Fd; Tenter Fd
(*v.* tentour); Town Fd; Walks (*v.* walk); West Moorhill; Wheat Earth *&*
Edge (*v.* ecg); Wholley Fd (cf. Buckley Wood *supra*, Woolley 310 *supra*);
Wine Fd; Withinshaw ('willow wood', *v.* wiðign, sceaga); Wood Bottom
1842 (*v.* botm); Wood (Green) Fd.

5. MOTTRAM IN LONGDENDALE (101–9995)

Mottrum 1211–25 Facs *et freq*, (*-in Longedonedale*) 1332 Plea, *-am*
(*in Longedenedale*) 1308 Pap *et freq*, *-e* 1547 *MinAcct*, *Motram*

1558 Pat, *Mottrom* (*-cum Longe-, -in Langedenedale*) c.1310,
1323 Pat
Moterum in Longedenedale 1339 Orm², *-am*(*e*) 1542 Pat, 1546 Dugd,
Motteram 1580 Sheaf, *-om* 1635 ib
Motterham 1456 Orm², *Moterham in Longdondale* 1548 Earw

This p.n. is the same as Mottram St Andrew 202 *supra*, *v.* mōtere.
Cf. Longdendale 2 *supra*.

BROADBOTTOM (BRIDGE & HALL) (101–9993), (*le*) *Brodebothem* 1286
Eyre, *-am* 1330 Earw (p), *le Brodbothum* 1360 *Rental*, *-am* 1394 Earw,
Brodebothome 1614 ib, *Broadbottom Bridge* 1831 Bry, *Besthill Bridge*
1880 Earw, 'the broad valley-bottom', *v.* brād, boðm. Cf. Besthill
Mill in Charlesworth Db, near Broadbottom Bridge. The origin
of *Besthill* is not known.

(THE) HAGUE, HAGUE BANK, (*le*) *Hagh*(*e*) 1339 Orm², 1360 *Rental*,
1394 *CoLegh*, 1419, 1438 *SocAnt*, 1439 ChRR (p), *Haghaghe* 1360
MinAcct, *Haigh* 1638 Earw, (*The*) *Hague* 1831 Bry, 1847 *TA*,
Mottromhawe 1345 *Eyre*, possibly the origin of the surname *del Hawe*
1285 Court 213, *del Haye* 1286 ib 224 (also lit. *-Hathe*), 'the hedged
enclosure', *v.* haga, cf. Littlehill *infra*.

BACKMOOR, *Little Moor* 1847 *TAMap*, *v.* back, mōr¹.   BROAD
MILLS, *Brodebothome Milne* 1614 Earw, *v.* myln, cf. Broadbottom
supra.   BROWNROAD, *Brown Road* 1847 *TAMap*, *v.* brūn¹, rod¹.
CARR HO, 1831 Bry, *v.* kjarr 'brushwood, marsh'.   DANIEL WELL.
EDGE LANE HO, cf. Harrop Edge 312 *supra*.   GORSEY BROW.
HAREWOOD LODGE, 1831 Bry, cf. *Harewode* 1271 *AddCh*, 'hoar wood',
v. hār², wudu.   HARRYFIELDS.   HILLEND, 1831 Bry, 'the end
of the hill'.   HODGE FOLD & PRINT WORKS, *þe Hodge Hall* 1655
Earw, *Hodge Mill* 1831 Bry, *v.* hall, fald, myln. The origin of *Hodge*
is unknown. Cf. *Hodg Croft* 158 *supra*.   HURSTCLOUGH (BROOK),
Hurst Clough 1845 *TA*, 'wood valley', *v.* hyrst, clōh.   LANE-ENDS,
a five-ways.   LEEBANGS ROCKS, '(rocks at) the meadow-banks',
v. lēah, banke, roke.   LIMEFIELD MILL, cf. *Lime Field* 1845 ib.
LITTLEHILL, *Hague* 1831 Bry, cf. Hague *supra*.   MAINSGRASS,
Mean Grass 1831 Bry, *Main Grass* 1845 *TA*, 'demesne-', or 'common
pasture', from main or (ge)mǣne and gærs.   MANOR HO.
MILE-END HO.   MOTTRAM HILL.   MOTTRAM MOOR, 1831 Bry,

v. mōr[1].   MOTTRAM NEW RD, cf. Old Road *infra.*   (LOWER) MUDD, *Higher & Lower Mud Meadow* 1845 *TA*, *v.* mudde 'mud'. OLD MILL FM, cf. *le Oldemulneton* 1313 *SocAnt*, 'the old mill enclosure', *v.* ald, myln, tūn.   OLD RD, cf. Mottram New Rd *supra.*   OVERDALE.   PADDOCK, 1845 *TA.*   PARSONAGE FM, *Rectory* 1831 Bry, *Parsonage Field, Green & Meadow* 1845 *TA.* PINGOT LANE, *v.* pingot.   PRIM'S PARLOUR, a secluded hollow in the woods on the north bank of the R. Etherow, *v.* parlur.   LOWER ROE CROSS, *Row Cross* 1785 Barnes[1], *Roe Cross Mill* 1831 Bry, cf. Roe Cross 311 *supra*, supposed to be named after Ralph de Stavelegh whose effigy, known locally as 'Sir Roe', lies in Mottram church (Orm[2] III 856), *v.* cros.   SILVER SPRING, a well-spring, *v.* spring, cf. 313 *supra.*   SUMMERBOTTOM, 1845 *TA*, 'valley-bottom used in summer', *v.* sumor, botm, cf. Winter Bottom 313 *supra.*   WARHILL, 1842 OS, *le Wharell'* 1360 *Rental* (p), *v.* quarrelle 'a quarry'. WARRASTFOLD BRIDGE, *v.* fald, cf. *Werehurst* 1401 Mere (p), 1406 ChRR (p), 'wooded-hill at a weir', *v.* wer, hyrst. The surname is still current, as *Warhurst*, imported into north-west La from Ch. WHITEGATES, *White Gate* 1842 OS.   WILLOW BANK.

FIELD-NAMES

The undated forms are 1845 *TA* 277. Of the others 1313 is *SocAnt*, 1337 *Eyre*, 1360 *Rental*, 1360[2] *MinAcct*, 1831 Bry.

(a) Apron Croft; Back Ridings (*v.* ryding); Backside; Bangs Fd, Bank Fd, Banks (cf. *del Baunk* 1337 (p), *v.* banke); Bent (*v.* beonet); Blade Fd; Boar Fd (*v.* bār[2]); Bone Dust Fd (*v.* bone-dust); Booth Mdw (*v.* bōth); Botany Mdw (perhaps a derogatory name, after Botany Bay, for a poor and remote piece of land); Bowden Mdw; Brick Mdw; Brook Fd; Brush Wd (*v.* brusshe); Butty Fd (*v.* butty); Bye Ho; Calf Croft; Catt Torr (*Cat Torr* 1831, 'wild-cat rock', *v.* cat(t), torr); Clough Fd (*v.* clōh); Clover Fd; Coal Pit Fd; Coat-, Cote Mdw (*v.* cot); Corn Fd; Cow Hey; Crinsey (perhaps an example of the el. discussed at *le Crymbe* 331 *infra*, with (ge)hæg); Crow Dole (*v.* crāwe, dāl); Dam Croft, Fd & Mdw; Dole (*v.* dāl); Dolley Mdw; Dover; Elder Walls Bank & Mdw (perhaps 'elder-tree springs', *v.* ellern, wælla); The Eyes ('the water-meadows', *v.* ēg); Flake Fd (*v.* flak); Flax Lands; Fodderings (*v.* fōdring); Foot Road Fd ('footpath field'); Georgy; Goyt Croft (*v.* gote 'a water-course'); Hadden Fd; Hall Fd; Hanging Acre (*v.* hangende); Hanneys Road (*v.* rod[1]); Hard Fd; Haven Wd (cf. *Haven House* 1831); Hem Mdw (*v.* hemm); High Road (*v.* rod[1]); Hyde Wd; Intake (*v.* inntak); Kershaw Brow (from the surname *Kershaw* and brū); Kiln Fd; Kinderdole (from the surname *Kinder* and dāl); Knott Fd & Mdw (*v.* knǫttr); Leach Fd (*v.* læc(c)); Little Hurst Fd (*v.* hyrst); Mail Fd; Marl Fd; Meg

Clough (v. meg, clōh); Mill Fd; Moor Croft, Fd & Mdw; Moss Mill; Mother Fd; Nettle Hall 1831; Noddy Banks; Old Gate (v. gata); Othart; Pinfold (v. pynd-fald); The Plunge (v. plunge); Rakes Eye (v. rake, ēg); Red Ground Wd; Riddings (v. ryding); Rough Heys; Rushy Croft & Fd (cf. *le Ruschiheie* 1313, v. riscig, (ge)hæg); Sandy Green; Shippon Croft; Sick Mdw; Slack Brow, Slacks (v. slakki); Slang (v. slang); South Fd; Spring Fd; Square Fd; Stone Fd; Tenter Fd (v. tentour); Thistley Fd; Three Corner'd Piece; Tithe Barn; Titterton Fd; Tongue Mdw & Sharp (v. tunge, cf. Tongue Sharp Wood 162 *supra*); Torkington; Town Fd; Triangle; Twin Fd (v. twinn); Wall Hey (perhaps from wælla 'a well, a spring' and (ge)hæg); Warth (v. waroð); Wednesoff Croft & Fd (v. Wedneshough 309 *supra*); Well Fd; Wheat Acre; Wood Fd; Woodcock Hey; Yellow Fd.

(b) *del Euese* 1313 (p) (v. efes 'an edge or border, a brow'); *Heleigh* 1313 (p) ('high clearing', v. hēah, lēah); *le Holehous* 1360 ('house in a hollow', v. hol[1], hūs); *le leg* 1313 (v. lēah); *le Maysterrudyng* 1313 ('the master's clearing', from ME *maister* and ryding); *Prestfeld* 1360[2] ('priest's field', v. prēost, feld); *le Rudiger* 1313 (probably 'reedy marsh', v. hrēodig, kjarr, cf. Redacre 132 *supra*); *Ruggeway* 1360 ('ridge way', v. hrycg, weg); *Sikenytleg* 1313 (first el. obscure, v. lēah).

6. NEWTON (101–9595)

Neutun e13 Facs, l13 *SocAnt* (p), -*ton* (*iuxta Hide*) 1288 *Eyre*, (-*iuxta Godelegh*) 1353 Plea, (-*in Longdenedale*) 1357 *ChFor*, (-*iuxta Dokynfeld*) 1362 Plea
Newton 1318 (17) Sheaf (p), 1394 *CoLegh* (-*in Longedenedale*) 1335 Plea

'New farm', v. nīwe, tūn, cf. Dukinfield, Godley, Hyde, Longdendale 276, 306, 279, 2 *supra*.

STREET-NAMES: BOTTOM ST., cf. *Bottoms* 1845 *TA*, v. botm 'a valley-bottom'; BROOK ST., cf. Johnson Brook 277 *supra*; COMMERCIAL BROW & ST., from *The Commercial* (p.h.) 1831 Bry, v. brū; HALLBOTTOM LANE, cf. *Hall Bottom* 1831 Bry, *Holebottom* 1847 *TAMap*, 'deep bottom', v. hol[2], botm; LODGE LANE, cf. *Newton Lodge* 1842 OS; MUSLIN ST., 1847 *TAMap*; OLD RD, *Old Lane* 1847 *TAMap*; SAWYER BROW, v. brū; SMITH ST., cf. *Smith's Fields* 1845 *TA*; THROSTLE BANK ST., cf. 279 *supra*; VICTORIA ST., 1860 White, *Back Lane* 1831 Bry, 'lane at the back', v. back.

BARNFIELD. BAYLEY FIELD MILL, *Bayley-field Colliery* 1860 White, cf. 279 *supra*. BRADLEYGREEN, 1831 Bry. CARRFIELD MILL, v. 279 *supra*. DUNKIRK (LANE & WOOD), *Dunkirk (Colliery)* 1831 ib, *Dunkirk Homesites* 1845 *TA*, cf. Dunkirk 331 *infra*, v. 329 *infra*. FLOWERY FIELD, 1845 *ib*, cf. 279 *supra*. THE GOODIERS,

Goodier House 1860 White.　　HARBOUR, *Harbor* 1831 Bry, *v.* here-
beorg.　HYDE MILL & PARK, cf. Hyde 279 *supra*.　　LYNE EDGE,
v. 278 *supra*.　　MOTTRAM RD, leading to Mottram 313 *supra*.
NEWTON BANK, 1845 *TA*, *v.* banke.　　NEWTON GREEN, -*Greene*
1647 Earw, *v.* grēne[2].　　NEWTON HALL, MOOR & WOOD, 1831 Bry,
cf. Newton Wood 278 *supra*.　　NEWTON HO, 1860 White.　　SEA-
COMBE PLACE.　　SHAWHALL, [ʃei c:], 1860 White, *Shaw Hole* 1845
TA, 'hollow at a wood', *v.* sc(e)aga, hol[1].　　VALE COTTAGES.

FIELD-NAMES

The undated forms are 1845 *TA* 291. Of the others 1286 is Court, 1831 Bry.

(*a*) Back Mdw ('meadow at the back'); Barley Croft; Bent (*v.*
beonet); Black Acre; Boat Croft (*v.* bōt); Brick Butts (*v.*
bryke, butte); Brick Kiln Fd; Broken Back (perhaps land hard to till, a back-breaking field); Brook Fd; Carrs (*v.* kjarr); Cock Hill; Cocker Mdw (*v.* cocker); Coal Pit Fd; Cowlane; Crooked Bottom (*v.* croked, botm); Doll's ith' Hole (probably 'belonging to Dorothy who lives in the hollow', from the fem. pers.n. *Doll* a pet-form of *Dorothy* and hol[1]); Eyes (*v.* ēg); Hay Bay (*v.* hēg, bay[2]); Hell Hole; Higgin Fd; Hollinwood (*v.* holegn); Homesites (*v.* 332 *infra*); Horsepool Mdw (*v.* hors, pōl[1]); Long Hey; Marl Fd; Merchant Flat; Moor Croft & Fd; Oxhey; Oxicrow (perhaps from prec. with crew); Pingot (*v.* pingot); Plain; Pye Oaks (1831, 'magpie oaks', *v.* pīe[2]); Ridgefield; Rough Fd & Hey; Rushy Fd; Springs Wd (*v.* spring); Stone Heyer (*v.* stān, cf. Blackeyer 265 *supra*); Wall Fd (*v.* wælla); Well Mdw.

(*b*) Grymesbothum, Grimesbothe 1286 ('Grim's valley-bottom and herds-man's hut', from the pers.n. ON *Grímr*, ODan *Grīm* and bōth, bōðm).

7. STAYLEY (101–9698)

　　Staue-, Stavel', -legh, -leg' e13 Facs (p), 1272 Earw, 1286 *Eyre et
　　freq* to 1402 (17) Sheaf[3] 18, -*ley* 13 (17) ib, 1348 *Eyre*, 1430, 1447
　　ib, 1532 Plea, (-*in Longdendale*) 1337 *Eyre*, (*Stayley alias-*) 1560
　　Earw, -*lay* m13 *SocAnt* (p), -*le* 1386 Plea, -*ly* 1399 ChRR (p),
　　Stafele n.d. (17) Sheaf (p)
　　Staflegh 13 (17) Sheaf[3] 18, *Stavlegh* 1471 *MinAcct*
　　Staleye 1285 *Eyre* (p), *Stalegh* 1351 *Dow*, 1377 *AddCh*, *Staley* 1559
　　Pat
　　Stallegh 1467 *MinAcct*
　　Steiley 1574 Sheaf[3] 21
　　Stayley 1560 Earw
　　Steal(e)y 1621 Orm[2], Earw, *Steeley* 1645 ib

'Wood where staves are got', v. stæf, lēah, cf. Staveley Db 301, La 29, Studies[1] 96. Since the nineteenth century the township has taken its name from the hamlet of Stalybridge *infra*.

STALYBRIDGE (101–9698), 1687 Earw, *Stayley Bridge* 1788 ib, 'the bridge at Stayley', v. brycg, cf. Stayley *supra*. This is probably the site of *Stalifford* 1332 Sheaf, v. ford. Stalybridge is the name of a hamlet in La, v. La 29, which extended to the Ch bank of R. Tame in the eighteenth century, and has since superseded Stayley as the township-name.

STREET-NAMES: ACRES LANE, 1850 *TAMap*, cf. Acres Brook *infra*, v. æcer; DEMESNE ST., 1850 *TAMap*, v. demeyn; KNOWL ST., *Knowle Street* 1860 White, v. cnoll; MOTTRAM RD, 1860 ib, leading to Mottram 313 *supra*; MOTTRAM OLD RD, 1860 ib, *Staley Lane* 1842 OS, cf. Stayley *supra*; NORTH-END RD, cf. North End Mills *infra*; STOCKS LANE, v. Stocks *infra*.

SIDEBOTTOM FOLD, 1850 *TAMap*, -botham- 1831 Bry, v. fald 'a fold', cf. the local surname *Sid(e)bothem*, -(u)me 1286, 1287, 1289 Court, *Sydebothom* 1398 ChRR, *Syd(e)bothum*, -ame, -ome 1577, 1586 Dow, and other forms in Bardsley 690, 'wide valley-bottom', v. sīd, boðm.

ACRES BROOK (R. Tame), cf. Acres Lane *supra*.   ALBION MILLS, 1831 Bry.   ASH HILL.   ASHES, 1831 ib, v. æsc.   ASHTONHILL CROSS, *Ashen Hill Cross* 1831 ib, 'cross at a hill growing with ash-trees', v. æscen.   BESOM LANE & Row, perhaps from dial. besom 'a slatternly woman', but cf. OE bes(e)ma 'broom' and Beesoms Hill 329 *infra*.   LOWER BOWER FOLD, *Poor End* 1831 ib, (*Lower*) *Boar Fold* 1840 TA, v. bār[2], fald.   BROOKFIELD TERRACE, *Brookfield* (*House*) 1860 White.   BRUSHES, 1770 Earw, *Bruches* 13 (17) Sheaf, 'lands newly broken out for cultivation', v. bryce.   BUCKTON GRANGE & VALE, named from Buckton Castle 323 *infra*; Buckton Vale was *Lawton Nook* 1831 Bry, v. nōk.   BURNHOUSEFOLD, *Burnt House Fold* 1840 TA, '(farmstead at) the burnt house', v. brende[2], hūs, fald.   CARRBROOK, *Car Brook* 1860 White, a hamlet named from Carr Brook 17 *supra*.   CASTLE CLOUGH, 1831 Bry, named from Buckton Castle 323 *infra*, v. castel(l), clōh.   CASTLE HALL MILL, *Stayley Mill* 1831 ib, cf. *Staueleymulne* 1430 Eyre, *Castle Hall* 1860 White, v. myln.   COCKERS, 1850 *TAMap*, *Arplet* 1831 Bry, cf. Harpley *infra*.   COCK WOOD, 1831 ib, v. cocc[2], cf. Cock Knarr 310 *supra*.   COPLEY, 1831 ib, *Coppelegh* 1345 Eyre (p), probably from copped but the OE pers.n. *Coppa* is possible, v. lēah 'a clearing'.

CROFT HO, 1860 White. CROWS I' TH' WOOD, 1850 *TAMap*,
Great Wood, Crows in the Wood 1831 Bry, *Crow ith' Wood* 1840 *TA*,
'cabins in the wood', *v.* crew (cf. creu), wudu. DRY CLOUGH,
1850 *TAMap*, cf. *le Dryeclough* 1357 *ChFor*, 'dry valley', *v.* drȳge,
clōh. EARLY BANK, 1860 White, cf. 277 *supra*. FIELDS.
FLASH, 1831 Bry, cf. *le Flaskes* 1403 *JRC*, *v.* flask, flasshe 'a swamp'.
FLAXFIELD, *Flax Fields* 1831 Bry. FOLD, 1831 ib. FOX HILL,
(*Further-*) 1840 *TA*. GALLOWS CLOUGH, *v.* 312 *supra*. (HIGHER
& LOWER) HARPLEY, (*Great- & Little-*) 1840 *ib*, *Arp(e)le(gh)* 1345
Eyre, from lēah 'a clearing, a woodland glade', with hearpe 'a harp',
in some undetermined sense. Lower Harpley is *Low Fold* 1831 Bry,
cf. Cockers *supra*. HARRIDGE HALL & PIKE, *Harridge Hall* 1831 ib,
Harridge (*Pike*) 1840 *TA*, 1842 OS, *v.* pīc[1]. Harridge may be 'high
ridge', *v.* hēah, hrycg, but it lies on the same boundary as Shire
Clough *infra*, and the first el. may be hār[2]. HARTLEY QUARRY &
TERRACE. HEAPS, 1850 *TAMap*. HEY HEADS, 1831 Bry, 'the
top ends of an enclosure', *v.* (ge)hæg, hēafod. HILL TOP, 1831 ib.
HUDDERSFIELD RD, 1860 White, leading to Huddersfield WRY.
HUSSEY QUARRY. HYDE GREEN, 1840 *TA*, (*Lower*) 1850 *TAMap*,
High Green 1831 Bry, *v.* hēah, grēne[2], cf. Hyde 279 *supra*. KER-
SHAW HEY, 1842 OS, from the surname *Kershaw* and (ge)hæg.
LITTLE BANK, 1831 Bry, cf. *Hollin & Under Bank* ib, *v.* banke,
holegn, under. LUKES FOLD, *Luke Fold* 1840 *TA*, *v.* fald.
MARLPIT, (a farm), cf. *Marlpits* 1850 *TAMap*, *v.* marle-pytt.
MILLBROOK, 1831 Bry. MOORGATE, 1831 ib, 'gateway to a moor',
v. geat. MOORLANDS & -SIDE. NAILORS, *Nailers* 1831 ib.
NORTH END MILLS, cf. Northend Rd *supra*. OAKFIELD, 1850
TAMap. OAKLANDS. OAKWOOD MILLS. PARKHILL, 1860
White. POTHILL, 1840 *TA*, *v.* pot(t). ROCK HALL, 1831 Bry.
SAUNDER'S GREEN, 1831 ib. SHAW BANK & MOOR, *Shaw Moor*
1831 ib, *Shaw Bank* 1860 White, 'bank and moor at a wood', *v.*
sceaga. SHIRE CLOUGH, 1831 Bry, *v.* scīr[1], clōh 'a valley'. This,
being the boundary between Stalybridge and that part of Hollingworth now included in Mossley La, is now a county boundary, but
it was anciently the boundary of the Duchy of Lancaster's territory
of Longdendale, cf. Harridge *supra*. SHUTTS LANE, cf. *Higher &
Lower Shutts* 1840 *TA*, *v.* scēat 'a corner of land'. SPRING BANK,
1831 Bry, 'well-spring bank', *v.* spring. SPRING-GROVE MILL,
1831 ib. STAYLEY HALL, 1579 Earw. STALY BROOK (R. Tame),
cf. Stayley *supra*. STALYHILL, *Dye House* 1831 ib. STOCKS

(Brook), *Stocks* 1850 *TAMap*, *-House* 1831 Bry, *v.* stocc.   Sun
Green, *Lower Green* 1842 OS.   Tonge Fold, *Tong* 1831 Bry, cf.
Tonge 1404 ChRR (p), and Tonge Ho 313 *supra*, '(fold at) the spit
of land', *v.* tong, fald.   Walkerwood, 1842 OS.   Wellbank,
1831 Bry.   Wild Bank, 1831 ib, *Wild Banks Hill* 1842 OS, *v.*
wilde.   Winter Hill, 1831 Bry, an exposed situation, *v.* winter.
The Wood, 1860 White.   Woodlands.

FIELD-NAMES

The undated forms are 1840 *TA* 367, the others are 1358 *MinAcct*, 1362
Eyre, 1827 Earw, 1831 Bry, 1842 OS, 1850 *TAMap* 367, 1860 White.

(*a*) Bone Dust Fd (*v.* bone-dust); Bottoms Fold Ho (*Bottoms* 1831, *v.*
botm); Bridge Eye 1860 (*v.* ēg, cf. Stalybridge *supra*); Broadhead Fd; Brook
Fold 1850 (*v.* fald); Broomfield; Buckleys Homesites & Wd (cf. *Buckley Hill*
1831, *Buckleys* 1842, from the surname *Bulkeley* or *Buckley*, *v.* 330 *infra*);
Carnock Hill; Causeway (*v.* caucie); Cinder Hill (*v.* sinder); Clod (*v.* clodd);
Clough Brow; Cote Mdw (*v.* cot); Cow Lane; Crooked Bottom (*v.* botm);
Dilitch Croft; Dock Fd (*v.* docce); Dog Hill; Dry Earth & Knowl (cf. Dry
Clough *supra*); Earnshaw 1831 (cf. *Erneshagh* 1358 (p), 'eagle wood', *v.*
earn, sceaga); Eddish (*v.* edisc); Fowler Mdw; Greaves (*v.* grǣfe); Green
Hill; Hanging Bank (*v.* hangende); Hard Land; Hay Shed; High Grounds
1831; Hollin Clough (*v.* holegn, clōh); Homesite(s) (*freq* in this township,
v. 332 *infra*); Hulmes (*v.* hulm); Laughing Stead (*v.* stede); Lead Fd;
Lighters Hill Clough (*v.* clōh. The appearance of this f.n. and *Jordansfeld*
infra, in the same township suggests identification of *Lighters* with *le
Ligtheker* 1347 *Eyre*, *Lyghtker* 1357 ChFor, 'light brushwood-marsh', *v.*
lēoht, kjarr, which in 1347 was an assart made by *Jordan* de Macclesfield,
cf. Jordangate (st.n.) 115 *supra*); Little Wd; Low Fd 1831; Lud Castle; Marl
Earth 1831; Mere Pasture (*v.* (ge)mǣre); Miller Hey (1842, 1850); New
Hays; Over Water (*v.* ofer[3]); Paunge Mdw; Pingot (*v.* pingot); Prince Croft;
Pudcock Wd 1831; Little Red; Rid Mdw (*v.* (ge)ryd(d)); Ridding Clough
(*v.* ryding, clōh); Riot; Shippon Mdw; Shroggs (*v.* shrogge); Slate Croft;
Sour Acre; Spout Fd (*v.* spoute); Stubble Mdw & Wd; Tansy Fd; Tenter
Fd (*v.* tentour); Three Gates 1850; Three Nook; Tunnel Mdw; Turpin
Flatt; Valley Mill 1827, 1831; Wedker Wd; Well Mdw; Whoms ('marshy
hollows', *v.* hvammr).

(*b*) *Jordansfeld* 1362 (from the ME pers.n. *Jordan*, and feld, cf. Lighters
Hill Clough *supra*).

8. Tintwistle (102–0297), locally [tinsl]

Tengestvisie 1086 DB, *Tengestwysel*, *-twissell* 1345 *Eyre*, 1360
MinAcct
T(h)engetuesile, *-tuwisel* m13 SocAnt, For, *T(h)enge-*, *Ty(e)nge-*,

Tinge(t)-, -twy-, -twisel(e), -el(l), -il, -ul 1286, 1287, 1288 *Eyre,*
1309, 1310 Cl, 1345, 1348 *Eyre,* 1358, 1360 *MinAcct,* 1455
ChRR, 1494 *SocAnt* (p), *Tyngetwesull, -ule* 1408 ChRR, Orm²,
-ill 1474 Earw, *Tyngetewesyll, -tewysyll* 1489 Pat
Tyngethysel, Tyntegthysel 1285 *For*
Tyngestwysel 1345 *Eyre*
Ty-, Ti-, Tengeltwy-, -twi-, -twesel(l) 1347, 1349, 1353 *Eyre*
Tingtwisel 1369 (17) Orm², *Tyngtwisell* 1574 Sheaf, *Tingtwistle*
1603 NotCestr
Tyngwysell 1378 *Eyre*
Tinchtil(l) or *Tingetwissel* c.1620 Orm²
Tintwizle near Woodhead c.1703 *Chol, Tintwistle* 1724 NotCestr
Longden 1724 NotCestr

The final el. is **twisla** 'a fork (of a river or valley)'. The village is
above the meeting of Arnfield Brook and R. Etherow. For the first
el., Ekwall (DEPN) suggests a Brit river-name identical with Teign
D 14, RN 398, which he would bring from a derivative of Brit
*tagnā 'sprinkling' (Welsh *taen*). The place was occasionally called
after Longdendale 2 *supra*. The *Tyngel-, Tingel-, Tengel-* forms
from *Eyre* probably represent mis-written *Tynges-* etc.

ARNFIELD (BROOK, CLOUGH, FLATS, GUTTER, LANE & MOOR)
(102–0198), *Arn(e)wayesfeld, -is-* 1350, 1351 *Eyre, Arn(i)es(s)feld* 1360
MinAcct, Arn(e)wayfeld 1358, 1362 *ib,* 1360 *Rental, (Magna & Parva)*
Arnefeld 1360 *Rental, Arnfield (Moor)* 1831 Bry, *Armfield* 1717 Sheaf,
(Mill) 1831 Bry, *(Brook, Clough, Moor)* 1842 OS, 'Arneway's, or
Earnwīg's, field', from the ME pers.n. and surname *Arneway* or its
original the OE pers.n. *Earnwīg, v.* feld, magna, parva. The surname
is borne by Alice *Arnewey* 1290 Court, at Macclesfield, and John
Ernwey, Arnewey mayor of Chester 1268–78, cf. Reaney s.n.
Arneway. The brook joins Hollingworth Brook 311 *supra*.

BRITLAND EDGE HILL, *Bretland Edge* 1819 Orm¹, 1831 Bry, *Brettelond*
1337 *Eyre, Bretland* 1345 *ib, -lond* 1359 *ib,* 1408 Orm² (p), the origin
of the surname *Bretland* of Thorncliff 309 *supra*, 'the land of the
Britons', *v.* **Brettas, land,** ecg; cf. WRY 2 269, Orm² III 872.

CROWDEN (BRIDGE, (GREAT & LITTLE) BROOK, HALL, (LITTLE)
MOOR & MEADOWS) (102–0799), *(molendinum de) Crowedene* 1350

Eyre, Crowden 1482 ChRR (p), *-Brook* 1831 Bry, *-Meadows &*
Factory, (Little) Crowden Moss, 1842 OS, *-Hall* 1860 White, *(Great)*
Croden Brook 1760 Earw, 1831 Bry, *Cradden Brook* 1697 Earw, cf.
Great Crowden Intake 1842 OS, *Hadfield Intakes* 1831 Bry, 'crow
valley', *v.* crāwe, denu. The hamlet was known as Crowden Brook
from the stream; the mill- and factory-site is drowned in Torside
Reservoir *infra.* The brook joins R. Etherow.

MICKLEHURST (101–9702), 1831 Bry, *Mikelhourst* 1345 *Eyre, Mukel-*
hurst 1358 *MinAcct, Muculhurst* 1360 *ib, Muccle-* 1362 *ib, Mulchurst*
1724 NotCestr, 'the great wooded-hill', *v.* micel, mikill, hyrst, cf.
Lytelhurst 1358 *MinAcct, Lit(t)el-* 1360, 1362 *ib, Rental, v.* lȳtel
'little'. Micklehurst is now included in Mossley La.

WOODHEAD (CHAPEL) (102–0899), *Wodehede* 1424 *Chol, Woodhede (in*
Londondale) 1548 Earw, 1550 *MinAcct, (the) Woodhead* 1488 (18)
Earw, c.1620, 1656 Orm², *-Chappel* 1659, 1689 Earw, 'the top of the
wood', *v.* wudu, hēafod, cf. *Longdene(dale) heved, Langedeneheved*
1285 *ChFor,* 'the head of Longdendale', *v.* 2 *supra.* The chapel is
mentioned in the will (1488) of its founder, Sir Robert Shaa (i.e.
Shaw), as 'a Chappell that I have made in Longden Dale' (Earw 1
416).

ABRAHAM'S CHAIR, 1842 OS.   ALPHIN (PIKE), 1842 OS, *v.* pīc¹ 'a
hill'.   ANCOTE HILL, *Hankeith Hill* 1842 OS, '(hill at) the lonely
cottage', *v.* āna, cot.   ARNFIELD COVERT, *Black Intake, Spring*
Intake 1842 ib.   AUDERNSHAW CLOUGH, *Audershaw Clough* 1842 ib,
'alder-wood dell', *v.* alor, sceaga, clōh.   BAREHOLME MOSS, *Bare*
Em Moss & End 1842 ib, 'bare marsh', *v.* bær¹, holmr, mos, ende¹.
BINNS (MOSS), *Binns Scar* 1831 Bry, probably from dial. *bing* 'a heap'
(cf. bing) and sker 'a scar'; but Professor Löfvenberg suggests the
first el. may be OE binn in the sense 'a hollow' adduced by Reaney
s.n. *Binne(s), Binns.*   BLACK GUTTER, *v.* goter.   BLACK HILL
(END), 1842 OS.   BLACK TOR, *v.* torr.   BOTTOMS RESERVOIR,
the site of *Bottom Lodge Mill* 1831 Bry, *Bottom* 1842 OS, *Bottoms*
Mill 1847 *TAMap, Bottoms Lodge* 1860 White, and of *Rhodes Mill(s)*
1831 Bry, 1847 *TAMap, v.* botm 'a valley-bottom', cf. Rhodeswood
infra.   BOWERCLOUGH HEAD, the head of Bower Clough in
Saddleworth WRY, *v.* hēafod.   BRICK MILL, 1831 Bry.   BRIDGE
MILL, 1860 White, named from Tintwistle Bridge *infra.*   FAR &

NEAR BROADSLATE, 1842 OS, tracts of moorland, 'broad sheep-pasture', *v.* slæget. BROCKHOLES WOOD, 1842 ib, *Brockholt Wood* 1831 Bry, 'badger(-holes) wood', *v.* brocc, holt, hol[1]. BROKEN GROUND, 1842 OS. BROOK HOUSES, named from Carr Brook 17 *supra.* BRUN, *The-* 1847 *TAMap*, *Bran* 1842 OS, 'hill-edge', *v.* brún[2]. BUCKTON CASTLE, 1767 Earw, *vnum castrum dirutum vocatum Buckeden* (*castell*) 1360 *Rental*, '(castle at) the buck-valley', *v.* bucc, denu, castel(l), cf. Castle *infra.* BUTTERLEY MOSS, 1842 OS. BYRNESS, perhaps from ME *burinesse* 'burial place', *v.* burgæsn. CADDING WOOD, cf. *Caddeneboth* c.1285 *For, Caeding Bottom* 1845 *TA*, '(herdsman's hut at) Cada's valley', from the OE pers.n. *Cada* and denu; bōth is replaced by botm 'a valley-bottom'. CARR, (*Wood*) 1845 *ib*, *Car* 1842 OS, *v.* kjarr 'brushwood, marsh', cf. Carr Brook 17 *supra.* CASTLE (CLOUGH), *Castle* 1598 Earw, (*The-*) 1847 *TAMap*, *Castle Clough & Houses* 1831 Bry, '(hamlet and valley near) the castle', *v.* castel(l), clōh, cf. Buckton Castle *supra.* This may be *Castelsted* 1347 *Eyre*, 'place at-' or 'site of a castle', *v.* stede. CASTLES, *Castle Moss* 1842 OS, *v.* castel(l), mos, referring to moorland outcrops of rock fancied to resemble ruined castles. CAT CLOUGH, 'wild-cat's valley', *v.* cat(t), clōh. CLOUD-BERRY KNOLL, *Cloudberry Hill* 1842 OS, 'rocky hill', *v.* clūd, beorg, cf. The Cloud 330 *infra.* CLOUGH (MILL), *Slough Mill* 1831 Bry, *Clough* 1842 OS, *v.* clōh. COCKERHILL. COOMBES CLOUGH, *Cowmes Clough* 1831 Bry, *Combs Clough* (*Head*) 1842 OS, *v.* cumb 'a hollow, a valley', clōh, hēafod. COTE, *The* 1847 *TAMap*, *v.* cot 'a cottage, a hut'. COWBURY DALE, 'valley where the cow-berry grows', *v.* dæl[1]. CROSSGATE, 1842 OS, *cf. Cross Gate Croft* 1845 *TA.* UPPER DEAD EDGE, *Dead Edge* (*End*) 1842 OS, probably dēad 'dead, a place of death' and ecg. DEER STONES, a scar, *v.* dēor, stān. DEVILS BRIDGE. DEWHILL NAZE, *Durehill Naze* 1831 Bry, from OE næs, a side-form of næss, 'a promontory', cf. DEPN s.n. *Naze.* DIDSBURY INTAKE, 1845 *TA.* DRYSIKE CLOUGH, '(valley at) the dried-up watercourse', *v.* drȳge, sík, clōh. DUN HILL, 1842 OS, on the boundary with Upperthong WRY 2 290, *v.* dūn or dunn, hyll. ENTERCLOUGH, 1723 Earw, (*Bridge*) 1831 Bry, *v.* clōh 'a valley, a dell'. A similar name is Enter House WRY 6 245 (*Enter Bottom* 1847, *v.* botm). FEATHERBED MOSS, 1819 Orm[1], *v.* mos 'a moss'. The name alludes to the soft spongy nature of the peat moss, cf. WRY 1 234, 2 283, 314, 6 98, Db 70, 373. GRAINS MOSS, 1842 OS, *v.* grein 'a branch, a fork' (dial. *grain* 'a small valley forking off from another'), mos. GREEN HILL, 1842 OS, *Good Greave* 1831 Bry, cf. Round Hill *infra*. GREEN HOLLOW. GREENTOP, 1847 *TAMap*, v. topp. GREYSTONE SLACK, cf. *Grey Stones (Edge)* 1842 OS, '(hollow and escarpment at) the grey rocks', v. grǣg[1], stān, slakki, ecg. HARE HILL (CLOUGH), *Hare Hill* 1842 ib. HAWTHORN CLOUGH, *Nether Head Clough* 1842 ib, cf. *Upper Head Clough* ib, 'the valley at the top end', v. hēafod, clōh; it lies at the head of Longdendale and leads the headwaters of R. Etherow, cf. Redhole Spring *infra*. HEY (CLOUGH, EDGE, MOSS & WOOD), *Hey (Edge & Wood)* 1831 Bry, *Hay Farm & Moss* 1842 OS, v. (ge)hæg 'an enclosure'. HEYDEN (BROOK, HEAD & MOOR), UPPER HEYDEN, *Heyden (Clough & Edge)* 1831 Bry, *(Bridge, Brook, Head & Moor)* 1842 OS, perhaps 'hay valley', v. hēg, denu, cf. Holme Moss *infra*. The brook joins R. Etherow 23 *supra*. HIGH-STONE ROCKS, HIGHSTONES, *High Stone* 1659 Earw, *-s* 1831 Bry, v. hēah, stān, roke. HOARSTONE EDGE, 1842 OS, *Woolstone Edge* 1831 Bry, v. hār[2], stān, ecg. HOLLINS (CLOUGH), *Hollins* 1692 Sheaf, *(the-)* 1699 Earw, *-Clough* 1842 OS, 'the hollies', v. holegn, clōh, cf. next. HOLLINS (FM), *Hollins (Mill)* 1831 Bry, 1842 OS, v. holegn, cf. prec. HOLME MOSS, 1709 WRY 2 269, 1842 OS, *Heyden Edge* 1831 Bry; the earlier name is from Holme WRY 2 269, the later one from Heyden *supra*, v. mos, ecg. HOLYBANK WELL, v. holegn, banke. HORSFIELD WOOD, *Horse-* 1842 OS. HOWARDS, 1847 *TAMap*. HOWEL'S HEAD, *Howells Hill* 1831 Bry, *Owls Head Hill* 1842 OS, cf. WRY 2 315, v. hēafod 'a promontory'. INTAKE, *The Intack* 1847 *TAMap*, v. inntak. GREAT & LITTLE INTAKE, 1842 OS. IRONBOWER MOSS & ROCKS, perhaps from hyrne 'a secluded nook' and būr[1], cf. Heronbridge 332 *infra*. KILN CLOUGH, *Kill Clough* 1842 ib, v. cyln, clōh. LADDOW MOSS & ROCKS, *Ledlow Rocks* 1831 Bry, *Ladder Moss & Rocks* 1842 OS, cf. WRY 2 315, where ladda 'a servant, a youth, a lad' is suggested, v. mos, roke. LAD'S LEAP, 1831 Bry, v. ladda, hlēp. LITTLE CLOUGH, 1842 OS. LOFTEND, LOFT INTAKE, *Little Crowden Intake* 1842 ib, *Intake Aloft, The Loft, Loft Wood* 1845 *TA*, v. lopt 'a loft, an upper chamber', here used of elevated land, cf. Crowden *supra*. LONG SIDE (MOSS), *Longside* 1831 Bry, v. sīde 'hillside'. LOW MOOR, 1831 ib. MEADOW CLOUGH, 1842 OS. MEADOWGRAIN CLOUGH, *Meadow Grain* 1842 ib, v. mǣd, grein (dial. *grain*) 'a small valley forking off from another'. MILLBROOK BRIDGE & HO, named from Hollingworth Brook 311 *supra* near Woolley Mill *infra*.

MILL POND, cf. *molendinum de Tyngetwysell'* 1358 *MinAcct.* MILL-
STONE ROCKS, 1842 OS, *v.* mylen-stān. MOOR EDGE RD, *Stayley
Street* 1880 Earw, marked as a Roman road 1842 OS. THE
MOORLANDS. MOUNT SKIP, 1842 ib, a moor. NOONSUN HILL,
Noon Sun 1842 ib. NORTH GRAIN (CLOUGH), *North Grain* 1842 ib,
'north forks', *v.* norð, grein, clōh. OAKEN CLOUGH (BROOK &
GRAINS), *Oaking Clough* (*Grains*) 1842 ib, 'brook and forks in an
oak-grown valley', *v.* ācen, clōh, grein. OAKSIDE BRIDGE &
CLOUGH, *Oak Sike Clough* 1842 ib, 'oak-tree watercourse', *v.* āc, sík.
OGDEN (BROOK & CLOUGH), (*Upper*) *Ogden, Ogden Meadows* 1831
Bry, *Ogden Clough & Pasture* 1842 OS, 'oak valley', *v.* āc, denu.
The brook becomes Hollingworth Brook 311 *supra.* ORMES
MOOR, cf. *Ormesty* 271 *supra.* OVERGREEN, *v.* uferra. PIKE-
NAZE (HILL & MOOR), *Pickenhurst* 1819 Orm², *Pike Naze Hill* 1831
Bry, *Pikenose Farm & Moor* 1842 OS, *Pikenaes* 1847 *TAMap*,
'pointed hill', *v.* pīc¹, næs (cf. Dewhill Naze *supra*), nōs(e). RAKES
MOSS & ROCKS, *Rakes Moss* 1842 OS, cf. *Small Croden Rakes* 1831
Bry and Valehouse Wood *infra*, 'moss and rocks at a narrow path',
v. rake. RAWKINS BROOK, 1847 *TAMap*, *Rowkins Brook* 1831
Bry. REDHOLE SPRING, *Red Hole source of R. Mersey* 1831 ib,
Red Hole Spring 1842 OS, *v.* rēad, hol¹. RED RATCHER, *-s* 1842 ib,
v. rēad, rocher. RESIDUUM LODGE. RHODESWOOD COTTAGE &
RESERVOIR, *Rhodes Wood* 1842 ib, cf. *Rodefeld* 1360 *Rental, v.* rod¹
'a clearing', feld. Cf. *Rhodes Mill*(*s*) 1831 Bry, 1847 *TAMap*, lost in
Bottoms Reservoir. Rhodeswood Reservoir covers *Great-, Redshaw-
& Ridings Wood* 1831 Bry, *v.* rēad, sceaga, ryding. RICHMOND
HO. ROBINSON'S MOSS & SPRING, *Robinson's Moss* 1831 ib.
ROUND HILL (MOSS), *Roundhill* 1842 OS, *Good Greave* 1831 Bry; the
older name extended to a tract of moorland including Green Hill
supra, and seems to be 'good wood', *v.* gōd², grǣfe. ROUND
INTAKE, 1845 *TA*. SALTER'S BROOK (BRIDGE), *Saltersbrooke* 1699
Earw, *Salter's Brook* 1750 Sheaf, cf. WRY 1 342, 'salt-merchant's
brook', *v.* saltere, brōc; a stream on the boundary of WRY at the
head of Longdendale, on Crump's saltway 'F', cf. 50 *supra*, Crump
132. SHEEPFOLD (2x), *Sheep Cote* 1842 OS. SLIDDENS (MOSS),
1842 ib. SOLDIERS LUMP, a hill on the boundary of Upperthong
WRY. SPAN (GUTTER), *Spond Moor* 1842 OS, *v.* spann¹, mōr¹,
goter, *v.* Sponds 200 *supra.* SPRING BANK MILLS. SQUIRE
MILL, *Doctor Mill* 1831 Bry. STABLE CLOUGH, 1842 OS.
STONEBRAKE QUARRIES. STONEFOLD. STONE LOW, *Stony Low*

1845 *TA*, 'stony hill', *v.* stānig, hlāw. TINTWISTLE BRIDGE, & -*Ford* 1831 Bry, *v.* ford. TINTWISTLE HALL, 1860 White. TINTWISTLE KNARR, 1842 OS, -*Norr* 1831 Bry, *v.* cnearr 'a rugged rock'. TOOLEYSHAW MOOR & MOSS, 1842 OS. TOP O' TH' GREEN, 1831 Bry. TORSIDE RESERVOIR, 1860 White, cf. Torside Db 71. TOWNHEAD FM, *Town Head* 1842 OS, *Town End* 1831 Bry, 'the top end of the town', *v.* toun, hēafod, ende[1]. TOP STONES. VALEHOUSE RESERVOIR, site of *Vale House (Mill)* 1831 ib, *v.* val, hūs, cf. foll. and Valehouse Fm in Glossop Db. VALE-HOUSE WOOD, *Rakes Wood* 1842 OS, *v.* rake, cf. prec. and Rakes Moss *supra.* VALE MILLS, 1860 White, *Greaves Mill* 1831 Bry, *v.* grǣfe, cf. prec. WARLOW PIKE, 1842 OS, *Horelouwe* 1348 *Eyre* (p), *Harelowe* 1468 WRY 2 317, 'boundary hill', *v.* hār[2], hlāw, pīc[1] 'a pointed hill'. It is on the county boundary, cf. WRY loc. cit. WARM HOLE, 1847 *TAMap*, *Wormall* 1831 Bry, cf. WRY 2 319. WESTEND MOSS, 1842 OS, *v.* west, ende[1]. WHITE GATE. WHITE LOW (SLACK), *Whitelow Slack* 1842 ib, '(hollow at) the white-hill', *v.* hwīt, hlāw, slakki. WIGGIN CLOUGH, 'mountain-ash dell', from dial. *wicken* (*v.* cwicen) and clōh. WIMBERRY MOSS. WINDGATE EDGE, *Whinnet Edge* 1831 Bry, *Windyate Edge* 1842 OS, 'wind-gap hill', *v.* wind-geat, ecg. WINTER HILL, 1845 *TA*, *v.* winter. WITHENS BROOK, EDGE & MOOR, *Withens Clough & Mouth*, *Withans Edge* 1831 Bry, *Withern Moor* 1842 OS, *v.* wiðign 'a willow copse', clōh, mūða 'a mouth, the opening of a valley', ecg, mōr[1], brōc. WOODBOTTOM FM, 1860 White, cf. *Wood Bottom* 1845 *TA*, 'wooded valley-bottom', *v.* wudu, botm. WOOLLEY MILL & LANE, *Wool(l)ey Mill* 1831 Bry, 1842 OS, cf. Woolley 310 *supra.*

FIELD-NAMES

Since the township is very extensive, the modern field-names are arranged by hamlets. The undated forms are 1845 *TA* 397. Of the others, 1286 is *Eyre*, Court, 1348, 1359, 1375 *Eyre*, 1358, 1360[1] *MinAcct*, 1360[2] *Rental*, 1831 Bry, 1842 OS, 1847 *TAMap*, 1860 White.

(*a*) ARNFIELD. Bank Acre; Bent (*v.* beonet); Black Hey; Bramwell Hey; Brassrich Fd, Mdw & Top; Bricker Head (*v.* hēafod); Butts Mdw (*v.* butte); Calf Hey; Coldhurst (*v.* cald, hyrst); Cote Field Top (*v.* cot); Croft Home-sites (*v.* 331 *infra*); Great Hey (*v.* (ge)hæg); Hawthorn; Hey Head (*v.* (ge)hæg, hēafod); Hopkin Fd; How Mdw (*v.* hōh); Intake; Lumber Hey (*v.* lumber); Marled Hey; Mickle Mdw (*v.* micel, mikill); Mill Hole; Millers Hole; Pannell; Patch; Penny Croft (*v.* pening); Pepper Hill (cf. Pepper St.

(Chester) 333 *infra*); Rough Hey; Rushy Croft; Stony Dole (*v.* dāl); Town Fd; Turf Pits 1842; Vincet Hey.

MICKLEHURST. Angle Mdw (*v.* angle); Beak Fd; Bean Fd; Bent (*v.* beonet); Blake Mdw (*v.* blæc); Breeze Hill 1860; Calf Hey; Carr (*v.* kjarr); Cat Holes; Clay Fd; Close Fd (*v.* clos); Cross Bank; Ditches; Elmanhurst ('elm-wood', *v.* elmen, hyrst); (Old & Upper) Folks Pasture; Granny Mdw; Hazles; Hey Bank, Heads, Top & Wd (*v.* (ge)hæg, hēafod); Hole Ho 1847; Inklebottom (*v.* botm); Knowl (*v.* cnoll); Lauton Intake, Lawton Nook 1831; Main Fd (*v.* main); Man Fd; Marled Earth; Mead (*v.* mǣd); Mellor Moor (cf. Db 145); Midge Hill 1842 (*v.* mycg, hyll); Mill Fd & Hey; Old Fd; Oldham Stair Mill 1831; Pingot (*v.* pingot); Pits Head (*v.* pytt, hēafod); Ridd (*v.* ryde); Riddings (*v.* ryding); Slid Wd; Smithy Bottom (*v.* botm); Spout Mdw (*v.* spoute); Tenter Croft & Fd (*v.* tentour); Vineyard (*v.* vinȝerd); Well Hole; The Wharf Garden (*v.* waroð, cf. Wharf 65 *supra*); Wheat Hey; White Fd; Whittle Fd (cf. Whitle Db 153, 'white hill', *v.* hwīt, hyll); Wood Fd; Worsted Brow.

TINTWISTLE. Acre; Angle Mdw (*v.* angle); Ash Fd; Bank (cf. *Bank Wood* 1831, 1842); Barn Bank Brow 1842; Beeley Intake (cf. *Beely Booth* 1842, *v.* bōth); Bent Mdw (*v.* beonet); Berry Mdw; Birches; Black Chew Head 1842 (on the county boundary, *v.* WRY 2 313); Bottom (*v.* botm); Break; Bridge End; Brink Moor 1842 (*v.* brink); Broad Bent Wharf (*v.* beonet, waroð, cf. Wharf Garden *supra*); Calf Hey; Chapel Fd & Wd (cf. Woodhead Chapel *supra*); Clay Dole (*v.* dāl); Clough Edge (*v.* clōh, ecg); Coldberry Stones 1831 ('(rocks at) the cold hill', *v.* cald, beorg); Corn Hey; Cote Fd (*v.* cot); Cow Pasture; Creak (*v.* creic); Dewsnaps Croft (*v.* dēaw, snæp, cf. 277 *supra*); Dry Earth; Eyes (*v.* ēg); Fiddle Case (from the shape of the field); Field Head; Flat Dole (*v.* flatr, dāl); Flatt (*v.* flat); Fullers Wd; Great Wd (1831, 1842, cf. Rhodeswood *supra*); Greave (*v.* grǣfe); Hemp Butts (*v.* hænep, butte); Hole; Hollin Hey (*v.* holegn); Hollingworth Intake (cf. Hollingworth 309 *supra*); Hough (*v.* hōh); How Day Head Mdw (*del Ewode* 1359 (p), *le Heewodeheggh, Ewodeheye* 1360², '(enclosure at) a wood by a river', *v.* ēa, wudu, hecg, (ge)hæg, cf. *Ewode* 213 *supra*, Ewood La 75, 91. *How Day Head* is 'the top end of *Ewodeheye*', *v.* hēafod); Hungry Hole (*v.* hungrig); Intake (*freq*, *v.* inntak); Jack Wd (*v.* jack); Kiln Hill; Knowl Hill; Lead Croft; Lenches (*v.* hlenc); Ley Bottom(s) & Fd (*v.* lēah or lǣge, botm); Leylands (*v.* lǣge, land); Leys (*v.* lǣs or lēah); Longhurst (*v.* hyrst); Longshutt (*v.* scēat); Lowside 1842 (*Lawside* 1831, 'hillside', *v.* hlāw, sīde); Main Dole (*v.* main, dāl); Marled Earth; Mayers (perhaps analogous with Blackeyer 265 *supra*); Mean Hey ('common enclosure', *v.* (ge)mǣne); New Hey; Nicker Mdw (*v.* nicor); Oaks; Oulers (*v.* alor); Paddock Leach (*v.* padduc, lǣc(c)); Patch; Peppercorn Hey (perhaps an enclosure held at a peppercorn rent); Pesters Hey; Pinfold (*v.* pynd-fald); Pingle (*v.* pingel); Plain; Prestors Leys; Redshaw Wd 1831 (*v.* rēad, sceaga, cf. Rhodeswood *supra*); Red Shores (*v.* rēad, scor(a)); Ridd (*v.* ryde); Riding Bank, Ridings Wd 1831 (*v.* ryding, cf. Rhodeswood *supra*); Rocher (*v.* rocher); Rushy Leys (*v.* lēah); Rye Fd; Slack Riding (cf. *The Slack* 1842, *v.* slakki); Springwell Wd 1842; Stony Dole, Hey & Wharf (*v.* dāl, (ge)hæg, waroð, cf. Garden

Wharf *supra*); Stubbing Wood, Stubbings (*v.* stubbing); Tang (*v.* tang); Top o' th' Lane 1831; Town Field Knowl; Turf Moss 1842; Wall Croft (cf. *le Wallecroft* 1360², *v.* wælla, croft); Warth (*v.* waroð); Water Rean (*v.* wæter, rein); Waterside (Mills) 1842, 1860 (cf. Waterside Db 105); West Fd; Wood Hey; Wood Top.

(*b*) *le Hertstoncloghouses* 1358, *Herstonclouhouses de Tyngettwysell* 1360¹, *Herstancloghous, le Herstoncloughouses* 1360² ('(houses at) the valley where hearth-stones are got', from ME *herth-ston* 'a hearth-stone', and clōh, hūs); *Holinfryth* 1348 ('holly wood', *v.* holegn, (ge)fyrhðe, but perhaps this is Holmfirth WRY 2 289); *Hollurbek* 1375 (p) ('alder stream or valley', from alor and bece¹ or bekkr); *Lytelhurst* (*v.* Micklehurst *supra*); *del Stonis* 1286 (p) ('the rocks', *v.* stān); *le Wallefeld* 1360² ('the spring field', *v.* wælla, feld); *Wileford* 1286 ('ford at a game- or fish-trap', *v.* wīl, ford, cf. Macclesfield Park 120 *supra*).

INDEX OF CROSS-REFERENCES

References in Part I of *The Place-Names of Cheshire*, to names and topics contained in subsequent Parts. Township- and parish-names are cited simply; other names are followed by the name of the township or parish in which they lie. The **bold figure** indicates the Part in which the name or subject will appear.

INDEX OF PARISHES
AND TOWNSHIPS IN PART I